Privacy and Personal Data Protection Law in Asia

Edited by
Adrian Mak
Ching Him Ho
and
Anselmo Reyes

•HART•
OXFORD • LONDON • NEW YORK • NEW DELHI • SYDNEY

HART PUBLISHING

Bloomsbury Publishing Plc

Kemp House, Chawley Park, Cumnor Hill, Oxford, OX2 9PH, UK

1385 Broadway, New York, NY 10018, USA

29 Earlsfort Terrace, Dublin 2, Ireland

HART PUBLISHING, the Hart/Stag logo, BLOOMSBURY and the Diana logo are trademarks of Bloomsbury Publishing Plc

First published in Great Britain 2025

A catalogue record for this book is available from the British Library.

A catalogue record for this book is available from the Library of Congress.

Library of Congress Control Number: 2024947284

ISBN: HB: 978-1-50996-547-2
ePDF: 978-1-50996-549-6
ePub: 978-1-50996-548-9

Typeset by Compuscript Ltd, Shannon
Printed and bound in Great Britain by CPI Group (UK) Ltd, Croydon CR0 4YY

MIX
Paper | Supporting responsible forestry
FSC® C013604

To find out more about our authors and books visit www.hartpublishing.co.uk. Here you will find extracts, author information, details of forthcoming events and the option to sign up for our newsletters.

To HL, Rachel, Jayden and Elvis

SERIES EDITORS' PREFACE

This is the fifth thematic volume of Hart's *Studies in Private International Law – Asia* series. It has three features that distinguish it from the preceding thematic volumes.

First, given its subject matter, the book essentially sets out and comments on regulatory laws within the Asian jurisdictions that it covers. This feature thus calls for an explanation as to why the book comes within a series dedicated to private international law. It is hoped that the justification given in the introductory chapter will persuade readers of a need to harmonise conflict of law rules relating to data protection across borders.

Second, rather than just covering the 15 Asian jurisdictions (China, Hong Kong, Taiwan, Japan, South Korea, Singapore, Malaysia, Vietnam, Cambodia, Myanmar, the Philippines, Indonesia, Thailand, Sri Lanka and India) that its predecessors canvassed, this book has ventured into two Central Asian countries (Uzbekistan and Kazakhstan). It is hoped that this greater, more inclusive, coverage of Asia will continue as a feature in future volumes.

Third, as a corollary to the first and second features, the authors of the 17 jurisdictional chapters of this book come from a more diverse range of occupations and industries than before. The list of contributors includes not just lawyers and law professors, but also persons who must grapple with data protection regulations as part of their day-to-day work for companies and other organisations. As data protection law must be inherently pragmatic in its approach, it is hoped that the insights of those who are engaged in controlling, processing, transferring, and safeguarding data as part of their routine work will significantly enhance the value of this book.

Previous volumes have proposed rudimentary principles upon which the private international law of Asian jurisdictions on a given subject, can be based, developed and ultimately harmonised. This volume is no different in that respect. It suggests that Asian states should look to the European Union's (EU) General Data Protection Regulation (GDPR) as a ready-made framework for their own data privacy laws. The precise application of elements within that framework might vary from state to state (for instance, countries may have differing notions on the scope of the national security exception to GDPR). However, it would make sense for Asia in general to adhere to a unified standard of data privacy and to offer a level of protection for data subjects which is at least equivalent to GDPR. The adoption of a robust single standard would facilitate the growth of the digital economy throughout Asia.

The Editors
Kyoto
12 August 2024

ACKNOWLEDGEMENTS

We are grateful to all contributors for the hard work put into their chapters. We would also thank the following for their assistance with the compilation of this volume: Ada Chung, Emily Lee, Ji En Lee, Hughes Tang, Sherson Ng and Zee Kin Yeong.

The Editors
Hong Kong
1 July 2024

CONTENTS

LIST OF CONTRIBUTORS

Adam Au is general counsel at Toys R Us Asia.

Khin Thitsar Aung is an Associate Professor in the Department of Law at Yangon University of Distance Education.

Eng Yi Chia is an Associate at Cecil Abraham & Partners in Malaysia.

Eung-Kyung Cho is an Attorney-at-Law in South Korea.

Sai Ramani Garimella is an Associate Professor at South Asian University in India.

Lanx Goh is Global Head of Privacy at Prudential Plc, Adjunct Associate Professor at the National University of Singapore, Adjunct Lecturer at the Singapore Management University, and Honorary Consul of the Republic of Bulgaria in Singapore.

Ching Him Ho is a barrister at Plowman Chambers in Hong Kong.

Abdulaziz Jurajonov is an Associate (Advocate) at Centil in Uzbekistan.

Joshua Kow is Corporate Counsel (Privacy & Data) at Sony Interactive Entertainment.

Mai-Thanh Le is a Professor at Thang Long University in Hanoi, Vietnam.

Lemuel Didulo Lopez is a Lecturer at RMIT University in Australia.

Adrian Mak is a Mediator based in Hong Kong and a Director of Kabishiki Kaisha Anselmo Reyes in Japan.

Haaris Moosa is an Advocate of the High Court of Kerala in Kochi, India.

Abdumalik Mukhtorov is an Advocate at Azizov & Partners in Uzbekistan.

Rothna Ngorn is a Senior Associate at Bun & Associates in Cambodia.

Tien-Duc Nguyen is a Research Fellow at the Institute of State and Law of the Vietnam Academy of Social Sciences.

Botagoz Omarova is a lawyer at Azizov & Partners and a Leading Researcher at the Institute of Legislation and Legal Information of the Ministry of Justice in Kazakhstan.

Priskila Pratita Penasthika is an Assistant Professor at the Faculty of Law of Universitas Indonesia.

Hemaka Perera is an Associate Counsel (Foreign) working with VK Rajah SC in Singapore.

Anselmo Reyes is an International Judge of the Singapore International Commercial Court.

Nobuyuki Sato is a Professor at Chuo Law School and Executive Vice-President of Chuo University.

Puthkarona Seng is a Senior Associate at Bun & Associates in Cambodia.

Noor Muzalifah Binti Shabudin is partner at Cecil Abraham & Partners in Malaysia.

Huang-Chih Sung is a Professor at the National Chengchi University Graduate Institute of Technology, Innovation and Intellectual Property Management in Taiwan.

Azizbek Suyunboev is Advocate at Azizov & Partners in Uzbekistan.

Ei Thandar Bo is an Associate Professor in the Department of Law at Yangon University of Distance Education.

Thaya Uthayophas is Group Data Protection Officer and Senior Privacy Counsel at LINE MAN Wongnai in Thailand.

Phoebe Woo is a DPhil Law Candidate at the University of Oxford and a Pre-Doctoral Fellow at the University of Hong Kong.

Arubegim Yerlankyzy is a lawyer at Azizov & Partners in Kazakhstan.

Yun Zhao is the Henry Cheng Professor in International Law and Associate Dean (Mainland Affairs) at the Faculty of Law of the University of Hong Kong.

LIST OF CASES

China

England

European Commission

Hong Kong

India

Japan

Malaysia

Philippines

Singapore

South Korea

Sri Lanka

Taiwan

Thailand

United States

Uzbekistan

LIST OF STATUTES AND INSTRUMENTS

International Instruments

Hague

Primary Legislation, Secondary Legislation and Other Materials

Cambodia

China

England

European Union

Hong Kong

India

Indonesia

Japan

Kazakhstan

Malaysia

Myanmar

Philippines

Singapore

Sri Lanka

Vietnam

Introduction

CHING HIM HO AND ANSELMO REYES

I. Overview

This chapter has several objectives. Its overall purpose is to introduce data privacy and protection law to readers who are unfamiliar with the subject. Section II will seek to justify the inclusion of a book on Asian data protection regulations in a series devoted to the conflict of laws in Asia. Section III is an initial attempt at identifying trends in the data protection regulations of Asian states. It will be suggested that a key trend is for Asian states to be influenced, to a greater or lesser extent, by the European Union's (EU) General Data Protection Regulation (better known as GDPR),[1] in the development of their data protection regimes. A more in-depth comparison of Asian data regimes will be found in the Conclusion to this book. The heart of this chapter is to be found in sections IV and V. As not all readers will be familiar with GDPR, section IV will summarise its basic provisions. Section V will then submit that the EU's principles can serve as a template against which to benchmark the 17 data protection regimes surveyed in the succeeding chapters of this book.

II. Data Protection and the Conflict of Laws

This is the fifth thematic volume within the *Studies in Private International Law: Asia* series. The thematic volumes are supposed to be studies of specific conflict of law in Asian jurisdictions. However, in contrast to previous thematic volumes which concentrated on the standard issues of private international law (jurisdiction, applicable law, the enforcement of judgments or awards across state borders, and the harmonisation of cross-border law), this book focuses on how 17 Asian states have sought to safeguard personal data in their domestic law.[2] Accordingly, a large part of this book concerns what might be characterised as purely regulatory law, prompting one to query how this book can purport to be a study of private international law.

We respond to the query by way of an intuitive examination of the notions of 'personal information or data', 'privacy', and 'protection' pervading this book. We suggest that, simply

[1] Regulation (EU) 2016/679 of the European Parliament and of the Council of 27 April 2016 on the Protection of Natural Persons with Regard to the Processing of Personal Data and on the Free Movement of Such Data, and Repealing Directive 95/46/EC (2016) OJ L119/1, available at gdpr-info.eu/.

[2] The Asian states are China, Hong Kong, Taiwan, Japan, South Korea, Singapore, Malaysia, Vietnam, Cambodia, Myanmar, the Philippines, Indonesia, Thailand, Sri Lanka, India, Uzbekistan and Kazakhstan.

on an intuitive level, three issues come straightaway to mind when one considers the notions highlighted.

The first issue is the scope of one's personal information or data. What qualifies as information or data that is personal to a human being (that is, a data subject)? As a matter of principle, every detail about oneself and how one interacts with the world at large should constitute one's personal information or data. On this footing, the ambit of personal information is wide, ranging from matter-of-fact details about a person (name, sex, marital status, address, occupation, nationality, race, birth date, height, weight, and level of education) to more intimate descriptions of one's habits and activities (tastes in music and literature, activities on social media, and spending patterns).

Given such a wide definition of what personal data comprises, the second issue is whether every datum or piece of information about oneself constitutes one's 'privacy'. In other words, to what extent is a data subject entitled to deny access to information about oneself, so that the world at large can only know such information if the individual consents. If not all one's personal data are to be regarded as off-limits in the absence of consent, how is the line to be drawn between what information is (and what information is not) entitled to be treated as private to oneself. What are the underpinning principles for personal information or data to be classified as off-limits to outsiders?

The third issue shifts from an understanding of the nature of personal data and privacy to an examination of regulatory regimes for permitting or denying access to such private data. The accounts of the data protection regimes in the 17 Asian states contained in this book focus on the following matters:

1) When may an individual's private information be:
   a) collected,
   b) processed,
   c) transferred to third parties, or
   d) stored,

   by data controllers and processors?
2) What conditions (if any) govern such collection, processing, transfer, or storage?
3) What remedies (if any) are available to data subjects whose information has been wrongly collected, processed, transferred, or stored?

Even on the intuitive understanding just sketched out, it will be apparent that cross-border issues inevitably arise, especially given the ubiquity of cyberspace and the vast amounts of personal data now being transmitted by individuals to corporations or natural persons over social media and the internet at every second of every day. The three matters identified in the previous paragraph readily give rise to a host of sub-questions which are analogous to the standard topics of private international law. This is because, although a country's data protection regimes purport to regulate the handling of personal information within its boundaries, in practice the regime must be extra-territorial to be effective. Cyberspace knows no territorial limits. It can be accessed from anywhere, so that a state's data protection regime must extend to regulating what is available over the internet anywhere and everywhere in the world.

There are consequently issues of jurisdiction and applicable law: (1) To what extent (if at all) will the data protection laws of state A apply to a data controller or processor in state B who has wrongly collected, processed, transferred, or stored the personal information of a data subject residing in state A?

There are issues of recognition and enforcement beyond a state's boundaries: (2) Suppose that state B has a more stringent regime for the protection of personal data than state A, can a data subject residing in state A invoke the protection of state B's laws against a data controller or processor who has wrongly exploited that individual's personal information? (3) What means (if any) are available to a data protection supervisory authority in state A to enforce state A's data protection laws against a data controller or processor in state B who maintains no (or no substantial presence) in state A? (4) What means (if any) are available to the data protection supervisory authority in state B to ensure that state A does not make unreasonable demands of what should (or should not be done) by state B's data privacy regulatory regime for the protection of the personal information of data subjects residing in state A?

There are issues of conflict and harmonisation: (5) Is the consequence of the answers to the foregoing sub-questions that, in practice, data controllers and processors will have to comply with the totality of data protection laws in the countries in which they operate or in which their services or products may be accessed? (6) What if those data protection laws are inconsistent with each other?

There are policy issues about where we are (or should be) heading with so many overlapping data protection and privacy regimes: (7) With ever-increasing regulation, what has become of notions such as the 'freedom of the internet commons' and 'access to information' that the advent of the web was supposed to usher?

In short, there are an abundance of conflict of law issues, which can only be approached through a study of different regulatory regimes and their interactions with one another.

III. Some Asian Trends

A divergence in how different Asian states categorise and regulate personal data renders the identification of common ground among them difficult. Nonetheless, we submit that the following common characteristics can be discerned.

In 1948, by Article 12 of the Universal Declaration of Human Rights, the UN acknowledged a human right of privacy: 'No one shall be subjected to arbitrary interference with his privacy, family, home or correspondence, nor to attacks upon his honour and reputation. Everyone has the right to the protection of the law against such interference or attacks'.[3] Since then, many states have recognised privacy as a fundamental right, despite uncertainties as to the precise meaning of the concept. Data privacy rights have been enshrined in constitutions, national law, administrative regulations, and case precedents, as a means of safeguarding the individual's right to privacy and the collection, use and transfer of an individual's personal data. Among the Asian jurisdictions studied here, Japan,[4] Hong Kong,[5]

[3] UN, Universal Declaration of Human Rights (1948), available at un.org/en/about-us/universal-declaration-of-human-rights.

[4] Constitution of Japan, Art 13.

[5] Hong Kong Basic Law, Art 30.

South Korea,[6] Myanmar,[7] Kazakhstan,[8] Vietnam,[9] and Thailand[10] have expressly identified privacy as a fundamental right in their constitutional documents. Other states (such as Sri Lanka,[11] Taiwan,[12] Cambodia,[13] Singapore,[14] and Indonesia[15]) have not explicitly referred in their constitutions to a person's right to privacy, but have acknowledged the right to privacy as a fundamental human right in their legislation or court decisions.

Among the 17 jurisdictions covered in this volume, most have enacted a data protection legal framework, with Myanmar and Cambodia being the exceptions. In general, data protection in such frameworks refer to protection against the unwanted disclosure of personal information.[16] Thus, doxing (that is, disclosure of others' personal data without consent) is typically criminalised. Among Asian states where data protection laws are in place, the relevant regimes mirror GDPR to a greater or lesser extent. Most states' legislation broadly prohibits the transfer of personal data from their jurisdiction to states which do not have data protection regulations affording a similar standard of protection.

Nonetheless, differences exist. Individual states have included special features in their data protection laws. In Taiwan, for instance, the restriction on international transfer of personal data applies only to non-public entities. The Personal Data Protection Acts of Singapore and Indonesia[17] exclude liability in the case of an individual acting in a personal or domestic capacity, or when the data concerned comprise 'business contact information'.[18] Hong Kong has a 'whitelist' regulation (that is, a requirement that data only be transferred to states having a similar level of protection). However, that has not yet come into operation, apparently due to a lack of consensus on the matter among the business community.[19] Consequently, although GDPR has provided the backbone for data protection regimes in Asia, each state has modified GDPR, adapting it to local circumstances and needs.

An individual's privacy and personal data may be governed by different sets of legislation within a state. One set of laws will deal with an individual's rights as a human being, highlighting paradigm situations of privacy violation and providing for compensation or some other remedy in case of infringement. A different set of laws will govern what others (natural or legal persons) can do with an individual's personal data, in particular regulating the collection, processing, transfer and storage of personal data. For instance, in Taiwan the right to privacy is regulated by the Civil Code, whereas the protection of personal data is covered by the Personal Data Protection Act. In Japan, the Act on the Protection of Personal Information specifically deals with the transfer of citizens' personal data but only tangentially covers a data subject's right to privacy.

[6] Constitution of the Republic of Korea, Art 17.
[7] Constitution of the Republic of the Union of Myanmar, Art 357.
[8] Constitution of the Republic of Kazakhstan, Art 18.
[9] Constitution of the Socialist Republic of Vietnam, Art 11.
[10] Constitution of the Kingdom of Thailand B.E. 2560 (2017), Art 32.
[11] Constitution of the Democratic Socialist Republic of Sri Lanka of 1978, Art 14A.
[12] Constitutional Interpretation No 585 (15 December 2004) (Taiwan).
[13] Constitution of Cambodia, Arts 31 and 40.
[14] Constitution of the Republic of Singapore (2020 Rev. Ed. Sing.), Art 9(1).
[15] Constitution of the Republic of Indonesia 1945, Arts 28G(1), 28H(4) and 28J.
[16] W Prosser, 'Privacy' (1960) *California Law Review* 48, 3, 384.
[17] Personal Data Protection Law (Indonesia), Art 56.
[18] Personal Data Protection Act 2012 (Singapore), s 4(4)b.
[19] Personal Data Protection Ordinance (Hong Kong), s 33.

For practical purposes, many Asian states have sorted personal data into categories to facilitate regulation. Some jurisdictions divide personal data into two large categories, depending on the nature of the pieces of information involved. One category (involving data which are more closely related to an individual's privacy) will typically be subject to stricter regulations. For example, in Taiwan, the collection of 'specific personal data' is prohibited unless prescribed conditions are met. This category of 'specific personal data' includes medical records, medical treatment data, genetic information, sexuality, health examination, and criminal record.[20] These are considered more intimate types of personal information. On the other hand, the collection and processing of 'general personal data' will often be less stringently regulated. Thailand has a near identical classification of personal data to Taiwan in this regard.[21] Japan also has a similar system of binary classification, but instead of labelling categories as 'specific' and 'general', personal data is sorted into 'sensitive personal information' and 'non-sensitive personal information'. Kazakhstan accords heightened protection to an individual's health, religion, and biometric information. By contrast, the legislation in other states, notably Singapore, does not define 'sensitive personal data' or contain special categories of personal data to which more stringent regulations are applied.

The characterisation of data as 'personal' is not immutable but can be modified or even eliminated altogether by appropriate means. Through processes of anonymisation (converting personal data into a form which cannot be used to identify an individual), pseudonymisation (substituting parts of personal data with made-up values), and de-identification (removing certain parts of personal data through which an individual can be identified), information can cease to be 'personal' and become more readily transferrable and freely accessible. Asian jurisdictions typically allow for such processes to de-personalise data.

In many Asian jurisdictions, just as under GDPR, the right to privacy is not absolute. The right is subject to interference in certain circumstances as, for instance, when national security or criminal investigations are concerned. In evaluating whether an interference with the right to privacy is legitimate, Asian jurisdictions apply legal tests of varying standards of stringency. Some states, like Taiwan, allow a safe zone to public authorities for infringement of a citizen's right to privacy, to the extent that a government's conduct was aimed at fulfilling a statutory duty or obligation.[22] Another test that may be applied is that of proportionality. In other words, where a complaint of personal data infringement is made against a government agency, a court or other authority considering the case might ask itself:

1. whether the relevant agency had the power to conduct itself as it did;
2. whether the agency exercised any such power for a legitimate purpose;
3. whether the agency's conduct was no more than what was necessary to achieve the identified purpose; and
4. whether on balance the infringement of the individual's right to privacy was justified by the need to achieve the purpose.

[20] Personal Data Protection Act (Taiwan), Art 6.
[21] Personal Data Protection Act BE 2562 (Thailand), Ch A(c)(iv).
[22] Art 6, Personal Data Protection Act (Taiwan), Art 6.

As for remedies, Asian courts have readily granted relief (notably monetary compensation, injunctions and declarations) to prevent the continued breach of an individual's right to privacy.[23] But the bases of data privacy infringement claims vary from state to state. Some jurisdictions (such as Singapore) classify an action for breach of personal privacy as a statutory tort (for example, under Singapore's Personal Data Protection Act).[24] Complexity can arise when a controller or processor in state B infringes the privacy of a data subject in state A. In such situation, there is no one-size-fits-all solution among different Asian states. Some civil law countries (such as Indonesia and Thailand) apply the principle of *actor sequitur forum rei* with the result that a complaint should be lodged in the court of the place where the defendant is domiciled. Other states, such as Japan,[25] take multiple factors into account, including the defendant's domicile, the place of performance of a relevant obligation, the defendant's place of business, and the place of the wrong, before reaching a conclusion on a court's jurisdiction to hear an infringement complaint.

Nevertheless, a significant obstacle to effective data protection is the lack of a clearly applicable law in the situation where a data breach occurs in cyberspace and has potential ramifications in multiple states. To date, most jurisdictions have yet to enact local legislation to address the issue of applicable law in cases of multinational data breach. Therefore, the existing data protection legislation of many Asian states remain silent as to the issue of the law applicable and there may be overlapping assertions of jurisdiction.

IV. Summary of GDPR

Having identified GDPR as a backbone of data protection regulation in many Asian jurisdictions, this section summarises the principles underlying GDPR for readers who are not familiar with its terms.

GDPR comprises a Preamble and nine Chapters. The Preamble consists of 173 paragraphs and takes up nearly half of GDPR. In effect, the 173 paragraphs set out general principles of data privacy and protection which serve as a commentary on the interpretation and implementation of the rights and obligations contained in GDPR's nine chapters. This section will focus on the Preamble, summarising its key principles. It will then more briefly outline the contents of GDPR's nine chapters.

A. Preamble

From the outset, paragraph (1) signals that GDPR is about 'the protection of natural persons in relation to the processing of personal data'.[26] That is because 'everyone has the right to

[23] See, eg, Personal Data Protection Act 2012 (Singapore), s 48O.

[24] ibid, s 32.

[25] Code of Civil Procedure (Japan), Arts 3–9.

[26] Para (14) stresses that GDPR does not cover the processing of data belonging to legal persons, such as companies or business associations. But it appears that an individual may appoint an non-governmental organisation to act on his or her behalf when seeking a remedy for breach of the GDPR (see para (142)). On the special protection needed for the personal data of children, see para (38). On the special measures and care needed in handling

the protection of personal data concerning him or her'.[27] Such entitlement is 'a fundamental right' as affirmed by Article 8(1) of the Charter of Fundamental Rights of the European Union and Article 16(1) of the Treaty on the Functioning of the European Union (TFEU). A consequence of this recognition is (as acknowledged in paragraph (2)) any principles relating to data privacy and protection must respect the rights and freedoms of natural persons regardless of nationality or residence. The aspiration is that the enactment of these principles will

> contribute to the accomplishment of an area of freedom, security and justice and of an economic union, to economic and social progress, to the strengthening and the convergence of the economies within the internal market, and to the well-being of natural persons.

However, the right to have one's personal data protected is not absolute. This emerges from paragraph (4) which recognises that the right 'must be considered in relation to its function in society and be balanced against other fundamental rights, in accordance with the principle of proportionality'. There are trade-offs to consider when GDPR is being applied.

GDPR requires in paragraph (10) that, within the EU, there be a '[c]onsistent and homogenous application' of rules, not just to provide a high level of protection for data subjects, but also to remove 'obstacles to flows of personal data' among states. This paragraph thus picks up the theme of proportionality, suggesting that there is a balance to be struck between safeguarding a person's data on the one hand and ensuring access to information on the other. Nonetheless, within 'several sector-specific laws in areas that need more specific provisions', states are allowed a 'margin of manoeuvre' to enact their own laws as to the handling of 'sensitive data'. GDPR accordingly confers each state with some latitude (for example) on the extent to which an individual's privacy may be infringed in the interests of national security and the prevention of criminal activity.[28]

information which is 'particularly sensitive in relation to fundamental rights and freedoms', see paras (51) to (54). Examples are personal data on race or ethnic origin (para 51) or details relating to employment, social welfare, and health (especially where communicable diseases are concerned) (paras (52) to (54)). On employment and collective agreements, see also para (155).

[27] For examples of the width of what is comprised by the expression 'personal data', see paras 34 (genetic data) and 35 (health data).

[28] See further para (16) which expressly states that GDPR does not apply to 'activities concerning national security' and para (19) which excludes the 'processing of personal data by competent authorities for the purposes of the prevention, investigation, detection or prosecution of criminal offences or the execution of criminal penalties, including the safeguarding against and the prevention of threats to public security and the free movement of such data'. Note also para (20) dealing with data processing by courts and other judicial authorities. The gist of it is that GDPR applies to their activities, so that judges should be aware of their obligation under GDPR and should respond to complaints in their handling of personal data. Individual states may 'specify … operations and … procedures in relation to the processing of personal data by courts and other judicial authorities'. But any such laws 'should not cover the processing of personal data when courts are acting in their judicial capacity, in order to safeguard the independence of the judiciary', enhance awareness among members of the judiciary of their obligations under this Regulation and handle complaints in relation to such data processing operations. Contrast the position in relation to '[p]ublic authorities to which personal data are disclosed in accordance with a legal obligation for the exercise of their official missions'. By para (31), such public authorities 'should not be regarded as recipients if they receive personal data which are necessary to carry out a particular inquiry in the general interest, in accordance with … law'. However, when requesting information, public authorities should always act in writing and provide reasons for their request. Their request 'should not concern the entirety of a filing system or lead to the interconnection of filing systems' and, in any event, processing of personal data by them 'should comply with the applicable data-protection rules according to the purposes of the processing'. In other words, although not treated as personal data recipients, public authorities are not entitled to be cavalier in the way that they handle information disclosed to them by individuals. They would still be under a duty to safeguard such information from wrongful disclosure or use.

Paragraph (13) introduces a different theme. It refers to the 'consistent monitoring of the processing of personal data' and 'equivalent sanctions in all Member States as well as effective cooperation between the supervisory authorities of different Member States'. This therefore provides that, to facilitate accountability in the handling of personal data, business enterprises should keep proper records of the data that they process.[29] Their records and record-keeping can then be monitored. Paragraph (15) adds that the record-keeping obligation must be technology neutral. The obligation arises regardless of whether an enterprise processes data by hand or automation.[30]

Paragraphs (22) to (25) have conflict of law implications. Paragraph (22) stipulates that GDPR should apply to any personal data processing by an establishment in the EU.[31] This is regardless of (1) whether such processing takes place in the EU or elsewhere and (2) whether the processing is done by a branch of the establishment or by a subsidiary with separate legal personality from the establishment. Paragraph (23) deals with the situation where the personal data of a data subject within the EU is processed outside the EU by a non-EU establishment.[32] In such case, GDPR will apply to processing activities 'related to offering goods or services to such data subjects irrespective of whether connected to a payment'. In determining whether the criterion for the application of GDPR has been met, one needs to consider the data processor's intentions, examining whether the establishment 'envisages offering services to data subjects in one or more Member States in the Union'. Paragraph (23) observes that the mere fact that an establishment's website may be accessed in the EU will not be enough to meet the criterion. Paragraph (24) adds that GDPR will also apply where the non-EU establishment is processing data for the purpose of 'monitoring … the behaviour of [EU] data subjects in so far as their behaviour takes place within the [EU]'. The test is whether the relevant EU data subjects are being 'tracked on the internet', including through 'profiling … particularly … to take decisions concerning her or him or for analysing or predicting her or his personal preferences, behaviours and attitudes'.[33]

[29] However, para (13) expressly exempts MSMEs (micro-, small and medium enterprises) having fewer than 250 employees from record-keeping obligations. Analogous exceptions from GDPR are found in para (18) (excluding 'the processing of personal data by a natural person in the course of a purely personal or household activity … with no connection to a professional or commercial activity').

[30] For more on record-keeping, see the discussion on para (82) below.

[31] In determining a data controller's main establishment, reference might be made to para (36). In short, one needs to pinpoint the place of 'effective and real exercise of management activities determining the main decisions as to the purposes and means of processing'. This will not necessarily be the place where data processing is carried out. The presence and use of technical means and technologies for processing personal data or processing activities do not, in themselves, constitute a main establishment and are therefore not determining criteria for a main establishment. Where relevant activities are carried out by several entities, the main establishment of the controlling entity should be regarded as the main establishment of the group, "except where the purposes and means of processing are determined by another undertaking".

[32] Para (80) stipulates that a non-EU establishment which processes the data of EU subjects must designate a representative (within the EU?) to serve as a point of contact with relevant EU public authorities. The representative In the case of breaches by the non-EU establishment, enforcement proceedings will be brought against the representative.

[33] On profiling, see also para (30): "Natural persons may be associated with online identifiers provided by their devices, applications, tools and protocols, such as internet protocol addresses, cookie identifiers or other identifiers such as radio frequency identification tags. This may leave traces which, … when combined with unique identifiers and other information received by the servers, may be used to create profiles of the natural persons and identify them." But this should be read as subject to para (70) (individual's right to object to being profiled, for the purpose of direct marketing). See further para (71) (discussed below).

Paragraph (25) concerns the application of GDPR to a non-EU establishment in a Member State's diplomatic mission or consulate.

Paragraphs (26), (28) and (29) deal with pseudonymisation and similar processes. GDPR will not apply where it is not possible to identify a person directly or indirectly from a data set because of pseudonymisation or similar processes.[34] This principle thus facilitates statistical research. Paragraph (27) adds that GDPR does not apply to the personal information of deceased persons.

Personal data may only be processed by a data controller or processor with the consent of the data subject or pursuant to some law (paragraph 40). Consent is defined in paragraph (32). It must be a 'freely given, specific, informed and unambiguous indication of the data subject's agreement to the processing of personal data relating to him or her'.[35] This covers consent conveyed by electronic means. A data subject should not be made to indicate consent by silence, pre-ticked boxes or inactivity. If a request for information is made for several purposes, consent should be given for each purpose. Moreover, individuals should be entitled to limit their consent to what is compatible with the purposes of a given research project (paragraph (33)).

When data is to be processed by consent, the principle of transparency requires that 'any information and communication relating to the processing of those personal data be easily accessible and easy to understand, and that clear and plain language be used' (paragraph 41).[36] Details that should be drawn to a data subject's subjection include (1) the data controller's identity, (2) the purposes of the data processing, and (3) 'further information to ensure fair and transparent processing'. The latter category might comprise information on the risks, rules and safeguards involved and the data subject's rights. Any personal data obtained should be 'limited to what is necessary for the purposes for which they are processed'. Thus, the period for which personal data is to be stored must be no more than what is necessary for the relevant processes. There must be means to enable correction of inaccuracies or errors in the personal information obtained. Further, suitable measures must be taken for the security and confidentiality of the personal data disclosed. Under paragraph (42), a data controller should be able to show that an individual has consented to the processing of his or her data. Standard form consents drafted by a controller should be 'in an intelligible and easily accessible form, using clear and plain language and it should not contain unfair terms'. Individuals should know who the data controller is and the purposes for which the personal data supplied are to be used are intended. Paragraph 42 warns: 'Consent should not be regarded as freely given if the data subject … is unable to refuse or withdraw consent without detriment'.

In contrast, where data is to be processed by a government authority in the public interest, it must be under a law authorising the operation and identifying its purpose (paragraph (45)). Further, the law

> could specify … general conditions … governing the … data processing, [such as] specifications for determining the controller, the type of personal data … subject to the processing, the data

[34] See also para (57) on obtaining further information to enable an anonymised data subject to be identified.

[35] However, in consequence of para (43), consent will not be treated as freely given (and cannot be taken as the basis for processing of personal data) where there is 'a clear imbalance between the data subject and the controller, in particular where the controller is a public authority'.

[36] On transparency, see further para (58).

> subjects concerned, the entities to which the personal data may be disclosed, the purpose limitations, the storage period and other measures.

In this regard, processing will be lawful and necessary when done to protect the life of the data subject or another natural person (paragraph (46)).

Paragraphs (46) to (50) provide instances of data processing that may be regarded as legitimate. This involves a balancing of the legitimate interests of a data controller with those of a data subject. For instance, a controller will have a legitimate interest to process data to obviate fraud (paragraph (47)). Interestingly, paragraph (47) suggests that processing for direct marketing purposes 'may' be a legitimate interest. Under paragraph (48), data controllers belonging to a group 'may' have a legitimate interest in sharing data with other members of the group for administrative reasons. By paragraph (49), data processing in the interests of network and information security also constitute a legitimate interest, if done proportionately. As for processing beyond the purposes for which consent has been given or beyond the authority conferred by law, that will only be possible 'where the processing is compatible with the purposes for which the personal data were initially collected' (paragraph (50)). Examples would be the archiving of data, the conducting of research, or the compilation of statistics. Another instance would be the disclosure of information to the police or other competent authority in criminal cases. But such transmission can be constrained by 'legal, professional or other binding obligation of secrecy'.

A corollary to transparency in data collection is the need for the implementation of a system whereby a data subject can readily obtain, correct or delete information about him or her. The requisites of such a system are covered by paragraphs (59) to (69). For instance, information need not be provided

> where the data subject already possesses the information, where the recording or disclosure of the personal data is expressly laid down by law, or where the provision of information to the data subject proves to be impossible or would involve a disproportionate effort (paragraph (62)).

Importantly, a data subject has the 'right to be forgotten' (that is, the right to have personal information deleted) when data is 'no longer necessary in relation to the purposes for which they [were] collected or otherwise processed', when consent for collection is withdrawn, or where there has been non-compliance with law (paragraph (65)).

Given rapid developments in the use of artificial intelligence (AI) in data processing, paragraph (71) should be noted. It confirms an individual's right 'not to be subject to a decision … evaluating personal aspects relating to him or her … based solely on automated processing and which produces legal effects concerning him or her'. Examples are the denial of an online credit or employment application without human involvement. But a balancing exercise is involved. If, for instance, a question of fraud or tax-evasion is involved, profiling may be permissible, subject to adequate protections.

Paragraph (82) returns to the theme of record-keeping. Data controllers and processors must keep records of their processing and cooperate with government authorities supervising their activities, including providing access to their records. Data controllers and processors need to consider the risks involved in their processing activities and take appropriate security measures (including encryption) to safeguard such processes and any information collected (paragraph (83). Measures include 'taking into account the state of the art and the costs of implementation in relation to the risks and the nature of the personal data to be protected'. Where the risks are high and the consequences of breaches of an individual's privacy are great, a 'data protection impact assessment' (DPIA) ought to be undertaken (paragraph (84)). If a DPIA concludes that the establishment's data processing entails 'a high risk which the controller cannot mitigate by appropriate measures in terms of available technology and costs of implementation',[37] reference should be made to the relevant supervisory authority on ways of mitigating the effects of data breaches.[38] In the event of a significant data breach, paragraph (85) states that 'the controller should notify … the supervisory authority without undue delay and, where feasible, not later than 72 hours after having become aware of it'. In addition, a data subject whose data has been compromised, should be informed of the breach as soon as possible, together with 'recommendations … to mitigate potential adverse effects' (paragraph (86)).

Paragraph (101) affirms the importance of '[f]lows of personal data to and from countries outside the [EU] and international organisations … [to] the expansion of international trade and international cooperation'. But flows should not compromise the data protection standards in GDPR, especially when personal data is passed to a non-EU state and from there to another state. Thus, without prejudice to treaties or conventions (see paragraph (102)), 'transfers to third countries and international organisations may only be carried out in full compliance with [GDPR]'. For this purpose, the European Commission is empowered to determine for all EU members whether a non-EU state has implemented 'an adequate level of data protection'. This is intended to provide certainty and uniformity within the EU as regards non-EU countries.

Paragraph (104) sets out the factors that the European Commission should take into account when making a determination. Factors include: (1) the 'fundamental values on which the [EU] is founded'; (2) respect for the rule of law in the non-EU state; (3) 'access to justice as well as international human rights norms and standards'; and (4) the non-EU state's 'general and sectoral law, including legislation concerning public security, defence and national security as well as public order and criminal law'. Paragraph 104 adds that the non-EU state should: (1) 'offer guarantees ensuring an adequate level of protection essentially equivalent to that ensured within the [EU]'; (2) 'ensure effective independent data protection supervision'; (3) 'provide for cooperation mechanisms with the Member States' data protection authorities'; and (4) provide data subjects with 'effective and enforceable rights and effective administrative and judicial redress'. The Commission is supposed to review its determinations regularly (paragraph (106)) and can decide that a non-EU state no longer meets the GDPR standard (paragraph (107).

Where a non-EU state does not meet GDPR standards, data controllers and data processors should 'compensate for the lack of data protection … by way of appropriate safeguards for the data subject' (paragraph (108)). Measures would include 'binding corporate rules, standard data protection clauses adopted by the Commission, standard data protection clauses adopted by a supervisory authority, or contractual clauses authorised by a supervisory authority'. In limited situations (such as legal necessity[39]), it should also be possible for data to be transferred to non-EU states where a data subject expressly consents (paragraph (111)). On the extraterritorial effect of legislation in non-EU states purporting

[37] Eg, this may be the situation where there is large scale data processing done on a regional, national or international level (see para (91)).
[38] On consultation with the supervisory authority generally, see further paras (92) to (96).
[39] For examples of legal necessity, see paras (112) and (113).

to affect data subjects within the EU, paragraph (115) provides that transfers of personal information should only be allowed where the requirements of GDPR are met. In this vein, paragraph (116) proposes the establishment of cross-border cooperation with data supervisory authorities outside the EU on a reciprocal basis.[40]

Paragraphs (119) to (123) deal with the independence, funding, resources, responsibilities and duties of supervisory authorities. However, paragraph (118) observes that supervisory authorities, no matter how independent, should be subject to judicial review. As an additional safeguard, a European Data Protection Board (EDPB) is to be set up to ensure GDPR's consistent application in the EU. Details of the EDPB are set out in paragraphs (140) and (141).

Paragraph (143) concerns applications by natural or legal persons to annul the EDPB's decisions on remedies (including damages[41] and penalties[42]) against actions by supervisory authorities. Paragraph (145) deals with proceedings against data controllers or processors. Except where the complaint is against a supervising authority, claimants may choose between commencing proceedings in the state where a controller or processor has an establishment or in the place where the data subject resides. General rules on jurisdiction within the EU are subject to the latter special jurisdictional rule (paragraph (147)). There may also be fines and criminal sanctions for infringements of GDPR (paragraph (148)).

Paragraph (153) highlights the need to balance the right to privacy against the right to freedom of expression. It states: 'Member States law should reconcile the rules governing freedom of expression and information, including journalistic, academic, artistic and or literary expression with the right to the protection of personal data pursuant to this Regulation'. It is left to Member States to decide how the balance between the competing rights is to be drawn. Where the resulting domestic laws are different, then 'the law of the Member State to which the controller is subject should apply'.

Paragraph (154) concerns personal information in official documents to which members of the public are granted access in the public interest. Paragraph (156) to (163) impose safeguards on data processing for archiving, historical, scientific and statistical purposes. Paragraph (165) preserves the constitutional rights of churches and religious associations.

Paragraphs (166) to (170) confer power on the Commission and the EU to implement specified measures in connection with data protection and privacy.

B. Chapters

The main body of GDPR is divided into 11 chapters, entitled: (I) General Provisions; (II) Principles; (III) Rights of Data Subject; (IV) Controller and Processor; (V) Transfers of Personal Data to Third Countries or International Organisations; (VI) Independent

[40] See also paras (124) to (138) on mechanisms of cooperation among supervisory authorities, where data protection in more than one state is involved, including on instituting a 'one-stop-shop mechanism' (especially paras (127) and (128)) and ensuring consistency (paras (135) and (136)). On a one-stop-shop, see further para (141): 'Every data subject should have the right to lodge a complaint with a single supervisory authority … in the Member State of his or her habitual residence, and the right to an effective judicial remedy … if the data subject considers that his or her rights under this Regulation are infringed'.

[41] See para (146).

[42] See para (148).

Supervisory Authorities; (VII) Cooperation and Consistency; (VIII) Remedies, Liability and Penalties; (IX) Provisions Relating to Specific Processing Situations; (X) Delegated Acts and Implementing Acts; and (XI) Final Provisions.

i. Chapter I (General Provisions)

Article 1 sets out the two principal norms which GDPR seeks to balance: (1) 'the rights and freedoms of natural persons and in particular their right to the protection of personal data' and (2) 'the free movement of personal data'. Article II affirms that GDPR is technology neutral and sets out what is excluded from the purview of GDPR. In that respect, data processing by a natural person as part of 'a purely personal or household activity' falls outside the scope of GDPR. Article 3, on the other hand, provides for GDPR's extraterritorial effect. GDPR will apply to data processing by a controller or processor within the EU, regardless of where the processing takes place. Conversely, it also applies to the processing of data belonging to data subjects in the EU, regardless of where a controller or processor is situated. For the purposes of Article 3, 'processing' involves

> (a) the offering of goods or services, irrespective of whether a payment of the data subject is required, to such data subjects in the Union; or (b) the monitoring of their behaviour as far as their behaviour takes place within the Union.

Article 4 defines terms (such as 'personal data', 'processing', 'controller', 'consent', and 'supervisory authority') used throughout GDPR.

ii. Chapter II (Principles)

The chapter sets out the key principles underlying data processing. Of primary interest is Article 5(1) which constrains the extent to which personal data may be processed, used and stored, to no more than what is necessary for a legally valid purpose:

Personal data shall be:

a) processed lawfully, fairly and in a transparent manner in relation to the data subject ('lawfulness, fairness and transparency');
b) collected for specified, explicit and legitimate purposes and not further processed in a manner that is incompatible with those purposes; further processing for archiving purposes in the public interest, scientific or historical research purposes or statistical purposes shall … not be considered to be incompatible with the initial purposes ('purpose limitation');
c) adequate, relevant and limited to what is necessary in relation to the purposes for which they are processed ('data minimisation');
d) accurate and, where necessary, kept up to date; every reasonable step must be taken to ensure that personal data that are inaccurate, having regard to the purposes for which they are processed, are erased or rectified without delay ('accuracy');
e) kept in a form which permits identification of data subjects for no longer than is necessary for the purposes for which the personal data are processed; personal data may be stored for longer periods insofar as the personal data will be processed solely for archiving purposes in the public interest, scientific or historical research purposes

or statistical purposes … subject to implementation of the appropriate technical and organisational measures required by this Regulation in order to safeguard the rights and freedoms of the data subject ('storage limitation');

f) processed in a manner that ensures appropriate security of the personal data, including protection against unauthorised or unlawful processing and against accidental loss, destruction or damage, using appropriate technical or organisational measures ('integrity and confidentiality').

Article 6 specifies when data processing is lawful. Essentially, processing is lawful if it is done with the consent of a data subject, pursuant to a legal obligation or duty, or as a matter of necessity in the public interest. Article 7 enumerates the conditions for a valid and binding consent by a data subject. Article 8 deals with consent by children, while Articles 9 and 10 deal with the processing of special categories of data (information about an individual's race, ethnic origin, political views, religion, health, sex life, orientation, and criminal record). Article 11 is about processing in cases where it is not necessary to identify individuals.

iii. Chapter III (Rights of Data Subject)

Chapter III is divided into five sections. The first four sections deal with specific rights of a data subject. Section 1 focuses on the right to transparency. Section 2 details a subject's right to be informed about processing operations relating to him or her (whether the personal data being processed has been obtained from the subject or not) and to have access to the personal data collected. Section 3 deals with a subject's right to rectification of personal data, the right to have the same erased (that is, the right to be forgotten), and the right to restrict the processing of personal data. Article 20 refers to portability, that is, the right to receive personal data in a 'structured, commonly used and machine-readable format and have the right to transmit those data to another controller without hindrance'. Section 4 confers a right to object to decisions being taken by automated processing, including by profiling.[43]

Section 5 implicitly acknowledges that the rights in the previous four sections are not absolute. Article 23(1) authorises the EU or Member States to limit such rights by legislation. But this is only provided 'the essence of the fundamental rights and freedoms' is respected, and the restriction is 'a necessary and proportionate measure in a democratic society' for safeguarding:

a) national security;
b) defence;
c) public security;
d) the prevention, investigation, detection or prosecution of criminal offences or the execution of criminal penalties, including the safeguarding against and the prevention of threats to public security;
e) other important objectives of general public interest of the Union or of a Member State, in particular an important economic or financial interest of the Union or of a Member State, including monetary, budgetary and taxation matters, public health and social security;

[43] GDPR, Art 4 defines 'profiling' as 'any form of automated processing of personal data consisting of the use of personal data to evaluate certain personal aspects relating to a natural person, in particular to analyse or predict aspects concerning that natural person's performance at work, economic situation, health, personal preferences, interests, reliability, behaviour, location or movements'.

f) the protection of judicial independence and judicial proceedings;
g) the prevention, investigation, detection and prosecution of breaches of ethics for regulated professions;
h) a monitoring, inspection or regulatory function connected, even occasionally, to the exercise of official authority in the cases referred to in points (a) to (e) and (g);
i) the protection of the data subject or the rights and freedoms of others; and
j) the enforcement of civil law claims.

Additionally, Article 23(2) stipulates that any restrictions must identify:

a) the purposes of the processing or categories of processing;
b) the categories of personal data;
c) the scope of the restrictions introduced;
d) the safeguards to prevent abuse or unlawful access or transfer;
e) the specification of the controller or categories of controllers;
f) the storage periods and the applicable safeguards taking into account the nature, scope and purposes of the processing or categories of processing;
g) the risks to the rights and freedoms of data subjects; and
h) the right of data subjects to be informed about the restriction, unless that may be prejudicial to the purpose of the restriction.

iv. Chapter IV (Controller and Processor)

Chapter IV deals with the duties and responsibilities of data controllers and processors. It is in five sections. Section 1 is on general obligations of controllers and processors. Article 30 imposes a duty to keep proper records, while Article 31 requires them to cooperate with supervisory authorities. Section 2 imposes duties on controllers and processors to maintain the security of personal data, 'taking into account the state of art'. Such duties include the duty to inform supervisory authorities and data subjects of significant breaches of personal data.[44] Section 3 concerns the need to carry out DPIAs. Section 4 requires controllers and processors to appoint data protection officers. Section 5 encourages Member States, supervisory authorities, the European Commission, the EDPB, and others (1) to draw up codes of conduct on the application of GDPR, and (2) to set up institutions and means for data protection certification as a way of establishing compliance with GDPR.

v. Chapter V (Transfers of Data to Personal Data to Third Countries or International Organisations)

Chapter V enacts rules for assessing whether data may be transferred to non-EU states or international bodies. The general principle is in Article 44:

> Any transfer of personal data which are undergoing processing or are intended for processing after transfer to a third country or to an international organisation shall take place only if … the conditions laid down in this Chapter are complied with by the controller and processor, including for onward transfers of personal data from the third country or an international organisation

[44] See Arts 33 and 34.

> to another third country or to another international organisation. All provisions in this Chapter shall be applied in order to ensure that the level of protection of natural persons guaranteed by this Regulation is not undermined.

In effect, the transfer of personal data to a non-EU state will require evidence that the transferee state has in place personal data laws affording a similar standard of protection as GDPR. Such standard will be met where the European Commission has determined that the relevant non-EU state provides equivalent protection (Article 45), or if a controller or processor has put in place suitable safeguards and 'on condition that enforceable data subject rights and effective legal remedies for data subjects are available' (Article 46). Conversely, where GDPR does not authorise a transfer to a non-EU state, then by Article 48:

> [a]ny judgment of a court or tribunal and any decision of an administrative authority of a third country requiring a controller or processor to transfer or disclose personal data may only be recognised or enforceable in any manner if based on an international agreement … in force between the requesting third country and the Union or a Member State ….

Article 49 lists exceptions to the strict rules in Chapter V, such as where the fully informed consent of a data subject has been obtained for a transfer.

vi. Chapter VI (Independent Supervisory Authorities) and Chapter VII (Cooperation and Consistency)

Chapter VI has two sections. The first concerns the independent statis of supervisory authorities, while the second specifies the competence, tasks and powers of the same. Chapter VII builds on Chapter VI by detailing how supervisory authorities are to cooperate with, and provide mutual assistance to, each other. Article 63 of Chapter VI sketches out a mechanism to ensure consistency in the way that GDPR is applied among states. In this respect, the EDPB[45] is to resolve disputes between supervisory authorities on the proper course of conduct (Article 65).

vii. Chapter VIII (Remedies, Liability and Penalties)

Chapter VIII identifies different avenues of redress for breaches of GDPR. Avenues include: (1) the right of the data subject to complain to the supervisory authority of one's habitual residence, one's place of work or the place of breach (Article 77); (2) the right to seek a remedy in a state court against the decision of the supervisory authority of that state (Article 78); and (3) the right to seek a remedy against a controller or processor (other than a statutory authority exercising a public power) in the court of a state in which the controller or process has an establishment or in the court of the state where the data subject habitually resides (Article 79). When seeking a remedy, Article 80 sets out that a data subject may be represented by

> a not-for-profit body, organisation or association which has been properly constituted in accordance with the law of a Member State, has statutory objectives which are in the public interest, and is active in the field of the protection of data subjects' rights and freedoms with regard to the protection of their personal data.

[45] Established under Section 3 of Chapter VI.

Article 81 deals with conflicts of jurisdiction, in which complaints involving the same subject are brought before two forums. In such cases, proceedings may be stayed in favour of the court first seized.

Article 82 deals with damages for the breach of GDPR. It confers a right on a person to claim compensation from a controller or processor for damages suffered. Liability may be joint and several where more than one controller or processor is involved. But a controller or processor will be exempt from liability if it proves that it is 'not in any way responsible for the event giving rise to damage'. Article 83 regulates administrative fines, while Article 84 covers penalties for 'infringements which are not subject to administrative fines pursuant to Article 83'.

viii. Chapter IX (Provisions Relating to Specific Processing Situations)

The specific situations upon which Chapter IX focuses are: (1) data processing for journalistic, academic, artistic or literary expression (Article 85); (2) data processing for official documents to which the public will have access (Article 86); (3) data processing in connection with national identity numbers (Article 87); (4) data processing for archiving in the public interest or for scientific, historical, or statistical research (Article 88); (5) data processing in connection with employees (Article 89); and (6) data processing done by churches and religious bodies (Article 91). In addition, Article 90 enables states to regulate the extent to which authorities may obtain personal data from controllers and processors subject to professional obligations of secrecy or confidentiality.

ix. Chapter X (Delegated Acts and Implementing Acts) and Chapter XI (Final Provisions)

Under Chapter X, the European Commission may delegate its powers. It may also be assisted by a committee established under Article 93. Chapter XI concerns (1) GDPR's relationship with an earlier directive (which is repealed), (2) a previous directive on processing for public electronic communications services, and (3) existing agreements with non-EU states and international organisations. Article 97 provides that GDPR is to be reviewed by 25 May 2020 and thereafter periodically every four years. Lastly, Article 99 made GDPR applicable from 25 May 2018.

V. GDPR and the Future of Data Protection in Asia

This section will put forward three observations on the GDPR's potential to shape the development of data privacy and protection in Asia going forward.

First, Professor Anu Bradford has discerned three regulatory models of data protection regime in the world today.[46] They are the US market-driven model, the Chinese state-driven model and the EU rights-driven model. The US model is premised on freedom of access to

[46] Anu Bradford, *Digital Empires: The Global Battle to Regulate Technology* (Oxford University Press, 2023).

information and the belief that regulation should be kept to a minimum so as not to stifle technological innovation and development within the private sector. The difficulty with the US model has been that, although successful in fostering unprecedented innovation, it has enabled very few companies (Google, Amazon, Apple, Meta, and Microsoft) to become dominant in the digital market, leading to a situation which 'compromises individuals' abilities to exercise their agency and participate in democracy'.[47] On the other hand, the Chinese model is government-led and 'seeks to maximize [China's] technological dominance while maintaining social harmony and control over its citizen's communications'.[48] Thus, at least initially, China exercised a light regulatory touch on the growth of its domestic digital economy, while capitalising on their resultant innovations to enhance state control and the authority of the Chinese Communist Party over aspects of social life within China. More recently, according to Professor Bradford, 'the Chinese government is increasingly adopting the view that the largest tech companies have grown too powerful'[49] and is now seeking to curtail their activities, albeit all along maintaining 'the fundamental goal of the Chinese government: cementing the state's control of the digital economy as a defining feature of China's regulatory model'.[50] In contrast, the EU model stresses human rights, that is, 'a human-centric approach to regulating the digital economy where fundamental rights and the notion of a fair marketplace form the foundation of regulation'.[51] The problem with this model, as identified by Professor Bradford, is that it can lead to a stifling of business initiatives. She points out that there are '[f]ew successful tech giants emerging from Europe'[52] She observes that, paradoxically, the EU model as exemplified by GDPR may in fact constrain the fundamental human right of free expression by too strictly regulating what may or may not be said over the web.

Each model plainly has its strengths and weaknesses. Different states may be attracted to one or other model or some combination of them, depending on the nature of their government. Professor Bradford observes that, at one end of the spectrum, jurisdictions having liberal economies may incline towards the US or EU model, while at the opposite end autocratic states may prefer the Chinese model.[53] For the purposes of this book, the authors would simply suggest that the EU model can serve (and has served) as a ready-made, but broadly comprehensive template for Asian jurisdictions seeking to develop a modern data privacy and protection regime. By adopting GDPR in whole or part, there would be no need to re-invent the wheel.

It is true that, in terms of government, Asian countries run the gamut from the liberal to the autocratic. But it is submitted that GDPR caters for this. It has already been noted that GDPR explicitly exempts certain areas (for example, national and public security, defence, and criminal investigation) from its scope. It would be up to individual Asian jurisdictions adopting GDPR or something like it, to decide how to define derogations from the ambit of their legislation, such as what activities would constitute processing for the purposes of

[47] ibid, 8.
[48] ibid.
[49] ibid.
[50] ibid, 8–9.
[51] ibid, 9.
[52] ibid, 10.
[53] ibid, 21–23.

security, defence and the fight against criminal conduct. Indeed, as is evident from the China chapter in this book, the Chinese Personal Information Protection Law (PIPL) contains many rules which are similar (if not identical) to those of GDPR. For Asian jurisdictions generally, the question would not then be so much whether the right to the protection and privacy of one's personal data are fundamental human rights. Few Asian countries today would seriously argue with that cornerstone of GDPR. The real issue is how the balance is to be struck among competing interests, including privacy, free expression, freedom of access to information, maintenance of social harmony, public security, and technological innovation. This would be for each Asian state to determine.

Second, on the assumption that Asian jurisdictions adopt something like GDPR as their framework for data protection, how might the conflict of law questions raised in Section 1 of this chapter be answered? We suggest that the answers would be along the following lines:

Question (1): To what extent (if at all) will the data protection laws of state A apply to a data controller or processor in state B who has wrongly collected, processed, transferred or stored the personal information of a data subject residing in state A?

Answer: If a remedy is sought before the court in state A, the law of state A would apply and be enforceable against the data controller or processor wherever situated. If an action is brought in the court of state B, the domestic law of state B would apply. But it would not have been permissible to transfer the data of the subject in state A to state B or elsewhere, unless it could be shown that the controller or processor in state B was subject to similar duties and responsibilities as controllers and processors in state A. Therefore, even if the law of state B is applicable, the data subject from state A should receive similar protection from that law as that afforded by state A's legislation.

Question (2): Suppose that state B has a more rigorous regime for the protection of personal data than state A, can a data subject residing in state A invoke the protection of state B's laws against a data controller or processor in state B who has wrongly exploited that individual's personal information?

Answer: See the previous answer. Given the data of the subject in state A has been processed or collected by a controller or processor in state B, the subject should be able to enforce claims against the latter before the court of state B applying the more stringent law of state B.

Question (3): What means (if any) are available to a data protection supervisory authority in state A to enforce state A's data protection laws against a data controller or processor in state B who maintains no (or no substantial presence) in state A?

Answer: In the absence of a multilateral convention or bilateral treaty, the effective enforcement of data protection laws across borders will require cooperation between supervisory authorities in different jurisdictions. The supervisory authority in state A can block the activities of a foreign controller or processor in state A. But, even then, data which the foreign controller and processor has collected may be stored in offshore servers and be accessible both within and outside state A. While the court in state A can grant an injunction purporting to have worldwide effect against a processor or controller, the injunction is unlikely to be effective against a controller or processor with only minimal presence in state A.

Question (4): What means (if any) are available to a data protection supervisory authority in state B to ensure that state A does not make unreasonable demands of what should (or should not be done) by state B's data privacy regulatory regime for the protection of the personal information of data subjects residing in state A?

Answer: From the previous answer, cooperation among supervisory authorities will be needed if state A's data protection laws are to be enforceable extraterritorially. If unreasonable demands are made by state A's supervisory authority, other authorities may refuse to cooperate, thereby making it difficult for state A to enforce its demands outside state A.

Question (5): Is the consequence of the answers to the foregoing questions that, in practice, data controllers and processors will have to comply with the totality of data protection laws of all countries in which they operate or in which their services or products may be accessed?

Answer: Given differing standards of data protection among the states in which a controller or processor wishes to do business, it will make economic sense for the controller or processor to comply with the data protection regime of the state having the most demanding standard. This is essentially a consequence of what Professor Anu Bradford has dubbed the *de facto* 'Brussels Effect'.[54] She points out that, despite the US having a less stringent data protection standard than GDPR, the major US technology companies (Google, Meta, Microsoft and Apple) have adopted GDPR as their standard because they wish to do business in the EU. Economies of scale mean that 'market forces and companies' business incentives alone are often sufficient to convert the EU's data privacy regulation into a global regulation'.[55]

Question (6): What if the data protection laws of Asian jurisdictions are inconsistent with each other?

Answer: Given that Asian countries will wish to sell their products and services abroad (including within the EU), Professor Bradford's *de facto* 'Brussels Effect' posits that the data protection laws of different Asian countries will gradually converge to some form of the GDPR model.[56] Consequently, although data protection may be uneven and at varying stages among Asian countries today, in the future they will likely mirror GDPR to a greater or lesser extent, despite the absence of a multilateral convention or a system of bilateral treaties.

Question (7): With ever-increasing regulation, what has become of notions such as the 'freedom of the internet commons' and 'access to information' that the advent of the web was supposed to usher?

Answer: As discussed at the start of Section IV, it will be for each Asian country to balance values such as free access to information, privacy of an individual's personal information, free speech, national security, and social harmony. This will be the case even if a majority of countries adopt GDPR or something like it. The free flow of and access to information will not be the same in every jurisdiction.

[54] ibid, 324.
[55] ibid, 325.
[56] ibid, 325–26.

Third, we do not wish to convey the impression that GDPR or something like it will answer all cross-border issues that arise in relation to data protection and privacy in today's world. At best, GDPR offers a framework for data protection regulations in Asia. As always, the devil will be in the details. Much of GDPR leaves it to individual states to come up with implementing strategies and legislation. There will be innumerable issues to which GDPR can only point the way to answer. It will be for governments, supervisory authorities, and courts in Asia to work out precisely what the principled responses should be to specific difficulties.

This book invites stakeholders including government officials, legislators, judicial officers, academics, legal practitioners and data processing conglomerates, to consider what needs to improve existing data protection laws and regulations in their state, by comparison with regimes elsewhere, especially the EU. In this vein, the authors of the various chapters were invited not only to describe and evaluate the privacy and personal data regimes in their state, but also to reflect on how those regimes might be strengthened internally and harmonised with the rest of the world. It is hoped that this book can be of assistance in tackling future problems.

1

China

YUN ZHAO

I. Introduction

Thanks to modern information technologies, China has developed rapidly in the process of informatisation and digitalisation in the past few decades. However, science and technologies are a double-edged sword. Whilst people enjoy the convenience brought about by modern technologies, the large amounts of data generated in the informatisation and digitalisation process are subject to arbitrary collection, illegal acquisition and excessive use, a situation that calls for a legal regime to ensure proper protection. To date, as many as 32 countries around the world have explicitly made data and information rights (ie the right to personal data and the right to information) fundamental rights for citizens when formulating and amending their constitutions.[1]

China does not have a strong tradition of data and privacy protection. However, with data increasingly becoming a valuable asset, the country has stepped up efforts to devise a proper regime for the protection of personal data and privacy. This chapter examines the relevant rules regulating data protection and privacy in China.

It is necessary to elaborate on two concepts – 'personal information' and 'personal data' – before delving further into the legal regime in China. Most countries equate the two concepts, and hence this chapter also uses the terms 'personal information' and 'personal data' interchangeably. However, it should be noted that there are a number of differences between the two, with the former possibly involving analytical processing.

II. General Legal Framework of International Data Transfers and Data Protection

A. Constitutional Protection for Data and Data Transfer

Although the Chinese Constitution does not specifically address the issue of data protection, it does touch upon the concept of privacy, acknowledging that the personal dignity

[1] Joseph Lee Riccardi, 'The German Federal Data Protection Act of 1977: Protecting the Right to Privacy' (1983) *Boston College International and Comparative Law Review* 6, 243.

of citizens is protected by law and that insults, libel, false charges or frame-ups are prohibited.[2] Some scholars have argued that in the Chinese rights system 'privacy is still a strange concept, and the right to privacy is not part of the right to personhood'.[3]

The Chinese Constitution also protects residences from trespass,[4] and further provides that

> no organizations or individuals may, for whatever reason, infringe upon citizens' freedom and privacy of correspondence, except in cases where to meet the needs of state security or of criminal investigation, public security or procuratorial entities are permitted to censor correspondence in accordance with the procedures prescribed by law.[5]

B. Statutory Frameworks for Data Transfer and Protection

With the Chinese Constitution providing a constitutional basis, China has further developed rules and institutional safeguards to ensure the realisation of data transfer and protection. At present, there are three foundational statutory frameworks for data and cybersecurity governance, ie the Cyber Security Law (CSL), the Personal Information Protection Law (PIPL) and the Data Security Law (DSL). As the first positive response to China's value choices for relatively strict localised data storage, the CSL was enacted on 7 November 2016 with the goal of strengthening data protection, data localisation and cybersecurity for the sake of national security. The law introduced a requirement for a security assessment for any data transfer out of China for commercial purposes. The country's preference for a relatively strict localised data storage regime seems to be in response to increasingly stringent national security considerations.[6]

The PIPL took effect on 1 November 2021, bringing with it many provisions of the European Union (EU) General Data Protection Regulation (GDPR). The new law prohibits private companies from misusing personal data, and for the first time offers complete protection for personal data in China. The PIPL clearly stipulates the requirements and conditions for the cross-border provision of personal information. It further subtly provides for the necessary extraterritorial application of the legislation to fully protect personal information rights and interests within China. Consequently, the PIPL is applicable to the handling within China of personal information processed outside China, and requires processors of personal information outside China to establish a special agency or appoint a representative in charge of personal information protection-related matters in China.

The DSL was enacted on 10 June 2021 and took effect on 1 September 2021. It does not provide detailed rules on the cross-border flow of data, but cites corresponding provisions of the CSL specifying that the State Council and State Department of Network Information

[2] The Constitution of the People's Republic of China ('PRC Constitution'), Art 38. The current Constitution of China, the PRC's fourth constitution, was adopted by the Fifth National People's Congress on 4 December 1982, and subsequently underwent five amendments: in 1988, 1993, 1999, 2004 and 2018.

[3] Paul de Hert and Vagelis Papakonstantinou, 'The Data Protection Regime in China' (2015) *Depth Analysis Brussels Privacy Hub Working Paper* 1(4).

[4] The PRC Constitution, Art 39.

[5] ibid, Art 40.

[6] CSL, Art 37.

shall formulate specific rules.[7] This comprehensive data legislation stipulates that the state has an obligation to protect the data-related rights and interests of individuals and organisations and that the public security and state security organs shall, in accordance with relevant state regulations and subject to strict approval procedures, retrieve data for the purpose of maintaining national security or investigating crimes in accordance with the law.

i. Data Protection Frameworks

a. Influence of International Data Protection Frameworks

With the introduction of the three aforementioned foundational frameworks, China has substantially narrowed the gap between national frameworks and international benchmarks. For example, the PIPL is very similar to the GDPR and other privacy agreements and laws in Europe and Asia. The PIPL requires companies handling personal data to conduct regular self-audits to assess their information security risks and implement corresponding policies and safeguards. The Information Security Technology – Guidance for Personal Information Security Impact Assessment[8] provides detailed specifications for multinational companies conducting data-processing operations in China and states that they must reconfigure their information technology systems to comply with the country's strict personal information security impact assessment.

b. Specific Provisions for Particular Sectors

China's data protection framework has long been piecemeal in nature, with numerous industry-specific legal instruments and, to a lesser extent, general laws. For example, the Chinese Ministry of Industry and Information Technology (MIIT) issued the Regulations on the Protection of Personal Information of Telecom and Internet Users[9] in 2013 in response to the need to implement the National People's Congress Standing Committee (NPCSC) Decision on Strengthening the Protection of Internet Information.[10] The personal information to which the Regulations apply is information collected from users by telecommunications service providers and Internet information service providers in the course of providing services and information from which users can be identified. Because the Regulations are by nature administrative rules, they set out only limited penalties and relatively low fines of a maximum of RMB100,000.[11] Such weak penalties are not conducive to punishing and preventing violations of users' personal information.

[7] DSL, Art 31.

[8] Standard Np.: GB/T 39335-2020, issued by the National Standardisation Management Commission on 19 November 2020.

[9] Adopted at the second Ministerial Meeting of the MIIT of the PRC on 28 June 2013 and promulgated by Order No. 24 of the MIIT on 16 July 2013, effective as of 1 September 2013.

[10] Adopted at the 30th Meeting of the NPCSC on 28 December 2012.

[11] Regulations on the Protection of Personal Information of Telecom and Internet Users, Arts 22–23. Penalties include warnings and fines of up to RMB100,000. China's Administrative Penalties Law stipulates only that the limits within which departmental regulations may set fines and penalties shall be set by the State Council, whilst the 2021 Notice on Further Implementation of the Law of the PRC on Administrative Penalties stipulates that where laws and administrative regulations have not yet been enacted and where fines are first set by departmental regulations in accordance with the law owing to urgent administrative needs, the maximum amount of fines

Other specific provisions pertain primarily to the private sector, such as the banking and legal sectors. For example, the People's Bank of China (PBC) issued the Implementing Measures for the Protection of the Rights and Interests of Financial Consumers.[12] This document, whilst incorporating the requirements of existing legal instruments on personal data protection, requires financial institutions to handle (including collecting, storing, using, processing, transmitting, providing and disclosing) consumer financial information in accordance with the principles of legality, propriety and necessity, and in strict accordance with the purposes and scope authorised by the user, and not to refuse to provide financial products or services simply owing to a financial consumer's refusal to provide non-essential information.[13] It also imposes strict conditions on financial institutions in relation to the safekeeping of consumer financial information, including implementing a system of remedial measures for information security incidents, as well as a reporting mechanism.[14]

In addition to the protection of user data in the financial sector, China also has specific provisions pertaining to the protection of other types of data, including health data, automotive data and children's data. In the health sector, the three major provisions are the Measures for the Management of Population Health Information (for trial implementation), the Regulations on Human Genetic Resources Management, and the Specifications for the Application and Management of Electronic Medical Records (for trial implementation). The State Internet Information Office (SIIO), the Development and Reform Commission, the MIIT, the Ministry of Public Security and the Ministry of Transport jointly issued the Certain Provisions on Automotive Data Security Management (for trial implementation) in 2021, and the SIIO enacted the Regulations on the Online Protection of Children's Personal Information in 2019.

c. Distinction and Interface between Data Protection and Privacy

In China, data protection and privacy are different but closely connected concepts. Data protection refers to the means taken to safeguard the security and confidentiality of personal data. In contrast, privacy refers to the rights of an individual to keep his or her personal information and activities secret.

The main legal framework for data protection in China is the CSL, which requires companies to implement measures to protect the security and confidentiality of personal data. The PIPL also has specific measures pertaining to the protection of personal information.

The Chinese Constitution and other laws and regulations safeguard privacy, including the General Principles of Civil Law and Criminal Law. The scope of privacy protection in China extends beyond data protection to include the protection of personal reputation and the confidentiality of communications.

set shall not exceed RMB100,000. The maximum amount of fines set by laws and administrative regulations for similar violations that involve the life, health or safety of citizens, including financial safety, and have harmful consequences shall not exceed RMB200,000. Although the penalty limit has increased, compared with the RMB30,000 limit in 1996, the Notice still emphasises that departmental regulations should set fines that adhere to the over-penalty equivalent.

[12] Adopted at the PBC's 6th meeting on 1 September 2020, taking effect from 1 November 2020.

[13] Implementing Measures for the Protection of the Rights and Interests of Financial Consumers, Arts 28–29.

[14] ibid, Art 34.

Data protection and privacy overlap in China because the protection of personal data is a component of the more extensive right to privacy. Privacy comprises a wider variety of rights and safeguards than does data protection, which focuses on the security and confidentiality of personal data.

d. Distinction between Data Users, Data Subjects, Data Processors and Data Subcontractors

Data users are persons or entities that acquire and use personal information, whereas data subjects are the persons whose personal information is collected and used. There is no fixed definition of the term 'data subjects' in China. However, a data subject is generally taken to be a natural person who is identified or identifiable directly or indirectly through personal data, such as his or her name, ID card number, personal biometric data, address, communication records, property data, travel data, accommodation data, health and physiological data, and transaction data. Data processors are persons or organisations that handle personal data on behalf of data consumers. Data subcontractors are data processors that are contracted to process personal data by other data processors.

Under Chinese data protection laws, data users and data processors have separate duties and obligations. Data subjects have the right to be informed, the right to access their data, the right to refuse the processing of their data, the right to data portability and the right to erase their data. In other words, the laws transplant many of the rules of the GDPR. Data processors are responsible for processing personal data in line with data users' instructions and for applying relevant security measures. In the event of a data breach, the processors of personal information must take immediate remedial actions and notify both the personal information protection authorities and the individuals concerned. As an extension of data processors, data subcontractors have the same duties with respect to the processing of personal data.

Foreign processors of personal information are required to establish designated agencies or appoint representatives in mainland China if they fall within the scope of the PIPL. These agencies or representatives are then responsible for matters relating to the protection of personal information. Processors of personal information that need to transfer the information out of the mainland must first carry out a personal information protection impact assessment.

e. Distinction between Personal and Non-Personal Data

The definition of personal data is dynamic and needs to take specific scenarios into account. In China, personal data refers to any information that may be used – directly or indirectly – to identify an individual and does not include anonymised information. The core is the identifiability of information, recorded electronically or in another form, relating to identified or identifiable natural persons. Such information includes a person's name, identification number, address, phone number and biometric data. In contrast, non-personal data refers to information that cannot be utilised to identify an individual. It may refer to data that has been anonymised or aggregated to the point that it cannot be associated with a particular person.

Personal data has three constituent elements: first, a subject who is a natural person; second, a certain carrier record; and, third, the identification of a specific natural person. The first two elements are objective elements, and thus are not controversial, whilst the third involves a subjective determination of 'specific natural person' and 'identification'. The Beijing Internet Court held in both the Tencent reading infringement case (*Huang v Tencent Holdings*) and Jitterbug personal information infringement case (*Ling v ByteDance*), both heard in 2020, that identifiability

> includes the identification of individual identity and also the identification of individual characteristics; the identification of individual identity determines who the subject of the information is, and the identification of individual characteristics determines what kind of person the subject of information is, i.e. the information is able to reveal the natural traces or social traces of the individual and outline the image of the individual personality.[15]

Accordingly, it is presumed that if more than one piece of information can accurately describe the characteristics of an individual and form a precise portrait of that individual, then it may constitute personal data. The scope of personal data is thus broad, with implications for the handling of personal data in such scenarios as personalised recommendations and digital marketing.

Although there are uniform rules in China for judging whether individual characteristics belong to the scope of the identification of personal data, as well as rules on the degree of identification required, Chinese law does not explicitly define 'non-personal data' even though laws such as the DSL should by definition cover it. Hence, at present, personal data are subject to various legal protections and duties under China's data protection regulations, but non-personal data are not. In general, the acquisition and use of personal data are subject to more stringent criteria and restrictions than the collection and use of non-personal data.

f. Distinction between Anonymised, Pseudonymised and Encrypted Data

The term 'anonymised data' refers to information that has been processed in such a way that it cannot be associated with a particular person. Such processing may entail the removal of identifying information or the aggregation of data in such a manner that no person can be identified. The PIPL also states that anonymisation is a process by which personal information is processed in such a way that it cannot be associated with a specific natural person and cannot be recovered.[16] The purpose of anonymisation is to process personal data in such a way that a specific personal information subject cannot be identified from the processed information even in combination with other additional information.

The term 'pseudonymised data' refers to data in which identifying information has been replaced with a pseudonym (a fictitious name). Such replacement can serve to protect a person's privacy while enabling his or her data to be used for certain objectives. The term 'encrypted data' refers to information that has been altered via an encryption technique, rendering it unintelligible without the correct decryption key. Encryption can ensure secrecy and guarantee that only authorised users can access the encrypted data.

[15] Beijing Internet Court, People.cn, legal.people.com.cn/n1/2020/0731/c42510-31805538.html.
[16] PIPL, Art 73.

The CSL imposes a number of restrictions on the handling of personal data, but also provides exceptions to these restrictions, ie 'the processing cannot identify a specific individual and cannot be recovered'.[17] Although Chinese law does not explicitly use the term 'anonymisation', Article 42 of the CSL draws on foreign regulations on anonymisation. The accompanying Personal Information Security Code further clarifies the irrecoverable nature of anonymisation and stipulates that anonymised information is no longer personal data.[18]

g. Distinction between Domestic and Cross-Border/International Transfers

Whilst the Internet is global, regulation is local.[19] The core of data flow regulation is data localisation. For a country with a low level of technological development, underdeveloped industries and imminent security threats, a tight data flow strategy – data localisation – may be the best option.

Here, domestic data transfers refer to the transmission of personal information inside China, whereas cross-border/international data transfers refer to the exchange of personal information between China and other nations. Cross-border/international data transfers are generally subject to tougher standards and restrictions than domestic data transfers under Chinese data protection legislation because personal data transmitted outside China may be more susceptible to abuse or unauthorised access. Therefore, firms that wish to transmit personal data worldwide may be required to take extra measures to guarantee their security and protect people's privacy.

According to the Administrative Measures for the Security Assessment of Outbound Data Transfer, a cross-border/international transfer is a 'data processor's provision of important data and personal information collected and generated in their operations within the territory of China to overseas recipients'.[20] The following two circumstances are clearly defined as data exit:

1. The data worker transmits and stores overseas … data collected and generated during … operations in China;
2. The data collected and generated by the data worker, notwithstanding [whether they are] stored in China, [are] allowed to be [queried], retrieved, downloaded, or exported by overseas institutions, organizations, or individuals.[21]

The difference between domestic and cross-border transfers lies in the identity of the recipient and the destination of transmission.

h. Power of Privacy Regulator

Different from the independent privacy regulator in the EU, there is no single specific such authority or agency in China. Chinese legislation collectively refers to the National

[17] CSL, Art 42.

[18] Personal Information Security Code, Art 3.14.

[19] Bret Cohen, Britanie Hall and Charles Wood, 'Data Localization Laws and Their Impact on Privacy, Data Security and the Global Economy' (2017) *Antitrust* 32, 107.

[20] Administrative Measures for the Security Assessment of Outbound Data Transfer, Art 2.

[21] Guidelines of the Cyberspace Administration of China for Application of Data Exit Security Evaluation, 1st edn (31 August 2022), Section 1.

Internet Information Department and 'relevant departments of local people's governments at or above the county level' as 'departments that perform personal information protection duties'.[22] However, the main focus of the National Internet Information Department is national data security rather than personal information protection, and the country therefore lacks a dedicated personal information protection regulator to achieve all-round ex-ante supervision.

The regulators in charge of the protection of personal information include the Cyberspace Administration of China (CAC), relevant State Council departments and relevant local government departments at the county level or higher. The CAC is the primary privacy regulator in China and is responsible for implementing the country's data protection and cybersecurity legislation. The CAC can investigate and prosecute entities that violate such legislation, and has the authority to levy fines and other punishments.

Apart from the CAC, several other governmental bodies are responsible for data security and privacy. For instance, the MIIT oversees/regulates the gathering and use of personal data by certain types of businesses. The public security authorities also have significant enforcement power, particularly with respect to crimes relating to the infringement of privacy. They have sanctioning powers according to law, including powers to order violators to take corrective action, issue warnings, confiscate illegal gains, order a suspension or termination, impose fines, record violations on credit files, and take disciplinary action.[23]

III. Legal Bases, Mechanisms and Exceptions for Cross-Border Data Transfers and Data Protection

A. International Data Transfer

i. 'Adequacy Findings', Whitelists and Blacklists

'Adequacy' is the term used by the EU in describing countries, regions, sectors or international organisations that it believes can provide substantially the same level of data protection as exists within the EU. An 'adequacy finding' is a conclusion by a data protection authority or other regulatory body that a particular country or territory has appropriate data protection laws and policies to safeguard personal information.[24] This conclusion may permit the transfer of personal information to the country or jurisdiction in question without the need for any additional consent or compliance procedures.

A 'whitelist' is a list of countries or jurisdictions with adequate data protection laws and practices in place to which personal data may be transmitted without further permission or compliance steps. A 'blacklist' is a list of countries or jurisdictions with inadequate data protection laws and practices in place to which personal data cannot be transmitted without further permission or compliance steps.

[22] PIPL, Art 60.
[23] ibid, Arts 66–68.
[24] GDPR, Art 45(1).

The notion of adequacy findings is unique to the EU and European Economic Area. Other nations and jurisdictions, like China, have their own criteria and procedures for evaluating the sufficiency of the data protection laws and practices of other nations.

ii. Consent of Data Subjects as an Exception to the Existence of Privacy Safeguards Overseas

Data subjects' consent may exempt international data transfers from data protection requirements, whereas personal data may be sent without authorisation only to countries with adequate data protection laws and practices. However, data subjects may assume that the provision of informed consent for international data transmission affords them sufficient privacy protection even though the destination country or jurisdiction lacks data protection laws and processes. It is essential that consent be informed, voluntary and purpose-specific. Data subjects must also be allowed to revoke consent.

The existence of privacy safeguarding technologies such as privacy computing and anonymisation has been used as a panacea for data security in Chinese legislation. The Chinese Civil Code provides exceptions to the protection of personal data, including in situations where 'it is not possible to identify a specific person after processing and cannot be recovered'.[25]

iii. Contracts

Contracts safeguard personal data during international transfers. Data protection regulations demand that measures be taken to protect personal data when they are transmitted internationally. One such measure is a data protection contract with the data receiver. A data protection contract can outline the reasons for using personal data, the parties' rights and duties, and the data protection measures in place. It may also specify methods of dispute resolution and the controlling legislation.

Given China's highly localised data policy, there are extremely limited means by which outbound data transmission can take place, and a security assessment and authentication are required. On 30 June 2022, the SIIO released draft provisions on the Standard Contractual Clauses (SCC) on outbound personal information with the aim of implementing relevant provisions in the PIPL.[26] Given insufficiencies in the level of personal information protection or law enforcement protection in the jurisdiction where the overseas recipient is located, the personal information protection requirements established by Chinese laws and regulations are translated into legally binding and enforceable contractual terms agreed between the domestic personal information processor and the overseas recipient.

Contracts respect the free will of the parties concerned. However, the draft SCC provisions have an overriding effect, which means that other contracts entered into by the

[25] Chinese Civil Code, Art 1038. Further reference can be made to Art 3.14 of Information Security Technology – Personal Information Security Specifications.

[26] PIPL, Art 38(1)(3) specifies that the processor of personal information should take necessary measures to ensure that the activities of the foreign recipient in handling that information meet the personal information protection standards set forth in the PIPL.

personal information processor and overseas recipient in relation to the outbound personal information must not conflict with the standard contract.[27]

iv. Asia-Pacific Economic Cooperation Cross-Border Privacy Rules System

As the world's largest regional economic cooperation organisation, the Asia-Pacific Economic Cooperation (APEC) has made significant efforts to promote the economic development of e-commerce in the Asia-Pacific region and to achieve the free and secure flow of data across borders within the region. The APEC ratified the APEC Data Privacy Pathfinder Agreement in 2007 and established the Data Privacy Pathfinder in the same year. Through the efforts of the Data Privacy Pathfinder and unanimous agreement of the heads of the APEC's 21 economies, the Cross-Border Privacy Rules (CBPR) system was officially adopted in 2011 with the objective of implementing the APEC Privacy Framework's requirements for the cross-border flow of personal data between APEC economies. In addition to the CBPR system, APEC has also established the Cross-Border Privacy Enforcement Arrangement to support the establishment of a cross-border data regime. China is involved in the Privacy Pathfinder programme.

The APEC's voluntary CBPR system facilitates cross-border data transfers while safeguarding privacy. It provides important institutional safeguards for the establishment of mechanisms to maintain balanced machinery for the cross-border flow of personal data and secure privacy under the APEC Privacy Framework. The CBPR system helps enterprises to comply with the Privacy Framework while transferring personal data. The Framework's nine principles define people's private data rights and organisations' data collection and usage duties. Participants in the CBPR system must preserve personal data and convey them securely and transparently.

The CBPR system is managed centrally through the joint oversight of the Data Privacy Group, which establishes a three-tier certification system of economies, responsible agents and applicant organisations. It provides mandatory effectiveness safeguards through cooperation among the privacy enforcement authorities in the APEC economies. A voluntary, enforceable and accountability-based privacy protection certification mechanism endorsed by the APEC economies has been established, and data controllers within the APEC economies can join the certification system after meeting the certification requirements to demonstrate their level of data protection to their counterparts in offshore transactions. Under the CBPR system, APEC established the Privacy Recognition of Processors system in 2015 to help the processors of personal information to demonstrate their ability to effectively meet the obligations of personal information controllers with respect to the processing of personal information.

v. Privacy Certification Schemes, Trust Marks and International Privacy Seals

A privacy seal is a seal of trust or trust mark granted by a third-party provider for display on a company's website. Companies pay an annual fee to have an image of the third-party

[27] SCC, Art 2(2). The SCC has not yet come into force, and hence the contract terms and conditions signed between the two companies in data outbound activities remain valid; once the SCC takes effect, terms and conditions that conflict with the SCC will be replaced with relevant provisions of the SCC.

provider's seal pasted onto their homepage or privacy policy page. Users who click on the seal are automatically redirected to the website of the web assurance seal service to verify its validity, thereby providing them with visual assurance that the site in question meets certain privacy standards. The European Commission recognises the EU–US Privacy Shield Framework for the transfer of personal data from the EU to the US as providing adequate data protection. ISO/IEC 27001 is an information security management standard that specifies recommended practices for protecting personal data. Furthermore, TRUSTe, a privacy seal programme, verifies companies' privacy procedures.

China has chosen not to apply for a privacy seal programme, but rather to adopt personal data protection certification as one of the legal paths for cross-border data transfers, somewhat similar to the data protection certification provided by the EU.[28] Prior to the publication of the Technical Specification for Safe Certification of Cross-Border Processing Activities of Personal Information (Certification Specification), relevant Chinese laws and regulations did not contain specific requirements for the certification of personal information protection or the application of standard contracts. The Certification Specification, whilst constituting only a technical specification, serves as a detailed regulation from the perspective of specific operations, not simply as an ideological guidance document. On 14 August 2020, the Ministry of Commerce issued the Notice on the Issuance of the General Plan for Comprehensively Deepening the Pilot Program for the Innovative Development of Trade in Services, which requires the Central Internet Information Office, the MIIT, the Ministry of Commerce, and other departments to support and guide pilot programmes for carrying out security assessments of cross-border data flows and establish data protection capability certification and other data security management mechanisms. In August 2021, Beijing municipal government proposed carrying out research and pilot projects on the third-party certification of cross-border data protection capabilities in specific areas of the city and establishing a data protection capability certification mechanism.

At present, the Certification Specification mainly provides guidance from the perspective of the cross-border processors of personal information rather than from that of the certification body with respect to the basic norms of certification.

B. International Data Protection and Liability

i. Specific Requirements or Policies for Data Processing and Retention

The DSL provides that both data processing and data retention constitute data processing in a broad sense.[29] For the network operators that engage in network data collection, storage, use, processing, transmission, provision, and disclosure and make use of data processing security technology, the GB/T 41479-2022 Network Data Processing Security Requirements

[28] See GDPR, Art 46.2(f). EU Member States, supervisory authorities and the EU Data Protection Board are required to promote the establishment of data protection certification mechanisms for companies to demonstrate compliance with the GDPR requirements. For third-country data controllers or processors that are not subject to the GDPR, obtaining certification enables them to demonstrate that they have adopted appropriate safeguards, including the use of contracts or other binding legal instruments to demonstrate that they have implemented the required safeguards for the protection of personal data and the rights of data subjects.

[29] DSL, Art 3.

make detailed provisions, as well as outline management requirements. The document applies to network operators to regulate network data processing, as well as to regulatory departments and third-party assessment agencies to supervise, manage and evaluate it. Network operators identify the data involved in data processing, including personal information and other important data, create a data protection directory and update it in a timely manner. The Network Data Processing Security Requirements stipulate that a network operator shall, in accordance with both relevant national standards and contractual provisions and business operation needs, classify and grade the management of identified data.

When carrying out data processing, network operators should comply with data security protection obligations in accordance with contractual agreements, laws and regulations;[30] strengthen risk monitoring to identify data security flaws, vulnerabilities and other risks;[31] and take encryption, desensitisation, backup, access control, audit and other technical or other necessary measures to strengthen data security protection to protect data from leakage, theft, tampering, destruction and improper use. Furthermore, for the protection of important data and sensitive personal information, network operators should carry out regular risk assessments in their data processing activities and submit risk assessment reports to the relevant competent authorities.[32] Each risk assessment report should include the type and quantity of the important data handled, the data processing activities conducted, and the data security risks identified and countermeasures taken. Moreover, a data security management responsibility and evaluation assessment system should be established, a data security protection plan should be formulated, security risk assessment should be conducted, security incidents should be dealt with in a timely manner, and education and training should be organised.[33]

The DSL further provides special rules for the processing of government data, stipulating obligations in the following areas: the collection and use of government data, security management, commission, and disclosure.[34]

ii. Regulations on Legal Ownership of Data Necessary

Data subjects have data protection and privacy rights in most jurisdictions. For example, they may have the right to access, delete or object to the use of their personal data. Data privacy and protection do not require ownership rights. Instead, data subjects are granted these rights independently of legal ownership.

Data are owned by the individual or data subject who produces and processes them entirely on his or her own without the involvement of other people. If more than one person is involved in the generation, collection, processing, transmission, modification or storage of data, each individual enjoys part of the rights and interests related to the data, or they jointly share ownership of the data in the case of difficulty quantifying the relevant data rights and interests.

[30] ibid, Art 8.
[31] ibid, Art 29.
[32] ibid, Art 31.
[33] ibid, Art 27.
[34] ibid, Arts 38–42.

'Doxxing', the searching for and publishing of private or identifying information about a particular individual on the Internet, typically with malicious intent, is prohibited by many laws and regulations. The GDPR, for example, forbids the illegal processing of personal data, including non-consensual publication. China has a number of legal documents that address doxxing. They include the 2019 Provisions on the Ecological Governance of Network Information Content, the Provisions of the Supreme People's Court on Several Issues concerning the Application of Law in the Trial of Cases involving Civil Disputes over Infringements upon Personal Rights and Interests through Information Networks, and the Interpretation of the Supreme People's Court and the Supreme People's Procuratorate on Several Issues concerning the Application of Law in the Handling of Criminal Cases of Infringing on Citizens' Personal Information.

Advocacy for the protection of private rights to personal data in China has gone through a process moving from privacy rights to property rights to personality rights. Early understanding of personal data was based primarily on the perspective of personal privacy not being interfered with, with personal data included within the scope of privacy protection. However, with the popularisation of the Internet, large amounts of private and sensitive personal data began being publicly shared on the Internet, and the commercial use of such data gradually began to proliferate. It therefore became necessary to explain the status of personal data from the perspective of property rights and to relate personal data to the concept of property rights. Further, owing to frequent infringements of personal data, personal dignity, personal freedom and other personal interests entailed in personal data subsequently began to attract widespread attention.

It can be seen that the process of protecting personal information in China is closely related to the widespread use of high technologies in the information age, and it is thus no longer in line with the trend of the times to incorporate personal data protection into privacy protection. First of all, in addition to private information, there are other types of personal information with economic value. For example, employee information used for cross-border sharing can affect the personnel management structure of an enterprise, and online companies collect information about the shopping preferences of consumers and use algorithm technology to deliver corresponding shopping advertisements to specific consumers. Second, the right to privacy as a specific personality right is stipulated in the field of private law, whilst the protection of personal information focuses on specific subjects' right to the free disposal of information that can identify them. The purpose of protection is thus not to restrict the use of personal information, but rather to ensure legal and compliant use by data processors. The development of e-commerce and the improvement of national governance capabilities encourage and even require the use of big data technology to scientifically collect and use personal information for future planning purposes. Last but not least, the right to privacy is a negative, defensive right, necessitating the use of largely ex post facto remedies after a rights infringement occurs. Today, such services as food delivery, ticket booking, shopping and travel require individuals to transfer their personal information to other parties in advance in the process of buying, selling, replacing, authorising, etc. They usually need to indicate their willingness to transfer the information by checking the 'User Notice' option when registering as a new member for the equivalent of the free use of the platform concerned. Hence, the protection of personal information should not be limited to ex post facto relief, but should emphasise ex-ante norms providing guidance on the data processing behaviour of enterprises or platforms.

China's current personal information rights system was created within the confines of private law, in parallel with the protection and governance of personal information. The PIPL ushered in an era of specific legislation on the protection of personal information. However, it is worth noting that neither the Civil Code nor the PIPL, nor any other relevant laws, establishes the rights and interests pertaining to personal information as a civil right. Rather, their aim is to protect the rights and interests of information subjects by regulating processing behaviour in the context of personal information processing activities. In other words, the normative model of personal information protection focuses not on the protection of identities as such, but rather on the regulation of relevant conduct in the data processing process.

In general, the PIPL provides effective protection for personal information rights and interests by granting data subjects a series of rights in personal data processing activities, such as the right to know, the right to decide, the right to copy, the right to access, the right to portability, the right to delete, the right to explain and the right to refuse automated decision-making.

iii. Extraterritorial Effect of Data Protection and Privacy Law

The extraterritorial impact of data protection and privacy legislation refers to their implementation outside the jurisdiction or jurisdictions in which they were implemented. In other words, such legislation may apply to the collection, use and/or processing of personal data regardless of where it occurs. Accordingly, a national law may be applicable to persons or organisations outside the nation's territory or to acts committed outside its territory.

The degree to which data protection and privacy rules apply extraterritorially depends on the particular legislation and nations or jurisdictions concerned. Specific regulations, such as the GDPR, may apply to the processing of the personal data of EU citizens by companies based outside the EU. Other regulations may have a more limited extraterritorial impact, applying only to the processing of personal data by entities with a physical presence in the nation or region in which they were established.

In China, the PIPL is applicable to the handling of personal data both within and outside the territory of the People's Republic of China (PRC).[35] Foreign organisations carrying out personal information processing activities in foreign countries for the offering of products or services to natural persons in the PRC, or for analysing and assessing the behaviours of natural persons in the PRC, are subject to the PIPL.

iv. Data Breach Notification

Data breach notification refers to the obligation of personal data controllers and processors to notify and report to relevant regulatory authorities regarding any breach. Data breaches may arise from network operators' system vulnerabilities or failure to update technical measures in a timely manner, deliberate attacks by hackers, illegal operations, or intentional leaks by internal managers.

[35] PIPL, Art 3.

In many countries and jurisdictions, the reporting of data breaches to privacy authorities and data subjects is mandated by law, although the criteria differ depending on the exact rules and nations or jurisdictions concerned. In the EU, enterprises must inform the appropriate supervisory body of a data breach 'without undue delay and, where feasible, not later than 72 hours after becoming aware of it'.[36] In addition, the affected data subjects must be informed without undue delay if the data breach is likely to result in great danger to their rights and freedom.

In China, the DSL provides that:

> network operators shall adopt technical measures and other necessary measures to ensure the security of personal information they gather and to prevent personal information from leaking, being destroyed, or lost. When the leak, destruction, or loss of personal information occurs, or might have occurred, remedial measures shall be immediately taken, and provisions followed to promptly inform users and to make a report to the competent departments in accordance with regulations.[37]

The PIPL provides a number of rules on data breach notification. The first is to clarify the scenarios in which the data breach notification obligation is triggered. The occurrence of data leakage, regardless of whether the personal data concerned are sensitive or general, may trigger the data breach notification system.[38] The PIPL does not stipulate the quantity of personal data that must have been compromised. Hence, there is no need to consider the quantity of data for initiation of the data breach notification system, but rather only the substantive criteria of whether there has indeed been a 'breach, correction and loss' and whether it has 'caused harm to the data subject'.

The second rule is to clarify the subjects of the data breach obligation. Similarly to the GDPR, the PIPL stipulates that 'personal information processors' are required to fulfil the obligation of data breach notification. In other words, it is the enterprises and individuals that have the right to and can independently decide the purpose and method of personal data processing that are the subjects of that obligation.

The third is to clarify the objects that need to be notified of data breaches. Referring to the experience of the GDPR legislation, China's PIPL also divides the objects of notification into two categories: the data supervision department (the department tasked with personal information protection duties) and data subjects themselves (individual users). However, the PIPL does not use the number and scale of data breaches as criteria for determining whether there is a need to notify the data regulatory authorities, as the GDPR does. Instead, it clearly stipulates that as long as a personal information leakage, correction or loss has occurred or may occur, the personal information processor must notify the regulatory authorities. There may be a need for the Chinese legal regime to provide further guidance in future in terms of the notification requirements and scope of the data regulatory authorities. With respect to whether it is necessary to notify the 'personal information subject', the PIPL provides certain exemptions. For example, if the personal information processor that has experienced a data breach is able to take timely measures to effectively avoid any harm caused by information leakage, correction or loss, then it may not need to notify the

[36] GDPR, Art 33(1).
[37] DSL, Art 42(2).
[38] PIPL, Art 57.

personal data subject. However, it should be noted that the PIPL is extremely strict in its application of this data breach notification exemption, requiring that the personal information processor has indeed taken immediate measures and that those measures have avoided damages to the personal data subject concerned. The exemption is also restricted in another way: when the department with responsibility for personal information protection believes that a data breach may cause harm, the corresponding data regulatory department has the right to require the personal information processor to notify the relevant data subject.

IV. Data Security and Data Localisation

A. Data Security or Localisation Requirements

Guided by the ideas of technological nationalism and overall national security, real security needs, industrial efficacy and technological development have become the main forces driving the localisation and the precise control of important local data through Internet sovereignty and the Government's institutionalised dominance of the data regime. China's data localisation is the result of Internet sovereignty.[39]

The PIPL establishes data security rules for enterprises that gather and use personal data. One of these enterprises' obligations is to deploy suitable security measures to safeguard personal data against unauthorised access, use and/or disclosure.

Certain enterprises, most notably the critical information infrastructure operators (CIIOs), are obliged by the CSL to establish security measures for their information systems and the personal data they handle. These measures may include encryption and other technological safeguards to protect the transfer and storage of sensitive data.

In addition to data security standards, the CSL also imposes data localisation obligations on several industries. Specific data must be kept inside China, and exporting certain types of data is prohibited. Typically, data localisation requirements apply only to the CIIOs, with the exception of data localisation rules that pertain to specific sectors. According to the requirements of the CSL, the CIIOs are required to maintain multi-level cybersecurity protection systems, the breach of which would damage national security, the national economy, people's lives and the public interest. In this regard, the CSL focuses on important industries and such sectors as public communication and information services, energy, transport, water, finance, public services and e-government.[40]

i. Data Security or Localisation Requirements for Particular Types of Data

Specific categories of data, such as state secrets, biological information and other sensitive data, are subject to data security and localisation laws in China. Not only has China

[39] Jinhe Liu, 'China's data localization' (2020) *Chinese Journal of Communication* 13(1) 84–103.

[40] CSL, Art 37 reconstructs the rules for cross-border data transmission, marking the beginning of China's legal restrictions on cross-border data transmission based on the principle of network sovereignty. This provision does not restrict the operations of major multinational companies in China, but requires their operations to comply with the law, reflecting the CSL's national security-oriented and legislative purpose of promoting development with security and security with development.

demonstrated concern over the malicious use of its own data, it has also shown a tendency towards a defensive Internet policy based on core national security interests. Relevant requirements are mandated by several statutes and rules, including the CSL and the PIPL.

In 2013, the State Council issued the Regulations on the Administration of the Credit Industry, which require the collation, preservation and processing of information collected by credit agencies in China to be carried out within China.[41] The Administrative Measures for the Management of Population Health Information (for Trial Implementation) issued by the Health and Welfare Commission stipulates that population health information should not be stored, hosted or leased on servers outside China.[42] Moreover, the data localisation requirement is also defined in the Notice on the Protection of Personal Financial Information by Banking Financial Institutions[43] and the Regulations on the Administration of Internet Publishing Services.[44]

The CSL requires in principle that all personal data and important data collected and generated by the CIIOs during their operations in China be stored within the country. Those that are provided outside China for business purposes should also undergo a security assessment in accordance with the measures established by the Chinese Internet Information Department and relevant departments of the State Council. The 'local storage, outbound assessment' system marks the first time for China to make uniform provisions for localised data storage across industries and to provide uniform guidance for data localisation legislation in various fields.

The CSL closely regulates the acquisition, use, and processing of state secrets and other sensitive data, which may be subject to different localisation and security restrictions. For instance, the CSL mandates that personal data about state secrets be retained in China and forbids the transfer of such data outside China without prior consent from the appropriate authorities.

Additionally, the PIPL imposes additional constraints on acquiring, using and processing sensitive data such as biological information. For instance, it mandates that companies obtain the express agreement of data subjects before collecting and using sensitive data and imposes extra security measures for storing and transferring such data.

V. Issues in Private International Law

A. Litigation Involving Cross-Border Data Protection and Privacy

Claimants and defendants in cross-border data protection and privacy cases may include individuals, organisations or government bodies. Damages, injunctive relief and other kinds of redress may be available to plaintiffs in such cases, depending on the applicable laws and the nations or jurisdictions concerned. Depending on the individual laws and nations or jurisdictions concerned, transnational data protection and privacy disputes may be decided

[41] Regulations on the Administration of Credit Industry, Art 24.
[42] Administrative Measures, Art 10(2).
[43] Issued by the People's Bank of China in 2011.
[44] Issued by the State Administration of Press, Publication, Radio, Film and Television and the Ministry of Industry and Information Technology in 2016.

by judicial or administrative authorities. Disputes may, in certain instances, be settled by international arbitration or other alternative dispute resolution processes.

Only the PIPL is pertinent to the data protection-related lawsuits filed in China thus far. With reference to public interest litigation for the protection of personal data rights established by the GDPR,[45] the Supreme People's Procuratorate of China in September 2020 issued Guidance on Actively and Steadily Expanding the Scope of Public Interest Litigation Cases, explicitly incorporating personal data protection into a new area of procuratorial work.

Civil and administrative public interest litigation has arisen from the personal data protection methods stipulated in the PIPL, the Civil Code and the CSL. The Civil Procedure Law recognises government authorities and related organisations as the subjects entitled to initiate civil public interest litigation,[46] whilst the Administrative Procedure Law specifies that the People's Procuratorate is entitled to initiate administrative public interest litigation.[47] The PIPL, which is based on these two procedure laws, further limits the eligible subjects for public interest litigation concerning personal data protection to the following entities: the People's Procuratorate, consumer organisations, as prescribed by law, and organisations determined by the SIIO.[48] This limitation shows that China upholds a strict restriction on the scope of eligible plaintiffs for public interest litigation. The Law on the Protection of Consumer Rights and Interests provides a useful reference by indicating the relevant consumer associations including the China Consumer Association and its subordinate associations.

The PIPL does not specify the role of the victims whose personal data rights and interests are directly infringed in public interest litigation. In the absence of specific regulations, the Civil Procedure Law applies to lawsuits concerning personal data protection filed by individuals. Whilst the Civil Procedure Law does not specify public interest litigation for personal data protection, it does not exclude this category of cases.[49] Accordingly, if the procuratorial authorities or other organisations fail to file a lawsuit, individuals can do so in a people's court. In addition, the Judicial Interpretation of the Supreme People's Court on the Application of the Civil Procedure Law also provides that the people's courts do not exclude the right of the victims of an infringement to sue in an ongoing public interest proceeding.[50]

It should be noted that tort law is very closely related to litigation involving cross-border data protection and privacy. The PIPL provides:

> Where a personal information processor infringes the rights or interests on personal information due to any personal information processing activity and cannot prove that the processor is not at fault, the processor shall assume the liability for damages and other tort liability. The liability for damage prescribed in the preceding paragraph shall be determined based on the losses of

[45] See GDPR, Art 80. Regardless of whether the data subject entrusts them to do so, EU Member States may grant certain public interest organisations the right to assert legal rights on behalf of a data subject against the Data Protection Authority and the controller and processor of the information concerned and, if necessary, to initiate proceedings.

[46] Civil Procedure Law, Art 55.

[47] Administrative Procedure Law, Art 25.

[48] PIPL, Art 70.

[49] Civil Procedure Law, Art 58.

[50] Judicial Interpretation of the Supreme People's Court on the Application of the Civil Procedure Law, Art 286.

> individuals incurred thereby and the benefits acquired by the infringing personal information processor; and where it is difficult to determine the aforementioned losses or the benefits, the amount of damages shall be determined based on the actual circumstances.[51]

The above provision is the same as the formulation of tort liability in the Tort Liability Division of the Civil Code, which includes cessation of the infringement, removal of the nuisance, elimination of the danger, restitution, restoration, continuation of performance, compensation for losses, payment of liquidated damages, elimination of adverse effects, rehabilitation of reputation and extension of apologies.[52]

B. Jurisdictional Issues involving Cross-Border Data Protection and Privacy

When the same behaviour violates the (data) laws of numerous states, the requirements for determining whether a court has jurisdiction may vary by rule and country. A court's jurisdiction depends on the parties, the dispute and the location of the relevant assets or events. If another case involves the same data protection or privacy problem, local courts may respond differently depending on the laws and nations or jurisdictions concerned. Courts may cooperate or wait until the other case is resolved, and courts sometimes make inconsistent decisions.

In China, the Civil Procedure Law is the main authority for determining the jurisdiction of the courts. The country has longstanding data localisation and strict Internet censorship policies for reasons of political stability and national security. China's choice of personal jurisdiction based on the location of the server is a territorially based jurisdictional rule. For example, cases involving domain name infringement disputes are subject to the jurisdiction of the people's court in the place where the infringing act was committed or where the defendant is domiciled; the place of infringement can be the location of the computer terminal or other equipment on which the plaintiff found the domain name.[53] The Civil Procedure Law, the Interpretation of the Supreme People's Court on the Application of the Civil Procedure Law of China, and the Interpretation of the Supreme People's Court on the Application of the Criminal Procedure Law of China all recognise this jurisdictional ground for online infringement cases.[54]

The situation is easy without the involvement of any third-party service providers, such as telecommunications network providers, access providers that provide storage and transmission services, or e-commerce platform providers. In the case of the latter, more factors need to be considered in determining the relevant location(s).

[51] PIPL, Art 69.

[52] Civil Code, Art 179.

[53] See the Judicial Interpretation of the Supreme People's Court on Several Issues Concerning the Application of Law in Hearing Civil Dispute Cases Involving Computer Network Domain Name (as amended in 2020) adopted on 26 June 2001. Article 2 provides that infringement disputes involving domain names are under the jurisdiction of the intermediate people's court in the place of infringement or place of the defendant's residence. If these places are difficult to determine, the location of the computer terminal and other equipment can be regarded as the place of infringement.

[54] See, eg, Judicial Interpretation for Criminal Procedure Law, Art 2.

C. Applicable law in Litigation Involving Cross-Border Data Protection and Privacy

The laws and nations involved may determine the relevant law in multijurisdictional matters where a court has jurisdiction. The parties, dispute issues and location of relevant assets or events are usually considered by a court while deciding on the appropriate legislation.

Connecting factors determine a case's jurisdiction. Data protection and privacy disputes often include the location of data subjects, controllers or data. Courts may use forum law instead if foreign law conflicts with public policy or obligatory regulations.

D. Recognition and Enforcement of Foreign Judgments Involving Data Protection and Privacy

No separate set of rules is in place to deal with the recognition and enforcement of foreign judgments concerning personal data and privacy. Thus, the general rules in the Civil Procedure Law apply.[55]

E. Obstacles to Effective Data Protection

Private international law rules in China may hinder data protection and privacy, depending on the laws and jurisdictions concerned. Cross-border data protection and privacy disputes may be complicated by private international law principles that decide which country's laws apply. For instance, such principles may leave it unclear whether a country's data protection and privacy laws apply to such a dispute, which may lead to inconsistent conclusions. Data gathered, utilised and processed internationally may compound these concerns.

China's Law on the Application of Laws on Foreign-Related Civil Relations does not have a specific provision for cross-border data transfer.[56] Hence, the country has adopted a special legislative model of enacting procedural provisions for the application of laws in a series of substantive laws on data protection or providing rules for the determination of the location of data servers in the Civil Procedure Law and Criminal Procedure Law.

China follows some private international law and privacy principles such as the Lisbon Guidelines. These principles explain how private international law applies to data protection and privacy conflicts and may be utilised by the courts and other authorities in China and other countries to determine which laws apply.

[55] Civil Procedure Law, Arts 541–45.

[56] Adopted by the 17th Meeting of the Standing Committee of the Eleventh National People's Congress of the PRC on 28 October 2010 and effective as of 1 April 2011. It was the first centralised conflict of laws regulation in China.

VI. Topical Issues and Prospects

A. Artificial Intelligence or AI-Generated Data

Strictly speaking, artificial intelligence (AI) can be divided into weak or strong AI. The nature of AI-generated data should be independent of the subject matter of information property rights. It is arguable whether AI-generated data belong to works under Copyright Law or are the object of neighbouring rights. In general, however, AI-generated data cannot meet the requirements of 'works' under Copyright Law, which involve intellectual activity that directly produces literary, artistic or scientific works. Similarly, AI-generated data are essentially a type of data, and thus there is no right to disseminate an AI-generated work covered by a neighbouring right.

China's data protection and privacy laws extend to AI-generated data. The PIPL governs the collection, usage and processing of personal data, including AI data, under Article 62(2). It requires enterprises to secure personal data, including AI-processed data, using technological and organisational means. The PIPL also requires the express agreement of data subjects for automated decision-making and profiling.

B. Potential Cooperation under Belt and Road Initiative

A key objective of China's Belt and Road Initiative (BRI) is to connect China with key countries in Eurasia and Africa through the development of infrastructure, including Internet infrastructure.[57] As of July 2022, China has signed more than 200 cooperation documents with 149 countries and 32 international organisations around the world to build the 'Belt and Road'.[58] The Digital Silk Road is designed to downplay the impact of China's industrial overcapacity[59] by absorbing some of its excess industrial capacity and facilitating the export of Chinese goods and surplus equipment through massive infrastructure development in less developed regions both with China and abroad, as well as through the expansion and restructuring of transnational manufacturing and trade networks. With the rise of Chinese Internet giants in both the domestic market and global market, the past few years have seen a growing number of public policies in China centring on the Digital Silk Road. The Online Silk Road, or Information Silk Road, has also become increasingly central to public policies. The concept was first introduced in a 2015 White Paper jointly issued by the National Development and Reform Commission, the Ministry of Commerce and the Ministry of Foreign Affairs.[60] The 13th Five-Year Plan released by the State Council in 2016 also

[57] Hong Shen, 'Building a Digital Silk Road? Situating the Internet in China's Belt and Road Initiative' (2018) *International Journal of Communication* 12, 19.

[58] See China Belt and Road Web, available at www.yidaiyilu.gov.cn.

[59] At the end of 2012, the capacity utilisation rates of China's steel, cement, electrolytic aluminium, flat glass and shipping industries were only 72%, 73.7%, 71.9%, 73.1% and 75%, respectively, significantly lower than international levels. Specific reference is made to the Guiding Opinions on Solving Serious Overcapacity Contradictions issued by the State Council in 2013.

[60] Jointly promote the construction of cross-border fibre optic cables and other communication trunk networks, improve the level of international communication interconnection, and open up the Information Silk Road.

emphasises the construction of sea and land fibre optic cable infrastructure, the Internet Silk Road between China and Arab countries, and the China-Association of Southeast Asian Nations (ASEAN) Information Port.[61] In addition, President Xi Jinping further reaffirmed the key role of the Digital Silk Road in the BRI at the first Belt and Road International Cooperation Summit held in Beijing from 14 to 15 May 2017.

C. Data Protection Post COVID-19 Pandemic

The COVID-19 pandemic has changed data transmission and privacy regulations in several nations. For the purposes of contract tracing and vaccination efforts, for example, several governments have temporarily allowed the gathering, use and exchange of personal data.

Since the outbreak of COVID-19, China has actively focused on the prevention and control principle of 'early detection and early isolation',[62] adopted a variety of means, including big data technology, to carry out the monitoring, early warning and statistical analysis of key populations, and used accurate, timely and comprehensive information as a weapon to fight the pandemic. At the same time, Beijing, Shanghai and other cities normalised regular nucleic acid testing, and government-designated medical institutions collected and analysed massive amounts of personal data every day, which posed a severe challenge to protecting personal information while effectively screening positive cases to curb the pandemic's spread. It can be seen that the collection, analysis, and utilisation of information and data are of self-evident significance to the prevention and control of an infectious disease epidemic. However, while protecting citizens' right to life and health, it is also important to balance their need for personal privacy protection. Therefore, China formulated a legal framework for the collection and utilisation of personal information in the context of the COVID-19 pandemic. The Emergency Response Law,[63] the Law on the Prevention and Control of Infectious Diseases[64] and the Regulations on Emergency Response to Public Health Emergencies,[65] combined with the relevant provisions of the CSL on emergency support and information disclosure and protection, provide necessary rules regarding the responsibilities and obligations of government departments, enterprises, organisations, and

Accelerate the construction of bilateral cross-border fibre optic cables, plan and build intercontinental submarine fibre optic cable projects, improve air (satellite) information channels, and expand information exchanges and cooperation. Specific reference is made to the Vision and Action for Promoting the Construction of the Silk Road Economic Belt and the 21st Century Maritime Silk Road announced on 28 March 2015.

[61] 'The State Council on the Issuance of Notice of the "Thirteenth Five-Year" National Informatization Plan' Guo Fa [2016] No 73, 27 December 2016, not in effect.

[62] The principle centres on the early detection and isolation of those infected with the virus, effectively stopping its spread; strengthening community grid management to ensure that prevention and control measures are implemented early and in detail; and further improving detection capacity, optimising the confirmation process, shortening the time to diagnosis confirmation, and implementing treatment at the same time as diagnosis. See, specifically, the State Council Joint Prevention and Control Mechanism triggered by the Notice on Further Strengthening the Implementation of Responsibility to Do a Good Job of Prevention.

[63] The Emergency Response Law of the PRC was adopted by the Standing Committee of the Tenth National People's Congress of the PRC at its 29th meeting on 30 August 2007, effective 1 November 2007.

[64] Revised for the first time on 28 August 2004 during the eleventh meeting of the Tenth National People's Congress Standing Committee; and for the second time on 29 June 2013 during the third meeting of the Twelfth National People's Congress Standing Committee.

[65] PRC State Council Decree No 376, published on 9 May 2003.

individuals in the context of epidemic prevention and control and offer basic guidelines on the rational use of relevant information during an epidemic.

The regulation of the physical public domain brought about by the COVID-19 pandemic prompted the public to shift from offline to online activities, rendering social life more dependent than ever on digital technology.[66] In the process of normalising the pandemic restrictions, the development of the digital economy and society ushered in a new round of development opportunities in Chinese society, with demand for online education, online medical care and online offices increasing significantly. However, the process of shifting to an online lifestyle has further highlighted the importance of personal information protection. In this context, the CAC issued the Notice on Doing a Good Job in Personal Information Protection and Using Big Data to Support Joint Prevention and Control, which clarifies that personal information collected for epidemic and disease prevention and control must not be used for any other purpose. Without the consent of the person whose information is being collected, no organisation or individual may disclose such personal information as a person's name, age, ID card number and so forth.

COVID-19 forced students to shift from offline learning to online distance learning, a new type of learning that allowed minors to continue to learn during the pandemic. However, it also increased their online contact, and hence exposure to online risk. Widespread data collection and privacy issues have become the most pervasive threats facing children and teenagers today. An increase in AI and machine learning applications may further compromise the privacy of minors through novel data collection and analysis processes that are not yet widely understood. Therefore, in 2020, China revised the Law on the Protection of Minors for the third time, creating a special chapter on 'Network Protection'[67] that focuses on network information management and creating a scientific, systematic and holistic online protection system for minors. Although the COVID-19 pandemic is not the only reason for the emergence of a special protection system for minors' information, the rise of online learning methods triggered by the pandemic was an important factor in its rapid implementation.

[66] Tanusree Sharma and Masooda Bashir, 'Use of Apps in the COVID-19 Response and the Loss of Privacy Protection' (2020) *Nature Medicine* 26(8) 1165–67.

[67] Twenty-second meeting of the thirteenth National People's Congress Standing Committee on 17 October 2020.

2

Hong Kong

ADAM AU AND PHOEBE WOO

I. Introduction

When acclaimed Director Mabel Cheung embarked on the ambitious, decade-long project of documenting the lives of a group of teenagers at the prestigious Ying Wa Girls' School in Hong Kong for the film *To My Nineteen-year-old Self*, it was met with great fanfare and hailed as a revealing look at how history becomes imbricated into the texture of Hong Kong's collective identity. However, few could have foreseen then that the film would one day become embroiled in a bitter publicity dispute. Despite being praised by critics leading up to its release, the documentary swiftly became mired in controversy over allegations that the production company had forced through public screening without obtaining proper consent. To quell the growing backlash, the film was hastily pulled from circulation.

Of all the consequential legal issues currently in dispute on a global scale, none is more divisive than the issues surrounding the domain of privacy. Striking a balance between the right to privacy and the right to access information lies at the heart of many of such debates. What muddied the water in the Ying Wa case was the issue of informed consent. Questions arose: what is sufficient consent? What is considered a sufficient legal basis for access to private information? At its core, the line between the two rights founded on opposing ideologies is elusive, and one that the judiciaries, policy-makers, government entities across the globe redraw from time to time. In charting the development of data protection and privacy law in Hong Kong, it is important to note that the law did not develop in short bursts, but through mediated, gradual cycles.[1] Instead of a straight line, such continuum loops back repeatedly like a curlicue, vacillating between tightened privacy and loosened disclosure based on societal tendencies. The contentious debate surrounding *To My Nineteen-year-old Self* then is not an isolated case. The uptick in high-profile data

[1] One can find analogy in the United States where the debate on privacy ebbed and flowed over the last century. While the First Amendment of its Constitution promises freedom of speech, press, and expression, the Supreme Court of the United States has yet to define exactly when the right to privacy should supersede the right to publish truthful information. This means that the lower courts can make their own interpretations on how to handle the conflict between privacy and press freedoms. The consequence of a lack of clear guidance on balancing these two essential rights has led to differing opinion on the matter.

breaches and misuses in recent years has placed privacy issues into sharper focus.[2] While relatively few in Hong Kong have brought such issues to open court, the term 'privacy' is now a regular fixture in the public discourse.

This chapter provides an overview of data protection and privacy regulations in Hong Kong. The chapter is divided into five parts. Following this Introduction, section II provides a general legal framework for data protection and privacy in Hong Kong. Section III examines the legal bases, mechanisms, and exceptions for cross-border data transfers and data protection under Hong Kong law. Section IV evaluates the development of Hong Kong data protection and privacy laws in the age of big data and artificial intelligence.

II. General Legal Framework of Privacy and Data Protection

A. Constitutional Protection

In Hong Kong, the right to privacy is guaranteed by Article 30 of the Basic Law and Article 14 of the Hong Kong Bill of Rights (BOR) under the Bill of Rights Ordinance (Cap 383) (BORO). The latter owes its genesis to Article 17(1) of the International Covenant on Civil and Political Rights (ICCPR). The right to privacy, however, is not absolute and qualified by restrictions.[3]

In determining whether a privacy-intrusive measure is justifiable, the four-step test as laid down by the Court of Final Appeal in *Hysan Development Company Limited v Town Planning Board*[4] shall be considered. When applying the test, it should be asked: (1) whether the measure in question pursues a legitimate aim; (2) if so, whether it is rationally connected to the legitimate aim identified; (3) whether the measure in question is no more than necessary for its purpose; and (4) whether there is a reasonable balance between the societal benefits of the encroachment and the rights of an individual which are constitutionally protected.[5] The Court implied that derogation from fundamental human rights such as privacy can only be done to 'the extent strictly required by the exigencies of the situation',[6] taking into account any detrimental impact on individuals.

[2] One of the most high-profile privacy breach incidents concerned the unauthorised access to personal data of approximately 9.4 million passengers of Cathay Pacific Airways Limited and Hong Kong Dragon Airlines Limited: Privacy Commissioner for Personal Data, Hong Kong (PCPD), 'Data Breach Incident Report: Cathay Pacific Airways Limited and Hong Kong Dragon Airlines Limited: Unauthorised Access to Personal Data of Passengers' (6 June 2019) Report Number: R19 – 15281, available at https://www.pcpd.org.hk/english/news_events/media_statements/files/PCPD_Investigation_Report_R19_15281_E.pdf.

[3] ICCPR and BORO respectively allow intrusive measures to be taken: ICCPR, Art 4(1) and BORO, s 5. Former Privacy Commissioner for Personal Data, Mr Stephen Kai-yi Wong also observed that 'privacy right is not absolute but subject to restrictions': Stephen Kai-yi Wong, 'Balancing Privacy Right Against Public Interests Amidst COVID-19 Pandemic' (Hong Kong Lawyer, 2020), available at www.hk-lawyer.org/content/balancing-privacy-right-against-public-interestsamidst- covid-19-pandemic.

[4] *Hysan Development Company Limited v Town Planning Board* (2016) 19 HKCFAR 372.

[5] ibid [134]–[135].

[6] BORO, s 5.

B. Personal Data (Privacy) Ordinance (Cap 486)

The Personal Data (Privacy) Ordinance (Cap 486) (PDPO) is the primary legislation which governs data protection and privacy in Hong Kong. It aims to 'protect the privacy of individuals in relation to personal data, and to provide for matters incidental thereto or connected therewith'.[7] While the right to privacy as enshrined in the Basic Law and BOR is broad enough to cover various interests in privacy, such as interests in freedom from surveillance and interests in freedom from interference of personal life,[8] the PDPO only focuses on the protection of personal data. It is 'not intended to establish general privacy rights against all possible forms of intrusion into an individual's private sphere'.[9]

i. Legislative Background

The basic tenets of data protection and privacy law development in Hong Kong can be readily identified through time. The origins can be traced back to 1989, when the initial building blocks of data protection and privacy law took shape under British colonial rule in Hong Kong. At that time, Hong Kong's Attorney General and Chief Justice instructed the Law Reform Commission to examine local laws affecting privacy, and to report on whether any measures were necessary to offer protection and provide remedies against persons whose privacy has been violated.[10] In August 1994, the Law Reform Commission published a report on the reform of personal data protection (LRC's Report), which considered the Organisation for Economic Co-operation and Development's Privacy Guidelines 1980, ICCPR, and the Commission of the European Communities' amended proposal for a Council Directive on the protection of individuals with regard to the processing of personal data and on the free movement of such data (1992).[11] The LRC's Report comprehensively covered a wide range of issues concerning data protection and privacy, which included the complex definition of 'privacy',[12] what the objective and scope of Hong Kong's data protection and privacy law should be,[13] how to regulate the collection, use and disclosure of personal data,[14] interactions between data protection law and other areas of law such as human rights and the law of confidence,[15] and trans-border data flow.[16] The LRC's Report was the blueprint for today's PDPO.

[7] PDPO, Long Title.

[8] *Eastweek Publisher Ltd v Privacy Commissioner for Personal Data* [2000] 2 HKLRD 83 [36], referring to Law Reform Commission of Hong Kong, 'Report: Reform of the Law Relating to the Protection of Personal Data' (Topic 27) (August 1994) [5]–[6], available at www.hkreform.gov.hk/en/docs/rdata-e.pdf.

[9] Law Reform Commission of Hong Kong, 'Report: Privacy and Media Intrusion' (December 2004) [9.39], available at www.hkreform.gov.hk/en/docs/rmedia-e.pdf; Office of the Privacy Commissioner for Personal Data (PCPD), Hong Kong, *Data Protection Principles in the Personal Data (Privacy) Ordinance – from the Privacy Commissioner's Perspective*, 2nd edn (2010) [3.27].

[10] Law Reform Commission of Hong Kong, Report (n 8) [1].

[11] ibid, [2.9]–[2.34].

[12] ibid, [3]–[8].

[13] ibid, Chapter 8.

[14] ibid, Chapters 9 and 10.

[15] ibid, Chapters 4 and 5.

[16] ibid, Chapter 17.

ii. Statutory Framework

PDPO is a distinctive legislation that is principle-based: '[i]ts core provisions are encapsulated in the six data protection principles, which are found in Schedule 1 to the Ordinance'.[17] Data users are not allowed to do any act, or engage in any practice, that contravenes any of the data protection principles (DPPs) unless the act or practice is required or permitted under the PDPO.[18]

Before looking into the DPPs, we should consider the definition of 'personal data', and the distinction between 'data subject' and 'data user' under the PDPO. To qualify as 'personal data' under the PDPO, the data in question should fulfil the following: first, the data must relate directly or indirectly to a living individual; second, it must be practicable for the identity of the individual to be directly or indirectly ascertained from the data and third, the data must be practicably accessible.[19]

Judicial interpretations in Hong Kong have demarcated the reach and confines of these parameters. Take the case *Wu Kit Ping v Administrative Appeals Board*[20] as an example. The complainant made a data access request for medical documents concerning her health from the data user, but the data user redacted parts of the documents. The redaction fell into three categories: (i) the names of writers and recipients of the documents, which were found by the court to be personal data of those individuals and not that of the complainant, making the redaction lawful; (ii) statements by a medical officer regarding the treatment of the complainant, which the court considered to be the complainant's personal data and thus should have been disclosed; and (iii) general statements unrelated to the complainant, which were found not to be the complainant's personal data and thus had been lawfully redacted. The court ruled that only the redactions of category (ii) should have been disclosed, as they were opinions directly related to the complainant. In relation to the second criteria under the definition of 'personal data', in *AAB No. 16/2000*, the Administrative Appeals Board upheld the decision of the Privacy Commissioner for Personal Data (PCPD) that 'practicable' should mean 'reasonably practicable'. The definition of 'personal data' carries great importance, as the DPPs exclusively pertain to personal data. Data that does not qualify as 'personal data' under the PDPO definition will not be subject to any safeguards under the DPPs.

Aside from the classification of 'personal data', the concepts of 'data subject' and 'data user' under the PDPO is likewise paramount. In relation to personal data, 'data subject' means 'the individual who is the subject of the data',[21] and 'data user' means 'a person who, either alone or jointly or in common with other persons, controls the collection, holding, processing or use of the data'.[22] Consider this hypothetical: Company X owns personal data of Person A. Person B obtains the personal data of Person A from Company X and passively transmitted such data to a third party. In this scenario, Person B would not be regarded as a data user as Person B did not control the collection, holding, or processing Person A's personal data.[23] What this case illustrates is that when determining who is the data user,

[17] PCPD (n 9) [1.1].
[18] PDPO (n 7), s 4.
[19] ibid, s 2.
[20] *Wu Kit Ping v Administrative Appeals Board* [2007] 4 HKLRD 849.
[21] PDPO (n 7), s 2.
[22] ibid.
[23] Similar facts can be found in *AAB No. 22/1997*. In that case, the Administrative Appeals Board held that a secretary who was only involved in the transmission of the documents concerned was not a data user as she did

the central question is, who wields control over the collection, holding, processing or use of such data. Simply amassing, retaining, or utilising data in some manner does not automatically confer control. The crux is to identify who dictates the terms of the data collection, holding, processing or use – that entity exercises true control.

The DPPs constitute foundational principles under the PDPO, delineating directives on how data users must collect, hold, and use personal data. DPP1 stipulates that data users shall not collect personal data unless the collection is 'for a lawful purpose directly related to a function or activity of the data user who is to use the data'.[24] DPP2 stipulates that data users should take reasonable steps to ensure that the personal data collected 'is accurate having regard to the purpose (including any directly related purpose) for which the personal data is or is to be used', and where they have reasonable grounds to believe that the personal data collected is inaccurate, they shall cease use of the data for that purpose, or erase the data.[25] DPP3 stipulates that data users shall not use personal data collected for a new purpose without the consent of the data subject.[26] DPP4 stipulates that data users shall take all possible steps to ensure any personal data they hold 'is protected against unauthorized or accidental access, processing, erasure, loss or use'.[27] DPP5 stipulates that data users shall take all practicable steps to ensure that a person can

> (a) ascertain a data user's policies and practices in relation to personal data; (b) be informed of the kind of personal data held by a data user; (c) be informed of the main purposes for which personal data held by a data user is or is to be used.[28]

DPP6 stipulates that data subjects shall be entitled to

> (a) ascertain whether a data user holds personal data of which he is the data subject; (b) request access to personal data [...]; (c) be given reasons if a request referred to in paragraph (b) is refused; (d) object to a refusal referred to in paragraph (c); (e) request the correction of personal data; (f) be given reasons if a request referred to in paragraph (e) is refused; and (g) object to a refusal referred in paragraph (f).[29]

The DPPs contain exemptions. Personal data held by data users for certain purposes, such as for the fulfilment of judicial functions,[30] for domestic purposes,[31] for staff planning in employment settings,[32] for security or law enforcement purposes,[33] for protecting the

not control the collection, holding, or processing of the data contained in the document. See also: Office of the Privacy Commissioner for Personal Data, Hong Kong, Data Protection Principles in the Personal Data (Privacy) Ordinance – from the Privacy Commissioner's perspective (2nd edn, 2010) [4.3].

[24] ibid, sch 1, DPP1(1). See also the landmark case of Eastweek Publisher Ltd v Privacy Commissioner for Personal Data (n 8). The statement from the judgment of Ribeiro JA (at 90I), which was repeated almost word for word in the judgment given by Godfrey VP (at 102D), clearly defined the meaning of 'collect': 'It is ... of the essence of the required act of personal data collection that the data user must thereby be compiling information about an identified person or about a person whom the data user intends or seeks to identify.'

[25] ibid, sch 1, DPP2(1).

[26] ibid, sch 1, DPP3(1).

[27] ibid, sch 1, DPP4(1).

[28] ibid, sch 1, DPP5(1).

[29] ibid, sch 1, DPP6(1).

[30] ibid, s 51A.

[31] ibid, s 52.

[32] ibid, s 53.

[33] ibid, ss 57–58.

physical or mental health of any individual,[34] for a news activity,[35] and for statistics and research purposes[36] are exempted from DPPs.

iii. Amendments to the PDPO

The PDPO has undergone two amendments since it took effect from December 1996. The first round of revisions occurred in 2012, enacted as a reaction to escalating public disapproval over the exploitation of personal information by major corporations in Hong Kong. In 2012, Octopus Holdings Limited, the issuer of Octopus cards, being the smart cards that most Hong Kong citizens use for daily transportation and consumption, was found to have over-stepped its data use privilege.[37] The Personal Data (Privacy) (Amendment) Ordinance 2012 introduced rules that govern the use of personal data in direct marketing. Under the new rules, data users must obtain the data subject's consent,[38] and take specified actions before using personal data in direct marketing.[39] Those specified actions include:

a) Inform the data subject that they intend to use the personal data and that they may not use the data unless the data subject has consented to the intended use.
b) Provide the data subject with information concerning the kinds of personal data to be used, and the classes of marketing subjects in relation to which the data is to be used.
c) Provide the data subject with a free channel to communicate his or her consent to the intended use.[40]

Data users must also notify the data subject when using personal data in direct marketing for the first time.[41] If a data user intends to provide a data subject's personal data to a third party for use by that third party in direct marketing, the data user must first obtain the data subject's consent,[42] and take the following actions:

a) Inform the data subject in writing its intention to do so and that it may not provide the data unless the data subject has consented to the intended provision in written form.
b) Provide the data subject with written information in relation to the intended provision.
c) Provide the data subject a free channel to communicate his or her consent to the intended provision in writing.[43]

[34] ibid, s 59.
[35] ibid, s 61.
[36] ibid, s 62.
[37] In July 2010, Octopus Cards Limited admitted that it had been selling personal data to third parties since January 2006, and had earned HK$44 million from the sale: 'Octopus Sold Personal Data of Customers for HK$44m' *South China Morning Post* (Hong Kong, 27 July 2010), available at www.scmp.com/article/720620/octopus-sold-personal-data-customers-hk44m. The PCPD soon carried out an investigation and found that Octopus Cards Limited had contravened DPP1(1), DPP1(3), and DPP3: PCPD, 'Report Published under section 48(2) of the Personal Data (Privacy) Ordinance (Cap. 486)' (18 October 2010) Report Number R10-9866, available at https://www.pcpd.org.hk/english/publications/files/R12_0080_e.pdf.
[38] PDPO (n 7), s 35E.
[39] ibid, s 35C.
[40] ibid.
[41] ibid, s 35F.
[42] ibid, s 35K.
[43] ibid, s 35J.

The second amendment of the PDPO was enacted in 2021, prompted by a proliferation of doxxing incidents. According to the PCPD, the term 'doxxing' (also known as 'doxing') refers to

> the gathering of the personal data of target person(s) or related person(s) (such as family members, relatives or friends) through online search engines, social platforms and discussion forums, public registers, anonymous reports, etc., and disclosure of the personal data on the Internet, social media or other open platforms (such as public places).[44]

In May 2021, a Legislative Council Paper noted that the PCPD had handled over 5,700 complaints concerning doxxing activities from June 2019 to April 2021.[45] It was further observed in an Information Note published by the Legislative Council Secretariat that around 60 per cent of the complaints handled by the PCPD involved members of the public, 36 per cent involved police officers and their family members, and the remaining 4 per cent involved government officials.[46]

At that juncture, the existing legislation contained two lacunae. First, the requirement to show that a defendant has not obtained consent from the data user prior to disclosure of personal data of a data subject under the old section 64(2) of the PDPO (now repealed)[47] created evidential difficulties for the prosecution.[48] Additionally, Hong Kong's criminal and tort law offered insufficient safeguards, as the offence of criminal intimidation under section 24 of the Crimes Ordinance (Cap 200) as well as the torts of intimidation and harassment failed to encompass all reprehensible doxxing conduct.[49]

When doxxing activities became rampant during the political movements of 2019, the Secretary for Justice and the Commissioner of Police sought an interim injunction order from the Court of First Instance to restrain any person from 'using, publishing, communicating or disclosing to any other person' the personal data of and concerning any police officers and their family members without the latter's consent; 'intimidating, molesting, harassing, threatening, pestering or interfering with' any police officers and their family members; and 'assisting, causing, counselling, procuring, instigating, inciting, aiding, abetting or authorising others' to commit any of the above two acts.[50] The Court granted the injunction and later extended it.[51]

Yet, even after the injunction was granted, intrusive doxxing activities remained pervasive. According to the 2021 Legislative Council paper, the PCPD referred 60 cases to the

[44] PCPD, 'Doxxing Offences', available at www.pcpd.org.hk/english/doxxing/index.html#:~:text=In%20general%2C%20doxxing%20refers%20to,personal%20data%20on%20the%20Internet%2C.

[45] Legislative Council Panel on Constitutional Affairs, *Proposed Amendments to the Personal Data (Privacy) Ordinance (Cap. 486)* (LC Paper No. CB(4)974/20-21(03)) [2].

[46] Research Office, Legislative Council Secretariat, *Information Note: Measures to Address Doxxing in Selected Places* (IN09/19-20) [2].

[47] The old s 64(2) of the PDPO stipulates that '[a] person commits an offence if – (a) the person discloses any personal data of a data subject which was obtained from a data user without the data user's consent; and (b) the disclosure causes psychological harm to the data subject.'

[48] For a detailed evaluation of the law before the 2021 amendment, see Chor Kiu Woo, 'Doxxing in Hong Kong – Way Forward' 4–7, available at www.pcpd.org.hk/english/news_events/events_programmes/others/files/2020_2021.pdf.

[49] ibid.

[50] *Secretary for Justice v Persons Unlawfully and Wilfully Conducting Etc* (HCA 1957/2019, 25 October 2019).

[51] Extension granted on 8 November 2019: *Secretary for Justice v Persons Unlawfully and Wilfully Conducting Etc* [2019] 5 HKLRD 500; and 13 November 2019: *Secretary for Justice v Persons Unlawfully and Wilfully Conducting Etc* [2020] 5 HKLRD 638.

Department of Justice on the ground of breaching the injunction.[52] In *Secretary for Justice and Yiu Ka Yu*,[53] for instance, the defendant was charged with civil contempt of court on the ground that she had posted the personal data of a police officer and his wife on a Telegram chat group. Although the defendant in the post asked others not to post or pass on the personal data shared, the Court held that 'the fact that the [defendant] gave the detailed residential address and specific mobile phone number [of the police officer and his wife] in a public chat group showed that she was facilitating others to intimidate, molest, harass and/or pester [the police officer] and his wife.'[54] The defendant was sentenced to an immediate custodial sentence of 21 days. In his judgment, Coleman J remarked that

> the deeply ugly behaviour of doxxing has not been limited to doxxing police officers, or doxxing activities by only one 'side' of the recent social unrest against the other 'side'. Any doxxing activity by any person or group against any other person or group is equally unacceptable, and equally seriously endangers society.[55]

In three other cases which involved the disclosure of personal data of police officers and their family members, the defendants were each given a suspended sentence.[56]

Considering the groundswell of bitter public sentiment against doxxing, the Personal Data (Privacy) Amendment Ordinance 2021 was passed in July 2021 and two new offence criteria were created to close the legal loopholes. A person commits an offence if he or she discloses any personal data of a data subject without the data subject's consent,

> (a) with an intent to cause any specified harm to the data subject or any family member of the subject; or (b) being reckless as to whether any specified harm would be, or would likely be, caused to the data subject or any family member of the data subject.[57]

A person also commits an offence if, in addition to fulfilling conditions (a) and (b) as just mentioned, disclosure actually 'causes any specified harm to the data subject or any family member of the data subject'.[58] Furthermore, the PCPD was empowered to carry out investigation and institute prosecution,[59] and to demand related persons to rectify doxxing contents.[60] In December 2022, a 27-year-old man became the first person to be charged under section 64(3A) of the PDPO on the ground that he had maliciously leaked the personal data of his ex-partner on social media. The Court convicted the defendant of seven charges of the doxxing offence upon his guilty plea and sentenced him to eight-months' imprisonment.[61]

[52] Legislative Council Panel on Constitutional Affairs (n 45) [4].
[53] *Secretary for Justice v Yiu Ka Yu* [2021] 1 HKLRD 607.
[54] ibid [17].
[55] ibid [50].
[56] *Secretary for Justice v Chan Oi Yau Riyo* [2020] 3 HKLRD 494; *Secretary for Justice v Cheng Lai King* [2020] 5 HKLRD 356; *Secretary for Justice v Chan Kin Chung* [2021] 1 HKLRD 563.
[57] PDPO, s 64(3A).
[58] ibid, s 64(3C).
[59] ibid, s 64C.
[60] ibid, Part 9A.
[61] PCPD, 'First Sentencing Case of the New Doxxing Offence' (15 December 2022), available at www.pcpd.org.hk/english/news_events/media_statements/press_20221215.html.

iv. Assessing the PDPO's Current Reach

The PDPO is not without dispute, to say nothing of its narrow focus on privacy in relation to personal data, but not privacy rights in general. Intrusiveness alone, without a data collection element tied to identifiable individuals, does not fall within the PDPO's scope and coverage.[62] Further, the legislation does not clearly differentiate between sensitive and non-sensitive personal data. In contrast, mainland China's latest Personal Information Protection Law (PIPL) treats biometric identification, religious beliefs, specific identities, healthcare, financial account, individual location tracking, etc, as well as personal information of minors under the age of 14 as sensitive personal information.[63] Personal information processors shall only process sensitive personal information if there is a specific purpose and when it is of sufficient necessity, and where stringent protective measures are in place.

Meanwhile, in the European Union (EU), under the General Data Protection Regulations (GDPR), data related to individual race, political views, religious beliefs, trade union membership, genetics and biometrics, health-related data, and data concerning a person's sex life or sexual orientation is treated as a 'special category', which must comply with stricter conditions.[64] In addition to this, mainland China and the EU mandate organisations that encounter data breaches to notify regulatory bodies within a stipulated timeline;[65] however Hong Kong currently lacks comparable legal provisions obligating reporting of such security incidents.

Furthermore, the rights afforded to data subjects in Hong Kong diverge substantially from those in mainland China and the EU across critical dimensions. Under the PDPO, data subjects are entitled to make a request to an organisation for access to their personal information, request copies of their data and request correction of any errors. In contrast, Article 47 of mainland China's PIPL stipulates that personal information handlers shall, actively or based on individual requests, delete personal information where certain prescribed circumstances occur.[66] Meanwhile, Article 17 of the GDPR gives similar rights to data subjects known as 'the right to be forgotten'. However, the PDPO does not expressly confer individuals the right to request deletion of their personal information. The PDPO only requires data users to take all practicable steps to erase personal data held by it where the data is no longer required or is inaccurate for the intended purpose under section 26 and DPP2(2). While the introduction of additional regulations over the doxxing activities was welcomed by the public, privacy advocates argue Hong Kong law still lags behind other jurisdiction in key areas.[67]

[62] By comparison, in mainland China, the Cyber Security Law and the Data Security Law along with the PIPL represent three pillars of the Chinese data protection legislation system and together form an overarching framework governing the data processing and cybersecurity issues.

[63] PIPL, Art 28.

[64] GDPR, Arts 4(13), (14) and (15) and 9, and Recitals (51) to (56).

[65] ibid, Art 33 and PIPL, Art 57.

[66] GDPR (n 64) Art 47.

[67] On 20 February 2023, in a briefing to the Legislative Council of Hong Kong, the PCPD proposed several amendments to the PDPO. These amendments include: (a) mandatory data breach notification mechanism; (b) direct regulation of data processors under the PDPO in relation to personal data retention and security obligations; (c) requirement for data users to formulate a clear personal data retention policy; and (d) express powers

C. Privacy Regulator: Privacy Commissioner for Personal Data

The PCPD is the only privacy regulator in Hong Kong. It was established pursuant to section 5 of the PDPO and came into force in 1996. The missions of the PCPD are to 'promote the protection and respect for personal data privacy through publicity and education', 'facilitate lawful and responsible use of personal data by providing guidance and best practices', 'monitor and supervise compliance through effective enforcement', and 'maintain the efficacy of the regulatory regime through continuous review and enhancement, taking into account global standards for the protection of personal data privacy'.[68]

Generally, upon receiving a complaint about contravention of any of the DPPs, the PCPD will first carry out an investigation.[69] Should the PCPD find that there has been a privacy violation, it will issue an enforcement notice to the offending data user.[70] The enforcement notice should state that the data user has contravened the PDPO, and then state the remedial actions that the data user must take.[71] Any data user who fails to comply with an enforcement notice commits an offence.[72] As mentioned earlier, by virtue of the amendment in 2021, the PCPD now also has the power to investigate complaints in relation to doxxing activities, prosecute any person who has committed any of the offences under section 64 of the PDPO and demand any person to rectify doxxing contents.[73]

During the onset of the COVID-19 pandemic in 2020, government authorities implemented various technological tools and policies to enforce quarantine restrictions. The authorities aimed to achieve an equilibrium between preserving civil liberties and defending public wellbeing. For example, they introduced a mobile application dubbed 'StayHomeSafe' to regulate home isolation protocols. In tandem with a Bluetooth-enabled wearable device, the smartphone platform could ascertain adherence to the quarantine mandate by the detainee, and flag authorities upon identification of any contravention. While there were public concerns that the mobile application had violated one or more of the DPPs,[74] the PCPD clarified that 'there are sufficient legal and justifiable bases' on which the Government may collect and use information with the aid of devices, applications, software, or super-computers to track potential COVID-19 carriers or patients to protect public health.[75]

by the Commissioner to impose administrative fines in addition to existing criminal fines. There may also be an option for fines based on annual turnover similar to the GDPR regulations, www.legco.gov.hk/yr2023/english/panels/ca/papers/ca20230220cb2-132-2-e.pdf.

[68] PCPD, 'What We Do', available at www.pcpd.org.hk/english/about_pcpd/our_role/what_we_do.html.

[69] PDPO (n 7) s 37.

[70] ibid, s 50.

[71] ibid.

[72] ibid, s 50A.

[73] ibid, s 64C and Part 9A.

[74] Shirley Zhao, 'Hong Kong Scraps Contact Tracing App That Raised Privacy Concern' (*Bloomberg UK*, London, 9 January 2023), available at www.bloomberg.com/news/articles/2023-01-09/hong-kong-scraps-contact-tracing-app-that-raised-privacy-concern; 'Contact Tracing Apps: A New World for Data Privacy' (Norton Rose Fulbright, February 2012), available at www.nortonrosefulbright.com/en-hk/knowledge/publications/d7a9a296/Kong#Hong.

[75] PDPO (n 7) s 59 stipulates situations where personal data may be exempted from the relevant DPPs if it is to be used to protect the physical or mental health of the data subject or others. Since personal data collected via the mobile application 'StayHomeSafe' would be used to stop the spread of COVID-19 and thus to protect

III. Legal Bases, Mechanisms and Exceptions for Cross-Border Data Transfers and Data Protection under Hong Kong Law

A. Safeguards for Cross-Border Transfers under the PDPO

i. Section 33 of the PDPO

As Hong Kong progresses into the digital epoch, the deliberation on adopting global privacy standards remains ongoing, especially as governance of transnational information flow has emerged as a polarising dilemma. Section 33 of the PDPO prohibits the transfer of personal data to places outside Hong Kong unless the data subject has consented to the transfer, or the jurisdiction has similar data protection legislation. Section 33 covers transfers from Hong Kong to a place outside Hong Kong and transfers between two other jurisdictions where the transfer is controlled by a Hong Kong data user.[76] According to section 33, the transfer of personal data to places outside Hong Kong is prohibited unless at least one of the below conditions is met:

a) The destination has been approved by the PCPD in writing.
b) The data user has reasonable grounds for believing that the place has laws which are substantially similar to, or serve the same purpose as, the PDPO.
c) The individual has consented in writing to the transfer.
d) The data user has reasonable grounds for believing that the transfer is for the avoidance or mitigation of adverse action against the data subject; it is not practicable to obtain the data subject's consent but, if practicable, such consent would be given.
e) The data are exempt from DPP3, which exempts personal data held for certain purposes such as domestic purposes, employment or staff planning, the prevention or detection of crime, the security or defence of Hong Kong, legal professional privilege, news activities etc.
f) The data user has taken all reasonable precautions and exercised all due diligence to ensure that the data will not be collected, held, processed, or used in any manner that would constitute a contravention of the PDPO if it occurred in Hong Kong.[77]

Section 33 has not been in force since the introduction of the PDPO in 1996. There have been intermittent discussions on its enforcement, and the PCPD has in the past commissioned consultancy studies on its enforcement suitability.[78] Despite rising focus on aligning with prevailing global standards, section 33 has, to date, remained inoperative.

public health, it is argued that the mobile application can be exempted from the DPP3 and DPP6: PCPD, 'The Use of Information on Social Media for Tracking Potential Carriers of COVID-19' (26 February 2023), available at www.pcpd.org.hk/english/news_events/media_statements/press_20200226.html.

[76] PCPD, 'Transfer of Personal Data Outside Hong Kong: Some Common Questions' (1 April 1997) Fact Sheet No 1, available at www.pcpd.org.hk/english/resources_centre/publications/guidance/fact1_intro_1.html.

[77] PDPO (n 7) s 33.

[78] Constitutional and Mainland Affairs Bureau, 'The Legislative Council Panel on Constitutional Affairs: Section 33 of the Personal Data (Privacy) Ordinance' LC Paper No. CB(2)1368/16-17(03), 15 May 2017, available at www.legco.gov.hk/yr16-17/english/panels/ca/papers/ca20170515cb2-1368-3-e.pdf.

ii. Other Safeguards under the PDPO

Supplemental to section 33, the PDPO institutes further risk controls regarding the transfer of information across borders. Such other safeguards include:

a) Disclosure and transfer are expressly included in the definition of 'use'.[79]
b) A requirement to adopt contractual or other means to prevent personal data transferred to data processors, whether within or outside Hong Kong, from being kept longer than is necessary for processing of the data (DPP2(3)).
c) A requirement to obtain the prescribed consent of data subjects for change of use of personal data collected (DPP3).
d) A requirement to adopt contractual or other means to prevent personal data transferred to data processors, whether within or outside Hong Kong, from unauthorised or accidental access, processing, erasure, loss, or use of the data being transferred for processing (DPP4(2)).

B. Intermittent Measures on Data Privacy

With safeguarding data privacy as a key legislative priority, the PCPD has regularly provided guidance and assembled a range of legal instruments to proactively tackle emerging privacy concerns. Pertinent events or recommendations made by the PCPD include the following:[80]

- In 1997, the PCPD claimed that the law of contracts and similar accords provide one of the viable mechanisms for moving data in line with the requirement of due diligence requirement of the PDPO. To create developments many have deemed necessary, the PCPD promulgated a model contract, adjusting a model drafted jointly by the Council of Europe, the European Commission, and the International Chamber of Commerce to meet the PCPD's expectations.[81] When asked when section 33 would go into effect, the PCPD said that there is no set date, but that the release of the model contract could make the process easier.[82]
- In September 2012, the PCPD published an advisory document about outsourcing the processing of personal data to data processors.[83] Given that the PDPO does not expressly regulate the role of a data processor, the document provides information on the data users' obligations to adopt contractual or other means to prevent unauthorised or accidental access, processing, erasure, loss, or use of the data transferred to the data processor for processing.
- In 2013, the PCPD engaged an outside consultant to develop a framework to evaluate whether personal data protection laws in other jurisdictions are comparable to the

[79] PDPO (n 7) s 2.
[80] Tanner De Witt, 'Data Transfers: The Curious Case of Cross-border Data Transfers in Hong Kong' (18 November 2022) available at www.tannerdewitt.com/cross-border-transfers-section-33/.
[81] PDPO (n 7) s 33.
[82] ibid.
[83] PCPD, 'Outsourcing the Processing of Personal Data to Data Processors' (September 2012), available at www.pcpd.org.hk/english/publications/files/dataprocessors_e.pdf.

objectives and standards of the PDPO. This research examined the data protection and privacy laws and regulations in 50 jurisdictions, 35 of which were deemed to have data protection standards sufficiently comparable to those in Hong Kong to be included on a 'whitelist' of approved destinations for cross-border data transfers.[84]

- In December 2014, the PCPD published its 'Guidance on Personal Data Protection in Cross-border Data Transfer', with recommended model clauses to be included in a data transfer agreement (2014 Guidance).[85] However, the model clauses to the Guidance remained optional.
- In tandem with the publication of the Guidance, the Constitutional and Mainland Affairs Bureau of the Hong Kong Government (CMAB) commissioned a consultant to assess the impact if data users fulfilled the requirements under section 33. In May 2017, CMAB reported to the Legislative Council Panel on Constitutional Affairs its preliminary findings of the 2013 consultancy study.[86] The report reiterated that Hong Kong is a jurisdiction made up of one single city. Given the small scale of the domestic market, cross-border business activities have always been buoyant and to date there was no indication that cross-border data transfers had undermined personal data privacy. It is therefore 'neither necessary nor appropriate' to introduce additional restrictions on top of the current regulatory framework.[87]
- In November 2018, a PCPD consultant offered solutions to issues identified in the business impact assessment study.[88] The study noted the uptick of local and global data breach incidents, coupled with the emerging impact from the implementation of the GDPR in 2018, put pressure on Hong Kong to revisit its data protection and privacy laws. Coupled with an increasingly data-driven economy, updated business models, digitalisation, and globalisation of data, as well as initiatives involving personal data privacy and other innovative practices concerning information and communications technology development, regulators around the world (including Hong Kong) have been reviewing their legislative frameworks to better protect personal data privacy rights.[89]
- Considering this, the PCPD contemplated a revision of the recommended model clauses in the 2014 Guidance to enhance the guidance and facilitate organisational data users by directly adopting the relevant clauses in data transfer agreements.[90] While the consultant's brief extended to updating the guidance itself, there was no specific timetable for enabling section 33.

[84] PCPD Fact Sheet No 1 (n 76) [7]–[11].

[85] PCPD, 'Guidance on Personal Data Protection in Cross-border Data Transfer' (December 2014), available at www.pcpd.org.hk/english/resources_centre/publications/files/GNcrossbordere.pdf.

[86] 'The Legislative Council Panel on Constitutional Affairs: Section 33 of the Personal Data (Privacy) Ordinance' (n 78) fn 1.

[87] ibid.

[88] Legislative Council Panel on Constitutional Affairs, 'Report on the Work of the Office of the Privacy Commissioner for Personal Data in 2019' LC Paper No. CB(2)815/19-20(04), April 2020 [47], available at www.pcpd.org.hk/english/resources_centre/publications/annual_report/files/anreport20_full.pdf.

[89] ibid [4].

[90] ibid [47].

- In January 2020, CMAB presented proposals to reform and modernise PDPO to the Legislative Council Panel on Constitutional Affairs. CMAB outlined six major proposed changes to the PDPO, but did not include any recommendations regarding the implementation or future status of section 33.[91]
- In May 2022, the PCPD issued a 'Guidance Note on the Recommended Model Contractual Clauses for Cross-border Transfers of Personal Data' ('2022 Guidance'). The 2022 Guidance has incorporated the prevailing standards expounded under the DPPs – arguably the regulatory backbone of the PDPO. While acknowledging section 33 is not yet in effect, the 2022 Guidance recommends organisations, especially small and medium-sized enterprises (SMEs), to voluntarily adopt the model contract clauses when transferring personal data across borders.

C. Why has Section 33 not been Implemented?

Some critics have questioned why Hong Kong has been tiptoeing around the weighty problem of section 33. The genesis of the debate predated even the GDPR with cross-border regulations being traditionally greeted by a penumbra of doubt. SMEs have been particularly vocal in their concern over the intended change. According to paragraph 11(a) of a paper published by the Legislative Council Panel on Consultation Affairs on section 33 of the PDPO, one of the justifications for resisting the implementation of section 33 was that: '[i]t is difficult for most companies, especially SMEs, to have sufficient resources for a professional assessment of the privacy protection laws of the destinations of intended data transfers'.[92]

According to its detractors, the straitjacket of section 33 would redirect vital resources to observe the new compliance requirements. Their coordinated lobbying and resistance to change put the plans of adoption on the back burner.

In 2014, following the issuance of recommendations regarding cross-border personal data flows, the PCPD observed:

> The situation of global data flows is markedly different today than in the 1990s when the Ordinance was enacted … Against this background, the issue of regulating cross-border data flows is becoming more acute than ever before. Countries worldwide are adopting a range of mechanisms to protect the personal data privacy of individuals in the context of cross-border data flows. It is high time for the Administration to have a renewed focus on the implementation of section 33 to ensure that the international status of Hong Kong as a financial centre and a data hub will be preserved.[93]

[91] These proposals include extending mandatory data breach notification mechanism, carefully stipulated data retention policy, enhanced sanctioning powers, regulation of data processors, broadened definition of personal data and the regulation of disclosure of personal data of other data subjects: Legislative Council Panel on Constitutional Affairs, 'Review of the Personal Data (Privacy) Ordinance' LC Paper No. CB(2)512/19-20(03), 20 January 2020, available at www.legco.gov.hk/yr19-20/english/panels/ca/papers/ca20200120cb2-512-3-e.pdf.

[92] 'The Legislative Council Panel on Constitutional Affairs: Section 33 of the Personal Data (Privacy) Ordinance' (n 78) [11(a)].

[93] PCPD, 'PCPD Publishes Guidance on Personal Data Protection in Cross-border Data Transfer' (29 December 2014), available at https://www.pcpd.org.hk/english/news_events/media_statements/press_20141229.html; Tanner De Witt, (n 80).

In a statement regarding data localisation in April 2020 (Data Localisation Media Response), while acknowledging the prominence of cross-jurisdiction data flow, the PCPD reiterated the position that

> [w]hen the PDPO came into effect in 1996, section 33 has not been brought into operation. The main reason is that at the material time, there had been fragmented privacy protection legislation in different jurisdictions, including the USA; and it was then not uncommon for overseas jurisdictions not to impose restrictions on cross-border / boundary data transfer.[94]

They continued:

> [t]he business sector (especially SMEs) has been wary of the implementation of section 33 as they anticipate difficulties in full compliance with the legal requirements (such as lack of human resources and requisite knowledge) and the adverse impact on the free flow of information which is pivotal to cross-jurisdiction business operations. But it has reviewed the latest global regulatory framework on cross-border/boundary data flow and communicated with the [Hong Kong government] on the ways forward which best suit the local circumstances in Hong Kong.[95]

Despite the above, section 33 implementation remained absent from the agenda of the legislative reform of the PDPO.

D. The Need to Implement Section 33

The rapid evolution of data protection and privacy laws across the globe, especially in mainland China, might bring changes to the future of section 33. Below we examine other salient arguments for the implementation of section 33.

i. Alignment with Global Trends

One of the contentions made by CMAB in its briefing to the Legislative Council Panel on Constitutional Affairs in May 2017 was that even though there are regulations on cross-border transfers of personal data in similar jurisdictions, such as those in the EU, data protection authorities in such jurisdictions have rarely encountered cases of enforcement concerned with provisions regulating cross-border transfers of personal data.[96] Along a similar vein, in the Data Localisation Media Response, the PCPD asserted that '[it] has not received any complaints from individuals or enterprises about the cross-border/ boundary data transfer provisions not coming into operation'.[97]

While legislative inertia has prevailed, changes in the international landscape suggest Hong Kong could ill afford to keep cross-border data transfer governance as a low priority, considering the region's economic dependence on data exchange. The judgment made

[94] PCPD, 'Response to Media Enquiry on Data Localisation' (15 April 2020), available at www.pcpd.org.hk/english/news_events/media_enquiry/enquiry_20200415.html.
[95] ibid.
[96] 'The Legislative Council Panel on Constitutional Affairs: Section 33 of the Personal Data (Privacy) Ordinance' (n 78) [12].
[97] PCPD (n 94).

by the Court of Justice of the European Union (CJEU) as well as a decision made by the European Commission best represents this issue.

The former is a 2021 case known colloquially as 'Schrems II'.[98] The case originated from an activist Maximilian Schrems who urged the Irish Data Protection Commissioner to rule that the standard contractual clauses employed by Facebook to transfer user data from EU member countries to its headquarters in the United States (US) were unlawful. Per Schrems' argument, acquisition of said personal information by United States intelligence entities would constitute a violation of the GDPR and additional EU legislation. The dispute centred on the discord between American surveillance statutes and the GDPR. The CJEU found that 'the requirements of US national security, public interest and law enforcement have primacy, thus condoning interference with the fundamental rights of persons whose data are transferred to that third country'.[99]

An essential aspect of the EU's GDPR posits that EU data subjects whose personal data are transferred to a third country relying on standard contractual clauses, must be afforded a level of protection equivalent to that guaranteed within the EU by the GDPR. This requires an assessment of both the contractual clauses agreed between the EU data exporter and the recipient of the transfer established in the third country. The relevant aspects of the legal system of the third country by the public authorities of that third country must also be assessed. In short, the CJEU ruled that the US did not provide equivalent or adequate protection to personal data that is offered by the EU.[100]

The second example involves a decision made by the European Commission on whether the data protection laws of the United Kingdom (UK), in the post-Brexit era, are 'adequate' in the opinion of the European Commission to protect EU personal data. After detailed assessment, the European Commission finally adopted adequacy decisions that permit personal data to flow freely from the EU to the UK, where data benefits from an essentially equivalent level of protection to that guaranteed under the GDPR.[101]

The European Commission thoroughly evaluated the statutory infrastructure of the UK in its determination. It states that '[a]s the UK GDPR is based on EU legislation, the data protection rules in the [UK] in many aspects closely mirror the corresponding rules applicable within the [EU]'. They concluded that 'the UK GDPR and the DPA 2018 ensure a level of protection for personal data transferred from the European Union that is essentially equivalent to the one guaranteed by Regulation (EU) 2016/679'.

[98] Case C-311/18 *Data Protection Commissioner v Facebook Ireland Limited and Maximillian Schrems* ECLI:EU:C:2020:559.

[99] CJEU, 'The Court of Justice Invalidates Decision 2016/1250 on the Adequacy of the Protection Provided by the EU-US Data Protection Shield' (16 July 2020), available at curia.europa.eu/jcms/upload/docs/application/pdf/2020-07/cp200091en.pdf.

[100] On 13 December 2022, the European Commission launched the process to adopt an adequacy decision for the EU-US Data Privacy Framework, which will foster trans-Atlantic data flows and address the concerns raised by the CJEU in its Schrems II decision of July 2020. The draft adequacy decision concludes that the US ensures an adequate level of protection for personal data transferred from the EU to the US. This is based on an in-depth assessment of the EU-US Data Privacy Framework itself and its obligations for companies, as well as the limitations and safeguards on access by the US public authorities to data transferred to the US, in particular for criminal law enforcement and national security purposes: European Commission, 'Questions & Answers: EU-U.S. Data Privacy Framework, Draft Adequacy Decision' (13 December 2022), available at ec.europa.eu/commission/presscorner/detail/en/qanda_22_7632.

[101] European Commission, 'Commission Finds that EU Personal Data Flows Can Continue with 11 Third Countries and Territories' (15 January 2024), available at https://ec.europa.eu/commission/presscorner/detail/en/ip_24_161 ('In June 2023, the EU adopted adequacy decisions for the United Kingdom').

This resolution underscores the stances embraced by a primary economic counterpart of Hong Kong in evaluating the aptitude of safeguards instituted by the data-receiving entity. The continued dormancy of section 33 is incongruous with the regulatory mechanisms enacted by other national bodies for cross-border data transmission. In pragmatic terms, the latest rulings stand to undermine Hong Kong corporations habitually tasked with intake of data from the EU or outbound transfer of sensitive EU user details beyond the bloc.

According to Article 45(2)(a) of the GDPR, when assessing the adequacy of the level of protection, the European Commission shall take account of:

> … rules for the onward transfer of personal data to another third country or international organization which are complied with in that country or international organization, case-law, as well as effective and enforceable data subject rights and effective administrative and judicial redress for the data subjects whose personal data are being transferred.[102]

The European Commission may determine that Hong Kong's current legislation is inadequate for protecting data transferred from the EU. Such an assessment could hinder commercial activities with EU entities, considering their growing reliance on cross-border data exchange and transmission. Since data flows bilaterally between parties, having parity in safeguards between the importer and exporter is prudent when handling sensitive information. The unregulated flow of data threatens the privacy, rights, and freedoms of individuals, as evidenced by many violations and misuses. Hong Kong's major economic partners such as the EU and UK may demand comparable privacy safeguards for personal data transferred under Hong Kong laws in the future.

ii. Harmonisation with Mainland China's Data Protection and Privacy Law

Mainland China has made sweeping changes to its data protection laws. The PIPL, China's first umbrella law on personal data protection, came into force on 1 November 2021. The PIPL provides comprehensive measures, including civil protection and administrative regulations in the field of personal information. The PIPL, together with two other fundamental laws on cybersecurity and data protection, the Chinese Cybersecurity Law 2016 (CSL) and the Data Security Law (DSL), opens a new chapter of data protection in China. The CSL is the fundamental law regulating cyberspace, covering personal information and data. The DSL is the fundamental legislation regulating data security, establishing a legal framework for data security. The PIPL marks the introduction of a comprehensive system protecting personal information in mainland China, which does not merely incorporate or replace rules already enshrined in other Chinese laws, but also draws inspiration from the GDPR.

The Chinese government acknowledged that cross-border data transfer is a crucial concern for international companies. The PIPL explicitly regulates cross-border data transfers. Operators of critical information infrastructure (CII) should complete a security assessment prior to any cross-border transfer of personal data. According to the PIPL, prior separate informed consent must be obtained from data subjects. The PIPL takes a very different approach to data transfer safeguards compared to the GDPR. Under the GDPR,

[102] GDPR, Art 45.

the jurisdiction where the personal data is being transferred to is the key factor in determining if adequate protections are in place. If the data transferee is in a jurisdiction with 'adequacy decisions', the cross-border transfer is deemed acceptable. If not, the transfer must rely on other safeguards provided under the GDPR.[103] Under the GDPR, the size or scale of the organisation transferring the data does not affect the requirements, nor does the actual amount of personal data being transferred.

Unlike the GDPR which focuses on the destination jurisdiction, the PIPL takes into account the size and scale of the data transferor. Specifically, if the entity transferring data out of China is a CII operator, or if the amount of personal data processed exceeds certain thresholds, additional oversight is required. In these cases, the data transferor must undergo a security assessment administered by the Cyberspace Administration of China (CAC) before transferring data abroad, regardless of the receiving jurisdiction. So while the GDPR emphasises adequate safeguards based on the location of the data recipient, the PIPL places more scrutiny on large Chinese companies and organisations exporting large quantities of personal data.

Minimising legal fragmentation between two highly integrated economies supports the case for Hong Kong to bring section 33 into force. With the passage of the new laws, mainland China's system will no longer represent a convenient counterargument against data protection. The cogency of this perspective also spotlights Hong Kong's position within the international sphere, as the jurisdiction has long functioned as a critical facilitator of communication between China and the global community, a role in which it has excelled for over half a century. Further, as many Hong Kong companies race for a competitive edge in mainland China, Hong Kong can no longer afford to operate in a self-enclosed state of stasis.

iii. Economic Integration with the Greater Bay Area

The promulgation of the Outline Development Plan for the Guangdong-Hong Kong-Macao Greater Bay Area (Plan) on 18 February 2019 signifies a milestone in the development of the Greater Bay Area.[104] According to the Plan, Hong Kong will 'proactively integrate into the overall national development, thereby expanding [the] scope of development and generating new impetus for growth to bring new development opportunities to different sectors of the community …'[105]

China has made significant progress in developing its legal framework and regulatory capabilities related to data, creating complexities for Hong Kong's distinct operating environment under 'one country, two systems'. While furthering interconnected markets and frictionless flow of goods and services is envisioned, reconciling the developmental incongruities between Guangdong, Hong Kong, and Macao remains a foundational challenge

[103] European Commission, 'What Rules Apply if my Organisation Transfers Data outside the EU?', available at ec.europa.eu/info/law/law-topic/data-protection/reform/rules-business-and-organisations/obligations/what-rules-apply-if-my-organisation-transfers-data-outside-eu_en#references.

[104] The Guangdong-Hong Kong-Macao Greater Bay Area also referred to as the Greater Bay Area is a megalopolis, consisting of nine cities and two special administrative regions in Southern China. It is envisioned as an integrated economic area aimed at taking a leading role globally by 2035.

[105] Constitutional and Mainland Affairs Bureau, 'Greater Bay Area – Overview' (2018), available at www.bayarea.gov.hk/en/about/overview.html.

integral to the Greater Bay Area. The Plan has placed an emphasis on deepening cooperation among the Greater Bay Area cities. As an example, Chapter 4 (Developing an International Innovation and Technology Hub) and Section 1 (Building an Open Community for Coordinated Innovation in the Region) stipulate that one of the development goals is:

> [t]o pursue the development of the 'Guangzhou-Shenzhen-Hong Kong-Macao' innovation and technology corridor, explore policy measures to facilitate the cross-boundary and regional flow of innovation elements such as talents, capital, information and technologies, and jointly develop a Greater Bay Area big data centre as well as platforms for international innovation.[106]

As evidenced by today's digital economy, the efficacy of digital information exchange and the success of 'deep integration of data'[107] is rooted in comparable legal safeguards. Without such safeguards, there are risks of damaged reputation and eroded trust with trade partners and allies. Section 33 might be considered as a *sine qua non* to reduce friction and strengthen coordination and compatibility among the different legal systems of the Greater Bay Area cities. Implementing Section 33 could help align Hong Kong with mainland China both economically and legally, notably embodying the key spirit of Greater Bay Area businesses under the strategic Plan. It might also help create a business environment in which domestic companies can have a legal basis to determine where and with whom to share the personal information in their possession.

As the discussion of fostering further integration among the cities of the Greater Bay Area gathers steam, efforts have been intensifying to strengthen Hong Kong's role as a 'digital metropolis'. In June 2022, the Hong Kong Government announced the establishment of the Digital Economy Development Committee chaired by the Financial Secretary to identify significant development trends, prominent drivers, key success factors, and development initiatives, to set directions, strategies, focus areas, priorities, and critical performance indicators, to formulate strategies and measures to enhance co-operation and co-ordination with stakeholders, to drive the growth of data services as an industry, to formulate strategies and measures to encourage the adoption of digitalisation by different industries, and to promote digital government.[108] To encapsulate the ever-accelerating shift from analogue to digital, the Legislative Council of Hong Kong held a meeting in November 2022 to discuss the establishment of a statutory body to oversee the development of 'Digital Hong Kong'. This rebranded moniker aims to connect Hong Kong and other cities in the Greater Bay Area to promote data interchange and develop cross-border e-commerce.[109] Presently, data integration and usage are land-mined by privacy risks that must be addressed. All such initiatives must therefore be evaluated against the backdrop of strengthening the protection

[106] ibid, 15.

[107] This is with reference to a remark made by President Xi Jinping in February 2021 where he was quoted: '[We should] focus on this new development path, and push for deep integration between big data and the real economy'. '[We must] nurture and strengthen [our] strategic and emerging businesses, and accelerate the modernization of our industries.': Ho M, 'Xi Jinping Sends Message on Growth through Innovation, Big Data in Guizhou' *South China Morning Post* (Hong Kong, 9 February 2021), available at www.scmp.com/news/china/politics/article/3121055/xi-jinping-sends-message-growth-through-innovation-big-data.

[108] Government of Hong Kong, 'Government Announces Establishment of Digital Economy Development Committee' (22 June 2022), available at www.info.gov.hk/gia/general/202206/22/P2022062200375.htm.

[109] 'Dr Hon Kennedy WONG's Motion on "Promoting Data Interchange in the Guangdong-Hong Kong-Macao Greater Bay Area and Developing Cross-Border E-commerce", LC Paper No. CB(3)811/2022(01), available at www.legco.gov.hk/yr2022/english/counmtg/motion/m_papers/cm20221130cb3-811-1-e.pdf.

of data protection as a matter of priority. Recently, in light of the growing demand for greater integration, the Innovation, Technology and Industry Bureau and the Cyberspace Administration of China signed the Memorandum of Understanding on Facilitating Cross-boundary Data Flow Within the Guangdong-Hong Kong-Macao Greater Bay Area (MoU) in Beijing on 29 June 2023, to jointly promote cross-boundary data flow in the Greater Bay Area. A key development was made in December 2023 of the 'Greater Bay Area Standard Contract for the Cross-boundary Flow of Personal Information within the Guangdong-Hong Kong-Macao Greater Bay Area (Mainland, Hong Kong)' (Standard Contract).[110] While the Standard Contract is a positive step, closer examination reveals substantial work remains. The two-party framework may present limitations in facilitating complex, multi-party data transfers typical between Hong Kong and mainland Chinese organisations, while its voluntary nature could limit adoption. It is unclear whether and how differences in data protection and privacy laws between the jurisdictions will eventually be reconciled. Ultimately, bridging this legal gap is crucial to enable seamless cross-border data flows.

IV. Development of Hong Kong Data Protection and Privacy Law in the Age of Artificial Intelligence

A. AI and Privacy

Emerging technologies like artificial intelligence (AI) and generative AI models, including large language models, have posed sustained challenges to data protection and privacy issues in Hong Kong. These technologies alter the logic of information exchange in unprecedented ways, transforming future regulatory frontiers.

The expansive potential of AI is enabled by the prolific generation of big data in the digital era. AI enables organisations to collect and analyse a variety of personal information from users regardless of their localities. As such, personal information commonly factors into the development and deployment of AI systems, especially modern implementations that derive intelligence through analysing massive datasets using sophisticated machine learning algorithms.

Consequently, AI poses formidable challenges to established data protection principles like transparency, data minimisation, and restricted use. Privacy risks intersect with broader ethical impacts as individuals subjected to algorithmic analysis can have their human rights, dignity, autonomy, and fairness undermined. If deployed irresponsibly, AI could erode consumer trust and enable unauthorised exploitation of personal data for competitive advantage or social control. Proactive governance is imperative to ensure ethical AI development that respects privacy and avoids disproportionate harms, particularly for vulnerable populations. Overall, the data-dependent nature of AI mandates evolving regulatory approaches to maintain data protection in an increasingly digitised society.

[110] Government of Hong Kong, 'Facilitation Measure on "Standard Contract for Cross-Boundary Flow of Personal Information Within the Guangdong-Hong Kong-Macao Greater Bay Area (Mainland, Hong Kong)" and its Early and Pilot Implementation Arrangements' (13 December 2023), available at www.info.gov.hk/gia/general/202312/13/P2023121300134.htm.

AI also raises questions about automated decision-making processes. With the analytical proficiency of algorithms advancing, such technologies can take over determinations traditionally requiring human discernment, including credit scoring and insurance risk appraisals. This raises ethical concerns around fairness and accuracy in decisions made without any meaningful input from users. The combination of vast databases,[111] Moore's Law enabling greater computing power, and sophisticated algorithms has created a perfect storm of risks. In response to these seismic shifts, in June 2024, the PCPD unveiled the 'Artificial Intelligence: Model Personal Data Protection Framework' (AI Framework) which offers guidance and recommended best practices to assist companies and organisations in Hong Kong with procuring, deploying, and utilising AI technology, including generative AI, in a manner that adheres to the PDPO.[112] The goal of the framework is to enable organisations to harness the advantages of AI while also safeguarding personal data privacy. By providing practical recommendations rooted in internationally recognised principles, the framework aims to promote the healthy maturation of AI in Hong Kong, support Hong Kong's aspirations to become an innovation and technology hub, and catalyse the growth of digital economies in both Hong Kong and the Greater Bay Area. In essence, the framework gives organisations in Hong Kong a toolkit to adopt AI responsibly in a way that spurs innovation while respecting privacy.

In general, the AI Framework covers four recommended measures:

- **Establish AI Strategy and Governance**: Organisations should formulate an AI strategy with governance considerations when procuring AI solutions. They should also establish an AI governance body and provide relevant AI training to employees;
- **Conduct Risk Assessment and Human Oversight**: Organisations should thoroughly assess AI risks and implement proportionate risk management measures based on the level of risk. This includes deciding on appropriate human oversight over AI systems;
- **Customisation of AI Models and Implementation and Management of AI Systems**: Organisations should properly prepare and manage data, test and validate AI models, ensure system and data security, and continuously monitor AI systems; and
- **Communication and Engagement with Stakeholders**: Organisations should regularly communicate and engage with stakeholders such as their staff, suppliers, customers and regulators to enhance transparency and trust.[113]

Guidance alone may not be enough. The expansive purview of AI will plausibly outgrow the boundaries of any governance frameworks meant to oversee it. To sufficiently govern AI's implications for privacy, regulators across the globe may ultimately be compelled to enact a full-fledged legislation emulating the EU's Artificial Intelligence Act.[114] In the interim,

[111] As billions of people interact daily online, their digital footprints create troves of data that algorithms can utilise to understand human behaviours and experiences. Looking ahead, generative AI models might one day be able to learn directly from live sensory feeds such as cameras and microphones. This enables access to a virtually unlimited supply of fresh training data captured from the environment in real-time without the need for manual human curation.

[112] PCPD, 'Artificial Intelligence: Model Personal Data Protection Framework' (June 2024), available at https://www.pcpd.org.hk/english/resources_centre/publications/files/ai_protection_framework.pdf.

[113] ibid.

[114] European Parliament, 'EU Artificial Intelligence Act', available at https://artificialintelligenceact.eu/ai-act-explorer/.

organisations must be cognisant of best practices, such as the use of encryption technology to safeguard users' information, along with stringent security policies governing internal usage.[115] A new realm of economic activity unconstrained by physical location has emerged in cyberspace. Though generating tremendous opportunities, the growth of cyber activities has eliminated geographic borders and left all stakeholders struggling to keep up with constant changes. This will be far from an easy transformation for legislators, not only for Hong Kong; the transformation will be global.

B. What does the Future Hold?

As a corollary to breakneck digital development, data protection and privacy issues has been elevated to the forefront of policy agendas. On ideological and practical fronts, the ascent of data privacy concerns clashes with the precipitous expansion of technology such as AI. The impact has reverberated beyond a cadre of policy-makers. It affects every stakeholder in the data market: multinational corporations, C-suites executives, and the many users sending data through the ever-multiplying digital channels. As the world tends toward the centralisation of authority over the use of data, Hong Kong might be pressured to follow suit.

On the other side of the divide, the rapid advancements of AI threaten to outpace and put under its thumb the rules and regulations that were designed to keep it in check. To address these arising challenges, data protection and privacy laws need to safeguard people's rights by establishing data stewardship and oversight principles. Many of such rights are already enshrined under the PDPO. For example, individuals have a right to access their data held by other organisations, as well as control how that information is used or disclosed.[116] Companies must obtain informed consent from the individual before using personal data for direct marketing purposes.[117]

In addition, companies must also take reasonable steps to protect collected personal information against unauthorised access, alteration, or disclosure. The PCPD encourages organisations to develop effective security policies and procedures for handling customer data and regularly align their policy. Organisations should have procedures for individuals to submit complaints about the use of personal data and pay attention to the treatment of data and abide by ethical standards. An agile regulatory framework has the capacity to adjust protections as novel issues arise. The PCPD frequently supplements existing regulations with timely guidance that helps identify protection gaps and addresses evolving changes. While such guidance does not hold the force of law, it nonetheless serves as a timely, salutary supplement.

Lastly, the defence of the sanctity of privacy must involve reading between the lines of the existing laws. In *To My Nineteen-year-old Self*, the production crew might have legitimately obtained consent – one of the fundamental legal bases to the use of personal information.

[115] The PCPD has promulgated a recommended privacy management programme: PCPD, 'Privacy Management Programme: A Best Practice Guide' (August 2018) 10, available at https://www.pcpd.org.hk//english/resources_centre/publications/files/PMP_guide_e.pdf.

[116] PDPO (n 7) sch 1, DPP6.

[117] ibid, ss 35E and 35K.

But what transpired subsequently defied the boundaries of the stipulated rules when the production company nevertheless acceded to the interviewees' demands. It is essential then that conflicting views are heard and thrashed out, bearing in mind the nuances of any situation when adhering to laws and regulations designed to safeguard personal information. Striking an equitable balance between legal accountability and social costs, and to build a citadel of privacy protection, often requires coordinated and thoughtful efforts from all stakeholders.

History has shown that leaving citizens in the self-policing hands of a few corporate custodians could lead to disastrous outcomes. This is not alarmism. With the rise of cyberattacks like ransomware, the social costs of breaches are far from insignificant.[118] As technology's onward march proceeds unchecked, existing legal scaffolds may crumble against novel methods of improper data collection and use.

Much of the world's commerce has now migrated into the cyberspace not subordinated to conventional rules, government oversight or territorial partitions. As the global outlook on privacy began to evolve, so too did the way people view their rights to privacy. The world is saturated with diametric debates on the stringent versus libertarian regulation of cross-jurisdiction data flow. While technology incessantly revolutionises the controller's tools, it simultaneously threatens to antiquate existing laws at an alarming speed. It remains to be seen how the ideological fault line between Hong Kong and the rest of the world will resolve.

Ultimately, technology and privacy, however contentious their relationship may sometimes be, are necessarily symbiotic. The real issue is that the more reverence citizens have for their own privacy, the more variance every jurisdiction disposes to interpret the scale of their own data protection systems. Thickening protection buffers and cracking down on misuse will not solve all the problems. Pushing boundaries and taking risks is in the nature of innovation; data use will always involve some degree of risk. But regularly updating regulations and providing timely guidance can serve as a lynchpin that elevates data protection standards to a comparable level with other leading data protection systems, such as those in the EU and mainland China, under the same frame of reference without necessarily compromising digital development. Although the specific trajectory of Hong Kong's data protection laws is still developing, it is clear that increased safeguards and technological advancement will need to be reconciled as these regulations progress, regardless of the precise direction they ultimately follow.

[118] There have been an increasing number of high-profile data breach incidents. For example, the PCPD conducted an investigation into a ransomware attack on the information systems of the Consumer Council in 2023: Investigation Report (2 May 2024), available at https://www.pcpd.org.hk/english/enforcement/commissioners_findings/files/r24_14749_e.pdf.

3

Japan

NOBUYUKI SATO

I. Introduction

On 1 April 2023, a new personal information protection system was launched in Japan, amending the previous system that was first introduced in 2003. Under the new system, the Act on the Protection of Personal Information (APPI),[1] an act of the Diet – the national legislature of Japan – provides a framework for protecting personal information based on common principles for both the private and public sectors. The APPI also delegates supervisory authority to the Personal Information Protection Commission of Japan (PPC) as a unified regulator for both the private and public sectors. Although the APPI does not protect privacy in general, it functions as a basic and general law in the area of personal information protection. This chapter outlines the current status of data protection and privacy in Japan, mainly focusing on the APPI and referring to other laws such as the Constitution of Japan,[2] the Civil Code,[3] and the Penal Code[4] as necessary.

In Japan, privacy was first recognised as a legal issue in the 1960s. In 1964, the Tokyo District Court held that

> the idea of individual dignity, which is one of the fundamental principles of modern law and the foundation of the Constitution of Japan, can only be firmly ensured when the personalities of individuals are mutually respected and their egos are protected from unfair interference. To that end, it is not permitted to disclose private affairs of others without adequate reasons. […] The right not to disclose one's private affairs is indispensable in today's society of mass communication to ensure the dignity of the individual and the pursuit of happiness.[5]

The Court added that

> the right to privacy is understood as a legal guarantee or right not to have one's private life disclosed without adequate reasons, and that, when it is infringed, the right to an injunction against the infringing act or damages for emotional distress should be allowed. Article 709 of the Civil Code provides that such a violation should be considered a tort.[6]

[1] The APPI was initially introduced as the Act No 87 of 2003. In 2021, the Diet amended it by the Act No 37 of 2021 which fully came into effect on 1 April 2023.

[2] Constitution 1946. English translations of the Constitution and key statutes are available at www.japaneselawtranslation.go.jp/.

[3] Act No 89 of 1896.

[4] Act No 45 of 1907.

[5] Tokyo District Court Decision on 28 September 1964, 15-9 Kaminshu 2317.

[6] ibid.

The case itself was not appealed to the Supreme Court, but in subsequent cases,[7] the Supreme Court has also recognised that information pertaining to privacy is subject to legal protection.[8] However, case law has established that the right to privacy as the right not to have private matters unnecessarily disclosed and did not explicitly state whether the collection, storage, processing, or use of personal information that does not result in disclosure constitutes an invasion of privacy. Therefore, the Diet has decided to establish a statutory system through the APPI and related statutes for the protection of such personal information apart from the protection of privacy.

When the APPI was originally enacted in 2003, it provided for a segmented personal information protection system. In other words, the APPI of 2003, as the basic law for the protection of personal information in Japan, set forth the objectives and basic concepts common to both the public and private sectors, while stipulating specific personal information protection mechanisms only for the private sector, leaving the public sector to be governed by separate acts. For the private sector, each minister was empowered by the APPI to supervise business operators handling personal information within the scope of their competent jurisdiction. On the other hand, in the public sector, each national organ was to protect personal information autonomously in accordance with acts such as the Act on the Protection of Personal Information Held by Administrative Organs[9] and the Act on the Protection of Personal Information Held by Incorporated Administrative Agencies.[10] Any person who was dissatisfied with the handling of personal information by a national organ could appeal to the Information Disclosure and Personal Information Protection Review Board ('Board'), but the Board had only the power to review individual appeals and did not have the authority to supervise the overall protection of personal information held by national organs. As for the more than 1,700 local governments on the province or town level throughout Japan, each of them was supposed to establish its own personal information protection system through its own ordinances, rather than adopting a unified national regulation.

In 2015, the Japanese Government submitted a bill to the Diet to amend the APPI on a large scale for the first time. After four months of debate, the bill passed in both houses of the Diet almost unanimously.[11] According to the commentary of the PPC about this amendment, there were three major elements behind this amendment: (1) increasing the possibility of using personal data due to the development of information technology – demand for clarifying the definition of 'personal information', (2) evolution of big data – demand for the appropriate use of 'big data' while protecting personal information, and (3) globalisation – demand for making rules about cross-border data transfer.[12] In addition to making significant revisions to meet these demands, the 2015 amendment also partially overhauled the segmented regulatory regime adopted in 2003. It established the PPC as a unified regulator for the private sector, transferring the powers previously held by

[7] Supreme Court Grand Bench Decision on 24 December 1969, 23-12 Keishu 1625; Supreme Court Second Bench Decision on 12 September 2003, 58-8 Minshu 973; Supreme Court First Bench Decision on 6 March 2008, 62-3 Minshu 665; Supreme Court First Bench Decision on 9 March 2023, 77-3 Minshu 627.

[8] English translations of key decisions of the Supreme Court are available at www.courts.go.jp/english/index.html.

[9] Act No 58 of 2003. Repealed on 1 April 2023 by the Act No 37 of 2021.

[10] Act No 59 of 2003. Repealed on 1 April 2023 by the Act No 37 of 2021.

[11] Act No 65 of 2015.

[12] See www.ppc.go.jp/files/pdf/280222_outline_v2.pdf.

ministers. However, it maintained the autonomous personal information protection system for national administrative organs and local governments based on laws and ordinances respectively.

In 2021, the latest APPI amendments were made.[13] This amendment, intended to reform the segmented Japanese personal information protection system into a unified one, was highly large-scale and was, therefore, implemented in several phases, with full enforcement on 1 April 2023. In a nutshell, the amendments aim to achieve the following four purposes: (1) they abolished two segmented regulatory acts for national organs, including the Act on the Protection of Personal Information Held by Administrative Organs and the Act on the Protection of Personal Information Held by Incorporated Administrative Agencies, and integrated them into the APPI, making the revised APPI a unified law covering the private sector and the public sector including the national and local governments by applying the amended Act to local governments; (2) they made the PPC a unified regulatory and supervisory body of the personal information protection system; (3) they made various adjustments following the integration of the laws; and (4) they made adjustments to harmonise with the European Union's (EU) General Data Protection Regulation (GDPR).

II. General Legal Framework of International Data Transfers and Data Protection

A. Constitutional Protection for Data Transfer and Protection

In Japan, there is no specific constitutional provision regarding the transfer and protection of information. However, it is understood that information relating to privacy is constitutionally protected by Article 13 of the Constitution of Japan which is further interpreted by case law.

In 1969, the Grand Bench of the Supreme Court stated that

> Article 13 of the Constitution provides as follows: 'All of the people shall be respected as individuals. Their right to life, liberty, and the pursuit of happiness shall, to the extent that it does not interfere with the public welfare, be the supreme consideration in legislation and in other governmental affairs.' This provision can be construed to mean that citizens' freedom in private life should be protected against the exercise of state power including police power. As part of such citizens' freedom in private life, any person has the right not to have his/her face or appearance photographed without consent or good reason.[14]

This decision was the first to recognise that information about a person's private life is protected by Article 13 of the Constitution. The Supreme Court has cited this decision in many cases involving personal information related to privacy. The Supreme Court has further explained the *ratio decidendi* of this decision that

> Article 13 of the Constitution provides that citizens' liberty in private life shall be protected against the exercise of public authority, and it can be construed that, as one of individuals' liberties in

[13] Act No 37 of 2021.

[14] Supreme Court Grand Bench Decision on 24 December 1969, 23-12 Keishu 1625.

> private life, every individual has the liberty of protecting his/her own personal information from being disclosed to a third party or made public without good reason.[15]

Therefore, in Japan, only personal information related to privacy can be protected under the Constitution with respect to international transfer and disclosure.

B. Statutory Frameworks for Data Transfer and Protection

The statutory framework for data transfer and protection in Japan is divided into two categories: one for personal information and the other for non-personal information. In this context, personal information is defined in the APPI as information which can be used to identify a specific living individual, regardless of whether the information is privacy-related or not. For personal information, the APPI establishes a uniform regulatory framework. For non-personal information, however, there is no general statute. Instead, some statutes regulate information for specific purposes. For example, the Unfair Competition Prevention Act[16] protects trade secrets. In addition, for both personal or non-personal information, if the handling of such information constitutes a tort, it is subject to damages or an injunction under the Civil Code.

This chapter focuses on the discussion of personal information, and non-personal information is mentioned only where necessary.

i. Definition of Key Legal Concepts

In this section, the structure of the APPI and other sub-legislations, including the Cabinet Order to Enforce the Act on the Protection of Personal Information ('APPI Cabinet Order'),[17] the Enforcement Rules for the Act on the Protection of Personal Information ('APPI Enforcement PPC Rules')[18] made by the PPC and the Guidelines of the PPC will be examined. Some statutory concepts will also be summarised below.

First, the APPI is a law governing the handling of personal information, in which personal information is defined under Article 2(1) as

> information relating to a living individual which falls under any of the following items: (i) information containing a name, date of birth, or other identifier which can be used to identify a specific individual; (ii) those containing an individual identification code.[19]

[15] Supreme Court First Bench Decision on 6 March 2008, 62-3 Minshu 665; Supreme Court First Bench Decision on 9 March 2023, 77-3 Minshu 627.

[16] Act No 47 of 1993.

[17] Cabinet Order No 507 of 2003.

[18] Rules of the Personal Information Protection Commission No. 3 of 2016.

[19] An 'individual identification code' is a character, number, symbol, or other code prescribed by Cabinet order that can identify a specific individual solely on the basis of information. See APPI, Art 2(2). Currently, biometric identification codes and official personal identification numbers are prescribed. On the other hand, credit card numbers, etc do not fall under '(ii) individual identification code'. However, they can be classified as '(i) information containing a name, date of birth, or other identifier which can be used to identify a specific individual' in a case.

Second, the APPI defines the following entities involved in the handling of personal information and sets forth their rights and obligations:

The APPI defines the person identified by personal information as an 'identifiable person'[20] and grants certain rights. This is roughly equivalent to what is called a 'data subject' in other jurisdictions. Because personal information is defined as 'information about a living individual', this 'identifiable person' does not include dead persons or legal entities.

'Business handling personal information' is that which belongs to the private sector and is regulated by the APPI. This is defined as 'a person that uses a personal information database or the equivalent for business'.[21]

'Administrative entity' means an organ or institution belonging to the public sector and is regulated by the APPI. This includes administrative organs, local government organs, incorporated administrative agencies or other prescribed corporations, local incorporated administrative agencies (Article 2(11)). It does not, however, include the Diet of Japan, local assemblies, and courts.

ii. Influence of International Data Protection Frameworks

Japanese law in this area has been strongly influenced by foreign law, especially the EU law. The discussion on protecting personal information in Japan began with the acceptance of the eight principles of the Organisation for Economic Co-operation and Development ('OECD') Privacy Guidelines of 1980[22] as an OECD member economy. In 1988, a limited protection statute focusing on personal information held by administrative agencies and processed by computer was enacted along with the eight principles.[23] For the private sector, on the other hand, protection of personal information has been achieved through soft law, such as guidelines, rather than statutes. For example, the Japan Information Processing and Development Centre (JIPDEC),[24] a non-governmental and non-profit organisation, released the Guidelines for Personal Information Protection in the Private Sector in 1988, and the 'PrivacyMark' certification system in 1998.

However, this approach of limited protection in the public sector and soft law regulation in the private sector was found to be weak in light of the 1995 EU Data Protection Directive.[25] This prompted the Government to introduce the APPI in 2003. The 2015 amendment introduced provisions to address cross-border transfers of personal data and established the PPC as a unified supervisory authority for the private sector. This was in

[20] APPI, Art 2(6).

[21] ibid, Art 16(2).

[22] Recommendation of the Council concerning Guidelines Governing the Protection of Privacy and Transborder Flows of Personal Data, available at legalinstruments.oecd.org/en/instruments/OECD-LEGAL-0188.

[23] Act on the Protection of Personal Information Electronically Processed and Held by Administrative Organs (Act No 95 of 1988).

[24] The Japan Information Processing and Development Center was established in 1967 as a public interest foundation. It changed its legal form to a general incorporated foundation in 2011. At the same time, it changed its official English name to JIPDEC.

[25] Directive 95/46/EC of the European Parliament and of the Council of 24 October 1995 on the protection of individuals with regard to the processing of personal data and on the free movement of such data [1995] OJ L281/31–50.

response to the EU's efforts at the time to strengthen the rules governing data transfers outside the EU, by amending the 1995 Data Protection Directive into the GDPR. The 2021 amendments made the PPC a supervisory authority not only for the private sector, but also for the public sector, including local governments. It also replaced the blanket exception for the academic sector in the previous law with individual exceptions.[26] All these changes were considered necessary in order to obtain EU adequacy recognition under the GDPR.

iii. Specific Provisions for Particular Sectors

The APPI of 2023, as amended in 2021, applies to both the public sector (administrative entities) and the private sector (business handling personal information). However, different rules may apply to the public and the private sectors. The basic concept of the Organisation for Economic Co-operation and Development (OECD) eight Principle-type rules regarding the handling of personal information, ie, specification of the purpose of use, use within the scope of the purpose, secure management, and the individual's rights to disclosure, correction, deletion, etc, is not significantly different for the two sectors. However, the specific rules take into account the differences in characteristics between the public sector, which handles personal information for public purposes and the private sector, which has a considerable difference in organisational structure and handles personal information according to their respective business purposes. Chapter 4 (Articles 16 through 59) applies only to the private sector and Chapter 5 (Articles 60 through 129) applies only to the public sector.

However, there are several exceptions to this framework. First, among the private sector, (1) journalistic organisations, (2) persons in the business of creating literary works, (3) religious organisations, and (4) political organisations are not subject to the entire provisions of Chapter 4 due to the constitutional value of their activities, when they handle personal information for their original purposes.[27] Instead, they should establish and publish their own internal regulations.[28] Second, entities like universities and other academic research institutes, when handling personal information for the purpose of providing it for academic research, without the consent of the individual, may use it beyond the original purpose of use,[29] acquire personal information requiring special consideration,[30] and provide it to third parties.[31] Third, national universities and national hospitals are classified as the private sector according to Article 2(11), but since they are also in the public sector, they are partially subject to the discipline of the public sector.[32] In addition, separate regulations are provided for the protection of personal information for the specific sectors including the Banking Act and the Telecommunications Business Act, but there is no special law that excludes the application of the APPI.

[26] Act No 37 of 2021, Art 50.
[27] APPI, Art 57(1).
[28] ibid, Art 57(3).
[29] ibid, Art 18.
[30] ibid, Art 20.
[31] ibid, Art 27.
[32] ibid, Art 58.

iv. Distinction and Interface between Data Protection and Privacy

In Japan, privacy protection and personal information protection are considered distinct concepts. Privacy is understood as a part of the 'right to life, liberty, and the pursuit of happiness' guaranteed by Article 13 of the Constitution of Japan, constituting a personal right, and its infringement constitutes a tort. On the other hand, Article 2(1) of the APPI defines personal information as

> information relating to a living individual which falls under any of the following items: (i) information containing a name, date of birth, or other identifier which can be used to identify a specific individual; (ii) those containing an individual identification code.

However, the article didn't consider whether the information pertains to personal interests.

The APPI is a law that demands the proper use of personal information in both the public and private sectors. However, violations of the APPI are only partially subject to administrative or criminal sanctions, whereas infringements of privacy resulting from violations of the APPI would lead to tort remedies[33] apart from the APPI itself.

Furthermore, the 2017 amendment to the APPI introduced additional protections for 'sensitive personal information' which could be seen as incorporating a privacy perspective into the APPI.[34] However, this does not transform the APPI into a privacy protection law.

v. Distinction between Personal and Non-Personal Data, and between Anonymised, Pseudonymised, or Encrypted

The APPI is intended to protect 'personal information'. However, there was a major controversy over the handling of information about living individuals that cannot be used to identify a specific individual (non-personal data). JR East, Japan's largest railway company, issues SUICA, a multi-purpose integrated circuit card used for small payments such as payment of train fares and records its usage data based on the individual's consent. In 2013, JR East planned to provide information to another company after converting cardholders' birth date from year, month, and day to year and month, and then converting the SUICA ID number to an irreversible different number. Since the converted data was no longer personally identifiable, it was not considered to be personal information, and thus the provision of this information was not considered illegal under the APPI at the time. However, SUICA users strongly criticised the plan, so JR East stopped providing this information.

In response, for the purpose of additional regulation, the Government introduced the 'anonymised personal information' system in the 2015 amendment to the APPI, and the 'pseudonymised personal information' system in the 2021 amendment.

Now under the APPI, 'anonymised personal information' is defined as 'information relating to an individual that can be prepared in a way that makes it not possible to identify a specific individual … and also make it not possible to restore that personal information'.[35]

[33] Civil Code, Art 709, the general law of torts, provides as follows: 'A person that has intentionally or negligently infringed the rights or legally protected interests of another person is liable to compensate for damage resulting in consequence.'

[34] APPI, Art 2(3).

[35] ibid, Art 2(6).

'Pseudonymised personal information' is defined as 'information relating to an individual that can be prepared in a way that makes it not possible to identify a specific individual unless collated with other information'.[36]

In other words, 'anonymised personal information' cannot be restored to personally identifiable 'personal information', but 'pseudonymised personal information' can be restored to 'personal information' by matching it with other information. Therefore, the regulations for the two are also different. Anonymised personal information that has been properly processed is no longer personal information and can be freely provided to third parties without the individual's consent. On the other hand, since pseudonymised personal information is still classified as personal information, the 'businesses handling personal information' can use it for a purpose different from the original purpose of use by changing the purpose of use,[37] but in principle cannot be provided to third parties.[38]

vi. Distinction between Domestic and Cross-Border/International Transfers

Under the APPI, the transfer of personal information to third parties is regulated separately depending on whether the holder of the personal information to be transferred is in the private or public sector.

a. Private Sector

The APPI establishes basic rules for transfers (provisions)[39] of personal information to domestic third parties, with additional rules for transfers to foreign third parties. For sensitive personal information, there are additional regulations for both domestic and foreign transfers.

For the domestic transfers of non-sensitive personal information, Article 27(1) requires, in principle, the prior consent of the identifiable person (opt-in), while allowing seven specific exceptions including cases involving law enforcement.[40] Article 27(2) also provides

[36] ibid, Art 2(5).

[37] ibid, Art 41(9).

[38] ibid, Art 41(6).

[39] Because the APPI uses the term 'provision' instead of 'transfer', this chapter also uses the term 'provision' when a strict interpretation of the statute is at issue.

[40] The seven exceptions are: (i) cases based on laws and regulations; (ii) cases in which there is a need to protect the life, wellbeing, or property of an individual, and it is difficult to obtain the consent of the identifiable person; (iii) cases in which there is a special need to improve public wellbeing or promote healthy child development, and it is difficult to obtain the consent of the identifiable person; (iv) cases in which there is a need to cooperate with a national government organ, local government, or person entrusted thereby with performing the functions prescribed by laws and regulations, and obtaining the consent of the identifiable person is likely to interfere with the performance of those functions; (v) cases in which the business handling personal information is an academic research institution or the equivalent, and providing the personal data for the purpose of publication of academic research results or teaching is unavoidable (excluding cases in which there is a risk of unjustly infringing on individual rights and interests); (vi) cases in which the business handling personal information is an academic research institution or the equivalent, and needs to provide the personal data for the academic research purpose (including cases in which a part of the purpose of handling the personal data is for academic research purposes, and excluding cases in which there is a risk of unjustly infringing on individual rights and interests) (limited to cases in which

for an 'opt-out' exception. The transfer of personal information to a third party without the prior consent of the identifiable person is permitted if three requirements are fulfilled when a business handling personal information (1) must notify the identifiable person of eight items, including the fact that providing the data to the third party constitutes the purpose of the use, or make these eight items readily accessible to the identifiable person, (2) must notify the PPC of the said items, and (3) must agree to cease to provide a third party with any personal data which can be used to identify the identifiable person, at the request of that person.

Article 28 introduces additional rules for the transfer of personal information to a third party located in a foreign country which in principle requires the prior consent of the identifiable person. This consent must be a consent to provide personal information to a third party in a foreign country. In addition, when obtaining consent, it is necessary to provide information on the personal information protection system of the foreign country and the personal information protection measures taken by the third party.[41]

However, three exceptions to this rule are listed in Article 28(1). If one of them applies, the consent of the identifiable individual is not required. First, the seven specific exceptions set forth in Article 27(1) can be applied in the same way even if the third party to whom the information is transferred is in a foreign country. The second exception applies when the third party is in a foreign country that has established a personal information protection system recognised by the PPC to have equivalent standards to that in Japan regarding the protection of individual rights and interests. Under this exception, third parties in the EU and the UK are currently treated the same as third parties in Japan, and personal information may be provided to them by using Article 27 instead of Article 28. The third exception applies when the third party in a foreign country meets the requirement that

> a person that establishes a system that conforms to standards prescribed by Order of the Personal Information Protection Commission as necessary for continuously taking measures equivalent to those that a business handling personal information must take concerning the handling of personal data pursuant to the provisions of [Section 2 of Chapter 4].

In this case, the third party in a foreign country is also treated the same as a third party in Japan and may be provided personal information under Article 27 instead of Article 28.

In this respect, the PPC has established two criteria for this exception in Article 16 of the APPI Enforcement PPC Rules. First, measures in accordance with the intent of the provisions of Section 2 of Chapter 4 of the Act are implemented between the business handling personal information and the third party to whom personal information has been given in an appropriate and reasonable manner regarding the handling of the said personal information by the said third party. Second, the third party to whom personal information is provided should be certified based on an international framework regarding the handling of personal information. These two points are discussed in more detail later in the chapter.

the business handling personal information and the third party jointly conduct academic research); (vii) cases in which the third party is an academic research institution or the equivalent, and the third party needs to handle the personal data for academic research purposes (including cases in which a part of the purpose of handling the personal data is for academic research purposes, and excluding cases in which there is a risk of unjustly infringing on individual rights and interests).

[41] APPI, Art 28(2).

The opt-out provision in Article 27(2) does not extend to sensitive personal information. As a result, the consent of the identifiable individual, whose information is to be provided to a third party, is necessary regardless of whether the third party is in Japan or in a foreign country with the seven exceptions listed in Article 27(1).

b. Public Sector

The transfer of personal information held by an administrative entity in the public sector to a third party is regulated in Chapter 5 of the APPI. Article 69(1) stipulates that 'An administrative organ's head or administrative entity must not personally use or provide other persons with personal information the administrative entity holds for any purpose other than the purpose of use, except cases based on laws and regulations.' This paragraph regulates use of personal information for any purpose other than the original purpose of use, and provision of it to the third party at the same time. Article 69(2) allows four limited exceptions to Article 69(1).[42] However, these exceptions shall be overridden if it is found that using that personal information personally or providing it to other persons for any purpose other than the purpose of use is likely to cause unjust prejudice to the rights or interests of the identifiable person or a third party.

In addition, the provision of personal information to third parties located in foreign countries is subject to almost identical restrictions as those on businesses handling personal information.[43]

vii. The Privacy Regulator and its Powers

The PPC, an external commission of the Cabinet Office under the authority of the Prime Minister, is the regulator of both the public and private sectors in the handling of personal information. Although it is not a privacy regulator in general, it is mandated to pursue ensuring the proper handling of personal information in order to protect individual rights and interests while ensuring smooth and proper management of the processes or services of administrative entities as well as ensuring due consideration of the value of personal information, and the fact that the proper and effective application of personal information contributes to the creation of new industries and the realization of a vibrant economic society and enriching quality of life for the Japanese public.[44]

[42] The four exceptions are: (i) if the personal information the administrative entity holds is used or provided with the identifiable person's consent, or if it is provided to the identifiable person; (ii) if the administrative entity uses personal information it holds within the organ only to the extent necessary for managing processes or services under the jurisdiction provided by laws and regulations, and there are reasonable grounds for the use of that personal information; (iii) if the personal information the administrative entity holds is provided to other administrative organ, incorporated administrative agency or other prescribed corporation, local government organ, or local incorporated administrative agency; the person that receives the information uses it only to the extent necessary for managing the processes or services under its jurisdiction provided by laws and regulations; and there are reasonable grounds for the use of that personal information; (iv) beyond what is set forth in the preceding three items, if the personal information the administrative entity holds is provided exclusively for statistical purpose or academic research purpose; provision of the information to other persons is obviously beneficial to the identifiable person; or there are other special grounds for providing that personal information.

[43] APPI, Art 71.

[44] ibid, Art 131.

To carry out these duties, the PPC is vested with certain powers. The main powers are: (1) supervisory authority over private sector businesses, including businesses handling personal information;[45] (2) supervisory authority over administrative entities;[46] and (3) supervisory authority over certified personal information protection organisations.[47]

The PPC's supervisory authority over private sector operators is structured in such a way that it can be exercised within a step-by-step process, which may take the form of requiring the submission of reports or materials, conducting on-site inspections, providing guidance and advice, recommending, or ordering the correction of violations of the law, and publicising violations of the order. On the other hand, the PPC does not have the power to issue orders to administrative entities. However, while recommendations to businesses in the private sector should be based on violations of the law, recommendations to administrative entities can be made for matters other than violations of the law. Reports on actions taken in response to the recommendations can also be requested.

'Certified Personal Information Protection Organizations' are private corporations that handle complaints and other matters to contribute to the proper handling of personal information, pseudonymised personal information, or anonymised personal information. The PPC may certify such organisations,[48] require them to report,[49] issue orders,[50] or revoke their certification.[51]

Therefore, the PPC does not have the authority to impose administrative sanctions. The APPI criminalises certain acts, such as the refusal of a business handling personal information to comply with the PPC's request to submit necessary information or material,[52] but it is for the courts to impose sanctions as opposed to the PPC.

III. Legal Bases, Mechanism and Exceptions for International Data Transfers and Data Protection

A. International Data Transfer

i. 'Adequacy Findings' or White Lists and Black Lists

The 1980 OECD Recommendation was originally formulated in anticipation of the expansion of cross-border transfers of personal information. The APPI enacted in 2003 was modelled on it but did not include provisions for cross-border transfers. At the time, the EU countries already had personal data protection laws in place under the Data Protection Directive which was supplemented by the 'Proposal for a Regulation of the European Parliament and

[45] ibid, Arts 146–52. In particular, Art 146(1) provides that the PPC may supervise a business handling personal information, a business handling pseudonymised personal information, a business handling anonymised personal information, a business handling information related to personal information, or other concerned person.
[46] ibid, Arts 156–60.
[47] ibid, Arts 153–55.
[48] ibid, Art 47.
[49] ibid, Art 153.
[50] ibid, Art 154.
[51] ibid, Art 155.
[52] ibid, Art 146.

of the Council on the protection of individuals with regard to the processing of personal data and on the free movement of such data (General Data Protection Regulation)' issued by the European Commission on 25 January 2012.[53]

In Japan, amendments to the APPI are urgently called for to keep the Japanese law in line with the principles of the GDPR, adopted in Article 25 of the Data Protection Directive, which allows the transfer of personal information from the EU only to countries with an 'adequate level of protection'. Therefore, the 2015 amendment to the APPI introduced regulations on the transfer of personal information to third parties located in foreign countries.

As noted above, the APPI is strongly influenced by the EU legal approach. The EU introduced the principle in Article 25 of the Data Protection Directive in 1995 to allow the transfer of personal data from the EU only to countries with an 'adequate level of protection'. The need to address this principle was one of the reasons for the adoption of the APPI in 2003.

Following amendments in 2015 and 2021, there are restrictions on the provision of personal information to third parties in foreign countries in Article 28 of the APPI for businesses handling personal information and in Article 71 of the APPI for administrative entities. The framework is that the provision of personal information to a third party in a foreign country requires the consent of the identifiable individual in principle, but that the provision of personal information to a third party in a foreign country that meets certain conditions, or to a third party that meets certain conditions, is treated the same as the provision of personal information to a third party in Japan, as an exception. In this case, businesses handling personal information or administrative entities may choose the 'opt-out' framework. This is deregulation based on the so-called 'whitelist' system.

Currently, the PPC lists 31 countries[54] as 'a foreign country that has established a personal information protection system recognised to have equivalent standards to that in Japan regarding the protection of individual rights and interests'. The PPC cooperates with foreign regulators, but no additions to the whitelist are planned.

Conversely, there is no 'blacklist' system in Japan, as the APPI permits the transfer of personal information to third parties in any country with the consent of the identifiable individual.

ii. Consent of Data Subjects as Exception to Existence of Privacy Safeguards Overseas

Although Japanese law does not have a blacklisting system, it allows cross-border data transfers with the consent of the identifiable person. This is a potential threat to the rights and interests of the identifiable person. Therefore, the APPI requires businesses handling personal information and administrative entities to provide information about both the foreign country and the third party when obtaining consent.[55] This is similar to Article 49(1)(a) of the GDPR, which requires the provision of risk information when making a decision and is an effective means of regulating cross-border data transfers. However,

[53] COM(2012)011 final, 25 January 2012, available at eur-lex.europa.eu/legal-content/EN/TXT/?uri=celex%3A52012PC0011.

[54] The 31 countries are Austria, Belgium, Bulgaria, Croatia, Cyprus, Czech Republic, Denmark, Estonia, Finland, France, Germany, Greece, Hungary, Iceland, Ireland, Italy, Latvia, Liechtenstein, Lithuania, Luxembourg, Malta, Netherlands, Norway, Poland, Portugal, Romania, Slovakia, Slovenia, Spain, Sweden, and the United Kingdom.

[55] APPI, Arts 28(2) and 71(2).

there are a number of operational difficulties with this approach, including the practical issues associated with using a cloud system.

In this regard, a frequent question is this – does using a cloud service with servers located outside of a country constitute providing information to a third party in a foreign country? And if so, where is the foreign country? First, the PPC states that whether or not uploading personal information to the cloud constitutes 'provision' of personal information depends on whether or not the cloud service provider 'handles' the uploaded personal information.[56] For example, if the service provided by the cloud only stores encrypted data, the cloud service provider is not considered to be handling personal information. On the other hand, if a school uses an external cloud education management system, the learning records uploaded to the cloud are handled by the service provider. In the latter case, this results in the provision of personal information to the third party. In this case, how should we determine whether the personal information is being provided to a third party in a foreign country or to a third party in Japan? There are several possible answers if one considers the location of the server, the location of the service, or the location of the service provider's office. As far as the personal information protection measures of a service provider are concerned, it is reasonable to consider the location of the service provider's office although it may be difficult to determine the location if the service provider operates in multiple countries. In such cases, from the perspective of protecting the interests of the identifiable person, it would be desirable to provide information for all possible jurisdictions. Since the obligation to present information about both the foreign country and the third party was introduced in 2022, no court decision has yet been rendered on this matter.

iii. Contracts

As mentioned above, according to Article 28(1) of the APPI and Article 16(1) of the APPI Enforcement PPC Rules, the personal information may be provided to the third party in a foreign country without the consent of the identifiable person if

> measures in accordance with the intent of the provisions of Section 2 of Chapter 4 of the Act are ensured to be implemented between the business handling personal information and the third party to whom personal information is provided in an appropriate and reasonable manner regarding the handling of the said personal information by the said third party.

The question then arises as to what constitutes an appropriate and reasonable manner. According to the PPC's interpretation, the third party in a foreign country of contracts, agreements, or memoranda may be required to comply with Articles 17–28, 33–38 and 40 of the APPI with exceptions that apply only to businesses in Japan.[57] Such contracts or agreements shall concern personal information provided by the business in Japan to the foreign third party.[58] With respect to other information held by the third party, the third party is not required to take any action consistent with the intent of the Japanese law.[59]

[56] Q&A 7-53. PPC, *Q&A Concerning the Guideline for the APPI*, available at www.ppc.go.jp/files/pdf/2312_APPI_QA.pdf.

[57] 4-1. PPC, *Guideline on the APPI (Provision to the Third Party in Foreign Countries)*, available at www.ppc.go.jp/files/pdf/231227_guidelines02.pdf.

[58] ibid.

[59] ibid.

The PPC also states that international consistency will be considered in determining compliance with the 'measures in accordance with the intent of the provisions of Section 2 of Chapter 4 of the Act'.[60] Therefore, when concluding a contract, it is possible to use a model contract from the EU, the Association of Southeast Asian Nations, or other international organisations. However, it is necessary for these model contracts to be substantially in accordance with Articles 17 to 28, 32 to 38, and 40 of the APPI. This determination will ultimately be made by the courts through contract interpretation, with the guidelines for interpretation of model contracts serving as an important reference.

In Japan, the interpretation of a contract should 'reasonably clarify the meaning of the contract, taking into account the purpose of the parties, the circumstances leading to the act in question, and the custom and practice in the transaction'.[61] The guidelines for the interpretation of model contracts are presumed to represent the unanimous interpretation of both parties unless there are special circumstances. However, if an interpretation according to the guidelines would result in non-compliance with the APPI, it is theoretically up to the discretion of the court whether to interpret the contract differently from the guidelines to comply with the APPI or to declare non-compliance.

iv. Asia-Pacific Economic Cooperation Cross-Border Privacy Rules System

Japan joined the Asia-Pacific Economic Cooperation (APEC) Cross-Border Privacy Rules (CBPR) System in 2014. In December 2016, the Japan Institute for Promotion of Digital Economy and Community ('JIPDEC', formerly known as the Japan Information Processing and Development Centre until 2011) was registered for the first time as an Accountability Agent (AA).

The CBPR system serves two functions in Japan. First, if a business handling personal information in Japan intends to provide personal information to a third party in a non-whitelisted country, and if the third party is certified by the AA under the CBPR system in its jurisdiction, the third party may receive the same treatment as a third party in Japan under Article 28(1) of the APPI and Article 16 item 2 of the APPI Enforcement PPC Rules because the PPC's interpretation on this matter clearly states that the CBPR system is one of the 'international framework(s)' of the APPI Enforcement PPC Rules.[62] This would reduce the burden on the Japanese business which intends to provide such personal information.

In addition, according to the PPC's interpretation,[63] even if the third party in a foreign country is NOT certified by the AA in its jurisdiction, and if the Japanese business which intends to provide personal information had been certified in Japan, it can also be expected that the applicability of the 'appropriate and reasonable manner' requirement of Article 16 of Item 1 of the APPI Enforcement PPC Rules is more likely to be recognised. This is because JIPDEC APEC CBPR Requirements 6.4[64] specifies the duty to supervise third parties as one

[60] 4-2. PPC, ibid.
[61] Supreme Court First Bench Decision on 19 July 1976, 118 Shumin 291.
[62] 4-2, *Guideline on the APPI (Provision to the Third Party in Foreign Countries* (n 57).
[63] Q&A 7-53. PPC, *Q&A Concerning the Guideline for the APPI* (n 56).
[64] See www.jipdec.or.jp/project/cbpr/JIPDEC_AOP_CBPR_005.pdf.

of the requirements for certification, and it is expected that such a duty will be reflected in the content of contracts with third parties in a foreign country.

The second is the case of information transfer in the opposite direction. If a Japanese business handling personal information receives personal information from a foreign entity that is subject to cross-border data transfer restrictions, the Japanese business can expect to reduce the procedural burden in the foreign country related to the transfer of personal information by being certified under the CBPR system. This expectation is not directly protected by the APPI but will be protected through the spread of the APEC CBPR system and the harmonisation of national laws. In Japan, JIPDEC is the only AA under the CBPR system and has certified four businesses handling personal information.

v. International Privacy Certification Schemes, Trustmarks or Privacy Seals

In Japan, the 'PrivacyMark' system and ISMS certification are widely used to visualise the data and privacy protection efforts of companies and other entities.

The 'PrivacyMark' system, which JIPDEC began operating in 1998, is a system that assesses the adequacy of an entity's personal information system and its operation and allows entities that meet the criteria to use the 'PrivacyMark' logo. Since it is based on the Japanese Industrial Standard 'JIS Q 15001:2017 Personal Information Protection Management Systems – Requirements', it focuses on the protection of personal information rather than the security of information systems in general. In addition, because it is designed to work in conjunction with the APPI, it is not international in nature but is a system specific to Japan.

The ISMS certification, on the other hand, certifies compliance with JISQ27001 which is the Japanese localisation of ISO/IEC27001. It is not limited to the protection of personal information but covers information security in general. The ISMS certification system in Japan was started by the JIPDEC in 2001. However, since 2018, the 'ISMS Accreditation Center' (ISMS-AC), an organisation independent of JIPDEC, has taken over the core of the system.[65] Unlike the PrivacyMark, ISMS certification is not performed by the ISMS-AC itself, but by private organisations called ISMS Certification Bodies. The ISMS-AC is responsible for accrediting that the ISMS certification body is competent to perform certifications according to the requirements of the international standards and that the certifications are performed in an impartial manner. The ISMS certification is international in nature as it is a conformance certification to the international standard ISO/IEC27001.

The number of registered entities is 17,222 for 'PrivacyMark' as of 30 September 2022[66] and 7,027 for ISMS certification as of 26 August 2022[67] with 'PrivacyMark' having more than twice as many users. One reason for this may be that 'PrivacyMark' was available earlier and was often used as a tender requirement by local governments. However, the number of ISMS registrations is also expected to increase due to the recent increase in the use of both or either as a tender requirement and the addition of Privacy Information Management System certification to ISMS certification (ISMS-PIMS).

[65] See isms.jp/english/about/overview.html.
[66] See privacymark.jp/certification_info/jdi6lq00000017af-att/pmark_data_20220930.pdf.
[67] See isms.jp/topics/news/20220901.html.

B. International Data Protection and Liability

i. Specific Requirements or Policies for Data Processing and Retention

A fundamental principle of information processing in Japan is to balance the protection of individual interests, such as the protection of personal information, with the protection of other interests. This is well illustrated by the purpose clause of the APPI, which provides as follows:

> Article 1 The purpose of this Act is to protect the rights and interests of individuals while ensuring the smooth and proper management of the processes or services of administrative entities, as well as to ensure due consideration of the value of personal information and the fact that the proper and effective use of personal information contributes to the creation of new industries and the realization of a vibrant economic society and an enriched quality of life for the Japanese public; [...][68]

Based on this fundamental principle, the APPI adopts the basic structure of first establishing a system to protect the rights of individuals, and then making exceptions to this system to secure other interests. The starting point is the specification of the purpose for which the personal information is to be processed. Article 17(1) of the APPI states that 'in handling personal information, the business handling personal information must specify as much as possible the purpose for which it uses that information'. In addition, Article 18(1) of the APPI states that 'A business handling personal information must not handle personal information beyond the scope necessary for achieving the purpose of use specified pursuant to the provisions of the preceding Article' and Article 19 of the APPI states that 'a business handling personal information must not utilise personal information in a way that there is a possibility of fomenting or inducing unlawful or unjust act'. These articles are designed to protect the rights and interests of individuals.

However, the APPI seeks to ensure that a balance is struck by making exceptions to these provisions in order to protect other rights and interests. Although the purpose of use may be altered, a business handling personal information must not alter it beyond the extent that can be appreciably linked to what it was before the alteration.[69] A business handling personal information can handle personal information beyond the scope necessary for achieving the purpose of use only with the prior consent of the identifiable person.[70] In addition, Article 18(3) of the APPI lists six situations where the application of Article 18(1) is exempted.[71]

[68] APPI, Art 1.

[69] ibid, Art 17(2).

[70] ibid, Art 18(1).

[71] The six situations are: (i) cases based on laws and regulations (including local ordinances; hereinafter the same applies in this chapter); (ii) cases in which there is a need to protect the life, wellbeing, or property of an individual, and it is difficult to obtain the consent of the identifiable person; (iii) cases in which there is a special need to improve public wellbeing or promote healthy child development, and it is difficult to obtain the consent of the identifiable person; (iv) cases in which there is a need to cooperate with a national government organ, local government, or person entrusted thereby with performing the functions prescribed by laws and regulations, and obtaining the consent of the identifiable person is likely to interfere with the performance of those functions; (v) cases in which the business handling personal information is an academic research institution or the equivalent, and needs to handle the personal information for the purpose of using it in academic research (hereinafter referred to as 'academic research purposes' in this chapter) (including cases in which a part of the purpose of handling the

ii. Regulations on Legal Ownership of Data Protection and Privacy Rights

As mentioned above, in Japan the right to privacy is protected by case law based on Article 13 of the Constitution of Japan and Article 709 of the Civil Code. On the other hand, the APPI does not entitle the right to privacy to individuals. However, the APPI recognises the following statutory rights of identifiable persons with respect to the handling of personal data concerning them:

1) the right to be informed of the purposes for which personal data are to be used;[72]
2) the right to request the disclosure of personal data;[73]
3) the right to request that personal data be corrected, added, or deleted if the content of the data is not factual;[74]
4) the right to request that personal data cease to be used or be deleted if it is used for purposes other than those specified (in violation of Article 18), if it is used in an inappropriate manner (in violation of Article 19) or if it is acquired in an inappropriate manner (in violation of Article 20);[75]
5) the right to request that personal data cease to be provided to a third party if it is provided in an inappropriate manner (in violation of Article 27(1) or Article 28);[76] and
6) the right to request that personal data cease to be used, deleted, or provided to a third party if it is no longer necessary for the business to use the personal data, if the personal data has been leaked, or if the handling of the personal data is likely to harm the rights and interests of an identifiable person.[77]

When an individual invokes these rights, ownership of the data is never an issue. Under the general principle of Japanese law, only tangible objects are subject to property rights.[78] Intangible objects, which are typically information, are subject to property rights only if there is a provision in the statute law. A typical example is the Copyright Act[79] which grants rights in one's own works separate from ownership of the media of one's works. However, the APPI does not contain any provisions regarding the ownership of personal information. In fact, the APPI does not even specify whether the ownership of personal information provided by an individual to a business or administrative entity under the APPI is subject to property rights.

The problem, therefore, is how to deal with new breaches such as doxxing. The APPI is based on regulating the relationship between individuals and businesses handling personal information and administrative entities and does not regulate individuals who engage in

personal information is for academic research purposes, and excluding cases in which there is a risk of unjustly infringing on individual rights and interests); (vi) cases in which personal data is provided to an academic research institution or the equivalent, and they need to handle the personal data for academic research purposes (including cases in which a part of the purpose of handling the personal data is for academic research purposes, and excluding cases in which there is a risk of unjustly infringing on individual rights and interests).

[72] APPI, Art 32(2).
[73] ibid, Art 33(1).
[74] ibid, Art 34(1).
[75] ibid, Art 35(1).
[76] ibid, Art 35(3).
[77] ibid, Art 35(5).
[78] Civil Code, Art 85 states: 'The term "things" as used in this Code means tangible objects.'
[79] Act No 48 of 1970.

acts such as doxxing. Theoretically it is not impossible to counteract doxxing by combining the rights under the APPI with the above rights, but in practice this is extremely difficult.

Therefore, under Japanese law, the right to privacy and personality rights recognised under general law, such as the Constitution and the Civil Code, are used to counter doxxing. However, the problem here is that doxxing, which typically involves the dissemination of personal information on the Internet without the consent of the person concerned, makes it difficult to identify the perpetrator itself, and therefore it is also difficult to resolve disputes through judicial proceedings.

This has prompted the Diet of Japan enacted in 2001 the Act on the Limitation of Liability for Damages of Specified Telecommunications Service Providers and the Right to Demand Disclosure of Identification Information of the Senders.[80] This law partially removes the obligation of confidentiality of communications that is generally owed by telecommunications service providers and allows them to provide information about the infringer to the person alleging that his or her rights have been infringed, while also allowing for limited damages. Its Article 4(1) provides that

> Any person alleging that his or her rights were infringed by distribution of information via specified telecommunications may … demand a specified telecommunications service provider to disclose identification information of the sender pertaining to said infringement of the rights possessed by said provider of disclosure-related service, (i) where there is evidence that the rights of a person demanding said disclosure were infringed by the distribution of the infringing information, and (ii) where said identification information of the sender is necessary for the person demanding said disclosure to exercise his or her rights to claim damages and where there is justifiable ground for said person to receive disclosed identification information of the sender.

However, its Article 3 provides that the provider itself will only be liable for damages in a limited number of cases, such as when it was aware that an infringement had been committed through a telecommunications service provided by the provider and could have prevented it.

A person whose interests have been infringed by doxxing will first use this law to identify the infringer and then seek removal of the information or compensation under Article 709 of the Civil Code. However, electronic data can be easily copied and it is common for data to remain on the Internet even after the infringer has deleted the information. The so-called 'right to be forgotten' is therefore an issue. However, the Japanese laws, including the APPI, do not provide for this. Therefore, it is again necessary to rely on the Constitution and the Civil Code, which are general laws not specifically targeting personal information. In a decision of 31 January 2017, the Supreme Court, in a case against Google in which a person sought to remove from search results news articles and commentaries about a crime he had committed several years earlier, did not generally deny the possibility of a removal order on the basis of an invasion of privacy, but held that such crime reports would not be removed on the grounds that the crime reports and commentaries were still of public interest.[81] This decision does not reject the 'right to be forgotten' *per se* but shows a comparative balance tilting towards the right to know and freedom of expression.

[80] Act No 137 of 2001.
[81] Supreme Court Third Bench Decision on 31 January 2017, 71-1 Minshu 63.

iii. Extraterritorial Effect of Data Protection Law

The 2021 Amendment to the APPI also extends to the extraterritorial application of the APPI and sets out its basic framework in its Article 171.

According to Article 171 of the APPI, the extraterritorial application applies to all four types of businesses covered by the Act in a foreign country. These are (1) a business handling personal information, (2) a business handling pseudonymised personal information, (3) a business handling anonymised personal information or (4) a business handling information related to personal information. Extraterritorial application occurs when any of the following four types of information is handled in a foreign country in relation to supplying a good or service to a person in Japan: (a) information by which that person in Japan is identifiable, (b) information related to personal information that is to be acquired as that personal information, (c) pseudonymised personal information prepared by using that personal information or (d) anonymised personal information prepared by using that personal information.

The most typical case is where an Internet retailer in a foreign country handles the personal information of a Japanese consumer in order to sell and deliver goods to the consumer (case (1) and (a)). Slightly more complex cases are where a foreign server operator (X), at the request of a Japanese company (Y), provides IP addresses (not personal information) from Japan accessing X's server, and Y matches these with Y's customer list containing the IP addresses of customers and uses the information for marketing purposes (case (4) and (b)), or where an Internet retailer in a foreign country handles anonymised personal information created from the personal information of Japanese consumers in order to analyse trends in relation to the sale of products to Japanese consumers (case (3) and (d)).

On the other hand, the handling of personal information of employees of a Japanese domestic subsidiary by its parent company in a foreign country solely for the purpose of managing information of employees of its group companies is not subject to extraterritorial application. However, in this case, the provision of personal information of employees of the Japanese subsidiary to the foreign parent company constitutes the provision of personal information to a third party in a foreign country and is regulated by the aforementioned Article 28.1.

iv. Data Breach Notification

Article 26 of the APPI requires businesses handling personal information to report to the PPC and to notify the identifiable person in the event of a personal data incident that meets certain conditions. Article 26(1) of the APPI and Article 7 of the APPI Enforcement PPC Rules provide that certain conditions are met where leakage, loss or damage has occurred or is likely to occur in relation to the following four types of data or situation: (1) personal data containing sensitive personal information; (2) personal data that may cause property damage due to wrongful use; (3) attacks on personal data that may have been carried out for wrongful purposes; and (4) data of more than 1,000 persons. Article 26(2) of the APPI and Article 10 of the APPI Enforcement PPC Rules provide that when a business handling personal information reports to the PPC and to notify the identifiable person as soon as possible, depending on the circumstances of the situation, unless notification is difficult and alternative measures are taken to protect the rights and interests of the person. Article 68 of the APPI and Articles 44 to 46 of the APPI Enforcement PPC Rules provide for the same obligations for administrative entities.

IV. Data Security and Data Localisation

A. Data Security and Localisation Requirements

In Japan, there is no statutory regulation for data localisation. The Japanese Government advocates Data Free Flow with Trust (DFFT) and has not adopted a policy to promote data localisation as a national policy. However, the Government has called for data localisation in the form of guidelines rather than legislation, as strengthening cybersecurity has become an important issue for Japan.

Pursuant to Article 26(1) of the Basic Act of Cybersecurity,[82] the Japanese Government has formulated the 'Unified Set of Standards for Cybersecurity Measures for Government Agencies' which includes the 'Guidelines for the Formulation of Standards for Measures for Government Agencies'. The 2023 version states that

> the information system security manager or the information security manager of the section office shall select the contractor by assessing the risk of laws and regulations other than domestic laws being applied to the information handled by the agency through the use of outsourced services, and, if necessary, the location where the agency's information is handled and the applicable laws and jurisdictions stipulated in the contract shall be included in the specification as well as in the selection conditions for the contractor.[83]

In the medical field, the 'Guidelines for Security Management of Medical Information Systems (Edition 6.0) – Planning and Management' also states that when medical information is stored off-site, 'it should be confirmed that the information equipment in which the medical information is stored is covered by Japanese laws'.[84]

B. Data Security or Localisation Requirements for Particular Types of Data

Japan does not have localisation legislation based on the type of information. However, the Act on the Protection of Specially Designated Secrets[85] is relevant in this regard. Until the enactment of this statute in 2013, there were few differences in legal protection based on

[82] Act No 104 of 2014.

[83] National Center of Incident readiness and Strategy for Cybersecurity (eds), *Guidelines for the Formulation of Standards for Measures for Government Agencies* (4 July 2023) 164, available atwww.nisc.go.jp/pdf/policy/general/guider5.pdf.

[84] Ministry of Health, Labour and Welfare eds. *Guidelines for Security Management of Medical Information Systems (Edition 6.0) – Planning and Management* (May 2023) 27, available at www.mhlw.go.jp/content/10808000/001102575.pdf.

[85] Act No 108 of 2013.

the nature of information in Japan. For example, Article 100 of the National Public Service Act[86] provides that 'an official shall not divulge any secret which may have come to his/her knowledge in the course of his/her duties' and its Article 109 provides for a penalty of up to one year's imprisonment or a fine of up to 30,000 yen for violation. Importantly, there is no difference in the duty of confidentiality or penalty depending on the nature of the leaked information.

After the enactment of the Act on the Protection of Specially Designated Secrets, it stipulates that information held by the Government that is 'not publicly undisclosed and whose leakage could seriously impede the security of Japan and therefore must be kept secret in particular'.[87] Specially designated secrets are not disclosed to the public until their designation is lifted, and their use for administrative purposes is restricted. Article 9 of the Act also provides that specially designated secrets may be disclosed to foreign governments or international organisations only in special cases. However, the Act does not provide for systematic localisation of data by directly prohibiting certain types of information from being taken out of the country.

V. Issues in Private and International Law

A. Litigations Involving Cross-Border Data Protection and Privacy

While there are many aspects to cross border data transfers and privacy disputes, this chapter focuses on online privacy disputes, which are structurally different from offline disputes. Disputes on the Internet may take the form of disputes between new types of parties due to the technical characteristics of the Internet. For example, while traditional invasions of privacy are two-party disputes between publishers and celebrities, doxxing invasions of privacy involve the difficulty of identifying the infringer and the fact that the harm cannot be remedied by deleting the information from the infringer's computer. Therefore, online service providers, search engine providers and platform providers are required to delete or make the information invisible. In Japan, due to constitutional protections, such requests can only be challenged in the judicial courts.

The issue is usually on jurisdiction and the extraterritorial application of the judgment. For example, in a recent case where Google was ordered by the Supreme Court of Canada to delete certain information worldwide, Google agreed to delete the information within Canada but refused to restrict access thereto from places outside of Canada.[88] Google's refusal in this regard gives rise to significant challenges against remedies for victims of data breaches. In fact, Google filed a lawsuit in the US District Court for the Northern District of California, seeking an injunction against the enforcement of a Supreme Court of Canada order in the United States. The Court issued an injunction on the grounds that

[86] Act No 120 of 1947.
[87] Act No 108 of 2013, Art 3(1).
[88] *Google Inc v Equustek Solutions Inc*, 2017 SCC 34. See also Nobuyuki Sato, 'Saibansho ni your Intanetto Jyoho no Sekaiteki Kisei no Kanousei – Google Inc.v Equustek Solutions Inc Kanada Saiko Saibansho Hanketsu o Keiki to shite-' in N Sato (ed), *Kenpo Riron no Saikochiku* (Keibundo, 2019).

the order violates Section 230 of the US Communications Decency Act[89] and threatens freedom of speech.[90]

In Japan, however, this issue is not as apparent and there have been no significant court decisions in cross-border disputes. This is because Japan is the only country where there is a concentration of native Japanese speakers, and there is a special situation where Google can effectively and practically resolve disputes by following the decisions of Japanese domestic courts. Of course, Japanese courts may face similar problems in the future. One scenario involves enforcing a foreign judgment in Japan ordering the deletion of data worldwide, and another requires a Japanese court to issue a judgment with worldwide effect.

With respect to the former, the 1997 Supreme Court decision[91] on enforcing foreign judgments in Japan has precedential value. In that case, the payment of punitive damages ordered by a California state court against a Japanese company had to be recognised and enforced in Japan under Article 118 of the Japanese Code of Civil Procedure. The Supreme Court denied the validity of the foreign judgment on the ground that it did not meet one of the four requirements for recognition of its validity: 'The content of the judgment and the litigation proceedings must not be contrary to public order or good morals in Japan.'[92] In other words, the Supreme Court denied punitive damages in Japan based on the fact that Japanese law strictly distinguishes between criminal penalties and civil remedies. In light of this precedent, whether the effect of a judgment ordering deletion of data worldwide extends to data on servers located in Japan must be determined by the court on a case-by-case basis. For example, in cases such as invasion of privacy or sexual expression, where coordination with freedom of expression is necessary, the court may be more inclined to find that the judgment is against public order and morality due to legal and cultural differences between countries. On the other hand, in cases such as intellectual property infringement, it may be assumed that expungement will be relatively easy to grant if the common ground is recognised worldwide. Although the Supreme Court's precedent,[93] emphasising the principle of territoriality, has held that an action in a Japanese court for the destruction of an infringing product in Japan based on a US patent right is not permitted, in 2023 the Intellectual Property High Court ruled for the first time that the Patent Act[94] can be applied extraterritorially.[95] Future developments in case law, including changes in precedent, should be closely monitored.

With respect to the latter scenario, Japanese courts have generally taken a cautious approach to the extraterritorial application of Japanese law. However, in 2017 the Supreme Court applied the Act on Prohibition of Private Monopolization and Maintenance of Fair Trade[96] extraterritorially.[97] The decision of the Intellectual Property High Court in 2023 marked a shift toward the extraterritorial application of patent law. Although these

[89] 47 USC § 230.
[90] Case No 5:17-cv-04207-EJD, 2017 WL 5000834 (ND Cal, Nov 2, 2017).
[91] Supreme Court Second Bench Decision on 11 July 1997, 51-6 Minshu 2573.
[92] Code of Civil Procedure, Art 118(iii).
[93] Supreme Court First Bench Decision on 26 September 2002, 56-7 Minshu 1551.
[94] Act No 121 of 1959.
[95] Intellectual Property High Court Grand Bench Decision on 26 May 2023, 15962 Tokkyo News 1 and 15963 Tokkyo News 1.
[96] Act No 54 of 1947.
[97] Supreme Court Third Bench Decision on 12 December 2017, 71-10 Minshu 1958.

extensions cannot be considered precedents for tort based privacy protection, as they are based on the interpretation of individual statutes, they represent a change in the Court's previous stance, and the future development of case law in this scenario should also be closely monitored.

B. Jurisdictional Issues Involving Cross-Border Data Protection and Privacy

The primary law for determining jurisdiction in multijurisdictional cases in Japan is Articles 3–2 to 3–12 of the Code of Civil Procedure.[98] However, their effect can be superseded by any arbitration agreement or exclusive jurisdiction agreement. In the absence of such an agreement, the above provisions will be applied to determine whether the Japanese courts have jurisdiction. As will be discussed hereinbelow, under Japanese law, even in the case of an international conflict of jurisdiction, the jurisdiction of the Japanese courts is recognised if one of the statutory grounds exists but jurisdiction will be denied when a special circumstance is recognised.[99]

As the Japanese law does not distinguish data breaches between online and offline, jurisdiction is determined based on the defendant's domicile, the place of the event and the nature of the dispute. If any of these provisions are applicable, Japan may be the place of jurisdiction. In cross-border data transfer and privacy disputes, the place of the defendant's domicile, the place of performance of the obligation, the place of business and the place of the tort are often determined. However, there are problems, for example, in the case of contracts entered into and completed entirely online, the place of performance cannot be contemplated. In such cases, a provision[100] is used which allows Japanese courts to have jurisdiction for the purpose of consumer protection. Since this provision can only be used in business-to-consumer cases, its applicability to consumer-to-consumer cases on the Internet is controversial.[101]

Even when the jurisdiction of Japanese courts is recognised, there are practical difficulties. Since judicial power constitutes a part of state sovereignty, in principle, it is not permissible for Japanese courts to conduct judicial proceedings in a foreign country. For example, under Article 223 of the Code of Civil Procedure, a Japanese court may issue an order with a sanction of a fine for disobedience, requiring a cloud service provider in Japan, whether a party or a third party, to submit documents. However, if the cloud service provider is located outside of Japan, this is not permissible as it would constitute a violation of the sovereignty of that foreign country. Therefore, a Japanese party and court must examine evidence using the framework of international judicial assistance. However, Japan is not a signatory to the Convention of 18 March 1970 on the Taking of Evidence Abroad in Civil or Commercial Matters,[102] to which 66 countries, primarily common law countries,

[98] Act No 109 of 1996.
[99] Code of Civil Procedure, Art 3–9.
[100] ibid, Art 3–4.
[101] See Takuya Shima, 'Online Service Provider o meguru Kokusaiteki na Ho Kiritsu: Teishoku Ho no Kanten kara no Kosatsu' (2022) 73(1) *Hokudai Hogaku Ronshu* 1.
[102] See assets.hcch.net/docs/dfed98c0-6749-42d2-a9be-3d41597734f1.pdf.

are signatories. Therefore, the examination of evidence outside of Japan must be conducted either by the court of a foreign country or by a Japanese consul stationed in a foreign country under the Convention of March 1954 on Civil Procedure,[103] or under a bilateral treaty or agreement between Japan and the country concerned. Due to the time constraints and enforceability issues associated with these procedures, parties often opt for a foreign court even in cases where a Japanese court may have jurisdiction. Consequently, practitioners are increasingly focusing on establishing a new framework that combines Alternative Dispute Resolution (ADR), including international commercial arbitration, with online dispute resolution.[104]

C. Applicable Law in Litigations Involving Cross-Border Data Protection and Privacy

The primary law for determining applicable law in multijurisdictional cases in Japan is the 'Act on General Rules for Application of Laws'.[105] This law uses a traditional connecting factor approach to determine the applicable law. The following are some of the most relevant in relation to cross-border data transfers and privacy violations:

1) Tort in general: A claim arising from a tort is governed by the law of the place where the result of the wrongful act occurred.[106]
2) Defamation (exception 1): A claim arising from a tort of defamation of others is governed by the law of the victim's habitual residence.[107]
3) Tort (exception 2): A claim arising from a tort is governed by the law of the place with which the tort is obviously more closely connected than the place indicated in the preceding three Articles, in light of that the parties had their habitual residence in the places governed by the same law at the time of the occurrence of the tort, that the tort was committed in breach of the obligation under a contract between the parties, or any other circumstances concerned.[108]
4) Juridical Act: A juridical act is governed by the law of the place chosen by the parties at the time of the act.[109]
5) Juridical Act: In the absence of a choice of law under Article 7, a juridical act is governed by the law of the place with which the act is most closely connected at the time of the act.[110]
6) Consumer Contracts: In the absence of a choice of law under Article 7, a Consumer Contract is governed by the law of the consumer's habitual residence.[111]

[103] See assets.hcch.net/docs/30f6092f-2a79-45f6-85a9-4f13c7c783c2.pdf.
[104] For example, see research projects of the Japan Institute of International Arbitration and Training, available at www.jiiart.com/en/.
[105] Act No78 of 2006.
[106] the Act on General Rules for Application of Laws, Art 17.
[107] ibid, Art 19.
[108] ibid, Art 20.
[109] ibid, Art 7.
[110] ibid, Art 8.
[111] Act on General Rules for Application of Laws, Art 11(2).

From the above applicable articles in the case of a data breach, it can be seen that there are differences depending on the type of data.

Similar to Article 19 of the Act on General Rules for Application of Laws which determines the applicable law based on the victim's domicile for defamation (which is an injury to personal interests among the torts), it would be logical to apply the same Article when the infringed data are personal data. This approach would also avoid the problem of the difficulty of identifying the place of origin of the consequences of the act committed in cases of infringements of personality on the Internet where the damage occurs worldwide. On the other hand, in the case of non-personal data, the principle of Article 17 the Act on General Rules for Application of Laws should apply. However, if the data concern both personal and non-personal interests, such as certain portrait data which is also subject to the right of publicity as a property right, it may be possible to consider that Article 17 should be applied instead of Article 19.[112]

On the other hand, there are also questions as to when contract law should be applied. Most cross-border data transfers are based on contracts, in which online service providers play an increasing role and the contractual relationship is becoming more complex. Apart from contracts of use with the provider, the purchase of goods and ancillary services on the provider's site with a person other than the provider is a daily occurrence, often involving a choice of law agreement that is highly disadvantageous to the user. In such cases, actions including the application of the consumer protection provisions of Article 11 should be taken.

D. Obstacles to Effective Data Protection

Although it is not a problem limited to Japanese law, there are inherent limitations in addressing new cross-border challenges such as data protection using the approach of resolving disputes with domestic laws of sovereign states. For instance, various services utilising blockchain technology inherently do not rely on the laws of any particular nation and can even be entirely contained within cyberspace. There are limitations to the traditional approaches of traditional private international law in addressing legal issues that arise in such contexts.[113]

E. Major Data Protection Cases and 'Data Scraping'

In Japan, while there has not yet been a significant ruling specifically on 'data scraping', the Supreme Court in 2023 ruled that a system which enables data matching of personal information by the Government was constitutional and was not in violation of the constitutional right to privacy. It is a pity that this decision did not address the issue of data ownership but

[112] See Kunifumi Saito, 'Conflict of Law around the Right of Publicity' (2014) 32 *Jyoho Tsushin Gkkai Shi* 2, available at www.jstage.jst.go.jp/article/jsicr/32/2/32_83/_pdf.

[113] See Mathias Audit, 'Le droit international privé confronté à la blockchain' (2022) 293 *Journal of Law and Politics* 135.

focused on the methods of data use and the risks associated with its use, concluding that the measures in place were sufficient to prevent privacy violations.

In 2013, the Diet of Japan enacted the 'Act on the Use of Numbers to Identify a Specific Individual in Administrative Procedures'.[114] This Act provides that each person registered in the Basic Resident Registry[115] will be assigned a personal number, commonly known as 'My Number', to be used to increase administrative efficiency and ensure fairness of benefits and burdens. In Japan, different numbers are used for different administrative activities, and identification between different procedures is generally carried out separately as required. For example, passport numbers and social security numbers are different numbers, and even if these two numbers are matched, the identity of the person identified by these numbers is unknown. 'My Number' was introduced as a new key number for matching to facilitate identification across procedures. As a result, several lawsuits were filed against the law, claiming that it violated the right to privacy guaranteed by Article 13 of the Constitution. This decision is the Supreme Court's first ruling on these claims. The appellants sought an injunction against the collection, keeping, use or provision of information about them through 'My Number' on the grounds that it violated their right to privacy guaranteed by Article 13 of the Constitution.

On 9 March 2023, the Supreme Court First Bench affirmed the constitutionality of the Individual Number system. In the decision, first, the Supreme Court, with reference to precedents, held that

> Article 13 of the Constitution provides that the freedom of the citizen to lead a private life is to be protected against the exercise of public authority, and it is understood that one of the freedoms of an individual to lead a private life is that every individual has the freedom not to have information concerning that individual disclosed or published to third parties without due cause.[116]

The Court then ruled that the law was constitutional and pointed out inter alia that the law only allows data matching in statutory cases despite the risk of improper data matching. The Court also highlighted that there are security controls in place and that My Number itself is a meaningless number.

VI. Topical Issues and Prospects

A. Artificial Intelligence or AI-Generated Data

The Copyright Act defines a work as 'a creatively produced expression of thoughts or sentiments that falls within the literary, academic, artistic, or musical domain'.[117] This definition, of course, presupposes the existence of a human being with free will and the act of creative expression. There is no restriction on the tools used for this creative expression so the use of computers is not an disputed issue. However, complex issues arise with current generative

[114] Act No 27 of 2021.

[115] The mayor of a municipality shall maintain a Basic Resident Registry that registers all persons, regardless of nationality, residing in the municipality. Article 3 of the Basic Resident Registry Act, Act No 81 of 1967.

[116] Supreme Court First Bench Decision on 9 March 2023, 77-3 Minshu 627.

[117] Copyright Act, Art 2(1), Item 1.

artificial intelligence (AI). When given a prompt, a generative AI performs probabilistic calculations based on learned data and outputs a plausible result. The output may appear to be a creative expression, but since the person giving the prompt has not performed a creative act, and at least the current 'weak AI' has no intention, its data output cannot be evaluated as a creative expression. As a result, the output of a generative AI is not a work at all and is not itself subject to copyright protection. In other words, the standard interpretation of current Japanese law is that the output of a generative AI does not belong to anyone.

But there are two problems with this interpretation. On one hand, even if the output of the generative AI is so similar to other works that it may have constituted copyright infringement if produced by a person, no one can be held legally liable. On the other hand, even if the output has economic value, legal protection would be difficult.

Therefore, the Agency for Cultural Affairs of Japan is seeking a legislative solution, including a revision of the Copyright Act. The current draft proposal seeks a solution that focuses on economic benefit sharing without addressing the issue of free will.[118] The future development of the legislation is still uncertain.

B. Potential Cooperation under Belt and Road Initiative

The Japanese Government has not signed any official documents on the Digital Silk Road or the Belt and Road Initiative in general. From Japan's perspective, cooperation on data transfer and data protection is important because China is its largest trading partner, and the volume of cross-border data transfer is extremely high. In this regard, it is often pointed out that both countries are members of the Regional Comprehensive Economic Partnership (RCEP) and that the framework includes ideas on data protection and the protection and regulation of cross-border data transfers. In particular, Article 12.14, entitled 'Location of Computing Facilities', states that 'No Party shall require a covered person to use or locate computing facilities in that Party's territory as a condition for conducting business in that Party's territory' and Article 12.15, entitled 'Cross-border Transfer of Information by Electronic Means', provides that 'A Party shall not prevent cross-border transfer of information by electronic means where such activity is for the conduct of the business of a covered person'.[119] These are seen as a starting point for potential cooperation between RCEP members, including Japan and China.

C. Data Protection Post COVID-19 Pandemic

In Japan, the COVID-19 pandemic brought about significant social changes, including a rapid acceleration of the digitisation of society, but had little impact on data transfer and privacy protection regulations. Although the APPI was amended during the pandemic period, its content had been discussed before and did not respond to the pandemic.

[118] The Agency for Cultural Affairs, *On AI and Copyright (Tentative Draft)* (15 January 2024), available at www.bunka.go.jp/seisaku/bunkashingikai/chosakuken/hoseido/r05_06/pdf/93988501_01.pdf.

[119] Regional Comprehensive Economic Partnership (RCEP) Agreement (15 November 2020), Arts 12.14 and 12.15.

This is because the PPC, as the authority of the APPI, dealt with the challenges by interpreting the APPI in a flexible manner and did not require amendments or new legislation.

The fact that a person is infected with COVID-19 is sensitive personal information that, in principle, cannot be collected or provided to third parties without the consent of the person. There is a case when a patient infected with COVID-19 was transferred from one medical institution to another, the former institution contacted the PPC to ask whether personal information could be transferred from the original institution to the new institution without the patient's consent. The PPC responded that if the purpose of use of personal information is posted in the hospital and no objection is raised, the information can be provided with the patient's implicit consent.[120] The PPC's interpretation is not that opt-out is allowed, but that consent, albeit implied, has been given. This is not an unlawful interpretation but it is certainly a very broad one. However, there was no strong criticism of this answer at the time, nor is there now. In this sense, it can be argued that COVID-19 has influenced the culture of legal interpretation in Japan in relation to data transfer and privacy protection, rather than legislation.

[120] Secretariat Office of the PPC, *Sharing of Personal Information between Medical Institutions in Relation to New Coronavirus Infections and the APPI* (28 April 2020), available at www.ppc.go.jp/files/pdf/iryoukikan.pdf.

4

South Korea

EUNG-KYUNG CHO

I. Introduction

South Korean data protection law sees its origin in several acts enacted in the 1990s and 2000s.[1] In parallel with the technological advances and the exponentially increasing rate of internet and smartphone penetration, the country's data protection regime evolved rapidly into a modern and unified framework. The evolution was marked in particular by the enactment of the Personal Information Protection Act (PIPA) in 2011 and most recently by its 2023 amendment which reinforced the data subjects' rights while further unifying and modernising the discipline.

Today, the country's data protection regime is commonly referred to as one of the strictest in the world. The robustness of this system is however paired with continuous efforts to perfect the rules, both through innovation and adaptation to global standards.

II. General Legal Framework of International Data Transfers and Data Protection

South Korea's data privacy protection derives both from the Constitution (A) and statutes (B). Case law also greatly contributed to shaping the country's data protection regime, as exposed throughout this chapter.

Beyond these main sources of law, the PIPA Presidential Decree and Implementing Regulations contain additional rules on the use, disclosure, and processing of personal data by governmental or private entities and individuals.[2] Public authorities also regularly publish non-binding guidelines to help with understanding the law, such as the Guide to the Interpretation of Data Protection Laws and Regulations issued by the Personal Information

[1] See, eg, the Act on Data Protection of Public Bodies, the Act on the Use and Protection of Credit Information, and the Act on the Protection and Use of Location Data. Unless specified otherwise, all sources cited in this chapter – articles, decisions, statutes, and public documents – are in Korean.

[2] Korea Legislation Research Institute's unofficial English translation available at: https://elaw.klri.re.kr/eng_service/lawView.do?hseq=63755&lang=ENG.

Protection Commission (PIPC),[3] the Handbook on the Psedonymisation of Personal Data,[4] and the Guidelines for the De-Identification of Personal Data.[5]

A. Constitutional Basis for Data Protection

South Korea's Constitution does not expressly provide for data protection or right to data privacy. The Constitutional Court however expressly declared the 'right to self-determination of personal data' as a fundamental right in 2005, on the basis of the right to privacy and the right to human dignity, worth, and pursuit of happiness enshrined respectively in Article 17 and Article 10(1) of the Constitution.[6] According to the Constitutional Court, the right to self-determination of personal data means that 'the data subject has the right to decide him/herself (i) when, (ii) to whom, and (iii) to what extent data concerning him/her may be known and used, meaning the right to decide him/herself on the disclosure and use of personal data'.[7] The constitutional protection of the right to self-determination of personal data has since been reiterated numerous times by the Court.[8]

The concept of right to self-determination of personal data and its constitutional origin was first alluded to by the Supreme Court in the 1990s. In 1998, the Supreme Court indeed stated that the purpose of Articles 10 and 17 is not only to recognise a 'passive right not to have one's privacy be violated or disclosed', but also an 'active right to control freely data concerning oneself in a highly digitalised modern society'.[9] This position was reiterated by the Court in 2011,[10] shortly before it expressly adopted the term of 'right to self-determination of personal data' in 2014.[11] In its 2014 decision, the Supreme Court also clarified that personal data which comes under the protection of the right to self-determination of personal data should be understood as

> a set of information which allows to identify an individual in that they characterise one's individual identity such as his/her body, beliefs, social status, and position, and must not be limited to data pertaining to an individual's inner scope but extend to personal data which was formed or has already been disclosed in one's public life.[12]

B. Statutory Framework for Data Transfer and Protection

i. *The Two Periods of Statutory Evolution*

From 1994 to 2011, South Korea's data protection law underwent a first set of substantial changes.[13] The statutory framework was initially scattered in several acts,[14] leading to

[3] PIPC, *Guide to the Interpretation of Data Protection Laws and Regulations* (2 December 2020).
[4] PIPC, *Handbook on the Psedonymisation of Personal Data* (5 February 2024).
[5] Ministry of the Interior and Safety, *Guidelines for the De-Identification of Personal Data* (2016).
[6] Constitutional Court Decision, 26 May 2005, Ja99Heunma513.
[7] ibid.
[8] See, eg, Constitutional Court Decision, 21 July 2005, 2003Heunma282; Constitutional Court Decision, 24 November 2022, 2021Heunma130; Constitutional Court Decision, 31 March 2016, 2015Heunma688.
[9] Supreme Court Decision, 24 July 1998, 96Da42789.
[10] Supreme Court Decision, 2 September 2011, 2008Da42430.
[11] Supreme Court Decision, 24 July 2014, 2012Da49933.
[12] Supreme Court Decision, 24 July 2014, 2012Da49933. See also Supreme Court Decision, 15 October 2015, 2014Da77970; Supreme Court Decision, 17 August 2016, 2014Da235080.
[13] Choi Kyung Jun et al, *Personal Information Protection Act* (Parkyoungsa, February 2024) 7.

discussions on the need for unification. In 2011, the PIPA was enacted to act as the single main instrument of data protection in matters of 'collection, generation, connecting, interlocking, recording, storage, retention, value-added processing, editing, searching, output, correction, recovery, use, provision, disclosure, and destruction of personal data'.[15]

Since 2020, additional revisions further modernised the discipline. Notably, the '3 Data Acts', namely the PIPA, the Act on the Promotion of Information and Communications Network Utilization and Information Protection (ICNA), and the Act on the Use and Protection of Credit Information (UPCIA), were all revised substantially in 2020 to introduce the notion of pseudonymised data and allow reasonable use of personal data in the absence of consent, among others. The PIPA underwent another large-scale revision more recently in 2023, recognising in particular data subjects' right to reject decisions based on fully automated personal data processing and to data portability, as well as introducing new rules on international data transfers. It is also during this second period of evolution that South Korea became one of the few Asia Pacific jurisdictions to receive the European Union's (EU) adequacy decision,[16] shortly after joining the Asia-Pacific Economic Cooperation's voluntary cross-border privacy rules (CBPR) in 2017.

ii. The PIPA

a. Purpose

In its initial version, Article 1 of the PIPA had described its purpose as

> regulating matters related to the processing of personal data in order to enhance the rights and interests of the citizens and realise the individual's dignity and worth by protecting secrets of private life from the collection, leakage, misuse and improper use of personal data.

This provision thus implied that the main purpose of the regulation of personal data processing was the 'protect[ion of] the secrets of private life'.

Following the 2014 revision of the PIPA, Article 1 was reformulated to provide that the Act aims to 'govern the processing and protection of personal data in order to safeguard the rights and freedom of individuals and further realise the dignity and worth of individuals'.[17] The purpose of personal data protection is therefore no longer limited to the protection of secrets of private life, but extends to guaranteeing the individual's liberty and rights.

[14] For a detailed description of the evolution of data privacy law in South Korea until 2011, see Kim Ju Young and Son Hyung Seob, *Geinjeongbobobeu Ihae* [*Understandung Personal Data Protection Law*], (Beobmumsa, 2012) 112–28.

[15] Article 2 of the PIPA 'Definitions'. Korea Legislation Research Institute's unofficial English translation, available at https://elaw.klri.re.kr/eng_service/lawView.do?hseq=53044&lang=ENG.

[16] The General Data Protection Regulation was an important model for the 2023 revision of the PIPA. See Kim Hyun Sook, 'A Comparative Study on Scientific Research in the Data Protection Laws between EU and Korea' (2020) *Journal of Korea Information Law* 115–148, 118.

[17] Article 1 of the PIPA 'Purpose'.

b. Scope of Application

Ratione materiae: personal data: According to Article 2(1) PIPA:

> [t]he term 'personal information' means any of the following information relating to a living individual:
>
> a. Information that identifies a particular individual by his or her full name, resident registration number, image, etc.;
> b. Information which, even if it by itself does not identify a particular individual, may be easily combined with other information to identify a particular individual. In such cases, whether or not there is ease of combination shall be determined by reasonably considering the time, cost, technology, etc. used to identify the individual such as likelihood that the other information can be procured;
> c. Information under items (a) or (b) above that is pseudonymized in accordance with subparagraph 1-2 below and thereby becomes incapable of identifying a particular individual without the use or combination of information for restoration to the original state.

According to the Guide to the Interpretation of Data Protection Laws and Regulations, there are no special restrictions as to the content or shape of 'personal data', such that any information which can identify an individual falls under the scope of the PIPA. This means all personal data, irrespective of its form or processing method – whether digital or in handwritten form, and whether automatic or manual. The mere existence of a link with the data subject suffices, whether objective – such as one's height, age, weight – or subjective – such as third parties' opinion of a given individual. Moreover, the information does not necessarily need to be a verified truth, and may thus be an inaccurate or false information.[18]

Personal data under the PIPA only concerns information on natural persons – including foreigners[19] – who are 'living'.[20] Information concerning deceased individuals may however qualify as personal data of family members of the deceased if they allow to identify the relationship between the deceased and family members, such as information on hereditary diseases.[21] information concerning embryos and fetuses before birth are in principle not considered as personal data under the PIPA.

Sensitive data, which are defined by Article 23 PIPA as 'including ideology, belief, admission to or withdrawal from a trade union or political party, political opinions, health, sex life, and other personal information that is likely to markedly threaten the privacy of any data subject',[22] may not be processed by data controllers, save for '[w]here the personal information controller informs the data subject of the matters provided for in Article 15 (2) or 17 (2), and obtains the consent of the data subject apart from the consent to the processing of other personal information', or 'where other statutes require or permit the processing of sensitive information'. The scope of this category is expected to grow and discussions are ongoing in particular with regard to information on the region of origin and whether one has been victim of certain crimes.[23] Wherever data controllers process

[18] Guide to the Interpretation of Data Protection Laws and Regulations (n 3) 11.
[19] Choi Kyung Jun et al (n13) 107.
[20] PIPA, Art 2(1).
[21] Guide to the Interpretation of Data Protection Laws and Regulations (n 3) 10.
[22] Enforcement ordinance of the PIPA, Art 18.
[23] For further developments, see Choi Kyung Jun et al (n 13) 277.

sensitive information based on data subjects' consent, they are required to 'take measures necessary to ensure safety pursuant to Article 29 so that the sensitive information may not be lost, stolen, divulged, forged, altered, or damaged'.[24] Since 2023, the PIPA provides an additional protection by stating that

> [w]hen a personal information controller determines that there is a risk of privacy invasion due to the inclusion of sensitive information of the data subject in the process of providing goods or services, the personal information controller shall inform the data subject of the possibility of disclosure and methods of choosing non-disclosure of sensitive information before providing the goods or services.

The notion of pseudonymous data was introduced in the PIPA in 2020. Article 28-2(1) PIPA provides that data controllers 'may process pseudonymized information without the consent of data subjects for statistical purposes, scientific research purposes, and archiving purposes in the public interest, etc' but 'shall not include information that may be used to identify a certain individual when providing pseudonymized information to a third party'. While anonymised data is not mentioned *per se* in the PIPA, its Article 58-2 provides that the PIPA 'shall not apply to information that no longer identifies a certain individual when combined with other information, reasonably considering time, cost, technology, etc.', which is understood by authors as referring to anonymised data.[25]

Exclusions: Article 58 PIPA reads that the following matters fall outside the scope of Chapters 3 to 8 of the PIPA (which provide for various safeguards and guarantees): '[p]ersonal information collected or requested to be provided for the analysis of information related to national security' and '[p]ersonal information collected or used for its own purposes of reporting by the press, missionary activities by religious organizations, and nomination of candidates by political parties, respectively'.

While the PIPA had initially added to these two exceptions '[p]ersonal information collected pursuant to the Statistics Act for processing by public institutions' as well as '[p]ersonal information processed temporarily where it is urgently necessary for the public safety and security, public health, etc.', they were deleted following the 2023 PIPA revision in order to enhance the protection of citizens' personal data.[26]

Ratione personae: data controller: The PIPA regulates data controllers' actions. A 'data controller' is defined in Article 2(5) PIPA as 'a public institution, legal person, organization, individual, etc. that processes personal information directly or indirectly to operate the personal information files for business purposes'.

According to the PIPA, 'personal data files' should be understood as 'a set or sets of personal information arranged or organized in a systematic manner based on a certain rule for easy search of the personal information'.[27] The legislator is however silent as to what is

[24] PIPA, Art 23(2).

[25] Shin Jong Chul, *Geinjeongbobohobobhesol* [*Commentary of the Personal Information Protection Act*] (Jinhan M&B, 2020) 29–32; Choi Kyung Jun et al (n 13) 309.

[26] Explanations on the reform, 17. For more developments on both categories of data, see Choi Kyung Jun et al (n 13) 91.

[27] PIPA, Art 2(4).

meant by 'information arranged or organized in a systematic manner based on a certain rule' and scholars have suggested referring to Article 4(6) of the General Data Protection Regulation (GDPR) for assessment.[28] The PIPA does not explain either what should be considered as processing 'for business purposes'. Here, scholars have turned to criminal case law rendered on the notion to understand it as

> actions which form part of business in which one engages continuously, based on his/her status at work or career, and are unrelated to whether it is remunerated or profit-seeking, and can be limited to a one time action insofar as there is an intention of repetition.[29]

As to 'data processing', it is defined in Article 2(2) PIPA as 'the collection, generation, connecting, interlocking, recording, storage, retention, value-added processing, editing, searching, output, correction, recovery, use, provision, disclosure, and destruction of personal information and other similar activities'. Personal data being processed by another person and one merely passing it on or transmitting will not be considered as 'processing'.[30]

Ratione loci: The PIPA does not explicitly address the issue of its territorial application. The prevailing view among scholars is however that the PIPA does apply to foreigners having entered the South Korean territory or residing in South Korea, so as to allow them to be protected by its provisions.[31] As to the situation where South Korean data subjects' personal data are collected abroad and/or processed by business located abroad, the question arises as to whether the data controller must abide by the requirements of the PIPA. There are views that the mere foreign nationality of the data controller should not exclude systematically the application of the PIPA insofar as the effects reach South Korea.[32]

Authors have also noted that Article 20 of the Act on Private International Law (PILA) may affect the scope of application of the PIPA.[33] The provision states that

> [t]he mandatory provisions of the Republic of Korea to govern the corresponding legal relationship, irrespective of the applicable law, in light of the purpose of legislation, shall also apply where a foreign law is designated as the applicable law under this Act.

The debate on whether the provisions of data protection law should be considered mandatory within the meaning of Article 20 of the PILA is however currently ongoing.[34]

[28] Choi Kyung Jun et al (n 13) 79.

[29] ibid 78.

[30] Kim Yong Hak, *Geinjeongbo Bohobob* [*Personal Information Protection Act*] (Chongho Books, 2021) 8; Choi Kyung Jun et al (n 13) 80.

[31] Choi Kyung Jun et al (n 13) 107.

[32] Lee He-Won, 'A Legal Research on The Scope of Application of the Personal Information Protection Act' (2022) *Journal of Korea Information law* 26–1, 293.

[33] Choi Kyung Jun et al (n 13) 108.

[34] ibid 112–14, 445, 453; Han Seungsoo and Choi Jihyun, 'The Dispute of the Personal Data Breach and the Governing Law in the Litigation' (2021) *The Journal of Legal Studies* 24–1, 3 90–92; Lee Jong Hyeok, 'A Preliminary Study on the Data Protection Litigations from the Perspective of Private International Law – With Focus on the Categories of the Data Protection Litigations and the Issue of International Adjudicatory Jurisdiction' (2019) *Journal of Korea International Trade Law Association*, 28–2, 139–72, 160–62. With regard to former Article 30(2)(4) of the ICNA, the Supreme Court confirmed in its recent 2023 decision that it was a mandatory provision in that it materialises the constitutional right to self-determination of personal data (Supreme Court Decision, 13 April 2023, 2017Da219232).

c. Principles of Data Protection

The PIPA is based on the following principles:

- The eight Organisation for Economic Co-operation and Development (OECD) privacy principles, ie the Collection Limitation Principle, Data Quality Principle, Purpose Specification Principle, Use Limitation Principle, Security Safeguards Principle, Openness Principle, Individual Participation Principle, Accountability Principle; and
- The seven GDPR principles, ie Lawfulness, fairness and transparency, Purpose limitation, Data minimisation, Accuracy, Storage limitation, Integrity and confidentiality (security), and Accountability.[35]

Taking into consideration the country's specificities, Article 3 PIPA further expressly states the following eight principles:

1. The personal information controller shall specify explicitly the purposes for which personal information is processed; and shall collect personal information lawfully and fairly to the minimum extent necessary for such purposes;
2. The personal information controller shall process personal information in an appropriate manner necessary for the purposes for which the personal information is processed, and shall not use it beyond such purposes;
3. The personal information controller shall ensure personal information is accurate, complete, and up to date to the extent necessary in relation to the purposes for which the personal information is processed;
4. The personal information controller shall manage personal information safely according to the processing methods, types, etc. of personal information, taking into account the possibility of infringement on the data subject's rights and the severity of the relevant risks;
5. The personal information controller shall make public its privacy policy and other matters related to personal information processing; and shall guarantee the data subject's rights, such as the right to access their personal information;
6. The personal information controller shall process personal information in a manner to minimize the possibility of infringing the privacy of a data subject;
7. If it is still possible to fulfil the purposes of collecting personal information by processing anonymized or pseudonymised personal information, the personal information controller shall endeavor to process personal information through anonymization, where anonymization is possible, or through pseudonymisation, if it is impossible to fulfil the purposes of collecting personal information through anonymization; and
8. The personal information controller shall endeavor to obtain trust of data subjects by observing and performing such duties and responsibilities as provided for in this Act and other related statutes.

The above principles are referred to when interpreting each provision of the PIPA and determining whether a breach has occurred.[36]

[35] Kim Ju Young and Son Hyung Seob (n 14) 167–68; Choi Kyung Jun et al (n 13) 10.
[36] Kim Yong Hak (n 30) 13–22; Choi Kyung Jun et al (n 13) 11.

d. Data Subjects' Rights

Data subjects' rights are listed in Article 4 PIPA which provides that

> [a] data subject has the following rights in relation to the processing of his or her own personal information:
>
> 1. The right to be informed of the processing of such personal information;
> 2. The right to determine whether or not to consent and the scope of consent regarding the processing of such personal information;
> 3. The right to confirm whether or not personal information is being processed and to request access (including the provision of copies; hereinafter the same applies) to such personal information;
> 4. The right to suspend the processing of, and to request correction, deletion, and destruction of such personal information;
> 5. The right to appropriate redress for any damage arising out of the processing of such personal information through a prompt and fair procedure; and
> 6. The right to reject decisions based on fully automated personal data processing or to request explanations with regard to such decisions.

These rights however do not benefit from unconditional protection, nor do they have priority over all other rights. For each of them, the legislator regulates more specifically the conditions and procedures for their exercise through Articles 35 to 39-2 PIPA.

The data subjects' rights also extend to the data controllers' obligation to notify 'without delay' data subjects of any leakage of personal data.[37] In a recent decision dated October 2023, the PIPC fined PayPal Holdings over ₩900 million (roughly $660 000) for delaying notification of data subjects of the leakage of their personal data and failing to take appropriate measures to protect their data.

e. Privacy Regulator

The main authorities in charge of data protection in South Korea are the PIPC, the Korea Communications Commission (KCC), the Korea Internet & Security Agency (KISA), and the Financial Services Commission (FSC). The PIPC, placed under the Prime Minister's office, acts as the main body overseeing personal data protection and shaping the relevant policies. Concretely, it enforces the rules of the PIPA, handles complaints or remedial procedures, as well as mediating data-related disputes.

These regulators have the authority to impose numerous administrative penalties including fines up to three per cent of total sales, corrective orders and penalty surcharges. As to the PIPC, it can impose administrative fines, penalty surcharges, corrective orders, and has the authority to suspend data transfers abroad. Public prosecutors may also investigate data breaches and impose criminal sanctions. Under the PIPA, penalties can reach up to ₩100 million and imprisonment up to 10 years.[38]

[37] Article 34 of the PIPA 'Data Breach Notification'.
[38] PIPA 'Penalty Provisions', Art 70.

iii. Specific Provisions for Particular Sectors

Credit information. The UPCIA regulates personal credit information, ie information 'necessary to determine the credit worthiness of the other party to financial transactions and other commercial transactions'.[39] The Act is enforced by the FSC and not by the PIPC.

Location data. The Location Data Act regulates the protection and use of location information of persons. It is enforced by the KCC.

Information and communications service. Initially, the processing of personal data by Information and Communications Service Providers (ICSPs) and recipients of such information was governed by the ICNA. Since the reform of 2020, most of these matters are now governed by the PIPA under the Chapter 'Special Provisions for ICSPs'. The ICNA however still applies to certain matters, such as commercial providers of information services, including those provided through telecommunications services.

III. Legal Bases and Mechanisms for International Data Transfers and Data Protection

South Korea's first data protection law of 1994 did not include any rules on international data transfers since it sought mainly to protect the rights and interests of the citizens with regard to personal data processed by public bodies. While provisions on international data transfers were included in the ICNA following the 2000 reform, their effect was limited to prohibiting information and communication service providers from signing international contracts which violate the ICNA in relation to personal data of users.[40] Later on in 2011, the PIPA also introduced rules allowing international transfers, but these only applied to data provided to third parties.

It is through the recent revision in 2023 PIPA that a unified and complete regulatory framework of international transfers was put in place, without distinctions being made between on/offline and public/private matters. Currently, the rules on international transfers of personal data may be found in Section 4 of the PIPA, entirely devoted to '*International Transfers of Personal Data*'. The revision also significantly modernised the applicable framework by expanding the situations where international transfers are permitted as well as the basis for such transfers.

Today, the PIPA provides five legal basis for international transfers which are developed in detail below, and maintains the prohibition on the conclusion of contracts on international transfers which violate the PIPA. The principle of reciprocity and the system of designation of domestic agent have been expanded and the PIPC has been given the authority to order the suspension of international transfers.

[39] UPCIA 'Definitions', Art 2. Korea Legislation Research Institute's unofficial English translation, available at https://elaw.klri.re.kr/eng_mobile/viewer.do?hseq=46276&type=part&key=23.

[40] Choi Kyung Jun et al (n 13) 405.

A. Basis for International Data Transfers

The PIPA prohibits international data transfers by principle. Article 28-8(1) indeed provides that:

> data controllers shall not provide, outsource processing, or store data abroad, except in one of the enumerated cases:
>
> 1. Where the data subject has given specific consent to the international transfer;
> 2. Where there is a specific regulation on international transfer in a statute, treaty to which the Republic of Korea is a party or other international agreements;[41]
> 3. Where the processing outsourcing or storage is required for the conclusion or performance of a contract with the data subject and where each of the matters enumerated in paragraph 2 have been disclosed following the procedures stated in Article 30 or where the data subject has been informed of each of those matters fby email or following the method fixed by presidential decree;
> 4. Where the recipient of the personal data has received certification from the PIPC such as certifications pursuant to Article 32-2, and where the measures necessary to protect personal data and to guarantee the data subjects' rights, as well as measures necessary to execute the certified matters in the country where the data is being transferred, have been adopted;[42]
> 5. Where the PIPC recognises that matters such as the system of protection, scope of guarantee of data subjects' right, and the process of remedying breaches of the country or international body to which the data is being transferred are substantially similar to the level of protection provided by the PIPA.

Scholars have remarked that, based on the current formulation of Article 28-8 PIPA which pertain to data being 'provide[d], processing outsource[ed], or store[d] abroad', there is a potential blind zone with regard to personal data which are collected and used abroad, which would not fall under the scope of Section 4 on international data transfers despite involving transfers of data abroad.[43]

i. Consent of Data Subjects as Exception to Existence of Privacy Safeguards Overseas

When requiring consent to an international data transfer, the data subject must be informed of the following:

- personal data being transferred;
- country, date, and method of transfer;

[41] International agreements may take various forms, such as a charter, statute, covenant, agreement, convention, protocol, exchanges of notes, memorandum of understanding or agency-to-agency arrangement (see Choi Kyung Jun et al (n 13) 431). In case of conflict between a provision of a treaty and that of domestic law, the principle of *lex speciali* mandates that the former prevail (Supreme Court Decision, 22 July 1986, 82Daka1372).

[42] As of March 2024, the only certification delivered by the PIPC is the Information Security Management System (ISMS-P) managed by the KISA' (*see* Articles 14–15 and Annex 2 of the Rules on the operation of international transfers of personal data).

[43] Choi Kyung Jun et al (n 13) 425.

- name of the party to which the data is transferred;
- recipient's purpose of use of the transferred data and duration of retention and use; and
- method and procedure of refusal of transfer and effects of such refusal.[44]

Should any of these elements be subject to subsequent changes, the data subject must be informed of the change and give consent to the said transfer.[45]

ii. Necessity for Conclusion and Performance of Contract with Data Subject

Article 28-8(1) of the PIPA provides an exception allowing international transfers of personal data where the processing outsourcing/storage of personal data is necessary for the conclusion and performance of a contract with the data subject. If the contract negotiations which involved processing outsourcing or storage of personal data ultimately fail, all personal data involved up to that moment must be immediately destroyed.[46]

Based on the duty of transparency,[47] the data controller must inform the data subject of the following:

- personal data being subject to processing outsourcing or storage;
- country, date, and method of such outsourcing and storage;
- name of the party in charge of processing outsourcing or storage of the data;
- purpose of use, duration of retention and use of the outsourced or stored data; and
- method and procedure of refusal of outsourcing and storage and effects of such refusal.

iii. Duties Imposed in Case of International Data Transfer

Data controllers are first bound to conform with provisions of the PIPA on international data transfers, such as the prohibition of conclusion of contracts in breach of the PIPA, the principle of reciprocity, and the rules on retransfers to third countries.[48]

In addition, data controllers must abide by Article 17 'Provision of Personal Information', Article 18 'Limitation to Out-of-Purpose Use and Provision of Personal Information', Article 19 'Limitation to Use and Provision of Personal Information on Part of Its Recipients', and Chapter 5 'Guarantee of Rights of Data Subjects', and put in place the protective measures determined by presidential decree.[49]

iv. Order to Suspend International Data Transfers

The newly-introduced Article 28-9 PIPA provides that, when the requirements of a lawful international transfer listed in Article 28-8(1) PIPA are not fulfilled, or when there is harm caused to the data subject or a significant risk that such harm will be caused due to the

[44] PIPA, Art 28-8(2).
[45] PIPA, Art 28-8(3).
[46] Choi Kyung Jun et al (n 13) 431.
[47] PIPA, Art 28-8(1)(3).
[48] See PIPA, Art 28-8(5), Arts 28-10, and Art 28-11.
[49] PIPA, Art 28-8(4).

fact that the party, country, or international body receiving the data does not provide the same level of protection of personal data as the PIPA, the PIPC may order the data controller to suspend the international transfer. The PIPC's authority is understood as being discretionary.[50]

According to the PIPA Enforcement ordinance, in assessing whether such breach has occurred, the PIPC shall take into account the following:

- The type and scale of the personal data which has been transferred abroad or in relation to which such transfer is predicted;
- The importance of the breach of Article 28-8(1), (4), or (5) PIPA;
- Whether the harm to be caused to the data subject or which is likely to be caused to the data subject is significant or difficult to repair;
- Whether it is beneficial to the data subject to order the suspension of the transfer than not to order it;
- Whether it is possible to protect and prevent the violation of personal data by measures provided in Article 64(1); and
- Whether there exist reasons to consider that it will be difficult to appropriately protect personal data due to signficiant breaches occurring in the country to which the data is transferred.

The PIPC is required to inform the data controller, in writing, of the content of the order to suspend, the reasons behind such order, the procedures and methods of objecting to the order, as well as other necessary matters.[51] The data controller may object within seven days from receipt of the order and, within 30 days, the PIPC may decide on whether to lift the order and must inform the data controller of its decision in writing.[52]

v. Data Security and Data Localisation

South Korea provides several data localisation requirements in various sectors. In particular, Article 16 of the Act on the Establishment, Management, Etc. of Spatial Data, prohibits that map data of a certain level of precision be taken abroad, due to national security reasons.[53] The Data Protection Standards for Cloud Computing Services Guidelines also provide that cloud computing networks serving public agencies shall be physically separate from networks serving the general public and use data centres in South Korea.

IV. Issues in Private International Law

Despite recent revisions of both the PIPA and the PILA,[54] neither of these acts nor any other South Korean statutes directly address the private international law issues which can arise in cross-border data protection litigation. The interplay between the two statutes – and

[50] Choi Kyung Jun et al (n 13) 449.

[51] Enforcement ordinance, Art 29-11(4).

[52] PIPA, Art 28-9(2) and Enforcement ordinance, Art 29-12(2).

[53] Korea Legislation Research Institute's unofficial English translation, available at https://elaw.klri.re.kr/eng_service/lawView.do?hseq=32771&lang=ENG.

[54] As developed above, the PIPA was substantially revised in 2023, while the PILA was last revised in 2022, by a significant reform introducing general statutory rules on conflicts of jurisdiction for the first time.

potentially other instruments – regarding applicable law, jurisdiction, and recognition of foreign judgments is thus currently unsettled and it remains to be seen whether the issues exposed briefly below will benefit from clarifications by courts or the legislator in the near future.

A. Litigations Involving Cross-Border Data Transfer and Privacy

While case law is not abundant on this issue yet, the following potential scenarios can be considered:[55]

- First, litigation may be commenced by data subjects against data controllers. This first category of litigation may occur before South Korean courts following their initiation by local data subjects against foreign data controllers or foreign data subjects against domestic businesses, or even by foreign data subjects against foreign businesses;
- Second, litigation may be commenced by associations on behalf of data subjects against data controllers. This category may involve the protection of a collective body of consumers which are data subjects, domestic and/or foreign, against domestic businesses or foreign businesses;
- Thirdly, litigation may also occur between data controllers. This typically concerns contracts for personal data transfers and claims between transferor and transferee, but claims may also originate from the data subject against either of them; and
- Fourthly, litigation may be commenced by data controllers against states. Such claims may moreover be based on the State Compensation Act,[56] irrespective of actions initiated based on the PIPA.[57]

B. Jurisdictional Issues Involving Cross-border Data Protection and Privacy

i. *Jurisdictional Clauses*

Pursuant to Article 42(3) PILA,

> [w]here the parties to a consumer contract reach an agreement on international jurisdiction under Article 8, such agreement shall be effective only in any of the following cases: (i) Where an agreement on international jurisdiction is reached after the occurrence of a dispute; (ii) Where an international jurisdiction agreement allows a consumer to file a lawsuit not only with the court, but also with a foreign court.[58]

In cases where the contract may not be regarded as a consumer contract, Article 14(1) of the Act on the Regulation of Terms and Conditions requires that the clause does not qualify as

[55] For a detailed analysis, see Lee Jong Hyeok (n 34).
[56] Korea Legislation Research Institute's unofficial English translation, available at https://elaw.klri.re.kr/kor_service/lawTwoView.do?hseq=15550.
[57] Lee Jong Hyeok (n 34)149–50.
[58] Korea Legislation Research Institute's unofficial English translation, available at https://elaw.klri.re.kr/eng_mobile/subjectViewer.do?hseq=60196&type=subject&key=13&pCode=182&pName=Immigrant%20by%20Marriage.

'[a] clause which prohibits customers from filing a lawsuit unreasonable disadvantageous to them or requires customers to agree to jurisdiction'.[59]

On the issue of jurisdictional clauses in data protection litigation, the Supreme Court rendered a significant decision in April 2023.[60] The case concerned a lawsuit filed by Korean users against Google LLC and Google Korea LLC requesting the disclosure of the domestic users' personal data which had been provided to a third party, and more specifically to US intelligence agencies as part of the PRISM data-collection programme.

In its decision of 13 April 2023, the Supreme Court held that the dispute did not fall under the exclusive jurisdiction of the South Korean courts and that, based on the fact that Google LLC is based in California and operates services from the same area, the agreement providing for the exclusive international jurisdiction of the Californian courts was valid. The Supreme Court however added that, with regard to users who used the emails services for personal purposes and were passive consumers having concluded the service contracts by being attracted by advertisements, the terms concluded with Google LLC were consumer contracts and that they could lodge their claim before the courts of the place of their habitual residence based on former Article 27 (now Article 47) PILA, despite the exclusive jurisdiction clause found in the agreement. The Supreme Court thereby reiterated the purpose of the provision and the importance of protecting consumers' interests.

ii. Rules of General and Special Jurisdiction

In the absence of any specific provision in the PIPA and the PILA regarding data protection litigation, the following rules of international jurisdiction may be relevant depending on the circumstances of the case.

Setting out the 'general principles of international jurisdiction', Article 2 PILA first states that

> '[t]he court of the Republic of Korea shall have international jurisdiction where a party or a case in dispute has a substantial connection with the Republic of Korea. In determining whether any substantial connection exists, the court shall adopt reasonable principles, compatible to the ideology of the allocation of international jurisdiction, which aims to achieve impartiality between the parties, and appropriateness, speediness, and economy of adjudication. Where there is no provision regarding international jurisdiction in this Act or in any other statutes or regulations, or treaties of the Republic of Korea, the court shall determine whether it has international jurisdiction, in consideration of the provisions of the domestic laws on jurisdiction, but shall give full consideration to the special nature of international jurisdiction, in light of the purport of paragraph (1).

The PILA then provides for a number of concrete rules of jurisdiction, some of which may be relevant in data-related cross-border litigations:[61]

[59] For further developments on this issue, see Lee Jong Hyeok (n 34) 155–56.

[60] Supreme Court Decision, 13 April 2023, 2017Da219232. See Lee Jong Hyeok, 'New Developments in Korean Private International Law' in Olivier Gaillard and Krista Nadakavukaren Schefer (eds), *Private International Law in East Asia, From Imitation to Innovation and Exportation* (Bloomsbury Publishing, 2024) 107–22, 114–15.

[61] For a detailed commentary of the rules in their recently-revised version, see Suk Kwang Hyun, *Gukjejepangwanhalbob – 2022nyeon gejeong gukjesabob hesol* [*International Adjudicatory Jurisdiction Law – Commentary of the 2022 Revised PILA*] (Parkyoungsa, 2022).

Article 3 General Jurisdiction:

(1) The court shall have international jurisdiction over a case involving a person who has habitual residence in the Republic of Korea. The same shall also apply where the habitual residence of a person does not exist in any country or cannot be identified, but the person has a residence in the Republic of Korea. [...]

(3) The court shall have international jurisdiction over a lawsuit involving a corporation or organization with its principal office, place of business, statutory seat, or place of central administration located in the Republic of Korea or a corporation or organization established under the law of the Republic of Korea.

Article 4 Special Jurisdiction over Locations of Offices or Places of Business:

(1) For a person, corporation, or organization that has an office or place of business in the Republic of Korea, a lawsuit in connection with the business affairs of such office or place of business may be filed with the court.

(2) For a person, corporation, or organization engaged in a continuous and systematic business or operating activities in or toward the Republic of Korea, a lawsuit in connection with such business or business activities may be filed with the court.

Article 42 Jurisdiction over Consumer Contracts[62]

(1) Where a consumer who has a habitual residence in the Republic of Korea concludes a contract for a purpose other than his or her occupation or business activities, he or she may file a lawsuit with the court against the other party to the contract (referring to a person who concludes a contract for his or her occupation or business activities; hereinafter referred to as 'business entity') in any of the following cases:

  1. Where a business entity engages in occupation or business activities, such as solicitation for transactions through advertising, before the conclusion of a contract in a country in which a consumer has a habitual residence (hereinafter referred to as 'country of habitual residence') or where a business entity engages in occupation or business activities, such as solicitation for transactions through advertising in a territory not included in the consumer's country of habitual residence toward the country of habitual residence, and where the contract falls under the scope of the business entity's occupation or business activities;
  2. Where a business entity receives an order from a consumer in the consumer's country of habitual residence;
  3. Where a business entity encourages a consumer to place an order in a country other than his or her country of habitual residence.

(2) Where the habitual residence of a customer is in the Republic of Korea, a business entity may file a lawsuit over a contract under paragraph (1) (hereinafter referred to as 'consumer contract') against the consumer in the court only.

[62] To be read in parallel with Article 47 'Consumer Contract':

(1) 'Even where the parties to a consumer contract choose the applicable law, the protection given to the consumer pursuant to the mandatory provisions of the country in which the habitual residence of the consumer is located shall not be deprived;

(2) Where the parties to a consumer contract do not choose the applicable law, the law of the habitual residence of the consumer shall govern, notwithstanding Article 46;

(3) Notwithstanding Article 31 (1) through (3), the method of a consumer contract shall be governed by the law of the habitual residence of the consumer.'

(3) Where the parties to a consumer contract reach an agreement on international jurisdiction under Article 8, such agreement shall be effective only in any of the following cases:

1. Where an agreement on international jurisdiction is reached after the occurrence of a dispute
2. Where an international jurisdiction agreement allows a consumer to file a lawsuit not only with the court, but also with a foreign court.

Article 41 Special Jurisdiction over Lawsuit Regarding Contract:

(1) A lawsuit regarding a contract may be filed with the court, if any of the following places is located in the Republic of Korea:

1. Place of delivery, in cases of a contract for the supply of goods;
2. Place of supply of service, in cases of a contract for the supply of services;
3. Place where the main part of the obligations is performed, in cases of a contract under which places of delivery and places of supply of services are multiple, or a contract, the purpose of which is to supply both goods and services

(2) A lawsuit regarding a contract, other than the contracts prescribed in paragraph (1), may be filed with the court, where the parties to the contract agree that the obligations that formed the basis of the claim were or are to be performed in the Republic of Korea.

Article 44 Special Jurisdiction over Lawsuit Regarding Torts:

A lawsuit regarding torts may be filed with the court, where a tort is committed in or toward the Republic of Korea or where the consequences thereof occur in the Republic of Korea: Provided, That the same shall not apply where it is impossible to predict that the consequences of the torts occur in the Republic of Korea.

As was the case in the 2023 Supreme Court decision,[63] most claims are however likely to be based on Article 42 PILA. This would in turn require a detailed analysis of whether its conditions of application have been met, in particular the issue of whether the business entity engaged 'in occupation or business activities' in the country in which the consumer has his/her habitual residence, notably by 'directing' its activities towards that country.

C. Applicable Law: In Litigations Involving Cross-Border Data Protection and Privacy

Similarly to the above, there are no rules in the PIPA or the PILA which regulated these matters in the context of data protection. The following general rules may be relevant in determining the applicable law in such context.

If the personal data breach leads to a tort action, one would first need to refer to any choice of law made by the parties.[64] Article 53 of the PILA indeed provides that

> the parties may choose, by agreement, the law of the Republic of Korea as the applicable law after the occurrence of management of affairs, unjust enrichment, or torts: Provided, That the right of a third party shall not be affected thereby.

[63] Supreme Court Decision, 13 April 2023, 2017Da219232.

[64] For a general study on the law applicable to damages claim for data breaches, see Han and Choi (n 34) 61–99.

This agreement may be implicit.[65] In the absence of an agreement, Article 52 of the PILA 'Torts' may become relevant and lead to the application of the law applicable to the legal relationship between the tortfeasor and the injured party, the law of the country where the habitual residences of the tortfeasor and the injured party are located, or the law of the place where it is committed or the consequences thereof occur.[66]

If the application of the above rules results in the application of a foreign law, Article 20 of the PILA has the effect of still imposing the application of mandatory rules of the Republic of Korea.[67] The issue of whether data protection provisions should be considered as mandatory within the meaning of Article 20 of the PILA is however currently still debated.[68]

As to the calculation of damages, Article 52 (4) of the PILA provides that

> [i]n cases of application of a foreign law under paragraphs (1) through (3), the right to claim compensation for damage resulting from a tort shall not be recognized, where the nature of such right is not evidently for the purpose of payment of due compensation to the injured party or where such right is exercised beyond the scope essentially necessary for the payment of due compensation to the injured party. This rule may however potentially enter into conflict with those of the PIPA dictating various caps to the amount of compensation which can be decided by the courts,[69] and an *in concreto* analysis will be necessary.[70]

[65] Suk Kwang Hyun, *Gukjesabeop haeseol* [*Commentary on Private International Law*] (Parkyoungsa, 2013) 392.

[66] Article 52 of the PILA (Torts):

1. 'A tort shall be governed by the law of the place where it is committed or the consequences thereof occur'.
2. Where the habitual residences of the tortfeasor and the injured party are in the same country while a tort is committed, the law of such country shall govern, notwithstanding paragraph (1). (3).
3. Where a tort violates an existing legal relationship between the tortfeasor and the injured party, the law applicable to such legal relationship shall govern, notwithstanding paragraphs (1) and (2).'

[67] Article 20 of the PILA (Mandatory Application of Law of Republic of Korea): 'The mandatory provisions of the Republic of Korea to govern the corresponding legal relationship, irrespective of the applicable law, in light of the purpose of legislation, shall also apply where a foreign law is designated as the applicable law under this Act.'

[68] Choi Kyung Jun et al (n 13) 112–14, 445, 453; Han and Choi (n 34) 90–92; Lee Jong Hyeok (n 34) 160–62. With regard to former Article 30(2)(4)of the ICNA, the Supreme Court confirmed in its recent 2023 decision that it was a mandatory provision in that it materialises the constitutional right to self-determination of personal data (Supreme Court Decision, 13 April 2023, 2017Da219232).

[69] Article 39(3) of the PIPA:

> 'Where a data subject suffers damage out of loss, theft, divulgence, forgery, alteration, or damage of his or her own personal information, caused by wrongful intent or negligence of a personal information controller, the Court may determine the amount of compensation for damage not exceeding five times such damage: Provided, That the same shall not apply to the personal information controller who has proved non-existence of his or her wrongful intent or negligence.'

Article 39-2 of the PIPA:

(1) 'Notwithstanding Article 39 (1), a data subject, who suffers damage out of loss, theft, divulgence, forgery, alteration, or damage of his or her own personal information, caused by wrongful intent or negligence of a personal information controller, may claim a reasonable amount of damages not exceeding three million won. In such cases, the said personal information controller may not be released from the responsibility for compensation if it fails to prove non-existence of his or her wrongful intent or negligence.
(2) In the case of a claim made under paragraph (1), the Court may determine a reasonable amount of damages not exceeding the amount provided for in paragraph (1) taking into account all arguments in the proceedings and the results of examining evidence.
(3) A data subject who has claimed compensation pursuant to Article 39 may change such claim to the claim provided for in paragraph (1) until the closure of fact-finding proceedings.'

[70] Han and Choi (n 34) 81.

For contractual breach claims, Article 45 PILA provides for the principle of parties' autonomy and Article 46 (Objective Connection to Determine Applicable Law) reads that 'where the parties to a contract do not choose the applicable law, the contract shall be governed by the law of the country most closely related to the contract' and follows up with a list of connecting factors.[71]

As to consumer contracts, the PILA provides specific rules[72] to protect consumers as weaker parties. According to Article 47 PILA, '[e]ven where the parties to a consumer contract choose the applicable law, the protection given to the consumer pursuant to the mandatory provisions of the country in which the habitual residence of the consumer is located shall not be deprived'. In its 2023 ruling, the Supreme Court reiterated the importance of protecting the interests of consumers and clarified that, even when the parties to a consumer contract have chosen a law other than that of the country of the consumer's habitual residence, the mandatory provisions of the law of the country of the consumer's habitual residence may not be excluded.[73]

V. Topical Issues and Prospects

A. Artificial Intelligence or AI-Generated Data

In statutory law, since its revision in 2023, Article 4(6) PIPA recognises data subjects' right to reject decisions based on fully automated personal data processing or to request explanations with regard to such decisions. This general provision is also developed in Chapter 5 'Guarantee of Data Subjects' Rights', Article 37-2(1) and (2)[74] which provide that data subjects have the right to 'reject decisions based on the processing of personal data through fully automated systems (including systems applying artificial intelligence technology) when such decisions have a significant influence on their rights or obligations', and moreover to request explanations from the data controller. Once the data subject has exercised his/her

[71] Article 46 of the PILA (Objective Connection to Determine Applicable Law)

(1) 'Where the parties to a contract do not choose the applicable law, the contract shall be governed by the law of the country most closely related to the contract.
(2) Where a party to a contract is to perform any of the following under the contract, the law of the country, in which the habitual residence of the party is located, at the time of the conclusion of the contract (the law of the country in which the principal office is located, where the party is a corporation or organization), shall be presumed to be most closely related: Provided, That where the contract is concluded in connection with the party's occupation or business activities, the law of the country, in which the place of business of the party is located, shall be presumed to be most closely related:
   1. In cases of assignment contracts, the performance as the assignor;
   2. In cases of use contracts, the performance as the party who provides objects or rights for use;
   3. In cases of delegation contracts, outsourcing contracts, or other similar contracts for the provision of services, the performance of the services.
(3) In cases of a contract on the right to immovable property, the law of the country, in which the immovable property is located, shall be presumed to be most closely related.'

[72] For developments on the assessment of whether a contract qualifies as a consumer contract, see Han and Choi (n 34) 85–56.

[73] Supreme Court Decision, 13 April 2023, 2017Da219232.

[74] Introduced in 2023 and entered into force in March 2024.

right, data controllers must abide by that decision by refraining from applying the disputed decision or providing the requested explanation, unless there is a valid reason, such as a risk of 'unfair violation of others' life, body, property or other interests'.

Another AI-related novelty concerns the creation in October 2023 of the 'Artificial Intelligence Privacy Team' within the PIPC. Its main missions consist in providing interpretations and applicable standards regarding the PIPA in AI matters and facilitating the communication and collaboration between the Government and the private sector.

B. Potential Cooperation under the Belt and Road Initiative

To this day, South Korea is not part of the Belt and Road Initiative.

C. Data Protection Post COVID-19 Pandemic

The COVID-19 pandemic led to a large number of personal data breaches as well as concerns of breaches voiced following the tracing of COVID-positive patients. This led the PIPC to include amendments of two provisions of the PIPA in 2023. Under Article 15(1) PIPA, data controllers are allowed to collect personal data in a number of cases and to use it within the scope of the purpose of collection. Article 15(2)(7) PIPA was added following the pandemic to allow for such collection and use 'when urgently required for the public safety and well-being, such as public health'. A similar provision was also added in Article 18(2)(10) PIPA with regard to the use and provision to third parties of data. While under Article 18(1) PIPA data controllers are prohibited from using or providing data to third parties beyond the specified scope, Article 18(2) provides exceptions to this rule in a number of cases and insofar as there are no risks of an unreasonable violation of the rights of a data subject or third party. In 2023, Article 18(2)(10) was introduced to allow such use or provision 'when urgently required for the public safety and well-being, such as public health'.[75] These novelties replace the much broader exception which existed under the older version of the PIPA whereby 'personal data processed temporarily where it is urgently required for the public safety and well-being, such as public health' fell outside the scope of all the rules prescribed by Chapters 3 to 7 of the PIPA. These rules included a set of general protections such as those applicable to the processing of personal data and guarantee of data subjects' rights.

The pandemic also raised issues related to the processing of data under the Act on the Prevention and Control of Infectious Disease (the 'Infectious Disease Prevention Act'). In September 2020, the Act underwent a revision to specify the standards applicable to the processing of personal data required for public safety.[76] Article 6(2) of the Infectious Disease Prevention Act provides that

[75] The notion of 'public safety and well-being' in both provisions is understood as including safety from disasters. See Choi Kyung Jun et al (n 13) 214.

[76] Infectious Disease Prevention Act, Art 76(2).

> [e]ach citizen shall have the right to know information on the situation of the outbreak of infectious diseases and the prevention and control of infectious diseases and how to cope therewith, and the State and local governments shall promptly disclose the relevant information.[77]

That being said, the exact scope of the 'relevant information' to be disclosed by public bodies is still being debated, especially with regard to whether it extends to information allowing to identify an individual, such as the movement of COVID-positive patients.[78]

[77] Official translation, available at: www.law.go.kr/LSW/lsInfoP.do?lsiSeq=172762&viewCls=engLsInfoR&urlMode=engLsInfoR&chrClsCd=010203#0000.

[78] Lee Joo Hee, 'A Study on Personal Information Protection Measures in the Covid-19 Era' (2020) *Science, Technology and Law* 11-2, 307–308.

5

Singapore

LANX GOH AND JOSHUA KOW*

I. Introduction

The Personal Data Protection Act 2012[1] (PDPA) was passed into law by the Parliament of Singapore on 15 October 2012, and obtained presidential assent shortly after on 20 November 2012. Following a 'sunrise' period where organisations[2] were encouraged to build towards compliance without penalty, specific provisions relating to a 'Do Not Call Registry' ('DNC Registry') for specified marketing messages came into force on 2 January 2014,[3] and all remaining key obligations in respect of collection, use, and disclosure of personal data more generally (the 'Data Protection Obligations') came into force on 2 July 2014.[4] The PDPA has been administered and enforced by the Personal Data Protection Commission (PDPC), a part of the Infocomm Media Development Authority (IMDA) under the Ministry of Communications and Information (MCI), ever since.

The PDPA is unique among privacy and data protection laws, both in the Asia-Pacific region and globally. Driven neither by the 'human-rights approached favoured in the European Union [EU] nor the "threat-technology-structure mix that has driven reform in the US"',[5] the PDPA is instead driven by 'the imperative of globalisation and the need to adopt standards that will afford trust in national institutions and seamless integration into global networks'.[6] Indeed, at the Second Reading of the PDP Bill,[7] Dr Yaacob Ibrahim,

* The authors are deeply grateful to Professor Anselmo Reyes, Mr Adrian Mak, and Mr Ching Him Ho for their helpful suggestions and comments on this chapter. All views expressed here are the authors' personal views only and should not be taken to represent the views or policy positions of their respective employers. Any mistakes are entirely the authors' own.

[1] Personal Data Protection Act 2012 (2020 Rev. Ed. Sing.), available at sso.agc.gov.sg/Act/PDPA2012.

[2] See below on the usage of the term 'organisation' as defined in the PDPA.

[3] PDPC, 'Do Not Call Registry & You', available at www.pdpc.gov.sg/overview-of-PDPA/do-not-call-registry/individual/do-not-call-registry-and-you.

[4] PDPC, 'Advisory Guidelines on Key Concepts in the PDPA' (Revised 16 May 2022) ('Key Concepts Guidelines') 2 [2.2], available at www.pdpc.gov.sg/-/media/Files/PDPC/PDF-Files/Advisory-Guidelines/AG-on-Key-Concepts/Advisory-Guidelines-on-Key-Concepts-in-the-PDPA-17-May-2022.pdf.

[5] Ken Chia, 'Jurisdictional Report: Singapore' in *Regulation of Cross-Border Transfers of Personal Data in Asia* (*Asian Business Law Institute*, 2018) 317 [8], available at abli.asia/abli-publications/regulation-of-cross-border-transfers-of-personal-data-in-asia-softcover/.

[6] ibid.

[7] Yaacob Ibrahim, 'Singapore Parliamentary Debates, Official Report' (15 October 2012) vol 89, available at sprs.parl.gov.sg/search/email/link/?id=023_20121015_S0003_T0002&fullContentFlag=false.

Minister for Information, Communication and the Arts, emphasised that the PDPA will '… enhance Singapore's competitiveness and strengthen our position as a trusted business hub. It will put Singapore on par with the growing list of countries that have enacted data protection laws and facilitate cross-border transfers of data'.

In language broadly emblematic of Singaporean society's pragmatism and business-friendliness, section 3 of the PDPA expressly states that the law's purpose is to

> govern the collection, use, and disclosure of personal data by organisations in a manner that recognises *both* the *right of individuals* to protect their personal data and *the need of organisations* to collect, use or disclose personal data for purposes that a reasonable person would consider appropriate in the circumstances [emphasis added].[8]

The recognition that a balance needs to be struck between individual rights and business needs[9] guides the PDPC's enforcement of the PDPA's 11 distinct but interrelated obligations,[10] positioning it as both an enabler of data use and enforcer of data protection standards.[11]

With limited exceptions,[12] the PDPA regulates virtually every aspect of the personal data life cycle in Singapore, commencing from collection and culminating in its disposal after processing. As a result of PDPA's comprehensiveness and its outsized impact on Singapore's data protection landscape, one might be tempted to think that familiarity with the PDPA is all that is required to understand privacy through a Singaporean lens. This cannot be further from the truth. The PDPA merely sets a baseline standard for personal data protection in Singapore,[13] and the provisions of other written laws (eg, sectoral regulation in the banking and/or insurance industries) prevail to the extent that the Data Protection Obligations are inconsistent with them.[14]

In this chapter, the authors will discuss and evaluate the various strands of legislation and regulation which, read together, comprise Singapore's approach to privacy and data protection. Apart from an introduction and discussion of the constitutional, common law, and statutory sources of privacy and data protection law in Singapore, specific attention will also be given to the PDPA, its key provisions, and its treatment of international data transfers as understood through the lens of the Transfer Limitation Obligation. Where appropriate, the authors will refer to case law from the Singapore Courts as well as enforcement decisions of the PDPC concerning the PDPA's Data Protection Obligations. Finally, the authors will make specific observations on topical issues such as artificial intelligence, changes brought about by COVID-19, and the international efforts undertaken by the PDPC and the Government to promote Singapore's interests in the region.

[8] Explanatory Statement to the Personal Data Protection Bill (Bill No 24/2012), Part I, Clause 3, available at sso.agc.gov.sg/Bills-Supp/24-2012/.

[9] See, eg, Key Concepts Guidelines (n 4) 33, [9.3]–[9.5].

[10] See, e., PDPC, 'Data Protection Obligations' for an overview of these 11 obligations, available at www.pdpc.gov.sg/overview-of-PDPA/the-legislation/personal-data-protection-act/data-protection-obligations.

[11] IMDA, 'The Driving Force behind Personal Data Protection' (25 January 2022), available at www.imda.gov.sg/resources/blog/blog-articles/2022/01/the-driving-force-behind-personal-data-protection.

[12] See, eg, PDPA, First, Second, Fifth and Sixth Schedules.

[13] PDPC, 'PDPA Overview – What is the PDPA?', available at www.pdpc.gov.sg/overview-of-PDPA/the-legislation/personal-data-protection-act. See also, PDPA, s 4(6)(b).

[14] PDPA, s 4(6)(b).

II. Constitutional, Common Law, and Other Statutory Protections

As a Commonwealth nation and common law jurisdiction, Singapore's approach to privacy and data protection may be best understood through the intersection and interaction of its constitutional liberties, common law jurisprudence, and through statutory laws including, but not limited to, the PDPA. We examine each in turn below.

A. Constitutional Protections

It is crucial to state upfront that the Singapore Constitution[15] does not contain any explicit provision for the protection of privacy as a fundamental right.[16] Although Article 9(1) of the Singapore Constitution enshrines a right not be deprived of 'life or personal liberty' save in accordance with law, the Court of Appeal, the highest court in Singapore's judicial system, expressly held in *Lim Meng Suang* that a right to privacy and personal autonomy cannot be read into this phrase.[17] Instead, the right not be deprived of 'life or personal liberty' merely referred to a person's freedom from 'an unlawful deprivation of life and unlawful detention or incarceration',[18] and that foreign cases that have conferred an expansive constitutional right to life and liberty should be 'approached with circumspection because they were decided in the context of their unique social, political and legal circumstances'.[19]

Of particular interest is the Court of Appeal's recognition of the fact that Article 9 of the PDPA was derived from Article 21 of the Indian Constitution.[20] Almost three years after *Lim Meng Suang* was delivered in Singapore, the Indian Supreme Court proceeded to recognise a distinct and fundamental right to privacy 'as an intrinsic part of the right to life and personal liberty' in *Puttaswamy v Union of India*,[21] read not only from Article 21 of the Indian Constitution but also from the broader Part III in which it is contained. Unfortunately, subsequent pronouncements by the PDPC in enforcement decisions indicate that the local courts are unlikely to adopt a similar approach as the Indian Supreme Court.[22]

For completeness, there are no other fundamental liberties[23] in the Singapore Constitution which may suggest a constitutional right to privacy in the manner argued in *Lim Meng Suang*, whether expressly or impliedly.

[15] Constitution of the Republic of Singapore (2020 Rev. Ed. Sing.), available at sso.agc.gov.sg/Act/CONS1963.
[16] *My Digital Lock Pte Ltd* [2018] SGPDPC [22].
[17] *Lim Meng Suang v Attorney-General* [2014] SGCA 53 [44] (Phang JA).
[18] ibid [46].
[19] ibid [48].
[20] ibid [47].
[21] *Justice KS Puttaswamy (Retd.) and ANR v Union of India and Ors*, Writ Petition (Civil) No 494 of 2012, available at indiankanoon.org/doc/127517806/.
[22] *My Digital Lock* (n 16) [24].
[23] See, eg, Singapore Constitution, arts 9–16, setting out the fundamental liberties of persons in Singapore.

B. Common Law and Other Statutory Protections

Absent any constitutional right relating to the protection of privacy as in India or other jurisdictions, the follow-on question is thus whether any similar or equivalent rights exist under the common law. By virtue of the Application of English Law Act (AELA),[24] the common law of England, so far as it was part of the law of Singapore immediately before 12 November 1993, continues to be a part of the law of Singapore.[25] While the Singapore Courts have not made any explicit pronouncements on the existence of a general tort of privacy,[26] it has been posited in an enforcement decision by the PDPC that there nevertheless exists in Singapore a 'framework of common law and statutory torts that *collectively* protect an individual's privacy'.[27] Decisions made by the PDPC are not de facto legally-binding, but may nevertheless be persuasive and/or cited with approval by judicial authorities vested with power to make binding legal decisions.[28]

In *My Digital Lock*, in explaining his exercise of discretion to discontinue certain investigations under section 50 of the PDPA in favour of separate ongoing legal proceedings, (former) Deputy Commissioner of the PDPC Yeong Zee Kin ('Deputy Commissioner Yeong') cited the privacy framework first proposed by William Prosser[29] with approval, referring to the right to privacy as comprising four separate 'rights':

a) the right to seclusion;
b) the right to prevent publication of private communication;
c) the right to prevent the appropriation of identity; and
d) the right to prevent false publicity.[30]

As concerns the right to seclusion, which involves an invasion of a victim's private space or affairs, Deputy Commissioner Yeong noted that the Singapore High Court had already cast doubt on the existence of such a common law right, and called for legislative intervention if such a right ought to be recognised.[31] This right now takes the form of a statutory tort of harassment, enshrined in the Protection from Harassment Act (POHA).[32] POHA also expressly abolished the common law tort of intentional harassment, and established that no civil proceedings shall be brought for the tort of harassment except as a statutory tort under section 14 of the POHA.

For completeness, POHA allows the Protection from Harassment Court, a specialised court dedicated to dealing with harassment matters and established on 1 June 2021,[33] to

[24] Application of English Law Act 1993 (2002 Rev. Ed. Sing), available at sso.agc.gov.sg/Act/AELA1993.
[25] ibid, s 3(1).
[26] *My Digital Lock* (n 16) [22]. See also, Lanx Goh and Jansen Aw, 'Data Protection Law in Singapore' in Simon Chesterman (ed), *Data Protection Law in Singapore: Privacy and Sovereignty in an Interconnected World*, 2nd edn (Academy Publishing, 2018) [4.10].
[27] *My Digital Lock* (n 16) [21].
[28] See, eg, *Reed, Michael v Bellingham, Alex* [2022] SGCA 60 [109], where the Court of Appeal cited *AIG Asia Pacific Insurance Pte Ltd & Toppan Forms (S) Pte Ltd* [2019] SGPDPC 2 and *Asia Pacific Insurance Pte Ltd* [2018] SGPDPC 8 with approval.
[29] William L Prosser, *Privacy* (1960) 48 *California Law Review* 383, 389.
[30] *My Digital Lock* (n 16) [26].
[31] *AXA Insurance Singapore Pte Ltd v Chandran s/o Natesan* [2013] 4 SLR 545 [8].
[32] Protection from Harassment Act 2014 (2020 Rev. Ed. Sing.), ss 3–4, available at sso.agc.gov.sg/Act/PHA2014.
[33] Ministry of Law, 'Press Release: Quicker, More Effective Remedies Against Harassment with New Protection from Harassment Court from 1 June 2021' (31 May 2021), available at www.mlaw.gov.sg/news/

have oversight of all criminal and civil matters which may relate to:[34] (a) harassment, alarm or distress, fear; (b) provocation or facilitation of violence; and (c) unlawful stalking, among others. The Protection from Harassment Court may, in appropriate cases, make several orders (eg, protection orders, correction orders, publication orders, etc) and/or award damages to victims. Between 1 June 2021 to 30 June 2022, a total of 676 cases involving harassment, cyber-bullying, and doxxing were filed with the Protection from Harassment Court.[35] As noted by Lanx and Jansen, 'POHA can be said to represent the clearest recognition of some right of seclusion from intrusion'.[36]

In contrast with the approach taken by Hong Kong with its Personal Data (Privacy) Amendment Ordinance 2021,[37] where new provisions were introduced to criminalise doxxing acts and provide the Hong Kong Privacy Commissioner for Personal Data (PCPD) with statutory powers to conduct investigations and serve cessation notices to cease or restrict disclosure,[38] there are no equivalent provisions or powers granted to the PDPC under the PDPA. Instead, the Singapore High Court has, in a case involving a web post concerning an applicant's alleged incompetence as a sports coach and alleged molestation of athletes, affirmed that 'harassing conduct on the Internet, such as those in the Web post in the present case would be covered by ss 3 and 4 of the POHA'.[39]

As concerns the right to prevent publication of private communication, Deputy Commissioner Yeong observed that case law in the United Kingdom had recognised this as a new cause of action[40] distinct from an action for breach of confidence, as traditionally defined in *Coco v AN Clark*.[41] However, he noted the Singapore Court of Appeal did not go as far, recognising the question of 'whether we should afford, like the courts in England and various other jurisdictions, protection to one's privacy by way of the law of confidence regardless of whether such a right is guaranteed under the Constitution … [the] extent to which we should adopt such jurisprudence, i.e., the circumstances under which the law of confidence would extend its protection to private information acquired without consent' gave rise to serious questions to be tried.

In these circumstances where the Court of Appeal had left open the question of whether such a common law tort should exist,[42] Deputy Commissioner Yeong observed that a private claimant could, in a case before the civil courts, plead *both* the common law tort to prevent publication of private information as well as pursue a private claim based on breaches of the PDPA to not only provide himself with a more comprehensive set of reliefs, but also to

press-releases/2021-05-31-quicker-more-effective-remedies-against-harassment-with-new-protection-from-harassment-court-from-1-june-2021/.

[34] See POHA, ss 3–10 for a list of criminal offences under POHA.

[35] Kasiviswanathan Shanmugam, Singapore Parliamentary Debates, Official Report, Session 1, Vol No 95, Sitting No 71 (5 October 2022).

[36] Lanx Goh and Jansen Aw (n 26) [4.40].

[37] Personal Data (Privacy) Amendment Ordinance 2021, Ord No 32 of 2021 (Hong Kong).

[38] See, eg, PCPD, 'Doxxing Offences: The Law', available at www.pcpd.org.hk/english/doxxing/index.html.

[39] *Benber Dayao Yu v Jacter Singh* [2017] SGHC 92 [25].

[40] *My Digital Lock* (n 16) [35], citing *Campbell v MGM Ltd* [2004] 2 AC 457 and *Douglas v Hello! Ltd* [2008] 1 AC 1.

[41] See *Coco v AN Clark (Engineers) Ltd* [1968] FSR 415, where Megarry J held that the three elements essential to a cause of action for breach of confidence were: (a) that the information was of a confidential nature; (b) that it was communicated in circumstances importing an obligation of confidence; and (c) that there was an authorised use of the information to the plaintiff's detriment.

[42] *My Digital Lock* (n 16) [37], citing *ANB v ANC* [2015] SLR 522 [23].

provide the Singapore courts with the opportunity to adopt the common law right identified in the United Kingdom.[43]

Turning then to the rights to prevent appropriation of identity (or right of publicity) and the right to prevent false publicity respectively, Deputy Commissioner Yeong opined that the former may be protected by the law of passing off in Singapore[44] but '[p]rivate individuals are likely to have more success in relying on the PDPA to prevent misuse or abuse of their identity on the basis of use or disclosure without consent'.[45] On the latter, he asserted it could possibly be protected within the law of defamation[46] although further stressed that defamation and data protection are distinct and cannot be conflated under the PDPA to recognise a form of false light publicity.[47] Deputy Commissioner Yeong continues to observe that it is in

> the area of personality rights that the area of overlap between the PDPA and common law rights is the greatest, since both operate on personal information. This is also the area where the contours between any common law right [...] and statutory rights under the PDPA have yet to come under judicial scrutiny in Singapore.[48]

He then proceeds to state that

> [p]erhaps the PDPA and the right of publicity are means to different ends – while the right of publicity seeks to protect the commercial value of the name or image of the individual, the PDPA seeks to hold organisations accountable for the proper and respectful handling of personal data, by imposing a standard of conduct that permits reasonable use, processing or disclosure while preventing misuse or abuse of personal data.[49]

Indeed, Lanx and Jansen observed 'that there has been criticism that the tort of publicity, along with the tort of false light publicity, "protect[s] other interests" besides privacy itself'.[50]

C. The Personal Data Protection Act (PDPA)

The PDPA governs the collection, use and disclosure of individuals' personal data by organisations in a manner that recognises both the right of individuals to protect their personal data and the need of organisations to collect, use and disclose personal data for purposes that a reasonable person would consider appropriate in the circumstances. In other words, the PDPA protects *informational privacy*,[51] and sits within the 'penumbra of laws protecting privacy'[52] such as those discussed above. It is not, by any means, an 'omnibus privacy legislation',[53] nor were there any other such laws prior to its enactment.

[43] ibid [40].
[44] ibid [43].
[45] ibid [50]. See also, Lanx Goh and Jansen Aw (n 26) [4.66].
[46] ibid [46], citing *Chiam See Tong v Xin Zhang Jiang Restaurant Pte Ltd* [1995] 1 SLR(R) 856.
[47] ibid [47]. See also, Lanx Goh and Jansen Aw (n 26) [4.74].
[48] ibid [48].
[49] ibid [50].
[50] Lanx Goh and Jansen Aw (n 26) [4.67].
[51] *My Digital Lock* (n 16) [51].
[52] *My Digital Lock* (n 16) [27].
[53] Gary Kok Yew Chan and Pey Woan Lee, *The Law of Torts Singapore*, 2nd edn (Academy Publishing, 2015) [16.011].

It is important to note that, unless expressly provided in the PDPA itself, the provisions of other written laws prevail to the extent that they are inconsistent with the Data Protection Obligations.[54] The provisions of the PDPA do not supersede existing statutes with sector-specific data protection requirements; for example, the banking secrecy requirements applicable to banks under section 47 of the Banking Act.[55]

The Data Protection Obligations in the PDPA may be broadly understood as comprising 11 distinct obligations,[56] namely the Accountability Obligation,[57] the Notification Obligation,[58] the Consent Obligation,[59] the Purpose Limitation Obligation,[60] the Accuracy Obligation,[61] the Protection Obligation,[62] the Retention Limitation Obligation,[63] the Transfer Limitation Obligation,[64] the Access and Correction Obligation,[65] the Data Breach Notification Obligation,[66] and the Data Portability Obligation[67] respectively. In the interests of brevity, the authors do not propose to discuss each obligation exhaustively in this chapter. Suffice to say, however, that Data Protection Obligations are broadly consistent with the data protection principles in the Organisation for Economic Co-operation and Development (OECD) Guidelines on the Protection of Privacy and Transborder Flows of Personal Data ('OECD Guidelines').

It is apposite to note that the Portability Obligation has not yet come into effect, and there remains no right to data portability under the PDPA which would require organisations to transmit personal data to another organisation upon an individual's request as of the date of this chapter's writing. The PDPC has, however, committed to introducing the Data Portability Obligation in phases through the issuance of Codes of Practice or similarly suitable regulatory instruments.[68]

Under the PDPA, 'personal data' refers to data, *whether true or not*, about an individual who can be identified:

a) from that data; or
b) from that data and other information to which the organisation has or is likely to have access.[69]

Individuals refer to natural persons, *whether living or deceased*. The PDPA applies to all organisations collecting, using, and/or disclosing personal data in Singapore, *whether*

[54] PDPA, s 4(6)(b).
[55] Banking Act 1970 (2020 Rev. Ed. Sing).
[56] PDPC, 'Data Protection Obligations' (n 10).
[57] PDPA, Part 3 and in particular, s 11(2) contained within.
[58] ibid s 20.
[59] ibid, s 13.
[60] ibid, s 18.
[61] ibid, s 23.
[62] ibid, s 24.
[63] ibid, s 25.
[64] ibid, s 26.
[65] ibid, ss 21, 22 and 22A.
[66] ibid, Part 6A.
[67] Proposed for future introduction into the PDPA, Part 6B but with no clear indication on the date of implementation.
[68] PDPC, 'Response to Feedback on the Public Consultation on Proposed Data Portability and Data Innovation Provisions' (20 January 2020) 12, [6.3].
[69] PDPA, s 2(1).

or not it has a physical presence or is registered as a company in Singapore. Therefore, an organisation is bound by the PDPA so long as personal data is collected from individuals located in Singapore (eg, through online platforms). For completeness, the PDPA also applies to personal data which has been collected overseas and subsequently transferred into Singapore.[70]

The PDPA does not apply to any individual acting in a personal or domestic capacity[71] which was further illustrated to be 'related to home or family'. Hence, an individual acts in a domestic capacity when undertaking activities for his home or family. Examples of such activities could include opening joint bank accounts between two or more family members or purchasing life insurance policies on one's child.[72] In comparison, on 13 May 2020, in a dispute between a mother and her daughter over the publication of photos of the grandchildren, the court held that it was impossible to establish with certainty that the posting of photos on social media fell under the 'household exemption' in Article 2(2)(c) of the General Data Protection Regulation (GDPR)[73] since it was unclear whether the photographs could be found through a search engine and ended up with third parties. The GDPR finding clearly contrasts with the PDPA position which focuses on the status of the actors (personal capacity vis-à-vis commercial capacity) rather than whether the personal data will end up with another third party.

Further, in contrast with other key data protection laws both in the region and globally, the PDPA does not contain a definition for 'sensitive personal data'[74] or special categories of personal data[75] (eg, racial or ethnic origin, sexual orientation, etc). Instead, the PDPC has, in advisory guidance, recommended that organisations 'implement robust policies and procedures for ensuring appropriate levels of security for personal data of varying levels of sensitivity'.[76] In a widely-known data breach of a cluster of public healthcare institutions, the PDPC took consideration of the fact that medical data is 'personal data of a sensitive nature which should be accorded a higher standard of protection'.[77] Other categories of personal data that have been regarded as more sensitive in nature include:[78]

a) National Registration Identity Card (NRIC) numbers and other national identification numbers (eg, birth certificate numbers, Foreign Identification Numbers (FINs), Work Permit numbers, and passport numbers);[79]

[70] Key Concepts Guidelines (n 4) 36, [11.1].

[71] PDPA, s 4(1).

[72] Key Concepts Guidelines (n 4) 23, [6.10].

[73] Regulation (EU) 2016/679 of the European Parliament and of the Council of 27 April 2016 on the protection of natural persons with regard to the processing of personal data and on the free movement of such data (2016) OJ L119/1, Art 2(2)(c).

[74] For comparison purposes, see Data Privacy Act of 2012, Republic Act No 10173 (Philippines) s 3(1) and Personal Data Protection Act 2010, Act No 709 (10 June 2010) (Malaysia) s 4.

[75] See, for comparison purposes, GDPR, Art 9.

[76] Key Concepts Guidelines (n 4) 114, [17.3(c)].

[77] *SingHealth & Anor* [2019] SGPDPC 3 [51].

[78] See also, Lanx Goh and Nadia Yeo, 'Sensitive Personal Data in the Singapore Context' [2019] *PDP Digest* 37, available at www.pdpc.gov.sg/-/media/files/pdpc/pdf-files/resource-for-organisation/2019-personal-data-protection-digest.pdf.

[79] PDPC, 'Advisory Guidelines on the Personal Data Protection Act for NRIC and Other National Identification Numbers' ('Advisory Guidelines') (31 August 2018), available at www.pdpc.gov.sg/-/media/Files/PDPC/PDF-Files/Advisory-Guidelines/Advisory-Guidelines-for-NRIC-Numbers---310818.pdf.

b) personal data of a financial nature such as bank account details, Central Depository account details, securities holdings, transaction and payment summaries, names of the policyholder's dependants or beneficiaries, the sum insured under the insurance policy, the premium amount and type of coverage, an individual's personal history involving drug use and infidelity, sensitive medical conditions;[80] and
c) personal data of minors.[81]

Concerning national identification numbers specifically, organisations are generally not allowed to collect, use, or disclose NRIC numbers unless required by law or used to verify identities to a high degree of fidelity.[82] The PDPC considers it necessary to accurately establish or verify the identity of an individual to a high degree of fidelity where the failure to do so may pose a significant safety or security risk (eg, visitor entry to preschools where ensuring the safety and security of young children is an overriding concern), or where inability to do so would pose a risk of significant impact or harm to an individual and/or the organisation (eg, fraudulent claims relating to healthcare, financial, or real estate matters).[83]

Interestingly, and in contrast with many other data protection regimes, the Data Protection Obligations of the PDPA relating to collection, use, and disclosure of personal data do not generally apply to 'business contact information'.[84] Such information includes an individual's name, position name or title, business telephone number, business address, business electronic mail address or business fax number and any other similar information about the individual, not provided by the individual *solely for his or her personal purposes*.[85] Information on a business name card that has been provided for the purpose of joining a mailing list at a corporate seminar, for example, would not fall within the scope of the Data Protection Obligations.[86] However, the definition of 'business contact information' is ultimately dependent on the purpose for which such contact information may be provided.[87]

Data that has been anonymised is no longer considered personal data for the purposes of the PDPA.[88] To this end, it bears mention that the PDPC has released a significant amount of guidance concerning personal data that has been anonymised and/or pseudonymised, and the implications of both techniques on PDPA compliance. In both its Selected Topics Guidelines and Basic Anonymisation Guide,[89] the PDPC makes a distinction between anonymisation (ie, conversion of personal data into data that cannot be used to identify any individual through applying anonymisation techniques and safeguards to prevent re-identification) and de-identification (ie, removal of identifiers that directly identify an individual),[90] although both terms may be used interchangeably in other

[80] *Aviva Ltd* [2017] SGPDPC 14 [17].
[81] ibid and PDPC, 'Advisory Guidelines on the Personal Data Protection Act for Selected Topics' ('Personal Data Protection Act Guidelines') (Revised 17 May 2022) 59, [8.12].
[82] Advisory Guidelines (n 79) 5, [3.1].
[83] ibid, 8–9, [3.13].
[84] PDPA, s 4(4)(b).
[85] ibid, s 2(1).
[86] Key Concepts Guidelines (n 4)18, [5.18].
[87] ibid, 19, [5.19].
[88] Personal Data Protection Act Guidelines (n 81) 11, [3.5].
[89] PDPC, 'Guide to Basic Anonymisation' ('Guide to Basic Anonymisation') (31 March 2022), availableatwww.pdpc.gov.sg/-/media/Files/PDPC/PDF-Files/Advisory-Guidelines/Guide-to-Basic-Anonymisation-31-March-2022.pdf.
[90] ibid, 7.

jurisdictions.[91] The PDPC considers de-identification to be one step in a five-stage process comprising: (a) knowing the data; (b) de-identifying the data; (c) applying anonymisation techniques; (d) computing risk; and (e) managing the risks, respectively.[92]

Notably, the PDPC considers pseudonymisation (ie, the replacement of identifying data with made-up values) to be a 'basic data anonymisation technique'[93] alongside other techniques like record suppression and character masking, to be applied as part of the anonymisation process.

The PDPA makes a distinction between two categories of users of personal data – 'organisations' and 'data intermediaries' respectively.[94] An organisation is defined as any individual, company, association, or body of persons, corporate or unincorporated, whether or not formed or recognised under the law of Singapore or resident, or having an office or a place of business, in Singapore. On the other hand, a 'data intermediary' refers to an organisation which processes personal data on behalf of another organisation but does not include an employee of that other organisation. These definitions are broadly similar, although not fully identical, to the concepts of 'data controller' and 'data processor' used in other privacy and personal data protection laws. There is no expressly stated definition of 'data sub-intermediary' in the PDPA that would be similar or equivalent to what other laws would consider a 'sub-processor'.

One way that the PDPA departs significantly from the data protection laws of other jurisdictions is the fact that it does not apply to public agencies, such as ministries of the Singapore Government.[95] Protection of personal data in the public sector is instead governed by:

a) the Public Sector (Governance) Act (PSGA), under which unauthorised disclosure and improper use of information are offences which carry fines not exceeding $5,000 and/or imprisonment terms not exceeding two years;[96] as well as
b) the Government Instruction Manual on Infocomm Technology & Smarts Systems Management ('IM on ICT&SS Management'), first enacted in 2018 to strengthen public sector data governance and setting out how the Singapore Government manages and protects data (including personal data) in its possession or control.[97] The IM on ICT&SS Management was most recently updated in 2019, with additional technical and process measures to protect data and prevent data compromise.[98]

D. Data Breach Notification under the PDPA

Recent amendments to the PDPA have also introduced a new 'Data Breach Notification Obligation',[99] which came into effect on 1 February 2021. Under the newly-introduced

[91] Personal Data Protection Act Guidelines (n 81) 10, [3.2].
[92] Guide to Basic Anonymisation (n 89) 14.
[93] ibid 34.
[94] PDPA, s 2(1).
[95] ibid, s 4(1)(c).
[96] PSGA, s 7(1).
[97] Smart Nation Singapore, 'Government's Personal Data Protection Laws and Policies', available at www.smartnation.gov.sg/about-smart-nation/secure-smart-nation/personal-data-protection-laws-and-policies/.
[98] Smart Nation Singapore, 'Government's Personal Data Protection Initiatives, available at www.smartnation.gov.sg/about-smart-nation/secure-smart-nation/personal-data-protection-initiatives.
[99] See PDPA, Part 6A.

provisions, unless an exception applies, organisations have a duty to assess data breaches that have occurred affecting personal data in their possession or under their control, and an obligation to notify the PDPC and affected individuals if certain prescribed thresholds are met. Organisations must notify the PDPC as soon as is practicable, but in any case no later than three calendar days after assessment.[100]

Under section 26A of the PDPA, a 'data breach' in relation to personal data means the unauthorised access, collection, use, disclosure, copying, modification or disposal of personal data, or the loss of any storage medium or device on which personal data is stored in circumstances where the unauthorised access, collection, use, disclosure, copying, modification or disposal of the personal data is likely to occur. A data breach is notifiable if it results in, or is likely to result in, significant harm to an affected individual or is, or is likely to be, of a significant scale.[101]

Under the Personal Data Protection (Notification of Data Breaches) Regulations 2021 ('PDP Breach Regulations'), data breaches are deemed to result in significant harm to an individual if they relate to:

a) the individual's full name or alias or identification number, and any of the personal data or classes of personal data relating to the individual set out in Part 1 of the Schedule of the PDP Breach Regulations,[102] subject to Part 2 of the Schedule of the PDP Breach Regulations;[103] or
b) all of the following personal data relating to an individual's account with an organisation:
   i. the individual's account identifier, such as an account name or number;
   ii. any password, security code, access code, response to a security question, biometric data or other data that is used or required to allow access to or use of the individual's account.

Similarly, a data breach is deemed to be of a significant scale if the number of affected individuals is 500 or more. This is a unique breach notification requirement only to be found under the PDPA and in the United States where states such as Alabama and California must notify their local Attorney General if the affected individuals cross 1000 and 500 respectively.

Section 26E of the PDPA provides that where an organisation is a data intermediary processing personal data on behalf of and for the purposes of a public agency and has reason to believe that a data breach has occurred in relation to that personal data, the organisation must, without undue delay, notify the public agency of the occurrence of the data breach.

In situations where a data breach involves more than one organisation, the Key Concepts Guidelines provide that each organisation involved is individually responsible for its own compliance with the Data Breach Notification Obligation in respect of that breach.[104] Nevertheless, organisations may agree between themselves for one organisation to take the

[100] ibid, s 26D.
[101] ibid, s 26B(1).
[102] These include the amount of any wages, salary, fee, commission, bonus, gratuity, allowance or other remuneration paid or payable to the individual by any person, whether under a contract of service or a contract for services, as well as the assessment, diagnosis, treatment, prevention or alleviation by a health professional of sexually-transmitted diseases, HIV/AIDs, schizophrenia or delusional disorder, or substance abuse and addiction, among others.
[103] These exclude personal data that is publicly available, and any personal data that is disclosed to the extent that is required or permitted under any written law.
[104] Key Concepts Guidelines (n 4) 132, [20.10].

lead in conducting the assessment to determine whether the breach is notifiable, although each organisation has to notify the Commission albeit using the same information where relevant.[105] There is nothing in the Key Concepts Guidelines suggesting that organisations outside of Singapore (eg, a foreign-incorporated corporation that collects and uses personal data of individuals in Singapore) cannot avail themselves of such a coordinated approach.

E. Right of Private Action under the PDPA

While enforcement of the PDPA is most frequently done by the PDPC in exercise of its powers to investigate[106] and subsequently issue directions and/or financial penalties,[107] it is perhaps unsurprising to note that individuals are empowered to institute civil proceedings under the PDPA as well. Specifically, persons who suffer loss or damage directly as a result of certain contraventions[108] of the PDPA by an organisation are entitled to a right of action for relief in civil proceedings pursuant to section 48O of the PDPA.[109] Reliefs that may be granted by a court include injunctions, declarations, damages, or any other relief as the relevant court thinks fit.[110]

In *Reed v Bellingham*,[111] the Court of Appeal had the opportunity to consider the appropriate interpretation of the phrase 'loss or damage', and specifically whether a plaintiff's emotional distress and loss of control of personal data fell within the scope of this phrase for the purposes of a civil claim.

By way of background, the respondent, Mr Alex Bellingham, was formerly an employee of IP Real Estate Investments Pte Ltd ('IP Real Estate'), itself a part of the 'IP Global' group of companies. His role involved managing an investment fund, the 'Edinburgh Fund', which was set up by the IP Global group. When the respondent left IP Real Estate for a new employer, Q Investment Partners Pte Ltd ('Q Investment'), he used the personal data of investors of the Edinburgh Fund (including their names, personal email addresses, and investment activities in the fund) to contact and market opportunities to them on behalf of Q Investment. IP Real Estate and another company in the IP Global group, IP Investment Management Pte Ltd ('IP Investment'), subsequently commenced proceedings in the District Court,[112] seeking an injunction to restrain Mr Bellingham from using, disclosing or communicating personal data of three customers of his ex-employer, and to destroy all copies of personal data obtained by him. Mr Michael Reed, an individual investor in the Edinburgh Fund who was approached by Mr Bellingham, was added as the third plaintiff to the proceedings.

While the District Judge found that the right of private action was not intended to be exercised by IP Investment and IP Real Estate,[113] he nevertheless proceeded to issue an

[105] ibid, [20.10]–[20.11].
[106] PDPA, s 50(1).
[107] ibid, ss 48I–48J.
[108] Namely, contraventions by an organisation of any provision of Part 4, 5, 6, 6A, or 6B, or contraventions by a person of any provision of Division 3 of Part 9 or section 4B(1), of the PDPA respectively.
[109] This right of private action was formerly enshrined at section 32(1) of the PDPA, prior to amendments under the Personal Data Protection (Amendment) Act 2020 which came into force on February 2021.
[110] PDPA, s 48O(3)(a)–(c).
[111] *Michael Reed v Alex Bellingham* [2022] SGCA 60.
[112] *IP Investment Management Pte Ltd and ors v Alex Bellingham* [2019] SGDC 207.
[113] ibid, [111].

injunction for the benefit of Mr Reed,[114] whom he found had the requisite standing to bring the action as it related to Mr Bellingham's use of his personal data. The decision of the District Judge was subsequently appealed against by Mr Bellingham, who argued that Mr Reed did not have a right of action given that he did not suffer any 'loss or damage'. This resulted in the injunction being set aside,[115] as the High Court found that the term 'loss or damage' was limited to the heads of loss or damage under common law, and did not include distress or loss of control over personal data.[116] The decision of the High Court was then appealed against by Mr Reed.

In restoring the orders first made by the District Court, the Court of Appeal held that, inter alia, section 32 of the PDPA is a statutory tort,[117] and the phrase 'loss or damage' can be purposively interpreted to include emotional distress.[118] Specifically, it found that the Singapore Parliament intended to displace the starting position at common law that emotional distress is not actionable, and that considering the scheme and purpose of the PDPA as a whole, excluding emotional distress from the scope of the private right of action would 'cut across Parliament's intention to promote the right of individuals to protect their personal data'.[119] Nevertheless, the Court of Appeal stopped short of providing a general standard of emotional distress, instead preferring a multi-factorial approach to determine whether emotional distress has been proved, with several non-exhaustive considerations:

a) The nature of the personal data involved in the breach;
b) The nature of breach;
c) The nature of the defendant's conduct;
d) Risk of future breaches of the PDPA causing emotional distress to the claimant; and
e) Actual impact of the breach on the claimant.[120]

Separate from the point on 'emotional distress' above, another issue on appeal was whether the 'loss of control' of personal data could qualify as another head of 'loss or damage' for the purposes of the private right of action. Agreeing with the High Court that 'every contravention of Part 4 to 6 of the PDPA inevitably involves some form of loss of control over personal data',[121] accepting 'loss of control' would therefore render the requirement of 'loss or damage' tautologous.[122] In the words of the Court of Appeal, 'Parliament shuns tautology and does not legislate in vain, and the courts should concomitantly endeavour to give significance to every word in an enactment', loss of control of personal data should not be actionable.[123]

There have, to date, been no other privacy or personal data protection-related appeals that have resulted in published decisions by the Court of Appeal.

[114] ibid, [162] and [172].
[115] *Bellingham, Alex v Reed, Michael* [2022] 4 SLR 512.
[116] ibid, [93].
[117] *Reed, Michael v Bellingham, Alex* (n 28) [60], citing *My Digital Lock* (n 16), [4.78].
[118] ibid, [68].
[119] ibid, [77].
[120] ibid, [115].
[121] ibid, [109], affirming *Bellingham, Alex v Reed, Michael* (n 115), [44]–[47].
[122] ibid, [109], citing *My Digital Lock* (n 16), [4.22].
[123] ibid, [110].

III. Legal Bases, Mechanisms and Exceptions for International Data Transfers and Data Protection

A. International Data Transfer and the Transfer Limitation Obligation

In a Parliamentary debate relating to positioning Singapore to be a global centre for data storage and services, Dr Janil Puthucheary, Senior Minister of State for Communications and Information, noted that

> with the world becoming more digitally connected, global data flows have surged. Cross-border data flows generate significant value and growth to economies. Singapore, like other countries, is also tapping on this opportunity to grow our digital economy, by strengthening our position as a key digital connectivity hub.[124]

In a more recent speech, Minister of Communications and Information, Mrs Josephine Teo, reaffirmed Singapore's commitment to facilitating cross-border transfers, stating that while '[there] are certainly datasets which no country will be comfortable falling into foreign hands, and which must be secured … [this should not] prevent the movement of non-sensitive data that supports business innovations'.[125]

By way of overview, section 26(1) of the PDPA provides that organisations must not transfer any personal data to a country or territory outside Singapore except in accordance prescribed under the PDPA, to ensure that organisations provide a standard of protection to personal data so transferred that is comparable to the protection under the PDPA. Although section 26(1) of the PDPA appears to limit transfer by default (resulting in this requirement coming to be known as the 'Transfer Limitation Obligation'), we take the view that the provisions of the PDPA relating to international data transfers are ultimately intended to be facilitative, rather than preventative, for organisations transferring personal data abroad.

The precise requirements of the Transfer Limitation Obligation are fleshed out in subsidiary legislation, namely the Personal Data Protection Regulations 2021 (PDPR)[126] issued by the Minister for Communications and Information in exercise of the powers conferred on him by section 65 of the PDPA. For completeness, several other regulations and notices have also been issued by the Minister, pursuant to section 65 of the PDPA as well as other provisions conferring related powers under the PDPA.[127]

Pursuant to Regulation 10(1) of the PDPR, a transferring organisation must, before transferring an individual's personal data to a country or territory outside Singapore on or after 1 February 2021, take appropriate steps to ascertain whether, and to ensure that, the recipient of the personal data in that country or territory outside Singapore (if any) is

[124] Janil Puthucheary, 'Parliamentary Debates, Official Report', vol 94, sitting no 59 (6 February 2018).

[125] Minister of Communications and Information, 'Speech by Minister of Communications and Information, Mrs Josephine Teo, at the Opening of the Personal Data Protection Week on 18 July 2023' (18 July 2023) [37], available at www.mci.gov.sg/media-centre/speeches/speech-by-minister-at-the-opening-of-the-personal-data-protection-week/.

[126] Personal Data Protection Regulations 2021, No S 63 (Made on 28 January 2021).

[127] These include, for example, the Personal Data Protection (Appeal) Regulations 2021, No S 65 (Made on 28 January 2021), the Personal Data Protection (Notification of Data Breaches) Regulations 2021, No S 64 (Made

bound by 'legally enforceable obligations' (in accordance with Regulation 11) to provide to the transferred personal data a standard of protection that is at least comparable to the protection under the Act.

What constitutes a 'legally enforceable obligation' for the purposes of Regulation 10(1) of the PDPR includes obligations imposed on recipients under any law, contract, binding corporate rules, or any other legally binding instrument.

Regulation 11(2) of the PDPR states that any such contract must require the recipient to provide a standard of protection for the personal data transferred to the recipient that is at least comparable to the protection under the PDPA and also specify the countries and territories to which the personal data may be transferred under the contract. For completeness, the PDPC has also taken the position that the Transfer Limitation Obligation requires the recipient to be bound by obligations that are legally enforceable by the transferring organisation (as opposed to by an unrelated third party), if it is relying on contract.[128]

The PDPC also recognises and encourages the use of the Association of Southeast Asian Nations' Model Contract Clauses ('ASEAN MCCs') to fulfil the Transfer Limitation Obligation. Although the ASEAN MCCs are intended to help parties ensure that the transfer of personal data is done in a manner that complies with the legal and regulatory requirements of ASEAN Member States (eg, countries with comprehensive privacy and personal data protection laws, such as Thailand and the Philippines) and to protect data subjects' personal data based on the principles of the ASEAN Framework on Personal Data Protection,[129] the PDPC has in a recent decision opined that they could also 'ease B2B transfers between Singapore and other jurisdictions such as Canada'.[130] This is because the ASEAN MCCs can also be used to fulfil the Transfer Limitation Obligation under the PDPA for countries with data protection regimes based on the OECD Privacy Guidelines as well, including those outside ASEAN.[131]

Significant efforts have been undertaken by the PDPC, in collaboration with other ASEAN regulators, to encourage the use of the ASEAN MCCs. These efforts include a collaborative effort with the European Union to publish a Joint Guide to ASEAN Model Contractual Clauses (MCCs) and EU Standard Contractual Clauses (SCCs) ('ASEAN-EU Joint Guide'),[132] which identifies commonalities between the two sets of templates, and which help foster a common understanding and facilitates contractual negotiations on data transfers between ASEAN and EU business partners.[133] An amendment to the ASEAN-EU

on 28 January 2021), and the Personal Data Protection (Prescribed Law Enforcement Agency) Notification 2020, No S 272 (Made on 31 March 2020).

[128] Benjamin Wong, 'Confidential Information and Data Protection' (2021) 22 *Singapore Academy of Law Annual Review of Singapore Cases* 267, [11.64], referring to PDPC's enforcement decision in *Belden Singapore Private Limited & Anor* [2021] SGPDPC 13.

[129] ASEAN, 'ASEAN Model Contractual Clauses for Cross Border Data Flows' (Final Copy Endorsed by the 2nd ASEAN Digital Senior Officials' Meeting, January 2021), 4, available at asean.org/wp-content/uploads/3-ASEAN-Model-Contractual-Clauses-for-Cross-Border-Data-Flows_Final.pdf.

[130] *Supernova Pte Ltd & Anor* [2022] SGPDPC 7.

[131] PDPC, 'Guidance for Use of ASEAN Model Contractual Clauses for Cross Border Data Flows in Singapore' (22 January 2021) 2, [3], available at www.pdpc.gov.sg/-/media/Files/PDPC/PDF-Files/Practical-Guidance-Provided-by-PDPC/Singapore-Guidance-for-Use-of-ASEAN-MCCs---010921.pdf.

[132] PDPC, 'Joint Guide to ASEAN Model Contractual Clauses and EU Standard Contractual Clauses Now Available' (24 May 2023), available at www.pdpc.gov.sg/news-and-events/announcements/2023/05/joint-guide-to-asean-model-contractual-clauses-and-eu-standard-contractual-clauses-now-available.

[133] Speech by Minister of Communications and Information (n 125) 42.

Joint Guide was subsequently announced during the fourth ASEAN Digital Ministers Meeting on 2 February 2024,[134] and now consists of an additional 'Implementation Guide' with examples of best practices for both controller-to-controller and controller-to-processor transfers under both ASEAN MCCs and EU SCCs.

Regulation 11(3) of the PDPR specifies that binding corporate rules must specify the recipients of the transferred personal data to which the binding corporate rules apply, the countries and territories to which the personal data may be transferred under the binding corporate rules and the rights and obligations provided by the binding corporate rules. Binding corporate rules may also only be used for recipients that are related to the transferring organisation; in other words, only recipients which, directly or indirectly, control or are controlled by the transferring organisation, or are under the control of a common person as the transferring organisation, may avail themselves of binding corporate rules as a means of transfer.[135]

A recipient is also taken to be bound by legally enforceable obligations to provide a standard of protection for the transferred personal data that is at least comparable to the PDPA if they hold a 'specified certification' that is granted or recognised under the law of that country or territory to which the personal data is transferred.[136] To this end, the PDPR was amended in June 2020[137] to recognise the Asia-Pacific Economic Cooperation Cross-Border Privacy Rules ('APEC CBPR') and Asia-Pacific Economic Cooperation Privacy Recognition for Processor ('APEC PRP') certification systems as satisfying legally enforceable obligations for transfer of personal data out of Singapore.

Where the recipient is an intermediary (ie, what would be considered a 'controller-to-processor' transfer), certifications of the recipient under the APEC PRP System or the APEC CBPR system would be taken as satisfying the Transfer Limitation Obligation. If the recipient is an organisation that will use the transferred personal data for its own purposes (ie, what would be considered a 'controller-to-controller' transfer), then only certifications of the recipient under the APEC CBPR system would suffice for the same purpose. No additional requirements would need to be met for the transfer of personal data to such recipients.

In addition to promoting the APEC CBPR and APEC PRP standards, it is crucial to note that Singapore continues to participate heavily in the Global Cross-Border Privacy Rules ('Global CBPR') Forum as a founding member.[138] The Global CBPR Forum seeks, among other objectives, to establish and promote adoption of the Global Cross-Border Privacy Rules System and Global Privacy Recognition for Processors System to facilitate data protection and free flow of data globally.[139] Singapore is represented on the Forum's leadership, and continues to build on the aforementioned APEC CBPR and APEC PRP

[134] PDPC, 'Two Guides Unveiled at ASEAN Digital Ministers' Meeting (ADGMIN) 2024' (2 February 2024), available at www.pdpc.gov.sg/news-and-events/announcements/2024/02/two-guides-unveiled-at-adgmin-2024.

[135] Personal Data Protection Regulations 2021, regs 11(3)(c) and 11(4).

[136] ibid, reg 12(1).

[137] See www.pdpc.gov.sg/news-and-events/announcements/2020/06/singapore-now-recognises-apec-cbpr-and-prp-certifications-under-PDPA.

[138] IMDA, 'Singapore Welcomes Establishment of the Global Cross-Border Privacy Rules (CBPR) Forum' (21 April 2022), available at www.imda.gov.sg/resources/press-releases-factsheets-and-speeches/press-releases/2022/singapore-welcomes-establishment-of-the-global-cross-border-privacy-rules-cbpr-forum.

[139] Global CBPR Forum, 'About the Global CBPR Forum', available at www.globalcbpr.org/about/.

systems so that certified organisations may transfer data seamlessly across borders to more economies, including non-APEC jurisdictions.[140]

Separately, of indirect relevance here is the Data Protection Trustmark (DPTM) certification[141] currently being administered by the IMDA. Despite being a 'certification scheme' recognised in Singapore, it is important to note that while the DPTM allows organisations to demonstrate accountable data protection practices,[142] and further that compliant overseas transfers are evaluated as part of the certification process,[143] the DPTM is not a 'specified certification' that would *ipso facto* mean that the certified organisation is a recipient that is bound by legally enforceable obligations under Regulation 10(1) of the PDPR similar to the APEC CBPR or the APEC PRP.

The PDPC encourages transferring organisations to rely on legally enforceable obligations or specified certifications especially when there is an ongoing relationship with the recipient as they provide better accountability.[144] Nevertheless, Regulation 10(2) of the PDPR may also be satisfied in certain circumstances when a transferring organisation is unable to rely on legally enforceable obligations or specified certifications:

a) subject to Regulation 10(3) of the PDPR, the individual consents to the transfer of the individual's personal data to that recipient in that country or territory ('Transfers by Consent');
b) the individual is deemed to have consented to the disclosure by the transferring organisation of the individual's personal data to that recipient under sections 15(3), (4), (5), (6), (7), or (8) of the PDPA;
c) the transfer of the personal data to the recipient is necessary for the personal data to be used or disclosed under Part 1 or paragraph 2 of Part 2 of the First Schedule to the PDPA, and the transferring organisation has taken reasonable steps to ensure that the personal data so transferred will not be used or disclosed by the recipient for any other purpose;
d) the personal data is data in transit[145] ('Transfers of Data in Transit'); or
e) the personal data is publicly available[146] in Singapore.

As concerns Transfers by Consent specifically, an individual is not taken to have consented if: (a) a reasonable summary in writing of the extent to which the personal data being transferred will be *protected* to a standard comparable to the PDPA; (b) the consent obtained was

[140] IMDA Press Release on Global CBPR Forum.

[141] IMDA, 'About the Data Protection Trustmark (DPTM)', available at www.imda.gov.sg/how-we-can-help/data-protection-trustmark-certification.

[142] See www.imda.gov.sg/how-we-can-help/data-protection-trustmark-certification.

[143] IMDA, 'DPTM Certification Checklist' 6, section D, available at www.imda.gov.sg/-/media/imda/files/programme/dptm/dptm-checklist.pdf.

[144] Key Concepts Guidelines (n 4) 124, [19.7].

[145] PDPR, reg 9 defines 'data in transit' as personal data transferred through Singapore in the course of onward transportation to a country or territory outside Singapore, without the personal data being accessed or used by, or disclosed to, any organisation (other than the transferring organisation or an employee of the transferring organisation acting in the course of the employee's employment with the transferring organisation) while the personal data is in Singapore, except for the purpose of such transportation. This would include, for example, data from overseas passing through servers within Singapore enroute to its destination overseas.

[146] PDPA, s 2(1) states that 'publicly available', in relation to personal data about an individual, means personal data that is generally available to the public. This includes personal data which can be observed by reasonably expected means at a location or an event at which the individual appears and that is open to the public.

required as a condition of providing a product or service, unless the transfer is reasonably necessary to provide the product or service to the individual; or (c) consent was obtained by providing false or misleading information about the transfers, or by using other deceptive or misleading practices.

As concerns Transfers of Data in Transit specifically, Regulation 9 of the PDPR defines 'data in transit' as personal data transferred through Singapore in the course of onward transportation to a country or territory outside Singapore, *without the personal data being accessed or used by, or disclosed to, any organisation* (other than the transferring organisation or an employee of the transferring organisation acting in the course of the employee's employment with the transferring organisation) while the personal data is in Singapore, except for the purpose of such transportation. Based on this definition, 'data in transit' should only be construed narrowly; for example, data from outside Singapore, passing through servers within Singapore, enroute to its destination outside Singapore.[147]

Notably, requirements for transfers of personal data under the PDPA do not include 'adequacy' requirements similar to those in the EU,[148] or in other Southeast Asian jurisdictions such as Thailand.[149] In the absence of the concept of a 'third country', or the power to 'blacklist' specific jurisdictions as contemplated in recently-passed Indian legislation,[150] the Transfer Limitation Obligation may therefore be viewed as jurisdiction-agnostic, focusing more on ensuring that recipient organisations will continue to protect the personal data that it has received to a standard that is comparable to that established in the PDPA, rather than on the jurisdiction where the personal data is transferred to *per se*.

For completeness, it bears mention that:

a) section 26(2) of the PDPA uniquely empowers the PDPC to exempt organisations from any requirement prescribed pursuant to section 26(1) of the PDPA in respect of any transfer of personal data. Any such exemption may be granted subject to conditions specified by the PDPC in writing, and may be revoked at any time;[151]
b) cross-border transfers of data in Singapore's banking industry are subject to additional requirements by virtue of the Monetary Authority of Singapore's (MAS) Guidelines on Outsourcing,[152] which are not superseded by the PDPA.

B. Other Relevant Obligations

As alluded to above, one of the PDPA's Data Protection Obligations is the 'Retention Limitation Obligation', which requires organisations to cease to retain documents containing personal data, or remove the means by which the personal data can be associated with particular individuals, as soon as it is reasonable to assume that the purpose for which that

[147] Key Concepts Guidelines (n 4), 129, [19.11].

[148] See, eg, GDPR, Art 44.

[149] See, eg, section 28 of Thailand's Personal Data Protection Act, B.E. 2562 (2019).

[150] See, eg, section 16 of the Digital Personal Data Protection Act 2023 (No 22 of 2023) (India), which empowers the Indian Central Government to restrict transfers to countries or territories outside India by way of notification.

[151] PDPA, s 26(3).

[152] MAS, 'Guidelines on Outsourcing' (5 October 2018), available at www.mas.gov.sg/regulation/guidelines/guidelines-on-outsourcing.

personal data was collected is no longer being served by retention of the personal data, and retention is no longer necessary for legal or business purposes.[153]

The PDPA does not specify a fixed retention period for personal data, instead leaving it to be determined based on reasonableness in consideration of the purposes for which the data was collected and retained, and/or other legal or specific industry-specific requirements which could apply. Nevertheless, as good practice, organisations are encouraged to prepare an appropriate personal data retention policy setting out their approach to retention periods for personal data.

In considering whether an organisation has ceased to retain personal data, the Commission will consider the following factors:

a) Whether the organisation has any intention to use or access the personal data;
b) How much effort and resources the organisation would need to expend in order to use or access the personal data again;
c) Whether any third parties have been given access to that personal data; and
d) Whether the organisation has made a reasonable attempt to destroy, dispose of or delete the personal data in a permanent and complete manner.[154]

Where a data intermediary processes personal data on behalf of and for the purposes of another organisation pursuant to a contract, the data intermediary will only be subject to the Protection Obligation (discussed below), the Retention Limitation Obligation, and the Data Breach Notification Obligation.[155] However, the data intermediary remains responsible for complying with all Data Protection Obligations in respect of all other activities.[156]

IV. Data Security and Data Localisation

Section 24 of the PDPA requires organisations to protect personal data in their possession or under their control by making reasonable security arrangement to prevent: (a) unauthorised access, collection, use, disclosure, copying, modification or disposal, or similar risks; and (b) the loss of any storage medium or device on which personal data is stored. This is frequently referred to as the 'Protection Obligation'.

Broadly in line with the push from a compliance-based to accountability-led approach, the PDPC has, in advisory guidance, stated that there is no 'one size fits all' solution for organisations to comply with the Protection Obligation.[157] Instead, organisations should adopt security arrangements that are reasonable and appropriate in the circumstances.

For example, in the employment context, the PDPC has found it reasonable to expect a greater level of security for highly confidential employee appraisals compared to more general information about the projects an employee has worked on.[158] The PDPC has also recently taken the position that, consistent with domestic and international developments

[153] PDPA, s 25(a)-(b).
[154] Key Concepts Guidelines (n 4), 120–121, [18.13].
[155] ibid, 24, [6.17].
[156] ibid.
[157] ibid, 114, [17.2].
[158] ibid.

(eg, in the UK, Canada, and Australia), two-factor authentication and multi-factor authentication (2FA/MFA) should be a baseline requirement for administrative accounts to systems that hold personal data of a confidential or sensitive nature, or large volumes of personal data, where a failure to implement could *ipso facto* amount to a breach.[159]

An overwhelming number of the PDPC's enforcement decisions to date concern the Protection Obligation. Additionally, the highest financial penalties ever imposed under the PDPA have also been in respect of the Protection Obligation – on 14 January 2019, the PDPC imposed a penalty of SGD 250,000 on Singapore Health Services Pte Ltd ('SingHealth'), a corporate cluster of healthcare institutions in Singapore, in respect of a cyber attack which compromised its patient database system and which affected more than 1.5 million individuals, including the country's Prime Minister. A penalty of SGD 750,000 was also imposed on Integrated Health Information Systems Pte Ltd ('IHiS'), the central national IT agency for the public healthcare sector in Singapore which was responsible for the development and maintenance of SingHealth's IT systems, in the same enforcement decision.[160]

Notably, these penalties were issued prior to amendments that came into force on 1 October 2022, which would allow the PDPC to impose financial penalties up to a maximum of ten per cent of an organisation's annual turnover in Singapore.[161] It remains to be seen if the PDPC will issue higher financial penalties in more egregious cases moving forward.

The PDPA does not contain express data localisation requirements (ie, requirements which require organisations to only store certain categories of personal data within Singapore). In another publication, we observed that data localisation requirements and transfer limitation requirements, such as Singapore's Transfer Limitation Obligation, may be thought of as different categories of essentially the same type of regulation.[162] In our view, Singapore's Transfer Limitation Obligation achieves similar policy goals as data localisation, without the attendant concerns of stifling innovation and preventing cooperation in an increasingly interconnected and data-driven world.[163]

V. Other Topics and Issues

A. Shift from Compliance to Accountability

Over and above mere compliance with the Data Protection Obligations, the PDPC has in recent years pushed organisations in Singapore to move away from a culture of 'check-box' compliance and towards one that fosters accountability. In a 2019 keynote speech, Deputy Commissioner Yeong stated that '[t]he principle of accountability forms the substratum of the PDPA', and that '[t]he Commission's shift from compliance to accountability is [...] not a shift in principle but a shift in emphasis'.

[159] *Lovebonito Singapore Pte Ltd* [2022] SGPDPC 3, [51(a)].

[160] *Singapore Health Services Pte. Ltd. & Anor* [2019] SGPDPC 3; *SingHealth* (n 77) 48, [135]–[138].

[161] By way of the Personal Data Protection (Amendment) Act 2020.

[162] Lanx Goh and Joshua Kow, 'Data Localisation: The Way Forward or Backward for Data Innovation?' [2020] *PDP Digest* 63, 66, available at www.pdpc.gov.sg/news-and-events/announcements/2020/09/pdp-digest-2020-now-available.

[163] ibid, 71, [17].

What was originally known as the 'Openness Obligation' in the original version of the PDPA that was passed in 2012 has since been aptly renamed the 'Accountability Obligation',[164] focusing instead on how an organisation discharges its responsibility for personal data in its possession or which it has control over. Satisfying the Accountability Obligation requires an organisation to appoint a Data Protection Officer who is sufficiently skilled, knowledgeable, and amply empowered to discharge his or her duties,[165] and to develop and implement internal and external policies and practices and train its staff on them,[166] among other obligations.

Examples of this gradual shift to accountability are aplenty. The introduction of the Data Breach Notification Obligation (among other amendments under the Personal Data Protection (Amendment) Bill 2020), for example, show that organisations that collect, use, and disclose personal data in Singapore will be held to a higher standard of accountability.[167]

B. Data Processing during COVID-19

At the height of the COVID-19 epidemic, the PDPC was proactive in its issuance of guidance concerning the collection, use, and disclosure of personal data relating to contact tracing and the use of SafeEntry and TraceTogether, the national applications for check-in and contact tracing respectively. For example, the PDPC clarified that in the event of a COVID-19 case, relevant personal data, including NRIC, can be collected, used and disclosed without consent to carry out contact tracing and other response measures, as this was necessary to respond to an emergency that threatened the life, health or safety of other individuals.[168]

On 5 February 2024, the Singapore Government announced that SafeEntry and TraceTogether were no longer in use,[169] and virtually all COVID-19 related personal contact tracing data derived from them have been deleted.[170] Both applications have been removed from mobile app stores, and backend infrastructure for both applications have also been dismantled. The decision to delete such data was made pursuant to section 82(8) of the COVID-19 (Temporary Measures) Act,[171] where the ministers of the relevant authorities have determined that both applications would no longer be required to prevent or control the spread of COVID-19.

[164] Key Concepts Guidelines (n 4), 151, [21.1], fn 82.
[165] PDPA, s 11(3).
[166] ibid, s 12(a) and 12(c).
[167] 2021 PDP Digest, Foreword by the Personal Data Protection Commissioner, 4.
[168] PDPC, 'Advisories on Collection of Personal Data for COVID-19 Contact Tracing and Use of SafeEntry' (4 January 2022), available at www.pdpc.gov.sg/Help-and-Resources/2021/05/Advisory-on-Collection-of-Personal-Data-for-COVID-19-Contact-Tracing.
[169] Smart Nation Singapore, 'Discontinuation of TraceTogether and SafeEntry', available at www.smartnation.gov.sg/media-hub/press-releases/20240105/.
[170] ibid, except in one instance where TraceTogether data pertaining to a 2020 murder case will be retained by the Singapore Police Force indefinitely.
[171] COVID-19 (Temporary Measures) Act 2020 (No 14 of 2020), available at sso.agc.gov.sg/Act/COVID19TMA2020.

C. Regulating Artificial Intelligence

According to a recent survey commissioned by Salesforce and conducted by YouGov, 40 per cent of Singaporean workers already use and experiment with artificial intelligence (AI) in their work, although many surveyed had a limited understanding of practices that promoted ethics and safety.[172] It is therefore unsurprising that Singapore is supportive of, but nevertheless takes a balanced view on, recent developments in the use of AI. On 9 May 2023, Minister of State for Communications and Information Dr Janil Puthucheary stated in no uncertain terms that 'Singapore supports the responsible development and deployment of Artificial Intelligence (AI), so that its benefits may be enjoyed in a trusted and safe manner'.[173] This was recently underscored by the Chief Executive of the IMDA, Lew Chuen Hong, who described Singapore's approach as a '... balanced approach to meet the twin goals of data protection and market innovation'.[174]

To this end, an Advisory Council on the Ethical Use of AI & Data was established in 2018, for the purpose of assisting the IMDA in engaging stakeholders to support the development of AI governance capabilities and frameworks, including ethics standards and reference governance frameworks. Additionally, the council will publish advisory guidelines, practical guides, and codes of practice for the industry's voluntary adoption, drawing on expertise from various fields and consumer and civil society representatives.[175] Similarly, in November 2019, Singapore published its National AI Strategy aimed at transforming the country into 'as a leader in developing and deploying scalable, impactful artificial intelligence (AI) solutions, in key sectors of high value and relevance to our citizens and businesses' by 2030.[176]

These early investments have since borne fruit. In relation to data protection and privacy, the IMDA launched its first comprehensive 'Trusted Data Sharing Framework' (TDR Framework') to help Singaporean companies overcome challenges in addressing digital trust between data providers and develop 'trusted data'.[177] The TDR Framework provides a common 'data-sharing language' and suggests a systematic approach to the broad considerations for establishing trusted data sharing partnerships, while incorporating content from existing PDPC guides on personal data anonymisation and sharing (among others)

[172] Jeanette Tan, '40% of Singaporeans use AI at work, 76% of them pass results off as their own: Survey' (*The Straits Times*, 20 September 2023), available at www.straitstimes.com/business/40-of-singaporeans-use-ai-at-work-75-of-them-pass-it-off-as-their-own-survey.

[173] Janil Puthucheary, Singapore Parliamentary Debates, Official Report of Parliament No 14 Session 2 Vol No 95 Sitting No 103 on 9 May 2023.

[174] IMDA, 'Opening remarks for PDPC Commissioner at IAPP Asia Privacy Forum' (19 July 2023), available at www.imda.gov.sg/resources/press-releases-factsheets-and-speeches/speeches/2023/opening-remarks-for-pdpc-commissioner-at-iapp-asia-privacy-forum.

[175] IMDA, 'The Full Composition of Singapore's Advisory Council on the Ethical Use of AI and Data (Advisory Council) was announced by Minister for Communications and Information Mr S Iswaran at AI Singapore's First Year Anniversary' (30 August 2018), available at www.imda.gov.sg/resources/press-releases-factsheets-and-speeches/archived/imda/press-releases/2018/composition-of-the-advisory-council-on-the-ethical-use-of-ai-and-data.

[176] Smart Nation Singapore, 'The Next Frontier of Singapore's Smart Nation Journey', available at www.smartnation.gov.sg/initiatives/artificial-intelligence/.

[177] IMDA, 'About the Trusted Data Sharing Framework' (4 April 2023), available at www.imda.gov.sg/how-we-can-help/data-innovation/trusted-data-sharing-framework.

and providing sample legal templates to enable contractual data sharing.[178] The TDR Framework itself is organised into four parts; namely, the data sharing strategy, legal and regulatory considerations, technical and organisation considerations, and considerations for operationalisation.[179]

In 2019, the PDPC introduced the Model AI Governance Framework to provide organisations with guidance on tackling ethical and governance issues when deploying AI solutions. The Model Framework promotes public understanding and trust in technologies through detailed and implementable guidance. The Model AI Governance Framework was subsequently updated in 2020 to add new considerations and refine its usability and relevance. Alongside this, the Implementation and Self-Assessment Guide for Organisations (ISAGO) was released as a companion guide to the Model Framework. ISAGO helps organisations align their AI governance practices with the Model Framework and provides industry examples to facilitate implementation.

As part of the aforementioned National AI Strategy, IMDA has also developed 'AI Verify', an AI governance testing framework and software toolkit based on 11 internationally recognised AI ethics principles, namely transparency, explainability, repeatability/reproducibility, safety, security, robustness, fairness, data governance, accountability, human agency and oversight, inclusive growth, societal and environmental well-being.[180] AI Verify helps organisations evaluate their AI systems' performance against these principles through standardised tests, fostering transparency for user companies. Notably, however, AI Verify does not establish ethical standards or assure total safety and freedom from biases in tested AI systems.[181] To enhance AI testing technologies, IMDA has also established the related 'AI Verify Foundation', which seeks to promote the use and development of AI testing frameworks and foster open collaboration on testing and governing AI, while also encouraging AI testing adoption through education and outreach. Several prominent members, including, Google, IBM, Microsoft, Red Hat, and Salesforce, help set the Foundation's strategic direction and development roadmap.[182]

The PDPC continues to remain at the forefront of local developments in AI, and has already begun considering whether further guidance should be provided under the PDPA in relation to topics such as the use of data to train generative AI models.[183] Following an announcement made at the recent IAPP Asia Forum 2023 held in Singapore, Singapore launched a public consultation for Proposed Advisory Guidelines on Use of Personal Data in AI Recommendation and Decision Systems,[184] which seek to address how organisations

[178] IMDA, 'Enabling Data-Driven Innovation Through Trusted Data Sharing in a Digital Economy' (28 June 2019), available at www.imda.gov.sg/resources/press-releases-factsheets-and-speeches/archived/imda/press-releases/2019/enabling-data-driven-innovation-through-trusted-data-sharing-in-a-digital-economy.

[179] IMDA & PDPC, 'Trusted Data Sharing Framework' (3 August 2023), available at www.imda.gov.sg/-/media/imda/files/programme/data-collaborative-programme/trusted-data-sharing-framework.pdf.

[180] PDPC, 'Singapore's Approach to AI Governance', available at www.pdpc.gov.sg/help-and-resources/2020/01/model-ai-governance-framework.

[181] ibid.

[182] ibid.

[183] IMDA, 'Opening Remarks for PDPC Commissioner at IAPP Asia Privacy Forum' (n 174) at [8].

[184] PDPC, 'Public Consultation for the Proposed Advisory Guidelines on Use of Personal Data in AI Recommendation and Decision Systems' (19 July 2023), available at www.pdpc.gov.sg/guidelines-and-consultation/2023/07/public-consultation-for-the-proposed-advisory-guidelines-on-use-of-personal-data-in-ai-recommendation-and-decision-systems.

may benefit from existing exceptions within the PDPA when they want to use personal data in the development of machine-learning AI models or systems, and how organisations may meet requirements under the consent, notification and accountability obligations under the PDPA when collecting personal data for use in machine learning AI systems for decisions, recommendations or predictions. These include, for example, the application of the 'Research Exception' at Division 3, Part 2 of the Second Schedule of the PDPA when developing AI systems,[185] and the extent to which datasets have to be anonymised when developing or training an AI system or machine learning model,[186] among other topical issues. As of the date of this chapter's writing, the final, published version of these Advisory Guidelines remain to be seen.

Internationally, Singapore continues to be actively involved in both regional and global efforts to establish and align on common principles for AI governance. On 2 February 2024, collaborative efforts by ASEAN Member States resulted in the creation and publication of the ASEAN Guide on AI Governance and Ethics,[187] which is intended to serve as a 'practical guide for organisations in the region that wish to design, develop, and deploy traditional AI technologies in commercial and non-military or dual-use applications', while focusing on encouraging alignment and interoperability of AI frameworks within ASEAN.[188] Collaborations with countries outside of ASEAN have also borne fruit, as exemplified by the joint mapping exercise conducted by IMDA and the US National Institute of Standards and Technology (NIST), which provides greater clarity on how businesses can meet requirements of both IMDA's 'AI Verify' and NIST's AI Risk Management Framework (RMF) respectively.[189] For completeness, Singapore also announced a proposed 'Model AI Governance Framework for Generative AI' ('MGF-GenAI')[190] at the 2024 World Economic Forum annual meeting held Davos, Switzerland, and is currently seeking international feedback on it at the time of writing.[191]

D. International Cooperation

In addition to efforts made to align on standards for cross-border transfers described above (eg, adopting the APEC CBPR and APEC PRP standards respectively), Singapore continues to enter into Digital Economy Agreements (DEAs) to establish digital trade rules and digital

[185] IMDA, 'Proposed Advisory Guidelines on use of Personal Data in AI Recommendation and Decision Systems' (Issued 18 July 2023), 8, [6.1]–[6.4], available at www.pdpc.gov.sg/-/media/Files/PDPC/PDF-Files/Legislation-and-Guidelines/Public-Consult-on-Proposed-AG-on-Use-of-PD-in-AI-Recommendation-and-Systems-2023-07-18-Draft-Advisory-Guidelines.pdf.

[186] ibid, 10–11, [7.7]–[7.11].

[187] ASEAN, 'ASEAN Guide on AI Governance and Ethics', available at asean.org/book/asean-guide-on-ai-governance-and-ethics/.

[188] ibid, 8, [1].

[189] MCI, 'Singapore and the US to Deepen Cooperation in AI', available at www.mci.gov.sg/media-centre/press-releases/singapore-and-the-us-to-deepen-cooperation-in-ai/.

[190] AI Verify Foundation & IMDA, 'Proposed Model AI Governance Framework for Generative AI: Fostering a Trusted Ecosystem' (Issued 16 January 2024), available at aiverifyfoundation.sg/downloads/Proposed_MGF_Gen_AI_2024.pdf.

[191] Goh Yan Han, 'S'pore Seeks International Feedback on New Governance Framework for Generative AI' (*The Straits Times*, 17 January 2024), available at www.straitstimes.com/singapore/s-pore-seeks-international-feedback-on-new-governance-framework-for-generative-ai.

economy collaborations with other countries. Through DEAs, Singapore aims to 'develop international frameworks to foster interoperability of standards and systems and support our businesses, especially SMEs, engaging in digital trade and electronic commerce'.[192]

Recognising that 'fragmented rules on data protection has also led to varying restrictions for personal data transfer and increased compliance costs', several decent DEAs concluded by Singapore have included specific provisions that address cross-border flows of personal data between signing parties. For example:

a) In the Digital Economy Partnership Agreement (DEPA)[193] concluded between Singapore, Chile, and New Zealand, parties have agreed that they 'shall pursue the development of mechanisms to promote compatibility and interoperability between their different regimes for protecting personal information [including] where practicable, appropriate recognition of comparable protection afforded by their respective legal frameworks' national trustmark or certification frameworks; or other avenues of transfer of personal information between the Parties',[194] and 'shall endeavour to mutually recognise the other Parties' data protection trustmarks as a valid mechanism to facilitate cross-border information transfers while protecting personal information';[195]
b) In the Singapore-Australia Digital Economy Agreement (SADEA),[196] concluded between Singapore and Australia, parties have agreed that they 'recognise that the CBPR System is a valid mechanism to facilitate cross-border information transfers while protecting personal information'.[197] In the Memorandum of Understanding (MOU) on Cooperation in Personal Data Protection (SADEA PDP MOU) included with and signed as part of SADEA, parties have reached the understanding that they will collaborate in: (a) active participation in and joint promotion of, the APEC CBPR; and (b) the exchange of information and sharing of experiences on the development and implementation of national trustmark or certification frameworks.[198]

VI. Conclusion

As established in this chapter, Singapore's approach to privacy and data protection may be best described as pragmatic and facilitative. Despite being enacted more than a decade ago, the PDPA continues to retain its forward-looking and technology-neutral character

[192] Ministry of Trade and Industry Singapore, 'What are Digital Economy Agreements (DEAs)?', available at www.mti.gov.sg/Trade/Digital-Economy-Agreements.

[193] Digital Economy Partnership Agreement (signed on 12 June 2020), available at www.mti.gov.sg/Trade/Digital-Economy-Agreements/The-Digital-Economy-Partnership-Agreement.

[194] ibid, Art 4.2(6)(a) and (d).

[195] ibid, Art 4.2(10).

[196] Singapore-Australia Digital Economy Agreement (signed on 6 August 2020, entered into force on 7 December 2020), available at www.mti.gov.sg/Trade/Digital-Economy-Agreements/The-Singapore-Australia-Digital-Economy-Agreement.

[197] ibid, Art 17(8).

[198] Singapore-Australia Digital Economy Agreement Cooperation in Personal Data Protection (signed on 23 March 2020), [2(1)(f)] and [2(1)(g)], available at www.dfat.gov.au/sites/default/files/australia-singapore-mou-artificial-intelligence.pdf.

through constructive public consultations and timely amendments. Clarificatory guidance is provided through case law, enforcement decisions, regulatory advisories and frameworks, while government participation in regional and global fora on key topics such as AI ensures that the overarching legal regime remains broadly aligned with international developments and standards.

As local and cross-border data flows become increasingly important parts of the digital economy, Singapore's approach to privacy and data protection augurs well for its ambition to be the technology capital of Asia. Amidst a sea of rapidly-changing laws and greater recognition of the geopolitical aspects of data, Singapore offers a lighthouse of clarity and opportunity.

6

Taiwan

HUANG-CHIH SUNG

I. Introduction

As a democracy with respect for human rights, Taiwan is committed to the protection of people's privacy and personal information. Privacy and personal data protection in the Taiwanese legal system are governed by two different sets of laws: the protection of privacy is mainly regulated by the Civil Code as a right of personality, while the protection of personal data is regulated by the Personal Data Protection Act.

In the Civil Code, the right to privacy is originally considered part of the right to personality, although there was no explicit provision in the law prior to the law amendment in 1999. Victims can petition to the courts to stop the violation and demand the offenders to pay damages if their right to privacy is violated. The Civil Code, as amended in 1999, formally listed privacy as one of the enumerated rights of personality, thereby strengthening the protection of privacy under civil law.

Taiwan has long placed a high priority on protecting and safeguarding personal information. As early as 1995, Taiwan enacted the Computer Personal Data Protection Act, which preceded the current Personal Data Protection Act, to regulate the handling of personal data by computers, prevent the violation of personal rights and promote the reasonable use of personal data.[1] The Personal Data Protection Act was subsequently amended on two occasions in 2010 and 2015, and the Third Amendment was completed on 16 May 2023.[2]

One of the key points of the Third Amendment is to establish a new Personal Data Protection Commission as the competent authority for the Personal Data Protection Act, acting as an independent supervisory authority to protect personal data.[3] The establishment of the Personal Data Protection Commission aims to create an independent supervisory mechanism[4] and is expected to bring a new dimension to personal data protection in Taiwan. At the time of writing of this jurisdiction report (20 July 2024),

[1] Computer Personal Data Protection Act, Art 1.

[2] National Development Council, 'The Legislative Yuan has passed the Third Amendment to the Personal Data Protection Act, which will increase penalties for leaks of personal data by companies and establish the Preparatory Office of the Personal Data Protection Commission as soon as possible', News Release (16 May 2023), available at www.ndc.gov.tw/nc_27_36901.

[3] Personal Data Protection Act, Art 1-1.

[4] Legislative justification of Article 1-1 of the Personal Data Protection Act.

this law amendment has not yet entered into force and the Personal Data Protection Commission is still in the pipeline.

Section II of this chapter covers the general legal framework for privacy and data protection in Taiwan, including the constitutional protection of privacy and personal data protection, the legal framework for privacy protection, and the legal framework for personal data protection. Section III presents the judicial practice of privacy and personal data protection in Taiwan, including an observation that 'reasonable expectation of privacy' has become an implicit legal requirement for personal data breaches in judicial practice, and introduces three leading cases. Section IV covers the legal bases, mechanisms and exceptions for international data transfers and data protection, including the legal framework for international data transfers and that of data protection. Section V presents the legal framework for data and cybersecurity in Taiwan, focusing on the regulations and practice of the Cybersecurity Management Act.

II. General Legal Framework of Privacy and Data Protection

A. Constitutional Protection for Privacy and Data Protection

The protection of privacy and personal data is not explicitly listed as a fundamental right in the Constitution. The intention of the Constitution to protect privacy and personal data has been progressively outlined in the successive interpretations of the Constitution by the Grand Justices.

Constitutional Interpretation No 509 of 2000 stated that while freedom of speech is a fundamental right of citizens, the law may impose reasonable restrictions on freedom of speech according to the nature of its dissemination in order to protect personal reputation, privacy and the public interest.[5] This is the first time that the Constitutional Interpretation of the Grand Justices has referred to the protection of privacy at the constitutional level. However, it only referred to privacy in the abstract and did not specify what kind of privacy people have.

Constitutional Interpretation No 585 of 2004 first declared that, although privacy is not an explicit constitutional right, it is a fundamental right based on human dignity, respect for the individual's subjectivity and the integrity of his or her personal development, the protection of the private sphere of one's life from intrusion by others, and autonomous control over one's personal data.[6] This is the first time that the interpretation of the Constitution by the Grand Justices has emphasised that the protection of privacy is one of the fundamental rights. Although this constitutional interpretation treated the autonomous control of personal data as part of the right to privacy, it did not specify what kind of personal data it referred to.

[5] Constitutional Interpretation No 509 (7 July 2000), available at cons.judicial.gov.tw/docdata.aspx?fid=100&id=310690.

[6] Constitutional Interpretation No 585 (15 December 2004), available at cons.judicial.gov.tw/docdata.aspx?fid=100&id=310766.

In 2005, the Grand Justices in Interpretation No 603 reaffirmed that privacy is one of the fundamental constitutional rights, and that the right to control personal data autonomously is also part of the right to privacy.[7] For the first time, the Grand Justices introduced the concept of 'information privacy right', defined as the right of individuals to control their personal data.[8] The 'information privacy right' protects the right of individuals to decide whether, to what extent, when, how and to whom their personal data are disclosed, to be informed about and to control the use of their personal data and to correct any inaccuracies in the data.[9] This interpretation specifies that protected personal data are fingerprints. When the Government collects fingerprints of individuals on a large scale and stores them in a database for a specific and important public interest purpose, the purpose of the collection should be specified by law, the collection should be closely related to the important public interest purpose, and the use of the fingerprints for purposes not specified by law should be expressly prohibited.[10] On this basis, the Grand Justices held that the requirement to provide fingerprints in order to apply for an identity card under the Household Registration Act was unconstitutional.[11]

The conflict between freedom of the press and individual privacy has long been an intractable problem in human society. Journalists often have to follow their subjects in order to report the news. However, according to Article 89 of Taiwan's Social Order Maintenance Act, 'a person who follows another person without proper reason and does not listen to advice' is subject to a fine of up to NT$3,000 or a reprimand. This has led to journalists being punished on a number of occasions. Whether or not this provision of the Social Order Maintenance Act impedes the freedom of the press and is therefore unconstitutional was a major legal issue in Grand Justices' Interpretation No 689 in 2011.[12] The Grand Justices ruled that freedom from intrusion into one's private life and the autonomy of personal data are, of course, constitutional rights.[13] In the public sphere, however, everyone has the freedom of movement guaranteed by the Constitution. In participating in the life of the community, the freedom of movement of individuals cannot be free from interference with the freedom of movement of others and must be tolerated within reasonable limits.[14] While in the private sphere an individual's privacy should be protected to a higher degree, in the public sphere an individual's freedom to claim non-intrusion is limited to what he can reasonably expect from others, ie not only must his expectation of non-intrusion be manifest, but this expectation must be considered reasonable by society as a whole.[15] This interpretation suggested for the first time that a person seeking privacy in public should have a 'reasonable expectation of privacy'.[16] This jurisprudence has underpinned many subsequent court decisions in Taiwan.

[7] Constitutional Interpretation No 603 (28 September 2005), available at cons.judicial.gov.tw/docdata.aspx?fid=100&id=310784&rn=20959.

[8] ibid.

[9] ibid.

[10] ibid.

[11] ibid.

[12] Constitutional Interpretation No 689 (29 July 2011), available at cons.judicial.gov.tw/docdata.aspx?fid=100&id=310870&rn=9808.

[13] ibid.

[14] ibid.

[15] ibid.

[16] ibid.

One of the issues in Interpretation No 756 in 2007 was whether the requirement to inspect and read a prisoner's correspondence under the Prison Act violated the freedom of confidential communication guaranteed by Article 12 of the Constitution.[17] Article 12 of the Constitution states that 'the people shall have the freedom of communication in confidence'. The purpose of this freedom is to ensure that people have the right to be free from arbitrary interference by the Government or others with the existence, purpose, time, manner and content of communications. In this interpretation, the Grand Justices appeared to regard the right to privacy, which is not enumerated in the Constitution, as a broader and higher fundamental right than the freedom to communicate in confidence. According to the Grand Justices,

> this freedom of secret communication is one of the specific forms of constitutional protection of the right to privacy, which is essential for the preservation of human dignity, the integrity of the individual's subjectivity and the development of his personality, the protection of the private sphere of life against arbitrary interference by the State and others, and the preservation of autonomous control over one's personal data'.[18]

Article 239 of Taiwan's Criminal Code states that 'anyone who has a spouse and commits adultery with another person shall be punished by imprisonment for a term not exceeding one year'. However, the constitutionality of the crime of adultery has long been controversial in Taiwanese society. In Interpretation No 791 of 2020, the Grand Justices held that the crime of adultery in Article 239 of the Criminal Code was unconstitutional and should be abolished.[19] In the opinion of the Grand Justices, marriage is a permanent union between two spouses entered into by their free will, which is the basis for the formation and development of the family and society and is guaranteed by the Constitution. However, with the development of a liberal and pluralistic society, the importance of personal autonomy (including sexual autonomy) in the marital relationship has been increasingly recognised and valued, and the social function of marriage has tended to be relativised.[20] The offence of adultery not only directly restricts people's sexual autonomy, but also interferes with their privacy in the process of prosecution and trial.[21] Most acts of adultery take place in the private sphere of a person's life and are not public. The process of detection, prosecution and adjudication inevitably interferes with the private sphere of a person's life and with the autonomous control of personal data, with the result that the public power of the Government is driven directly into the very private sphere of people and seriously interferes with their privacy.[22] It is therefore clear that the restrictions imposed by the offence of adultery are more harmful than the interests they are intended to protect and are therefore disproportionate.[23]

[17] Constitutional Interpretation No 756 (1 December 2017), available at cons.judicial.gov.tw/docdata.aspx?fid=100&id=310937.

[18] ibid.

[19] Constitutional Interpretation No 791 (29 May 2020), available at cons.judicial.gov.tw/docdata.aspx?fid=100&id=310972.

[20] ibid.

[21] ibid.

[22] ibid.

[23] ibid.

B. Statutory Framework of Privacy Protection

The right to privacy is one of the rights of personality.[24] Taiwan's early Civil Code did not explicitly protect the privacy of individuals, and those whose privacy was violated could only seek protection under an abstract right of personality. Article 18 of the Civil Code states that

> in the event of an infringement of rights of personality, a person may apply to the court for an injunction to stop the infringement or, if there is a risk of an infringement, for an injunction to prevent the infringement; damages or compensation may be claimed only if there are special provisions in this law.

As the old Civil Code did not contain specific provisions on the protection of privacy, a person whose privacy had been violated could only apply to the court for an injunction to prevent the violation and could not claim damages.

The problem was not resolved until the Civil Code was amended in 1999 to include the protection of privacy in Article 195. The current Article 195(1) of the Civil Code provides that

> if a person unlawfully injures another person's body, health, reputation, freedom, credit, privacy or chastity, or unlawfully interferes with another person's legal interests to a significant extent, the victim may claim an equivalent amount in damages, even if the damage is not to property. Equivalent damages for the restoration of honour may also be claimed by a victim whose honour has been violated.

Accordingly, a person whose privacy has been infringed may not only seek an injunction to prevent the infringement, but may also claim damages.

In addition to the Civil Code, there are a number of types of offence under the Criminal Code that constitute a violation of a legal interest relating to the private sphere. In other words, the Criminal Code also provides a certain level of protection for the privacy of individuals.

The privacy of an individual's home is invaded by the unlawful entry or trespass to his or her home.[25] For this reason, Article 306 of the Criminal Code therefore states:

> Anyone who enters another person's house, building, land or vessel without a valid reason shall be punished by imprisonment for up to one year or a fine of up to NT$9,000; the same applies to anyone who remains in the house without a valid reason or who remains there after being asked to leave.

An unlawful search of a person's body or home by a law enforcement officer is also an invasion of privacy.[26] Hence, Article 307 of the Criminal Code therefore states that 'anyone who searches another person's body, house, building, boat, vehicle or aircraft without complying with the law shall be punished by imprisonment for up to two years, detention or a fine of up to NT$9,000'.

[24] J Angelo Corlett, 'The Nature and Value of the Moral Right to Privacy' (2002) 16 *Public Affairs Quarterly* 329, 330.

[25] Zaied Shouran, Ahmad Ashari and Tri Kuntoro Priyambodo, 'Internet of Things (IoT) of Smart Home: Privacy and Security' (2019) 182 *International Journal of Computer Applications* 3, 3.

[26] George E Edwards, 'International Human Rights Law Challenges to the New International Criminal Court: The Search and Seizure Right to Privacy' (2001) 26 *Yale Journal of International Law* 323, 327.

Anyone who uses a tool to spy on another person's non-public activities or physical privacy without a valid reason is in breach of that person's privacy.[27] Thus, Article 315-1 of the Criminal Code therefore states that

> any person who does any of the following shall be punished by imprisonment for up to three years, detention or a fine of up to NT$300,000: (1) Any person who uses an instrument or device to spy on or eavesdrop on the non-public activities, speech, conversation or private parts of the body of another person without a valid reason; (2) Any person who uses an audio, photographic, video or electromagnetic recording to eavesdrop on the non-public activities, speech, conversation or private parts of the body of another person without a valid reason.

In summary, Taiwan's Criminal Code protects the privacy of people's homes, non-public activities and intimate parts of their bodies through the threat of criminal sanctions.

C. Statutory Framework of Personal Data Protection

The purpose of the Taiwan Personal Data Protection Act is to regulate the collection, processing and use of personal data of natural persons and to promote the rational use of personal data.[28]

Taiwan's first personal data protection law was enacted in 1995 under the title 'Computer Personal Data Protection Act'. This law did not apply to all sectors, but was limited to eight sectors, namely credit bureaus, hospitals, schools, telecommunications, finance, securities, insurance and mass communications.[29] The Act was substantially amended in 2000 to extend the regulation to all industries and was renamed the 'Personal Data Protection Act'.[30] After 15 years, the Personal Data Protection Act was again substantially amended and the competent authority was changed from the Ministry of Justice to the National Development Council.

The third amendment to the Personal Data Protection Act was finalised on 16 May 2023.[31] In addition to increasing the penalties for violations of the law, the most important point of this amendment is the establishment of a new Personal Data Protection Commission as the competent authority for the Personal Data Protection Act, acting as an independent supervisory authority for the protection of personal data.[32]

The personal data protected by this law are the name, date of birth, national identity card number, passport number, features, fingerprints, marriage, family, education, occupation, medical records, medical treatment information, genetic information, sexuality, medical examinations, criminal records, contact details, financial situation, social

[27] Kelly Freund, 'When Cameras Are Rolling: Privacy Implications of Body-Mounted Cameras on Police' (2015) 49 *Columbia Journal of Law & Social Problems* 91, 97.

[28] Personal Data Act, Art 1.

[29] General Description of the 2000 Amendments, available at db.lawbank.com.tw/GetFile.ashx?pfid=0000242877.

[30] ibid.

[31] National Development Council, 'The Legislative Yuan has passed the Third Amendment to the Personal Data Protection Act, which will increase penalties for leaks of personal data by companies and establish the Preparatory Office of the Personal Data Protection Commission as soon as possible' News Release (16 May 2023), available at www.ndc.gov.tw/nc_27_36901.

[32] Personal Data Protection Act, Art 1-1.

activities and other data that can directly or indirectly identify a natural person.[33] The subjects protected by the Personal Data Protection Act are natural persons who are still alive and not those who are deceased.[34] Non-personal information, such as the name of a company, is not protected by the Data Protection Act.[35]

Of all these types of personal data, social activities have the broadest scope, including records of telephone messages and communications,[36] records of inquiries made by the debtor to the tax authorities,[37] interpersonal relationships,[38] records of e-Tag tracking,[39] records of GPS tracking of a vehicle,[40] and information on immigration.[41]

'Indirectly identifiable', as defined in the Personal Data Protection Act, means that the entities holding the information cannot directly identify the individual on the basis of that information alone, but must compare, combine, link, etc with other information in order to identify that particular individual.[42] Although the anonymised data is no longer personal data that cannot be protected under the Personal Data Protection Act, the pseudonymised data, which can be re-identified by cross-referencing with other databases, may still be protected under the Personal Data Protection Act.[43]

The subjects regulated by this Act include public authorities and non-public entities. Public authorities are central or local authorities or administrative bodies that exercise public powers under the law,[44] including public hospitals[45] and public schools.[46] Non-public entities are natural persons, legal entities or other entities other than public authorities,[47] including notaries[48] and private schools.[49]

The activities regulated by this law are the collection, processing and use of personal data. Data collection means the acquisition of personal data by any method and means.[50] Data processing means the recording, inputting, storing, editing, correcting, copying, retrieving, deleting, exporting, linking or internal transmission of data for the purposes of creating or using a personal data file.[51] Data use means the use of collected personal data for purposes other than processing.[52] Under the Personal Data Protection Act, the collection, processing or use of personal data shall respect the rights and interests of the

[33] ibid, Art 2(1)
[34] Enforcement Rules of the Personal Data Protection Act, Art 2.
[35] Interpretation issued by the Ministry of Justice, No 10403509940, dated 7 August 2015.
[36] Interpretation issued by the Ministry of Justice, No 10203504230, dated 7 April 2013.
[37] Interpretation issued by the Ministry of Justice, No 10303501350, dated 29 January 2014.
[38] Taipei High Court, Criminal Judgment No 2294, Shang Yi Zi, 2014.
[39] Interpretation issued by the Ministry of Justice, No 10403513240, dated 23 October 2015.
[40] Taipei District Court, Criminal Summary Judgment No 2135, 2021; Taipei High Court, Criminal Judgment No 352, Shang Yi Zi, 2015.
[41] Shihlin District Court, Criminal Judgment No 84, 2019.
[42] Enforcement Rules of the Personal Data Protection Act, Art 3.
[43] Huang-Chih Sung, 'Legal Risks and Management Implications of Big Data Transactions – Focusing on the Reidentification of Personal Data' (2018) 37 *Management Review* 121, 123.
[44] Personal Data Protection Act, Art 2(7).
[45] Interpretation issued by the Ministry of Justice, No 10403500490, dated 30 January 2015.
[46] Interpretation issued by the Ministry of Justice, No 10103109040, dated 1 November 2012.
[47] Personal Data Protection Act, Art 2(8).
[48] Interpretation issued by the Ministry of Justice, No 10303510940, dated 25 September 2014.
[49] Interpretation issued by the Ministry of Justice, No 10103109040, dated 1 November 2012.
[50] Personal Data Protection Act, Art 2(3).
[51] ibid, Art 2(4).
[52] ibid, Art 2(5).

data subjects, be carried out in good faith and in a trustworthy manner, not exceed the scope necessary for the specific purpose, and be appropriate and reasonably related to the purposes for which it was collected.[53]

When a public authority or a non-public entity collects personal data from a data subject, it shall clearly inform the data subject of the following:

1) the name of the public authority or the non-public entity;
2) the purposes of the data collection;
3) the categories of personal data involved;
4) the duration, scope, subject and methods of use of the personal data collected;
5) the rights that the data subject may exercise and how to exercise them; and
6) the data subject's freedom to choose whether or not to provide the personal data and the implications of not providing the data for the data subject's rights and interests.[54]

However, the collection of personal data may be exempted from the said notification if:

1) the notification may be waived in accordance with the law;
2) the collection of personal data is necessary for the public authority to fulfil its statutory duties or for the non-public entity to exercise its statutory obligations;
3) the notification would interfere with the performance of the public authority's statutory duties;
4) the notification would be detrimental to the public interest;
5) the data subject knows what should be disclosed; and
6) the collection of personal data is not for profit and has no obvious adverse effect on the data subject.[55]

The so-called 'statutory obligations' refers to the obligations of non-public entities under laws or regulations that are specifically authorised by law. For example, Taiwanese companies are required to prepare a list of their shareholders under the Corporate Law.[56] A company will definitely not be able to fulfil its statutory obligation if it does not collect the personal data of its shareholders. Therefore, a company's collection of shareholders' personal data is necessary to comply with its legal obligations and does not constitute an infringement of personal data.[57]

At the request of data subjects, public authorities or non-public entities shall respond to requests to provide access to, or copies of, the personal data they hold within 15 days. However, this provision shall not apply in any of the following cases where the response would:

a. interfere with national security, diplomatic and military secrets, general economic interests or other vital national interests;
b. interfere with the exercise of the official duties of a public authority; and
c. interfere with the vital interests of the collecting authority or a third party.[58]

[53] ibid, Art 5.
[54] ibid, Art 8(1).
[55] ibid, Art 8(2).
[56] Corporate Law, Art 210(1).
[57] Interpretation issued by the Ministry of Justice, No 10500077090, dated 3 May 2016.
[58] Personal Data Protection Act, Arts 10 and 13(1).

Public authorities or non-public entities shall maintain the accuracy of personal data and correct or supplement them on their own initiative or at the request of the data subjects.[59] If the accuracy of personal data is in dispute, public authorities or non-public entities shall, on their own initiative or at the request of the data subjects, cease to process or use the data, unless it is necessary for the exercise of their duties or business, or with the written consent of the data subjects and subject to a note indicating the dispute.[60] When the specific purpose for which personal data were collected has ceased to exist or the time limit has expired, public authorities or non-public entities shall, on their own initiative or at the request of the data subject, erase, cease to process or use personal data, unless it is necessary for the exercise of their duties or business or with the written consent of the data subjects.[61] Where a public authority or non-public entity receives such a request, it shall decide whether or not to refuse the request within 30 days; where necessary, this period may be extended by a further period not exceeding 30 days, and the reasons for the extension shall be notified in writing to the applicant.[62]

If a public authority or non-public entities violates the Personal Data Protection Act so that the collected personal data is stolen, leaked, or falsified, the data subjects shall be informed in an appropriate manner after investigation.[63]

The protected personal data mentioned above can be divided into two categories: specific personal data and general personal data. Medical records, medical treatment data, genetic information, sexuality, health examinations and criminal records are specific personal data.[64] Medical records include: (1) medical records prepared by physicians in accordance with the Medical Practitioners Act; (2) examination and test reports; and (3) records prepared by various other medical personnel in the course of their duties.[65] It is worth noting that information such as addresses and telephone numbers in medical records are still general personal data rather than specific personal data.[66] Medical treatment information refers to medical treatment and other personal data prepared by a physician or other healthcare professional for the purpose of treating, correcting or preventing disease, injury or disability or for other medically justifiable reasons, or for the purpose of prescribing, administering, performing surgery on or disposing of personal data based on the results of such examination.[67] Genetic information refers to a segment of the human body made up of deoxyribonucleic acid (DNA), a single piece of genetic information that controls a specific function of the body.[68] Personal data relating to sexuality refers to personal information about one's sexual orientation or sexual habits.[69] Personal data relating to health examination is data generated by a medical procedure that is not intended for the diagnosis or treatment of a specific disease.[70] A criminal record is

[59] ibid, Art 11(1).
[60] ibid, Art 11(2).
[61] ibid, Art 11(3).
[62] ibid, Art 13(2).
[63] ibid, Art 12.
[64] ibid, Art 6.
[65] Enforcement Rules of the Personal Data Protection Act, Art 4(1); Medical Care Act, Art 67(2).
[66] Interpretation issued by the Ministry of Justice, No 10203511120, dated 31 October 2013.
[67] Enforcement Rules of the Personal Data Protection Act, Art 4(2).
[68] ibid, Art 4(3).
[69] ibid, Art 4(4).
[70] ibid, Art 4(5).

a record of a deferred prosecution order, a record of a non-prosecution order made by a prosecuting authority, or a record of a conviction imposed or enforced by a court.[71]

The specific personal data should, in principle, not be collected, processed or used unless the following specific conditions are met:

1) it is expressly provided for by law;
2) to the extent necessary for public authorities to carry out their statutory duties or for private parties to fulfil their statutory obligations, and with appropriate safeguards in place before or after the fact;
3) personal information provided by the individual or lawfully disclosed;
4) where it is necessary for statistical or scientific research by public authorities or academic research institutes for medical, health or crime prevention purposes and the data are processed by the provider or the collector and no specific individual can be identified from the manner in which the data are disclosed;
5) to assist public authorities in the performance of their statutory duties or to the extent necessary for the public authorities to perform their statutory duties, and where appropriate safeguards are in place before or after such disclosure; or
6) with the written consent of the data subject. However, with the exception of personal data that exceeds what is necessary for a specific purpose or is otherwise restricted by law, personal data may only be collected, processed or used with the written consent of the data subject or where consent is obtained against his or her will.[72]

The inability to identify a particular individual referred to above means that the personal data will be encrypted, anonymised, partially hidden or otherwise processed in such a way that the particular individual cannot be identified.[73]

Any person who unlawfully collects, processes or uses the aforementioned specific personal data with the intention of unlawfully benefiting himself or a third party to the detriment of another person shall be punished with imprisonment of up to five years and a fine of up to NT$1,000,000.[74] If a non-public entity unlawfully collects, processes or uses the above-mentioned specific personal data, it shall be fined between NT$50,000 and NT$500,000 by the relevant industry authority of the central government or the local government, and shall be ordered to rectify the situation within a specified period of time; if the situation is not rectified within the specified period of time, the penalty shall be imposed repeatedly.[75]

Personal data other than specific personal data may, in principle, be collected, processed and used provided that the strict standards of the Personal Data Protection Act are observed. The Personal Data Protection Act distinguishes between public authorities and non-public entities with regard to the collection, processing or use of general personal data.

As far as public authorities are concerned, the collection or processing of personal data should be for a specific purpose and meet one of the following conditions: (1) to the extent necessary for the performance of their statutory tasks; (2) with the consent of the

[71] ibid, Art 4(6).
[72] Personal Data Protection Act, Art 6.
[73] Enforcement Rules of the Personal Data Protection Act, Art 17.
[74] Personal Data Protection Act, Art 41.
[75] ibid, Art 47.

data subject; (3) without infringing the rights and interests of the data subject.[76] The use of personal data by public authorities is limited to what is necessary for the performance of their statutory duties and is consistent with the specific purpose for which it was collected. The use of personal data for purposes other than those specified may be permitted only in exceptional circumstances, such as with the consent of the data subject or when necessary for statistical or scientific research in the public interest after de-identification.[77]

Where a public authority maintains personal data files, it should designate a person responsible for maintaining security to prevent personal data from being stolen, manipulated, destroyed, lost or leaked.[78] Public authorities should make available to the public, on computerised websites or by other appropriate means, the following information and any subsequent changes thereto:

1) the name of the personal data file;
2) the name and contact details of the holding authority;
3) the basis and specific purposes for which the personal data file is held; and
4) the nature of the personal data.[79]

For non-public bodies, personal data should only be collected or processed for a specific purpose and in one of the following circumstances: (1) it is expressly provided for by law; (2) there is a contractual or similar relationship with the data subject and appropriate safeguards have been put in place; (3) the personal data is provided by the data subject or otherwise lawfully disclosed; (4) it is necessary for statistical or scientific research in the public interest by an academic research institution and where the data has been processed by the provider or collected in such a way that no specific individual can be identified; (5) it is with the consent of the data subject; (6) it is necessary to further the public interest; (7) the personal data is obtained from generally available sources; (8) there is no infringement of the rights of the data subject.[80]

In principle, non-public entities may only use the personal data they collect to the extent necessary for the specific purpose for which it was collected. For example, it is consistent with the Personal Data Protection Act for a company to reward employees to the extent necessary by publishing the names of award winners on the Honour Roll for specific personnel management purposes.[81]

The collected personal data may be used for purposes other than the original specific purpose for which it was collected only in the following exceptional cases: (1) it is expressly provided by law; (2) it is necessary to promote the public interest; (3) it is for the purpose of eliminating danger to the life, limb, liberty or property of the data subject; (4) it is for the purpose of preventing substantial harm to the rights and interests of others; (5) it is necessary for statistical or scientific research in the public interest by a public authority or scientific research organisation, provided that the data have been processed by the provider or the collector does not have the possibility to identify the specific individuals in the

[76] ibid, Art 15.
[77] ibid, Art 16.
[78] ibid, Art 18.
[79] ibid, Art 17.
[80] ibid, Art 19.
[81] Interpretation issued by the Ministry of Justice, No 10203502790, dated 27 March 2013.

manner in which the data have been disclosed; (6) it is with the consent of the data subjects; (7) it is in the interest of the data subjects.[82]

For example, financial institutions regularly use the information system set up by the Taiwan Depository and Clearing Corporation to check the customer information they hold against the anti-money laundering (AML) control list. The purpose is to maximise the effectiveness of the AML control list database in preventing money laundering. This measure may qualify for the 'necessary to promote the public interest' exception, which allows financial institutions to use the personal data collected for purposes other than those for which they were collected.[83]

If a non-public entity violates the Personal Data Protection Act, in addition to imposing a fine in accordance with the provisions of the Personal Data Protection Act, the relevant industry authority of the central government or the local government may impose the following penalties:

1) prohibit the collection, processing or use of personal information;
2) order the deletion of personal data files that have been processed;
3) confiscation or destruction of personal data collected in violation of the law; or
4) publication of the situation of violation of the law by the non-public entity, as well as the names and persons responsible.[84]

In summary, both public authorities and non-public entities must have a specific purpose and comply with certain legal conditions before they collect or process personal data. Once a public authority or non-public entity has obtained personal data, it can in principle only use them for the specific purpose for which they were originally obtained, and if it wishes to use them for a purpose other than the specific purpose, it must comply with the legal requirements. At this stage, it is generally not easy to find the data subjects to obtain their written consent. The most common and feasible method is to de-identify the personal data.

Public authorities or non-public entities are liable for damages if they violate the Personal Data Protection Act and cause the unlawful collection, processing, or use of personal data of other persons. Public authorities shall be liable for damages for the unlawful collection, processing or use of personal data in violation of the provisions of this Act, unless the damage is caused by natural disasters, accidents or other force majeure.[85] Non-public entities are also liable for damages caused by illegally collecting, processing or using personal data of others in violation of the Personal Data Protection Act, unless they can prove that they did not act intentionally or negligently.[86] Victims of unlawful data collection, processing and use may claim equivalent compensation, even if the damage is not material. If their reputation has been damaged, they may also claim appropriate damages to restore their reputation.[87] If victims cannot prove the actual amount of damages, they can apply to the court for calculation of damages in accordance with the circumstances of the assault at a rate of between NT$500 and NT$20,000 per person per incident.[88]

[82] Personal Data Protection Act, Art 20.
[83] Interpretation issued by the Ministry of Justice, No 10603501350, dated 26 January 2017.
[84] Personal Data Protection Act, Art 25(1).
[85] ibid, Art 28(1).
[86] ibid, Art 29(1).
[87] ibid, Arts 28(2) and 29(2).
[88] ibid, Arts 28(3) and 29(2).

The Personal Data Protection Act sets an upper limit on the amount of compensation for damages caused by the infringement of other people's personal data. Where the rights of a plurality of parties are infringed for the same cause, the maximum aggregate amount of damages claimed by the parties shall be limited to NT$200 million, unless the benefit of the personal data infringement to the person who unlawfully collects, processes or uses other people's personal data exceeds NT$200 million.[89] For those who unlawfully collect, process or use other people's personal data, this compensation cap significantly reduces their liability in tort. In many cases, it prevents the victims from being compensated for the damage they have suffered.

In addition, there may be criminal liability for the unlawful collection, processing, use or international transfer of another person's personal data. Any person who unlawfully collects, processes, uses or internationally transfers personal data of another person with the intention of unlawfully benefiting himself or a third party or to the detriment of another person shall be punished by imprisonment for up to five years and a fine of up to NT$1 million.[90]

Furthermore, non-public entities may be subject to administrative liability for the unlawful collection, processing, use or international transfer of other person's personal data. If a non-public entity illegally collects, processes, uses or internationally transfers personal data of others, the central government or local government shall impose a fine of NT$50,000 to NT$500,000 and order the entity to make corrections within a specified period of time. If the non-public entity fails to rectify the situation by the end of the period, it shall be subject to the repeated penalties.[91]

To ensure that the impact of the Personal Data Protection Act is not overwhelming, the Act itself contains a fair use clause. Article 51 of the Personal Data Protection Act states that

> the provisions of this law do not apply to the following cases: (1) a natural person collects, processes or uses personal data for the purpose of purely personal or family activities; and (2) audiovisual data collected, processed or used in public places or public activities that are not combined with other personal data.

Therefore, it is not an infringement of personal data for people to post personal information, such as photos or videos of their relatives or friends, on social platforms solely for personal activities.[92]

III. Judicial Practice of Privacy and Personal Data Protection

A. 'Reasonable Expectation of Privacy' Becomes Implicit Legal Requirement for Personal Data Breaches in Judicial Practice

As mentioned above, privacy and personal data protection in Taiwan are governed by two separate and seemingly unrelated legal regimes.

[89] ibid, Arts 28(4) and 29(2).
[90] ibid, Art 41.
[91] ibid, Art 47.
[92] Interpretation issued by the Ministry of Justice, No 10203502790, dated 27 March 2013.

However, many court decisions on personal data breaches have used the plaintiff's (victim's) 'reasonable expectation of privacy' as an element of the defendant's personal data breach, creating an element that is not found in the Personal Data Protection Act. In other words, the court held that even if the defendant had unlawfully collected, processed or used the plaintiff's personal data, as long as the plaintiff did not have a reasonable expectation of privacy in his or her personal data, the defendant had not committed a personal data breach.

The author suggests that there are two possible reasons for the courts' decisions to consider invasion of privacy as a legal requirement for a personal data infringement. First, the courts may have been influenced by previous interpretations by the Grand Justices, in particular the 'information privacy right' in Interpretation No 603 and the 'reasonable expectation of privacy' in Interpretation No 689, both of which introduced the concept of privacy into the adjudication of personal data protection disputes. These interpretations by the Grand Justices have led lower court judges to consider the violation of privacy as a legal prerequisite for the violation of personal data protection.

Second, the Personal Data Act protects a wide range of data, including name, date of birth, national identity card number, passport number, physical characteristics, fingerprints, marriage, family, education, occupation, medical records, medical treatment, genetics, sex life, medical examination, criminal record, contact details, financial situation, social activities and other data that can directly or indirectly identify an individual. Social activities, in particular, encompass almost all aspects of people's daily lives, leading to concerns about breaches of other people's personal data in everyday activities. Thus, by making the plaintiff's 'reasonable expectation of privacy' a prerequisite for an invasion of personal data, which is not in the law though, judges may be attempting to limit the scope and power of the Personal Data Protection Act.

Despite the court's approach above, the author disagrees with the courts' reliance on a 'reasonable expectation of privacy', which is not required by law, as a prerequisite for determining an infringement of personal data. As judges have a duty to follow the law in deciding cases, the use of 'reasonable expectation of privacy' as a prerequisite for finding an infringement of personal data is clearly inconsistent with the law. The author will illustrate her viewpoint with the following case studies.

B. Case Study 1: Student Information Case

In this case, the plaintiff requested a university to provide and disclose information on students who applied for tuition fee waivers from 2001 to the present, including gender, year of admission, department and college of admission, admission route, high school graduation school, and county and municipality of residence, in accordance with the Government Information Disclosure Act. The plaintiff's case was based on academic research and argued that this research could raise public concern about the selection mechanisms of top universities and prompted national universities to review their selection mechanisms. The plaintiff also argued that if student information did not meet the criteria for de-identification, it should be de-identified first.[93]

[93] Administrative Judgment No 283 of 2017 of the Taipei High Administrative Court.

However, the university refused to provide the information on two grounds: (1) the Government Information Disclosure Act gives people the right to ask government agencies for government information prepared or obtained within the scope of their authority, but it does not give people the right to ask government agencies to reduce the administrative activities of government agencies to writing and to prepare reports or statistical analyses according to their intentions;[94] (2) the tuition waiver application information includes gender, year of enrolment, department and college of enrolment, route of enrolment, school of high school graduation, and city of residence. Even after the de-identification process, which removes personal names and student numbers, the information may still indirectly identify a specific individual through cross-referencing with other information, so there is still a risk that a specific student could be identified.[95]

In this dispute, the university acknowledged the risk of re-identification when de-identifying personal data, and believed that even if individual names and student IDs were removed, they could be matched with other data to identify a particular student. Because student information includes gender, year of enrolment, department and college of enrolment, route of enrolment, high school graduation school, and county and city of residence, students from certain remote villages or remote high schools may be at particularly high risk of being re-identified because few students from those villages or high schools are enrolled at the university each year. Therefore, there is a high probability that some students will be identified after cross-matching information such as gender, year of entry, faculty and college of entry, and route of entry.

The plaintiff appealed the administrative decision, but the appeal was also dismissed. The plaintiff then brought the present administrative action before the Taipei High Administrative Court. The Taipei High Administrative Court accepted the university's first argument and held that the defendant had not produced or obtained the relevant information as alleged and requested by the plaintiff under Article 3 of the Government Information Disclosure Act, and that the plaintiff had no right to request the defendant to produce the relevant information as alleged by the plaintiff.[96] The Taipei High Administrative Court therefore dismissed the plaintiff's case. With regard to the second ground raised by the university, the Taipei High Administrative Court found that there was no need to address it further. It is a pity that such an excellent opportunity was missed to examine and discuss whether the de-identified data could be cross-referenced with other data and thus pose a risk of re-identification.

C. Case Study 2: Health Insurance Database (Supreme Administrative Court)

This is one of the most interesting decisions of the Supreme Administrative Court of Taiwan on the issue of de-identification of personal data.[97] Taiwan has had a national

[94] ibid.
[95] ibid.
[96] ibid.
[97] The plaintiff appealed to the Supreme Administrative Court, and on 13 November 2014, No 600 of the Supreme Administrative Court issued Administrative Judgment of 2014, reversing the original judgment and remanding

health insurance scheme since 1995. By paying a monthly health insurance premium, people pay only a small fee and is deductible when they seek medical care from a medical institution. The medical institution submits the medical records to the Central Health Insurance Bureau for insurance coverage. Its superior, the Ministry of Health and Welfare, established the National Health Insurance Database, which has accumulated nearly 30 years of national medical data. The Ministry of Health and Welfare has de-identified the medical data and opened it up to academic institutions for academic research, making it one of the most important databases for international medical and public health research.

This case arose when, in 2012, eight members of the public (the plaintiffs) sent a letter of attestation to the Central Health Insurance Bureau of the Ministry of Health and Welfare stating that they refused to allow the Central Health Insurance Bureau to disclose their personal health insurance data to third parties for purposes other than health insurance-related matters.[98] The plaintiffs' main concern was that the Central Health Insurance Bureau had provided their health insurance data to the Ministry of Health and Welfare for the establishment of the Scientific Centre for Health and Welfare Data and to the National Institutes of Health for the establishment of the National Health Insurance Database for academic and commercial use.[99] However, the plaintiffs' claim was rejected by the Central Health Insurance Bureau and they appealed the decision. The appeal was also rejected, and they filed an administrative lawsuit with the Taipei High Administrative Court.[100]

The plaintiffs argued that the collection, processing or use of medical records and personal medical data by the Central Health Insurance Bureau was subject to the Personal Data Protection Act to the extent necessary for the performance of its statutory functions and for the specific purpose of the collection.[101] In this case, the Central Health Insurance Bureau provided the unencrypted and directly identifiable personal data of the National Health Insurance to the Ministry of Health and Welfare and the National Institutes of Health to create a database. This was not in line with the original purpose of the data collection and was not in accordance with the Central Health Insurance Bureau's statutory duties.[102] Furthermore, the use of the databases by academics for academic research to be published in academic journals could not be directly considered to be in the public interest. The Central Health Insurance Bureau was required to de-identify health insurance data in accordance with the Personal Data Protection Act. Although the Ministry of Health and Welfare encrypted the health insurance data before creating the database, it only replaced the personal identification numbers in the health insurance data with a set of random codes. This allowed the health insurance data to be matched with other databases to identify specific individuals. Therefore, the Ministry of Health and Welfare's approach did not truly de-identify the health insurance data and violated the norms of the Personal Data Protection Act.[103]

the case to the original trial. On 19 May 2016, No 120 of the Taipei High Administrative Court issued Administrative Judgment of 2014, which was again appealed to the Supreme Administrative Court. On 26 January 2017, the Supreme Administrative Court issued Administrative Judgment No 54 of the Supreme Administrative Court of 2017, dismissing the appeal.

[98] No 54 of the Administrative Decision of the Supreme Administrative Court of 2017.

[99] ibid.

[100] ibid.

[101] ibid.

[102] ibid.

[103] ibid.

The defendant, the Central Health Insurance Bureau, argued that it had already encrypted the health insurance data twice before handing it over to the National Health Institute for the creation of the National Health Insurance Database.[104] In addition to deleting the name and date of birth from the health insurance data (only the month and year of birth were retained), the identity card number was also encrypted. It was part of the Central Health Insurance Bureau's statutory duties to contribute to the development of healthcare by using the database for academic research and publishing the results in national and international journals.[105] The Central Health Insurance Bureau encrypted the database before making it available to the public so that the health insurance database could no longer be used to identify specific individuals, in accordance with the provisions of the Personal Data Protection Act.[106]

In its decision, the Supreme Administrative Court first noted that the way in which the Central Health Insurance Bureau had de-identified health insurance data had been significantly reduced, but not to the extent of 'completely severing the link between the health insurance data and the particular data subject'.[107] The Supreme Administrative Court did not question whether the removal of the patient's names from the health insurance data and the encryption of the patient's ID numbers by the Central Health Insurance Office was sufficient to de-identify the patient, but rather who performed the de-identification.[108] Both the Central Health Insurance Bureau and the Ministry of Health and Welfare admitted that the so-called 'encrypting the patient ID card numbers' was not carried out by the Central Health Insurance Bureau (the data provider), but by the Ministry of Health and Welfare (the data recipient). The Ministry of Health and Welfare sent its staff to the Central Health Insurance Bureau to encrypt the health insurance data, and then brought the encrypted health insurance data back to the Ministry of Health and Welfare to establish the National Health Insurance Database. This mode of operation left the recipient, the Ministry of Health and Welfare, in sole control of decryption and enabled the Ministry to link health insurance data to individual patients. Therefore, it did not meet the standard of de-identification.[109]

However, the Supreme Administrative Court dismissed the appeal primarily on the ground that the Ministry of Health and Welfare should have the authority to collect and process health insurance data.[110] As a higher authority than the Central Health Insurance Bureau, it could have complied with the de-identification requirements of the Personal Data Protection Act by slightly improving the encryption process (ie the encryption process was carried out by the Central Health Insurance Bureau rather than the Ministry of Health and Welfare sending staff to the Bureau).[111] Finally, the Supreme Administrative Court stated that the plaintiffs, who claimed that their right to information was at risk of being violated, should have indicated the extent and likelihood of the violation. However, they never specifically argued this in the appeal.[112]

[104] ibid.
[105] ibid.
[106] ibid.
[107] ibid.
[108] ibid.
[109] ibid.
[110] ibid.
[111] ibid.
[112] ibid.

In summary, the decision of the Supreme Administrative Court is significant on two levels. First, on a substantive level, the Supreme Administrative Court confirmed, or at least did not actively deny, that the de-identification requirement could be achieved by removing the personal names from the personal data and encrypting the identity card numbers. Second, the Supreme Administrative Court was more concerned with procedural issues, ie whether the encryption of the personal data identifiers was carried out by the data provider or by the data recipient. The Supreme Administrative Court clarified that the encryption of personal data may not be carried out by the recipient of the data, otherwise the recipient would be able to restore the link between the data and the data subjects.

D. Case Study 3: Health Insurance Database (Constitutional Court)

The eight plaintiffs in the previous administrative case were not satisfied with the decision of the Supreme Administrative Court. They asked for a constitutional interpretation, arguing that the academic research exception for the specific personal data in the Personal Data Protection Act was unconstitutional.[113] They claimed that the Personal Data Protection Act allows the Government to compulsorily collect, process or use people's general or private sensitive personal data, or to compulsorily collect, process or use personal data on a large scale, or to compulsorily retain personal data outside the original purpose of collection, on the basis of organisational law alone, in violation of the principle of legal reservation.[114]

The Constitutional Court ruled in 2022 that the National Health Insurance Act lacked clear provisions on the supervision and protection mechanism for the Central Health Insurance Bureau to store personal data in a database and make it accessible for research.[115] For the Central Health Insurance Bureau to provide personal data to academic research institutions for use beyond the original purpose of collection, the current law also lacked relevant provisions to allow citizens to request the cessation of such use.[116] Therefore, the National Health Insurance Law violated the Constitution's intention to protect people's right to privacy, and the relevant authorities must amend the law within three years.[117]

The author disagrees with the decision of the Constitutional Court and argues that allowing people to opt out of the health database would create problems with the representativeness of ethnic groups, potentially leading to biased results in subsequent studies. While privacy is an important constitutional right, its protection should be balanced with the right to life and public health. The Constitutional Court's decision may seriously harm medical research by tipping the balance towards privacy protection alone.

[113] Constitutional Judgement No 13 of 2022.
[114] ibid.
[115] ibid.
[116] ibid.
[117] ibid.

IV. Legal Bases, Mechanisms and Exceptions for International Data Transfers and Data Protection

A. Legal Framework for International Data Transfers

International data transfers under the Personal Data Protection Act are defined as the processing or use of personal data across national borders.[118]

According to the Personal Data Protection Act, the relevant industry authority of the central government may restrict the international transfer of personal data by a non-public entity in any of the following cases: (1) where there are overriding national interests; (2) where there are special provisions in international treaties or agreements; (3) where the recipient country does not have adequate provisions for the protection of personal data, which may jeopardise the interests of the data subject; and (4) where this Act is circumvented by transferring personal data to third countries (regions) in a roundabout way.[119]

According to this provision, the international data transfer is restricted only to the non-public entities, but not to the public authorities. No specific reasons were given in the explanatory memorandum of the legislation.

In principle, under existing Taiwan law, it is permissible for a non-public entity that holds personal data to transfer lawfully collected personal data across national borders. This provision is intended to empower the relevant industry authority of the central government, at its discretion, to restrict the right and freedom of non-public entities to make international data transfers when one of the above situations arise.[120]

At the time of writing (21 July 2024), Taiwan has not signed a safe harbour agreement with any other country. Instead, the relevant industry authority of the central Government has full discretion to approve or disapprove the international transfer of data by non-public entities, even if the recipient country does not have adequate provisions for the protection of personal data. In this respect, when compared to other jurisdictions, it may be reasonable to say that the Personal Data Protection Act has yet to meet the international standard of protection of the interests of data subjects.

If the relevant industry authority of the central Government or local governments deems it necessary to inspect the security of data files, data processing methods, international transmission restrictions or other routine business inspections, it may send its personnel to enter the non-public entities with proof of their duties to conduct inspections, and may order the relevant personnel to provide the necessary explanations, cooperation measures or relevant supporting information.[121] When the relevant industry authority of central or local government carries out an inspection, it may work with information, telecommunications or legal experts.[122] Non-public entities and their personnel shall not avoid, obstruct or refuse the inspection.[123] Of course, the personnel involved in the

[118] Personal Data Protection Act, Art 2(6).
[119] ibid, Art 21.
[120] Interpretation issued by the Ministry of Justice, No 10203503330, dated 13 May 2013.
[121] Personal Data Protection Act, Art 22(1).
[122] ibid, Art 22(3).
[123] ibid, Art 22(4).

inspection shall be subject to a duty of confidentiality if, as a result of the inspection, they have access to information about the non-public entities under inspection.[124]

The relevant industry authority of the central Government or local governments may, in the course of an inspection of a non-public entity, withhold or make copies of personal data or its files that may be seized or used as evidence. The relevant industry authority of the central Government or local governments may require the owner or custodian to provide the personal data to be withheld or copied. If the non-public entity refuses to deliver or resists the seizure or copying without good reason, the relevant industry authority of the central Government or local governments shall compel it by the means least prejudicial to the interests of the non-public entity.[125]

The unlawful international transfer of other person's personal data may result in criminal liability. Any person who unlawfully internationally transfers other person's personal data with the intention of unlawfully benefiting himself or a third party or to the detriment of another person shall be punished by imprisonment for up to five years and a fine of up to NT$1 million.[126]

In addition, non-public entities may be subject to administrative liability for the illegal international transfer of personal data of others. If a non-public entity illegally transfers personal data of others internationally, the central Government or local government shall impose a fine of NT$50,000 to NT$500,000 and order the entity to make corrections within a specified period of time. If the non-public entity fails to rectify the situation by the end of the period, it shall be subject to the repeated penalties.[127]

B. Data Protection on an International Level

In order to actively work on measures related to the European Union's (EU) General Data Protection Regulation (GDPR) and coordinate negotiations with the EU on the adequacy certification of cross-border data transfers, Taiwan's National Development Council established a project office for personal data protection on 4 July 2018.[128] The National Development Council had already completed Taiwan's GDPR adequacy self-assessment report at the end of 2018, and asked the Ministry of Foreign Affairs to forward it to the EU's Directorate General for Justice.[129] Tiina Astola, Director General of the EU's Directorate General for Justice, formally replied to Taiwan in March 2019, stating that the Directorate General was still in the process of analysing the adequacy self-assessment report submitted by Taiwan and that the Directorate General would start a technical dialogue with Taiwan on issues related to the protection of personal data.[130]

According to the official press release of the National Development Council, Taiwan and the EU would hold the second round of consultations in spring 2020. Upon completion

[124] ibid, Art 22(5).
[125] ibid, Art 22(2).
[126] ibid, Art 41.
[127] ibid, Art 47.
[128] National Development Council, 'EU Welcomes Dialogue between Taiwan and Europe on Adequacy of GDPR Data Protection' (News Release, 11 March 2019), available at www.ndc.gov.tw/nc_27_32174.
[129] ibid.
[130] ibid.

of all consultations, the National Development Council planned to submit a draft amendment to the Personal Data Protection Act within three months of the EU's submission of a formal assessment report to Taiwan, with a view to obtaining adequacy recognition as soon as possible.[131]

However, in the year and a half since then, the National Development Council has not issued any news or information on amendments to the Personal Data Protection Act or the adequacy of the GDPR.

Until 26 May 2021, there was a media report questioning what progress was actually being made on GDPR adequacy recognition. On the same day, the National Development Council responded to the media report, noting that it had been working with the EU on the GDPR adequacy finding consultation since 2018. Although the EU side prioritised issues such as the adequacy finding for the UK's exit from the EU, both sides continued to engage in bilateral consultations.[132] In addition to continuing negotiations with the EU on the adequacy of the GDPR, the National Development Council also emphasised that it would promote domestic training on the Personal Data Protection Act and coordinate the implementation of the Personal Data Protection Act with the relevant industry authority of the central Government.[133]

V. Legal Framework for Data and Cybersecurity

In order to actively promote national cybersecurity policies and accelerate the construction of a national cybersecurity environment to safeguard national security and protect the public interest of society, Taiwan enacted the Cybersecurity Management Act in 2018.[134]

Cybersecurity in this Act refers to the protection of cyber systems or information from unauthorised access, use, control, disclosure, destruction, tampering, damage or other compromise to ensure their confidentiality, integrity and availability.[135]

The Cybersecurity Management Act applies to both public authorities and certain non-public organisations. Public authorities are central authorities, local authorities or public corporations exercising public power under the law, but excluding military authorities and intelligence agencies.[136] Specified non-public organisations are essential facilities providers, public utilities and government-owned consortia.[137]

With regard to the cybersecurity management of public authorities, they should comply with the requirements of their respective cybersecurity responsibility levels and formulate, revise and implement cybersecurity maintenance plans, taking into account the types,

[131] National Development Council, 'The National Development Council is Promoting the Amendment of the Personal Data Protection Act, and is Seeking Recognition of GDPR Adequacy' (News Release, 29 December 2019), available at www.ndc.gov.tw/nc_27_33660.

[132] National Development Council, 'Statement by the National Development Council in response to the News Report on the EU General Data Protection Regulation and the Harmonisation of the Implementation of the Personal Data Protection Act' (News Release, 26 May 2021), www.ndc.gov.tw/nc_27_35015.

[133] ibid.

[134] Cybersecurity Management Act 2018, Art 1.

[135] ibid, Art 3(3).

[136] ibid, Art 3(5).

[137] ibid, Art 3(6).

amount and nature of information they hold or handle, as well as the size and nature of their cyber systems.[138]

In order to implement the Cybersecurity Management Act, public authorities shall appoint a director of cybersecurity, who should be appointed by the head of the organisation as deputy head or an appropriate officer, to be responsible for promoting and overseeing matters relating to cybersecurity within the organisation.[139]

Public authorities should provide information on the implementation of cybersecurity maintenance plans to their superiors or regulators on an annual basis.[140] They should also audit the implementation of the cybersecurity maintenance plan of their subordinate or supervising authorities.[141]

With respect to the cybersecurity management of specified non-public organisations, the relevant industry authority of the central Government shall, after consulting with relevant public authorities, private organisations, experts and scholars, designate the providers of essential facilities, report to the public authority for approval, and notify the approved providers of essential facilities in writing.[142]

The approved providers of essential facilities should comply with the requirements of their respective cybersecurity responsibility levels and consider the type, amount and nature of information they maintain or handle, as well as the size and nature of their cyber systems, to formulate, revise and implement a cybersecurity maintenance plan.[143]

The relevant industry authority of the central Government shall supervise the providers of essential facilities. In this regard, the Cybersecurity Management Act requires the providers of essential facilities to submit information on the implementation of the cybersecurity maintenance plan to the relevant industry authority of the central Government.[144]

The relevant industry authority of the central Government shall audit the implementation of the cybersecurity maintenance plan submitted by the providers of essential facilities. If there are any deficiencies, the authorities shall require the providers to submit an improvement report.[145]

In addition, the specified non-public organisations, other than the providers of essential facilities, should also meet the requirements of their respective security responsibility levels and formulate, amend and implement cybersecurity maintenance plans, taking into account the type, amount and nature of the information they maintain or handle, as well as the size and nature of their information systems.[146]

Similarly, the relevant industry authority of the central Government may also request these non-public organisations to provide information on the implementation of the cybersecurity maintenance plan. In the event that deficiencies or improvements are found,

[138] ibid, Art 10.
[139] ibid, Art 11.
[140] ibid, Art 12.
[141] ibid, Art 13(1).
[142] ibid, Art 16(1).
[143] ibid, Art 16(2).
[144] ibid, Art 16(3).
[145] ibid, Arts 16(4) and 16(5).
[146] ibid, Art 17(1).

the specified non-public organisations under audit should also be required to submit an improvement report by a certain date.[147]

If the specified non-public organisations fail to provide information on the implementation of the cybersecurity maintenance plan or fail to submit an improvement report by a certain date, the relevant industry authority of the central Government shall require the organisations to remedy the situation within a specified period of time. If the specified non-public organisations fail to make corrections within the specified period of time, they shall be subject to a fine of between NT$100,000 and NT$1,000,000 per occurrence.[148]

In addition, specified non-public organisations should establish a notification and emergency response mechanism for cybersecurity incidents. They should notify the relevant industry authority of the central Government when they become aware of a cybersecurity incident.[149] If a specified non-public organisation fails to report a cybersecurity incident, the relevant industry authority of the central Government shall impose a fine of between NT$300,000 and NT$5 million and order the organisation to make corrections within a specified period. Furthermore, the specified non-public organisation shall be subject to successive penalties if it fails to make corrections within the specified period.[150]

VI. Conclusion

The essence of privacy and personal data protection is to strike a balance between the protection of rights and the innovative use of data. This is an important issue in both academic research and judicial practice in Taiwan.

According to the third amendment to the Personal Information Protection Act, Taiwan will soon establish an independent Personal Information Protection Commission. It is worth anticipating and continuing to pay attention to its functions and role.

Taiwan should consult with other countries as soon as possible to reach a consensus on the protection and regulations of the international transfers of personal data.

[147] ibid, Arts 17(2) and 17(3).
[148] ibid, Art 20.
[149] ibid, Arts 18(1) and 18(2).
[150] ibid, Art 21.

7

Malaysia

NOOR MUZALIFAH BINTI SHABUDIN AND CHIA ENG YI

I. Introduction

The Personal Data Protection Act 2010 (PDPA) Malaysia was enacted in 2010 and came into force on 15 November 2013.[1] This piece of legislation marks a significant advancement for Malaysia in aligning with international data protection standards. It seeks to regulate personal data processing in commercial transactions, safeguarding the rights and interests of individuals whilst accommodating business requirements.

This chapter is divided into five sections. The first provides an overview of Malaysia's legislative framework for data protection through the enactment of the PDPA. The second explores legal bases, mechanisms, and exceptions for international data transfer and data protection under the PDPA. The third examines specific data security measures required under the PDPA and the impact of data localisation on businesses in Malaysia. The fourth analyses the PDPA in the context of private international law, including its applicability to foreign entities and cross-border enforcement of data protection rights. The final section addresses current issues and prospects, such as the integration of specific provisions for Artificial Intelligence under the PDPA, the effects of the COVID-19 pandemic and upcoming or anticipated regulatory updates.

In summary, this chapter aims to explore the complex landscape of data protection in Malaysia, offering an analysis of its legal frameworks, mechanisms, and the ongoing and future challenges in data protection under the PDPA.

II. General Legal Framework of International Data Transfers and Data Protection

A. Constitutional Protection for Data and Data Transfer

In Malaysia, the Federal Constitution of Malaysia (FC) does not explicitly outline or recognise the right to data protection. However, an implicit right to privacy arguably exists in

[1] Personal Data Protection Act 2010 (Act 709) (Malaysia) (PU(B) 464/2013).

Malaysia arising from (i) the broad interpretation of Article 5(1) of the FC and (ii) various statutes and regulations incorporating the term '*privacy*'. This includes the Births and Death Registration Act 1957, the Child Act 2001, the Law Reform (Marriage and Divorce) Act 1976, the Penal Code, the Private Healthcare Facilities and Services Act 1998 and the Private Hospitals Regulations 1973.

Article 5(1) of the FC reads as follows: 'No person shall be deprived of his life or personal liberty save in accordance with law.' Over the years, Article 5(1) has been interpreted on various occasions by the Malaysian courts including the apex courts, on the interpretation and scope of the word '*life*' In this regard, judicial precedents have broadly interpreted the word '*life*' to include several rights such as the right to privacy and the right of an aggrieved person to seek relief from the court,[2] The right to seek and maintain employment is protected, provided any termination must be justified and follow a fair process.[3]

In 1996 the Court of Appeal of Malaysia in *Tan Tek Seng v Suruhanjaya Perkhidmatan Pendidikan & Anor*[4] speaking through Justice Gopal Sri Ram held that Article 5(1) encompasses all aspects integral to life and those matters which go to form the quality of life. Article 5(1) does not expressly mention the right to privacy resulting in conflicting decisions regarding its recognition in Malaysia.[5]

In *Ultra Dimension Sdn Bhd v Kook Wei Kuan*,[6] the High Court held that the appellant's conduct in using a photograph of the respondent in an open area for advertisement purposes did not violate privacy rights. The respondent was found to not have the right to sue for invasion of privacy. This decision was also upheld by the Court of Appeal in *Dr Bernadine Malini Martin v MPH Magazine Sdn Bhd & Ors and Another Appeal*.[7] It was held that Malaysia does not recognise invasion of privacy as an actionable wrongdoing.

On the other hand, the right to privacy was first recognised by the Federal Court of Malaysia being the apex court in the case of *Sivarasa Rasiah v Badan Peguam Malaysia & Anor*.[8] In this case, the Federal Court held that 'It is patently clear from a review of the authorities that "personal liberty" in Article 5(1) includes within its compass other rights such as the right to privacy.' Nevertheless, this passage is merely obiter dicta as the issue before the Federal Court concerned the right to be a member of a statutorily created and regulated professional body.

Subsequently, in *Lew Cher Phow @ Lee Cha Paw & Ors v Pua Yong Yong & Anor*,[9] Justice Vernon Ong held that even though right to privacy is not explicitly mentioned in the FC, it does not preclude the court from recognising it as a legitimate right. The learned Judge emphasised that the right to privacy is recognised globally as a fundamental human right.

In the same vein, the Court of Appeal in *Muhammad Juzaili bin Mohd Khamis & Ors v State Government of Negeri Sembilan & Ors*[10] referred to the *Sivarasa* case, reiterated that 'personal liberty' under Article 5 of the FC included the right to privacy. Although this

[2] *Sugumar Balakrishnan v Pengarah Imigresen Negeri Sabah & Anor* [1998] 3 MLJ 289, CA.
[3] *Tan Tek Seng v Suruhanjaya Perkhidmatan Pendidikan & Anor* [1996] 1 MLJ 261, CA.
[4] *Tan Tek Seng v Suruhanjaya Perkhidmatan Pendidikan & Anor* [1996] 2 CLJ 771.
[5] *Toh See Wei v Teddric Jon Mohr & Anor* [2017] 11 MLJ 67, HC, [55].
[6] *Ultra Dimension Sdn Bhd v Kook Wei Kuan* [2004] 5 CLJ 285.
[7] *Dr Bernadine Malini Martin v MPH Magazine Sdn Bhd & Ors and Another Appeal* [2010] 7 CLJ 525.
[8] *Sivarasa Rasiah v Badan Peguam Malaysia & Anor* [2010] 2 MLJ 333.
[9] *Lew Cher Phow @ Lee Cha Paw & Ors v Pua Yong Yong & Anor* [2011] 1 LNS 1528.
[10] *Muhammad Juzaili bin Mohd Khamis & Ors v State Government of Negeri Sembilan & Ors* [2015] 3 MLJ 513.

case was reversed on appeal to the Federal Court on procedural grounds, the Federal Court did not disturb the findings of the Court of Appeal on this issue.[11] Therefore, the right to privacy is still recognised in Article 5(1) for all intents and purposes.[12]

In addition, in *Maria Chin Abdullah v Ketua Pengarah Imigresen & Anor*,[13] Justice Tun Tengku Maimun, the Chief Justice of Malaysia, in delivering the dissenting judgment of the Federal Court, emphasised that the right to privacy exists although not explicitly mentioned in the FC. It is important to note that this is a dissenting judgment of the Federal Court, and the judicial pronouncement is considered obiter dicta.

Notably, the High Court in *Genting Malaysia Bhd v Pesuruhjaya Perlindungan Data Peribadi & Ors*[14] reaffirmed the right to privacy as one of the constitutional rights in Malaysia. In this case, the Inland Revenue Board of Malaysia (IRB) requested personal data from Genting Malaysia Bhd (Genting Malaysia), a publicly listed company, to expand its tax base under section 81 of the Income Tax Act 1967 (ITA). Genting Malaysia refused, arguing it would violate section 39 of the PDPA, but the IRB obtained a letter from the Deputy Commissioner of Data Protection allowing the disclosure. Genting Malaysia then initiated judicial review proceedings before the High Court. The High Court allowed the judicial review application and held inter alia that the PDPA must take precedence over the ITA.

The decision of the High Court in *Genting Malaysia Bhd* affects data users in the following manner:

i. all data users, including Genting Malaysia Bhd are required to comply with the seven personal data protection principles defined in the PDPA, with specific regard to the Disclosure Principle outlined in sections 8, 39, and 45 of the PDPA;
ii. data users must carefully examine any data disclosure requests from government authorities or regulators, as these entities are generally not permitted to demand extensive amounts of personal data indiscriminately; and
iii. prior to fulfilling any data requests, data users must verify that the requests are lawful and satisfy the necessary criteria set by the High Court in the aforementioned case.

Notwithstanding the conflicting decisions on the recognition of privacy rights under the FC, several recent Federal Court decisions are consistent and instructive.[15] These decisions underscore a judicial commitment to protecting fundamental rights by inclusively interpreting the FC. This also indicates a trend towards acknowledging and reinforcing the right to privacy, demonstrating a clear judicial intent to align domestic legal principles with evolving international human rights norms. This approach not only solidifies the status of privacy as a key constitutional guarantee but also reflects the Court's proactive role in advancing and safeguarding individual liberties in the face of contemporary challenges.

[11] *State Government of Negeri Sembilan & Ors v Muhamad Juzaili bin Mohd Khamis & Ors* [2015] 6 MLJ 736, FC.

[12] Sheila Ramalingam, 'The Case for the Tort of Privacy in Malaysia [2023] 1 MLJ xlv' (2023) *Malayan Law Journal*, available at www.researchgate.net/publication/367654096_THE_CASE_FOR_THE_TORT_OF_PRIVACY_IN_MALAYSIA.

[13] *Maria Chin Abdullah v Ketua Pengarah Imigresen & Anor* [2021] 1 MLJ 750, FC.

[14] *Genting Malaysia Bhd v Pesuruhjaya Perlindungan Data Peribadi & Ors* [2022] 4 CLJ 399.

[15] *Maria Chin Abdullah* (n 13). *Zaidi bin Kanapiah v ASP Khairul Fairoz bin Rodzuan and other cases* [2021] 3 MLJ 759, FC.

Notwithstanding this, on 29 April 2024, the Court of Appeal overturned the decision of the High Court by way of Civil Appeal No W-01(A)-449-08/2021. On 28 May 2024, aggrieved by the decision of the Court of Appeal, Genting Malaysia applied for leave to appeal to the Federal Court against the entire decision of the Court of Appeal. There is also an application for a stay arising from the decision of the Court of Appeal. The questions of law posed in the leave question that pertain to the PDPA are inter-alia as follows:

1. Whether the Director General of Inland Revenue (hereinafter referred to as 'DGIR') can compel a 'data user', such as the Applicant (hereinafter referred to as 'Data User'), to disclose personal data (hereinafter referred to as 'Personal Data') pertaining to its customers (hereinafter referred to as 'Customers'), which falls within the definition of 'personal data' in Section 4 of the Personal Data Protection Act 2010 (hereinafter referred to as 'PDPA'), under Section 39(b)(i), Section 39(b)(ii) or Section 45(2)(a) of the PDPA read together with Section 81 of the Income Tax Act 1967 (hereinafter referred to as '**ITA**') without obtaining the prior, specific and express consent of the Customers (hereinafter referred to as 'Customers' Consent');
2. Whether the DGIR can disregard the Personal Data Protection Principles provided under Section 5(1) of the PDPA (hereinafter referred to as 'the Protection Principles'), by requesting or demanding access to, or disclosure of, Customers' Personal Data from Data Users such as the Applicant, or to otherwise process such Personal Data (hereinafter referred to as 'the DGIR's Demands'), without obtaining the Customers' Consent or without having demonstrated the existence of a reasonable suspicion by the DGIR that any specific, identified and/or identifiable Customer had not complied with any material provision of the ITA relating to the assessment or collection of tax warranting a disclosure of such Personal Data of that particular Customer, and/or without the DGIR establishing that there is no real, actual or substantive prejudice against the purposes for which such Personal Data had been collected by the Applicant to the satisfaction of the High Court as evidenced by an appropriate court order for disclosure to the DGIR;
3. Whether the Protection Principles, in particular Section 8 of the PDPA, require Data Users such as the Applicant to reject the DGIR's Demands made under Part V/Section 81 of the ITA, until and unless the Customers' Consent is obtained by the DGIR or the DGIR has demonstrated that there is reasonable suspicion that any specific, identified and/or identifiable Customer had not complied with any material provision of the ITA relating to the assessment or collection of tax warranting a disclosure of the Personal Data of that particular Customer, and/or the DGIR has established that there is no real, actual and substantive prejudice against the purposes for which such Personal Data had been collected by the Applicant to the satisfaction of the High Court as evidenced by an appropriate court order for disclosure to the DGIR;
4. Whether the DGIR's various requests or demands for the Personal Data was a blanket request with the sole intention of 'fishing' for the Customers' Personal Data since it was not supported by any reasonable suspicion of any misconduct or criminal conduct on the part of any particular/identified Customer of the Applicant;
5. Whether the DGIR may request information other than a taxpayer's tax returns under Section 81 of the ITA, which section is contained in Part V of the ITA with the heading 'Returns';
6. Where Section 81 of the ITA is capable of two alternative meanings, whether the construction most favourable to taxpayers should be adopted, in light of the Court of Appeal's decision in Exxon Chemical (M) Sdn Bhd v. Ketua Pengarah Hasii Dalam Negeri [2006] 1 MLJ 428;

7. Whether the Federal Court's decision in Bar Malaysia v. Ketua Pengarah Hasil Dalam Negeri [2018] 9 MLJ 557 (hereinafter referred to as 'Malaysian Bar case') which found that the DGIR had used the ITA as an 'engine of fraud' and held that the DGIR should not be allowed to use the provisions of the ITA to go on unlawful 'fishing expeditions', is binding upon the DGIR in this case;
8. Whether disclosures of personal data under Section 39(b)(i) of the PDPA are only permitted if the Data User is able to demonstrate the necessity for preventing or detecting a crime or for the purposes of investigations;
9. Whether disclosures of personal data under Section 39(b)(ii) of the PDPA are only permitted if the Data User is able to demonstrate that it is required or authorised by law to disclose such Personal Data;
10. Whether Section 45(2)(iii) of the PDPA applies to the DGIR;
11. Whether the choice/prerogative as to whether or not to disclose the Personal Data under Section 39 and/or Section 45 of the PDPA ought to be exercised by the Data User or the requesting administrative authority such as the DGIR;
12. Whether the Latin maxim 'generalia specialibus non derogant' (the provisions of a specific Act prevail over the provisions of a general Act to the extent of any inconsistency), which was applied in the Malaysian Bar case, applies to the present scenario such that the relevant PDPA provisions, being the provisions of a specific Act enacted for the protection of Personal Data, should prevail over the general provisions of the ITA including Section 81;
13. When in doubt or in the case of conflict, whether priority should be given to the ITA or the PDPA, which is a specific legislation enacted much later than the ITA;
14. In the event Section 81 of the ITA prevails over the Protection Principles under the PDPA, whether the rights and interests of individuals whose Personal Data is being processed (hereinafter referred to as 'Data Subjects') would be prejudiced and whether such interpretation can stand by virtue of the supremacy of Article 5 of the Federal Constitution which protects privacy rights;
15. Whether the DGIR, as a tax collector, is competent to make decisions relating to Personal Data or to interpret the PDPA;
16. Whether acceding to the DGIR's Demands would defeat the mandatory Protection Principles legislated expressly to protect Data Subjects and cause the Data Users to be in breach of the mandatory obligations under the PDPA, including the Protection Principles;
17. Whether the refusal or failure to accede to the DGIR's Demands can subject the Data User to penalties and/or other sanctions under another piece of legislation, such as the ITA; and
18. Whether the Commissioner would be able to properly fulfil their statutory duty and function under the PDPA, including its duty and responsibility to implement and enforce the PDPA pursuant to Section 48 of the PDPA, if the Personal Data is released en masse to the DGIR, without obtaining the Customers' Consent or without the DGIR having demonstrated the existence of a reasonable suspicion that any specific, identified and/or identifiable Customer had not complied with any material provision of the ITA relating to the assessment or collection of tax warranting a disclosure of such Personal Data of that particular Customer, and/or without the DGIR establishing that there is no real, actual or substantive prejudice against the purposes for which such Personal Data had been collected by the Applicant to the satisfaction of the High Court as evidenced by an appropriate court order for disclosure to the DGIR.

It remains to be seen whether the Federal Court will allow the application for leave to appeal and eventually, the appeal.

B. Statutory Frameworks for Data Transfer and Protection

The PDPA serves as Malaysia's primary legislation for protecting personal data. Key provisions of the PDPA include:

i. the requirement for consent before processing personal data, the necessity of informing data subjects about the purpose of data collection and restrictions on data disclosure without the data subject's consent.[16]
ii. data users must take appropriate security measures to protect personal data from loss, misuse, unauthorised access, modification or disclosure.[17]
iii. data should not be retained longer than necessary[18] and data subjects have the right to access and correct their personal data.[19]
iv. imposes strict conditions on the transfer of personal data outside Malaysia, ensuring that the data remains protected.[20]

Furthermore, several subsidiary legislations have been enacted and passed including the following:

i. the Personal Data Protection Regulations 2013, in force from 15 November 2013 (PDP Regulations 2013);[21]
ii. the Personal Data Protection (Class of Data Users) Order 2013, in force from 15 November 2013 (PDP Class Order 2013);[22]
iii. the Personal Data Protection (Registration of Data User) Regulations 2013, in force from 15 November 2013;[23]
iv. the Personal Data Protection (Fees) Regulations 2013, in force from 15 November 2013;[24]
v. the Personal Data Protection (Compounding of Offences) Regulations 2016, in force from 15 March 2016;[25]
vi. the Personal Data Protection (Class of Data Users) (Amendment) Order 2016, in force from 16 December 2016;[26] and
vii. the Personal Data Protection (Appeal Tribunal) Regulations 2021, in force from 15 April 2021.[27]

Apart from the PDPA and the subsidiary legislations above, the Personal Data Protection Commissioner, as defined under section 47 of the PDPA, issued the Personal Data Protection Standard 2015 (PDP Standard 2015).

[16] PDPA, ss 6 to 11.
[17] ibid, s 9.
[18] ibid, s 10.
[19] ibid, ss 12 to 17.
[20] ibid, ss 129 to 133.
[21] PU(A) 335/2013.
[22] PU(A) 336/2013.
[23] PU(A) 337/2013.
[24] PU(A) 338/2013.
[25] PU(A) 60/2016.
[26] PU(A) 326/2016.
[27] PU(A) 168/2021.

In addition, several other statutes and guidelines contribute to the data protection landscape in Malaysia. The Communications and Multimedia Act 1998 (CMA) regulates the communications and multimedia industry in Malaysia, addressing issues related to data privacy and security in electronic communications. The Computer Crimes Act 1997 addresses cybercrimes, including unauthorised access to computer material and modification of computer contents, indirectly supporting data protection efforts. Additionally, regulatory bodies such as the Central Bank of Malaysia (BNM) and the Securities Commission (SC), have issued guidelines incorporating data protection provisions relevant to their sectors.

It is important to note that the PDPA, with its limited scope and broad exemptions, applies directly to data users and indirectly to personal data in commercial transactions. Section 2(1) states that the PDPA governs anyone who processes or controls personal data, including both manual and electronic data linked to natural persons. The PDPA applies to all commercial transactions including formal and informal agreements.[28]

The PDPA applies to data users in Malaysia including local users who outsource data processing and foreign users with local equipment as long as they have a representative in Malaysia.[29] However, companies merely transiting personal data through Malaysia are exempted from the PDPA as provided under section 2(2)(b) of the PDPA.

C. Data Protection Frameworks

i. Influence of International Data Protection Frameworks

The PDPA is founded on seven fundamental data protection principles. General Principle,[30] Notice and Choice Principle,[31] Disclosure Principle,[32] Security Principle,[33] Retention Principle,[34] Data Integrity Principle[35] and Access Principle.[36] These principles are greatly influenced by the European Union (EU) Data Protection Directive (DPD), which has been repealed and was replaced by the European Union's (EU) General Data Protection Regulation (GDPR) on 14 April 2016.[37] These principles have been further explained in the PDP Regulations 2013.

Besides that, the PDPA is also influenced by the Asia-Pacific Economic Cooperation Privacy Framework (APEC). According to section 10 of APEC, personal data used in connection with an individual's personal, family or household affairs is excluded from the regulations.

[28] ibid, s 4.
[29] ibid, s 2(2).
[30] ibid, s 6.
[31] ibid, s 7.
[32] ibid, s 8.
[33] ibid, s 9(1).
[34] ibid, s 10.
[35] ibid, s 11.
[36] ibid, s 12.
[37] Directive 95/46/EC of the European Parliament and of the Council of 24 October 1995 on the protection of individuals with regard to the processing of personal data and on the free movement of such data [1995] OJ L281/31.

In other words, affairs that are not commercial are excluded from the ambit of the act. This principle can be seen in section 45(1) of the PDPA, where the act has exempted personal, family and household affairs for recreational purposes from its application. For instance, a personal telephone notebook containing the names and phone numbers of friends, relatives or others will fall under this exemption.[38]

In addition, the PDPA aligns with the EU's GDPR in granting data subjects several rights. These include the right to be informed about data processing activities, mainly when it involves profiling-based decision-making. In such cases, the data controllers must explain that the processing requires profiling and making decisions based on the generated profiles.[39] Data subjects also have the right to access their personal data used for profiling,[40] rectify inaccuracies,[41] request data erasure,[42] and object to processing, including profiling.[43]

ii. Specific Provisions for Particular Sectors

PDP Class Order 2013 delineates 13 distinct classes of data users required to register under the PDPA Malaysia including sectors such as communications, banking, financial institutions, insurance, health, tourism, hospitality, transportation, education, direct selling, service providers, real estate, utilities, pawnbrokers and moneylenders. These classifications are informed by the relevant governing legislation specific to each sector.

Section 21 of the PDPA provides that the Commissioner is empowered to designate an organisation as a data user forum for a specific class of data users, setting out the conditions within which it operates. following this designation, the data user forum is authorised to independently develop, or at the request of the Commissioner, a code of practice as outlined in section 23 of the PDPA. As of the latest update, codes of practice have been established for the following sectors:

i. the Code of Practice on the Personal Data Protection for the Insurance and Takaful Industry in Malaysia, in force from 23 December 2016;
ii. the Personal Data Protection Code of Practice for the Malaysia Aviation Sector, in force from 21 November 2017;
iii. the Personal Data Protection Code of Practice for the Utilities Sector (Electricity), in force from 23 June 2016;
iv. the Personal Data Protection Code of Practice for the Banking and Financial Sector, in force from 19 January 2017;
v. the Personal Data Protection Code of Practice for the Utilities Sector (Electricity) 2.0, in force from 21 January 2020;
vi. the Personal Data Protection Code of Practice for the Utilities Sector (Water); and
vii. the Personal Data Protection Code of Practice for Private Hospitals in the Healthcare Industry.

[38] Ali Alibeigi and Abu Bakar Munir, 'Malaysian Personal Data Protection Act, a Mysterious Application' (2020) *University of Bologna Law Review*, available at ssrn.com/abstract=3792672.

[39] GDPR, Art 13(2)(f).

[40] ibid, Art 15.

[41] ibid, Art 16.

[42] ibid, Art 17.

[43] ibid, Art 21(1).

For data users not covered under section 23 PDPA, Section 24 allows the Commissioner to issue a code of practice, contingent on meeting certain requirements. On 15 December 2022, the Commissioner issued the General Code of Practice for Personal Data Protection. Paragraph 1.2 of the General Code provides that non-compliance is punishable by a fine of up to RM100,000.00 and/or imprisonment for a term not exceeding one year.

Apart from the PDPA, data protection in Malaysia is governed by other regulations and guidelines including the Credit Reporting Agencies Act 2010 (CRRA),[44] the General Consumer Code of Practice for the Communications and Multimedia Industry Malaysia (GCC), and Guidelines on Data Management (DM) and Management Information System (MIS) Framework.

Under section 4 of the PDPA, personal data processed by credit reporting agencies are exempted from the application of the PDPA. These credit reporting agencies fall under the jurisdiction of the CRRA. Recently, the High Court in *Genting Malaysia Bhd* case affirmed that the PDPA excludes credit information handled by such agencies as per section 4 of the PDPA and section 76 of the CRRA, however, the High Court's decision has been overturned by the Court of Appeal.

GCC is a guideline issued by the Malaysian Communications and Multimedia Commission (MCMC) in October 2003. It seeks to provide model procedures for the protection of consumer information.[45] The GCC applies to all licensed and non-licensed service providers who are members of the consumer forum as defined by the CM.[46]

In 2020, the Communications and Multimedia Consumer Forum of Malaysia (CFM), established under section 189 of the CMA by MCMC in 2001, proposed amendments to the GCC.[47] The revised GCC, detailed in CFM's 2020 Annual Report, was submitted to MCMC for approval on 30 November 2020 and officially registered in November 2022.

Significant updates include enhanced protections for consumers with special needs,[48] a requirement for service providers to disclose direct carrier billing charges,[49] and mandatory notification to subscribers before contract renewal or variation.[50]

The Guidelines on DM and MIS Framework mandate that development financial institutions (DFIs) implement effective data management and management information systems in line with their business and risk strategies.[51] As required under the Development Financial Institutions Act 2002,[52] these guidelines encompass principles of data governance, architecture, and internal controls.[53] To protect data, DFIs must secure data integrity, establish data classification policies, restrict access based on necessity, and ensure compliance with privacy laws through rigorous monitoring and legal safeguards for third-party access.

[44] Credit Reporting Agencies Act 2010 (Act 710) [PU(B) 12/2014].
[45] GCC 2003, cl 5.1(d).
[46] ibid, cl 6.
[47] 'Public Consultation for General Consumer Code of Practice for the Communications and Multimedia Industry 2020' (Bernama, 3 March 2020), available at www.kkd.gov.my/en/public/news/16563-bernama-03-march-2020-public-consultation-for-general-consumer-code-of-practice-for-the-communications-and-multimedia-industry-2020.
[48] GCC 2022, cl 2.3.
[49] ibid, cl 3.2.1(d)(iii).
[50] ibid, cl 4.5.
[51] Guidelines on DM and MIS Framework, cl 4.2.
[52] ibid, cl 2.1.
[53] ibid, cl 4.1.

iii. Distinction between Data Protection and Privacy

The FC or the PDPA do not expressly distinguish data protection from privacy. However, data protection and privacy concepts are closely connected. The right to privacy in Malaysia extends beyond data protection under the PDPA. For instance, the invasion of privacy may include the unauthorised publication of an individual for commercial purposes. This can be seen in the case of *Dr Bernadine Malini Martin v MPH Magazine Sdn Bhd and another appeal* [2010] 5 MLJ 75. Despite the acknowledgment by the Court of Appeal that the authorised publication amounts to an invasion of privacy, the appeal was dismissed since an invasion of privacy is not an actionable tort.

iv. Distinction between 'Data Users', 'Data Subjects', and 'Data Processors'

The terms 'data user', 'data subject' and 'data processor' are defined in section 4 of the PDPA as follows:

i. 'Data user' means a person who either alone or jointly or in common with other persons processes any personal data or has control over or authorises the processing of any personal data, but does not include a data processor;
ii. 'Data subject' means an individual who is the subject of the personal data; and
iii. 'Data processor' means in relation to personal data, means any person, other than an employee of the data user, who processes the personal data solely on behalf of the data user, and does not process the personal data for any of his own purposes.

Based on the interpretation above, the distinction between a data user, data subject, and data processor is primarily based on their roles and responsibilities in handling personal data. A data user is an entity or an individual who controls, authorises, or processes personal data, making decisions about its use, but does not act as a data processor. In contrast, the data subject is the individual to whom the personal data pertains, possessing rights over their data such as access and correction. A data subject is also an individual who is the personal data subject, which suggests that a data subject is a natural living person and cannot be a corporation. This can be seen in *Newlake Development Sdn Bhd v Zenith Delight Sdn Bhd & Ors*,[54] where the High Court held that disclosure of the bank statements by the first defendant was not an offence under the PDPA. The first defendant was a corporate entity. Hence, the PDPA does not apply according to section 4 of the PDPA.

Meanwhile, data processor processes personal data solely on behalf of the data user, following their instructions without any independent control or use of the data for their purposes, typically functioning as a third-party service provider. Therefore, it is noted that the PDPA imposes duties and obligations upon the data user and not the data processor. Thus, for data users who outsource some of their operations involving personal data processing, it is essential to ensure that the data processor complies with the law. Consequently, the data user can be held liable for an action by the data processor as evident in section 9(2) of the PDPA.

[54] *Newlake Development Sdn Bhd v Zenith Delight Sdn Bhd & Ors* [2021] 11 MLJ 729.

v. Distinction between Personal and Non-Personal Data

The 'personal data' in section 4 of the PDPA includes 'expression of opinion about the data subject'. The Oxford English Dictionary defines 'opinion' as 'what or how one thinks about something, judgment or belief'. Opinions embody aspects of feelings or thoughts about a matter rather than a systematic analysis of facts or data. By its definition, some human input is required.[55]

For data to be classified as 'personal data', according to section 4 of the PDPA, the data must relate directly or indirectly to a data subject, who is identified or identifiable from that information or other information in the possession of a data user. To determine whether data (electronic or manual) is 'personal data', several questions should be posed, among others: Can an individual be identified from the data or the data in the possession of the data user? An individual is 'identified' if someone has been distinguished from other group members. If the answer is 'yes', it is likely that the data is personal data.[56] Examples of personal data include name, age, date of birth, physical and email addresses, telephone number, national registration identity card number, employees' provident fund number, passport number, social security organisation number, driving licence number, bank card number and internet protocol address.[57]

vi. Distinction between Domestic and Cross-Border/International Transfers

Section 129 of the PDPA prohibits the transfer of personal data outside Malaysia unless protection is guaranteed.[58] The PDPA does not define transfer. The Organisation for Economic Co-operation and Development (OECD) Guidelines use the term 'transborder flows of personal data', which refers to movements of personal data across national borders.

In Malaysia, the Minister will specify the countries where personal data can be transferred through a 'white list'. In 2017, the Minister drafted a 'white list' through the Public Consultation Paper (PCP) Personal Data Protection (Transfer of Personal Data to Places Outside Malaysia) No 1/2017. Several countries had been listed in this draft white list, including European Economic Area (EEA) member countries, the United Kingdom (UK), the United States of America (US), Canada, Switzerland, and New Zealand.

It is important to note that the Minister is required to follow the conditions laid down in section 129(2) of the PDPA before choosing the country. The conditions are: (a) the country has a law that is 'substantially similar to' the PDPA, or that 'serves the same purposes' as the PDPA, or (b) the country otherwise ensures a level of protection about the processing of personal data that is 'at least equivalent to the level of protection afforded' by the PDPA.

[55] Tay Pek San, 'The Impact of the Personal Data Protection Act 2010 on Data Analytics in the Retail Industry' (2020) *The Malayan Law Journal* lxii–lxxxiii.

[56] Abu Bakar Munir and Siti Hajar Mohd Yasin, *Personal Data Protection in Malaysia Law and Practice* (Sweet & Maxwell Asia, 2010).

[57] Tay Pek San (n 54).

[58] See PDPA, s 129(1): 'A data user shall not transfer any personal data of a data subject to a place outside Malaysia unless to such place as specified by the Minister, upon the recommendation of the Commissioner, by notification published in the Gazette'.

Until the white list is finalised and published in the Gazette, data users must continue to rely on the exemptions provided in section 129(3) of the PDPA when transferring personal data outside Malaysia. At present, Malaysia has not gazetted any white list of certified countries for data transfer beyond the borders.[59]

vii. Privacy Regulator and its Sanctioning Powers

The Department of Personal Data Protection (DPDP) is led by a Commissioner whom the Minister appoints under section 47(1) of the PDPA. The Commissioner is entrusted with certain powers to enforce the PDPA, including preparing functional procedures and policies.[60] Aside from the appointment, the Minister also has the right to revoke the appointment of the Commissioner. Thus, the Minister has the power to hire and replace the Commissioner. Under section 49 of the PDPA, the Commissioner shall have the power to perform all things essential, convenient, incidental or consequential to perform his functions under the PDPA.

Sections 104 and 105 of the PDPA granted the Commissioner the ability to investigate possible breaches of the PDPA upon a complaint from an individual or on its initiative. While section 104 requires the complaint to be written in writing, section 105 allows the Commissioner, on its initiative, to investigate if there are reasonable grounds to believe such contravention existed. In contrast with section 105, the investigation under section 106(1) is not mandatory due to the term 'may'. Section 106(1) of the PDPA further provides a long list covering the situation where the Commissioner may refuse to investigate an incident initiated by a complainant.

Under section 108(1) of the PDPA, the Commissioner may serve the data user an enforcement notice if he believes that the data user has breached the provisions under the PDPA. It is undisputed that section 108(2) of the PDPA mentioned that the Commissioner must consider whether the data subject suffered any damages following the data user's breach of the PDPA before serving the enforcement of notice. However, the decision to serve the data user with an enforcement notice is entirely at the discretion of the Commissioner.[61]

Moreover, the Commissioner may exercise numerous other powers, including refusing registration for a data user,[62] refusing to renew the registration,[63] revoking registration for the data users,[64] carrying out inspections on the personal data systems of the data users,[65] and publishing reports setting out the recommendations resulting from the inspection users.[66]

In a similar vein, the Commissioner's authorised public officers are also empowered with certain powers, such as conducting investigations of any offence under the PDPA users,[67]

[59] Nurkhairina Binti Noor Sureani and others, 'The Adequacy of Data Protection Laws in Protecting Personal Data in Malaysia' (2021) *Malaysian Journal of Social Sciences and Humanities* 6, 10.

[60] PDPA, s 48(2).

[61] Abu Bakar Munir and Siti Hajar Mohd Yasin (n 55).

[62] PDPA, s 16(1)(b).

[63] ibid, s 17(3).

[64] ibid, s 18(1).

[65] ibid, s 101.

[66] ibid, s 103.

[67] ibid, s 112.

conducting search and seizure on equipment, systems, electronic data, records and properties of the data user with or without a warrant,[68] requiring the production of any computer, book, account, computerised data or other document kept by the data user or any other person and to inspect, examine and to download from them, make copies of them or take extracts from the data users,[69] and arresting any alleged person without a warrant who has allegedly committed or attempted to commit an offence under the PDPA.[70]

III. Legal Bases, Mechanisms and Exceptions for International Data Transfers and Data Protection

A. International Data Transfer

i. Adequacy Findings or White Lists

Section 129 of the PDPA governs the transfer of personal data to jurisdictions outside Malaysia.[71] Unlike the GDPR, which maintains an official 'white list' of countries with adequate data protection standards, as stated above, Malaysia does not have a pre-approved list of jurisdictions deemed to have equivalent data protection laws. In this regard, section 129 of the PDPA prohibits any transfer of personal data outside of Malaysia unless the protection of the personal data is guaranteed.

Under section 129(1), a data user is prohibited from transferring personal data abroad unless the destination is specified by the Minister. Section 129(2) of the PDPA provides the consideration to be taken into account by the Minister in making this determination as follows:

i. there is in that specified place by the Minister in force any law which is substantially similar to the PDPA, or that serves the same purposes of the PDPA; or
ii. the specified place by the Minister ensures an adequate level of protection in relation to the processing of personal data which is at least equivalent to the level of protection afforded by the PDPA.

In 2017, the Minister published a draft 'white list' for public consultation, which included EU/EEA countries, the UK, the US, Canada, Switzerland, and New Zealand. However, as of 3 June 2024, this list has not been finalised or published in the official Gazette. Until then, data users must rely on the exceptions under section 129(3) when transferring personal data abroad.

In view of the foregoing, section 129 of the PDPA, which regulates the transfer of personal data outside Malaysia, underscores the country's commitment to maintaining high data protection standards. Unlike the GDPR, Malaysia does not have a pre-approved list of countries with equivalent data protection laws, placing the responsibility on the

[68] ibid, ss 113 and 114.
[69] ibid, s 121.
[70] ibid, s 127.
[71] ibid, s 129.

Minister to designate acceptable jurisdictions. This case-by-case approach ensures that each foreign jurisdiction is carefully evaluated to meet or exceed the protection levels provided by the PDPA. By focusing on substantial similarity or equivalent protection, Malaysia aims to uphold rigorous data privacy standards, providing robust protection for personal data transferred abroad while allowing for tailored assessments that ensure compliance with national regulations. However, this process may introduce some uncertainty and potential delays for businesses needing to transfer data internationally. These issues may be mitigated by the exceptions outlined in section 129(3) of the PDPA – which are the exceptions to section 129(1) of the PDPA, which will be discussed further below.

ii. Consent of Data Subjects

Section 129(3)(a) of the PDPA stipulates that a data user, defined as any person who processes personal data or has control over or authorises the processing of personal data, is permitted to transfer personal data to a location outside of Malaysia. This transfer is legally permissible provided that the data subject, the individual to whom the personal data belongs, has given their explicit consent to the transfer. The consent from the data subject must be informed, meaning they should be fully aware of the nature of the data being transferred, the destination of the transfer, and any potential risks involved in such a transfer.

The provision in section 129(3)(a) of the PDPA ensures that the data subject's consent can override certain restrictions on data transfers, thus granting them significant control over their personal data. This provision is particularly important in the context of international data transfers, as it provides a clear legal pathway for data users to transfer personal data across borders with the explicit approval of the data subjects.

This consent-based transfer mechanism operates alongside the regulatory framework established under section 129(1) of the PDPA. Section 129(1) grants the Minister the authority to specify and periodically update a list of locations outside Malaysia that are approved for data transfers. These locations are deemed by the Minister to have adequate levels of data protection in place. Consequently, data transfers to these specified locations can occur without requiring additional consent, as they are pre-approved destinations based on their data protection standards.

However, the exception provided in section 129(3)(a) allows for greater flexibility. Even if a destination is not on the list of approved locations specified by the Minister, the transfer can still take place if the data subject consents to it. This provision acknowledges the autonomy of data subjects, allowing them to make informed decisions about their personal data irrespective of the Minister's list. This dual mechanism ensures both regulatory oversight and personal autonomy in the context of international data transfers, balancing the need for data protection with the facilitation of global data flows.

iii. Contracts

Section 129(3)(b) and (c) of the PDPA provide additional circumstances under which personal data can be transferred outside of Malaysia. Specifically, section 129(3)(b) allows for such a transfer when it is necessary for the performance of a contract between the data subject and the data user. This means that if an individual has entered into an agreement with a company or organisation that necessitates the transfer of their personal data to a foreign location for the fulfilment of contractual obligations, such a transfer is permissible under the PDPA. This provision underscores the practical need for data mobility in an increasingly globalised economy where services and obligations often cross national borders.

Furthermore, section 129(3)(c) extends the scope of permissible data transfers to include scenarios where the transfer is necessary for the conclusion or performance of a contract between the data user and a third party, provided this is at the request of the data subject or in their interest. This clause is significant because it acknowledges the complexities of modern contractual relationships, which frequently involve multiple parties across different jurisdictions. By allowing data transfers that facilitate these complex arrangements, the PDPA accommodates the operational realities of multinational business engagements, ensuring that data flows can support rather than hinder commercial activities and contractual obligations.

Critically, these provisions reflect a balance between the need for stringent data protection and the practical necessities of international commerce. While they provide necessary flexibility for businesses to operate efficiently on a global scale, they also ensure that such data transfers are justified and aligned with the interests of the data subject. This balance is crucial in maintaining the integrity of personal data protection while not stifling economic activity. However, the reliance on the necessity of contractual performance as a basis for data transfer places a significant onus on businesses to demonstrate this necessity, which may require robust documentation and clear contractual terms to avoid potential legal disputes.

To ensure clarity and legal certainty in contracts, it is essential to explicitly specify the governing law and dispute resolution mechanisms. This will clarify whether the PDPA or a foreign law applies, define the legal framework for the contractual obligations and designate the arbitration seat or jurisdictional court. Such specifics help avoid jurisdictional conflicts, streamline dispute resolution and ensure that disputes are resolved in a predetermined forum. This approach not only mitigates risks but ensures compliance with data protection standards and addresses potential conflicts with foreign laws.

B. International Data Protection and Liability

i. Specific Requirements or Policies for Data Processing and Retention

The PDPA sets out specific requirements for data processing and retention to ensure that personal data is handled in a manner that respects the rights of data subjects and maintains the integrity and security of the data. These requirements encompass various stages of the data lifecycle, from collection and processing to storage and eventual disposal.

Under the PDPA, personal data must be processed fairly and lawfully. Organisations are required to obtain the data subject's consent before processing their personal data, except in specific circumstances where consent is not necessary (eg, for the performance of a contract or compliance with legal obligations). Additionally, organisations must ensure that the data is processed for purposes directly related to the purpose for which the data was collected and that the processing is proportionate to that purpose.

The PDPA mandates that personal data should not be retained longer than necessary to fulfil the purpose for which it was collected. Organisations must establish and implement data retention policies that specify the retention period for different categories of personal data. Once the retention period has expired, the data must be securely deleted or anonymised to prevent unauthorised access or misuse.

ii. Data Subjects' Entitlement to Data Protection and Privacy Rights

The PDPA grants data subjects in Malaysia several rights concerning their personal data. These rights empower individuals to control and protect their personal information and to seek redress for any misuse or unauthorised processing of their data.

Data subjects must be informed about the collection and use of their personal data, as outlined in section 7 of the PDPA. This section requires data users to provide clear information on the purpose of data collection, the sources of the data, and any third parties to whom the data may be disclosed. This transparency helps individuals understand how their personal information is being used and shared.

Additionally, section 30 of the PDPA grants data subjects the right to access their personal data held by data users. This includes the right to obtain a copy of their data and details about the processing activities. Data users are required to respond to access requests within 21 days, ensuring that individuals can review their data promptly and maintain transparency.

Furthermore, section 34 of the PDPA allows data subjects to request corrections to their personal data if it is inaccurate, incomplete, misleading, or outdated. This provision ensures that data users maintain accurate and up-to-date information about data subjects, which is crucial for both the data subject's interests and the integrity of the data user's operations.

Section 38 of the PDPA provides that a data subject may by notice in writing, withdraw his consent to the processing of personal data in respect of which he is a data subject. Sections 42 and 43 of the PDPA provide data subjects with the right to prevent processing that is likely to cause substantial and unwarranted damage or distress. Data subjects can request the cessation of such processing, and data users must take appropriate action to mitigate any adverse effects.

Section 43(1) of the PDPA specifically allows data subjects to object to the processing of their personal data for direct marketing purposes. This empowers individuals to control how their data is used for marketing and ensures they are not subject to unsolicited marketing communications.

Lastly, section 93 of the PDPA and subsequent sections detail the process for data subjects to lodge complaints with the Personal Data Protection Commissioner if they believe their rights under the PDPA have been violated. This provides a mechanism for data subjects to seek redress and hold data users accountable for non-compliance.

As the PDPA was enacted based on the GDPR, consequently the rights outlined earlier mirror to an extent those under the GDPR.

iii. Anti-Doxxing Regulations

While Malaysia does not have specific anti-doxxing laws, the PDPA and other relevant legislation provide mechanisms to address the unauthorised publication of personal data.

Doxxing, which involves the malicious release of someone's private information without consent, can lead to harassment, identity theft, and other harmful consequences.

In this regard, section 130(1) of the PDPA stipulates that a person shall not knowingly or recklessly, without the consent of the data user: (a) collect or disclose personal data that is held by the data user; or (b) procure the disclosure to another person of personal data that is held by the data user. Additionally, section 130(5) of the PDPA provides that a person who commits an offence under section 130 shall be liable to a fine not exceeding RM500,000.00, or imprisonment for a term not exceeding three years, or both fine and imprisonment.

These provisions are designed to protect the personal data handled by data users (typically organisations and businesses) from unauthorised access and dissemination. By prohibiting the unauthorised collection and disclosure of personal data, these sections of the PDPA help ensure that personal data is kept secure and used appropriately, thus indirectly addressing concerns related to doxxing. However, it is important to note that while the PDPA provides mechanisms to safeguard personal data, as stated above, the PDPA is more focused on data protection in a commercial context and may not specifically target individual actions such as doxxing.

The MCMC can also take action against individuals who engage in doxxing under CMA. In this regard, section 233(1) of the CMA prohibits the improper use of network facilities or services, including the publication of obscene, indecent, false, menacing, or offensive content. Doxxing, which often involves the dissemination of harmful or malicious content, can be addressed under these provisions. Section 233(3) further provides that a person who commits an offence under section 233 shall be liable to a fine not exceeding RM50,000.00 or to imprisonment for a term not exceeding one year or to both and shall also be liable to a further fine of RM1,000.00 for every day during which the offence is continued after conviction.

iv. Extraterritorial Effect of Data Protection Laws

The extraterritorial application of data protection laws is a critical consideration in the context of global data flows. The PDPA primarily applies to data users established in Malaysia, meaning that Malaysian organisations must comply with its provisions when processing personal data. However, the PDPA also has limited extraterritorial effect, extending its reach to certain foreign entities.

Section 2(2) of the PDPA provides that the PDPA applies to a person in respect of personal data if:

i. the person is established in Malaysia and the personal data is processed, whether or not in the context of that establishment, by that person or any other person employed or engaged by that establishment; or
ii. the person is not established in Malaysia but uses equipment in Malaysia for processing personal data otherwise than for the purposes of transit through Malaysia.

The term 'person' is not defined in the PDPA. Reference is made to section 3 of the Interpretation Acts 1948 and 1967 (Act 388), which provides that 'person' includes a body of persons, corporate or unincorporated. Accordingly, the PDPA is applicable to any individual or corporate entity in Malaysia if the personal data is processed within the country.

For foreign individuals or corporate entities, the PDPA applies if they use equipment in Malaysia for processing personal data.

The PDPA applies to foreign entities that process personal data in Malaysia. This includes situations where a foreign organisation collects, stores, or processes data within Malaysian territory. For instance, if a foreign company operates a data centre in Malaysia or uses Malaysian-based service providers to process personal data, it must comply with the PDPA's requirements.

Enforcing data protection laws extraterritorially presents several challenges. Firstly, the jurisdictional reach of the PDPA is limited by principles of international law and sovereignty. Malaysian authorities may face difficulties in compelling foreign organisations to comply with the PDPA or in enforcing penalties against non-compliant entities. Secondly, differences in legal frameworks and regulatory approaches between countries can complicate the enforcement of extraterritorial data protection provisions.

To address these challenges, Malaysia can engage in international cooperation and establish mutual legal assistance agreements with other jurisdictions. These agreements facilitate cross-border enforcement of data protection laws by enabling information sharing, joint investigations, and coordinated enforcement actions. Additionally, participating in international data protection frameworks, such as the APEC Cross-Border Privacy Rules (CBPR) system, can enhance Malaysia's ability to ensure compliance with its data protection standards on a global scale.

v. Data Breach Notification

The PDPA does not currently mandate data breach notification, but proposed amendments to the PDPA aim to introduce such requirements. This shall be discussed further below.

IV. Data Security and Data Localisation

A. Data Security or Localisation Requirements

Under section 9 of the PDPA, data users are required to implement robust security measures to protect personal data from loss, misuse, unauthorised access, disclosure, or alteration.[72] Section 9(1) of the PDPA outlines practical steps for consideration as part of security measures to protect personal data including but not limited to considerations of data nature and potential harm for breaches, storage locations, equipment security, personnel reliability and secure data transfer. These steps are not mandatory. Data users must adopt measures that proportionately address the risks and costs associated with their data processing activities. Section 9 allows flexibility in balancing these costs against the potential risks and impacts of a security breach.[73]

[72] Janet Toh Yoong San, Boo Cheng Xuan, and Yee Yong Xuan, 'Data Residency and Retention Requirements in Malaysia' (*Lexology*, 2023), available at www.lexology.com/library/detail.aspx?g=58e24e92-df92-4d11-bba1-9507c9552bf9.

[73] Atiqah Binti Azman and others, 'Privacy in the Era of Big Data: Unlocking the Blue Oceans of Data Paradigm in Malaysia' (2021) 6 *Malaysian Journal of Social Sciences and Humanities* 203, available at doi.org/10.47405/mjssh.v6i5.780.

Section 10 of the PDPA provides that data should only be retained for as long as necessary. However, expeditious measures for data disposal including destruction or permanent deletion must ensue once the data ceases to be relevant for its designated purpose.[74]

Section 129 of the PDPA imposes data localisation requirements, prohibiting the transfer of personal data outside Malaysia unless the destination is specified by the Minister.[75] This requirement aims to ensure that personal data remains subject to Malaysian data protection laws and oversight.

Notwithstanding this, the transfer of personal data to a place outside Malaysia is permissible if any of the situations as provided by section 129(3) of the PDPA applies, which, among others, include the following situations:

i. the data subject has given his consent to the transfer;
ii. the transfer is necessary for the performance of a contract between the data subject and the data user; or
iii. if it could be ensured that the personal data transferred abroad will not be processed in any manner, which, if it was Malaysia, would be a contravention of the PDPA.

These exceptions help to balance the need for data protection with the practical realities of international commerce and global data flows.

B. Data Security or Localisation Requirements for Particular Data

In Malaysia, specific categories of data, such as government-related, health, accounting, and tax data, are governed by particular laws.

It is undisputed that the PDPA does not apply to the Federal Government and state governments pursuant to section 3 of the PDPA. Nevertheless, the Official Secrets Act 1972 classifies any government-related data as 'top secret', 'secret', 'confidential', or 'restricted'.[76] Notably, only the Minister or the relevant public officials may declassify any top-secret documents pursuant to section 2C of the Official Secrets Act 1972. This principle has been affirmed by the High Court in *Minister of Energy, Water and Communication & Anor v Malaysian Trade Union Congress & Ors*.[77] In this case, it was held that the Court should not usurp the power of the Minister concerned or the public officer charged with the responsibility of such declassification. The High Court in the *Minister of Energy* case referred to the case of *See Kok Kol @ See Liong Eng v Chong Kui Seng & Ors*,[78] where the Court of Appeal determined that if a document is designated and treated as an official secret by its creator, the law protects it as such, even if it contains information generally known to the public.

Under the PDPA, sensitive personal data refers to

> any personal data consisting of information as to the physical or mental health or condition of a data subject, his political opinions, his religious beliefs or other beliefs of a similar nature, the commission or alleged commission by him of any offence or any other personal data as the Minister may determine by order published in the Gazette.[79]

[74] PDPA, s 10(2).
[75] ibid, s 129.
[76] Official Secrets Act 1972, s 2.
[77] *Minister of Energy, Water and Communication & Anor v Malaysian Trade Union Congress & Ors* [2013] 1 MLJ 61.
[78] See *Kok Kol @ See Liong Eng v Chong Kui Seng & Ors* [2010] 2 CLJ 481.
[79] PDPA, s 4.

As such, health data may be regarded as personal data. The Code of Practice for Private Hospitals in The Healthcare Industry (Code of Practice) was established according to section 23 of the PDPA.

The Code of Practice sets data retention guidelines for private hospitals: seven years for adults and 25 years for newborns from their last visit. The accounting and tax-related data are governed under the ITA and the Companies Act 2016, respectively. Under section 82(1)(a) of the ITA, the taxpayers must keep sufficient records for seven years from the end of the year to which income from the business relates. This is consistent with the Court of Appeal's decision in *Ketua Pengarah Hasil Dalam Negeri v Lai Keng Chong & Anor*,[80] where the Court held that it was the taxpayer's statutory obligation under section 82(1)(a) of the ITA to keep sufficient records for seven years. Moreover, all documents that relate to any business in Malaysia shall be kept and retained in Malaysia pursuant to section 82(8) of the ITA.

Concerning accounting data, section 245 of the Companies Act 2016 requires a company, the directors and managers of a company to keep the accounting and other records for two purposes: (i) to sufficiently explain the transactions and financial position of the company and enable accurate and fair profit and loss accounts and balance sheets and any documents required to be attached to it to be prepared; and (ii) to enable the accounting and other records to be conveniently and appropriately audited.

A company must retain the records referred to above for seven years after completing the transactions or operations to which the entries relate.[81] The records referred to above must be kept at the company's registered office or at such other place as the directors think fit and shall always be open for inspection by the directors.[82] The company may keep the accounting and other records of operations outside Malaysia at a place outside Malaysia, provided that such accounting and other documents are sent to and kept at a place in Malaysia and are always made available for inspection by the directors.[83]

V. Issues in Private International Law

A. Litigation Involving Cross-border Data Protection and Privacy

Cross-border data transfers refer to the movement of personal information across international boundaries via various technologies and digital infrastructures. These transfers are crucial in the modern age of globalisation, where global data flow is the cornerstone of digital economy. The future of modern data processing has been shaped by the demands of multinational business operations, the entertainment industry, global communication network and so forth.

While such transfers have significantly driven the growth of modern businesses and economies, they also pose risks related to potential breaches of privacy and security.

[80] *Ketua Pengarah Hasil Dalam Negeri v Lai Keng Chong & Anor* [2012] 4 MLJ 184.
[81] Companies Act 2016, s 245(3).
[82] ibid, s 245(4).
[83] ibid, s 245(5).

Different countries have varying levels of data protection regulations, leading to inconsistencies in how personal data is safeguarded. Therefore, policymakers and organisations must take into account ethical elements, especially when dealing with private and personal data. Transparency in handling data, obtaining informed consent, and maintaining accountability are imperative in the context of cross-border data transfers.

Potential claimants and defendants in cross-border data transfer litigation can range from private individuals to government agencies, financial institutions, and service providers, depending on the circumstances. Claimants are typically those who suffer from data breaches or leaks of private information and seek to recover losses from the responsible parties. Defendants are usually organisations or entities authorised to handle personal data. Common wrongful acts that expose these entities to litigation include unauthorised data transfers, non-compliance with data protection laws, data breaches, and neglecting the rights of data subjects.

The adjudication of cross-border data protection and privacy disputes in Malaysia involves both judicial and administrative bodies. The Malaysian courts, such as the High Court and the Federal Court, serve as the judicial authorities for addressing data protection litigations. These courts interpret the provisions outlined in the PDPA, evaluate the evidence presented by parties and provide legal remedies. The judgments of the courts can significantly influence the development of jurisprudence concerning data protection.

Given the boundless nature of data transfers, a party may seek a globally effective injunction to adequately safeguard the data subject. Although case law in this specific area remains sparse, Malaysian courts have often issued worldwide injunctions to freeze assets outside the jurisdiction.[84] In these instances, the courts consider several factors including the strength of the case, the clear justification for the freezing order and whether there is risk of asset dissipation. Although Malaysian courts have yet to address worldwide injunctions specifically for data protection, they are likely to evaluate relevant factors on a case-by-case basis before exercising judicial discretion.

Under the PDPA, the appointment of a Personal Data Protection Commissioner aims to enforce its provisions.[85] The Commissioner serves as the primary administrative entity responsible for upholding data protection laws in Malaysia. It possesses the authority to investigate complaints, conduct inquiries, and impose penalties for breaches of the PDPA.

According to the Personal Data Protection Regulations 2013, the Commissioner holds the authority to inspect systems utilised in personal data processing. Data users are mandated to make these systems accessible for inspection by the Commissioner or designated inspection officers at reasonable times. Based on the Department of Personal Data Protection, the remedies provided by the PDPA take the form of criminal offence.[86] As such, breaches of the PDPA and certain provisions within the Personal Data Protection Regulations 2013 carry criminal liability. Penalties may involve fines, imprisonment, or both.[87] To ensure a

[84] See *Khidmas Capital Sdn Bhd & Anor v NRB Holdings Ltd and other appeals* [2006] 4 MLJ 194; *Securities Commission v Lee Kee Sien, Albert and Others* [2009] MLJU 117.

[85] PDPA, s 48.

[86] Official Portal of Department of Personal Data Protection FAQs, 'What Remedies are Available to Data Subject?' (*Department of Personal Data Protection*, 2021), available at www.pdp.gov.my/jpdpv2/frequently-asked-questions/?lang=en.

[87] PDPA, s 5.

balanced approach between administrative enforcement and judicial oversight, decisions made by the Commissioner can be contested within the judicial system. A data user holds the right to initiate a judicial review of the decision in the High Court if he is dissatisfied with a ruling from the Personal Data Protection Advisory Committee.[88]

Alternate dispute resolution mechanisms, such as international arbitration, play a vital role in resolving cross-border data transfer disputes. Parties can choose arbitrators with expertise in data protection and privacy laws to adjudicate disputes efficiently and effectively. The governing data protection law in cross-border disputes often depends on where the breach occurred or what was pre-agreed by the parties, such as a contractual clause specifying the applicable law.

B. Jurisdictional Issues Involving Cross-Border Data Protection and Privacy

Before proceeding further, in Malaysia, Article 121 of the FC explicitly states the existence of the two High Courts in Malaysia, namely the High Court of Malaya and the High Court of Sabah and Sarawak. Each court has jurisdiction over its respective geographical region.

As a general rule, the High Court handles cases and disputes occurring within the jurisdiction of Peninsular Malaysia, while the High Court of Sabah and Sarawak addresses cases within the jurisdictions of Sabah and Sarawak.[89] The High Court possesses the authority to hear all civil proceedings where: the cause of action arose; the defendant resides or conducts business; where the facts on which the proceedings are based exist; or any land the ownership of which is disputed is situated within the High Court's local jurisdiction.[90]

In the case of *Jaya Sudhir a/l Jayaram v Nautical Supreme Sdn Bhd & Ors*,[91] the Federal Court held that upon identifying duplicative proceedings, the courts will generally consider two primary factors: the desire of courts in upholding the agreements made by commercial parties and the desire of courts in preventing disruption through multiplicity or duplicity of litigation. This approach aims to avoid parallel proceedings, inconsistent findings, and inconvenience to third parties. The Federal Court also acknowledged that courts might refrain from enforcing exclusive jurisdiction or arbitration clauses if third-party interests are at stake or if there is a risk of parallel proceedings and inconsistent outcomes arising from the conduct of arbitration.

Based on this notion, in situations involving multiple litigations across different jurisdictions on the same matter, including data protection issues, courts can exercise their inherent powers[92] to issue orders such as staying proceedings until the resolution of the parallel case in another jurisdiction or granting an anti-suit injunction if necessary.

[88] See also 'What You Need to Know' (*Ministry of Communications of Malaysia and Personal Data Protection Commissioner Malaysia*, 2019), available at www.pdp.gov.my/jpdpv2/assets/2019/09/WhatYouNeedToKnow.pdf.

[89] 'Jurisdiction of High Court' (*The Official Portal of State Court of Kuala Lumpur*, 2023), available at kl.kehakiman.gov.my/en/jurisdiction-high-court.

[90] Courts of Judicature Act 1964, s 23.

[91] *Jaya Sudhir a/l Jayaram v Nautical Supreme Sdn Bhd & Ors* [2019] MLJU 523 at [60] to [61], FC.

[92] Rules of Court 2012, Order 92, r 4.

To date, no specific case law is readily available on how Malaysian courts will reconcile the principle of territoriality in relation to the cross-border nature of data cloud services. Nevertheless, the courts can exercise their discretion under Order 24, Rule 7A of the Rules of Court 2012 to order non-party disclosure to add the parties involved in a matter. An order for discovery will only be granted if the court is satisfied that such disclosure is necessary to resolve the case fairly or to save costs. Additionally, Order 24, Rule 8 of the Rules of Court 2012 provides that if the court finds discovery is not necessary or premature, it may dismiss or adjourn the application and refuse to make such an order. In cases where the data or documents are stored outside the jurisdiction, applicants are encouraged to apply for third-party disclosure to be served on a respondent outside Malaysia. This framework ensures that the principles of relevance, necessity, and jurisdiction are carefully balanced in the context of cross-border data issues.

C. Applicable Law in Litigation Involving Cross-border Data Protection and Privacy

As mentioned in the previous section, the principle of determining whether local civil courts have jurisdiction to hear a case is subject to section 23 of the Courts of Judicature Act. The case of *Siti Nur Aishah bt Ishak v Golden Plus Holdings Bhd* affirms this principle, indicating that it is sufficient for plaintiffs to show that their action falls within any of the sub-paragraphs of section 23(1).[93] Following this principle, the courts in establishing a connecting factor for data will likely identify the jurisdiction with the closest connection to the data or the parties involved. This could be the jurisdiction where the data was collected, processed, or stored, or where the data subjects or data controllers are located.

Malaysian courts demonstrate a willingness to consider international precedents in personal data protection cases. This can be seen in *Genting Malaysia Bhd v Pesuruhjaya Perlindungan Data Peribadi & Ors*,[94] where the High Court referenced the case of *Digital Rights Ireland Ltd v Minister for Communications, Marine and Natural Resources (C-293/12)* ('*Digital Rights Ireland*') to determine whether the operator of an integrated resort with a casino could disclose customer personal data to the Inland Revenue Department. The *Digital Rights Ireland* case, decided by the Grand Chamber Apex of the European Court of Human Rights, emphasised the primacy of the right to privacy in the context of personal data access requests by national agencies.[95] The Malaysian Court cited this case in its judgment, stating that 'general sweeping attempts or measures to secure disclosure of personal data are unacceptable to the court'.[96] However, the High Court's decision was overturned by the Court of Appeal and is now pending further determination in the Federal Court.

[93] *Siti Nur Aishah bt Ishak v Golden Plus Holdings Bhd* [2017] 3 MLJ 701 at [24], COA.

[94] *Genting Malaysia Bhd v Pesuruhjaya Perlindungan Data Peribadi & Ors* [2022] 11 MLJ 898.

[95] Court of Justice of the European Union, Judgment of 8 April 2014, Case C-293/12, *Digital Rights Ireland Ltd v Minister for Communications, Marine and Natural Resources and Others and Kärntner Landesregierung and Others* ECLI:EU:C:2014:238.

[96] *Genting Malaysia Bhd* (n 93) at [91] to [101], HC.

It is crucial to note, however, that in this instance, the Court did not directly consider data protection laws from other jurisdictions, as the issue at hand did not require such a consideration. This case illustrates the Malaysian courts' willingness to draw on foreign law as persuasive authority to inform their decisions, particularly regarding the balance between privacy rights and regulatory access to personal data.

In the case of *PT Sandipala Arthaputra v Muehlbauer Technologies Sdn Bhd*, the High Court provided clarity on when local courts will deny recognition of a foreign judgment.[97] The Court emphasised that the public policy consideration for recognising a foreign judgment under the common law rule focuses primarily on the nature of the judgment. Judgments based on laws that are objectively disgraceful or produce repellent outcomes, such as those obtained by fraud or corruption, will be denied recognition as they are against the public good and public interest in Malaysia.

This case underscores the importance of public policy in the recognition of foreign judgments by Malaysian courts that only complaints blatantly offensive to public conscience or injurious to public welfare will be upheld, thus ensuring that Malaysia's legal standards and public policy are maintained.

D. Recognition and Enforcement of Foreign Judgments Involving Data Protection and Privacy

There are no specific regulations for recognising and enforcing foreign judgments concerning personal data and privacy. Thus, the general rules on recognising and enforcing foreign judgments are applicable.

In Malaysia, the enforcement of foreign judgments can be achieved either through statutory enforcement or common law principles. For judgments obtained in countries listed in the First Schedule of the Reciprocal Enforcement of Judgments Act 1958 (Revised 1972) Act 99 (REJA), enforcement is possible by applying to register the foreign judgment in the High Court.[98] The party seeking to enforce the foreign judgment from countries that are not listed in the First Schedule can do so by initiating a fresh suit in court.

In the case of *PT Sandipala Arthaputra v Muehlbauer Technologies Sdn Bhd*,[99] Justice Choo Kah Sing held that when recognising a foreign judgment under common law, the courts will consider these factors: (i) whether the foreign judgment is final and conclusive; (ii) whether the foreign court had jurisdiction according to Malaysian private international law; and (iii) whether any defences against its recognition exist.[100] If these conditions are met, the local court will recognise the foreign judgment.

[97] *PT Sandipala Arthaputra v Muehlbauer Technologies Sdn Bhd* [2021] MLJU 1063 at [55] to [56] and [58], HC.

[98] Reciprocal Enforcement of Judgments Act 1958 (Revised 1972), s 4.

[99] *PT Sandipala Arthaputra v Muehlbauer Technologies Sdn Bhd* [2021] MLJU 1063 at para [14], HC.

[100] 'In an action on the judgment at common law, one or more of the following defences may be raised – (1) that the foreign court had no jurisdiction; (2) that the judgment was obtained by fraud; (3) that the judgment would be contrary to public policy, and (4) that the proceedings in which the judgment was obtained were opposed to natural justice.' Judgement by Supreme Court Judge Mohamed Azmi in *See Hua Daily News Bhd v Tan Thien Chin & Ors* [1986] 2 MLJ 107, SC.

E. Obstacles to Effective Data Protection

Due to the complexities of private international law, Malaysia faces significant challenges in ensuring effective data protection and privacy. Data breaches often involve cross-border data transfers which could complicate enforcement efforts. Different countries have varying standards and regulations making it difficult to determine the appropriate legal framework that applies. For instance, the PDPA may differ significantly from the data protection laws of other countries which can create confusion and compliance difficulties for multinational entities. Enforcing Malaysian data protection laws in other jurisdictions is also a problem as it often requires cooperation with foreign data protection authorities and experts to address specific issues, demanding considerable time and effort.

In addition, navigating the intricate legal processes involved in private international law is daunting and resource-intensive. Different countries have varied procedural rules, litigation procedures, evidentiary standards, and the availability of legal remedies, all of which can hinder the effective protection of data privacy.

The PDPA incorporates several key principles and concepts from the GDPR such as data subject rights and data protection by design, adapting these concepts to fit local requirements.[101] Both regulations address fundamental aspects of data protection, such as the lawful bases for data processing, requirements for record-keeping, and the rights of data subjects, including access, rectification, erasure, and restriction of processing. Similar to the GDPR, the PDPA also grants investigatory, corrective, and advisory powers to regulatory authorities. Additionally, both frameworks mandate the submission of an annual report by relevant organisations to demonstrate compliance with data protection requirements.

Despite these similarities, the two legislative frameworks have distinct differences. For example, the protection of children is approached differently in the PDPA and the GDPR. While the GDPR establishes a specific age limit for children's consent regarding data processing, the PDPA does not explicitly address such provisions.

Unlike the GDPR, the PDPA does not expressly define vendor privacy contracts, Data Protection Impact Assessments, or the requirement for appointing Data Protection Officers. Additionally, the handling of data breach reporting differs between the two regulations. The GDPR mandates prompt notification of data breaches to both supervisory authorities and affected individuals, whereas the PDPA does not specify such requirements. Furthermore, the PDPA does not directly define or refer to anonymisation or pseudonymisation of personal data, which are crucial elements for ensuring data privacy and security under the GDPR.

While the PDPA and the GDPR share common objectives and principles regarding data protection, they also demonstrate notable differences in their scope and approach. Policy-makers in Malaysia should consider these distinctions and refer to the GDPR when amending the PDPA to enhance its effectiveness and alignment with international standards.

[101] Regulation (EU) 2016/679 of the European Parliament and of the Council of 27 April 2016 on the protection of natural persons with regard to the processing of personal data and on the free movement of such data, and repealing Directive 95/46/EC (General Data Protection Regulation) [2016] OJ L119/1.

VI. Topical Issues and Prospects

A. Artificial Intelligence or AI-Generated Data

The Malaysian Government is actively promoting the implementation of artificial intelligence (AI) throughout the country. The Ministry of Higher Education recently inaugurated the first AI faculty at the University of Technology Malaysia (UTM)[102] during the Malaysia Artificial Nexus 2024 (My AI Nexus) event. The Prime Minister of Malaysia also launched the Malaysia Artificial Intelligence Consortium and the AI Talent Roadmap for Malaysia 2024–30 as part of the My AI Nexus.[103] These initiatives by the Government aim to boost digital transformation and AI adoption in Malaysia, fostering innovation, productivity, and competitiveness, while also serving as benchmarks to attract foreign investment.

Nevertheless, Malaysia currently demonstrates a relatively lower adoption of explicit AI policies and frameworks compared to other countries globally. According to the Global AI Index published in June 2023, Malaysia is ranked 44th out of 62 countries.[104] Consequently, it is not surprising that Malaysia has yet to enact specific legislation regulating AI. Instead, the prevailing laws concerning data protection, contracts and computer crime could potentially be extended to cover AI despite the complexity and potential disputes regarding their applicability. To date, there has been a lack of case law in Malaysia's jurisdiction that could guide in terms of AI and its legal definition.

While AI is often heralded as a transformative technology, it also raises significant concerns. In an article by *The Malaysian Reserve*,[105] experts highlighted several threats and challenges posed by AI. Science, Technology and Innovation Minister Chang Lih Kang emphasised ethical issues such as data privacy violations and potential biases in AI algorithms, which could lead to prejudicial outcomes. He advocated for the federal Government to implement new regulations and policies to safeguard individuals and ensure the ethical use of AI, as data privacy breaches can undermine public trust in both businesses and governments, while algorithmic biases can exacerbate systemic inequalities.

Additionally, Nicholas Lim, the Chief Technology Officer of Soft Space Sdn Bhd, warned against blindly trusting AI-driven correlations without human oversight. He noted that this could inadvertently result in the denial of services to certain customer segments. Lim stressed the importance of human judgement in verifying AI insights and ensuring fair treatment, advocating for continuous review and evaluation of AI models to identify and rectify any emerging biases.

To address the potential risks associated with the growing use of AI tools like ChatGPT, the Malaysian Government issued an advisory document titled 'ChatGPT and Security

[102] See 'UTM Faculty of Artificial Intelligence' (*UTM*, 2024), available at fai.utm.my.

[103] See Analysts, 'Various Initiatives Prove Government's Seriousness in Driving AI Development' (*Sinar Daily*, 12 May 2024), available at www.sinardaily.my/article/217987/focus/national/various-initiatives-prove-governments-seriousness-in-driving-ai-development---analysts.

[104] 'The Global AI Index' (*Tortoise Media*, 28 June 2023), available at www.tortoisemedia.com/intelligence/global-ai/#rankings.

[105] Akmar Annuar 'Threats and Challenges of AI' (The Malaysian Reserve, 5 June 2023), <themalaysianreserve.com/2023/06/05/threats-and-challenges-of-ai/> accessed on 5 June 2024.

Best Practices'.[106] This comprehensive document, released by the Malaysia Computer Emergency Response Team (MyCERT) under the Ministry of Communications and Digital, outlines best practices for the safe and responsible use of ChatGPT. The advisory covers various aspects, including security and privacy considerations, limitations of the technology, and user awareness.

Additionally, the Malaysian Qualifications Agency released a guide on the application of generative AI in higher education.[107] The advisory suggests that universities should create clear guidelines for both faculty and students on using generative AI tools in teaching, research, and academic writing. It also emphasises the importance of regularly reviewing and updating policies and practices related to the use of generative AI to enhance academic standards and administrative structures.

However, a significant change to Malaysian data protection legislation is underway. The Malaysian Government intends to reshape its technology landscape by emphasising AI and data integration through proposed amendments to three key legislations: revising the PDPA, introducing a new cybersecurity bill and planning the enactment of the Omnibus Data Protection Act.[108] The amended PDPA will primarily address regulations within the private sector while the Omnibus Data Protection Act will predominantly focus on government affairs and additionally facilitate the regulation of data transferability among government entities.

Given the Government's public announcement of upcoming legislative and policy changes to enhance data protection and cybersecurity in Malaysia,[109] the impact of AI regulation on businesses will vary depending on the industry and the specific applications of AI. Organisations and businesses adopting AI must be prepared to allocate funds for expertise and technology necessary to meet regulatory standards. However, these efforts will lead to significant benefits. The public will feel safer knowing that AI systems are governed by strict laws, fostering confidence that these technologies operate within safe and ethical boundaries.

B. Potential Cooperation under the Belt and Road Initiative

The Belt and Road Initiative (BRI) introduced by the Chinese President Xi Jinping in 2013 includes the China's Digital Silk Road (DSR) which incorporates digital technology into

[106] 'MA-912.022023: MyCERT Advisory – ChatGPT and Security Best Practices' (*MyCERT Malaysia*, 2024) <www.mycert.org.my/portal/advisory?id=MA-912.022023> accessed 3 June 2024.

[107] 'Advisory Note No. 2/2023: AI Generatif' (*Malaysian Qualifications Agency*, 31 March 2023) <www.mqa.gov.my/new/document/2023/edited/MQA%20Advisory%20Note%20No.22023-%20AI%20Generatif.pdf> accessed 3 June 2024.

[108] 'These three bills will act as the fundamental basis for a lot of the work in terms of data unification data usage, but still safeguarding issues around data sovereignty and data protection', Economy Minister Rafizi Ramli told a press conference at the Malaysia Digital Expo 2023 Grand Finale at Malaysia International Trade and Exhibition Centre on 6 November 2023. See 'Getting Malaysia Ready for the Rise of AI' (*Malaysia Investment Department Authority*, 6 November 2023), available at www.mida.gov.my/mida-news/getting-malaysia-ready-for-the-rise-of-ai/.

[109] See also S Joan Santani, 'Malaysia Coming up with AI Governance and Code of Ethics' (*Business Times*, 9 January 2024), available at www.nst.com.my/business/corporate/2024/01/998905/malaysia-coming-ai-governance-and-code-ethics.

various sectors to enhance global trade and economic growth between China and its participating countries.[110] Since then, Malaysia has been a key player in the DSR by signing several Memorandum of Understanding (MOU) with leading tech giants in China. This strategic move aims to enhance Malaysia's digital infrastructure and foster technological collaboration, reinforcing its position as a significant participant in the DSR initiative.[111]

Notable collaborations include an agreement between Malaysia's leading automotive manufacturer, DRB-HICOM Bhd and China's Zhejiang Geely Holding Group, a prominent global mobility technology company from China. This agreement focuses on developing and promoting the Automotive HiTech Valley in Tanjong Malim, Perak aiming to establish a hub for the new energy vehicle industry.[112]

Additionally, in April 2023, Kairous Capital, a Malaysian venture capital firm signed two MOUs with Digital Way Group and China Silk Road Group to establish the Malaysia-China Digital Cooperation Council and the Malaysia-China Digital Cooperation & Development Fund fostering digital innovation between the two nations.[113]

Another notable project is the Alibaba Cloud's Malaysia City Brain programme in Kuala Lumpur, a collaboration with China's Alibaba Group, Malaysia's digital economy development agency, Malaysia Digital Economy Corporation and the country's city council, Dewan Bandaraya Kuala Lumpur. The Malaysia City Brain is the first time Alibaba Cloud's smart city AI product is deployed outside of China and it leverages AI and big data to enhance urban management and public services such as traffic control and emergency response systems.[114]

The increasing collaborations between Chinese and Malaysian enterprises, including prominent tech corporations like Alibaba, Tencent[115] and Huawei[116] underscore the growing strength of Malaysia's digital economy system. Given China's status as Malaysia's largest trading partner since 2009,[117] these technological and economic collaborations are set to promote further growth and development in both countries.

[110] See also 'Xi Jinping to Host 37 World Leaders at Belt and Road Forum' (*The Straits Times*, 20 April 2019), available at www.straitstimes.com/asia/east-asia/xi-to-host-37-world-leaders-at-belt-and-road-forum.

[111] Indonesia, Singapore and Malaysia remain the top three destinations of China's DSR investments in Southeast Asia, collectively securing 52.3% of all DSR projects. See Wang Zheng, 'China's DSR in Southeast Asia: Progress and Challenges' (*Fulcrum Analysis on Southeast Asia*, 23 January 2024), available at fulcrum.sg/chinas-digital-silk-road-dsr-in-southeast-asia-progress-and-challenges/.

[112] 'Geely Holding Group and DRB-HICOM Sign Agreement on Development of New Energy Vehicle Industry Hub in Malaysia' (*Zhejiang Geely Holding Group Media Centre*, 1 April 2023), available at zgh.com/media-center/news/2023-04-01/?lang=en.

[113] Team AsiaTechDaily, 'Kairous Capital Establishes Malaysia-China Digital Cooperation Council for Tech investment' (*AsiaTech Daily*, 4 April 2023), available at asiatechdaily.com/kairous-capital-malaysia-china-digital-cooperation/.

[114] 'Alibaba Cloud Launches Malaysia City Brain to Enhance City Management' Alibaba Cloud '(*Alibaba*, 29 January 2018), available at www.alibabacloud.com/en/press-room/alibaba-cloud-launches-malaysia-city-brain-to-enhance-city-management?_p_lc=1#:~:text=Kuala%20Lumpur%2C%20January%2029%2C%202018, Kuala%20Lumpur%20(DBKL)%2C%20the.

[115] Liew Jia Teng 'Tech: Tencent Cloud Offers Path to China for Malaysians Firms' (*The Edge Malaysia*, 17 April 2024), theedgemalaysia.com/node/707605.

[116] 'Huawei and Time Collaborate to Pioneer Srv6 Technology Rollout in Malaysia' (*Huawei*, 20 May 2024), available at www.huawei.com/my/news/my/2024/huawei-time-collaborate-pioneer-srv6-technology-malaysia#:~:text=KUALA%20LUMPUR%2C%2020%20MAY%202024,Malaysia's%20telecommunications%20industry%20to%20make.

[117] 'Malaysia External Trade Statistics for the Year 2023' (*Ministry of Investment, Trade and Industry*, 2022), available at www.matrade.gov.my/en/component/joomdoc/Trade%20Statistics/Malaysias%20Trade%20Performances/Malaysias%20Trade%20Performance%202022/PR202212_ENG.pdf/download#:~:text=China%20%E2%80%93%20Exports%20Surpassed%20RM200%20Billion,13%20billion%20compared%20to%202021.

C. Data Protection Post COVID-19 Pandemic

The COVID-19 pandemic has highlighted critical issues in data protection and privacy, particularly through the use of the MySejahtera application in Malaysia.[118] Developed by the Malaysian Government for contact tracing, the application gathers extensive personal and health information but arguably lacks clear privacy policies and legal safeguards.[119]

Section 40 of the PDPA allows for the processing of personal data without the individual's explicit consent if it is necessary to protect the vital interests of the data subject or another person.[120] It can be argued that processing personal and sensitive data during the COVID-19 outbreak for pandemic control purposes concerns matters of life and death, thereby falling under the scope of section 40. However, the precise application of this provision remains to be seen due to the lack of judicial interpretations of section 40.

Nonetheless, it is crucial to acknowledge that section 40 of the PDPA does not grant private businesses or organisations the unrestricted authority to misuse or retain personal data beyond what is essential.[121] In this context, businesses and private organisations are advised to exercise caution when processing private and sensitive data ensuring, for instance, that the identity of the infected individuals is not disclosed unless necessary.

The Malaysian Bar has called for legal reforms in response to these challenges to bolster the accountability of government agencies in the event of data breaches.[122] This is especially so after a significant data breach was revealed in the 2021 Auditor-General's Report Series 2 which highlighted the presence of a 'super admin' account that had accessed and downloaded three million sets of data from multiple IP addresses from the MySejahtera application.[123] This revelation has raised significant concerns about data breaches within the country despite it being denied by the then Health Deputy Minister.[124]

It appears that the current provisions are insufficient to protect personal data, particularly in the context of the extensive data processing undertaken by the Government during the pandemic. This is in stark contrast to countries like France, which has implemented more detailed and stringent privacy policies for its COVID-19 contact tracing application.[125] The absence of stringent government guidelines on privacy policies, especially during the pandemic, significantly heightens the risk of data breaches. Without robust

[118] See 'MySejahtera' (*Ministry of Health Malaysia*, 2022), available at mysejahtera.moh.gov.my/en/.

[119] See 'MySejahtera's Private Policy' (*Government of Malaysia*, 2024), available at mysejahtera.moh.gov.my/en/about-mysejahtera/privacy-policy.

[120] ibid, ss 40(1)(b)(ii) and (iii).

[121] ibid, ss 10.

[122] Karen Cheah Yee Lynn, 'Press Release: Transparent and Protection of Privacy Crucial for Personal Data Collected through the MySejahtera Application' (*Malaysian Bar*, 27 February 2023), available at www.malaysianbar.org.my/article/about-us/president-s-corner/pressstatements/press-release-transparency-and-protection-of-privacy-crucial-for-personal-data-collected-through-the-mysejahtera-application.

[123] Mazwin Nik Anis and Ragananthini Vethasalam 'AG's report: MySejahtera was Target of 1.12 million Cyber Attacks' (*The Star*, 2023), available at www.thestar.com.my/news/nation/2023/02/16/auditor-general-report-mysejahtera-was-target-of-112-million-cyber-attacks.

[124] Shahrin Aizat Noorshahrizam 'Deputy Minister: Three million MySejahtera Users' Data Downloaded to Protect them from Hackers' (*The Malay Mail*, 27 February 2023), available at www.malaymail.com/news/malaysia/2023/02/27/deputy-minister-three-million-mysejahtera-users-data-downloaded-to-protect-them-from-hackers/57002.

[125] 'Contract Tracing Apps in France' (*Norton Rose Fulbright*, 2 December 2020), available at www.nortonrosefulbright.com/-/media/files/nrf/nrfweb/contact-tracing/france-contact-tracing.pdf?revision=73eb9585-be68-4fde-82fd-d5362607b90.

regulatory frameworks to enforce comprehensive privacy protections, individuals must remain vigilant about the potential risks of data misuse.

D. Upcoming Proposed Amendments to the PDPA 2010

Although the PDPA represents a critical step in safeguarding data privacy, the PDPA arguably has significant enforcement weaknesses. It appears to be inadequately holding telecommunications companies and government bodies accountable for data breaches. According to the Mid-Year Threat Landscape Report 2023[126] by CyberSecurity Malaysia, telecommunications hold the largest percentage of data breaches, followed by the Government, logistics and transportation, and banking sectors. These sectors are particularly vulnerable to data breaches due to the volume and sensitivity of the data they handle. The weak oversight of the PDPA contrasts sharply with stricter international data privacy laws like the GDPR, allowing companies to misuse consumer data with minimal repercussions.

The GDPR provides a robust framework for data protection, emphasising individual rights to manage personal data, which includes access, correction, erasure and restriction on processing. This ensures accountability and transparency in data handling by companies, with strict compliance required and substantial fines for violations. In contrast, the PDPA arguably offers weaker individual data control and less stringent enforcement, resulting in milder penalties and less proactive measures. This marks a significant gap in PDPA's effectiveness in safeguarding consumer data compared to GDPR.

In February 2020, the Commissioner released a public consultation paper entitled 'Public Consultation Paper No. 01/2020', identifying 22 areas for potential amendments to the PDPA.[127] The suggested amendments include clarifying consent requirements, enforcing the right of data subjects to be informed about third parties who have received their personal data, and establishing clear policies on endpoint security technologies, such as encryption, to reduce data breach risks. However, the draft bill was not tabled before the Malaysian Parliament dissolved in October 2022. The new Minister of Communications and Digital has since taken responsibility for the PDPA 2010 amendments.

As of October 2023, the Deputy Communications and Digital Minister announced that the department is finalising the bill, aiming to present it in March 2024. On 10 July 2024, the Personal Data Protection (Amendment) Bill 2024 (PDPA Amendment Bill) was tabled at the House of Representatives of the Malaysian Parliament for its first reading, with the introduction of significant amendments to the PDPA including but not limited to the introduction of a mandatory appointment of a data protection officer, compliance obligations on data processors including the imposition of penalties for breach, mandatory personal data breach notification, right to data portability, increased penalties for

[126] 'Mid-Year Report Threat Landscape 2023' (*CyberSecurity Malaysia*, 2023), available at www.cybersecurity.my/data/content_files/26/2511.pdf.

[127] 'Public Consultation Paper No. 01/2020' (*Personal Data Protection Commissioner*, 12 February 2020), available at www.pdp.gov.my/jpdpv2/assets/2020/02/Public-Consultation-Paper-on-Review-of-Act-709_V4.pdf.

breach of personal data protection principles, the removal of the whitelist regime for cross-border data transfers, etc. On 16 July 2024, the PDPA Amendment Bill was passed during its second and third readings in the House of Representatives of the Malaysian Parliament without any additional amendments.

On 22 July 2024, the PDPA Amendment Bill was tabled in the Senate of the Malaysian Parliament for its first reading. On 31 July 2024, the Senate passed the PDPA Amendment Bill after its second and third readings, also without any further amendments. Therefore, the PDPA Amendment Bill will come into force in Malaysia once it receives Royal Assent and is published in the Federal Gazette, or on a date specified in the law itself or appointed by the Minister via notification in the Federal Gazette.

These amendments aim to enhance data privacy safeguards. Additionally, it is anticipated that some of the PDPD is developing guidelines to restrict the use of AI in processing public personal data.

8

Vietnam

MAI-THANH LE AND TIEN-DUC NGUYEN

I. Introduction

Vietnam's legal framework on data protection remains in its infancy stage, despite the issue of data protection garnering growing public attention in recent years. The controversial Law on Cybersecurity ('2018 Law on Cybersecurity') approved by the National Assembly in 2018 stirred bewilderment among enterprises and individuals regarding the data localisation requirements, which would make compliance costs soar, and limit the space for free expression in cyberspace.[1] However, it has taken several years for the promulgation of Decree No 53/2022/ND-CP which provided guidance on the implementation of the 2018 Law on Cybersecurity. The Personal Data Protection Decree (PDPD) of 2023 could drastically transform the data protection and privacy framework in Vietnam. The decree was initially slated for promulgation in 2019, but it experienced significant delays. This decree represents the first comprehensive regulation of personal data protection in the country. Given the paramount importance of data protection, the Chairman of the National Assembly, Vuong Dinh Hue, has indicated that this decree could lay the groundwork for the eventual promulgation of a dedicated law on the matter.[2] However, it remains somewhat perplexing why the decree would not be directly adopted as a law from the outset.

Vietnam's engagement with matters of data protection and privacy is notably extensive. The nation ranks highly on its degree of internet penetration, being among the countries with the greatest internet coverage. As of September 2022, the country recorded 72.1 million regular internet users, representing 73.2 per cent of the nation's total population, and placing it twelfth globally in terms of internet usage.[3] In the realm of cross-border data flows, Vietnam ranked the seventh highest worldwide in 2019.[4] According to a survey, Vietnamese

[1] 'Người dân nhiều địa phương xuống đường gây náo loạn' ['People in Many Localities took to the Streets to Cause Chaos'] (*Vnexpress*, 10 June 2018), available at www.vnexpress.net/nguoi-dan-nhieu-dia-phuong-xuong-duong-gay-nao-loan-3761525.html.

[2] Thanh Chung, 'Dự thảo nghị định bảo vệ dữ liệu cá nhân 'mới, khó, cần xem xét tính cấp bách'' ['The Draft Decree on Personal Data Protection is "Novel, Demanding, and Necessity to be Considered'] (*Tuoi tre*, 13 February 2023), available at www.tuoitre.vn/du-thao-nghi-dinh-bao-ve-du-lieu-ca-nhan-moi-kho-can-xem-xet-tinh-cap-bach-20230213092235398.htm.

[3] Lưu Quý and An Thu, '25 năm phát triển Internet Việt Nam' ['25 Years of Vietnam Internet Development'] (*Vnexpress*, 13 February 2023), available at www.vnexpress.net/25-nam-phat-trien-internet-viet-nam-4536367.html.

[4] Nguyen Anh Duong, 'Time for Vietnam to Get Cracking on CPTPP Reforms' (*East Asia Forum*, 13 January 2022), available at www.eastasiaforum.org/2022/01/13/time-for-vietnam-to-get-cracking-on-cptpp-reforms/.

citizens were found to spend an average of six hours and 38 minutes online daily.[5] The omnipresence of the Internet in contemporary Vietnamese society can be attributed in part to the COVID-19 pandemic and the consequent shift to virtual platforms. The Government has promoted the development of e-governance and smart cities as one of its flagship development projects, which necessitate extensive use of technological devices.[6] A substantial number of public services are expected to transition to entirely online platforms, eliminating the need for face-to-face interactions and thereby reshaping the government-citizen dynamic.[7]

The seemingly insatiable demand for technological transformation has a dark side – cyberattacks on the system of information and communication technology in Vietnam have surged considerably over the years. As many as 9,700 cyberattacks were recorded in 2021, an increase of 42.4 per cent compared to the prior year.[8] The National Cyber Security Center of Vietnam cites a lack of vigilance and a deficit in cybersecurity awareness among stakeholders as the primary drivers of this trend.[9] Alarmingly, only one in 10 computers in Vietnam is furnished with anti-virus software.[10] The situation is further exacerbated by the ease with which personal data can be purchased online, often only a few search engine clicks away.[11] Approximately 80 per cent of Vietnamese internet users have reportedly been victims of data breaches and leaks.[12] In 2021, information on illegal large-scale personal data collection and trading was brought to light.[13] These developments revealed profound institutional inadequacies and systemic vulnerabilities in Vietnam's legal infrastructure.

This chapter endeavours to elucidate Vietnam's legal framework concerning cross-border data transfers and data protection. Despite the mounting concerns on data protection from state and non-state actors alike, the relevant laws have remained primitive. In detailing the data protection regulations, this chapter will highlight the influence of foreign laws, particularly the European Union's (EU) General Data Protection Regulation (GDPR), which have shaped Vietnam's omnibus legislative approach to data protection and security. The chapter will also discuss the multifaceted values and policy concerns underpinning the drafting of the pertinent laws. This includes striking a balance between

[5] ibid.

[6] Decision No 950/QD-TTg of the Prime Minister approving scheme for development of smart sustainable cities in Vietnam in the 2018–2025 period with orientations by 2030 (Promulgated on 1 August 2018).

[7] Van Anh, 'Important Transition For Digital Government As Public Services Go Online' (*Vietnamnet*, 8 February 2022), available at www.vietnamnet.vn/en/important-transition-for-digital-government-as-public-services-go-online-814110.html.

[8] 'Cyberattacks On The Rise' (*Vietnam News*, 9 April 2022), available at www.vietnamnews.vn/economy/1172361/cyber-attacks-on-the-rise.html.

[9] 'Cyberattacks Rise in Vietnam' (*MIC*, 14 October 2022), available at https://english.mic.gov.vn/Pages/TinTuc/155362/Cyberattacks-rise-in-Vietnam.html.

[10] Minh Nga, 'Vietnam Records Over 5,400 Cyberattacks in Five Months' (*Vnexpress*, 10 June 2022), available at https://e.vnexpress.net/news/news/vietnam-records-over-5-400-cyberattacks-in-five-months-4474118.html.

[11] Trong Dat and Van Anh, 'Personal Data of 10,000 Vietnamese Offered for Sale Online' (*Vietnamnet*, 17 May 2021), available at www.vietnamnet.vn/en/personal-data-of-10000-vietnamese-offered-for-sale-online-737456.html.

[12] 'Dữ liệu người Việt đang bị rò rỉ như thế nào?' ['How is Vietnamese People's Data Being Leaked?'] (*Vnexpress Podcast*, 31 March 2023), available at www.vnexpress.net/du-lieu-nguoi-viet-dang-bi-ro-ri-nhu-the-nao-4587579.html.

[13] 'Illegal Trading Of Personal Data Difficult To Control' (*Vietnamnet*, 8 June 2021), available at www.vietnamnet.vn/en/illegal-trading-of-personal-data-difficult-to-control-742262.html#:~:text=According%20to%20the%20Penal%20Code,VND40%20million%20to%20VND70%20million.

encouraging growth in the personal data sector, safeguarding individual rights to privacy and freedom from unlawful data harvesting and trading,[14] and the Government authorities' unease about losing control over cyberspace activities.[15] Consequently, the legal framework for data transfers and protection is expected to embody a blend of commitments and values.

II. General Legal Framework of International Data Transfers and Data Protection

A. International and Constitutional Protection for Data Transfer and Protection

Vietnam recognises the higher legal effect of international treaties over domestic legislation, excluding the Constitution.[16] Consequently, an examination of both the Constitution and the international conventions to which Vietnam is a signatory is vital. This precedes a detailed discussion on the domestic statutory provisions related to data protection and transfers.

The constitutional history of Vietnam firmly establishes an individual's right to privacy.[17] Liberal ideals have significantly influenced the country's foundational moment. Chapter II of the 1946 Constitution enshrines the duties and rights of citizens, of which Article 11 provides that the residence and correspondence of a person shall not be violated by anyone contrary to law.[18] This affirmation on the integrity and confidentiality of personal home and correspondence was further reiterated in Article 28 of the 1959 Constitution.[19] The 1980 Constitution expanded on the specific content of this guarantee under Article 71, specifically safeguarding telephone conversations and telegrams as part of the individual right to privacy. Similar provisions were found in Article 73 of the 1992 Constitution (as amended in 2001).[20] The terms 'personal privacy', together with 'personal secrecy' and

[14] Đỗ Thoa, 'Quốc hội thảo luận về dự thảo Luật An ninh mạng' ['The National Assembly Discussed the Draft Law On Cyber Security'] (*Dang cong san*, 23 Nov 2017), available at www.www.dangcongsan.vn/thoi-su/quoc-hoi-thao-luan-ve-du-thao-luat-an-ninh-mang-462975.html. See further, Quoc-Tan-Trung Nguyen, Thi-Hong-Ninh Bui, and Hong-Thanh Phung, 'Human Right Concerns in Vietnam's Cybersecurity Law: From International Discourse to a Comparative Perspective' (2022) 14(3) *Journal of Human Rights Practice* 968.

[15] For arguments on the regulatory characteristics of Vietnam's cybersecurity law, see Ngoc Son Bui and Jyh-An Lee, 'Comparative Cybersecurity Law in Socialist Asia' (2022) 55 *Vanderbilt Journal of Transnational Law* 631.

[16] The Law on International Treaties (2016) No 108/2016/QH13, Art 6. It bears noting that the Law on conclusion, accession to and implementation of treaties (2005) No 41/2005/QH11 which preceded the 2016 law provided that international treaties took priority over domestic laws without mentioning the Constitution, implying that Vietnam fully embraced the monist approach when it came to any inconsistency between the two sources. However, the 2016 law has impliedly amended this stance by explicitly singling out the primacy of the Constitution in the hierarchy.

[17] See, eg, Tien-Duc Nguyen and Pasquale Viola, 'Constitutional Rights in Socialist East Asia' (2022) 40(2) *Nordic Journal of Human Rights* 320.

[18] 1946 Constitution of the Democratic Republic of Vietnam (Adopted on 9 November 1946).

[19] 1959 Constitution of the Democratic Republic of Vietnam (Adopted on 31 December 1959).

[20] 1980 Constitution of the Socialist Republic of Vietnam (Adopted on 18 December 1980).

'familial secrecy', were adopted for the first time under Article 21 of the 2013 Constitution.[21] The constitutional safeguards extend to 'other forms of exchange of personal information', effectively encompassing electronic collection and processing of personal information on virtual platforms. One subtle difference between the 2013 Constitution and its predecessors lies in the holder of this right to privacy. While earlier versions of the Constitution presupposed Vietnamese citizens as the sole right-holders,[22] the 2013 Constitution adopted a naturalist approach, recognising every individual's right to privacy.[23] This shift effectively broadens the protective scope of privacy rights.

Despite limited enforceability, the constitutional enshrinement of the individual right to privacy serves two significant purposes: symbolic and normative.[24] Symbolically, the incorporation of this right highlights the progressive evolution of the constitution-makers and communicates the recognition of such rights (among others) by the ruling party to both foreign and domestic audiences.[25] Normatively, the constitution, as the supreme law of the land, acts as a guiding beacon for legitimate state conduct.[26] This includes the promulgation of laws and sub-laws to actualise constitutional principles and values.

On the supranational plane, the International Covenant on Civil and Political Rights of 1966 (ICCPR) is pertinent, given Vietnam's membership since 1982.[27] Article 17 of the ICCPR protects the human right to privacy against 'arbitrary or unlawful interference'. While 'unlawful' dictates that every interference must have a legal basis, not all law-based interferences may be justified. Hence, lawfulness is a necessary but not sufficient condition in determining the justifiability of any interference. In particular, a 'lawful' meddling into individual right to privacy which contradicts the core aims and objectives of the ICCPR and is unreasonable in nature, is considered 'arbitrary' and thereby violates the ICCPR.[28] The ICCPR has instituted a judicial mechanism under Part IV of the text, and the First Optional Protocol for resolving differences in its interpretation and application. However, Vietnam has not explicitly accepted or acknowledged the competence of the Human Rights Committee in handling individual complaints. This refusal is not unique. In fact, save for international investment treaties, Vietnam has consistently dodged international procedures entailing legally binding decisions.[29] The main causes of such non-compliance could be the country's cognisance of the disparity between international and national standards,

[21] 1992 Constitution of the Socialist Republic of Vietnam (Adopted on 15 April 1992, amended in 2001).

[22] See, eg, 1992 Constitution of the Socialist Republic of Vietnam (Adopted on 15 April 1992) ('1992 Constitution') Chapter 5.

[23] 2013 Constitution of the Socialist Republic of Vietnam (Adopted on 28 November 2013) ('2013 Constitution'), Art 21.

[24] For a more detailed discussion, see Tom Ginsburg and Alberto Simpser, *Constitutions in Authoritarian Regimes* (Cambridge University Press, 2014) 2–3.

[25] Bui Ngoc Son, 'Globalization of Constitutional Identity' (2017) 26 *Washington International Law Journal* 463.

[26] 2013 Constitution (n 23), Art 119.

[27] Nguyễn Thị Tuyết Giang, 'Việt Nam hoàn thành việc nộp Báo cáo giữa kỳ Công ước quốc tế về các quyền dân sự và chính trị' ['Vietnam Completed the Submission of the Inter-Term Report of the International Covenant on Civil And Political Rights'] (Ministry of Justice), available at www.moj.gov.vn/tttp/tintuc/Pages/cong-uoc-quoc-te.aspx?ItemID=9.

[28] UN Human Rights Committee, 'CCPR General Comment No. 16: Article 17 (Right to Privacy), The Right to Respect of Privacy, Family, Home and Correspondence, and Protection of Honour and Reputation' (8 April 1988), available at www.refworld.org/docid/453883f922.html.

[29] Trinh Hai Yen, 'Viet Nam' in Simon Chesterman, Hisashi Owada and Ben Saul (eds), *Oxford Handbook of International Law in Asia and the Pacific* (Oxford University Press, 2019) 492–95.

a lack of confidence in the impartiality of international tribunals, and potential adverse impacts on its reputation.[30]

Yet, interacting with the international community has positively influenced Vietnam's understanding of international human rights standards. The drafting of the 2013 Constitution, followed by an array of codes and laws, exemplifies Vietnamese legislators' efforts to bridge the gap between international and domestic human rights standards.[31] Vietnam has generally complied with reporting obligations under the frameworks of the ICCPR and the Universal Periodic Review, albeit frequently delayed. Notably, the state of Vietnam's legal regime for data protection and privacy in cyberspace has triggered the concern of many interlocutors in such dialogue rounds.[32] Moreover, colloquiums on data protection and privacy has helped familiarise Vietnamese state actors with the relevant international standards, such as the Council of Europe's Convention on the Protection of Personal Data and the GDPR.[33] Accordingly, it is anticipated that Vietnamese national laws will reflect an adequate degree of protection.

Regarding its multilateral frameworks, Vietnam has not acceded to the APEC Cross-border Privacy Enforcement Agreement. However, it has ratified the Comprehensive and Progressive Trans-Pacific Partnership (CPTPP) and the EU – Vietnam Free Trade Agreement (EVFTA). These new-generation free trade agreements contain provisions on e-commerce, cross-border data transfers and data localisation requirements. The loose wording of CPTPP and EVFTA appear to give Vietnamese authorities considerable discretion in developing a legal framework on data protection and localisation requirements, subject to key requirements such as non-discrimination in form and application.[34] However, the ambiguity of the data localisation requirements of Vietnam's 2018 Law on Cybersecurity has raised significant concerns among some CPTPP signatories, as it could potentially conflict with the CPTPP's e-commerce regulations.[35] After a four-year period, Vietnam enacted the highly anticipated implementing document, Decree No 53/2022/ND-CP, in 2022, which defined to limit the applicability of the Cybersecurity Law on data localisation. The content of Decree No 53 will be analysed below.

[30] Tien-Duc Nguyen and Thu-Thuy Thi Tran, 'The Limits of Vietnam's Incrementalism towards the Abolition of Capital Punishment for Drug Offenses' (2022) 17(2) *Asian Journal of Comparative Law* 222.

[31] Nguyen and Viola (n 17) 320–23.

[32] See, eg, 'Vietnam's Cybersecurity Law Sparks Concerns From Businesses' (*Nikkei Asia*, 12 June 2018), available at https://asia.nikkei.com/Politics/Vietnam-s-cybersecurity-law-sparks-concerns-from-businesses#:~:text=HO%20CHI%20MINH%20CITY%20%2D%2D,15%20against%2C%20with%2028%20abstaining; 'Vietnam Stands By its Cybersecurity Law Amid US Criticism' (*Vnexpress*, 20 July 2018), available at https://e.vnexpress.net/news/news/vietnam-stands-by-its-cybersecurity-law-amid-us-criticism-3781011.html.

[33] Waewpen Piemwichai, 'Socialist Republic of Viet Nam' in Clarisse Girot (ed), *Regulation of Cross-Border Transfers of Personal Data in Asia* (Asian Business Law Institute, 2018) 399; See also Hội thảo về bảo vệ dữ liệu cá nhân trên không gian mạng (*MPS*, 9 December 2020), available at www.bocongan.gov.vn/tin-tuc/hoi-thao-ve-bao-ve-du-lieu-ca-nhan-tren-khong-gian-mang-t29200.html.

[34] Oliver Massmann and Nguyen Thi Lang, 'Vietnam – Cybersecurity – Comparing Vietnam's Cybersecurity Law with its Commitments Under the CPTPP, EVFTA' (Duane Morris, 22 September 2021), available at https://blogs.duanemorris.com/vietnam/2021/09/22/vietnam-cybersecurity-comparing-vietnams-cybersecurity-law-with-its-commitments-under-the-cptpp-evfta/.

[35] These included Japan and Canada, see 'Time for Vietnam to Get Cracking on CPTPP Reforms' (Vietnam National Trade Repository, 29 December 2023), available at https://vntr.moit.gov.vn/vi/news/time-for-vietnam-to-get-cracking-on-cptpp-reforms. For more, see James Fox, 'How are Foreign Investors Responding to Vietnam's New Data Localization Regulation' (*Vietnam Briefing*, 23 September 2022), available at www.vietnam-briefing.com/news/how-are-foreign-investors-responding-to-vietnams-new-data-localization-regulation.html/.

B. Legal Framework for Data Protection and Transfers

Vietnam has taken substantial measures to enact a plethora of legal instruments addressing the transfer and protection of personal data. A comprehensive, 'omnibus law' to govern data protection remains absent. It is noteworthy, however, that a government decree, the PDPD, was introduced in mid-2023 to pilot the framework for personal data protection, paving the way for a formal law to be enacted later. The PDPD is not subordinate to any existing law. It is considered as an independent, 'headless' document, serving as an experimental precursor to a more comprehensive legislative framework expected in the future. To attain legal status, the draft decree had to receive the approval of the Government, and be approved by the Standing Committee of the National Assembly.

In general, there are key national statutes governing data protection and transfer. In addition, sub-laws on data protection and transfers include:

- Decree No 52/2013/ND-CP dated 16 May 2013 on e-commerce, as amended and supplemented by Decree No 85/2021/ND-CP dated 25 September 2021.
- Decree No 72/2013/ND-CP dated 15 July 2013, on the management, provision, and use of internet services and online information, as amended and supplemented by Decree No 27/2018/ND-CP dated 1 August 2018.
- Decree No 15/2020/ND-CP dated 3 February 2020, providing penalties for administrative violations concerning postal, telecommunication, information technology, radio frequency areas and e-transactions, as amended and supplemented by Decree No 14/2022/ND-CP dated 27 January 2022.
- Decree No 91/2020/ND-CP dated 14 August 2020 on spam messages, spam emails and spam calls.
- Decree No 53/2022/ND-CP dated 15 August 2022 on the implementation of provisions of the 2018 Cybersecurity Law.

Article 38 of the 2015 Civil Code reaffirms the constitutional right to privacy as follows:

1. Private life, personal privacy and family privacy are inviolable and protected by law.
2. The collection, storage, use, and publication of information related to the private life or personal privacy of an individual must have the consent of that person, and the collection, storage, use, and publication of information related to family privacy must have the consent of the family members, except where otherwise prescribed by law.
3. The safety of the mail, telephone, telegraph, electronic database and other forms of private electronic information exchange of an individual shall be ensured and kept confidential. The opening, control and seizure of the mail, telephone, telegraph, electronic database and other forms of private electronic information exchange of another person may only be conducted in the cases provided by law.
4. A party to a contract may not disclose information on the private life, personal privacy or family privacy of the other party(ies) known to it during the process of contract establishment and performance, unless otherwise agreed.[36]

Article 38 applies to all forms of personal information in relation to both public and private sectors in which the owner of the information is involved. A notable dispute arose

[36] Civil Code No 91/2015/QH13 ('Civil Code 2015') (Adopted on 24 November 2015).

concerning whether communications in a work email account were considered personal and confidential.[37] The Vietnamese court interpreted Article 38 as affirming a company's right to access and disclose its employee's emails at a meeting without the employee's consent. On the facts of the case, the company implemented a 'computer policy' which was aimed at preventing personal use of the company-sponsored email service, which designated the email account as 'labour tool' subject to the 'labour contract' between two parties. The computer policy included an express statement that the company reserved the right to access and monitor the contents of emails. The Vietnamese court agreed with the company's submission that the well-established company policies, compounded by the employee's lack of objection at the time that the labour contract was concluded, could be construed as a prior, implicit consent of the employee to the 'computer policy' of the company.[38]

In terms of industry-specific laws, the 2005 Law on Electronic Transactions provides that agencies and organisations shall not use, provide, or disclose part or all of the information related to private and personal affairs or information of individuals which they can access or control in e-transactions without securing their prior consent unless otherwise provided by law.[39] This provision has been removed from the 2023 Law on Electronic Transactions, which came into effect on 1 July 2024, since the issue of personal data protection would be subject to a specialised legal regime.[40]

The 2010 Law on Credit Institutions prescribes the obligation of credit institutions and foreign bank branches in maintaining confidentiality of information relating to accounts, deposits, deposited assets, and transactions of their clients.[41]

The 2010 Law on Protection of Consumers requires that consumer information be kept secure and confidential upon making transactions and using goods or services. In cases of collection, use and transfer of consumer information, a goods or service trader shall:

a. Clearly and publicly notify consumers in advance of the purposes of collection and use of their information;
b. Obtain consumers' consent before using their information for the purpose already notified to consumers;
c. Ensure security, accuracy and completeness of consumer information during collection, use and transfer;
d. Update and correct information, or take measures to enable consumers to update and correct inaccurate information;
e. Obtain consumers' consent before transferring their information to a third party, unless otherwise provided by law.[42]

Unlike its predecessor, the new 2023 Consumer Protection Law, which came into effect on 1 July 2024, clearly defines 'consumer information', which is beyond the concept of personal data and encompasses details about purchases, product use, and other transaction-related matters.[43] The new Law also enshrines more detailed provisions on the protection of

[37] See more Graham Greenleaf, *Asian Data Privacy Laws: Trade & Human Rights Perspectives* (Oxford University Press, 2017) 361–70.
[38] ibid.
[39] Law on Electronic Transactions No 51/2005/QH11 (Adopted on 29 November 2005), Art 46(2).
[40] Law on Electronic Transactions No 20/2023/QH15 (Adopted on 22 June 2023).
[41] Law on Credit Institutions No 47/2010/QH12 (Adopted on 16 June 2010), Art 14(2).
[42] Law on Protection of Consumers No 59/2010/QH12 (Adopted on 17 November 2010), Art 6(2).
[43] Law on Protection of Consumers No 19/2023/QH15 (Adopted on 20 June 2023), Art 3(3).

consumer information.[44] This broader scope is expected to strengthen consumer protection.[45] Most consumer information protection principles in the new Law align with established personal data protection regulations. These include informing consumers, obtaining their consent, and ensuring data security. Despite overall compatibility, differences remain regarding specific personal data protection requirements. Examples include the notification method and timing when security incidents occur. It is unclear which provision takes precedence in such cases and would require further clarification to ensure seamless and consistent consumer protection.

The 2016 Law on Children recognises the right to privacy of a child for his or her best interests.[46] Children are legally defined as those aged under 16, and not considered as having legal capacity to give full consent to the collection and processing of their data.[47] Additional consent must be secured from their parents or guardians.[48] His or her personal information is protected from all unlawful interferences. The law also prohibits the sharing and disclosure of 'information on personal lives or secrets of children without the consent of children who have reached full 7 years of age and of their parents or guardians'.[49] The providers of information and communications products or services in the cyberspace are obligated to ensure the safety and personal privacy of children.[50]

The 2015 Law on the Security of Network Information prescribes network information security activities, the rights and responsibilities of agencies, organisations, and individuals in ensuring: network information safety; civil cryptography; standards and technical regulations on network information security; doing business in the field of network information security; developing human resources for network information security; and state management of network information security.[51]

The 2018 Law on Cybersecurity seeks to safeguard national security and ensure social order and safety in cyberspace, and thus prescribes responsibilities of relevant agencies, organisations, and individuals.[52] There is a conceptual distinction between the Cybersecurity Law and the Law on Network Information Security. While the former aims to secure electronic data from attacks from relevant devices, such as computers, servers, networks or phones, the latter focuses on the confidentiality, integrity, and availability of (such) information.

The 2010 Law on Postage safeguards the confidentiality of postal parcels.[53] In practice, compliance is varied. It is not unusual for postal service providers to inspect packages to examine whether the contents meet national postal regulations. For example, many books and journals ordered from international sources are required to obtain a clearance certificate from the Ministry of Information and Communications. Therefore, a notification will be sent to the recipient before the parcel can be delivered.

[44] ibid, Arts 15–21.

[45] Giang Thi Huong Tran and Thomas J Treutler, 'Significant Aspects of Vietnam's New Consumer Protection Law' (*Tilleke & Gibbins*, 3 November 2023), available at www.tilleke.com/insights/significant-aspects-of-vietnams-new-consumer-protection-law/.

[46] Law on Children No 102/2016/QH13 (Adopted on 5 April 2016), Art 21(1).

[47] ibid, Art 1.

[48] ibid, Art 6(11).

[49] ibid, Art 6(11).

[50] ibid, Art 54(2).

[51] Law on the Security of Network Information No 86/2015/QH13 (Adopted on 19 November 2015).

[52] Law on Cybersecurity No 24/2018/QH14 (Adopted on 12 June 2018).

[53] Law on Postage No 49/2010/QH12 (Adopted on 17 June 2010), Art 4.

The 2022 Law on Cinematographic, the 2012 Law on Publication, and the 2016 Law on Press embody prohibitions on the disclosure of personal privacy and information.[54]

As per the 2015 Criminal Code, crimes related to personal privacy include infringement of confidentiality or safety of correspondence, telephone or telegraph communications or the exchange of other private information of others,[55] illegal provision or use of information on computer networks and telecommunications networks, including acts related to the lawful information of agencies, organisations, or individuals, without permission.[56]

The 2015 Criminal Procedure Code lays out the procedural steps for the search, sequestration and collection of private mails, telephones, telegrams, electronic data and other forms of the exchange of personal information.[57] The 2015 Criminal Procedure Code authorises the use of certain special investigation measures, such as secret recording and videotaping, wiretapping, and secret collection of electronic data.[58] Under certain circumstances provided for by law a special investigation may be launched.[59] The information gathered from authorised special investigation measures shall only be accepted as evidence if its collection complies with law, is only meant for deterring crime.[60] Decree No 25/2014/ND-CP empowers specialised agencies of the Ministry of Public Security and the Ministry of National Defense to request information technology and telecommunications enterprises to provide information about customers and users when there are signs of legal infringement.[61]

C. Data Protection Frameworks

Generally, the terms 'data protection' and 'data privacy' are employed broadly and often interchangeably, but there is an important conceptual distinction between the two. Data protection primarily focuses on protecting information from unauthorised access, whereas data privacy delineates those who have authorised access.[62] Put another way, data protection proactively safeguards against (external) threats, whereas data privacy assesses the internal data management practices within an organisation.[63] The contrasting EU and US approaches to this issue are an example of such a distinction.[64] However, this feature is not clear in Vietnam's legal context as it is commonplace to witness the interchangeable usage of the two terms in ordinary discourse. Influenced by the EU's GDPR, Vietnam is striving to adopt a privacy-by-design model for data protection.

[54] Law on Cinematographic No 05/2022/QH15 (Adopted on 15 June 2022), Art 9(1)(g); Law on Publication No 19/2012/QH13 (Adopted on 20 November 2012), Art 10(1)(c); Law on Press No 103/2016/QH13 (Adopted on 5 April 2016), Art 9(5).

[55] Criminal Code No 100/2015/QH13 (Adopted on 27 November 2015), Art 9(5).

[56] ibid, Art 288.

[57] Criminal Procedure Code No 101/2015/QH13 (Adopted on 27 November 2015), Art 195.

[58] ibid, Art 223.

[59] ibid, Arts 224–26.

[60] ibid, Art 227(1).

[61] Decree No 25/2014/ND-CP, Art 14.

[62] 'Data Privacy vs. Data Protection: Understanding The Distinction In Defending Your Data' (*Forbes*, 19 Dec 2018), available at www.forbes.com/sites/forbestechcouncil/2018/12/19/data-privacy-vs-data-protection-understanding-the-distinction-in-defending-your-data/?sh=652602ea50c9.

[63] Rick Robinson, 'Data Privacy vs. Data Protection'(*Ipswitch*, 31 January 2020), available at www.ipswitch.com/blog/data-privacy-vs-data-protection.

[64] For a detailed comparative evaluation, see James Q Whitman, 'The Two Western Cultures of Privacy: Dignity Versus Liberty' (2004) 113 *The Yale Law Journal* 1151.

In Vietnamese law, the term 'personal data' is not used consistently. Article 3(15) of the 2015 Law on the Security of Network Information defines 'personal information' (*thông tin cá nhân*) as any information relating to the identification of an individual. Meanwhile, Article 3(16) of Decree No 72/2013/ND-CP on the implementation of provisions of the 2006 Information Technology Law defines 'personal information' as any information relating to 'the identification of an individual's identity including name, age, address, ID number, phone number, e-mail address, and others as provided for by law'. Decree No 52/2013/ND-CP on e-commerce further expands this definition:

> [P]ersonal information is any information contributing to identifying a specific person, including their name, age, home address, phone number, medical information, account number, information on personal payment transactions, and other information that the individual would like to keep confidential.

In the context of the 2018 Law on Cybersecurity, Decree No 53/2022/ND-CP defines 'data on personal information' (*dữ liệu về thông tin cá nhân*) as any data relating to information in forms of symbols, letters, numbers, images, sounds or those in kind for the identification of an individual's identity. The PDPD is the first legal document to use the term 'personal data' (*dữ liệu cá nhân*), which is understood as any data about a natural person or relating to an identified or identifiable individual.[65] Essentially, the definitions of 'personal information', 'data about personal information', and 'personal data' seem to overlap and denote any information relating to an identified or identifiable person. The adoption of 'personal data' as provided in the PDPD shows the influence of the GDPR on Vietnam's data protection law.[66]

The existing legal framework does not meaningfully distinguish between personal and non-personal data. Industry-specific laws govern and protect relevant personal information. For example, healthcare regulations ensure the protection of personal medical records and transmittable disease status, while banking regulations safeguard the privacy of banking clients. The PDPD sets out two types of personal data: basic and sensitive. Basic personal data includes an individual's name, date and place of birth, blood type, gender, residential address, hometown, address, email, ethnicity, nationality, phone number, ID number, driving licence, individual tax number, social security number, status of marriage, browsing history in cyberspace, etc.[67] Notably, some of the personal data genres enshrined in Decree No 52 and Decree No 72 have been re-classified as sensitive in the PDPD. Sensitive personal data comprises political, religious, sex life, sexual orientation information, health data, genetic data, biometrical data, criminal records, financial data, social relationships, and other sensitive information as provided for by law. It seems that the two-tier categorisation of personal data imposes a more onerous duty related to the processing of sensitive data, which includes appointing a data protection officer (DPO) and a built-in data protection department (DPD) and informing data subjects about the processing of their sensitive personal data, unless specific exemptions as provided in the PDPD.[68] However, with no

[65] PDPD, Art 2(1).

[66] GDPR, Art 4(1) provides that '"personal data" means any information relating to an identified or identifiable natural person …'.

[67] PDPD, Art 2(3)(4).

[68] ibid, Arts 26–28.

specific provision on non-personal data, it remains unclear what legal rules will apply where personal and non-personal data are intertwined and inseparable.

The PDPD introduces novel concepts such as 'data subjects', 'data users', 'data controllers', 'data processors' and 'data controller-processors'. Accordingly, the 'data subject' is defined as an individual identified from the personal data.[69] The 'data controller' means an entity or individual that determines the purposes and means of processing personal data.[70] The 'data processor' refers to an entity or individual that processes data on behalf of the data controller through a contract or agreement.[71] The 'data controller-processor' is identified as an entity or individual that simultaneously decides the purpose, means and directly processes personal data.[72] Any entity not classified as a data subject, controller, processor, or controller-processor assistant involved in the processing of personal data is considered a third party.[73] By and large, the controllers and controller-processors are under heavier responsibility for personal data protection.[74]

In addition, the PDPD, with its ambitious and extensive governing scope, sets forth eight overarching principles.[75] The principle of Lawfulness is intended to facilitate the collection of personal data in cases of necessity, while ensuring compliance with the law. The principle of Purpose allows personal data to be processed for registered or announced purposes. The principle of Data Minimisation allows the collection of personal data within the scope necessary to achieve the particular purposes. The principle of Restricted Use permits the use of personal data only with the consent of the data subject or the authorisation of the competent authority. The principle of Data Quality ensures personal data be kept up-to-date and complete for data-processing purposes. The principle of Security mandates that safeguards be applied to personal data during theprocessing. The principle of Individuality requires that data subjects must be aware and informed of activities related to the processing of their personal data. Finally, the principle of Confidentiality requires that personal data be kept confidential during the processing. While the implementation of the PDPD is in its infancy, the textual adoption of the novel concepts and principles in the PDPD is somewhat unprecedented and highlights the incorporation by the Vietnamese Government of lessons from the GDPR model.

Vietnamese law does not currently recognise the concepts of anonymisation, pseudonymisation, and encryption. A notable exception is that banking regulations require classified information be encrypted prior to either domestic or international transfer.[76] The draft PDPD introduced the phrase 'de-identification of personal data', which referred to the process of anonymisation, erasing or pseudonymisation of information relating to identification of an individual, thus generating new data which may not be traced to a specific individual.[77] Yet, it is unclear what the legal ramifications of data anonymisation

[69] ibid, Art 2(6).
[70] ibid, Art 2(9).
[71] ibid, Art 2(10).
[72] ibid, Art 2(11).
[73] ibid, Art 2(12).
[74] ibid, Arts 38–40.
[75] ibid, Art 3.
[76] Circular No 31/2015/TT-NHNN regulating safety and confidentiality of banking information technology systems (2015), Art 35(2).
[77] Draft PDPD, Arts 2(13), 17(1).

might be, such as whether anonymisation of such data would exclude it from the governing scope of personal data laws. However, given its novelty the final text of the PDPD has left out this issue. Perhaps, the Government wishes to adopt the PDPD as the experimental scheme on personal data protection issue and takes stock of it step by step before making any further changes.

Previously, Vietnamese law treated domestic and cross-border data transfers equally. The decisive factor in both scenarios governing the lawful collection, recording, storage, use, disclosure, and dissemination of personal data by a third party is consent.[78] Consent must be obtained prior to any processing and transfers. There were no legal requirements for data exporters to seek prior authorisation from, or make a filing with, the Vietnamese authorities. Regulations governing the consent requirement emerged in certain sectors, such as the e-commerce sector, where consent must be in an express form.[79] These obligations, however, did not extend to all sectors. There were certain circumstances where the collection of personal information might be exempted from the consent requirement.[80]

The PDPD heralds a significant change in this respect, setting higher standards for cross-border data transfer. This is examined in the following section.

Data protection enforcement in Vietnam is a shared responsibility among several governmental agencies, with the scope of their involvement varying according to their respective fields of specialisation. The Ministry of Information and Communications (MIC) is the most relevant supervisory body, which has competence to monitor, investigate, settle complaints and denunciations, and manages data privacy violations relating to telecommunications, the Internet and Information Technology. The Ministry of Industry and Trade has the authority to investigate violations of data privacy relating to e-commerce. Data protection and privacy issues in the banking sector fall under the jurisdiction of the Vietnamese State Bank. The Ministry of Public Security (MPS) supervises the protection of state secrets, addresses cybercrimes, and other issues related to national security and social order. Where necessary, agencies, organisations, and individuals are required to work with the MPS and the Ministry of National Defense in investigating criminal offences concerning information security, and threats to national security.

Institutional changes do not materialise with the promulgation of the new legal document on personal data protection. The specialised regulatory agency, the Personal Data Protection Commission (PDPC), as proposed in the Draft PDPD, was removed from the final text of the PDPD. The PDPC would have 17 mandates as laid out in Article 24 of the Draft PDPD. Among other competencies, the PDPC would have the authority to make a request to the Director General of the Department of Cyber Security and High-Tech Crime Prevention and Control (under the MPS) to inspect and supervise the activities of personal data protection within an agency or organisation. In addition, the PDPC would evaluate and rate the reliability of personal data protection of agencies and organisations and publish this information on the National Personal Data Protection Portal. Given the pilot characteristic of the PDPD, the establishment of PDPC will resurface once the PDPD status is re-examined and upgraded to a law.

[78] Piemwichai (n 33) 404–405.
[79] Decree 52/2013/ND-CP on e-commerce (Adopted on 16 May 2013), Art 32(3).
[80] Piemwichai (n 33) 402.

III. Legal Bases, Mechanisms and Exceptions for International Data Transfers and Data Protection

A. International Data Transfers

The international transfer of personal data within the Vietnamese context has been largely liberal, with minimal state intervention. As noted above, except for the e-commerce sector, which necessitates express consent of data subjects for transfer of information, the specific form of consent required in other fields remains legally ambiguous. This lack of clarity led to different interpretations and mixed practices.[81] In addition, the 2006 Information Technology Law prescribes obligations to notify owners regarding the form, scope, place and purpose of the collection, processing or use of personal information.[82] However, there is no designated template to guide the fulfilment of this obligation.[83] The Law on Network Information Security places an obligation on organisations or individuals handling personal information to adopt and publicise their policies relating to the handling and protection of personal information.[84] Beyond these requirements however, the role of Vietnamese authorities in overseeing cross-border data transfers and ensuring compliance with the notification duties is relatively limited.

Considering the vast quantities of data transferred internationally from Vietnam annually, and the ensuing privacy risks as well as economic potentials, the Vietnamese Government has had strong incentive to tighten controls on data transfers.[85] This is one of the urgent matters that the PDPD aims to address. Accordingly, international/cross-border data transfer has been defined in the PDPD as the use of cyberspace or electronic devices/technology to transfer Vietnamese citizens' personal data outside Vietnam's territory.[86]

The PDPD introduces a substantial reform of the existing consent rules. Firstly, consent must be express and voluntary given that the data subject is fully informed about: (i) the genre of personal data to be processed; (ii) the purpose of the personal data processing; (iii) the authorised entities to process personal data; and (iv) the data subject's rights.[87] Silence, or a non-response of the data subjects would no longer be legally treated as implied consent. Secondly, consent shall be obtained on a granular basis, signifying that distinct purposes of data utilisation must be presented in a manner that allows data subjects to grant opt-in consent to individual purposes or a combination thereof. Additionally, the provision of partial or conditional consent may afford data subjects a degree of agency over their personal information. Moreover, consent must be granted in a printable or copyable format. The PDPD also clarifies that data subjects may rescind their consent at any time.[88]

[81] Piemwichai (n 33) 402.
[82] Law on Information Technology No 67/2006/QH11 (Adopted on 29 June 2006), Arts 1, 4(3)(4).
[83] Piemwichai (n 33) 402.
[84] Law on Network Information Security No 86/2015/QH13 (Adopted on 19 November 2015), Arts 3(17), 16(3).
[85] IPS, 'Dam bao dong chay du lieu an toan vat u do cho phat trien kinh te so' ['Ensuring a Safe and Free Flow of Data for the Development of a Digital Economy'] (IPS, August 2021), available at www.ips.org.vn/thu-vien/du-lieu-xuyen-bien-gioi-va-van-de-bao-ve-du-lieu-ca-nhan-ct225.html.
[86] PDPD, Art 2(14).
[87] ibid, Art 11.
[88] ibid, Art 12.

In the event of a dispute, the burden of proof regarding the grant of consent will rest with the data processor.

An ambiguity exists within Vietnamese personal data regulations regarding the potential legality of personal data trading. While Article 3(4) of the PDPD appears to impose a blanket ban on such transactions, stating that personal data 'cannot be bought or sold in any form', Article 22(2) seemingly takes issue with this by suggesting that 'buying and selling personal data without the consent of the data subject is a violation of the law'. This discrepancy is left open for interpretation, raising the question of whether consent could potentially legitimise data trading under certain circumstances.[89]

Under existing law, an individual's consent may not be relevant to the collection and processing of personal information in four circumstances: where (i) the information has already been published on e-commerce websites; (ii) for the signing, and/or performing of contracts for the sale and/or purchase of goods and services; (iii) for calculating prices or charges for use of information, products and services online;[90] and (iv) for performing other obligations as provided for by law.[91] The exemptions to the consent rule are broadened by the PDPD. Accordingly, Article 17 of the PDPD sets out five circumstances that a data subject's consent would not be necessary for processing personal data:

1. The processing is to protect the life and health of the data subject or others in an emergency situation. Data Controllers, Data Processors, Data Controller-Processors, and Third Parties are under the burden of proof.
2. The disclosure of personal data is in accordance with the law.
3. The processing of data is performed by competent state agencies in the event of a state of emergency related to national defence, national security, social order and safety, major disaster, or dangerous epidemic; when there is a threat to security and national defence but not to the extent that a state of emergency must be declared; or when the processing is to prevent and combat riots and terrorism, crimes, and law violations in accordance with law.
4. The processing is to perform the contractual obligations of the data subject with relevant agencies, organisations, and individuals as prescribed by law.
5. The processing is to serve the activities of state agencies prescribed by sector-specific laws.

The interplay of these grounds of exemptions with the broad applicability of the consent requirement may be further clarified in the future. For instance, the life and health of the data subject or other individuals may be a permissible ground to circumvent privacy rights of the data subject, even against their will. States of emergency concerning national defence, national security, social order and safety, dangerous events such as natural disasters or contagious pandemics can also legitimately limit such rights in light of Article 14 of the 2013 Constitution. The generality of certain prescribed exemptions may also give cause for concern. For instance, the catch-all phrase 'to prevent and combat crimes and

[89] Anh Hoai Nguyen, Giang Thi Huong Tran and Waewpen Piemwichai, 'A Closer Look at Vietnam's First-Ever Personal Data Protection Decree' (*Tilleke & Gibbins*, 21 April 2023), available at www.tilleke.com/insights/a-closer-look-at-vietnams-first-ever-personal-data-protection-decree/.

[90] Decree No 52/2013/ND-CP on e-commerce, Art 70(4).

[91] Law on Information Technology (n 82), Art 21(3)(c).

law violations' appears overly broad and subject to state agencies' divergent interpretations, thereby inherently engendering ambiguity about privacy rights. Despite remaining ambiguities, the provision on the processing of personal data without consent for the purposes of contractual obligations demonstrates the influence of the GDPR.[92]

Under Article 25 of the PDPD, entities that wish to transfer personal data outside Vietnam must prepare a comprehensive 'Dossier of Impact Assessment for Cross-Border Transfer of Personal Data' ('TIA Dossier'). Essential elements of the TIA Dossier include:

i. Identification and contact information of the transferor and recipient, including organisational details and responsible individuals.
ii. A detailed explanation of the intended purpose for processing personal data abroad.
iii. The types of personal data to be transferred.
iv. Demonstration of adherence to relevant PDPD regulations and outline implemented data protection measures.
v. A thorough evaluation of potential risks and negative consequences associated with the transfer, outlining strategies to mitigate such impacts.
vi. Verifiable consent from individuals whose data is subject to transfer.
vii. Documented agreements that clarify responsibilities and data protection commitments between the transferor and recipient.

The PDPD mandates an ex-post reporting approach. It requires the TIA Dossier be readily available for inspection and assessment by Vietnamese authorities. Within 60 days upon transfer completion, the transferor shall submit an original TIA Dossier to the Department of Cybersecurity and Hi-tech Crime Prevention within the MPS. Upon successful transfer, the transferor must promptly notify the relevant agency, providing necessary details and contact information. The authority reserves the right to review the TIA Dossier and request adjustments for completeness and compliance. The MPS holds the power to halt cross-border data transfers under specific circumstances, including: (i) violation of Vietnamese national security interests; (ii) incomplete or non-compliant TIA Dossiers; (iii) unauthorised disclosure or loss of Vietnamese citizen data. Noteworthy caveats regarding national security interests remains broadly defined, potentially impacting transfer approvals.

The embryonic stage of the overall framework of law for personal data protection in Vietnam is also reflected in the significantly underdeveloped privacy assessment regime. The existing legislation lacks any provisions on 'adequacy decision' that evaluates whether a third country, territory, specific sector in a third country, or an international organisation possesses a data protection law that offers adequate or comparable standards to that of Vietnam. Absent are whitelists and blacklists, which indicate jurisdictions to which cross-border transfer of personal data could potentially be made without adhering to consent or other compliance requirements. Furthermore, this matter goes almost entirely unmentioned in the Draft PDPD, except for the conditions for permissible cross-border data transfers. The Draft PDPD also does not clarify the position of the Vietnamese Government on this matter. Considering that one of the mandates of the PDPC is to advise the Government on

[92] Waewpen Piemwichai, Giang Thi Huong Tran and Trung Bao Tran, 'Vietnam's Personal Data Protection Decree Takes Important Step toward Issuance' (*Tilleke & Gibbins*, 8 February 2023), available at www.tilleke.com/insights/vietnams-personal-data-protection-decree-takes-important-step-toward-issuance/.

data protection policies, 'adequacy findings' may be deliberated upon subsequently, when the PDPC works out the provisions of the draft Decree in practice.

Contracts for cross-border data transfers between data exporters and importers are not required under Vietnamese law. Nonetheless, Vietnamese banking regulations impose a higher burden by compelling a written agreement prior to the transfer of data, irrespective of the place of transfer. Legal obligations and duties of all parties must be detailed in written agreements, including provisions setting out measures for handling data breaches and stipulating compensation for loss and damage.[93]

International certification plays very little role in Vietnam's data protection practices. In 2020, the country was reported to be considering joining the APEC Cross-Border Privacy Rules (CBPR).[94] It appears that the consideration process is still ongoing, without any definitive date for a final decision. As noted by Piemwichai, several issues need to be addressed before the formal process of joining the CBPR may be initiated.[95] Among other prerequisites, the promulgation of a comprehensive data protection legal framework is the first step. Consultations with data privacy and protection experts are also crucial for the assessment of organisational accountability and data protection management.

Trustmark schemes exist in Vietnam for the purposes of boosting consumers' confidence and facilitating e-commerce businesses.[96] However, in terms of privacy and data protection, trustmark schemes or privacy seals are little known to the public. Preliminary steps are being taken by the MIC to better inform internet users of the electronic services and virtual platforms they access within Vietnam. In particular, the MIC's National Cyber Security Center is developing a certification scheme (tinnhiemmang.vn) to rate the reliability and security of four categories, including: (i) organisations and agencies; (ii) websites; (iii) devices; and (iv) network systems.[97] The scheme aims to help users identify accurate information sources and preventing phishing attacks, whilst also assisting organisations and businesses to increase their professional reputation and consumer-friendliness In addition, the PDPC established under the Draft PDPD could be an important development. This agency has, among others, a mandate to assess and rank the reliability of data protection of agencies, organisations, and publicise it on the National Information Portal on data protection. After its adoption, the Draft PDPD will likely shift the attention of a significant portion of stakeholders to this issue. Thus, conditions facilitating a thriving marketplace for trustmark schemes and privacy seals may emerge.

B. International Data Protection and Liability

As noted above, the requirements for the collection, processing and retention of personal information are often dependent on sector-specific regulations. For example, unauthorised collection, copying, exchange, provision, transfer of state secrets are strictly prohibited

[93] Circular No 31/2015/TT-NHNN, Art 30(2).

[94] 'APEC Cross-Border Privacy Rules System Poised for Expansion' (*Hunton*, 26 Oct 2016), available at www.huntonprivacyblog.com/2016/10/26/apec-cross-border-privacy-rules-system-poised-expansion/.

[95] Piemwichai (n 33) 407–408.

[96] Greenleaf (n 37) 370.

[97] For more, see 'Tín nhiệm Mạng: Giới Thiệu' (*National Cyber Security Center VN*, 2021), available at https://tinnhiemmang.vn/gioi-thieu.

in any form.[98] State secrets must be encrypted before transfer, whether domestically or internationally.[99]

With the introduction of new entities relating to the processing of personal data, the PDPD further clarifies responsibilities of such actors. Accordingly, the Personal Data Controller shall demonstrate compliance with personal data protection laws through comprehensive organisational and technical measures, including security safeguards.[100] These measures must be regularly reviewed and updated as needed. The Controller shall promptly report any personal data breaches to the relevant authorities.[101] The Personal Data Processor shall engage in processing of personal data only upon a valid contractual agreement detailing the scope and purpose of data processing activities established with the designated Personal Data Controller.[102] The Controller and the Processor bear full legal responsibility for any damages arising from the processing of personal data and shall actively cooperate with the Ministry of Public Security and other relevant state agencies in safeguarding personal data, providing necessary information for investigations and handling any violations of personal data protection laws.[103]

Owners of personal information are entitled to privacy rights, and the confidentiality and integrity of their information shall be safeguarded in accordance with the 2013 Constitution and sectoral laws. The rules for the collection, storage, processing, use, disclosure, and publication of personal data are set out in the 2015 Civil Code. The Law on Network Information Security lays out several obligations and duties of data processors in relation to subjects of personal information.[104]

Upon the promulgation of the PDPD, the rights of data subjects are put together in a single statutory provision. Accordingly, Article 9 of the PDPD enshrines a set of 11 rights, meticulously crafted to empower data subjects and safeguard their personal information. These rights act as foundational pillars, enabling individuals to meaningfully engage with the processing of their data and assert their autonomy in the digital landscape. These include the right to be informed, right to consent, right to access, right to rescind consent, right to erasure, right to restriction, right to data portability, right to object to the processing of personal data for specific purposes, right to lodge a complaint to a competent authority, right to damages, right to self-defence. This set of rights seemingly draws inspiration from the GDPR.[105]

Violations of the data protection regulations will be punishable administratively and criminally. Decree No 15/2020/ND-CP, as amended by Decree No 14/2022/ND-CP, provides penalties for administrative violations in the fields of postage, telecommunications, radio frequency, information technology, and e-transactions. The collection of personal information without the consent of the owner entails a fine of VND 10–20 million.[106] Providing, sharing, disseminating, or selling the information of a person without his or her consent to

[98] Law on Safeguarding State Secret No 29/2018/QH14 (Adopted on 15 November 2018), Art 5.
[99] Law on Cipher No 05/2011/QH13 (Adopted on 26 November 2011), Art 9.
[100] PDPD, Art 38(1).
[101] ibid, Art 38(3).
[102] ibid, Art 39(1)(2).
[103] ibid, Arts 38(6)(7), 39(4)(5)(6).
[104] Law on Network Information Security 2015 (n 84), Arts 17–18.
[105] GDPR, Arts 12–23.
[106] Decree No 15/2020/ND-CP, Art 84(1).

a third party entails a fine between VND 20–30 million.[107] Failure to verify, rectify, or delete personal information upon a request from the owner can carry a fine of between VND 5–10 million.[108] Offenders may also be held criminally liable under Article 159 of the 2015 Criminal Code for violations of confidentiality and integrity of a person's correspondence, mail, telephone, or other forms of communication. Potential sanctions range from a fine, to non-custodial reform of three months, to imprisonment of up to three years. Victims are entitled to reparation under Article 13 of the 2015 Civil Code. Following the promulgation of the PDPD, the Ministry of Public Security will also be drafting a decree to detail administrative penalties for the violations in the field of cybersecurity.[109]

The administrative and criminal approaches of handling data-related violations also possess an extraterritorial dimension. Article 20 of the 2012 Law on Handling of Administrative Violations (as amended through 2020) empowers a competent authority to sanction any Vietnamese organisation and citizens committing an administrative violation outside the territory of Vietnam. Article 6(1) and (2) of the 2015 Criminal Code imposes criminal liability on any Vietnamese legal person or citizen residing outside Vietnam committing an offence under the Criminal Code. Any foreign legal person or individual can be held to criminal account under the Criminal Code for violations of legitimate rights and interests of Vietnamese citizens and the state of Vietnam, or pursuant to an international convention to which Vietnam is a party. Thus, while the prescriptive jurisdiction of the state in administrative cases is based on the nationality principle, in criminal cases subject to strict state competence, it is based on both the nationality principle and the territoriality principle. In addition, Article 6(3) of the 2015 Criminal Code provides universal jurisdiction for Vietnam to prosecute criminal cases that take place on the high seas or outside the country's airspace, in accordance with the international convention to which it is a party.

In the event of a data breach, the law requires data administrators – a role equivalent to a data controller who administers an information system[110] – to report the breach that has gone beyond their control to one or more of the members of the National Cyber Information Security Incident Response Network, including the Vietnam Computer Emergency Response Team.[111] However, it is worth noting that this obligation is not accompanied by a statutory timeframe for implementation. Furthermore, it is uncertain if this obligation is imposed on offshore information system operators. Businesses offering cyber services in Vietnam are obligated to notify users of data breaches or the risks thereof. There are no exceptions to this notice obligation. Nevertheless, the enforcement of this provision is far from effective, since the laws do not provide details on the timing or the method of such notice.[112] In the e-commerce sector, if information theft or potential information

[107] ibid, Art 84(2).

[108] ibid, Art 102(2)(c).

[109] The draft Decree on Penalties for Administrative Violations in The Field of Cybersecurity has been open for public consultation, available at https://thuvienphapluat.vn/van-ban/Cong-nghe-thong-tin/Nghi-dinh-quy-dinh-xu-phat-vi-pham-hanh-chinh-trong-linh-vuc-an-ninh-mang-488693.aspx.

[110] Law on Network Information Security (n 84) Art 2(5); Circular No 03/2017/TT-BTTTT.

[111] Yee Chung Seck and Thanh Son Dang, 'Vietnam: Regulatory Framework Regarding Reporting and Responding to Cyber Information Security Incidents – Decision No. 05 and Circular No. 20' (*Global Compliance News*, 24 November 2017), available at www.globalcompliancenews.com/2017/11/24/vietnam-cyber-security-incidents-20171124/.

[112] 'General Data Security Breach Notification Requirements: Vietnam: Global Data Privacy & Security Handbook: Baker McKenzie Resource Hub' (*Baker Mckenzie*), available at https://resourcehub.bakermckenzie.

loss occurs, the organisation storing the information shall be responsible for notifying the regulator within 24 hours after the detection of the breach.[113] As for banking regulations, credit institutions, foreign bank's branches, and intermediary payment service providers are mandated to report cybersecurity incidents to the State Bank of Vietnam within 24 hours of detection, along with an update on its resolution within five working days of its conclusion.[114]

IV. Data Security and Data Localisation

One of the fiercely controversial issues during the drafting of the 2018 Law on Cybersecurity concerned the introduction of the data localisation requirements.[115] In addition to the local presence requirement, Article 26 of the Cybersecurity Law compels service providers – both domestically and internationally – that collect, use, analyse, and process certain types of data on telecom networks, internet and value-added services in Vietnam's cyberspace to store that data in Vietnam for a fixed time period. Opinions on this data localisation requirement varied widely, from staunch opposition, to cautious support, to firm endorsement. Detractors, including some foreign governments, non-governmental organisations, and business associations,[116] argued that data localisation could infringe on human rights in cyberspace and hurt business interests.[117] For example, before and during its Universal Periodic Review in 2019, Vietnam faced severe criticism from foreign governments, including the US, for introducing data localisation requirements that could undermine free speech and privacy rights.[118] At a National Assembly deliberation session on the draft Cybersecurity Law, some deputies were sceptical of the enforceability and opportunity costs of such requirements.[119] On the other hand, proponents argued that such requirements were in line with international law and national law. It would be in the national interest to control the flow of data generated by Vietnamese service users or within the territory of Vietnam.[120] The 2018 Law on Cybersecurity was eventually approved by the National Assembly on 12 June 2018, despite the opposition. However, the exact application of the data localisation requirement was unclear. It was only in August 2022 when the Government's Decree No 53/2022/ND-CP was promulgated that the enforcement of such requirements was clarified.

com/en/resources/global-data-privacy-and-cybersecurity-handbook/asia-pacific/vietnam/topics/breach-notification-requirements.

[113] Decree No 52/2013/NĐ-CP on e-commerce, Art 72(3).

[114] Circular 18/2018/TT-NHNN dated 21 August 2018 regulating the information system in banking activities, Art 53(1).

[115] For more background information, see Nguyen, Bui & Phung (n 14).

[116] ibid.

[117] ibid, 3–7.

[118] ibid, 5.

[119] Bảo Hà, 'Đại Biểu Quốc Hội Tranh Luận về Dự Thảo Luật an Ninh Mạng' ['National Assembly Delegates Debate on Draft Law on Cyber Security'] (*Vnexpress*, 29 May 2018), available at https://vnexpress.net/dai-bieu-quoc-hoi-tranh-luan-ve-du-thao-luat-an-ninh-mang-3756101.html; Võ Hải, 'Tranh Luận Việc Buộc Facebook, Google Đặt Máy Chủ ở Việt Nam' ['Debate on Forcing Facebook and Google to Set Up Servers in Vietnam'] (*Vnexpress*, 23 November 2017), available at https://vnexpress.net/tranh-luan-viec-buoc-facebook-google-dat-may-chu-o-viet-nam-3674621.html.

[120] 'Đại Biểu Quốc Hội Tranh Luận về Việc Ban Hành Luật An Ninh Mạng' ['National Assembly Deputies Debate the Promulgation of the Law on Cyber Security'] (*Tạp chí Cộng sản*, 23 November 2017), available at

According to Decree No 53/2022/ND-CP, three types of personal data are required to be stored locally: (i) data identifying a person (personal data of service users in Vietnam); (ii) data generated by service users in Vietnam including the account name for use of services, duration of use of services, credit card information, email address, IP addresses for the latest login and logout, and registered telephone number attached to the account or data; and (iii) data reflecting the relationship between service users and others in Vietnam. These three types are referred to 'regulated data' within the context of Decree No 53.

Both domestic and foreign enterprises fall under this decree's jurisdiction, with domestic enterprises required to store the data in Vietnam regardless of their core businesses.[121] This broad mandate potentially conflicts with Article 26 of the Cybersecurity Law, which only requires localised storage by 'domestic service providers who collects, uses, analyses, processes certain types of data on telecom networks, internet and value-added services in Viet Nam's cyberspace'.[122] Meanwhile, 10 types of foreign enterprises may be subject to data localisation and local presence requirements. These include those which provide: (i) telecom services; (ii) services of data storage and sharing in cyberspace (cloud storage); (iii) supply of national or international domain names to service users in Vietnam; (iv) e-commerce; (v) online payment; (vi) intermediary payment; (vii) service of transport connection via cyberspace; (viii) social networking and social media; (ix) online electronic games; and (x) services of providing, managing, or operating other information in cyberspace in the form of messages, phone calls, video calls, email, or online chat. Two additional thresholds must be met:

i. The services provided by the overseas entity have been used by the service users to commit acts of violating the Cybersecurity Law; and
ii. The Department of Cybersecurity and High-Tech Crime Prevention (an authority under the Ministry of Public Security) has sent a written notice to an entity requesting coordination, prevention, investigation and handling of such violation acts, which has not been fully complied with.

Hence, despite legal ambiguity, some legal professionals argue that foreign entities must store the data locally and establish a branch or representative office if four conditions are met: (1) the data is regulated data; (2) the services are regulated services; (3) the use of the services is in violation of Vietnamese law; and (4) there has been a failure to cooperate upon a written request of the MPS.[123] Foreign entities shall have 12 months from the date of the MPS's request to establish a local presence in the form of a branch or representative office and localise the regulated data. It is up to the overseas entity to decide the form of data storage, with the minimum storage time of 24 months from the date of request receipt date. Non-compliance may result in strict penalties. In cases of *force majeure*, where

www.tapchicongsan.org.vn/web/guest/hoat-ong-cua-lanh-ao-ang-nha-nuoc/-/2018/48123/dai-bieu-quoc-hoi-tranh-luan-ve-viec-ban-hanh-luat-an-ninh-mang.aspx.

[121] Decree No 53/2022/ND-CP, Art 26(2).

[122] VCCI, *The Flow of Business Law 2022* (Industry and Commerce Publisher, 2022) 35.

[123] 'Decree 53 Guiding Cybersecurity Law' (*Pricewaterhousecoopers*, 8 September 2022), available at www.pwc.com/vn/en/publications/2022/220908-pwc-vietnam-legal-newsbrief-decree-53.pdf; Giang Thi Huong Tran, Waewpen Piemwichai and Trung Bao Tran, 'Decree 53 Provides Long-Awaited Guidance on Implementation of Vietnam's Cybersecurity Law' (*Tilleke & Gibbins*, 12 October 2022), available at www.tilleke.com/insights/decree-53-provides-long-awaited-guidance-on-implementation-of-vietnams-cybersecurity-law/.

it is impossible for the entity to observe the request, it must notify the Ministry within three working days for verification and may be granted an extra 30 days to seek a corrective alternative.

V. Issues in Private International Law

A. Litigations Involving Cross-Border Data Transfer and Privacy

Litigations involving cross-border data protection and privacy in Vietnam may be pursued through civil, administrative, and criminal routes. In civil and administrative cases, the claimants are typically information owners who believe their legitimate rights and interests are being infringed. This category includes both Vietnamese and foreign persons, agencies, and organisations, as well as international organisations and their representative offices.[124] In criminal cases, the Vietnamese procuracy drives the litigation before the courts. Defendants can range from individuals to agencies and organisations who have violated the confidentiality and integrity of personal information as protected by the law.

Notably, the concept of class actions does not have a solid legal basis in Vietnam. The 2015 Civil Procedure Code allows courts to combine similar cases into a single proceeding,[125] yet provides little procedural guidance to address lawsuits involving a large number of claimants.[126] In principle, social organisations and associations may act on behalf of consumers to bring a public interest lawsuit.[127] However, no such action relating to consumers' information protection and privacy has been documented. The Vietnam Consumers Protection Association (VICOPRO) has had minimal involvement in representing consumers before courts in cases of personal information breaches.[128] This lack of action can be partly attributed to the fact that, despite being authorised to represent consumers in related lawsuits, VICOPRO lacks the necessary resources to adequately perform such tasks, leaving consumers' privacy rights vulnerable to violations.[129]

[124] Civil Procedure Code No 92/2015/QH13 (Adopted on 25 November 2015), Art 465(1).

[125] ibid, Art 42.

[126] One example is the Vedan company case, where thousands of residents and farmers along the Thi Vai River suffered loss of livelihood and health hazards due to the company's discharge of untreated wastewater into the river. The Vedan case was eventually settled outside the court. Many lawyers and legal scholars have suggested that if the court took this case, it would have been overwhelmed by a massive workload, and the immaturity and ambiguities of the law, causing the case to be dragged out for many years, delaying the justice sought by the victims. See 'Lessons Learned from Vedan: A Call for Class Action Suits in Vietnam' (*Vietnam Law Magazine*, 9 January 2010), available at https://vietnamlawmagazine.vn/lessons-learned-from-vedan-a-call-for-class-action-suits-in-vietnam-3633.html.

[127] Law on the Protection of Consumers' Legitimate Rights and Interests 2010, Art 29.

[128] Until mid-2021, VICOPRO succeeded only one case in the protection of consumers' rights, see 'Vai trò quan trọng và một số kết quả đạt được của Hội Bảo vệ Người tiêu dùng Việt Nam (VICOPRO) trong công tác bảo vệ quyền lợi người tiêu dùng ở Việt Nam' ['The Important Role and Some Achievements of the Vietnam Consumer Protection Association (VICOPRO) in Protecting Consumer Rights in Vietnam'] (*Vietnam Competition and Consumer Authority*, 15 October 2021), available at www.vcca.gov.vn/default.aspx?page=news&do=detail&id=a0e74908-e948-4163-98c9-9615fa60f94f.

[129] Nguyễn Đình Hiệp, 'Tổ Chức Xã Hội Tham Gia Bảo vệ Quyền Lợi Người Tiêu Dùng Được Quy Định Như Thế Nào?' ['How are Social Organizations Involved in Protecting Consumer Rights Regulated?'] (*Luật Hoàng Anh*, 31 January 2023), available at https://luathoanganh.vn/thuong-mai/to-chuc-xa-hoi-tham-gia-bao-ve-quyen-loi-nguoi-tieu-dung-duoc-quy-dinh-nhu-the-nao-lha7261.html.

Civil law channels are often utilised to seek monetary compensation for damages, as provided under Articles 13–15 of the 2015 Civil Code. Additional restitutive and satisfactory measures to protect privacy rights may include orders for the compulsory termination of the violating act, public apology or correction, the performance of unfulfilled obligations, or the revocation of the illegal decision of a competent person, agency or organisation.[130] However, Vietnamese courts are generally apathetic towards civil cases dealing with personal information protection and privacy.[131] Losses related to reputational damage, which are considered enigmatic and cumbersome, are seldom awarded.[132] Public apologies, or negotiated monetary settlements are more common.

Within their competence and duties, state administrative bodies and officials are empowered to impose administrative penalties against violations related to data protection and privacy.[133] Principal administrative sanctions include warnings and fines. Offenders may have additional sanctions imposed including a withdrawal of their business licence, a business suspension for up to two years, confiscation of crime-related exhibits and instruments, and expulsion of foreign offenders. The penalty brackets for administrative breaches are scattered across legal documents, such as Decree 15/2020/ND-CP in the field of telecommunications, information technology, and e-transaction. The inspectorate department of an authority may investigate a possible legal violation and decide to conduct a thorough investigation where appropriate. As of the time this chapter was written, the MIC's Inspectorate has launched a close inspection of telecommunications carriers, postal businesses, and social networks regarding the collection, processing, and protection of personal information.[134]

Depending on the nature and seriousness of a violation, criminal charges may be brought forward. In the Vietnamese justice system, the principal penalties for individuals include warnings, fines, non-custodial reform, expulsion, fixed-term or life imprisonment, and the death penalty. Conversely, legal persons may face fines, or have their business suspended for either a fixed period of time or indefinitely.[135] Auxiliary penalties may also be considered. Individuals may face bans from holding certain posts, practising occupations or doing certain jobs, confiscation of property, and expulsion. Legal persons may face bans from certain businesses and confiscation of capital. For example, according to Article 288 of the 2015 Criminal Code, the crime of illegally distributing or using information on computer networks or telecommunications networks may entail monetary penalties and/or prison time; the maximum penalty is either seven years in prison, or a fine of VND 20–200 million. In cases with aggravating circumstances, the maximum fine is VND one billion. Article 159 of the 2015 Criminal Code also penalises 'the crime of infringing upon the secrecy or safety of correspondence, telephone calls, telegrams or other forms of exchange of private information of others', which entails a fine ranging from VND 20–50 million, non-custodial reform for up to three years, or one to three years of imprisonment, depending on the severity of the offence.

[130] Civil Code 2015 (n 36), Art 11.
[131] Piemwichai (n 33) 410.
[132] ibid.
[133] Law on Handling of Administrative Violations 2012 (amendments through 2020), Art 52.
[134] 'Thanh tra toàn diện các nhà mạng về vấn đề bảo vệ dữ liệu cá nhân' (Laodong) (4 Nov 2022), available at https://laodong.vn/thoi-su/thanh-tra-toan-dien-cac-nha-mang-ve-van-de-bao-ve-du-lieu-ca-nhan-1112794.ldo.
[135] Criminal Code 2015 (n 55), Arts 32–33.

It should be noted that legal scholars and practitioners argue that administrative and criminal penalties under Vietnamese laws are relatively lenient.[136] In a case where the breach of personal privacy resulted in the suicide of a teenager, for example, the sanction was considered inadequate for the deterrent purposes.[137]

B. Jurisdictional Issues Involving Cross-Border Data Protection and Privacy

Civil cases related to cross-border data transfers and personal data protection are under the common or non-exclusive jurisdiction of Vietnamese courts. This is the case except where the parties' agreement states otherwise, or where international convention(s) to which Vietnam is a signatory, apply. The criteria for determining the common competence of Vietnamese courts in these matters are laid out in Article 469 of the 2015 Civil Procedure Code, of which five are relevant to data-related disputes. The five criterion are as follows: (i) the defendant is an individual who resides, works or lives long-term in Vietnam; (ii) the defendant is an agency or organisation which is headquartered in Vietnam or the defendant is an agency or organisation which has a branch or a representative office in Vietnam, applicable to cases related to the operation of the agency/organisation's branch or representative office in Vietnam; (iii) where the defendant has properties in Vietnam; (iv) civil cases related to civil relations which are established, changed or terminated in Vietnam, objects of which are properties in Vietnam or acts performed in Vietnam; (v) civil cases related to civil relations which are established, changed or terminated in Vietnam, but involve rights and obligations of Vietnamese agencies, organisations and individuals or agencies, organisations and individuals that are headquartered or reside in Vietnam.

Once the court decides to accept the petition, any subsequent changes in certain circumstances, such as a foreign court concurrently taking on the case, will not result in a change in the jurisdiction of the court.[138] The case will continue to proceed in the Vietnamese court. However, where there is an ongoing lawsuit on the same privacy matter already being considered by a foreign court, the Vietnamese court will refuse jurisdiction and return the petition to the plaintiff.[139]

C. Applicable Law: In Litigations Involving Cross-Border Data Protection and Privacy

The choice of law applicable to personal data breach associated with pecuniary remedies may be made in pursuance to the rules governing conflict of laws, as provided in the international agreements on mutual legal assistance in civil matters between Vietnam

[136] Chu Thi Hoa, 'Còn những khoảng trống pháp luật về bảo vệ dữ liệu cá nhân' (*Ministry of Information and Communication*, 1 June 2022), available at mic.gov.vn/mic_2020/Pages/TinTuc/152653/Con-nhung-khoang-trong-phap-luat-ve-bao-ve-du-lieu-ca-nhan.html.

[137] ibid.

[138] Civil Procedure Code 2015 (n 124), Art 471.

[139] ibid, Art 472.

and other nations.[140] It bears noting that before 2010 Vietnam's mutual judicial assistance agreements had included circumstances where courts might apply foreign laws in specific civil matters, including marriage, family, inheritance (limited to movable assets), contracts, non-contractual damages, and labour contracts. However, this is no longer the case. This shift reflects a policy change in Vietnam's approach to mutual legal assistance agreements.[141] Post-2010 agreements primarily focus on procedural aspects, such as delivering documents, collecting evidence, and recognising/enforcing foreign court judgments, while provisions on determining applicable law in cross-border cases are absent.

The 2015 Civil Code allows the parties to choose the law applicable to compensation for non-contractual or tort damages, a provision which is applicable to breaches of protected personal data rights.[142] An exception is where the breaching party and the breached party have their domicile (in the case of individuals), or place of establishment (in the case of legal persons) in the same nation, in which case, the law of that nation shall apply.[143] Absent an agreement between the parties, the applicable laws shall be those of the country where the consequences of the breach arise. In addition, Article 670 of the 2015 Civil Code makes clear that foreign law shall not apply in cases where: (i) the result of applying such a law contradicts the fundamental principles of the Vietnamese law; or (ii) despite taking necessary measures under the procedural law, the contents of the foreign law cannot be determined.

However, in practice, the utility of these provisions is rather mixed.[144] The lack of clarity surrounding the responsibilities and subjects tasked with gathering and interpreting foreign laws in a proceeding results in low applicability of such laws due to heavy reliance on the goodwill of the courts.[145] For various reasons the courts are typically reluctant to resort to foreign laws especially in the field of data protection, and generally decide to apply Vietnamese law for dispute resolution instead.[146]

D. Recognition and Enforcement of Foreign Judgments

The 2015 Civil Procedure Code of Vietnam provides a framework for the recognition and enforcement of foreign judgments in several key areas. Articles 27(5), 29(9), 31(4),

[140] Lê Mạnh Hùng, 'Vấn đề áp dụng pháp luật nước ngoài trong giải quyết các vụ việc dân sự tại tòa án Việt Nam' ['The Issue of Applying Foreign Law in Resolving Civil Cases in Vietnamese Courts'] (*Tap chi toa an*, 20 July 2021), available at https://tapchitoaan.vn/van-de-ap-dung-phap-luat-nuoc-ngoai-trong-giai-quyet-cac-vu-viec-dan-su-tai-toa-an-viet-nam; For a list, see 'Danh Sách Hiệp Định Tương Trợ Tư Pháp Việt Nam Đã Ký Với Các Nước' ['List of Mutual Legal Assistance Agreements Vietnam Has Signed with Other Countries'] (*Luật sư Đà Nẵng – Luật sư FDVN*, 29 January 2019), available at https://fdvn.vn/danh-sach-hiep-dinh-tuong-tro-tu-phap-viet-nam-da-ky-voi-cac-nuoc/.

[141] Lê Mạnh Hùng, ibid.

[142] Civil Code 2015 (n 36), Art 687(1).

[143] ibid, Art 687(2).

[144] Nguyen Hung Quang, 'Thực tiễn áp dụng pháp luật nước ngoài trong xét xử dân sự ở Việt Nam và những khó khăn, thách thức – Góc nhìn của luật sư' ['Practical Application of Foreign Law in Civil Trials in Vietnam and Difficulties and Challenges – A Lawyer's Perspective'] (2020) 7 Thông tin Khoa học pháp lý, available at www.vnlawfind.com.vn/thuc-tien-ap-dung-phap-luat-nuoc-ngoai-trong-xet-xu-dan-su-o-viet-nam-va-nhung-kho-khan-thach-thuc-goc-nhin-cua-luat-su/.

[145] Lê Mạnh Hùng, 'Áp dụng pháp luật nước ngoài trong giải quyết các vụ việc dân sự có yếu tố nước ngoài' ['Apply Foreign Law in Resolving Civil Cases With Foreign Elements'] (*Tap chi toa an*, 20 July 2021), available at https://tapchitoaan.vn/ap-dung-phap-luat-nuoc-ngoai-trong-giai-quyet-cac-vu-viec-dan-su-co-yeu-to-nuoc-ngoai.

[146] ibid.

and 33(3) of the Civil Procedure Code explicitly mention the potential recognition of judgments related to civil, matrimonial, commercial, and labour matters. This expansive scope is further reinforced by Article 423 of the Civil Procedure Code. Accordingly, a foreign court's judgment on civil, marriage, family, trade, business, labour-related matters, decision, or decisions concerning property in criminal and administrative matters shall be recognised and enforced in Vietnam. The ground for such recognition and enforcement is based on either an international treaty to which both Vietnam and such country are signatories or the principle of reciprocity. Importantly, while Chapter XXXIV of the Civil Procedure Code is titled 'Procedure for the Recognition and Enforcement of Foreign Civil Judgments', its broader applicability to personal data protection-related judgments can be inferred from its substantive content and Article 423 itself.

On 25 September 2020, the Vietnamese Ministry of Justice released a critical dataset concerning the recognition and enforcement of foreign court judgments and arbitral awards.[147] This data encompasses 26 foreign court judgments and 83 foreign arbitral awards adjudicated by Vietnamese courts between 1 January 2012 and 30 September 2019. Notably, seven of the 26 court judgments addressed commercial disputes; three of which were not recognised and enforced.[148] The data also reveals a nuanced trend, with 30 out of 83 arbitral awards (36 per cent) facing non-recognition or enforcement.[149] None of the court judgments and arbitral awards concerned personal data protection. Among others, recognition and enforcement of foreign judgments and arbitral awards are most frequently resisted in circumstances where there are serious due process concerns and where fundamental principles of Vietnamese law are deemed to be compromised.[150] It bears noting that the legal concept of 'fundamental principles' functions analogously to 'public policy' in other jurisdictions.[151] However, its broad and undefined nature creates ambiguity, hindering the effective recognition and enforcement of foreign court judgments.[152] This situation would definitely be complicated by the introduction of the PDPD with the emergence of data subjects' rights and personal data protection principles. With the growing importance of personal data protection and the promulgation of the PDPD, Vietnam will soon see the rise in the number of disputes pertaining to cross-border data transfer and personal data protection as well as the need for recognition and enforcement of foreign judgments in this regard.

[147] 'Công bố cơ sở dữ liệu thi hành các bản án của tòa nước ngoài tại Việt Nam' ['Launching the Database of Enforcement of Foreign Court Judgments in Viet Nam'] (*Tuoi tre*, 25 September 2020), available at https://tuoitre.vn/cong-bo-co-so-du-lieu-thi-hanh-cac-ban-an-cua-toa-nuoc-ngoai-tai-viet-nam-20200925202830875.htm.

[148] See more Database of Enforcement of Foreign Court Judgments (Ministry of Justice), available at https://moj.gov.vn/tttp/Pages/dlcn-va-th-tai-Viet-Nam.aspx?fbclid=IwAR1wTsvb5Sl_61pjUiNMLqyP3XoWsNlzAi_GgZCsp1D44t0a8Rl5eF4pqAM.

[149] ibid.

[150] Truong Nhat Quang, Nguyen Duy Duong and Vu Tuan Duc, 'Foreign Court Judgments and Arbitral Awards in Vietnam' (*YKVN*, 6 January 2021), available at https://ykvn-law.com/foreign-court-judgments-and-arbitral-awards-in-vietnam/.

[151] Nguyen Ngoc Minh, Tran Ha Han and Nguyen Thi Thu Trang, 'Vietnam' in Anselmo Reyes (ed), *Recognition and Enforcement of Judgments in Civil and Commercial Matters* (Hart Publishing, 2019) 198–99.

[152] ibid.

9

Cambodia

ROTHNA NGORN AND PUTHKARONA SENG

I. Introduction

Data protection and privacy is of paramount concern in today's digital age. Many countries have been developing a comprehensive legal framework dedicated to the protection of personal data and privacy, which are both highly exposed to violation, especially online violation. Cambodia, nevertheless, does not have a specific law on data protection, which focuses on the protection of personal data and privacy, at present. In the absence of a specific law and regulation, issues pertaining to data protection and privacy are broadly governed by the Constitution of Cambodia (Constitution),[1] the Civil Code of Cambodia (Civil Code),[2] the Criminal Code of Cambodia (Criminal Code),[3] and through the fragmented collection of sector-specific regulations in the fields of banking and finance, telecommunications, insurance, electronic commerce and health.[4]

The Constitution guarantees the right to privacy, inviolability of residence and confidentiality of correspondence of every Cambodian citizen.[5] The Civil Code provides a general principle of respect of personal rights which includes the rights to life, personal safety, health, freedom, identity, dignity, privacy, and other personal benefits or interests.[6] The Criminal Code penalises the act of intercepting or recording private conversations, or recording a person's image in a private location, without his/her consent,[7] as well as the breach of professional confidentiality and other offences relating to automated data.[8]

As for the sectorial laws, the applicable laws and regulations in the banking and financial sector, telecommunications or health sectors contain some provisions on secrecy obligations; while the Law on Electronic Commerce (E-Commerce Law) provides compliance

[1] Constitution of Cambodia (1993) (Constitution).
[2] Civil Code of Cambodia (2007) (Civil Code).
[3] Criminal Code of Cambodia (2009) (Criminal Code).
[4] The same conclusion in: See Keo Sothie, 'Cambodia's Culture and Laws on Privacy and Data Protection, and the Future' in the Law Talks Series 'Law in the Digital Age: Protection of Consumer Rights' (Konrad Adenauer Stiftung, November 2021), available at www.kas.de/en/web/kambodscha/single-title/-/content/law-in-the-digital-age-protection-of-consumer-rights; Sovath Phin, 'Privacy and Data Protection in the Digital Age: A Holistic Approach to Privacy and Data Protection in Cambodia' (*Konrad Adenauer Stiftung*, 2021), available at www.kas.de/en/web/kambodscha/single-title/-/content/law-in-the-digital-age-protection-of-consumer-rights.
[5] Constitution, Art 40.
[6] Civil Code, Art 10.
[7] Criminal Code, Arts 301, 302, and 318.
[8] ibid, Art 427.

obligations for electronic service providers,[9] and intermediaries of electronic commerce,[10] as well as some basic rights for owners whose private information is collected while using the electronic commerce platforms.

To deal with the increasing challenge of data protection and privacy, the Royal Government of Cambodia has recently established a government data exchange platform through the adoption of Sub-Decree No 164 on Data Exchange via Cambodia Data Exchange platform (CamDX) on 24 August 2021 (Sub-Decree No 164). Having a limited scope, the Sub-Decree is only applicable to any transaction of data exchange via CamDX[11] in public sectors such as those associated with the Ministry, Institution, similar public entities, administrative public institutions, public institutions, other financial autonomous units and sub-national administrative as well as private sectors that are members of the CamDX. For this reason, the Sub-Decree No 164 will not be at the centre of our discussion in this chapter.

Besides the existing legal framework pertaining to data protection and privacy, Cambodia is preparing a draft law on personal data protection with the aim of providing a clear and comprehensive legal framework on the protection of personal data. Rather than being inspired by cultures of privacy for liberty or dignity, the preparation of the draft law is more likely to be driven by 'globalization – the need to adapt to changes in the world economy, catch up in legal and technological developments, and attract foreign direct investment'.[12] The motive behind the preparation of the draft law is not unusual because it is generally observed that 'reforms and laws in Cambodia have been adopted on a need-basis'[13] – which is the economic considerations in the context of privacy and data protection. Under this pragmatic approach, the objectives of having a law on personal data protection can be broadly categorised: first, with the focus on building a vibrant digital economy, society and digital government, the draft law, once adopted, would facilitate the visions of the Royal Government of Cambodia to encourage all involved stakeholders, including public institutions, private enterprises, and citizens to embrace the digital transformations with confidence and trust. Second, in the era of the Industry 4.0, by having the law on personal data protection, it would enable Cambodia to align with the global and/or regional trend in relation to data interoperability with the ultimate aim being to create a favourable environment for investment and promotion of socio-economic development.[14]

Even though the content of the draft law and the tentative timeline for adoption have not been made available to the public, it has been made known that public consultations

[9] Law on Electronic Commerce (2019) (Law on E-Commerce), Art 8. 'Electronic Service Provider' is defined as persons who use electronic means to supply goods and/or services, except for insurance institutions.

[10] ibid. 'Intermediary of Electronic Commerce' is defined as persons providing services of sending, reception, transmission, temporary or permanent storage of electronic communication; or a person providing other services related to electronic communication.

[11] CamDX is an information technology (IT) platform of the Cambodian Government, which is initiated for exchanging data by using the Application Programming Interface of a computer program between one IT system with another IT system between the public sector and private sector which is a member of CamDX with safety via internet system or other digital interconnected network. See 'CamDX – Cambodia Data Exchange' (Government of the Kingdom of Cambodia, 2020), available at www.camdx.gov.kh/.

[12] In this sense, see See Keo Sothie (n 4) 45.

[13] ibid.

[14] See Cambodia Digital Economy and Social Policy Framework 2021–2035 (2021) and Cambodia Digital Government Policy 2022–2035 (2022).

with the involved stakeholders, including civil society organisations and private companies, have taken place as part of the law-making process in Cambodia. Once the public consultation has materialised, it subsequently requires the submissions to be made to the General Assembly, Senate for review and approval before being promulgated by the King. However, this is not expected to take shape within 2024 or early 2025.

In addition, a draft law on cybercrime has also been in the pipeline:

> This draft law initially aimed to define the awareness measures, to prevent and combat against all cybercrimes to ensure law enforcement concerning cybercrimes, as well as to ascertain safety and legal benefits in using and improving information and communication technology.[15]

This draft law also calls for the establishment of the National Anti-Cybercrime Committee, which will be delegated with broad power as to the investigation into suspected cybercrime offences. In its current form, the draft law on cybercrime has received both positive and negative comments by the local and international community alike.[16] Several negatives concern the interference into the freedom of expression of the citizens and the unnecessary expansion of power of the Cambodian Government to seize computer systems from companies in permitted circumstances.[17] With its controversial nature, the timeline of the draft law cannot be anticipated.

As for a data protection regulator, Cambodia does not have one at present. Consequently, the competent courts of Cambodia and relevant competent authorities/regulators in specific sectors are empowered to oversee data protection matters under their respective competency, including the Ministry of Commerce, the Ministry of Post and Telecommunications (MPTC), the Ministry of Interior (MOI), the National Bank of Cambodia(NBC), and the Telecommunication Regulator of Cambodia.

II. General Legal Framework of International Data Transfers and Data Protection

A. Constitutional Protection for Data Transfer and Protection

Personal data is not expressly mentioned in the Constitution. However, the right to privacy, inviolability of residence and confidentially of correspondence are constitutionally protected in Cambodia.

Article 40 of the Constitution guarantees the right to the inviolability of residence and to the confidentiality of correspondence by mail, telegram, fax, telex and telephone. Hence, the privacy of residence and confidentiality of correspondence are recognised as constitutional rights for Cambodian citizens.

In addition, Article 31 of the Constitution provides that Cambodia recognises and respects human rights as enshrined in the United Nationals Charter, the Universal Declaration

[15] See https://mptc.gov.kh/en/laws-regulations/instructions/13631/.

[16] See Sar Socheath, 'Ministry of Interior Finalising Draft Law on Cybercrime' *Khmer Times* (27 October 2022).

[17] Fiona Kelliher, 'Leaked Law Proposal would Give Cambodia Expanded Powers to Censor Critics' (*rest of world*, 2020), available at https://restofworld.org/2023/cybersecurity-law-draft-cambodia-elections/.

of Human Rights and all the treaties and conventions related to human rights, women's rights and children's rights. Consequently, the protection of privacy, family, home or correspondence as recognised in Article 12 of the Universal Declaration of Human Rights is constitutionally protected under the Cambodian legislation.

While these constitutional provisions secure the confidentiality of communications and sanctity of the home, the protection of personal data per se is not explicitly enumerated. This lack of direct constitutional recognition of data protection has generated academic discussions on whether interference with personal data constitutes infringement of a fundamental human right in Cambodia.[18] Advocates of an expansive interpretation argue that the right to privacy and confidential correspondence may reasonably be extended to personal data. However, the countervailing view is that explicit constitutional safeguards are required given the exigencies of the digital age. Irrespective of doctrinal arguments, the absence of unambiguous constitutional personal data protection remains a key gap in Cambodia's legal framework.

B. Statutory Frameworks for Data Transfer and Protection

In the absence of a specific law on data protection and privacy comparable to the European Union's (EU) General Data Protection Act (GDPR), Cambodia's legal framework provides some protections on personal data under general and sector-specific statutes. For example, the recent Law on Civil Status, Civil Statistics and Identification ('Law on Civil Status'),[19] contains provisions concerning personal data in the context of civil registries. Data issues beyond the application scope of the Law on Civil Status are regulated by general laws such as the Civil Code and Criminal Code, and by some provisions of sectorial laws.

i. Law on Civil Status

Promulgated on 1 July 2023, the Law on Civil Status determines the rules and procedures for civil registration, residence registration, management of civil status statistics, registration of personal identification, and management of population registry.[20] The Law has however, a broad application and scope and applies to all persons living in the territory of Cambodia and Cambodians living abroad.

Concerning the personal data, the Law on Civil Status defines 'Personally Identifiable Data' as referring to any identifiable information of a person, such as name, sex, date and place of birth, nationality, residential address, contact information, etc. The Law also defines 'Privacy' as referring to the private condition of life that each person has the right to the legal protection of.[21] The elements of biometric data are also enumerated as including digital image, fingerprints, iris scans, and other biometric data as determined by the National Authority for Management of Population Identification.[22] Such personally

[18] See Sovath Phin (n 4) 68.
[19] Law on Civil Status Statistics and Identification (2023) ('Law on Civil Status').
[20] Sub-Decree No 103 on Civil Status (2020) (Civil Registration).
[21] See ibid, Annex, providing a glossary of the key terms of the law.
[22] See ibid, Art 148.

identifiable data and biometric data in the centralised Population Registry is afforded protection by the state. The modification, correction or update of such data shall be determined by the instruction of the National Authority for Management of Population Identification.

However, a closer look into the Law on Civil Status reveals that the matter of data privacy safeguards in such law is limited to the Population Registry, with uncertain implications for extension to the private sector data processing. It is interesting that the Law on Civil Status contains Chapter 7 on the use of data, privacy protection and data security.[23] Furthermore, Article 156 allows public service entities and private services providers to utilise the Registry for identity verification. The verification is however, limited to the confirmation on whether the relevant data is correct or incorrect and would not trigger any sharing of data in the Registry. The necessity and proportionality tests shall be adhered to when the utilisation has taken place by those public and private service entities.

Concerning privacy protection, the Law on Civil Status contains some privacy protections of unclear scope. Article 159 appears to indicate that personal identification data falls under the umbrella of privacy safeguards. Such interpretation is, nevertheless, not confirmed by any guideline or judicial precedent.

Similarly, as to data security, Article 160 mandates that collection, transmission, use and storage of personally identifiable data shall be carried out in a manner that could ensure security, accuracy and correctness of data, and shall protect the data against unauthorised use and loss. It requires determining specific procedures through the instruction of the MOI or other relevant ministries/authorities. Moreover, Article 160 mirrors Article 32 of the E-Commerce Law concerning general data protection duties. This consistency across sectoral laws shows promise. Yet, robust common standards are still lacking. The lack of further details or implementation mechanisms renders the obligation under Article 160 broad and theoretical. Ultimately, uncertainty persists regarding the Law on Civil Status' privacy safeguards for the Population Registry, let alone private sector data processing.

ii. Civil Code

While not explicitly defining 'personal data' or 'privacy', the Civil Code elaborates certain protections that may encompass these concepts under Articles 10 to 13.

According to Article 10 of the Civil Code, personal rights include the rights to life, personal safety, health, freedom, identity, dignity, privacy, and other personal benefits or interests. Violations of such enumerated rights are actionable through court-ordered injunctions and damages. Article 11 establishes rights to enjoin infringements, and Article 12 further provides the right to demand elimination of effect of violation of personal right, while Article 13 allows claims for any harm or prejudice under tort provisions.

Read together, these Articles have been interpreted as recognising privacy and personal data as protected 'personal rights', enforceable through injunctive and compensatory relief.[24] The broad construction of 'personal rights' under Article 10 reflects the evolving recognition of interests in data privacy in Cambodia's civil law jurisprudence. However, ambiguity persists due to the lack of clear definitions. Fully realising these emerging data

[23] ibid, Art 152.
[24] The same conclusion is provided in Sovath Phin (n 4) 63.

protections requires concrete statutory definitions and rights tailored to the exigencies of the digital age.

iii. Criminal Code

While not expressly regulating personal data protection, Cambodia's Criminal Code contains provisions that prohibit unauthorised collection and misuse of private information. The Code penalises the act of intercepting or recording private conversations, or recording a person's image in a private location without consent. Imprisonment and fines are imposed, foregrounding individual rights against intrusive data gathering. The consent is presumed to be given if the affected person is informed of the recording of conversation or the picture-taking and he/she was not opposed to it.[25]

In addition, the Code also mandates any person bound by professional secrecy obligation from disclosing secret information to an unauthorised third party, unless such disclosure is permitted by the law. The breaches of professional secrecy are punishable by an imprisonment from one month to one year and a fine from 100 thousand to two million Riels.[26] The breadth of 'secret information' allows application to personal data, though definitions depend on the laws and regulation applicable to each relevant profession.

Prohibitions on accessing or maintaining access to an automated data processing system, obstructing the operation of an automated data processing system, and fraudulent introduction, deletion or modification of data in an automated data processing system under Articles 427–429 also offer related protection. Such breaches are similarly punishable by an imprisonment and fine.

Pending the adoption of the draft law on cybercrime, the provisions of the Criminal Code as cited above would serve as a legal basis for combatting some forms of cybercrime and would allow the personal data involved in these crimes to be protected to some extent. However, it is expected that the draft law on cybercrime would fill the gaps of the Criminal Code in preventing and combatting other kinds of offence committed by computer systems (the 'cybercrime'[27]), either committed in Cambodia or outside Cambodia and having an effect on the interests of the legal entity or natural person in Cambodia.[28] The draft law covers a wide range of offences committed by computer systems such as 'illegal connections to others' computers, data interferences, child pornography production and distribution systems, fraud via computer as well as other offenses which affect national independence, integrity and security, etc'.[29] In addition, 'the dissemination of any information contents affecting national traditional values such as inciting racism; discriminating against religion; slander; defamation; insult; etc. will be counted as cyber offenses'.[30] As of this date, the adoption of the draft law on cybercrime remains a controversial topic among

[25] Criminal Code, Arts 301 and 302.

[26] ibid, Art 314.

[27] The broad definition of cybercrime could be retrieved from the provision of Article 1 of the draft law on Cybercrime (Draft V1-unofficial English translation), available at www.article19.org/wp-content/uploads/2018/02/Draft-Law-On-CyberCrime_Englishv1.pdf.

[28] ibid, Article 2.

[29] Ministry of Post and Telecommunications, Clarification on Draft of Cybercrime Law, available at https://mptc.gov.kh/en/laws-regulations/instructions/13631/.

[30] ibid.

relevant stakeholders[31] and some reports claim that 'there remain significant concerns that the Law, as currently drafted, restricts the freedom of expression and violates the right to privacy of Cambodians'.[32]

C. Data Protection Frameworks

i. *Influence of International Data Protection Frameworks*

Cambodia lacks a comprehensive data protection law drawing from global frameworks. The pending legislation offers an opportunity to align with international benchmarks, but current influences remain uncertain. Once enacted, Cambodia's draft law on personal data protection should be assessed on its adherence to globally recognised principles and standards.

ii. *Specific Provisions for Particular Sectors*

Absent omnibus regulation, sectoral laws fill gaps providing limited data protections for areas like electronic commerce, banking, telecommunications and healthcare. While reinforcing norms of confidentiality and consent, these fragmented protections fall short of a systematic rights-based approach seen in mature data protection regimes.

a. Electronic Commerce

The Law on Electronic Commerce (E-Commerce Law), adopted on 3 November 2019, contains several data protection provisions applicable to e-commerce entities. Its purpose is to govern domestic and cross-border electronic commerce in Cambodia, create legal certainty in the civil and commercial transactions by electronic system, and give confidence to the public in the usage of electronic communication.

Article 32 mandates E-Commerce Service Provider[33] and Intermediary of E-Commerce[34] storing electronic record of private information to implement reasonable and appropriate safeguards when storing private electronic records, to avoid the unauthorised loss, access, use, modification, leak or disclosure of such information.

[31] See: Business & Human Rights Resources Center, 'Cambodia: Civil Society Claims that Draft Law on Cybercrime Restricts Free Expression & Privacy of Individuals', available at www.business-humanrights.org/en/latest-news/cambodia-civil-society-claim-that-draft-law-on-cybercrime-restricts-free-expression-privacy-of-individuals/; Gerald Flynn and Phuong Vantha, 'Cambodia's Online Freedoms under Threat from Draft Cybercrime Law' (*Cambodianess-ThmeyThmey*, 22 October 2020); Nov Sivutha, Draft Law on Cybercrime Fast-Tracked' *The Phnom Penh Post* (28 June 2022).

[32] ICNL, 'Legal Analysis: Cambodia, Draft Law on Cybercrime' (2022), available at https://data.opendevelopmentcambodia.net/dataset/0224f751-51b2-4660-877a-e2082977b972/resource/d5cd7a30-4359-48b5-8ba2-7190965d300f/download/cambodia-cybercrime-analysis_final.pdf.

[33] Law on E-Commerce (n 9), Art 8. 'E-Commerce Service Provider' is defined as persons who use electronic means to supply goods and/or services, except for insurance institutions.

[34] ibid, Art 8. 'Intermediary of E-Commerce' is defined as persons providing the service of sending, reception, transmission, temporary or permanent storage of electronic communication; or a person providing other services related to electronic communication.

Additionally, Article 25 requires an intermediary of E-Commerce services to remove information likely to cause civil or criminal responsibility, while preserving records for evidentiary purposes and notifying the MPTC and other relevant competent authorities.

According to some reports, the relevant provisions of the E-Commerce Law were introduced urgently, arising from the need for economic reform; thus, such provisions are vague and not comprehensive enough. However, relevant provisions on data protection of the E-Commerce Law may still serve as a basis for developing a more comprehensive regulation of data protection in Cambodia.[35]

b. Banking and Finance

Cambodia's banking and financial sector law contain confidentiality provisions that offer partial data privacy protections. Article 47 of the Law on Banking and Financial Institution (Banking Law) mandates non-disclosure of customer information by banks and employees, including any confidential information pertaining to statement, facts, acts, figures or the contents of accounting or administrative documents. Though the scope of 'account content' is undefined, such content likely includes identifiable information of customer account-holders and the personal data of customers.[36]

Similarly, Article 221.1 of the Law on Negotiable Instrument provides that the bank is bound by secrecy and shall not disclose any information on the accounts to anyone, except where:

i. Disclosure is under compulsion by law.
ii. The interest of the bank requires disclosure.
iii. Disclosure is made with the express consent of the customer.
iv. Disclosure is under an opinion of the customer given in the ordinary course of business to another bank in response to the specific enquiry of the other bank.
v. The customer defaulted on his obligation to the bank.[37]

The 'bank' is broadly defined and covers any institution licensed to carry out banking operations under the Banking Law, and any other institution or entity authorised by law to take deposits or participate in payment transactions on behalf of customers.[38] However, the Law on Negotiable Instrument does not elucidate what 'information on the account' includes under Article 221.1. The question as to whether the provision of Article 221.1 could be interpreted to extend protection to the personal data of customers remains unanswered and the uncertainty persists around precisely what customer data merits protection.

c. Telecommunications

The Telecom Law of Cambodia is applicable to all telecommunications operations in Cambodia. While the Law lacks a specific provision on data protection, there is a general

[35] See Keo Sothie (n 4) 47–48.
[36] Law on Banking and Financial Institution (1999) ('Law on Banking').
[37] Law on Negotiable Instruments and Payment Transactions (2005) ('Law on Negotiable Instruments').
[38] Law on Banking (n 36), Art 2.

principle of privacy, security and safety of using telecommunications services. Under Article 65.b, subscribers shall have basic rights, among others, to privacy, security and safety of using the telecommunications service, except as otherwise determined by other specific law.

d. Health Sector

Cambodia's health sector laws and regulations contain confidentiality protections that partly uphold informational privacy rights of patients. Confidentiality of medical records and information is provided under the following laws and regulations: (i) the Law on the Management of Health Profession Practitioners;[39] (ii) Sub-decree No 61 on Physicians' Code of Ethics;[40] and (iii) Law on the Prevention and Control of HIV/AIDS.[41] In addition, the Ministry of Health also issued Operation Guidelines for Client's Rights and Providers' Rights-Duties in 2007 ('Operational Guidelines') to provide further explanation as to what patients' rights are and how to protect patients' information and keep them confidential.

The Law on the Management of Health Profession Practitioners requires that all health professionals including, among others, physicians, dentists, midwives, nurses, pharmacists, laboratory specialists, physical therapists, dental specialists, radiologists and other health professionals, shall comply with the code of ethics and professional standards. This includes the obligation to ensure confidentiality of medical record and information under the Sub-Decree No 61 on Physicians' Code of Ethics. The confidential obligation also mandates measures to either protect patients' identity or to obtain consent for the use of patients' records and information for preparing scientific publications or education.

Moreover, the Operational Guidelines also provide patients with the right to confidentiality of all information relating to their health. In this respect, the Guidelines requires that hospital, healthcare centres, clinics and other health facilities shall ensure the safety and security of patients' health data and information.

The Law on the Prevention and Control of HIV/AIDS also requires all professionals, data encoders, custodians of medical records related to HIV/AIDS to maintain confidentiality in handing medical information, especially the identity and personal status of persons with HIV/AIDS. Failure to protect patients' confidentiality is punishable.

iii. Distinction and Interface between Data Protection and Privacy

Cambodia's legal framework lacks clear delineation between privacy and data protection, reflecting its nascent development. The Constitution and the Civil Code focus on protection for general privacy interests, rather than specifically addressing the protection of personal data. Legal privacy concepts were reintroduced by the Constitution, wherein Article 31 explicitly refers to the Universal Declaration of Human Rights.[42] However, the legal concept of personal data protection is not clearly defined under any specific law.

[39] Law on the Management of Health Profession Practitioners (2019).
[40] Sub-Decree No 61 on Physicians' Code of Ethics (2003).
[41] Law on the Prevention and Control of HIV/AIDS (2002).
[42] See Keo Sothie (n 4) 45.

This ambiguity allows divergent interpretations on the coverage of data protection under privacy rights. 'The right to privacy plays an important role to entail the protection of a person (data subject) with regard to the processing of his or her personal data by another person or state'.[43] Further, 'the right to privacy has been also a basis for data protection under the UN international legal framework. Thus, data protection can be interpreted to fall in the right to privacy [.]'.[44]

The new Law on Civil Status evinces emerging distinction, defining 'Personally Identifiable Data' and 'Privacy'.[45] As per Article 159, the protection of privacy appears to cover the personal identification data, suggesting potential convergence. However, in the absence of an authoritative or judicial interpretation on the issue, the precise interface remains uncertain.

iv. Distinction between 'Data Users', 'Data Subjects', 'Data Processors' and 'Data Sub-Contractors'

The laws and regulations of Cambodia do not define or distinguish data users, data subjects, data processors and data sub-contractors.

v. Distinction between Personal and Non-Personal Data

The Cambodian data protection regime lacks distinction between personal data and non-personal data. However, emerging definitions provide clues to potential boundaries. Sub-Decree No 252 on the Management, Use, and Protection of Personally Identifiable Data defines the principles and procedures for the management, use, and protection of 'personally identifiable data' collected and stored by the MOI. Sub-Decree No 252 marks the first time that the term 'personally identifiable data' has been used in Cambodia's legal lexicon, defining it as information that can be used to determine the identity of an individual. Examples include name, sex, date of birth, place of birth, current place of residence, ethnicity, nationality, biometric data, as well as other data relating to the identity of an individual. But its limited applicability to data held by the MOI, and not all personally identifiable data, leaves overall uncertainty.

The Civil Status Law contributes a similar definition, covering any identifiable information of a person. This suggests a distinction from non-identifiable, and hence non-personal, data. Nonetheless, absent authoritative interpretation or precedent, it remains uncertain whether or not and how this definition of 'personally identifiable data' will be taken into consideration by the competent courts, authorities and/or regulator for distinguishing between personal and non-personal data.

vi. Distinction between Anonymisation, Pseudonymisation, and Encryption

Cambodia's legal framework is silent with respect to the distinction between data anonymisation, data pseudonymisation and encryption for the purposes of collecting,

[43] See Sovath Phin (n 4) 65.
[44] ibid.
[45] See Law on Civil Status (n 19).

storing, and transferring personal data. However, the Law on E-Commerce's broad provision on 'Security Procedure' offers clues to potential categorisation. According to the Annex, these procedures are used for verifying that the signature, communication or operation in the electronic system belongs to a person, or for detecting any errors or modifications. They may require the use of algorithms, formulas, codes, passwords or other security tools.

This expansive definition suggests that data anonymisation, data pseudonymisation and encryption could be considered as different types of Security Procedure under the Law on E-Commerce. Each offer graduated levels of protection tailored to data sensitivity. Anonymisation removes identifiers, pseudonymisation replaces them with pseudonyms, while encryption transforms data into coded form.

Nevertheless, absent explicit definitions or guidance, uncertainty persists regarding precise boundaries and legal implications of these notions in Cambodia. As Cambodia drafts its data protection law, defining and differentiating these procedures will enable proportionality in processing personal data.

vii. Distinction between Domestic and Cross-Border/International Transfers

The Cambodia data protection regime does not distinguish between domestic and cross-border data transfer. All data transfer – be it domestic or cross-border – is required to comply with the legal requirements under the applicable laws and regulations pertaining to data protection as described above. For instance, the Law on E-Commerce mandates security for electronic records without specifying domestic or international transfer.

This uniform approach follows from the lack of comprehensive data protection legislation delineating a comprehensive transfer and access regime. Most mature data regimes restrict cross-border data flows to protect domestic privacy rights and national security. By contrast, Cambodia's agnostic stance reflects its nascent data governance.

viii. Privacy Regulator

Cambodia currently lacks a centralised data protection authority, instead dispersing oversight across institutions. In the absence of a comprehensive law, privacy governance is fragmented. The competent courts of Cambodia hear cases relating to violation of personal rights or privacy and decide on civil compensation for damages caused to data subjects and/or criminal penalty in accordance with the relevant applicable laws. Sectoral regulators like the MOI handle cyber incidents, while the MPTC monitors e-commerce entities. The NBC supervises financial data practices.

This multi-agency model reflects Cambodia's incremental legal development. While bringing relevant expertise, coordination challenges can arise without consolidated supervision. As Cambodia's data regime matures, it is expected to establish an integrated regulator to harmonise standards and enforcement.

III. Legal Bases, Mechanisms and Exceptions for International Data Transfers and Data Protection

A. International Data Transfers

i. 'Adequacy Findings', Whitelists and Blacklists

Under the Cambodian data protection regime, there exists no 'adequacy findings' or designated jurisdiction whitelists and blacklists regulating international data transfers. Instead, a general consent requirement applies regardless of destination.

ii. Consent of Data Subjects as Exception to Existence of Privacy Safeguards Overseas

As a general rule, in order for any international transfer to take place, the consent must be obtained from the data subject in Cambodia – irrespective of the jurisdiction to which the international transfer is made.

iii. Contracts

Cambodia's data protection framework does not prescribe specific forms of consent for international data transfers. Written consent is not strictly mandated, potentially allowing implied consent. It is mainly a privately-driven sector and ultimately depends on accepted industry standards/practices.

In practice, prior written consent for collection, use or disclose of personal data is often incorporated into online terms of service and privacy policies. Accepting these contractual provisions by clicking on the button 'Acceptance of Terms and Conditions of Service' may constitute blanket authorisation for data collection, use and overseas transfer per stated terms.

iv. Privacy Certification Schemes, Trustmarks or International Privacy Seals

At present, there exist no privacy certification schemes, trustmarks or privacy seals that guarantee that a company or organisation complies to a pre-determined standard of data security.

B. International Data Protection and Liability

i. Specific Requirements or Policies for Data Processing and Retention

Unlike other countries where personal data protection law is in place, Cambodia's data protection framework currently lacks specific requirements or policies for data processing and retention. The absence of an omnibus law means key concepts like data processing are undefined, and no economy-wide standards exist.

Some sectoral retention periods are prescribed. In the banking and financial sector, a regulation of the NBC, ie a Prakas on Credit reporting, provides different data retention periods for different types of data involved in credit reporting activities, which is 10 years for positive credit information, three years for negative credit information, five years for bankruptcy data, and three years for court judgment. In addition, the Anti-Money Laundering Law promulgated in 2020 requires reporting entities such as the banks, non-banking financial institutions, insurance companies and credit cooperatives to store customer data for at least five years. However, comprehensive data lifecycle governance remains limited, in contrast with most mature regimes which mandate tailored retention linked to purposes, minimising storage.

ii. Regulations on Legal Ownership of Data Protection and Privacy Rights

Under the existing legal framework on data protection and privacy of Cambodia, there is no pre-determined list of data subjects' rights. However, certain privacy and personal data protections suggest embryonic rights. The Constitution and the Civil Code uphold the right to respect of privacy and personal rights, while sectoral laws recognise rights to telecom privacy and data accuracy.

But the scope and exercise of these nascent rights remain uncertain absent clear elaboration. And comprehensive user empowerment mechanisms seen in mature data protection regimes are yet to develop. Issues of data ownership and controller accountability also lack firm legal grounding.

iii. Extraterritorial Effect of Laws on Data Protection and Privacy

The extraterritorial applicability of Cambodia's data protection laws remains ambiguous due to the fragmented, sectoral approach. Each regulation has a different scope, complicating jurisdictional reach analysis. For example, the Telecommunications Law is applicable to all telecommunication operators operating in Cambodia;[46] while the E-Commerce Law may have extraterritorial scope as the law has the purpose to govern both domestic and cross-border electronic commerce in Cambodia.[47]

Absent clear provisions or interpretive precedents, practical questions around extraterritoriality lack authoritative answers. Persisting uncertainty leads to debate among legal experts regarding when offshore entities must comply with Cambodian data rules.

iv. Data Breach Notification

The legal framework on data protection imposes no legal obligation to notify the relevant regulators and/or the data subjects of data breach that may have occurred. However, voluntary notification, report and/or complaint to relevant competent courts or authority is encouraged in practice.

[46] Telecommunications Law, Art 3.
[47] E-Commerce Law, Art 1.

IV. Data Security and Data Localisation

A. Data Security and Localisation Requirements

There is no data localisation requirement under the current legislation for any sector. Data can be transferred cross-border to and from Cambodia provided that prior consent of the data subject is obtained. The lack of prescribed localisation reflects Cambodia's embrace of free data flows befitting its digital integration.

Nonetheless, some data security obligations are emerging. Article 32 of the E-Commerce Law provides that

> any person that holds personal information in electronic form shall use all means to ensure that the information is protected by such security safeguards as it is reasonable in every circumstance to avoid the loss, access, use, modification, leak or disclosure of those information, except with the permission of the owner of the information or any other party authorised by law.[48]

Thus, reasonable security safeguards must be put in place for the storing of personal data. Nevertheless, many uncertainties may hinder an effective and uniform implementation of data security safeguards provided under Article 32 of the E-Commerce Law. Firstly, there is no clear elaboration on what 'all means (of safeguards)' encompass or what 'reasonable circumstance (as provided under the Article 32)' is.[49] Secondly, 'there is no mention about when or how private parties must disclose their data collection practices, how long data is to be retained, or how data breaches are to be reported'.[50] Overall, it is uniformly understood that what constitutes reasonable security safeguards is undefined under the E-Commerce Law; however, this shows early sensitivity to protection needs.

B. Data Security and Localisation Requirements for Particular Types of Data

In Cambodia, there is no distinction between different types of data. As a general rule, the applicable laws and regulations pertaining to data protection do not contain specific provision on localisation requirements.

Regarding biological information which forms part of the personally identifiable data in the Population Registry, the Law on Civil Status requires that such information shall be stored in the record of the National Authority for Management of Population Identification. This means that the biological information collected and registered in the Population Registry by the competent authority shall be stored in Cambodia. Nevertheless, it is still unprecedented as to whether the localisation requirement provided under the Law on Civil Status would be extended to the biological information collected and/or processed by persons operating in the private sector.

[48] Law on E-Commerce (n 9), Art 32.
[49] See Keo Sothie (n 4) 47.
[50] ibid.

Concerning state secrets, the applicable laws and regulations pertaining to the data protection of Cambodia are silent with respect to the localisation requirements. However, Article 445 of the Criminal Code penalises the act of supplying the foreign state with information prejudicial to national defence. According to this Article, the act of supplying or making accessible to a foreign state or its agents information, processes, objects, documents, computerised data or files which are liable to prejudice the national defence shall be punished by imprisonment from seven to 15 years.

In addition, Article 446 of the Code provides the crime of collecting information prejudicial to national defence. According to this Article, the act of receiving or collecting information, processes, objects, documents, computerised data or files, with a view to supplying them to a foreign state or its agents which are liable to prejudice the national defence shall be punishable by imprisonment from five to 10 years.

A combination of Articles 445 and 446 would lead to an understanding that information, files or documents considered a national secret shall not be communicated or provided to foreign states or agents. Thus, it is reasonable to interpret that national or state secrets shall be stored in Cambodia under the strict supervision of competent authorities.

For other types of sensitive date, the applicable laws and regulations pertaining to the data protection of Cambodia do not contain specific requirements of localisation. This situation is another loophole in the Cambodian legal framework pending the adoption of the draft law on the protection of personal data.

V. Topical Issues and Prospects

A. Artificial Intelligence or AI-Generated Data

Similar to other countries, the rise of artificial intelligence systems (AI) raises novel data protection concerns for Cambodia. As private and public sectors acknowledge the growth and potential of AI, guidelines on legally classifying and governing rights over machine-generated data will be needed. Evidently, the Ministry of Industry, Science, Technology & Innovation in its National Research Agenda 2025 encourages the promotion of research in AI to ultimately facilitate the legal and policy framework of the Government.[51]

B. Potential Cooperation under the Belt and Road Initiative

As Cambodia develops its legal frameworks for data protection and privacy, the Belt and Road Initiative and Digital Silk Road could facilitate constructive exchange and harmonisation efforts. Some areas of collaboration could include supporting the development of comprehensive data protection legislation in Cambodia, technical exchanges on issues like data localisation, consent requirements, and enforcement approaches, and promoting

[51] Royal Government of Cambodia, 'National Research Agenda 2025' (2023), available at www.misti.gov.kh/public/file/202302191676819231.pdf.

joint research initiatives between experts to study data governance gaps, challenges and solutions suited to Cambodia's context.

Overall, constructive cooperation under the Belt and Road Initiative could support Cambodia in shaping a modern data protection regime attuned to its realities and across dimensions of law, governance, research and business. At the same time, technical exchange and assistance from diverse jurisdictions like the EU will also be valuable, given their experience in implementing comprehensive data protection legislation like the GDPR. Drawing lessons from diverse global practices while ensuring local adaptiveness will enable Cambodia to craft an optimal data governance model.

C. Data Protection Post COVID-19 Pandemic

The COVID-19 pandemic has accelerated digital adoption in Cambodia, highlighting data protection needs. Increased collection of health data and reliance on digital services raise privacy and security risks. Post-pandemic, efforts to govern data usage for public health while safeguarding individual rights will be vital.

10

Myanmar

EI THANDAR BO AND KHIN THITSAR AUNG

I. Overview

Data protection and privacy laws play a crucial role in safeguarding the privacy of data subjects. The primary aim of such legislation is to regulate the collection, storage, and use of a data subject's personal information by data controllers and processors. Numerous countries (as evidenced by the chapters of this book) have implemented laws requiring establishments to secure and safeguard data to prevent unauthorised access by third parties. These laws are intended to establish clear guidelines for government authorities and establishments engaged in the gathering, storage, and sharing of personal data obtained through information and communication technologies (ICTs) during online transactions. Additionally, sector specific laws will address how governments are to gather such information for essential services, such as voter registration, healthcare, or tax-related matters. By having stringent regulations in place, users' rights to privacy can be protected and the responsible handling of personal data enforced.

Currently, Myanmar lacks a comprehensive (as opposed to piecemeal) data protection law. There are no immediate plans to introduce such comprehensive legislation. The political situation in Myanmar today means that the Government is having to deal with a multitude of pressing concerns and data protection is not a priority. But, in line with its obligations as a member of the Association of Southeast Asian Nations (ASEAN), Myanmar is supposed to enact legislation and guidelines that are reflective of best practice in data protection and privacy. This would contribute significantly to the development of Myanmar and its integration into the ASEAN Economic Community (AEC). The situation relating to data protection in Myanmar is therefore worth monitoring, as the implementation of data protection laws and guidelines (as Myanmar has undertaken to do) will mark a major step toward ensuring individuals' rights to privacy and the security of personal information within Myanmar. It is hoped that, in due course, the area of data protection can receive more attention in Myanmar and there will be greater progress in this field.

II. Frameworks for Data Protection

A. Constitutional Framework

There is an express protection of the right to privacy, but only an oblique provision relating to the protection of personal data transfers, in the Constitution of the Republic of the Union of Myanmar 2008.[1] Section 357 of the Constitution reads: 'The Union shall protect the privacy and security of home, property, correspondence and other communications of citizens under the law subject to the provisions of this Constitution'. The reference to 'correspondence and other communications of citizens' can be construed as referring to the transmission of information relating to an individual from one party to another. Section 357 in fact reflects the text of Article 12 of the Universal Declaration of Human Rights (UDHR) which affirms that '[n]o one shall be subjected to arbitrary or unlawful interference with his privacy, family, home or correspondence, nor to unlawful attacks on his honour and reputation'. Myanmar was one of the 48 countries that voted in favour of the UDHR when it was put to the UN General Assembly for approval in December 1948 as Resolution A/RES/217(III)A.

Section 357 thus mandates the Myanmar Government to protect privacy and an individual's communications of personal information, and this offers individuals a general measure of protection in respect of their personal information. But Myanmar has no comprehensive law safeguarding people's personal information at present. Section 357 says little specific about safeguarding the transfer of personal information. It is therefore insufficient by itself to regulate the control and processing of personal data.

B. International and Regional Framework

Mention has been made of Myanmar's obligations as a member of ASEAN. Myanmar is a party to the 'ASEAN Framework on Personal Data Protection'[2] adopted at the ASEAN Telecommunications and Information Technology Ministers (TELMIN) Meeting on 25 November 2016. By the ASEAN Framework, all ASEAN states (including Myanmar) 'endeavour to take into account and implement in their domestic laws and regulations [nine] Personal Data Protection Principles'. The nine Principles are:

1) An organisation should not collect, use or disclose personal data about an individual unless:
   i. the individual has been notified of and given consent to the purpose(s) of the collection, use or disclosure of his/her personal data; or
   ii. the collection, use or disclosure without notification or consent is authorised or required under domestic laws and regulations.

[1] Constitution of the Republic of the Union of Myanmar (2008), available at www.myanmar-law-library.org/spip.php?page=pdfjs&id_document=64.

[2] ASEAN Telecommunications and Information Technology Ministers (TELMIN), Framework on Personal Data Protection, available at asean.org/wp-content/uploads/2012/05/10-ASEAN-Framework-on-PDP.pdf.

2) An organisation may collect, use or disclose personal data about an individual only for purposes that a reasonable person would consider appropriate in the circumstances.
3) The personal data should be accurate and complete to the extent necessary for the purpose(s) for which the personal data is to be used or disclosed.
4) The personal data should be appropriately protected against loss and unauthorised access, collection, use, disclosure, copying, modification, destruction or similar risks.
5) Upon request by an individual, an organisation should:
   i. provide the individual access to his/her personal data which is in the possession or under the control of the organisation within a reasonable period of time; and
   ii. correct an error or omission in his personal data, unless domestic laws and regulations require or authorise the organisation not to provide access or correct the personal data in the particular circumstances.
6) Before transferring personal data to another country or territory, the organisation should either obtain the consent of the individual for the overseas transfer or take reasonable steps to ensure that the receiving organisation will protect the personal data consistently with these Principles.
7) An organisation should cease to retain documents containing personal data, or remove the means by which the personal data can be associated with particular individuals as soon as it is reasonable to assume that the retention is no longer necessary for legal or business purposes.
8) An organisation should be accountable for complying with measures which give effect to the Principles.
9) An organisation should, on request, provide clear and easily accessible information about its data protection policies and practices with respect to personal data in its possession or under its control. An organisation should also make available information on how to contact the organisation about its data protection policies and practices.

There are exceptions to the Principles. Paragraph 4 of the ASEAN Framework excludes from the instrument's ambit: (1) 'measures adopted by a Participant to exempt any areas, persons or sectors from the application of the Principles' and (2) 'matters relating to national sovereignty, national security, public safety, public policy and all government activities deemed suitable by a Participant to be exempted'.

Reference should also be made to the Nay Pyi Daw Declaration of 28 January 2022 entitled 'Digital Transformation: The Engine for ASEAN Economic Recovery from COVID-19'. This was the outcome of the second ASEAN Digital Ministers' Meeting which took place online in January 2022. By the Nay Pyi Taw Declaration, ASEAN members undertook (among others) to '[e]nhance ASEAN's cybersecurity and cyber wellness through continued cooperation in cybersecurity, personal data protection, capacity building and digital certification activities' and '[s]trengthen regulatory coherence of data policies to build trust in the use and sharing of data within and across borders in ASEAN through the ongoing implementation of the ASEAN Framework on Digital Data Governance and Related Initiatives'.[3]

[3] For the 'ASEAN Framework on Digital Data Governance and Related Initiatives' as adopted by TELMIN in Bali on 6 December 2016, see asean.org/wp-content/uploads/2012/05/6B-ASEAN-Framework-on-Digital-Data-

ASEAN frameworks apart, Myanmar is not to date a party to any international data protection treaty or multilateral agreement. This inevitably leads to uncertainty, given a growing reliance within Myanmar as elsewhere in the world on digital technologies and online communication methods.[4] If Myanmar is to attract foreign investment and develop economically in the future, it will have at some point to adopt and be influenced by international data protection standards and best practices, as exemplified by the EU's General Data Protection Regulation (GDPR).[5] The Principles of the ASEAN Framework are fully compatible with the GDPR. Therefore, adopting the GDPR as a template for a comprehensive data protection law would probably be the quickest way for Myanmar to comply with its undertaking in the ASEAN Framework.

The Asia-Pacific Economic Cooperation (APEC) Cross-Border Privacy Rules (CBPR) constitute a voluntary framework for facilitating the secure and seamless flow of personal data across borders in participating APEC member economies.[6] Based on internationally recognised privacy standards, the CBPR operates through a set of privacy principles on prevention of harm, giving of notice, collection limitations, use choices, integrity, security safeguards, access and correction, and accountability. Organisations can demonstrate adherence to CBPR through an independent third-party assessment and certification process, enabling them to transfer personal data across borders within participating APEC economies. Currently, nine APEC economies (Australia, Canada, Japan, Mexico, South Korea, Singapore, Taiwan, the Philippines, and the United States) have joined the CBPR system, with others encouraged to align their privacy frameworks accordingly. A key feature of the CBPR is mutual recognition, where APEC economies accept certifications issued by authorised accountability agents from other APEC economies, fostering trust and privacy protection in cross-border data transfers. Additionally, cooperation and capacity building initiatives are undertaken to enhance understanding and implementation of the CBPR framework among participating economies. Myanmar has not formally adopted the CBPR system. Its position on joining this framework remains unclear.

Governance_Endorsedv1.pdf. The following paragraphs of the latter document are worth noting in the context of what needs to be done in Myanmar in respect of data protection:

18. Data flows should be accompanied by assurances that safeguards are in place to protect and secure the information regardless where the data goes. These safeguards should be harmonised to prevent the development of fragmented regulatory regimes, which may negatively impact data flows and increase business compliance costs.
19. It should be emphasised that not all requirements imposed on cross border data flows are detrimental to the economy. Requirements may exist to ensure that there are safeguards to accord the necessary protection for the data being transferred. It is important for individual ASEAN Member States to review and minimise restrictions to cross border data flows against the backdrop of its overall impact to data innovation and the goal of fostering a vibrant data ecosystem.

[4] On the Myanmar digital economy generally, see Oxford Business Group, 'Myanmar's New Digital Strategy Improves ICT Development and Network Readiness' (2020), available at oxfordbusinessgroup.com/reports/myanmar/2020-report/economy/connection-roadmap-new-digital-strategy-for-government-trade-and-investment-to-improve-sector-development-and-network-.readiness#:~:text=Digital%20Roadmap&text=The%20plan%20lists%2014%20goals,bn%20over%20the%20same%20period. The blog posting comments: 'Myanmar ranks among the lowest in ASEAN on four indicators of digital readiness: ICT development, e-government development, network readiness and cybersecurity'.

[5] Regulation (EU) 2016/679 of the European Parliament and of the Council of 27 April 2016 on the Protection of Natural Persons with Regard to the Processing of Personal Data and on the Free Movement of Such Data, and Repealing Directive 95/46/EC (2016) OJ L119/1, available at gdpr-info.eu/.

[6] See www.apec.org/docs/default-source/Groups/ECSG/CBPR/CBPR-PoliciesRulesGuidelines.pdf.

C. Statutory Frameworks

Here and there, existing Myanmar laws contain provisions on data privacy and protection. Examples are the Electronic Transactions Law 2004, the Law Relating to Private Healthcare Services 2007, the Telecommunications Law 2013, the Competition Law 2015, the Banking and Financial Institutions Law 2016, and the Law Protecting the Privacy and Security of Citizens 2017 (the Privacy Law). Some of the foregoing legislation is sector specific.

The Electronic Transactions Law was enacted by State Peace and Development Council Law No 5 of 2004 on 30 April 2004. It was amended by the Law Amending the Electronic Transactions Law No 6 of 2014 of 25 February 2014 and State Administration Council (SAC) Law No 7 or 2021 of 15 February 2021.[7] It regulates the use of electronic signatures, electronic records, and digital certificates and has sections prohibiting unauthorised access to computer systems and interception or alteration of electronic communications. It applies to any kind of electronic record and electronic data message used in the context of commercial or other activities, including domestic and international dealings, transactions, arrangements, agreements, contracts, and exchanges and storage of information.

The purpose of amending the Electronic Transactions Law was to improve cybersecurity measures and protect personal information in digital form. To provide clarity and an effective framework for dealing with personal data and to prevent cyberthreats, key definitions and requirements are defined in this law. For instance, the amended definition of 'personal data' in section 2(l) clarifies that the phrase encompasses 'any information that identifies or is capable of identifying an individual'. This broad definition ensures coverage of all identifying information.

Section 27 *bis* of the amended statute sets out the detailed responsibilities of an organisation's Personal Data Management Officer (PDMO)[8] in ensuring secure handling of personal data. It stipulates:

> 27 *bis* (A) The Personal Data Management Officer shall:
>
> (i) systematically store, protect and process personal data that he is responsible for according to its type, and level of security in accordance with the Law;
>
> (ii) prohibit the examination, disclosure, informing, dissemination, transmission, alteration, destruction, copying, or submission as evidence of the personal data of an individual without the consent of such individual, or the permission by the provision of an existing law to any individual or organization;
>
> (iii) refrain from processing personal data contrary to the objectives set out in this Law;
>
> (iv) systematically destroy all personal data that are retained, within a retention period, after the designated period expires.

[7] For an unofficial translation of the consolidated text of the Electronic Transactions Law, see www.myanmar-responsiblebusiness.org/pdf/electronic-transactions-law_consolidated_2014-and-2021_en.pdf. The text of Chapter 10 quoted here is taken from the foregoing translation.

[8] Section 2(m) of the amended Electronic Transactions Law defines a PDMO as 'the person and staff authorised by a governmental department or an organisation to be responsible for collecting, retaining, and using personal data in accordance with the law, or any existing laws'.

(B) The investigation team, or the person mandated or instructed to act on their behalf, who receives information that includes personal data in accordance with the existing laws, shall keep the information confidential except when disclosing the information to persons permitted in accordance with the Law.

(C) The provisions relating to the management of personal data shall not apply in the following scenarios:

(i) prevention, search and enquiry, investigation, or providing evidence before a court by a governmental department authorised by the Central Committee, the Investigative Team or a rule of law team in relation to cybersecurity, cyber-attacks, Cyber Terrorism, Cyber Misuse and cyber accidents or Cyber Crimes;

(ii) search and enquiry, investigation, gathering information, filing a charge, or providing evidence before a court by a governmental department authorised by the Central Committee, the Investigative Team or a rule of law team mandated to work on a criminal matter;

(iii) enquiry, investigation, gathering information or coordination of information is undertaken if cybersecurity and Cyber Crimes issues are of concerns to the state sovereignty, peace and stability or national security;

(iv) when carrying out activities set out in sub-section (iii), either the Central Committee, a relevant department, or organization assigned by the Central Committee having a separate authority and working on it in accordance with such standards.

Note that the PDMO must destroy personal data once the retention period expires. On the other hand, personal data obtained for the purposes of an investigation, are to be kept confidential, with disclosure only allowed when the law permits.

Section 38 *bis* of the amended statute is likewise significant. This section imposes penalties for various data-related offences. By sub-section (A), the failure to manage personal data in accordance with law can result in imprisonment for a maximum of three years, a fine of no more than 10 million kyats (about US$3,600), or both. Under sub-section (B), persons found guilty of unlawfully obtaining, disclosing, utilising, destroying, altering, distributing, or transferring personal data to a third party without authorisation, may be sentenced to between one- and three-years imprisonment, a fine of no more than five million kyats (about US$1,800), or both. Sub-section (C) prohibits the spreading of false or misleading material online with the intention of inciting social discord, public fear, or distrust. An offence is punishable by up to three years in prison, a fine of no more than five million kyats, or both. Sub-section (D) penalises the perpetrators of cyberattacks aimed at undermining national security, sovereignty, peace, stability, the rule of law, or national unity. Conviction carries a sentence of between two to five years, a fine of no more than 30 million kyats (US$10,800), or both. Finally, under sub-section (E), there are heavy penalties for obtaining illegal access to or hacking cyber facilities, with the intention of harming Myanmar or other nations or of advancing the interests of foreign states. A conviction carries a maximum sentence of seven years, a fine of 50,000,000 kyats (US$18,000), or both.

The Law Relating to Private Healthcare Services was enacted by State Peace and Development Council Law No 5 of 2007 on 5 April 2007. While the statute focuses on the regulation of healthcare services (including administrative orders relating to the same and the imposition of penalties for contraventions), there are aspects that indirectly intersect with data protection frameworks. Chapter XIII, section 25(1), for instance, imposes a duty on healthcare service providers to keep confidential patients' health information, except where there is an official request for the same by a government department or organisation.

Chapter XIII, on the other hand, deals with the issue, suspension, or cancellation of licences for private healthcare services by supervisory bodies. The grant of a licence may involve considerations of data protection compliance. This means that a failure to comply with confidentiality requirements could lead to administrative action.

The Telecommunications Law was enacted by Pyidaungsu Hluttaw No 31 of 2013 on 8 October 2013. It was amended by Pyi Htaung Su Hluttaw Law No 26 of 2017 on 29 August 2017.[9] It has provisions protecting the privacy of communications and the confidentiality of personal information (including data). Section 13 requires individuals, departments, and organisations, whether local or foreign, to obtain a licence from the Ministry of Communications and Information Technology, if they 'keep in possession or use' telecommunications equipment. While the provision does not directly concern data protection, it implies the existence of a regulatory framework (that is, the possibility of licensing conditions) that could include terms for the protection of personal information. In this vein, section 17 requires telecommunications service licensees to keep secure: (1) information transmitted or received through their service; and (2) confidential personal information of users. Such information is not to be disclosed to third parties 'except where allowed in accord with the existing laws'.

Other sections of the amended Telecommunications Law of interest from the viewpoint of data protection would be the following:

1) Section 31: This outlines the requirements and procedures for obtaining and renewing telecommunications licences. It emphasises the importance of compliance with regulatory standards to ensure service quality and user privacy.
2) Section 65: This addresses the obligations of telecommunications service providers to protect user data. It includes provisions for data encryption, secure storage, and measures to prevent unauthorised access.
3) Section 66: This details the penalties and legal consequences for breaches of user confidentiality and data protection regulations. It specifies fines, licence suspensions, and other disciplinary actions for non-compliance.
4) Section 69: This focuses on monitoring and auditing processes for telecommunications providers. It ensures that regular checks are conducted to verify compliance with data protection regulations and service standards.

The State Law and Order Restoration Council enacted the Banking and Financial Institutions Law by State Law and Order Restoration Council Law No 16 of 1990 on 4 July 1990. The legislation imposes restrictions on financial institutions. Banks are required under section 81 to keep confidential information relating to the affairs, accounts, records, and transactions of customers. There are limited exceptions in section 82 to the duty to maintain secrecy, including disclosure of information to the Central Bank of Myanmar or disclosure to comply with a court order or other legal requirement.

The Privacy Law was enacted by Union Parliament Law 5/2017 in March 2017 to protect the privacy and security of Myanmar citizens. It was amended by State Administration Council Law 4/2021 on 13 February 2021. The amendments came into effect less than

[9] For an English translation of the Telecommunications Law, see www.ptd.gov.mm/Uploads/Services/Attach/22018/2096121422018_2.%20Telecom%20Law(Eng).pdf.

two weeks after the military Government came to power. The amendments chiefly concerned the Government's power to conduct searches, seizures, and arrests and to extend detention without judicial oversight. The amendments also empowered the Government to conduct a broad range of surveillance and investigation activities that could intrude on individual privacy. The amendments accomplished this by suspending various sections of the Privacy Law for as long as the State Administration Council is in power.

III. Conclusion

By way of conclusion, we make five general observations on the frameworks identified in this chapter.

First, under section 2(1) of the Electronic Transaction Law, the expression 'personal data' refers to information that identifies or is capable of identifying an individual. That apart, as far as Myanmar law is concerned, none of the frameworks enumerated here define what constitutes or does not constitute 'personal data'. Nor do the frameworks clearly define or explain terms such as 'data users', 'data subjects' and 'data processors'.

Second, taken as a package, section 357 of the Myanmar Constitution, the Privacy Law (prior to its amendment), the Telecommunications Law and the Electronic Transactions Law come closest to implementing a rudimentary data privacy and protection regime in Myanmar today. But there are shortcomings.

The issue of e-Commerce Guidelines[10] by Myanmar's Ministry of Commerce on 5 September 2023 underscores the need for the systematic protection of personal data within the country's e-commerce landscape. While the Guidelines reinforce the need for data protection in alignment with the Constitution of Myanmar, the Telecommunications Law, the Electronic Transactions Law, and the Privacy Law, the Guidelines do not mandate the obtaining of prior consent from a data subject in respect of all forms of data processing. This omission is a gap in Myanmar's rudimentary regulatory framework, especially in comparison to international practice whereby obtaining explicit consent is a routine measure for ensuring data privacy and security.

The amended Electronic Transactions Law, which has extraterritorial jurisdiction, touches on the need for consent in relation to the handling of personal data. Thus, under section 27 *bis* (a)(ii), the PDMO shall seek the consent of the owner of data before any transfer of the latter's information. The law indicates that consent can serve as a legal basis for cross-border data transfers in the absence of comprehensive data protection laws. But, by itself, the law lacks the robustness seen in other jurisdictions, such as the EU, whereby consent must be explicit, informed, and revocable and where additional safeguards are in place to ensure that consent is truly voluntary.

Accordingly, the absence of a dedicated data protection law in Myanmar creates challenges not only for domestic data privacy, but also for international trade. As neighbouring countries, like Thailand, adopt stringent data protection laws modelled after GDPR, Myanmar's lack of similar legislation could hinder its ability to engage in cross-border

[10] For an English translation of the Guidelines' text, see www.lincolnmyanmar.com/wp-content/uploads/2023/09/E-Commerce-Guidelines-Primer-12.9.2023.pdf.

e-commerce. Countries with robust data protection frameworks may be reluctant to trade with those countries lacking such safeguards. Myanmar needs to develop a comprehensive data protection regime to align with global standards, ensuring both the protection of its citizens' personal data and the facilitation of international trade.

Third, cross-border or international data transfers involve the movement of personal data across national borders from Myanmar to other countries or vice versa. This happens when a company with operations in Myanmar transfers data to overseas affiliates or when an organisation outside Myanmar collects personal data from individuals located in another country. Despite the absence of a comprehensive data protection law in Myanmar, international data transfers are also subject to the data protection laws of a destination country. Myanmar organisations must comply with the latter laws when processing data originating from, or transferring data to, the destination country. For cross-border data transfers, it will be essential for Myanmar establishments to ensure that the data is adequately protected during transmission and processing in accordance with the data protection laws of all relevant jurisdictions. That will be the case even if a destination country's data privacy laws are stricter than those of Myanmar.

To make up for a deficiency in Myanmar's laws, Myanmar data controllers or processors may need to insert provisions such as the ASEAN Model Contractual Clauses (ASEAN MCCs) into international commercial contracts involving the collection, processing, transfer and storage of personal data outside Myanmar.[11] The incorporation of the ASEAN MCCs by Myanmar data controllers or processors will mean that their obligations relating to personal data will be on a par with those required by (for example) GDPR,[12] regardless of the current state of data protection in Myanmar. In other words, the lack of a dedicated data protection law in Myanmar thus poses challenges for day-to-day international data transfers, making it crucial for Myanmar organisations to implement their own contractual measures to ensure compliance with both local and international data protection standards. As other countries with robust data protection laws may be reluctant to engage in data exchanges with Myanmar, adopting best practices and internal policies akin to Binding Corporate Rules could help mitigate risks and facilitate smoother international data transfers.

[11] For the ASEAN MCCs, see 'ASEAN Model Contractual Clauses for Cross Border Data Flows' (2021), available at https://asean.org/wp-content/uploads/3-ASEAN-Model-Contractual-Clauses-for-Cross-Border-Data-Flows_Final.pdf.

[12] For a comparison of the ASEAN MCCs with the EU's Standard Contractual Clauses, see 'Joint Guide to the ASEAN Model Contractual Clauses and EU Standard Contractual Clauses' (2024), available at asean.org/wp-content/uploads/2024/02/Joint-Guide-to-ASEAN-Model-Contractual-Clauses-and-EU-Standard-Contractual-Clauses.pdf. The Introduction to the document states at p 4: 'The [ASEAN MCCs] and EU Standard Contractual Clauses … are model data protection clauses ("clauses") that can be incorporated by data exporters and importers in their contractual arrangements as a basis to allow the transfer of personal data across borders. The clauses are a voluntary tool to ensure personal data continues to benefit from a high level of protection in cases of international transfers, and to ensure compliance with applicable legal requirements for international data transfers in this regard. This concerns requirements following the ASEAN Member States' legal frameworks and the General Data Protection Regulation (GDPR) for the ASEAN MCCs and EU SCCs respectively. The clauses reflect the core data protection requirements that follow the ASEAN Framework on Personal Data Protection (2016) and the GDPR, which are increasingly recognised internationally. Through their standardisation and pre-approval, model data protection clauses become "ready-made" and easy-to-implement tools. Both MCCs and SCCs contain certain optional clauses that can be used where applicable'.

Fourth, Myanmar does not presently have a data protection supervisory authority or privacy commissioner. If Myanmar establishes a data privacy and protection regulator in the future, it is foreseeable that, just as in other countries, the regulator will have sanctioning powers to enforce those laws. For the time being, it is uncertain how breaches of any of the frameworks mentioned in this chapter will be dealt with by the Government or the courts.

Fifth, what is the prognosis for Myanmar data protection in the future? The use of blacklisting and whitelisting[13] in Myanmar, particularly following the military coup in February 2021, illustrates the Government's strategy to control information and communication. The military's initial reliance on blacklisting aimed to disrupt social media platforms and messaging apps like Facebook and Twitter and to stifle dissent and control the narrative. This approach forced citizens to use virtual private networks to access restricted sites. But it also significantly impacted on the country's digital economy by disrupting digital payment systems and other online services. Despite these efforts, protestors continued to find ways to communicate and mobilise, indicating the limited effectiveness of blacklisting in completely silencing dissent.

In contrast, the subsequent implementation of whitelisting allowed for the partial restoration of internet services, specifically for essential applications like digital banking, while maintaining blocks on major social media platforms. This approach was intended to mitigate economic damage. But it failed fully to revive the digital economy or restore freedom of expression. The selective allowance of internet services highlighted the regime's attempt to balance control with economic functionality. Overall, the shift from blacklisting to whitelisting reflected a tactical adaptation to sustain critical digital services while continuing to restrict broader access to information. However, these measures have drawn international criticism for violating human rights, particularly the right to freedom of expression.[14]

Given Myanmar's current political and legislative context, it is unlikely that its data protection legislation will closely mirror GDPR any time in the proximate future. The military regime prioritises control and censorship over transparent data protection laws, and significant political change towards democracy will be necessary for such alignment with GDPR or anything like it. Myanmar currently lacks the legal and institutional capacity to develop and enforce GDPR-style regulations. That sort of development requires substantial investment in capacity building and legal reform. Regional influences from ASEAN and APEC may promote some harmonisation, although the resulting standard within Myanmar may still be less stringent than GDPR. International pressures and economic incentives might push for clearer and more rigorous regulations on data protection and privacy. But effective implementation and enforcement depend on overcoming local, cultural and institutional challenges.

[13] Blacklisting designates forbidden cyber-sites, while whitelisting identifies government approved cyber-sites.

[14] See further https://netmission.asia/2021/06/03/netmission-insight-what-are-blacklist-and-whitelist-a-recent-case-of-myanmar/.

11

The Philippines

LEMUEL DIDULO LOPEZ

I. Introduction

The protection of privacy is well established in the Philippine Constitution.[1] The right to privacy, however, was for a long time not explicitly extended by legislation to data privacy. Statutes, like the Civil Code, can be used to broadly protect data privacy,[2] but none provided a comprehensive set of data protection rules similar to those existing in major global economies. There were also judicial decisions which further defined the scope of the right to privacy, but these cases were decided in the context of administrative issuances,[3] criminal proceedings,[4] search and seizures,[5] and public access to information.[6] Nonetheless, a primary motivation towards developing a more robust and comprehensive legal framework for data protection came with the need to protect the lucrative business processing outsourcing (BPO) industry, which the Philippines is a global leader.[7] Hence, the Data Privacy Act (DPA) was passed in 2012, bringing into Philippine law both the approaches of the European Union (EU) and the Asia Pacific Economic Cooperation (APEC).[8]

Notably, the principles of transparency, legitimate purpose, and proportionality form the foundation of the DPA.[9] Transparency means that the person whose personal information is being processed is aware of the nature, purpose, and extent of such processing.[10]

[1] *Morfe v Mutuc* (1968) 22 SCRA 424, 444–45.

[2] Civil Code 1949, Arts 26, 32 and 723 ('Civil Code'); Revised Penal Code 1930, Arts 128, 229, 290–92, 280 (RPC); Anti-Wiretapping Act 1965; Bank Secrecy Law 1955; Intellectual Property Code 2001.

[3] *Ople v Torres* (1998) 293 SCRA 141, 153–70.

[4] *People v Reyes* (1974) 60 SCRA 126, 127; *People v Morial* (2001) 363 SCRA 96, 124.

[5] *Lim v Ponce de Leon* (1975) 66 SCRA 299, 306; *Lopez v Commissioner of Customs* (1975) 68 SCRA 320, 326; *People v Briñas* (1999) 320 SCRA 22, 58; *Nocum v Laguna Tayabas Bus Co* (1969) 30 SCRA 69, 74.

[6] *Morfe* (n 1) 444–45; *Hilado v Reyes* (2006) 496 SCRA 282, 299–300; *Lagunzad v Soto Vda de Gonzales* (1979) 92 SCRA 476, 487; *Ayer Productions Pty Ltd v Capulong* (1988) 160 SCRA 861, 870–76.

[7] Bernie Cahiles-Magkilat, 'Lack of Legislation on Data Privacy Protection Worries Investors JFC', *Manila Bulletin* (Manila, 7 June 2011), archived at www.investphilippines.info/arangkada/lack-of-legislation-on-data-privacy-protection-worries-investors-%E2%80%93-jfc/.

[8] National Privacy Commission, *NPC Advisory Opinion No 2017-27*, 23 June 2017; see also Marck Joseph Macaraeg, 'From Atoms to Bits: Personal Data Privacy and Security in the Information Society' (2017) 62(1) *Ateneo Law Journal* 223, 238.

[9] Data Privacy Act 2012 (DPA), ch 3, s 11.

[10] Implementing Rules and Regulations of Republic Act 10173 also known as the 'Data Privacy Act of 2012' 2016 ('DPA IRR'), rule IV, s 18(a).

Legitimate purpose, on the other hand, means that the processing of information should be compatible with a declared and specified purpose which must not be contrary to law, morals or public policy.[11] Lastly, proportionality means that the processing of information should be adequate, relevant, suitable, necessary and not excessive in relation to a declared or specified purpose.[12] These principles have guided the implementation of the DPA and ushered into the Philippines a new era of active protection of data privacy.

II. General Legal Framework of International Data Transfers and Data Protection

A. Constitutional Protection for Data and Data Transfer

The Philippine Supreme Court has declared in *Morfe v Mutuc* that the right to privacy is protected by the Philippine Constitution.[13] *Ople v Torres* has confirmed that this constitutional protection to privacy is likewise present in the current 1987 Philippine Constitution,[14] particularly in the Bill of Rights.[15] The constitutional protection, however, focuses on the privacy of communication and correspondence, and does not explicitly mention data transfers and data protection. Nonetheless, in *Disini v Secretary of Justice*,[16] the Supreme Court, citing the United States case of *Whalen v Roe*,[17] stressed that privacy can be broadly classified into two: (1) decisional privacy or the right to independence in making certain important decisions; and (2) informational privacy or the interest in avoiding disclosure of personal matters. Furthermore, informational privacy has two aspects: the right not to have private information disclosed, and the right to live freely without surveillance and intrusion. Hence, data protection is understood as an aspect of the right to informational privacy.

Since the right to privacy has been described as a fundamental human right which is protected under the Philippine Constitution, it has since then become the basis for statutes mandating data protection.[18] Furthermore, the Supreme Court has promulgated the Rules on the Writ of Habeas Data,[19] which is aimed to provide an independent and summary remedy to protect the right to privacy as guaranteed by the Philippine Constitution.[20]

[11] ibid, rule IV, s 18(b).
[12] ibid, rule IV, s 18(c).
[13] *Morfe* (n 1) 444–45.
[14] *Ople* (n 3) 156.
[15] Constitution 1987 (Constitution), Art III, ss 1, 2, 3(1), 6 and 8; *Ople* (n 3) 156–57; Lemuel Lopez, 'The Right to Privacy in Inquiries in Aid of Legislation' (2003) 78(1) *Philippine Law Journal* 162, 171.
[16] *Disini v Secretary of Justice* [2014] GR Nos 203335, 203299, 203306, 203359, 203378, 203391, 203407, 203440, 203453, 203454, 203469, 203501, 203509, 203515 & 203518.
[17] *Whalen v Roe* (1977) 429 US 589, 599–600.
[18] DPA, ch 1, s 2; see also Department of Information and Communications Technology Act 2015, s 2(l); Financial Products and Services Consumer Protection Act 2022 (FPSCPA), s 2(d); Community Based Monitoring Act 2018, s 2; Philippine Identification System Act 2017, s 2.
[19] *Supreme Court Administrative Matter No 08-1-16-C 2008* ('Writ of Habeas Data').
[20] ibid, s 1; *Manila Electric Company v Lim* (2010) 632 SCRA 195, 202–203; *Lee v Ilagan* (2014) 738 SCRA 59, 64–67.

B. Statutory Frameworks for Data Transfer and Protection

The DPA is the primary and baseline legislation that regulates and protects data transfer and protection in the Philippines. The statute has two main goals: (1) to protect the fundamental right of privacy of data subjects; and (2) to ensure the free flow of information necessary to promote innovation and growth.[21] To achieve this, it regulates and protects the processing of personal information of data subjects falling within the DPA's scope. Processing of personal information includes, but is not limited to, the collection, recording, organisation, storage, updating or modification, retrieval, consultation, use, consolidation, blocking, erasure, or destruction of data.[22] Processing also includes the sharing and transfers, including international transfers,[23] of personal information, sensitive or privileged personal information.[24]

The DPA broadly applies to both natural and juridical persons, including those in the government and private sectors, who are engaged in the processing of personal information. This is regardless of the entity's type of organisation, size, or income. Hence, the DPA can apply to sole proprietors, individual professionals, or contractors, including those which are unorganised and informal.[25] Notably, the DPA covers transfers of personal information within the Philippines by persons or entities, regardless of their citizenship or residency.[26] Furthermore, the DPA applies to cross-border or international transfers of personal information belonging to Philippine citizens and residents.[27]

Despite its breadth, the DPA has a number of exceptions. For example, it excludes certain personal information about government officials[28] and government service providers,[29] personal information relating to permits and licences given by the Government,[30] and personal information required to carry out government functions.[31] It also excludes personal information processed for journalistic, artistic, literary or research purposes.[32] Lastly, it also excludes personal information needed by financial and banking institutions including those necessary to comply with the provisions of the Anti-Money Laundering Act (AMLA).[33] Notably, the statute excludes from its application the processing in the Philippines of personal information which were originally collected from residents of foreign jurisdiction in accordance with the laws of those foreign jurisdictions.[34]

[21] DPA, ch 1, s 2.
[22] ibid, ch 1, s 3(j).
[23] ibid, ch 1, s 21; DPA IRR, rule X, s 44(1)(b) and rule XII, s 50.
[24] DPA IRR, rule I, ss 3(f) and s 19; rule IV, s 19(a)(2) and 20; rule VI, s 26(1); rule VII, s 32; rule X, s 44; rule XI, s 49; rule XII, s 50.
[25] Aiken Larisa Serzo, 'Cross Border Data Regulation for Digital Platforms: Data Privacy and Security' (Discussion Paper No 2020-47, Philippine Institute for Development Studies, December 2020) [1.2.1].
[26] DPA, ch 1, s 4.
[27] ibid, ch 1, s 6.
[28] ibid, ch 1, s 4(a).
[29] ibid, ch 1, s 4(b).
[30] ibid, ch 1, s 4(c).
[31] ibid, ch 1, s 4(e).
[32] ibid, ch 1, s 4(d).
[33] ibid, ch 1, s 4(f).
[34] ibid, ch 1, s 4(g).

Furthermore, a number of statutes which were passed subsequent to the DPA explicitly require compliance with the DPA.[35] Nonetheless, there are also statutes modifying the DPA's application.[36] These statutes usually deal with personal information excluded from the DPA's scope and reflects the Philippine approach that certain types of data, like data gathered in the government and financial sector, are subject to special rules. Nonetheless, the DPA still applies to these types of data to the extent not explicitly provided by the special rules. Moreover, a number of penal statutes also modify the DPA's application, and this approach usually reflect the much higher public interest involved. For example, the Special Protection of Children in Situation of Armed Conflict Act allows data and information sharing between government and non-governmental organisations so both can remain informed and updated of the status of released children and to assess and address their needs.[37] Likewise, owners, lessors, and hotel operators have the obligation to notify law enforcement authorities when the relevant premises are used for human trafficking, and such sharing of information shall not be considered a violation of the DPA.[38]

Arguably, certain statutes which are aimed to protect the broader right to privacy could also cover data transfers and data protection.[39] These statutes include the Rape Victim Assistance and Protection Act of 1998 which recognises both the offended party and accused's right to privacy.[40] Similarly, any HIV-related information (for example, that a person has undergone a HIV-related test, has HIV infection or HIV-related illnesses, or has been exposed to HIV) is classified as confidential and protected by the owner's right to privacy; thus, its disclosure without the owner's consent is unlawful.[41] Similarly, whilst all healthcare practitioners and health institutions are required to report to the Rare Disease Registry diagnosed cases of rare disease and provide reports on the status of patients, the reporting is still subject to the patient's right to privacy.[42] Moreover, the Anti-Photo and

[35] Free Internet Access in Public Places Act 2016, s 9; Mobile Number Portability Act 2016, s 6(g); Permanent Validity of the Certificate of Live Birth, Death and Marriage Act 2022, s 7; Foundling Recognition and Protection Act 2022, s 28; Motorcycle Crime Prevention Act 2018, s 6; Philippine Energy Research and Policy Institute Act 2021, s 4(i); Philippine HIV and AIDS Policy Act 2018; Tax Amnesty Act 2018, s 22; Expanded Solo Parents Welfare Act 2022, s 16; Domestic Administrative Adoption and Alternative Child Care Act 2022, ss 29 and 38; Department of Migrant Workers Act 2021, s 18; Instituting a Policy of Inclusion and Services for Learners with Disabilities in Support of Inclusion Act 2022, s 16(d); Subscriber Identity Module Registration Act 2022, s 9; Covid-19 Vaccination Program Act 2021, ss 4 and 12; Anti-Online Sexual Abuse or Exploitation of Children and Anti-Child Sexual Abuse or Exploitation Materials Act 2022, ss 9(5) and 37 ('Anti-Online Sexual Abuse Act'); Strengthening the Policies on Anti-Human Trafficking in Persons, amending for the Purpose Republic Act 9208 as Amended, s 8; Tax Reform for Acceleration and Inclusion 2017, s 74.

[36] FPSCPA, s 8(e)(g); Community-Based Monitoring Act 2018, s 10; Philippine Identification System Act 2017, s 6(b)(c)(1); Telecommuting Act 2018, s 6.

[37] Special Protection of Children in Situation of Armed Conflict Act 2018, s 23(c) ('Children in Armed Conflict Act').

[38] Strengthening the Policies on Anti-Human Trafficking in Persons, amending for the Purpose Republic Act 9208 as Amended, s 8.

[39] Civil Code, Arts 26, 32 and 723; RPC, Arts 229, 290–292, 280, 128; Anti-Wiretapping Act 1965; Bank Secrecy Law 1955; Intellectual Property Code 2001 (Philippines); Revised Rules on Evidence, rule 130 (c), s 24; Children in Armed Conflict, ss 7(n) and 19(b); Anti-Online Sexual Abuse Act, s 21; Foundling Recognition and Protection Act 2022, s 21(f); Domestic Workers Act or Batas Kasambahay 2012, s 7; Electronics and Communication Engineering Law of the Philippines, s 35(h); Microfinance NGOs Act 2015, s 5(e); Expanded Anti-Trafficking in Persons Act 2012, s 10; Anti-Violence Against Women and Their Children Act 2004, s 44; Safe Spaces Act 2018, s 12; Juvenile Justice and Welfare Act 2006, s 5(h).

[40] Rape Victim Assistance and Protection Act 1998, s 5.

[41] Philippine HIV and AIDS Policy Act 2018, s 44(a)(b).

[42] Rare Diseases Act of the Philippines 2015, s 9.

Video Voyeurism Act prohibits the copying and distribution of private and sexual images or videos, without the consent of the persons involved.[43]

In addition, the Cybercrime Prevention Act (CPA) was passed to complement the DPA.[44] It introduces a set of cybercrime offences, including illegal access,[45] illegal interception,[46] data interference,[47] system interference,[48] cyber-squatting,[49] computer-related forgery,[50] computer-related fraud,[51] computer-related identity-theft,[52] thus, making criminally liable those who may have committed unlawful data transfers or breaches of protected data. Notably, a Philippine court would have jurisdiction if any of the elements of the foregoing cybercrime offences was committed within the Philippines or committed with the use of any computer system wholly or partly situated in the country, or when by such commission any damage is caused to a natural or juridical person who, at the time the offence was committed, was in the Philippines.[53] The CPA also introduces new investigation mechanisms by creating the cybercrime unit of the Philippine National Police and National Bureau of Investigation,[54] which can require the disclosure of computer data[55] and conduct search and seizures of computer data[56] after availing a court warrant.[57] Furthermore, instruments on international cooperation in criminal matters and domestic laws, to the widest extent possible for the purposes of investigations or proceedings concerning criminal offences related to computer systems and data, or for the collection of evidence in electronic form of a criminal, offence shall be given full force and effect.[58]

In addition, one can also apply for remedies like the Writ of Habeas Data or cite the Rules of Evidence, especially those concerning privileged communications, to enforce data privacy. The Writ of Habeas Data is a remedy available to any person whose right to privacy in life, liberty or security is violated or threatened by an unlawful act or omission of a public official or employee, or of a private individual or entity engaged in the gathering, collecting or storing of data or information regarding the person, family, home and correspondence of the aggrieved party.[59] It protects 'a person's right to control information regarding himself, particularly in the instances where such information is being collected through unlawful means in order to achieve unlawful ends'.[60] Clearly, the writ can be availed of in cases of illegal transfers of data and breaches of protected data. However, an important limitation is that the writ may not be availed in order to protect purely property or commercial concerns.[61]

[43] Anti-Photo and Video Voyeurism Act 2009, s 4.
[44] Cybercrime Prevention Act 2012 (CPA), s 2.
[45] ibid, s 4(a)(1).
[46] ibid, s 4(a)(2).
[47] ibid, s 4(a)(3).
[48] ibid, s 4(a)(4).
[49] ibid, s 4(a)(6).
[50] ibid, s 4(b)(1).
[51] ibid, s 4(b)(2).
[52] ibid, s 4(b)(3).
[53] ibid, s 21.
[54] ibid, s 10.
[55] ibid, s 14.
[56] ibid, s 15.
[57] ibid, ss 12 and 14–16.
[58] ibid, s 22.
[59] Writ of Habeas Data, s 1.
[60] *Roxas v Macapagal-Arroyo* (2010) 630 SCRA 211, 239.
[61] *Lee* (n 20) 65.

Meanwhile, the Rules on Evidence may be invoked to disqualify the testimonies of spouses, lawyers and their client, medical doctors and their patients, religious priests and ministers, and public officers (when public interest requires it) as to matters learned in confidence.[62]

i. Data Protection Frameworks

a. Influence of International Data Protection Frameworks

Because the Philippines is a global leader in the BPO industry, there has always been a strong call to align its legal framework on data protection with international standards.[63] When the DPA was drafted, two sources were considered[64] – the EU Data Protection Directive[65] and the APEC Privacy Framework.[66] Hence, the EU data privacy framework continues to influence the contemporary interpretation of the DPA. For example, the guidelines for the designation and the corresponding duties of the Data Protection Officer issued by the National Privacy Commission (NPC), the Philippines' privacy regulator, effectively aligns the requirements under the DPA with EU's General Data Protection Regulation.[67]

As an APEC member, the Philippines also has a strong incentive to align its data protection legislation with the APEC Privacy Framework. The APEC Privacy Framework, however, is less stringent and non-prescriptive (voluntary) as regards implementation and enforcement, albeit its core principles are similar to the EU Data Protection Directive. The APEC Privacy Framework's influence is seen in the DPA's adoption of key principles and in not explicitly allowing restrictions on data exports to countries without APEC-compliant laws. Likewise, the APEC Privacy Framework remains relevant especially given the recent participation of the Philippines in the APEC Cross-Border Privacy Rules system (CBPR). The Philippines' participation in the CBPR is led by the NPC and is aimed to allow Filipino businesses to enter larger markets within the Asia-Pacific by minimising dataflow barriers and adopting data privacy standards consistent with other jurisdictions.[68]

Likewise, as an Association of Southeast Asian Nations (ASEAN) member state, the Philippines actively participates in the organisation's data protection initiatives. Hence, the NPC has promoted the adoption and use within the Philippines of the ASEAN Model Contract Clauses (ASEAN MCCs) and ASEAN Data Management Framework.[69]

Moreover, in December 2016, the Philippines acceded to the Budapest Convention on Cybercrime. While the accession came after the CPA's enactment, a perusal of the law

[62] Revised Rules on Evidence rule 130 (c), s 24.

[63] Bernie Cahiles-Magkilat (n 7).

[64] *NPC Advisory Opinion No 2017-27* (n 8); see also Marck Joseph Macaraeg (n 8)238.

[65] Directive 95/46/EC of the European Parliament and of the Council of 24 October 1995 on the protection of individuals with regard to the processing of personal data and on the free movement of such data [1995] OJ L281/31.

[66] Asia Pacific Economic Cooperation, 'Data Privacy Framework' (Reports, December 2005), available at www.apec.org/publications/2005/12/apec-privacy-framework.

[67] National Privacy Commission, *NPC Advisory No 2017-01*, 14 March 2017; Ivy Patdu and Jamael Jacob, 'The Data Privacy Act and the National Privacy Commission's Five Pillars of Compliance' (2018) 63(1) *Ateneo Law Journal* 120, 131.

[68] 'CBPR System: An Overview' (*National Privacy Commission*), available at www.privacy.gov.ph/the-apec-cbpr-system-an overview/#:~:text=The%20Philippines%20formally%20joined%20the,standards%20consistent%20with%20other%20jurisdictions.

[69] National Privacy Commission, *NPC Advisory No 2021-03*, 5 November 2021.

reveals that the Budapest Convention has influenced the introduction of new cybercrime offences. Furthermore, the Department of Justice (DOJ) has explicitly recognised that the Budapest Convention is set to widen the mechanisms available for cybercrime investigation and prosecution and would influence the interpretation of the international cooperation provision of the CPA.[70]

ii. Specific Provisions for Particular Sectors

The DPA contains specific provisions for particular sectors. These include the government, banking, and finance institutions, and for those engaged in journalistic, artistic, literary and research purposes.

a. Government

The exemptions concerning the Government in the DPA reflect the general principle in the Philippine Constitution that a public office is a public trust.[71] Hence, the right to privacy may be more limited or may not be invoked when government sector data is involved. The term, 'government' is understood to include any government branch or body or entity, including national government agencies, bureaus, or offices, constitutional commissions, local government units, government-owned and controlled corporations, government financial institutions, state colleges and universities.[72] Hence, the DPA does not cover certain types of information about a public officer or government employee. This includes: the (1) fact that the person is a public officer or employee; (2) his position and office details; (3) details about his responsibilities, remuneration, and benefits; and (4) his name appearing in official documents.[73] Similarly, personal information about contractors performing services for the Government, including the terms of relevant contracts, are also excluded.[74] Lastly, personal information provided in relation to the government grant of licences and permits are likewise excluded.[75]

Nonetheless, this approach towards government sector data also reflects the fact that a number of legislations and administrative rules have already dealt with government-sector data. In fact, even the Constitution recognises the right of the people to information on matters of public concern.[76] Particularly, '[a]ccess to official records, and to documents, and papers pertaining to official acts, transactions, or decisions, as well as to government research data used as basis for policy development', is guaranteed to every Filipino.[77] Executive Order No 2016-02 operationalises this freedom of information by allowing access to official documents in the Executive branch, albeit subject to numerous exceptions.[78] Nonetheless,

[70] Christopher Lloyd Caliwan, 'DOJ Chief Welcomes PH Inclusion to Cybercrime Convention' (*Philippine News Agency*, 4 March 2018), available at www.pna.gov.ph/articles/1027338.
[71] Constitution, Art IX, s 1.
[72] See National Privacy Commission, *NPC Circular No 2016-01*, 10 October 2016, s3(G), ('Security of Personal Data in Government Agencies').
[73] DPA, ch 1, s 4(a)(1)–4(a)(4).
[74] ibid, ch 1, s 4(b).
[75] ibid, ch 1, s 4(c).
[76] Constitution, Art III, s 7.
[77] ibid.
[78] Executive Order No 2 2016, ss 2–3.

disclosure of personal information of public officials and employees is allowed only if it is material or relevant to the subject-matter of the request and its disclosure is permissible under law or administrative regulation.[79] Furthermore, under the Code of Conduct and Ethical Standards for Public Officials and Employees, government officials and employees are required to file a statement of assets and liabilities and financial disclosure, which necessarily include their personal information.[80] This statement shall be made available for inspection, including by the public for 10 days after its filing.[81]

However, with respect to personal data obtained by the Government which is not covered by any of the exemptions under section 4 of the DPA or other laws, these pieces of personal information should be processed in accordance with the DPA. In fact, a number of NPC issuances specifically deal with government-held data.[82] For example, data transfers by email are required to be encrypted.[83] Furthermore, access and transfer of personal data under the custody of a government agency to a third party, including another branch of the Government, for the purpose of performing government functions, should be covered by data sharing agreements.[84] However,

> there should always be a basis in law which mandates the sharing of information for a public function or service. This requirement may not be dispensed with by the mere fact that government agencies have executed data sharing agreements amongst themselves.[85]

Moreover, transfers to and processing by third parties located outside the Philippines are allowed, subject to cross-border arrangement and cooperation.[86] Furthermore, when law

[79] ibid, s 7(a).

[80] Code of Conduct and Ethical Standards for Public Officials and Employees 1989, s 8(A).

[81] ibid, s 8(C).

[82] Security of Personal Data in Government Agencies (n 72); *NPC Circular 2016-02*, 10 October 2016('Data Sharing Agreements Involving Government Agencies'); *NPC Advisory No 2022-01*, 29 January 2021 ('Guidelines on Requests For Personal Data of Public Officers'); *NPC Advisory No 2021-03*, 5 November 2021 ('Guidelines on the Processing of Personal Data For Election Campaign or Partisan Political Activity'); *NPC Advisory No 2017-02*, 3 April 2017 ('Access to Personal Data Sheets of Government Personnel'); *NPC Advisory Opinion No 2022-026*, 23 November 2022 ('Re: Disclosure of Personal Data Through the Database of Individuals Barred from Taking Civil Service Examinations and from Entering Government Service (DIBAR)'); *NPC Advisory Opinion No 2022-025*, 22 November 2022 ('Re: 201 Files of Government Employees'); *NPC Advisory Opinion No 2021-043*, 16 December 2021 ('Re: Data Sharing with the Philippine National Police'); *NPC Advisory Opinion No 2021-031*, 5 August 2021 ('Re: Processing for due Diligence, Quality Control, and Compliance Checks Pursuant to the Requirements of the Government Procurement Reform Act'); *NPC Advisory Opinion No 2021-018*, 18 June 2021 ('Re: PNP Request for Personal Information from Employers'); *NPC Advisory Opinion No 2021-007*, 5 March 2021 ('Re: Data Sharing Arrangements of the Philippine Veterans Affairs office With Other Government Agencies'); *NPC Advisory Opinion No 2021-006*, 5 March 2021('Re: Data Classification for the Disclosure of Procurement-related Document'); *NPC Advisory Opinion No 2020-051*, 26 November 2020 ('Re: Request for Personal Data by the National Bureau of Investigation and the Philippine Army'); *NPC Advisory Opinion No 2020-031*, 6 August 2020 ('Re: Access to Files and Records of Anti-illegal Drugs Operations of the Philippine Drug Enforcement Agency'); *NPC Advisory Opinion No 2020-012*, 19 February 2020 ('Re: Disclosure of Insurance Policy Details to the National Bureau of Investigation'); *NPC Advisory Opinion No 2020-002*, 6 February 2020 ('Re: Publication of the Full Content of Bureau of Internal Revenue (Bir) Rulings in the Bir Website'); *NPC Advisory Opinion No 2019-018*, 11 March 2019 ('Data Collection Surveys by Government Agencies'); *NPC Advisory Opinion No 2018-025*, 4 May 2018 ('Request for Information from Law Enforcement Agencies'); *NPC Advisory Opinion No 2017-054*, 11 September 2017; *NPC Advisory Opinion No 2017-038*, 14 August; *NPC Advisory Opinion No 2017-028*, 23 June 2017.

[83] Security of Personal Data in Government Agencies (n 72), s 24.

[84] ibid s 23; DPA IRR. s 20; National Privacy Commission, *NPC Advisory Opinion No 2017-054*, 11 September 2017; *NPC Advisory Opinion No 2017-038*, 14 August 2017; *NPC Advisory Opinion No 2017-028*, 23 June 2017.

[85] National Privacy Commission, *NPC Advisory Opinion No 2017-028*, 23 June 2017.

[86] Security of Personal Data in Government Agencies (n 72) s 10.

enforcement agencies including the Philippine National Police and the Philippine Army, in the performance of their public functions, request personal information, the same is subject to the test of legitimate purpose and proportionality. Hence, the 'request for and release of "pertinent information/data on the 28,000 Chinese National Retirees" as requested by the Army may be overly broad'.[87]

b. Finance

Special data privacy rules apply to the financial sector. Notably, the DPA excludes personal information needed by the Philippines' central monetary authority and chief financial regulator, the Bangko Sentral ng Pilipinas (BSP) and the other agencies regulating the financial sector,[88] as well as those needed for complying with the anti-money laundering laws.[89] On the other hand, the DPA applies to any other personal information other than those excluded under section 4(c) of the DPA.

The exclusion of certain financial-sector data is also because a number of laws already regulate the processing of personal information, along with other banking and finance-related data. The Bank Secrecy Law, for example, emphasises the absolute confidentiality of all bank deposits regardless of its nature and may not be examined, inquired, or looked into by any person or by the Government, except with the consent of the depositor, or in impeachment proceedings, or by court order.[90] Personal information related to these deposits are necessarily confidential. A similar provision also applies to foreign currency deposits.[91] Moreover, the AMLA allows the Anti-Money Laundering Council (AMLC) to examine bank deposits, which would necessarily include personal information of the depositor, when there is probable cause that such account has been involved in a money laundering offence.[92] Nonetheless, when reporting covered or suspicious transactions to the AMLC, covered institutions and their officers are prohibited from disclosing the fact that a covered or suspicious transaction report was made, the contents thereof, or any other information in relation thereto.[93]

Nonetheless, the NPC has issued a number of circulars that are particularly relevant to the financial sector.[94] These cover those types of financial sector data which are not excluded from the scope of the DPA.

[87] National Privacy Commission, *NPC Advisory Opinion No 2020-051*, 26 November 2020.
[88] DPA, ch 1, s 3(e).
[89] ibid, ch 1, s 3(f).
[90] Bank Secrecy Law 1955, s 2.
[91] Foreign Currency Deposit Act 1974, s 8.
[92] Anti-Money Laundering Act 2001 (AMLA), s 11.
[93] Implementing Rules and Regulations of Republic Act No 9160 2003 (AMLA IRR), rule 9.3.d.
[94] National Privacy Commission, *NPC Circular No 2020-01*, 14 September 2020 ('Guidelines on the Processing of Personal Data for Loan-Related Transactions'); *NPC Circular No 2022-02*, 1 December 2022 ('Amending Certain Provisions of NPC Circular No 20-01 on the Guidelines on the Processing of Personal Data for Loan-Related Transactions'); *NPC Advisory Opinion No 2021-026*, 12 July 2021 ('Re: Data Privacy Implications for Financial Services Industry Initiatives on Data Sharing'); *NPC Advisory Opinion No 2022-013* ('Re: Online Lending Mobile Application Permissions'); *NPC Advisory Opinion No 2021-036*, 23 September 2021('Re: Disclosure of Loan Documents Pursuant to a Legal Claim'); *NPC Advisory Opinion No 2021-033*, 13 August 2921 ('Re: Internal Dissemination of Information Regarding Bank-related Crimes'); *NPC Advisory Opinion No. 2021-012*, 16 April 2021('Re: Documentary Requirements for Accreditation as Financial Institution'); *NPC Advisory Opinion No 2020-050*, 26 November 2020 ('Re: Disclosure by Fintech, Digital Payment Platforms, and Telecommunications Entities of

Furthermore, the BSP has also issued regulations dealing with privacy and data protection. These regulations apply to banks and other financial institutions, such as payment service providers and microfinance and small to medium-sized enterprise lending institutions. Under BSP Circular No 707 (Loans and Credit Accommodations) 2010 and Circular No 754 (Credit Card Operations) 2012, the personal data of the borrower, cardholder or consumer shall be kept strictly confidential by banks, except when consent to disclose is given, when disclosure is ordered by a competent court, or when disclosed to counsels. However, when the DPA was passed, the BSP reinforced the DPA's application by qualifying the exceptions usually given to financial institutions. For example, BSP Circular No 1048 now requires banks to inform their consumers about how personal data will be used. Banks are also required to get the consent of their consumer before sharing information to third parties, unless expressly exempted by law or another BSP regulation. Notably, when the Financial Products and Services Consumer Protection Act (FPSCP) 2022 was passed, the right of financial consumers to data protection was statutorily recognised.

c. Journalism, Arts, Literature and Research

Personal data used by journalists and those used for artistic, literary and research purposes are also excluded from the DPA's application.[95] Notably, the DPA expressly states that the protection given to journalistic sources is not diminished in any way.[96] The NPC has issued several advisory opinions dealing with this exception.[97]

iii. Distinction and Interface between Data Protection and Privacy

In the Philippines, the right to privacy is understood to be the broader right, under which data protection is located. The Supreme Court has articulated this, as discussed earlier, in *Disini v Secretary of Justice*, which confirmed that data protection is an aspect of the right to informational privacy, which is, in turn, one of the two broad classifications of the right to privacy.[98]

Personal Data for Fraud Investigation'); *NPC Advisory Opinion No 2020-039*, 30 October 2020 ('Re: Disclosure or Sharing of Bank Transaction Information for Fraud Investigations'); *NPC Advisory Opinion No 2020-021*, 29 May 2020 ('Re: Automated Retrieval of Bank Transaction History'); *NPC Advisory Opinion No 2019-041*, 23 October 2019 ('Credit Card Fraud Investigation'); *NPC Advisory Opinion No 2019-040*, 17 October 2019 ('Anti-Money Laundering Council Request'); *NPC Advisory Opinion No 2019-014*, 5 March 2019 ('Proposed Bangko Sentral ng Pilipinas and Department of Interior and Local Government Join Memorandum Circular'); *NPC Advisory Opinion No 2018-060*, 30 August 2018 ('Disclosure of Personal Information to the Bangko Sentral ng Pilipinas'); *NPC Advisory Opinion No 2017-031*, 28 June 2017 ('Consent on the Sharing of Mobile Number of Bank Clients for Credit Scoring').

[95] DPA, ch 1, s 4(e).

[96] ibid, ch 1, s 5.

[97] National Privacy Commission, *NPC Advisory Opinion No 2021-023*, 5 July 2021 ('Re: Processing of Personal Data for Research Without Ethics Clearance'); *NPC Advisory Opinion No 2019-017*, 5 March 2019 ('Research and the Data Privacy Act of 2012'); *NPC Advisory Opinion No 2019-006*, 4 January 2019 ('Use of Clinical Data in Research').

[98] *Disini* (n 16).

iv. Distinction between 'Data Users', 'Data Subjects', 'Data Processors', and 'Data Sub-Contractors'

A 'data subject' is an individual whose personal information is processed.[99] On the other hand, 'data users' are known under the DPA as 'personal information controllers' (PIC). They refer to a person or organisation who controls the collection, holding, processing or use of personal information, including a person or organisation who instructs another person or organisation to collect, hold, process, use, transfer or disclose personal information on his or her behalf.[100] The term excludes: (1) a person who performs such functions as instructed by another person or organisation; and (2) an individual who collects, holds, processes or uses personal information in connection with the individual's personal, family or household affairs.[101] Furthermore, 'data processors,' known as 'personal information processors' (PIP) under the DPA, refer to any natural or juridical person to whom the PIC may outsource the processing of personal data pertaining to a data subject.[102]

A 'data sub-contractor' is not expressly mentioned in the DPA, although the statute expressly allows a PIC to sub-contract the processing of personal information.[103] Presumably, the party to whom the PIC sub-contracts the processing is the 'data sub-contractor,' who in effect, could be the PIP. Likewise, the Implementing Rules and Regulations of the DPA (DPA IRR) recognises 'data sub-contractors' under the concept of 'data sharing' or the sharing, disclosure or transfer to a third party of personal data under the custody of a PIC to one or more other PIC(s).[104] Under the DPA IRR, a PIC may sub-contract or outsource the processing of personal data provided proper safeguards, which may be contractual or otherwise, are put in place to ensure confidentiality, integrity and availability of personal data processes.[105] The DPA IRR also considers the situation where it is the PIP who has sub-contracted the processing of personal information. In such situations, data sharing is only allowed if the processing is carried out on behalf of the PIC and in accordance with his instructions as contained in the sub-contracting agreement.[106]

v. Distinction between Personal and Non-Personal Data

Under the DPA IRR, personal data refers to all types of personal information and sensitive personal information.[107] 'Personal information' is any information whether recorded in a material form or not, from which the identity of an individual is apparent or can be reasonably and directly ascertained by the entity holding the information, or when put together with other information would directly and certainly identify an individual.[108] Sensitive personal information, on the other hand, is a type of personal information: (1) about an

[99] DPA, ch 1, s 3(c).
[100] ibid, ch 1, s 3(h).
[101] ibid.
[102] ibid, ch 1, s 3(i).
[103] ibid, ch 3, s 14.
[104] DPA IRR, rule I, s 3(f).
[105] ibid, rule X, s 43.
[106] ibid, rule I, s 3(f).
[107] ibid, rule I, s 3(j).
[108] DPA, ch 1, s 3(g); DPA IRR, rule I, s 3(l).

individual's race, ethnic origin, marital status, age, colour, and religious, philosophical or political affiliations; (2) about an individual's health, education, genetic or sexual life of a person, or to any proceeding for any offence committed or alleged to have been committed by such individual, the disposal of such proceedings, or the sentence of any court in such proceedings; (3) issued by government agencies peculiar to an individual which includes, but is not limited to social, social security numbers, previous or current health records, licences or its denials, suspension or revocation, and tax records; and (4) specifically established by an executive order or an act of Congress to be kept classified.[109]

An advisory opinion has clarified that only natural persons can become a data subject.[110] Hence, the DPA only applies to data which falls within the definition of personal information[111] or personal data as defined under the DPA IRR. Nonetheless, such non-personal data (eg, data relating to corporations) may still be protected under another statute, administrative rule, or by the rules of procedure.

vi. Distinction between Anonymised, Pseudonymised, or Encrypted Data

Information is anonymous when it 'does not relate to an identified or identifiable natural person or to personal data rendered anonymous in such a manner that the data subject is not or no longer identifiable'.[112] In Advisory Opinion No 2017-27, the NPC clarified that 'anonymized data, in its truest sense, is not considered as personal information and thus, falls outside of the ambit of the DPA'.[113] However, when only some identifiers are removed (eg, patient and physician names, contact information, and location), this is not sufficient to anonymise the data.[114] 'Anonymization may necessitate additional measures to guarantee that the anonymity of the information is irreversible.'[115]

Pseudonymisation has been defined as

> the processing of personal data in a manner that the personal data can no longer be attributed to a specific data subject without the use of additional information, provided that such additional information is kept separately and is subject to technical and organizational measures to ensure that the personal data are not attributed to an identified or identifiable natural person.[116]

In Advisory Opinion No 2018-29, the NPC clarified that 'pseudonymization of personal data does not change the nature of the data – it remains to be personal data'; thus, would still fall within the DPA's scope.[117]

[109] DPA IRR, rule I, s 3(t).

[110] See National Privacy Commission, *NPC Advisory Opinion No 2017-06*, 5 January 2016.

[111] DPA, s 4; DPA IRR, rule I, s 4.

[112] *NPC Advisory Opinion No 2017-27* (n 8) citing Regulation 2016/679 of the European Parliament and of the Council of 27 April 2016 on the protection of natural persons with regard to the processing of personal data and on the free movement of such data, and repealing Directive 95/46/EC (General Data Protection Regulation) [2016] OJ L119/1, recital 26.

[113] *NPC Advisory Opinion No 2017-27* (n 8).

[114] National Privacy Commission, *NPC Advisory Opinion No 2018-68*, 20 November 2018.

[115] ibid.

[116] National Privacy Commission, *NPC Advisory Opinion No 2018-029*, 6 June 2018 citing Regulation 2016/679 2016, Art 4(5).

[117] ibid.

Encryption protects data by encoding the information in such a way that it is only accessible to authorised parties or individuals.[118] The encryption of personal data does not change the nature of data. It remains as personal data, and thus, still protected under the NPA. In fact, the NPC recommends in NPC Circular No 2016-01 (Security of Personal Data in Government Agencies), that 'all personal data that are digitally processed must be encrypted, whether at rest or in transit'.[119]

vii. Distinction between Domestic and Cross-Border/International Transfers

Processing of personal information within the Philippines, including data transfers, are understood as domestic transfers, and the DPA applies to them as a general rule. Hence, as long as the processing of personal information happens within the Philippines, the DPA applies regardless of the citizenship or residency of the person or entity processing the information. However, the DPA does not apply to personal information being processed in the Philippines but were originally collected from residents of foreign jurisdiction in accordance with the laws of those foreign jurisdictions.[120]

Furthermore, although the DPA distinguishes between domestic and cross-border or international transfers, it provides for no restrictions on cross-border data transfers from a PIC to a PIP located overseas, 'so long as … proper safeguards are in place to ensure the confidentiality, integrity and availability of the personal data processed, and prevent its use for unauthorized purposes'.[121] Moreover, the DPA applies to cross-border or international transfers where the personal information being processed belongs to a Philippine citizen or resident,[122] regardless of where they are located. Hence, entities located offshore may still be subject to the DPA. Nonetheless, cross-border arrangements and cooperation may qualify the PIC's responsibility for personal information.[123]

viii. National Privacy Commission

The NPC was established to administer and implement the DPA,[124] and primarily, to ensure compliance of the PIC.[125] Notably, it can receive complaints, institute investigations, facilitate settlement of complaints through the use of alternative dispute resolution (ADR) processes, adjudicate, award indemnity on matters affecting any personal information.[126] It can issue cease-and-desist orders, and impose a temporary or permanent ban on the processing of personal information upon finding that the processing will be detrimental to national security and public interest.[127] It can even compel any entity, including government

[118] See DPA, s 23(3); DPA IRR, s 31(b)(2)(c); National Privacy Commission, 'Data Security', available at www.privacy.gov.ph/implementing-privacy-and-data-protection-measures/data-security/#7.
[119] Security of Personal Data in Government Agencies (n 72) rule II, s 8.
[120] DPA, ch 1, s 4(g).
[121] National Privacy Commission, *NPC Advisory Opinion No 2018-057*, 20 September 2018.
[122] DPA, ch 1, s 6.
[123] ibid, ch 6, s 21.
[124] ibid, ch 2, s 7.
[125] ibid, ch 2, s 7(a).
[126] ibid, ch 2, s 7(b).
[127] ibid, ch 2, s 7(c).

agencies and instrumentalities to abide by its orders or take action on a matter affecting data privacy.[128] Likewise, it can recommend the prosecution and imposition of penalties in relation to the criminal offences contained in the DPA.[129]

III. Legal Bases, Mechanisms and Exceptions for Cross-Border Data Transfers and Data Protection under Philippine Law

A. International Data Transfers

i. Adequacy Findings or Whitelists and Blacklists

The DPA does not recognise or consider the data protection regulations in the country of destination. Hence, the DPA does not adopt a system which recognises adequacy findings, whitelists or blacklists.

Instead, the DPA adopts the principle that the PIC is accountable for personal data that have been outsourced or transferred for personal processing to third parties and PIP.[130] Particularly, the PIC is tasked to comply with the DPA, by entering into contractual or other reasonable means, to ensure a comparable level of protection while the information is processed by a third party.[131] Notably, the PIC is accountable even when he or the PIP is located outside the Philippines.

ii. Consent of Data Subjects as Exception to Existence of Privacy Safeguards Overseas

Personal information can be processed lawfully if the data subject has given his consent.[132] This consent has to be: (1) freely given; (2) specific; (3) informed; (4) an indication of will; and (5) evidenced by written, electronic or recorded means.[133] Moreover, consent remains valid 'as long as the purpose, scope, method and extent of the processing remain to be the same as that disclosed to the date subject when consent was given'.[134] Hence, when the processing of personal information involves transferring or sharing of the data subject's personal information to another party located overseas, as long as the consent meets the standards set by the DPA and the purpose, scope, method and extent of such processing were disclosed and remains the same, the data subject's consent shall remain valid regardless of whether another set of data privacy safeguards apply overseas. Nonetheless, the PIC shall always be accountable for complying with the DPA requirements and is required to use contractual and other reasonable means to ensure a comparable level of protection while the information is being processed overseas by the other party.[135]

[128] ibid, ch 2, s 7(d).
[129] ibid, ch 2, s 7(i).
[130] ibid, ch 6, s 21.
[131] ibid, ch 6, s 21(a).
[132] ibid, ch 3, s 12.
[133] ibid, ch 3, s 3(b).
[134] National Privacy Commission, *Advisory Opinion No 2018-58*, 26 October 2018.
[135] DPA, ch 6, s 21(a).

iii. Contracts

Fulfilling a legal obligation, including those arising from contracts, is another ground or basis to process personal information,[136] including those involved in international data transfers. Lawful processing on the basis of a legal obligation, however, is contingent on the law from which the legal obligation is derived.[137] Hence, since the law which is applicable to the contract determines the contractual rights and obligations, the same law also determines whether the PIC is allowed to lawfully process personal information, whether the processing that the PIC performs is necessary to comply with the legal obligation, and whether all the conditions imposed by the legal obligation for the processing of the personal information have been complied with.[138] However, the processing of personal information pursuant to a contract is circumscribed by the same limitation which applies to any contract (ie, they should not be contrary to 'law, morals, good customs, public order, or public policy'[139]). In that sense, mandatory requirements under the DPA should not be undermined by the foreign applicable law.

In 2021, the NPC issued an advisory on the use of ASEAN MCCs as part of the ASEAN Framework on Digital Data Governance.[140] The ASEAN MCCs provide standards for the transfer of personal data from one ASEAN member state to another. The use of ASEAN MCCs is voluntary and does not create any additional legal rights and obligations, which are determined by the law applicable to the contract.[141] Nonetheless, the NPC encourages ASEAN-based businesses to adopt the ASEAN MCCs as baseline standards in their data-related business operations.[142]

iv. APEC CBPR System

In 2020, the Philippines joined the APEC CBPR system, thus allowing Philippines-based entities to freely transfer personal data to all CBPR member states. The CBPR requires member states to establish third-party accountability agents whose main task is to certify that the data privacy policies and practices of participating businesses are compliant with the APEC Privacy Framework. Being CBPR-certified means that the data privacy policies and practices of the participating business comply with the APEC Privacy Framework. The NPC notes that '[t]he CBPR builds trust among customers by demonstrating an organizational commitment to privacy. Having a CBPR certification is an indication that appropriate technical and organizational measures to safeguard personal data are well in place'.[143] Furthermore, the NPC also notes that '[t]he CBPR System provides for baseline privacy and data protection standards and facilitates the cooperation of privacy enforcement authorities through the Cross-border Privacy Enforcement Arrangement (CPEA)'.[144]

[136] ibid, ch 6, s 12(c).
[137] *RLA v PLDT Enterprise* [2021], NPC Case No 18-010, 24.
[138] ibid.
[139] Civil Code, Art 1306.
[140] National Privacy Commission, *NPC Advisory No 2021-02*, 28 June 2021 ('Guidance for the Use of the ASEAN Model Contract Clauses and ASEAN Data Management Framework').
[141] ibid, s 5(A)(1).
[142] ibid.
[143] National Privacy Commission, 'The APEC CBPR System: An Overview', available at privacy.gov.ph/the-apec-cbpr-system-an-overview/.
[144] ibid.

v. International Privacy Certification Schemes, Trustmarks or Privacy Seals

In 2021, the NPC launched the Philippine Privacy Trust Mark (PPTM), 'which aims to increase trust and confidence in businesses and public offices as the mark offers the highest level of assurance on data privacy compliance and secure cross-border data transfers'.[145] The certification process involves evaluating an organisation's operational compliance with the DPA through risk management and assess an organisation's demonstration of having the proper organisational, physical, and technical security measures to ensure data protection.[146] In October 2023, the NPC released NPC Circular No 2023-05 which lists the requirements in getting the PPTM. Under the Circular, a PIC or PIP must be certified under the ISO/IEC 27001 (information security management system or ISMS) and ISO/IEC 27701(privacy information management system or PIMS) before applying for PPTM certification.[147] The circular also allows third-party certification bodies which, aside from getting certified under the same standards as the PIC or PIP, must also be certified under the ISO/ IEC 17021-1.[148]

B. International Data Transfer and Liability

i. Requirements and Policies for Cross-Border Data Processing and Retention

The DPA allows international data transfers through data sharing, sub-contracting, or outsourcing arrangements. Data sharing is defined as the disclosure or transfer to a third party of personal data under the PIC's control or custody.[149] It can happen as part of a data sharing agreement between two or more PICs with different processing objectives.[150] In all instances, data sharing must comply with the conditions under section 20 of the DPA IRR, which requires adequate safeguards for data privacy and security, and adherence to the principles of transparency, legitimate purpose, and proportionality.[151] Furthermore, when data sharing happens in the private sector, the data subject's consent is required.[152] Likewise, the PIC should inform the data subject about the following: identities of the relevant PICs/PIPs, purpose of data sharing, categories of personal data, intended recipients, rights of data subjects, information on the nature and extent of data sharing and manner of processing.[153]

Notably, government agencies can also transfer personal data across borders. Section 10 of NPC Circular No 2006-02 allows this as long as these transfers are covered by a data

[145] National Privacy Commission, 'NPC Launches Ph Privacy Trust Mark to Add Value to Business, Boost Trust in Cross-Border Data Transfers' (11 November 2021), available at privacy.gov.ph/npc-launches-ph-privacy-trust-mark-to-add-value-to-business-boost-trust-in-cross-border-data-transfers/.

[146] ibid.

[147] National Privacy Commission, *NPC Circular 2023-05*, 25 October 2023, s 4.

[148] ibid, s 5.

[149] National Privacy Commission, *NPC Circular 2016-02*, 10 October 2016, s 3(D); *NPC Circular 2020-03*, 23 December 2020, s 2(F).

[150] National Privacy Commission, *NPC Circular 2016-02*, 10 October 2016, s 3(D); *NPC Circular 2020-03*, 23 December 2020, s 2(G).

[151] DPA IRR, rule IV, s 20(a)(b).

[152] ibid, rule IV, s 20(b)(1).

[153] ibid, rule IV, s 20(b)(3).

sharing agreement.[154] Furthermore, like in the private sector, unless exempted by law, the PIC should obtain the data subject's consent,[155] and provide him with the same information required under section 20(b)(3) of the DPA IRR. Moreover, the data sharing agreement must state the purpose(s), type of personal data that will be shared, types of processing that is allowed to be performed, remedies available to the data subject, details of the data protection officer or compliance officer, duration of the agreement (no longer than five years[156]), general description of the security measures, and method and timeline for the secure return, destruction or disposal of the shared data.[157]

A sub-contracting or outsourcing agreement may also facilitate international data transfers. Here, the PIC discloses or transfers personal data to a PIP in order for the latter to perform certain outsourced activities.[158] The outsourcing agreement should explicitly indicate the terms and conditions of the processing to be performed by the PIP.[159] In this arrangement, the PIP does not have its own purpose for processing, but merely carries out the instructions given by the PIC.[160] Notably, the PIC is required to use contractual or other reasonable means to ensure that proper safeguards are in place, to ensure the confidentiality, integrity and availability of the personal data processed, and to prevent its use for unauthorised purposes, and generally, to comply with the DPA and related issuances.[161]

Because the DPA and DPA IRR do not prohibit the transmission of personal data outside the Philippines, personal data may still cross borders even though processing remains within the same entity. In such instances, no data sharing or outsourcing agreement is necessary. This may happen, for instance, when data processing involves using cloud infrastructures or M2M applications.[162] Nonetheless, the PIC and/or PIP concerned must still comply with the provisions of the DPA, DPA IRR, and NPC issuances.[163]

In all instances of international data transfers, the PIC is responsible for the personal information under its control or custody, including information that have been transferred to a third party for processing. Nonetheless, cross-border arrangements and cooperation may modify the extent of this responsibility.[164]

One must note that the DPA does not cover personal information originally collected from residents of foreign jurisdictions in accordance with relevant foreign laws, even though they are being processed within the Philippines.[165] Hence, if the international data transfers involve personal information about foreign residents collected under the relevant foreign law, the DPA will not apply.

[154] ibid, rule IV, s 20(d).
[155] National Privacy Commission, *NPC Circular 2016-02*, 10 October 2016, s 4.
[156] ibid, s 6(c).
[157] ibid, s 6.
[158] National Privacy Commission, *NPC Advisory Opinion No 2017-57*, 3 October 2017.
[159] ibid.
[160] ibid.
[161] DPA IRR, rule X, ss43 and 44(b).
[162] National Privacy Commission, *NPC Advisory Opinion No 2017-012*, 6 February 2017.
[163] ibid.
[164] DPA, ch 6, s 21; DPA IRR, rule XII, s 50.
[165] DPA, ch 1, s 4(g).

ii. The Rights of Data Subjects

Because the right to privacy is described as fundamental,[166] and data protection is considered an aspect of one's right to privacy,[167] data subjects need not establish data ownership to invoke data protection and privacy rights. Moreover, data subjects have the right to be informed, right to access, right to object, right to erasure and blocking, right to rectify, right to file a complaint, right to damages and right to data portability.[168] In certain instances like incapacity, these rights can be exercised by the data subject's lawful heirs and assignees.[169] Similarly, the data subject may authorise another person to exercise his rights, provided the authorisation must be specific and supported by appropriate documents.[170]

The DPA contains a number of anti-doxxing provisions, particularly sections 32 and 33, to penalise malicious and unauthorised disclosure of personal information.[171] Similarly, the various crimes under the CPA like illegal access, computer-related identity theft or cyber libel may also be used.[172] Similarly, Article 364 of the Revised Penal Code may be invoked if the disclosure was with the intent of blemishing the honour or reputation of a person. If the acts involving the non-consensual disclosure occurred with direct hostility and in the context of a grade school or secondary school, the Anti-Bullying Act of 2013 applies. In addition, Article 2176 of the Civil Code may be invoked in instances where the non-consensual disclosure happened because of fault or negligence.

iii. DPA's Extraterritorial Effect

The DPA has extraterritorial application if:

(a) The act, practice or processing relates to personal information about a Philippine citizen or a resident;
(b) The entity has a link with the Philippines, and the entity is processing personal information in the Philippines or even if the processing is outside the Philippines as long as it is about Philippine citizens or residents such as, but not limited to, the following:
  (1) A contract is entered in the Philippines;
  (2) A juridical entity unincorporated in the Philippines but has central management and control in the country; and
  (3) An entity that has a branch, agency, office or subsidiary in the Philippines and the parent or affiliate of the Philippine entity has access to personal information; and
(c) The entity has other links in the Philippines such as, but not limited to:
  (1) The entity carries on business in the Philippines; and
  (2) The personal information was collected or held by an entity in the Philippines.[173]

[166] *Morfe* (n 1) 444–45.
[167] *Disini* (n 16).
[168] DPA, ch 4, ss 16 and 18.
[169] ibid, ch 4, s 17.
[170] National Privacy Commission, *NPC Advisory No 2021-01*, 29 January 2021, s 3.
[171] DPA, ch VIII, ss 32 and 33.
[172] CPA, s 4.
[173] DPA, ch 1, s 6.

iv. Data Breach Notification

Personal data breach is 'a breach of security leading to the accidental or unlawful destruction, loss, alteration, unauthorized disclosure of, or access to, personal data transmitted, stored, or otherwise processed'.[174] The PIC shall promptly notify the NPC and affected data subjects when an unauthorised person acquires sensitive personal information or other information that may be used to enable identity fraud 'and the [PIC] or the [NPC] believes that such unauthorized acquisition is likely to give rise to a real risk of serious harm to any affected data subject'.[175] The notification must describe the: (1) nature of the breach; (2) sensitive personal information possibly involved; and (3) measures taken to address the breach.[176] Notably, notification may be delayed only when necessary to determine the scope of the breach, to prevent further disclosures, or to restore reasonable integrity to the information and communications system.[177]

NPC Circular No 2016-03 further explains that notice is required when: (1) the personal data involves sensitive personal information or any other information that may be used to enable identity fraud; (2) there is reason to believe that the information may have been acquired by an unauthorised person; and (3) the PIC or NPC believes that the unauthorised acquisition is likely to give rise to a real risk of serious harm to any affected data subject.[178] When the PIC is uncertain whether notice is required, he shall first consider the likelihood of harm or negative consequences on the affected data subjects and how notification could reduce the risks arising from the personal data breach.[179] In addition, he should also consider whether the: (1) information would likely affect national security, public safety, public order, or public health; (2) whether the breach involved at least 100 individuals; (3) whether particular laws require confidentiality; and (4) whether the breach involved personal data of vulnerable groups.[180] Furthermore, notice should be given within 72 hours upon knowledge of or reasonable belief that data breach has occurred.[181] Nonetheless, the NPC may not require notification after considering the: (1) security measures preventing use of personal data by any unauthorised person; (2) subsequent measures preventing the risk of harm or negative consequence from materialising; and (3) based on age or legal capacity of the affected data subjects.[182]

C. Data Security and Data Localisation

i. Data Security or Localisation Requirements

Under section 20 of the DPA, the PIC has to undertake organisational, physical and technical measures 'intended for the protection of personal information against any

[174] DPA IRR, rule 1, s 3(k).
[175] DPA, ch 5, s 20(f).
[176] DPA IRR, rule IX, s 39.
[177] ibid, s 40.
[178] National Privacy Commission, *NPC Circular No 2016-03*, 15 December 2016, s 11.
[179] ibid, s 13.
[180] ibid.
[181] ibid, ss 17 and 18.
[182] ibid, s 19.

accidental or unlawful destruction or processing',[183] including those against natural dangers.[184] The specific measures should consider the nature of the personal data, size of the organisation, complexity of operations, current privacy best practices and cost of security implementation.[185] In all instances, the implemented security measures should include: (1) safeguards to protect its computer network against accidental, unlawful or unauthorised usage or interference; (2) a security policy for the processing of personal information; (3) a process for identifying and accessing vulnerabilities in its computer networks, and for taking preventive, corrective and mitigating action against possible security breach; and (4) regular monitoring for security breaches and a process for taking preventive, corrective and mitigating action against possible security breach.[186]

Under the DPA IRR, the PIP is similarly imposed with an obligation to implement reasonable and appropriate security measures.[187] Hence, organisational, physical, and technical security measures should include having compliance officers, data protection policies, maintaining records of processing activities and review systems;[188] having office spaces which provides privacy to anyone processing personal data, measures preventing mechanical destruction of files and equipment;[189] and having a security policy and safeguards protecting the computer network against accidental, unlawful or unauthorised use, measures upholding the confidentiality, integrity, availability and resilience of processing systems, and regularly monitoring security breaches.[190]

As regards localisation requirements, the DPA does not have specific rules mandating data to be stored exclusively within the country. The DPA even contemplates that data may be stored elsewhere even when the PIC may be based in the Philippines.[191] Sector-specific rules found in other laws and administrative issuances may, however, have certain localisation requirements as discussed below.

ii. Government Sector

Under Executive Order No 2016-02, each government office is required to protect personal information under its custody or control by providing reasonable security arrangements against leaks or premature disclosure of personal information.[192] NPC Circular No 2016-07 echoes this by requiring all personal data being processed by a government agency to be stored in a data centre.[193] Access to all data centres owned and controlled by a government agency shall be restricted to agency personnel with the appropriate security clearance.[194] Encryption is legally required for government agencies, regardless of whether personal data is at rest or in transit.[195]

[183] DPA, ch 5, s 20(a).
[184] ibid, ch 5, s 20(b).
[185] ibid, ch 5, s 20(c).
[186] ibid.
[187] DPA IRR, rule VI, s 25.
[188] ibid, rule VI, s 26.
[189] ibid, rule VI, s 27.
[190] ibid, rule VI, s 28.
[191] National Privacy Commission, *NPC Advisory Opinion No 2017-012*, 6 February 2017.
[192] *Executive Order No 2016-02* s 7(b).
[193] Security of Personal Data in Government Agencies (n 72) s 7.
[194] ibid, s 9.
[195] ibid, s 8.

Furthermore, when sensitive personal information is involved, the government office has to provide additional security measures. Particularly, all sensitive personal information maintained by the government office shall be secured using the most appropriate standard recognised by the ICT industry and NPC.[196] Furthermore, only those government employees with security clearance from the head of the government agency shall have access to sensitive personal information.[197] Moreover, such sensitive personal information may not be transported to an off-site location unless with the agency head's approval and in accordance with the DPA (for example, only a maximum of 1,000 records at a time may be transferred).[198] Furthermore, government offices should require the NPC registration of their contractors' personal information processing system.[199]

iii. Banking and Finance

The FPSCP Act requires financial services providers to adopt and implement information security standards.[200] Furthermore, BSP Circular No 982 provides that financial institutions should put in place a robust, resilient, and enterprise-wide framework for their Information Security Risk Management supported by effective information security governance and oversight mechanism.[201] As such, financial institutions should maintain a comprehensive, well-designed and effective information security programme that is commensurate with its operational and IT profile complexity.[202]

iv. Health Sector

Compliance with the data security measures set under the DPA is usually required when dealing with health-related data. Hence, national cancer registries and monitoring systems and hospital-based cancer registries,[203] health information systems maintained by health service providers,[204] and COVID-19 pandemic contact tracing and information sharing arrangements of local government units should all comply with the standards under the DPA.[205]

Nonetheless, stricter standards may be enforced by legislation. This approach ensures a higher level of protection especially when the health sector-related data involves sensitive personal information. For example, the Mandatory Reporting of Notifiable Diseases and Health Events of Public Health Concern Act states that only authorised Department of Health (DOH) personnel can perform data collection, analysis, and dissemination of information from official disease surveillance and response systems.[206] The data collected may only be used for public health concern purposes and are exempted from the provision

[196] DPA, s 22.
[197] ibid, s 23(a).
[198] ibid, s 23(b).
[199] ibid, s 24.
[200] FPSCPA, s 8(g).
[201] Bangko Sentral ng Pilipinas, *BSP Circular No 982*, 2 November 2017, s 4.
[202] ibid, s 4.
[203] National Integrated Cancer Control Act 2018, s 28.
[204] Universal Health Care Act 2018, s 36.
[205] Bayanihan to Recover as One Act 2020, s 4(rrr).
[206] Mandatory Reporting of Notifiable Diseases and Health Events of Public Concern Act 2018, s 6(d).

of DPA on accessibility of data.[207] Similarly, any HIV-related information is classified as confidential which is protected by the owner's right to privacy, and any disclosure without the consent of the owner's consent is unlawful.[208]

Notably, several NPC issuances also deal with the required security measures for data gathered by private establishments while monitoring the COVID-19 pandemic. For example, physical health declaration and contact tracing forms, COVID testing registration forms, quarantine reports and other pertinent documents and information should be kept in a secure place at the end of business hours.[209] Establishments should also implement an access control policy which shall identify and limit the personnel with access to the personal data collected for the COVID-19 response.[210] Appropriate policies protecting computer networks or physical records against accidental, unlawful or unauthorised use or access are also required.[211] A monitoring system for security breach should also be available.[212]

Moreover, the NPC and DOH have issued joint guidelines requiring certain security measures for COVID-19-related data gathered by public and private healthcare providers.[213] For example, only authorised healthcare personnel and DOH officers can access records of COVID-19 patients.[214] Furthermore, only aggregate health information, or pseudonymised or anonymised detailed health information may be disclosed for public communication.[215] Health practitioners engaged in telemedicine should implement minimum organisational, physical and technical security standards and measures as set by the NPC and the Department of Information and Communications Technology.[216]

D. Data Security and Localisation Requirements for Particular Types of Data

As provided in Executive Order No 2016-02, public access to information possessed by the Government is regulated and subject to numerous exemptions.[217] Particularly, since state secrets are classified as among the exceptions,[218] there may be special security and localisation requirements applicable to them. Notably, the President has a right to withhold documents that might reveal military or state secrets, identity of government informers in some circumstances, information related to pending investigations, and those involving foreign relations.[219] As such, state secrets may involve personal data about government

[207] ibid.
[208] Philippine HIV and AIDS Policy Act 2018, s 44(a)(b).
[209] National Privacy Commission, *NPC Advisory No 2020-03*, 30 October 2020, s 5(D).
[210] ibid.
[211] ibid.
[212] ibid.
[213] National Privacy Commission and Department of Health, *Joint Memorandum Circular No 2020-0002*, 24 April 2020.
[214] ibid, VI (C)(1).
[215] ibid, VI (D)(3).
[216] ibid, V(5).
[217] Executive Order No 2016-02, s 4.
[218] Executive Secretary, *Memorandum from the Executive Secretary*, 24 November 2016, attachment.
[219] *Neri v Senate Committee on Accountability of Public Officers and Investigations* (2008) 549 SCRA 77, 120.

officials and private individuals. Accessing these pieces of information may require getting relevant security clearances.[220] However, state secrets bearing on military, diplomatic and similar matters may not even be available for disclosure.[221]

As discussed earlier, sensitive personal information under government custody is subject to special security measures.[222] In contrast, the DPA does not explicitly provide for special data security or localisation requirements for sensitive information which are in the possession of private entities and individuals, except those that may be implemented pursuant to section 29. Significantly, section 29 mandates that the nature of the personal data that requires protection and the risks posed by the processing should be considered in determining the appropriate level of security. Hence, given the nature of sensitive personal information and the higher risks involved when such information is unlawfully accessed or disclosed, higher level of security measures can be reasonably expected when private entities process sensitive personal information. Notably, this much higher degree of security measure is also reflected in section 20(f) of the DPA which requires the PIC to promptly notify the NPC when the breach involves sensitive personal information.

E. Issues in Private International Law

i. Categories of Litigation

The DPA does not contain rules specific to cross-border breaches of data protection and privacy rules. Instead, the DPA adopts the approach of making the PIC responsible for personal information under its control or custody, including those that have been transferred to a third party for processing, whether domestically or internationally.[223] Hence, should the PIC or third parties breach their obligations under the DPA, the PIC is necessarily accountable, and therefore, is usually a party to litigation. Furthermore, the individual(s) accountable for the organisation's compliance with the DPA and/or the third parties may also be included as parties. Of course, in instances where the breach involves a third party who is unauthorised to process the personal information, such third party may be included as defendant.[224]

The plaintiff can be the data subject, whose privacy rights may have been violated.[225] Furthermore, the NPC may also become a complainant in a criminal complaint before the DOJ. However, should the DOJ decide that a criminal case be filed before the court against the individual(s) recommended by the NPC for criminal prosecution, the DOJ prosecutors shall prosecute the criminal case on behalf of the 'People of the Philippines'.

The DPA provides for civil, criminal, and administrative liability for breaches of the DPA's provisions, including those involving cross-border data transfers and other violations of data privacy. Notably, remedies may be availed of before the NPC or the courts

[220] See, eg, *Almonte v Vasquez* (1995) 244 SCRA 286, 295; *Chavez v Presidential Commission on Good Government* (1998) 299 SCRA 744, 764.
[221] *Neri* (n 219) 183.
[222] DPA, ch 7, ss 23–24.
[223] ibid, ch 6, s 21.
[224] ibid, ch 8, s 25.
[225] National Privacy Commission, *NPC Circular No 2021-01*, 28 January 2021, rule 2, s 1.

depending on the breach involved. As mentioned, the NPC has the power to issue compliance or enforcement orders,[226] institute investigations,[227] facilitate or enable settlements,[228] award indemnity,[229] issue cease and desist orders,[230] impose temporary or permanent ban,[231] recommend to the DOJ criminal prosecution,[232] compel, or petition any entity to abide by its orders,[233] and to impose administrative fines.[234] The 2021 Rules of Procedure of the National Privacy Commission as amended provides for the procedural rules on how to avail these administrative remedies.[235]

On the other hand, criminal complaints involving the penal provisions of the DPA[236] are first filed with the DOJ for preliminary investigation. If the DOJ establishes probable cause (ie, there is 'sufficient [evidence or] ground to engender a well-founded belief that a crime has been committed and the respondent is probably guilty thereof, and should be held for trial'[237]), it proceeds to file a criminal information with the court and prosecutes the criminal case on behalf of the 'People of the Philippines'. The criminal proceedings may lead to imprisonment of the accused, and/or award of damages or imposition of fines. The court may also provide provisional remedies, including an injunction, attachment, among others.[238]

Moreover, aside from the remedies available pursuant to the DPA, certain remedies may also be available under the Constitution and other statutes. These remedies are usually granted by the courts. An example is the Writ of Habeas Data which can be availed of for violations of the constitutional right to privacy. Depending on the cause of action, the other forms of relief available may include damages, specific performance, restitution, injunction, and restraining orders.

Furthermore, parties may also choose to have their dispute resolved through ADR. Notably, the settlement agreements or arbitral awards arising from the ADR may be binding and enforceable on the parties.[239]

ii. Jurisdictional Issues

The DPA does not mention whether the NPC has the exclusive jurisdiction to hear and decide on matters involving violations of the provisions of the DPA. There is good reason, however, to interpret this silence as well as the existence of remedies from courts within the DPA (eg, those providing for criminal penalties), to mean that such jurisdiction is not

[226] DPA, ch 2, s 7(a); DPA IRR, rule III, s 9(f)(1).
[227] DPA, ch 2, s 7(b); DPA IRR, rule III, s 9(f)(1).
[228] DPA, ch 2, s 7(b); DPA IRR, rule III, s 9(f)(3).
[229] DPA, ch 2, s 7(b); DPA IRR, rule III, s 9(e)(3).
[230] DPA, ch 2, s 7(c); DPA IRR, rule III, s 9(f)(2).
[231] DPA, ch 2, s 7(c); DPA IRR, rule III, s 9(f)(3).
[232] DPA, ch 2, s 7(i); DPA IRR, rule III, s 9(f)(4).
[233] DPA, ch 2, s 7(d); DPA IRR, rule III, s 9(f)(5).
[234] DPA IRR, rule XIII, s 65; National Privacy Commission, *NPC Circular No 2022-01*, 8 August 2022.
[235] National Privacy Commission, *NPC Circular No 2021-01*, 28 January 2021; National Privacy Commission, *NPC Circular No 2024-01*, 26 January 2024.
[236] DPA, ch 8, ss 25–32.
[237] Rules of Court, rule 112, s 1.
[238] ibid, rule 127, ss 1–2.
[239] Alternative Dispute Resolution Act 2004, ss 17 and 40–44.

exclusively granted to the NPC.[240] This implies that the Regional Trial Court (RTC) should also provide remedies for violations of the DPA, distinct from those granted under the penal provisions of the DPA. Under section 19 of the Judiciary Reorganization Act of 1980, the RTC shall have jurisdiction '[i]n all cases not within the exclusive jurisdiction of any court, tribunal, person or body exercising judicial or quasi-judicial functions'. Hence, the RTC may also grant an injunction, award damages and other appropriate remedies when dealing with data and privacy protection cases.

Notably, the NPC or the courts should be able to assume jurisdiction over cases where the same act or omission may involve breaching the (data) laws of more than one state, provided the case falls within the scope of the DPA's application (for example, when the Act relates to the processing of personal information about a Filipino citizen[241]). This is because the DPA grants subject-matter jurisdiction over these matters. In addition, the NPC or the courts should also acquire jurisdiction over the person of the defendant or respondent through proper service of summons. If both subject-matter jurisdiction and personal jurisdiction are present, the NPC or court can proceed to hear and try the case even if the case involves activities which constitute breach of data laws of more than one state.[242]

Nonetheless, the NPC or the court may refuse to exercise their jurisdiction under the principle of *forum non conveniens*. In the Philippines, a court may 'refuse impositions on its jurisdiction where it is not the most "convenient" or available forum and the parties are not precluded from seeking remedies elsewhere'.[243] However, one must note that when foreign laws apply to the dispute, this is insufficient, on its own, to establish that the local court is not the most convenient forum.[244]

Furthermore, when another case concerning the same facts is already pending in a foreign court, the NPC or the court may also use the principle of *forum non conveniens* to desist from hearing the case since '… forum non conveniens is a means devised to address parallel litigation arising in multiple jurisdictions'.[245] The pendency, however, of a foreign action can be pleaded as a distinct ground under the principle of *litis pendentia*. For *litis pendentia* to apply, the following must concur: (a) identity of the parties or at least such as to represent the same interest in both actions; (b) identity of rights asserted and relief prayed for, the relief being founded on the same acts; and (c) the identity in the two cases should be such that the judgment which may be rendered in one would, regardless of which party is successful, amount to res judicata in the other.[246]

The DPA is silent as to whether parties can choose foreign courts to resolve data privacy disputes including those arising from the DPA or where Philippine law applies. Nonetheless, there is no mandatory jurisdictional rule in favour of Philippine courts or the NPC even for disputes falling under section 6 of the DPA, which is arguably a mandatory substantive rule. Because choice of law issues are recognised in the Philippines as

[240] See *Hernaez v Balmores*, AC No 13114, 30 August 2023, where a lawyer faced a disciplinary complaint at the Supreme Court for violating the DPA.
[241] DPA, ch 1, s 6(a).
[242] *Raytheon International, Inc v Rouzie, Jr* (2008) 546 SCRA 555, 564.
[243] ibid.
[244] *Saudi Arabian Airlines (Saudia) v Rebesencio* (2015) 746 SCRA 140, 168–69.
[245] ibid, 162.
[246] *Bank of America NT&SA v Court of Appeals* (2003) 400 SCRA 156, 170.

distinct from jurisdictional issues,[247] there should be no reason why data privacy disputes where Philippine law applies, including those falling under section 6 of the DPA, could not be heard by foreign courts. As such, parties should be able to choose foreign courts. Nonetheless, the Rules of Court requires that such choice should be exclusive and in writing for them to be recognised in the Philippines.[248]

iii. Applicable Law

The process of determining the applicable law involves answering two important questions: '(1) [w]hat legal system should control a given situation where some of the significant facts occurred in two or more states; and (2) to what extent should the chosen legal system regulate the situation'.[249] Before determining the applicable law, however, one should first determine whether a 'conflicts' situation exists, ie '[w]here the factual antecedents satisfactorily establish the existence of a foreign element ….'[250] The relevant foreign element may include parties with foreign nationality or domicile, a contract between foreign nationals, or properties situated in another country.[251]

After a 'conflicts' situation has been determined, the next step is characterisation. Here, 'it is necessary … to determine under what category a certain set of facts or rules fall'.[252] 'The purpose of "characterization" is to enable the forum to select the proper law'[253] to resolve the dispute. Hence, at this stage, the court looks at 'a factual situation, event, or operative fact',[254] and determines what area(s) of law are triggered and to what extent such law may determine the legal issue(s). For example, if the set of facts triggers legal issues relating to torts, the conflict of law rule which will be used would be the one applicable to torts, ie, the law of the state which has the most significant relationship to the tortious act.[255] Significantly, privacy violations can be characterised as torts.[256] In these instances, the connecting factors generally relevant to torts may be used to identify the proper law or the law which has the most significant relationship. This may include the: (1) nationality of the parties; (2) seat of a legal or juridical person; (3) place where an act has been done, the *locus actus*; (4) the place where an act is intended to come into effect and; (5) the place where judicial or administrative proceedings are instituted or done.[257] Notably, the Supreme Court has yet to identify any specific connecting factor(s) which may be considered significant or decisive in tort cases involving violations of privacy and data protection.

Alternatively, a privacy-related violation may also be characterised as breach of contract especially when parties have entered into an agreement on data protection. Here, the dispute would be limited to the parties to the contract and the court would apply the choice

[247] *Raytheon* (n 242) 564.
[248] Rules of Court, rule 4, s4(b).
[249] *Saudi Arabian Airlines v Court of Appeals* (1998) 297 SCRA 469, 489–90.
[250] ibid, 484–85.
[251] ibid.
[252] *Saudi Arabian Airlines* (n 249) 471.
[253] ibid.
[254] ibid 490.
[255] *Alcala Vda de Alcañeses v Alcañeses*, GR No 187847, 30 June 2021.
[256] *Ople* (n 3), 157.
[257] *Alcala* (n 255).

of law rule applicable to the contract. In the Philippines, formal validity is determined by the law of the country where the contract has been executed[258] or Philippine law. As regards substantive validity, this would be the law chosen by the parties and if no law was chosen, the law which has the closest connection to the contract.[259] Notably, the Supreme Court has recognised that Article 1306 of the Civil Code allows parties to choose foreign law as the law applicable to the contract.[260]

There are a number of exceptions to the application of foreign law. One is when the local law provides for its mandatory application. In regards to this, the DPA is considered to include mandatory provisions. The NPC appears to interpret the provisions requiring the extraterritorial application of the DPA as providing for the mandatory application of the DPA to any act or practice falling under section 6, whether done within or outside of the Philippines.[261] The NPC, for example, has opined that the DPA applies to a data processing agreement between the Department of Agriculture and the Food and Agriculture Organization because 'the personal data involved in the sharing is that of the beneficiaries who are Philippine citizens'. In other words, immunities and privileges given to a UN organisation by an international treaty which the Philippines is a party, should not in any way diminish the DPA's application as the act involved sharing the personal data of Philippine citizens, a situation which is covered by section 6(a) of the DPA.[262] The natural corollary is that if the matter involved is not among those listed under section 6 or if the matter falls among the exceptions to the DPA's application as provided under section 4, foreign law may be chosen as the applicable law.

Furthermore, the court may refuse to apply foreign law when such application is contrary to public order or public policy,[263] or when public interest requires it. 'It is a conflict of law policy that foreign law ordinarily applicable will not be applied if to do so would violate domestic public policy.'[264]

In the Philippines, when foreign law is chosen as the applicable law, it is treated as a question of fact. This law-as-fact treatment of foreign law gives rise to two important requirements: (1) foreign law must be pleaded; and (2) foreign law must be proven in evidence. Under rule 8, section 1 of the Rules of Court, a party should state '... a plain, concise and direct statement of the ultimate facts, including the evidence on which the party pleading relies for his claim or defence, as the case may be'. Hence, if a party is relying on foreign law for their claim or defence, they have to state this in their pleading. 'A foreign law is considered to be pleaded if there is an allegation in the pleading about the existence of the foreign law, its import and legal consequence on the event or transaction in issue.'[265] Failure

[258] Civil Code, Art 17.
[259] *Philippine Export and Foreign Loan Guarantee Corporation v VP Eusebio Construction Inc* (2008) 434 SCRA 202, 215.
[260] ibid.
[261] National Privacy Commission, *NPC Advisory Opinion No 2017-005*, 5 January 2017; *NPC Advisory Opinion No 2017-012*, 6 February 2017; *NPC Advisory Opinion No 2018-022*, 30 April 2018; *NPC Advisory Opinion No 2023-009*, 27 February 2023.
[262] National Privacy Commission, *NPC Advisory Opinion No 2023-009*, 27 February 2023.
[263] *Tenchavez v Escaño* (1965) 15 SCRA 355, 362; *Mijares v Ranada* (2005) 455 SCRA 397, 420–21; *Bankruptcy Estate of Mitich v Mercantile Insurance Co, Inc*, GR Nos 238041 & 238502, 15 February 2022.
[264] *Bankruptcy Estate of Mitich*, ibid.
[265] *Wildvalley Shipping Co, Ltd v Court of Appeals* (2000) 342 SCRA 213, 223.

to plead the foreign law would allow the court not to apply 'foreign law' even if the choice of law process points to the application of foreign law.[266] Furthermore, the party who is relying on foreign law should provide evidence of foreign law. This is because the party invoking the foreign law has the burden of proving the foreign law.[267] Failure to provide evidence of foreign law or when the evidence presented is insufficient (for example, when the evidence provided only points to the existence of the foreign law but not to how it should be applied or interpreted) allow the court to resort to processual presumption wherein the content of the foreign law is assumed to be identical or similar as it appears in Philippine law.[268] 'Where a foreign law is not pleaded or, even if pleaded, is not proved, the presumption is that foreign law is the same as ours.'[269]

iv. Recognition and Enforcement of Foreign Judgments

The Philippines is not a party to any treaty dealing with the recognition and enforcement of foreign judgments. Nonetheless, Philippine courts recognise and enforce foreign judgments pursuant to rule 39, section 48 of the Rules of Court. In *Asiavest Merchant Bankers (M) Berhad v Court of Appeals*, the Supreme Court explained that 'rules of comity, utility and convenience of nations' have allowed the recognition and enforcement of 'final judgments of foreign courts of competent jurisdiction … under certain conditions that may vary in different countries'.[270] In the same case, the Supreme Court has articulated the specific requirements:

> [A] valid judgment rendered by a foreign tribunal may be recognized … so long as it is convincingly shown that there has been an opportunity for a full and fair hearing before a court of competent jurisdiction; that the trial upon regular proceedings has been conducted, following due citation or voluntary appearance of the defendant and under a system of jurisprudence likely to secure an impartial administration of justice; and that there is nothing to indicate either a prejudice in court and in the system of laws under which it is sitting or fraud in procuring the judgment.[271]

Notably, under rule 131, section 3(n) of the Rules of Court, the foreign court which has issued the foreign judgment enjoys the presumption that it was acting in the lawful exercise of its jurisdiction. Hence, once the authenticity of the foreign judgment is proven, the party attacking a foreign judgment is tasked with the burden of overcoming its presumptive validity.[272] Specifically, the judgment may be assailed by evidence of want of jurisdiction, want of notice to the party, collusion, fraud, or clear mistake of law or fact.[273] Likewise, when the foreign judgments is against mandatory laws, public order, public policy and good customs of the Philippines, they may not be enforced or recognised.[274]

[266] ibid.
[267] *ATCI Overseas Corporation v Echin* (2010) 632 SCRA 528, 534.
[268] See *Northwest Orient Airlines, Inc v Court of Appeals* (1995) 241 SCRA 192, 200.
[269] *ATCI Overseas Corporation* (n 267) 534–35.
[270] *Asiavest Merchant Bankers (M) Berhad v Court of Appeals* (2001) 361 SCRA 489, 497.
[271] ibid, 497–98.
[272] ibid, 498.
[273] Rules of Court, rule 39, s 48; *Asiavest* (n 270) 496.
[274] Civil Code, Art 17.

However, the presumption of validity of the foreign judgment shall apply only after it has been presented and admitted in evidence. Notably, Philippine courts could not take judicial notice of foreign judgments. Foreign judgments need to be proven in evidence in accordance with rule 132, sections 24 and 25 of the Rules of Court. These rules have recently been amended and now reflect the Philippines' accession to the Apostille Convention,[275] which entered into force in the Philippines on 14 May 2019. Prior to the said amended rules, official or certified copies of the foreign judgments should be authenticated by the Philippine embassy or consulate. Under the current version of the rules, with respect to public documents from countries which are parties to the Apostille Convention, the need for authentication could now be dispensed with.[276] Instead, an apostille may be issued by the designated competent authority of the foreign country.[277] Notably, the apostille only certifies the authenticity of the signature, the capacity in which the person signing the document has acted and the identity of the seal or stamp which the document bears.[278]

There are no rules as regards the recognition and enforcement of foreign judgments that particularly applies to foreign judgments relating to data protection and privacy.

v. *Obstacles to Effective Data Protection and Privacy*

The DPA was drafted based on the best practices on data privacy found in the EU and APEC. It was envisioned to provide an effective regime of data and privacy protection.[279] Hence, privacy matters which fall within its scope could expect the baseline protection provided by the DPA. Nonetheless, the DPA removes from its scope 'personal information originally collected from residents of foreign jurisdictions in accordance with the laws of those foreign jurisdictions'.[280] Hence, in this particular situation, the applicable law would be the foreign law under which the personal data has been collected. This approach can, however, lead to an ineffective protection of data and privacy. For example, if the foreign law requires a degree of data protection that is lower than what the DPA provides, a Philippine court would not be able to avoid the application of such foreign law absent showing of the usual exceptions to the application of the foreign law (for example, being contrary to public interest).

Furthermore, the DPA does not prohibit the PIC, PIP, and any third-party processors from locating in other countries. Although the Philippines adopts an approach rooted on the accountability of the PIC, the rules on personal jurisdiction requiring service to the defendant located overseas may cause complications. Notably, the Philippines is not a party to any treaty on the service of process. The complexities relating to the service requirements is exacerbated when multiple parties and causes of action, counterclaims, and crossclaims are involved. Plaintiffs and complainants may be prevented from getting full remedy because they are unable to satisfy the service requirement when the defendants are located

[275] The Hague Convention Abolishing the Requirement of Legalisation for Foreign Public Document, opened for signature 5 October 1961, 527 UNTS 189 (entered into force 24 January 1965) ('Apostille Convention').
[276] ibid, Art 2.
[277] ibid, Art 3.
[278] ibid, Arts 3 and 5.
[279] DPA, ch 1, s 2.
[280] ibid, ch 4, s 4(g).

overseas or may be discouraged to proceed with litigation because of the additional costs and complexity to the legal issues involved.

Notably, the DPA also does not prohibit the parties to data privacy-related agreements like data sharing agreements from choosing foreign law as the law applicable to their contract, except to the extent that the effect of such foreign law may be limited by the mandatory application of section 6 of the DPA. This situation raises at least two important issues: (1) whether Philippine courts may fully enforce the scope of the chosen applicable foreign law; and (2) whether the parochial approach of section 6 would truly benefit the data subjects when the protection given by the foreign law is better. As regards the first issue, whilst there is no doubt that the parties' choice of foreign law could be given effect, the extent to which a choice of law clause would be given effect may be tested when parties have provided for the application of foreign law on non-contractual based causes of action, like torts. The inclusion of non-contractual related causes of action is highly possible given that data breaches may also be characterised as torts, and also to cover situations where third parties are liable for the data breach. Extending the scope of the chosen applicable law to causes of action that are not contractual in nature, like torts, pushes the usual understanding of the scope of the parties' freedom of contract. Most likely, in this situation, given the choice of law rule for torts, the contractual choice of foreign law will not bind the court *per se* but such choice would be considered as a strong factor in favour of the foreign law.

As regards the second issue, the NPC is clear that the DPA applies to matters listed under section 6 of the DPA. This parochial approach, however, may diminish the possibly much higher protection given by the contractually chosen foreign law. Related to this issue, parties to a privacy-related contract may be discouraged from seeking protection before the NPC and Philippine courts as that would lead to the application of section 6 of the DPA on matters falling within its scope. In both instances, this may lead to ineffective data and privacy protection.

Moreover, as discussed, the DPA also does not limit the ability of parties to agree on a different forum or ADR in settling their privacy-related disputes. The choice of a foreign forum may be motivated by a number of reasons, like better privacy rules, remedies, and enforcement mechanisms. However, there had been cases where courts override the parties' chosen forum, especially when words indicating exclusivity of choice are not stated, or when other factors relating to the administration of justice are considered more important.[281] This approach on the choice of forum clause raises questions on the effectiveness of such choice by the parties.

Furthermore, one must note that even when such choice of foreign jurisdiction is locally recognised, a Philippine court may only be able to assist at the enforcement stage of the foreign judgment or final order. Currently, there is no procedural mechanism, except in cross-border insolvency-related matters,[282] which may allow foreign issued interlocutory measures to be recognised and enforced in the Philippines. Hence, an interlocutory

[281] *Hongkong and Shanghai Banking Corp v Sherman* (1989) 176 SCRA 331; see also Lemuel Lopez, 'When Choice of Forum Clauses are Challenged: Key Lessons from Asian Jurisdictions' (PhD Thesis, The University of Melbourne, 2019) 195–201.

[282] Financial Rehabilitation and Insolvency Act 2010, ss 140–41.

injunction ordered by a foreign court requiring the immediate cessation of activities violating data privacy in the Philippines may not be given effect by a Philippine court. The aggrieved party may also be prevented from applying for interlocutory protection in the Philippine courts or NPC through a fresh proceeding because such application may amount to a breach of their choice of forum clause.

At the moment, the Philippines is not adopting or being influenced by any private international law guidelines in relation to data protection or privacy like the Lisbon Guidelines on Privacy.

F. Topical Issues and Prospects

i. Data Privacy and Artificial Intelligence

The use of artificial intelligence (AI) in the processing of personal information of data subjects is contemplated in the concept of automated access and processes under the DPA. In such a situation, data subjects have the right to be furnished with information about the methods utilised for automated access,[283] and the right to access information on automated processes where the data will or will likely be made as the sole basis for any decision significantly affecting or will affect the data subject.[284]

The DPA IRR articulates further the use of AI in processing personal information by introducing the terms, automated decision-making[285] and profiling.[286] In this regard, the DPA IRR confirms that the data subject has the right to be informed of the existence of automated decision-making and profiling,[287] right to be notified and furnished with information about the methods utilised for automated access,[288] right to object to the processing of his or her personal data, including processing for direct marketing, automated processing or profiling,[289] right to reasonable access to, upon demand, information to automated processes,[290] and right to obtain from the PIC a copy of personal information data being processed based on consent or contract, for commercial purpose, or through automated means.[291] Further, the DPA IRR requires the PIC to notify the NPC of automated processing operations where the processing becomes the sole basis of making decisions that would significantly affect the data subject.[292] Notably, no decision with legal effects concerning a data subject shall be made solely on the basis of automated processing without the consent of the data subject.[293]

[283] DPA, ch 4, s 16(b)(5).
[284] ibid, ch 4, s 16(c)(6).
[285] ibid, ch 8, s 34(a)(1).
[286] ibid, ch 1, s 3(p).
[287] DPA IRR, rule VIII, s 34(a)(1).
[288] ibid, rule VIII, s 34(a)(2)(f).
[289] ibid, rule VIII, s 34(b).
[290] ibid, rule VIII, s 34(c)(6).
[291] ibid, rule VIII, s 36.
[292] ibid, rule IX, ss 46 and 48.
[293] ibid, rule IX, s 48(b).

The NPC Circular No 2022-04 implements these rights of the data subject by requiring mandatory registration of automated decision-making or profiling data processing systems where the PIC or PIP has at least 250 employees, is processing sensitive personal information of at least 1,000 individuals, or where the processing of data will likely pose a risk to the rights and freedoms of data subjects.[294] Likewise, the PIC or PIP who carries out any automated decision-making operation or profiling shall indicate in its registration record and identify the data processing system involved in the automated decision-making or profiling operation.[295] Furthermore, the NPC may request from the PIC or PIP additional information and documents pertaining to its automated decision-making or profiling operation.[296] The NPC may issue a cease and desist for non-compliance with the registration and notification rules under NPC Circular No 2022-04.[297]

In addition to the DPA, the CPA's provisions on computer-related fraud,[298] identity theft,[299] as well as those offences against the confidentiality, integrity and availability of computer data and systems,[300] may also be used to deal with cybercrimes that may have been committed through the use of AI. Likewise, various provisions of the Civil Code[301] and even the Constitution[302] may be used.

ii. International Privacy-related Cooperation Agreements

With the goal of exchanging best practices in data governance, the Philippines has bilateral partnerships with Singapore's Personal Data Protection Commission,[303] the United Kingdom's Information Commissioner's Office[304] and the Hong Kong Office of the Privacy Commissioner for Personal Data.[305] These arrangements may further impact the interpretation and implementation of the DPA.

iii. Other Future Developments

House Bill No 898 was filed in 2022 at the House of Representatives, the lower chamber of Philippine Congress, with the goal of introducing provisions addressing some challenges

[294] National Privacy Commission, *NPC Circular No 2022-04*, 5 December 2022, s 5.
[295] ibid, s 26.
[296] ibid, s 28.
[297] ibid, s 38.
[298] CPA, s 4(b)(2).
[299] ibid, s 4(b)(3).
[300] ibid, s 4(a).
[301] Civil Code, Arts 19–21, 26, 2176.
[302] Constitution, Art III, s 3(1).
[303] National Privacy Commission, PH, Singapore Renew Stronger Ties in Personal Data Protection' (15 September 2022), available at https://privacy.gov.ph/ph-singapore-renew-stronger-ties-in-personal-data-protection/.
[304] National Privacy Commission, 'Privacy Commission Firms up Collaboration with UK Counterpart in Sharing Best Privacy Practices' (14 January 2021), available at https://privacy.gov.ph/privacy-commission-firms-up-collaboration-with-uk-counterpart-in-sharing-best-privacy-practices/.
[305] National Privacy Commission, 'PH, HK Sign MOU on Personal Data Protection' (22 May 2023), available at privacy.gov.ph/ph-hk-sign-mou-on-personal-data-protection/.

arising from cross-border data transfers. The bill seeks to introduce new categories of personal data like biometric and genetic data,[306] a wider definition of data breach,[307] additional exemptions from the scope of the DPA when dealing with cross-border crimes,[308] a wider scope for the extraterritorial application of the DPA,[309] additional powers for the NPC, and more rights granted to data subjects,[310] among others. The bill, however, has been pending since July 2022.

306 House Bill No 898 2022, s 1.
307 ibid.
308 ibid, s 2.
309 ibid, s 3.
310 ibid, s 9.

12

Indonesia

PRISKILA PRATITA PENASTHIKA*

I. Introduction

The Indonesian Personal Data Protection Law, Law Number 27 of 2022, (PDP Law) was approved by the House of Representatives of the Republic of Indonesia on 20 September 2022. On 17 October 2022, the President of the Republic of Indonesia gave assent to the law, which signifies its enactment and coming into force. Until the enactment of the PDP Law, data protection regulations in Indonesia had been provided across scattered sectoral regulations, making navigation potentially troublesome for businesses in an ever-convergent digital world. The PDP Law also comes at the right time, amidst various high-profile data breaches in Indonesia that have recently put data management and protection in the headlines.[1] The unified approach under the PDP Law is expected to provide more clarity and consistent personal data protection across all sectors in Indonesia.

Unlike the earlier laws and regulations on personal data protection, which only cover personal data processed through an electronic system, the PDP Law applies to personal data processed either through electronic systems or non-electronic systems. In addition, the PDP Law sets out normative provisions for personal data protection instead of detailed or practical rules. In this regard, the Government will have to issue implementing regulations to regulate the provisions in the PDP Law in greater detail.[2]

The PDP Law does not revoke the provisions of any earlier laws and regulations on personal data protection. Nevertheless, if any such provisions are at variance with it, the PDP Law provisions will prevail. On this account, this chapter encompasses the provisions on personal data protection stipulated in the PDP Law and the laws and regulations issued prior to the enactment of the PDP Law. In this way, this chapter also highlights the concordant and conflicting provisions of the earlier laws and regulations with those in the PDP Law.

* Assistant Professor in Private International Law at the Faculty of Law – Universitas Indonesia.

[1] The recent data breach cases in Indonesia, among others, are: (i) the personal data of 279 million users of the Agency of Social Security for Healthcare in Indonesia was compromised and sold on an online forum in May 2021; (ii) in October 2021, the website of the Indonesian Child Protection Commission was hacked which resulted in the leaking of its data; (iii) in September 2022, the personal data of 105 million Indonesians were allegedly leaked after the General Elections Commission was believed to be compromised; and (iv) the most recent occurrence was the leak of personal data of 3.2 billion users of the application of the COVID-19 contact tracing and vaccination record in Indonesia (*PeduliLindungi*).

[2] At the time of writing, the drafting process of the implementing regulations is still ongoing.

II. General Legal Framework of International Data Transfers and Data Protection

A. Constitutional Protection for Data Transfer and Protection

The 1945 Constitution of the Republic of Indonesia ('Constitution')[3] does not expressly mention the right to data protection and privacy. Nevertheless, the PDP Law invokes Articles 28G(1), 28H(4), and 28J of the Constitution to base the rights to data protection and privacy in Indonesia.

Article 28G(1) reads,

> Every person shall be entitled to the protection of his/her self, family, honour, dignity, and property under his/her control, as well as be entitled to feel secure and be entitled to protection against any threat of fear to do or omit to do something being his/her fundamental right.

Meanwhile, Article 28H(4) states, 'Every person shall be entitled to personal property, and such property right shall not be taken over arbitrarily by whomsoever.' Lastly, Article 28J(1) stipulates, 'Every person shall respect human rights of the other in the order of life of the society, nation, and state.' Its paragraph (2) further reads that

> In the exercise of his/her rights and freedom, every person shall abide by the limitations to be stipulated by the laws to solely guarantee the recognition as well as respect for the rights and freedoms of the others and in order to comply with just demands in accordance with considerations for morality, religious values, security, and public order in a democratic society.

B. Statutory Frameworks for Data Transfer and Protection

On account of its enactment on 17 October 2022, the primary legislation on data transfer and protection in Indonesia is the PDP Law. This law applies to individuals,[4] corporations, public bodies,[5] and international organisations that perform legal acts recognised under the law (1) in the Indonesian jurisdiction and (2) outside of the Indonesian jurisdiction, provided that such legal acts result in legal consequences (a) in the Indonesian jurisdiction, and/or (b) to a personal data subject of Indonesian nationality outside of the Indonesian jurisdiction.

The PDP Law defines personal data as any data concerning individuals, whether identified or may be identified independently or combined with other information, either directly or indirectly, through an electronic or non-electronic system.[6]

[3] *Undang-undang Dasar Negara Republik Indonesia Tahun* 1945 [The 1945 Constitution of the Republic of Indonesia]. The Constitution was amended four times, lastly in 2002.

[4] For the purpose of simplicity, the pronoun 'he' is used throughout this chapter when referring to an individual.

[5] PDP Law, Art 2. The term 'public bodies' is defined as '... executive, legislative, judicative and other bodies whose function and main duties are related to the organising of the state, where part or all of its funds originate from the state budget and/or the regional budget, or non-governmental organisations that part or all of its fund originates from the state budget and/or the regional budget, the contribution from the society and/or from offshore sources'. See PDP Law, Art 1(9).

[6] ibid, Art 1(1).

The PDP Law provides a foundation for personal data processing activities and protection in Indonesia. However, it also stipulates that the existing regulations on personal data protection remain applicable to the extent that they are not in conflict with its provisions.[7] In other words, if any provisions of the existing regulations on personal data protection are inconsistent with the PDP Law, the PDP Law provisions will prevail. It is worth noting that the PDP Law obliges data controllers, data processors, and any party involved in personal data processing to make necessary adjustments to comply with its provisions within two years from the date of its enactment.[8]

The Official Elucidation of the PDP Law further asserts that its provisions are the general standards for personal data protection. It allows the existence of other sectoral personal data protection regulations that would fit the characteristics of the relevant sectors. Thus, the current statutory framework on personal data transfer and protection in Indonesia also relies on separate regulations enacted prior to the PDP Law. The separate regulations on personal data protection are detailed below.

i. Electronic Information and Transactions

A set of statutory frameworks on electronic information and transactions touches upon personal data protection. Prior to the enactment of the PDP Law, these regulations served as the primary authority for the personal data protection regime in Indonesia. They are, among others:

a) Law Number 11 of 2008 on Electronic Information and Transactions, as amended by Law Number 1 of 2024 ('EIT Law');
b) Government Regulation Number 71 of 2019 on Implementation of Electronic Systems and Transactions ('Government Regulation 71/2019');
c) Regulation of the Minister of Communication and Information Number 20 of 2016 on the Protection of Personal Data in Electronic Systems ('MCI Regulation 20/2016'); and
d) Regulation of the Minister of Communication and Information Number 10 of 2021 on the Change of MCI Regulation Number 5 of 2020 on Private Electronic System Providers ('MCI Regulation 10/2021').

Article 26(1) of the EIT Law states, 'Unless otherwise provided by laws and regulations, use of any information through electronic media that involves personal data of a Person must be made with the consent of the Person concerned.' The Official Elucidation of the Law further asserts that the protection of personal data is a part of the right to privacy, which encompasses (i) the right to enjoy a private life and be free from any invasion, (ii) the right to communicate with other people without surveillance, and (iii) the right to inspect access to information about the personal life of and data on individuals.[9]

As implementing regulations, Government Regulation 71/2019 and MCI Regulation 20/2016 reaffirm the concepts of personal data protection encapsulated in the EIT Law. Both

[7] ibid, Art 75.
[8] ibid, Art 74.
[9] EIT Law, Art 26(1) and its Official Elucidation. The term 'Person' in the EIT Law encompasses Indonesian nationals, foreigners, and legal persons. See also Art 1(21).

regulations stipulate that the processing of personal data must respect the privacy of the personal data owner and be based on valid consent from the personal data owner or according to the regulations.[10] Government Regulation 71/2019, together with MCI Regulation 10/2021, further lay down provisions with regard to data localisation and Electronic System Providers (ESPs) and their obligations in Indonesia.[11]

Taking into consideration the aforementioned regulations on information and electronic transactions, it is also important to draw attention to Law Number 14 of 2008 on Disclosure of Public Information ('DPI Law'). Article 6 of the DPI Law prescribes that public bodies have the right to refuse to provide information that is excluded or does not accord with the law and regulations. These Articles specify that information with respect to privacy rights is information that should not be disclosed by public bodies.[12]

Article 17(g) and (h) of the DPI Law further itemise the information relating to individual privacy that must not be disclosed by public bodies. They concern information about: (i) the contents of an authentic personal deed and the last will or testament of an individual; (ii) the history and condition of a family member; (iii) the history, condition and care, physical medical treatment, and mental state of an individual; (iv) the financial condition, assets, income, and bank account of an individual; (v) the evaluation results and recommendation of the capacity and ability of an individual; and (vi) notes of an individual pertaining to his formal and non-formal education activities.

ii. Citizens' Administration and Archives Management

Law Number 23 of 2006 on Citizens Administration, as amended by Law Number 24 of 2013 ('CA Law'), ensures the safekeeping and confidentiality of citizens' personal data and documents. As the responsible authority concerning citizens' administration matters, the Minister of Home Affairs grants access rights to citizens' data to officers responsible for handling such matters. These officers are prohibited from circulating citizens' data that is not by their authority.[13]

The implementing regulation of CA Law, Government Regulation Number 40 of 2019 ('GR 40/2019'), further provides the citizens' data that shall be protected are: (i) information concerning physical and/or mental disabilities; (ii) fingerprint; (iii) iris; (iv) signature; and (v) other data elements that pertain to someone's disgrace.[14] The protection shall encompass the protection of access and confidentiality of such data.

Citizens' data shall be stored in the databases of the Ministry of Home Affairs and the offices of the Agency of Citizenship and Civil Registration at the provincial, regency, and city levels.[15] Any ministries, institutions, and Indonesian legal persons shall obtain an approval from the Minister of Home Affairs, governor, regent, or mayor of the relevant scope of the needed data in order to have access to citizens' personal data. The obtained personal data can only be used according to the requirements detailed in the approval. In the interest of

[10] Government Regulation 71/2019, Art 14(3); MCI Regulation 20/2016, Arts 8–9.
[11] See section IV below for details on data localisation and ESPs.
[12] DPI Law, Arts 6(1) and (3)(c). The term 'public bodies' in DPI Law is defined the same as in the PDP Law.
[13] CA Law, Art 79(1)-(3).
[14] ibid, Art 84; GR 40/2019, Art 54.
[15] GR 40/2019, Art 55.

state security and law enforcement, the protected citizens' data can only be accessed with the approval of the Minister of Home Affairs.[16]

As to archives management, Law Number 43 of 2009 on Archives ('Archives Law') lays down that the archive creator may restrict access to the archive because if it is opened to the public, it can reveal confidential and personal data.[17]

iii. Banking and Finance

In the banking and financial service sectors, it is essential to highlight Law Number 21 of 2011 on the Financial Services Authority (*Otoritas Jasa Keuangan/OJK*), as amended by Law Number 4 of 2023 on the Development and Strengthening of Financial Sector ('DSFS Law'). This law underlies the establishment of the Financial Services Authority, which has supervisory authority over all financial service providers in Indonesia. In this regard, the relevant provisions on personal data protection can be found in the Regulation of Financial Services Authority Number 6/POJK.07/2022 on Customer and Public Protection in the Financial Services Sector ('OJK Regulation 6/2022') and Circular Letter of Financial Services Authority Number 14/SEOJK.07/2014 on Confidentiality and Security of Consumer Personal Data and/or Information ('OJK Circular Letter 14/2014'). These instruments require financial services providers to protect the confidentiality and security of their customers' personal data. This obligation may be exempted only in the case of written consent given by the customers or an obligation required by law.[18]

The DSFS Law also obliges commercial banks,[19] sharia banks, and the affiliated parties to keep the information concerning bank customers and their savings confidential.[20] Nevertheless, this obligation may be exempted by: (i) the interest of law enforcement; (ii) a request of a receiver in the case of receivership; (iii) a written request by the customer or the legitimate heir of the customer; (iv) exchange of information among banks; (v) compliance in the framework of mutual legal assistance in criminal matters; (vi) a request for tax purposes; (vii) the interest of other institution for the purpose of state administration; (viii) the interest of policies in monetary, macroprudential, and payment system by the Bank of Indonesia; (ix) the interest of duty of the Indonesia Deposit Insurance Corporation; and (x) the enforcement of cooperation agreements among countries.

In addition, Regulation of Financial Services Authority Number 11/POJK.03/2022 on Implementation of Information Technology by Commercial Banks ('OJK Regulation 11/2022') obliges commercial banks to ensure the protection of customers' data. In a situation that potentially increases the risk for the owner of personal data, banks are required to carry out an impact assessment on the application of the principles of personal data protection.[21]

[16] ibid, Art 56.

[17] Archives Law, Art 44(1)(h). The term 'archive creator' is defined in this law as a party with independence and authority in carrying out functions, duties, and responsibilities in archive management. See also Art 1(19).

[18] OJK Regulation 6/2022, Art 11; OJK Circular Letter 14/2014.

[19] This chapter uses the term 'commercial banks' as opposed to the term 'sharia banks'.

[20] DSFS Law, Art 14. The affiliated parties encompass: (i) commissioners, directors, sharia supervisory board, or bank employees; (ii) any party that provides service to banks, among others, public accountants, surveyors, legal consultants, and any other consultants; (iii) any party that controls or is controlled, directly or indirectly, by banks; or (iv) any party that participates in the bank management according to the Financial Services Authority.

[21] OJK Regulation 11/2022, Art 44.

iv. Health

Upon the enactment of the PDP Law, the confidentiality and protection of personal data in health services are stipulated in Law Number 17 of 2023 on Health ('Health Law'). This recently enacted law serves as the integrated law for health services in Indonesia. Prior to the issuance of the Health Law, the confidentiality and protection of personal data were prescribed in scattered laws, which primarily focus on medical privacy and patients' medical records.

Article 4(1)(i) of the Health Law stipulates that every person has the right to obtain confidentiality over his health data and information. Following the provisions of the PDP Law, the Health Law also requires the Health Information System Operators to ensure the protection of every individual's health data and information. The processing of one's health data and information should be based on the consent of the person concerned and/or on other bases in accordance with the laws and regulations.[22]

According to the Health Law, the confidentiality of health data and information is to be curtailed in the case of: (i) complying with a request of law enforcement officers in the context of law enforcement; (ii) handling outbreaks, epidemics, or disasters; (iii) limited educational and research interests; (iv) efforts to protect against dangers for the safety of other people individually or in society; (v) interests of health maintenance, treatment, recovery, and patient care; (vi) the patient's request; (vii) the interests of administrative, insurance payments, health financing guarantees; and/or (viii) other interests regulated in statutory regulations.[23]

C. Data Protection Frameworks

i. Influence of International Data Protection Frameworks

Many of the core aspects of the PDP Law, including definitions of covered data and entities, lawful grounds, processing obligations, accountability measures, and controller-processor relationships, are modelled on the EU's General Data Protection Regulation (GDPR). However, there are a few notable provisions unique to the Indonesian context. For example, the PDP Law includes a broad extraterritorial scope provision that will apply to entities as long as their personal data processing activities have legal consequences in Indonesia or to an Indonesian national outside of the Indonesian jurisdiction.[24]

The PDP Law is not the first instrument that refers to the GDPR. An earlier reference to the GDPR in the Indonesian personal data protection regime was embodied in Government Regulation Number 80 of 2019 on E-Commerce ('Government Regulation 80/2019'). This regulation is one of the sectoral regulations that remain in force in the framework of personal data protection provided in the PDP Law. Article 59(1) of Government Regulation 80/2019 stipulates that business actors are obliged to store personal data in accordance with

[22] Health Law, Art 351.
[23] ibid, Art 4(4).
[24] PDP Law, Art 2(1).

the standards or the prevailing prevalence of business practices. Furthermore, the Official Elucidation of Article 59(2) of Government Regulation 80/2019 explicates that the standard of personal data protection in the context of trading through electronic systems in Indonesia shall consider the European standard of personal data protection. In addition to the GDPR, the Official Elucidation also refers to the Asia-Pacific Economic Cooperation (APEC) Privacy Framework as the standard of personal data protection.[25]

ii. Specific Provisions for Particular Sectors

According to Article 2(2), the PDP Law is not applicable to the processing of personal data by individuals in private or household activities. The PDP Law is silent as regards the activities that might be regarded as private or household activities.[26]

The PDP Law specifies that data subjects have the right to object to Automated Decision-Making (ADM), including profiling that gives rise to legal consequences or significantly impacts the personal data subject. This provision mirrors the GDPR and does not seem to be construed as a general prohibition against qualifying ADM. The PDP Law is silent regarding the ambit of legal consequences and significant impact on the personal data subject. Nevertheless, if the use of ADM significantly impacts the personal data subject, the data controller may need to conduct a data protection impact assessment. Similar to many other provisions set forth therein, the PDP Law states that further details regarding the procedure of filing an objection to ADM will be regulated in implementing regulations.[27]

The PDP Law allows the use of facial recognition technology or the installation of visual data processing devices in public places only for the purposes of security, disaster prevention, or traffic information analysis. There must be a notification to the public that such technology is in use in areas where they have installed the devices. Additionally, the installation of visual data processing devices shall not be used to identify a person. However, the last two requirements do not apply to the activities of prevention of criminal offences and law enforcement.[28]

With respect to the classification of personal data as detailed in section V below, the PDP Law obliges special procedures for processing the personal data of children and persons with disabilities.[29] Processing the personal data of children shall be subject to consent from the parents and/or the child's legal guardian. The PDP Law does not specify an age threshold for children. Therefore, Law Number 23 of 2002 on Child Protection as amended by Law Number 35 of 2014 ('Child Protection Law'), which stipulates that a child is any person

[25] 'APEC Privacy Framework (2015)' (*APEC*, 2017), available at www.apec.org/publications/2017/08/apec-privacy-framework-(2015).

[26] In November 2022, this provision was challenged by an Indonesian national for a judicial review to the Constitutional Court, case number 108/PUU-XX/2022. The Constitutional Court Judges ruled that the petitioner's petition was legally unjustifiable in its entirety. The Court views the personal data processing stipulated in Article 2(2) of the PDP Law as activities carried out in the private domain and non-commercial in nature. Thus, they should be excluded from the PDP Law's scope for the protection of human rights. See 'Personal Data Protection Law Regulates Control over Legal Entity's Personal Data' (*The Constitutional Court of the Republic of Indonesia*, 2023), available at https://en.mkri.id/news/details/2023-04-14/Personal_Data_Protection_Law_Regulates_Control_over_Legal_Entity%E2%80%99s_Personal_Data.

[27] PDP Law, Art 10. See section V below for more details about the data protection impact assessment.

[28] ibid, Art 17.

[29] ibid, Arts 25–26.

under 18 years old, serves as a reference for this matter.[30] As to persons with disabilities, the PDP Law requires the processing of their data to be carried out through specific communication means according to the regulations. Such personal data processing is also subject to the consent of the person with disabilities and/or his legal guardian. In this regard, implementing regulations on this matter is expected to specify the definition of persons with disabilities and the communication means to be used by data controllers to communicate with persons with disabilities.

As noted earlier, Article 11 of OJK Regulation 6/2022 stipulates that a financial service actor is not allowed: (i) to transfer consumers' personal data and/or information to third parties; (ii) to require consumers to agree to share their personal data and/or information as a condition of using a product and/or a service; (iii) to utilise consumers' personal data and/or information who have terminated or withdrawn from the application to use a product and/or service agreement; (iv) to make use of consumers' personal data and/or information whose application to use a product or service has been refused by the financial service actor itself; and (v) to make use of personal data and/or information of potential consumers who withdrew their application to use a product or service. These prohibitions may only be exempted if the consumer has provided written consent or laws and regulations require such an exemption. These prohibitions apply to both domestic and international data transfers. With the aim of protecting consumers and society, the Indonesian Financial Services Authority can impose sanctions on financial service actors in case of non-compliance with the personal data rules.[31]

As to personal data protection in the electronic system, MCI Regulation 20/2016 requires ESPs to provide a form in the Indonesian language to request approval from the intended personal data owner in order to acquire, collect, process, analyse, store, display, announce, transfer, circulate, grant access, and destroy personal data.[32] In addition, this regulation also requires that the personal data stored in the electronic system must be in the form of encrypted data.[33]

iii. Distinction and Interface between Data Protection and Privacy

In Indonesia, personal data protection is interconnected with the concept of privacy, that is the idea of maintaining integrity and personal dignity. Privacy rights are understood as an individual's ability to determine the person to handle his data and how such data is used. Unlawful personal data collection and circulation is a violation of privacy rights.

MCI Regulation 20/2016 further states that the nature of personal data is private and confidential.[34] Thus, the owner of personal data has the freedom to declare his data

[30] Child Protection Law, Art 1(1).

[31] OJK Regulation 6/2022, Art 55.

[32] ibid, Art 6. This provision is consonant with Law Number 24 of 2009 on the National Flag, Language, State Symbol, and National Anthem, and its implementing Regulation, Government Regulation Number 63 of 2019 on the Use of the Indonesian Language. These regulations oblige the use of the Indonesian Language on any agreement involving agencies of the Government of Indonesia, Indonesian state and private institutions, or individuals of Indonesian nationality. For details, see Priskila Pratita Penasthika, 'The Mandatory Use of National Language in Indonesia and Belgium: An Obstacle to International Contracting?' (2019) *Indonesia Law Review* 9 number 2, 83–104.

[33] MCI Regulation 20/2016, Art 15(2).

[34] MCI Regulation 20/2016, Arts 2(2)(a) and 34(1)(b).

confidential or non-confidential unless otherwise stipulated by the laws and regulations. In addition, the acknowledgement of and respect toward the private and confidential nature of personal data are evidenced by the freedom of the data owner to amend, add, or update his data.[35]

iv. Distinction between 'Data Users', 'Data Subjects', 'Data Processors', and 'Data Sub-Contractors'

a. Personal Data Subjects

After been modelled on the GDPR, the PDP Law introduces the term 'personal data subject', translated into Indonesian as *subjek data pribadi*. Article 1(6) of the PDP Law defines 'personal data subject' as any individuals to whom personal data is attached. The earlier regulations on personal data protection use the term 'personal data owner' (*pemilik data pribadi*).[36] It is noteworthy that the introduction of the term 'personal data subject' in distinction to 'personal data owner' is considered to indicate the Government's determination to step up its data protection regime with international standards.

One of the highlights of the PDP Law is that personal data subjects have the right to withdraw their consent for the processing of their data that has been granted to the personal data controller and are also entitled to cease, to postpone, and/or to limit the data processing, to delete and/or to destroy their data. Personal data subjects can exercise these rights by submitting a recorded request, delivered either electronically or non-electronically, to the personal data controller.[37]

b. Personal Data Controllers and Personal Data Processors

The PDP Law also introduces the concept of personal data controllers and processors in Indonesia. Similar to the concept of personal data subjects, personal data controllers and processors are also inspired by the GDPR. A personal data controller is defined as any individual, corporation, public body, or international organisation acting individually or jointly to determine the objectives and to exercise control over the processing of personal data.[38] Meanwhile, a personal data processor is any individual, corporation, public body, or international organisation acting individually or jointly to process personal data on behalf of a personal data controller.[39]

Taking into account the definitions above, a personal data processor cannot determine the objectives and exercise control over the personal data processing by himself. A personal data processor can only process personal data after being appointed by and on behalf of the data controller. On this account, any party that acts as a data controller must be cautious in appointing a data processor because it will affect compliance requirements and liabilities.

[35] ibid, Art 8(1)-8(3).
[36] For the purpose of consistency and clarity, this chapter uses the term 'personal data subject' when discussing the PDP Law and the term 'personal data owner' when discussing the laws and regulations on personal data protection enacted prior to the PDP Law.
[37] PDP Law, Arts 8–11, 14.
[38] ibid, Art 1(4).
[39] ibid, Art 1(5).

However, if a data processor conducts personal data processing beyond the orders and objectives set by the data controller, the responsibility for the personal data processing shall shift to the data processor.[40]

Several obligations of personal data controllers set out in the PDP Law also apply to personal data processors. These obligations, among others, are: (i) to ensure the accuracy, completeness, and consistency of personal data in accordance with the prevailing laws and regulations; (ii) to maintain a record of all personal data processing activities; and (iii) to protect and to ensure the security of the processed personal data.[41]

Personal data controllers are exempted from their obligations in situations relating to: (i) national security interest; (ii) law enforcement interest; (iii) public interest for the purpose of state administration; (iv) supervisory interest in the sector of financial services, monetary and payment systems, and financial system stability carried out in the context of state administration; and (v) other exceptions carried out for the purpose of implementation of provisions of law.[42]

c. Personal Data Protection Officers

Personal data controllers and processors are required to appoint a data protection officer responsible for ensuring data privacy compliance and mitigating the risk of data privacy breaches. This applies to personal data controllers and processors that: (i) process personal data for the purpose of public service; (ii) have core activities that require systematic and orderly monitoring of large-scale personal data; and (iii) process specific personal data or personal data relating to crimes on a large scale.[43] No thresholds are yet prescribed to determine what amounts to large-scale personal data processing. The implementing regulations of the PDP Law are expected to specify this matter.

Data protection officers have the duty to advise on data privacy requirements and compliance, to ensure the fulfilment of that compliance, to advise on personal data protection impact assessment, to oversee the performance of the data controller and processor, and to act as a contact person for issues related to the processing of personal data. In addition, a personal data protection officer can be an existing employee of the personal data controller and personal data processor or outsourced.[44]

The PDP Law does not require a data protection officer to be specifically certified. It only mentions that a data protection officer is appointed based on, among other things, their professionalism, legal knowledge, and capability in the area of data privacy practice.[45] Nevertheless, the Ministry of Communication and Information (MCI) is accelerating the certification requirements for data protection officers.[46] It is also noteworthy that training and certification for data protection officers have begun to take place in practice. The Indonesian Data Privacy Professionals Association (IDPPA), one of the existing professional

[40] ibid, Art 51(6).
[41] ibid, Art 52.
[42] ibid, Art 50.
[43] ibid, Art 53(1).
[44] ibid, Arts 53(3) and 54.
[45] PDP Law, Art 53(2).
[46] 'Kominfo Siapkan Sertifikasi Kerja dan Kompetensi PPDP' (*Kominfo*, November 2022), available at aptika.kominfo.go.id/2022/11/kominfo-siapkan-sertifikasi-kerja-dan-kompetensi-ppdp/.

associations with regard to personal data protection, organises training and issues certification for data protection officers.[47]

v. Distinction between Personal and Non-Personal Data

Unlike the earlier regulations on personal data that do not distinguish types of personal data, Article 4 of the PDP Law categorised personal data into general and specific personal data. General personal data includes generic information, such as name, gender, nationality, religion, marital status, and/or any personal data that are combined to identify a person.[48] Specific personal data includes detailed information such as health data, biometric data, genetic data, criminal records, children's and personal financial data. The Official Elucidation of Article 4(1)(a) of the PDP Law underlines that specific personal data is personal data which, if processed, may result in a more significant impact, among others, acts of discrimination and a considerable loss to the personal data subject.

Apart from the special procedures for facial recognition technology, personal data processing for children and persons with disabilities, and the rights of personal data subject to object to ADM noted above, the PDP Law is silent concerning any specific treatment required for handling specific personal data. Nevertheless, Article 34 of the PDP Law requires a personal data controller to conduct a data protection impact assessment (DPIA) if the personal data processing carries a high potential risk for the personal data subject. Processing specific personal data qualifies as high potential risk personal data processing. However, the PDP Law has not yet specified the procedures to conduct a DPIA or stated whether there would be any penalties for non-compliance. Such matters are expected to be further regulated in the implementing regulations.

vi. Distinction between Anonymised, Pseudonymised, or Encrypted

The PDP Law is silent regarding the issues of anonymisation, pseudonymisation, and data encryption. An exception is MCI Regulation 20/2016, which requires all ESPs to store personal data in encrypted form.[49] Nevertheless, according to the PDP Law, one of the requirements for data to be considered personal data and protected by law is that the data are identified or identifiable, either directly or indirectly, to an individual. If anonymisation, pseudonymisation or data encryption causes the data to be unidentifiable to an individual, then the data may fall beyond the application of the PDP Law. To date, there is no guidance on the interpretation and utilisation of anonymisation, pseudonymisation, and data encryption in Indonesia.

[47] 'Pelatihan Pejabat Pelindungan Data Pribadi Bersertifikat' (*Association of Indonesian Data Protection Practitioners* (*AIDPP*), 2024), available at appdi.org/sertifikasi-dpo/. AIDPP is another professional association. These two associations have the same abbreviations for their official name in Indonesian, which misleads the public into perceiving them as one entity. Nevertheless, unlike the IDPPA, the AIDPP decided not to organise training and issue certification for data protection officers due to the absence of competency benchmarks issued and approved by the Government. See also 'Tentang APPDI' (*AIDPP*, 2024), available at appdi.or.id/.

[48] The Official Elucidation of Article 4(3)(f) of the PDP Law clarifies that a phone number and IP address are examples of personal data that are combined to identify a person.

[49] MCI Regulation 20/2016, Art 15(2).

vii. Distinction between Domestic and Cross-Border/International Transfers

The PDP Law distinguishes between domestic and cross-border personal data transfers. As will be detailed below, the PDP Law lays down some requirements for cross-border personal data transfers, which are not applicable to domestic ones.

It is also important to underline that with regard to international personal data transfer in the electronic system, the ESPs are obliged to coordinate with the MCI or the authorised officials/institutions. This obligation applies to the cross-border transfer of personal data in relation to governmental institutions, citizens, and/or private entities domiciled in Indonesia. The coordination with the MCI encompasses: (i) submitting an implementation plan for personal data transfer, which must at least contain the full name of the target country, the full name of the recipient, the date of transfer, and the reasons/purposes of transfer; (ii) requesting advocacy, if necessary; and (iii) submitting an implementation report.[50] It is understood that the purpose of conducting coordination with the MCI before transferring personal data outside Indonesia is to allow the Government of Indonesia (GoI) to oversee the outward flow of information.

Since the PDP Law does not revoke any earlier regulations on the matter, the aforementioned requirements remain applicable for cross-border personal data transfers in the electronic system.

viii. The Privacy Regulator and its Powers

The MCI is currently the supervisory authority on the operation of electronic system operators, including matters relating to personal data protection compliance. Nevertheless, Article 58 of the PDP law introduces a specific data protection authority, though it does not expressly refer to the MCI as the authority nor provides the name of the authority.

The personal data protection authority will be established by the President and be obliged to report directly to him. This authority will have extensive duties and responsibilities, from formulating and stipulating policies and strategies on personal data protection, supervising compliance with personal data protection requirements, to facilitating alternative dispute resolution for personal data protection disputes. The PDP Law also authorises the personal data protection authority to impose administrative sanctions on violations of the provisions of the PDP Law by personal data controllers or processors.

Further provisions regarding the personal data protection authority and its duties are to be regulated in government regulations. It is nonetheless expected that the data protection authority will be established by the President within the two-year grace period of the PDP Law.[51]

In the context of personal data protection and security, it is important to note the role of the National Cyber and Crypto Agency (*Badan Siber dan Sandi Negara*) (BSSN). BSSN is a government agency under the authority of and directly responsible to the President. BSSN is a merger of two institutions, the National Crypto Agency and the Directorate of Information Security and the Directorate General of Informatics Applications at the MCI.

[50] ibid, Art 22.
[51] PDP Law, Art 74.

Thus, BSSN now handles all duties and functions in the field of encryption, as well as information security, secures the use of internet protocol-based telecommunications networks and the security of the existing telecommunications network and infrastructure at the MCI.[52]

III. Legal Bases, Mechanism and Exceptions for International Data Transfers and Data Protection

The PDP Law applies primarily to the 'processing of personal data', which refers to the 'collecting, managing, analysing, storing, revising, updating, displaying, announcing, transferring, disseminating, disclosing, deleting, and/or destroying of personal data'.[53] The PDP Law provides a closed list of what constitutes processing.

Prior to the PDP Law, consent was the primary legal basis for personal data processing. Whilst this approach might be intended as the ultimate form of protection by giving the personal data subjects control over the use of their personal data, the practical implementation of this requirement was considered problematic. It is because, in some circumstances, obtaining consent from a personal data owner is not always straightforward. The PDP Law attempts to resolve this issue by reintroducing several legal bases for personal data processing.[54] They are as follows:

i. Consent – with recorded, expressed, and valid consent from the personal data subject.
ii. Contractual obligations – to fulfil contractual obligations to which the personal data subject is a party or to fulfil the request of the personal data subject upon entering into an agreement.
iii. Legal obligations of the personal data controller – to comply with legal obligations of the personal data controller pursuant to statutory provisions.
iv. Interests of the personal data subject – to fulfil the vital interests of the personal data subject. The Official Elucidation of Article 20(d) of the PDP Law explains that vital interest is related to the survival of the personal data subject. For example, when the processing of personal data is required for severe medical treatment.[55]
v. Public interest – to fulfil the personal data controller's duty in the context of public interest, public service, or the implementation of his authority pursuant to the law and regulations.
vi. Other legitimate interest – fulfilment of other legitimate interests by taking into account the purposes, needs, and balance of the interest of the personal data controllers and the rights of the personal data subject.

These legal bases of personal data transfers were already stipulated in Article 14(4) of Government Regulation 71/2019. However, as Government Regulation 71/2019 only governs personal data transfers relating to electronic systems and transactions, it is conceivable that

[52] Presidential Regulation Number 28 of 2021 on the National Cyber and Crypto Agency.
[53] PDP Law, Art 16(1).
[54] ibid, Art 20(2).
[55] Referring to Art 14(4) of Government Regulation 71/2019, 'vital interest' is also understood as the need to protect fundamental matters about an individual's existence.

the PDP Law reintroduces these legal bases to expand their application to cover personal data transfers in non-electronic systems and transactions.

Moreover, these legal bases are modelled after those stipulated in the GDPR. Similar to the GDPR, the aforementioned legal bases are placed on an even level – no single legal basis takes precedence over any other. Nevertheless, implementing these requirements demands voluntary compliance and obliges every related party to determine and to assess the most relevant legal basis for personal data processing. In this regard, the implementing regulations specifying guidelines on assessing the applicability of each lawful basis are expected to shed some light on this matter.

A. International Data Transfer

i. 'Adequacy Findings' or Whitelists and Blacklists

Prior to the PDP Law, cross-border data transfers were only subject to the general requirements of: (i) coordinating with the MCI by submitting a cross-border personal data transfer report; and (ii) complying with the requirements specified in the relevant laws and regulations.

The PDP Law introduces layered requirements for international personal data transfers. A personal data controller sending data overseas must ensure that the receiving country has an equal or higher mechanism of personal data protection. This requirement may only be exempted if the sending data controller can ensure that adequate and binding personal data protection is available in the receiving country. In the event neither of these two requirements can be satisfied, the sending data controller must obtain consent from the personal data subject to transfer the personal data abroad.[56] The future implementing regulations are expected to detail international data transfer requirements. It is noteworthy that similar requirements on the adequacy of protection for transferring personal data abroad have previously been introduced in the context of e-commerce under Government Regulation 80/2019.[57]

While the requirements for international data transfer stipulated in the PDP Law seem straightforward, several matters need further clarification. First, the PDP Law only uses the term 'personal data controller' for international data transfers, which might suggest that only data controllers are allowed to transfer personal data abroad. Second, it remains to be seen which countries are deemed to have an equivalent or higher level of personal data protection and which institution will be given the duty to determine the list of such countries. In this regard, the PDP Law indicates that the personal data protection authority has the power to assess the fulfilment of the requirements for cross-border personal data transfer. Since the personal data protection authority is yet to be set up, it is also uncertain which institution would bear that duty. The MCI conceivably is the authority that holds the duty until the personal data protection authority is set up or designated. Third, it remains unclear whether such an assessment would be done as part of the notification to the MCI

[56] PDP Law, Art 56.
[57] Government Regulation 80/2019, Art 59(2)(h).

before the transfer or as part of the report after the transfer. It is expected that the implementing regulations mandated by the PDP Law will clarify these issues. It also remains to be seen whether the forthcoming implementing regulations will also include whitelists and blacklists of particular jurisdictions, standardised contractual language, and particular data processing activities such as pseudonymisation and encryption for international data transfer purposes.

Since the PDP Law does not revoke any earlier regulations on the matter, and the obligation to coordinate with the MCI as regards international data transfer stipulated in Article 22 of the MCI Regulations 20/2016 is not contradictory to the PDP Law, it is plausible that data controllers must still report pre- and post-offshore data transfers to the MCI for transferring data abroad.

ii. Consent of Data Subjects as Exception to Existence of Privacy Safeguards Overseas

As mentioned earlier, expressed consent from the personal data subject is one of the legal bases for the personal data controller to carry out data transfers. The consent from the data subject must be provided explicitly in written or recorded form. The consent may be submitted either electronically or non-electronically. The consent itself shall be self-explanatory, in an accessible format, and written in straightforward language. It is important to note that consent shall be made in the Indonesian language. The consent will be declared null and void if these requirements are not satisfied.[58]

In obtaining consent from the personal data subject, the personal data controller is required to provide the following information: (i) confirmation that the data processing shall be carried out for lawful purposes; (ii) the purposes of the data processing; (iii) the type and relevance of the personal data to be processed; (iv) the retention period for documents containing personal data; (v) details regarding the information collected; (vi) the period for processing personal data; and (vii) the rights of the personal data subject. In the event that there is a change of information related to these seven aspects, the data controllers must notify the personal data subject prior to the change of such information.[59]

The PDP Law allows personal data transfers to be carried out to fulfil obligations under an agreement to which the personal data subject is a party or to fulfil the data subject's request upon entering into an agreement.[60] The agreement, which includes a request for the processing of personal data but does not contain explicit valid consent from the data subject, will be declared null and void.[61]

iii. APEC Cross-Border Privacy Rules System

As a member of the APEC, Indonesia and the other 20 members have developed the APEC Cross-Border Privacy Rules (APEC CBPR). In 2011, together with the other APEC Leaders,

[58] PDP Law, Art 22 and its Official Elucidation.
[59] ibid, Art 21.
[60] ibid, Art 20(2)(b).
[61] ibid, Art 23.

the President of Indonesia at that time, Susilo Bambang Yudhoyono, endorsed the APEC CBPR. Nevertheless, to date, Indonesia has yet to submit a Notice of Intent to participate in the APEC CBPR.[62] In addition, Indonesia has not indicated her interest in joining the APEC Cross-Border Privacy Enforcement Arrangement (CPEA).[63]

The PDP Law asserts that the GoI may conduct international cooperation with other countries or international organisations concerning personal data protection.[64] Thus, it is expected that Indonesia will involve more at the regional and international levels regarding endeavours in protecting personal data.

iv. International Privacy Certification Schemes, Trustmarks or Privacy Seals

MCI Regulation 20/2016 requires ESPs to certify the electronic system they use for personal data processing.[65] In a different vein, Government Regulation 71/2019 obliges ESPs to obtain an electronic certificate. Simply put, according to Government Regulation 71/2019, the certification is not for the electronic system used by the ESPs, but for the ESPs themselves. The obligation to obtain an electronic certificate especially applies to SSL Encryption. In addition, this government regulation also provides that electronic system users may be obliged to obtain an electronic certificate for electronic transactions. ESPs and electronic system users shall apply to the Indonesian Electronic Certification Operator to obtain an electronic certificate.[66]

As to electronic certification operators operating in Indonesia, Government Regulation 71/2019 and MCI Regulation Number 11 of 2018 on Organising Electronic Certification ('MCI Regulation 11/2018') distinguish Indonesian and foreign electronic certification operators. Both Indonesian and foreign electronic certification operators are required to be acknowledged by MCI.[67]

B. International Data Protection and Liability

i. Specific Requirements or Policies for Data Processing and Retention

As noted earlier, the PDP Law is not applicable for personal data processing by individuals on private or household matters. Unfortunately, the law is silent on what those activities are. This matter is expected to be elaborated on in the implementing regulations.

As also addressed previously, the PDP Law states that processing children's data shall be subject to consent from the parents and/or the child's legal guardian. As to persons with disabilities, the PDP Law requires the processing of their data to be carried out through

[62] 'Participation in the APEC Cross-Border Privacy Rules (CBPR) System Affords Asia-Pacific Economic Cooperation Members a Unique Opportunity to work' (*CBPRs*, 2024), available at cbprs.org/government/.

[63] 'APEC Cross-Border Privacy Enforcement Arrangement' (*APEC*, 2024), available at www.apec.org/groups/committee-on-trade-and-investment/digital-economy-steering-group/cross-border-privacy-enforcement-arrangement#:~:text=The%20APEC%20Cross%2Dborder%20Privacy,an%20APEC%20economy%20may%20participate.

[64] PDP Law, Art 62.

[65] MCI Regulation 20/2016, Art 28(a).

[66] Government Regulation 71/2019, Art 51(1)-(4) and its Official Elucidation.

[67] ibid, Art 53 and its Official Elucidation; MCI Regulation 11/2018, Art 4.

specific communication means according to the regulations. Such personal data processing is also subject to the consent of the person with disabilities and/or his legal guardian.

There are also partial exemptions in the PDP Law. For example, particular personal data subject's rights can be derogated when the purpose of the processing of personal data is for: (i) national defence and security purposes; (ii) law enforcement; (iii) public interest purposes in the context of state administration (citizenship administration, social security, customs, taxation, licensing); (iv) supervision in the financial services sector, monetary and payment systems, and financial system stability carried out in the context of state administration, which falls under the supervision of Bank Indonesia, Indonesian Financial Services Authority, and Indonesian Deposit Insurance Agency; or (v) statistical and scientific research purposes.[68]

The PDP Law regulates that personal data controllers must cease personal data processing once the data retention period has been reached and subsequently destroy or delete the personal data.[69] Nevertheless, the PDP Law is silent concerning a timeframe for data retention or a maximum retention period. In this regard, Article 15(3)(b) of the MCI Regulation 20/2016 states that personal data are stored in an electronic system for a minimum period of five years. In addition, Archives Law is another regulation that can be referred to as regards the retention period for personal data. The Archives Law sets out that concealed archives may be declared to be retained for a maximum of 25 years.[70]

ii. Regulations on Legal Ownership of Data Protection and Privacy Rights

As pointed out above, protecting personal data is considered part of human rights protection. Article 5 of the PDP Law specifies that personal data subjects are entitled to information about the clarity of identity, the basis of legal interests, the purpose of requesting and using personal data, and the accountability of the party requesting their personal data. In addition, as to data protection in the electronic system, MCI Regulation 20/2016 specifies that personal data protection shall be carried out according to respect towards data as one's privacy. This privacy is perceived as the freedom of personal data owners either to declare confidentiality or to disclose their data, unless otherwise indicated according to the laws and regulations.[71]

Article 65(2) of the PDP Law provides that everyone is prohibited from unlawfully revealing personal data that does not belong to him. This provision serves as an anti-doxxing regulation in Indonesia.

iii. Extraterritorial Effect of Laws on Data Protection and Privacy

Article 2(1)(b) of the PDP Law confirms its extraterritorial scope as it would cover any individuals, corporations, public bodies, and international organisations that carry out legal acts stipulated in the PDP Law outside the jurisdiction of Indonesia, provided that such legal conduct has legal consequences in Indonesia and/or to an Indonesian personal data

[68] PDP Law, Art 15.
[69] ibid, Arts 16(2)(g) and 42(1).
[70] Archives Law, Art 66(1).
[71] MCI Regulation 20/2016, Arts 2(2)(a), 2(3), 8, and 9.

subject outside of the Indonesian jurisdiction. The extraterritorial provision provided in the PDP Law implies that any offshore entity that processes personal data in any of the aforementioned manners will also be subject to the PDP Law. However, it remains to be seen how the thresholds of the term 'legal consequences' will be regulated in the implementing regulations of the PDP Law.

The extraterritoriality application of the PDP Law offers more certainty for the Indonesian personal data protection regime. Earlier regulations on personal data protection are not always straightforward as regards their extraterritoriality effect. Only the EIT Law, which provides rules on data protection in the electronic information and transactions sector, expressly lays down its extraterritoriality application. According to Article 2, the EIT Law applies to every individual or legal entity who commits legal acts regulated under the Law, either in or outside of the Indonesian jurisdiction, which has legal consequences in the Indonesian jurisdiction and/or outside of the Indonesian jurisdiction and is detrimental to Indonesia's interest. The Official Elucidation of Article 2 of the EIT law further emphasises that the provision encompasses the legal acts carried out in or outside Indonesia by Indonesian national and legal entities, as well as foreign nationals and legal entities. Furthermore, according to the Official Elucidation, the phrase 'detrimental to Indonesia's interest' should be construed to include, but not be limited to, detriments to national economic interests, strategic data protection, the dignity of the nation, state defence and security, state sovereignty, citizens, as well as Indonesian legal entities.

iv. Data Breach Notification

In the event of a security breach, the PDP Law requires personal data controllers to submit written notification to the affected personal data subject and to the data protection authority no later than three days. The notice must contain the personal data involved in the breach, when and how the breach occurred, and any remedial measures taken by the data controller to mitigate harm.[72] In certain cases, personal data controllers may be obliged to inform the public about the data breach. Further guidance and implementing regulations specifying additional information on this matter are anticipated.

The provision concerning data breach notification stipulated in the PDP Law is a stricter requirement than that provided in the earlier regulations, for which the deadline to notify the personal data subject is 14 days after becoming aware of such breach.[73] As the stipulation in the earlier regulation is contradictory to that in the PDP Law, the provision on data breach notification in the PDP Law prevails.

IV. Data Security and Data Localisation

A. Data Security and Localisation Requirements

The PDP Law states that personal data controllers are required to adopt security measures to protect and ensure the security of the personal data they process. The security measures

[72] PDP Law, Art 46.
[73] MCI Regulation 20/2016, Art 28(c)(3).

shall include preparing and implementing technical and operational measures and employing a risk-based approach to determine the level of appropriate security for the personal data.[74] Personal data controllers also have to maintain the confidentiality of the data and to prevent them from being accessed unlawfully.[75] However, the PDP Law does not specify the required security measures. Therefore, the implementing regulations of the PDP Law are expected to provide the details for such matters.

In the electronic systems and transactions sector, Government Regulation 71/2019 distinguishes ESPs into two categories, Public ESPs and Private ESPs.[76] Public ESPs are defined as (i) state administration agencies and (ii) institutions appointed by state administration agencies to operate electronic systems on behalf of the appointing state administration agencies.[77] Meanwhile, Private ESPs are individuals, business entities, and the public that (i) are regulated or supervised by the ministries or institutions based on laws and regulations[78] and (ii) provide portals, sites, or applications via the Internet that are used for particular purposes, such as providing, managing, operating offers, and trading of goods and services. This definition encompasses ESPs whose electronic system is used or offered in Indonesia.[79]

Furthermore, Government Regulation 71/2019 requires Public and Private ESPs to be registered. Such registration should take place before the electronic system is made available for public use. The registration should be filed to the MCI and will be processed through an electronic integrated business licensing service, known as Online Single Submission (OSS).[80] The obligation to register also applies to Private ESPs established and domiciled abroad as long as they provide services, conduct business, and/or provide an electronic system that is used or offered in Indonesia.[81]

Although Public and Private ESPs must be registered, the data localisation requirement is applied differently. As to this matter, Government Regulation 71/2019 regulates that Public ESPs are required to process and to store electronic data and systems in Indonesia. Exemptions apply if the technology for processing and storing electronic data and systems is unavailable in Indonesia. A committee established by the MCI has the duty to determine the non-availability of such technology[82] so that a Public ESP is allowed to process and store electronic data and systems abroad.

On the other hand, Private ESPs may process and store electronic data and systems in or outside Indonesia. It implies that Private ESPs are allowed to maintain and store their data in an offshore data centre. Nevertheless, Private ESPs are still obliged to ensure that the GoI can effectively supervise the Private ESPs' processing and storing of such electronic data and systems. For this purpose, Private ESPs are required to give access to their electronic

[74] PDP Law, Art 35.
[75] ibid, Arts 38–39.
[76] Government Regulation 71/2019, Arts 1(5) and 2(2).
[77] Article 1(35) of the Government Regulation 71/2019 defines 'state administration agencies' as legislative, executive, and judiciary institutions at the central and regional levels, and other agencies formed by laws and regulations.
[78] For example, ESPs are supervised by the Indonesian Financial Services Authority.
[79] Government Regulation 71/2019, Arts 1(6) and 2(5) and the Official Elucidation.
[80] Government Regulation 71/2019, Art 6; MCI Regulation Number 5/2020, as amended by MCI Regulation 10/2021, Art 2.
[81] MCI Regulation Number 5/2020, as amended by MCI Regulation 10/2021, Art 4.
[82] Government Regulation 71/2019, Art 20(1)-(5).

systems and data upon receiving a written request from a relevant ministry, government agency, or law enforcement authority.[83]

Specific provisions on data localisation apply to the financial sector in Indonesia. OJK Regulation 11/2022 requires commercial banks to locate their electronic system in data centres and disaster recovery centres in Indonesia. Nevertheless, commercial banks, with permission from the Financial Services Authority, are allowed to locate their electronic system in data centres and disaster recovery centres abroad.[84]

In a similar vein, the Regulation of Financial Services Authority Number 4/POJK.05/2021 on the Implementation of Risk Management in the Use of Information Technology by Non-Bank Financial Service Institutions ('OJK Regulation 4/2021') states that non-bank financial service institutions that have data centres and disaster recovery centres[85] are required to locate their electronic system in the data centres and disaster recovery centres in Indonesia. An approval from the Financial Services Authority is a prerequisite for the non-bank financial service to locate their electronic system in the data centres and disaster recovery centres outside of Indonesia.[86]

B. Data Security or Localisation Requirements for Particular Types of Data

Law Number 17 of 2011 on State Intelligence ('SI Law') addresses the protection of information qualified as intelligence secrets. Article 25 of the SI Law stipulates that intelligence secrets are part of state secrets. Intelligence secrets are categorised to be those that might:

i. endanger the country's defence and security;
ii. reveal Indonesia's natural wealth classified as confidential;
iii. harm the resilience of the national economy;
iv. harm the interests of foreign policy and foreign relations;
v. disclose memorandum or letters which, according to its nature, necessary to be kept confidential;
vi. endanger the state intelligence system;
vii. endanger access, agents, and sources related to the implementation of intelligence functions;
viii. endanger the safety of state intelligence personnel; or
ix. reveal plans and implementation relating to the intelligence functions.

Intelligence secrets are subject to a retention period valid for 25 years. This retention period may be extended after obtaining approval from the House of Representatives of the Republic of Indonesia. Intelligence secrets may be disclosed prior to the end of its retention period,

[83] ibid, Art 21.
[84] OJK Regulation 11/2022, Art 35.
[85] Non-bank financial service institutions with assets between 500 billion and one trillion rupiahs are required to have a data centre. Meanwhile, non-bank financial service institutions are required to have a disaster recovery centre if their asset exceeds one trillion rupiahs, or the majority of their business operation relies on information technology. See OJK Regulation 4/2021, Art 22(2) and (4).
[86] OJK Regulation 4/2021, Art 23.

limited only to the interest of a court proceeding, and such a proceeding is closed to the public. In this regard, the retention period shall revive after the court proceeding concludes.

The legal instrument pertaining to the security of intelligence data is Regulation of the Prosecutor's Office of the Republic of Indonesia Number 5 of 2021 on the Intelligence Data and Information Management System of the Prosecutor's Office of the Republic of Indonesia ('PO Regulation 5/2021'). This instrument prescribes that intelligence data and information are archived in the Intelligence Data Bank. The security of the Intelligence Data Bank is carried out by utilising information technology support. Nevertheless, this regulation does not specify the technology to be used or the localisation requirements. This regulation also only concerns the safekeeping of intelligence data related to the duties of the Indonesian Prosecutor's Office.

V. Issues in Private and International Law

A. Litigations Involving Cross-Border Data Protection and Privacy

The PDP Law does not provide provisions specifically for cross-border data protection and privacy litigations. Nevertheless, referring to the scope application of the PDP Law,[87] any personal data subject, regardless of his country of origin and place of residence, is the potential claimant in the litigation proceedings in Indonesia if (1) his data is violated in the Indonesian jurisdiction or (2) outside of the Indonesian jurisdiction, provided that the data violation has legal consequences (a) in the Indonesian jurisdiction and/or (b) to an Indonesian personal data subject outside of the Indonesian jurisdiction.

On the other hand, any individuals, corporations, public bodies, and international organisations, regardless of their origin and residence, whether they act as personal data controllers or processors, are the potential defendants for their wrongdoing to the rights of a data subject, provided that their wrongdoing occurred (1) in the Indonesian jurisdiction or (2) outside of the Indonesian jurisdiction, resulting in legal impacts (a) in the Indonesian jurisdiction or (b) to an Indonesian personal data subject outside of the Indonesian jurisdiction.

It is also interesting to point out that any individuals, corporations, public bodies, and international organisations may still be brought as defendants if they violate the rights of a data subject according to the PDP Law, although they do not act as personal data controllers or processors. They can be sued if their misconduct occurred in the Indonesian territory or outside of Indonesia but have legal consequences in Indonesia or to an Indonesian personal data subject outside of Indonesia.

According to the PDP Law, personal data protection disputes are settled through arbitration, courts, or other alternative dispute resolution institutions.[88] The PDP Law imposes administrative and criminal penalties for violations in personal data processing. As addressed earlier, the anticipated data protection authority[89] will be the authority to impose

[87] PDP Law, Art 2.
[88] ibid, Art 64.
[89] ibid, Art 58.

administrative sanctions. The administrative sanctions may be in the form of: (i) a written warning; (ii) temporary suspension of processing activities; (iii) forced deletion of personal data; and/or (iv) administrative fines of a maximum of two per cent of annual revenue or sales of the personal data controllers. A detailed fine structure and guidance on the process for disputing or appealing are to be specified in the implementing regulations of the PDP Law.[90]

As to criminal liability, it will be imposed if (i) one illegally acquires, collects, discloses, or uses personal data that does not belong to them to benefit themselves or other persons at the harmful expense of a data subject,[91] and (ii) one intentionally creates false personal data to benefit themselves or other persons which may result in a loss for other persons.[92] These crimes are punishable by maximum imprisonment ranging from four to six years or a maximum fine ranging from four to six billion rupiahs.[93] While corporations may only be fined for criminal offences, it can be increased to 10 times of the maximum fines applicable to individual offenders. In addition, the management, the authority, the beneficial owner of a corporation could be incarcerated and fined for their actions for and on behalf of the corporation.[94]

In addition, according to Article 12 of the PDP Law, a personal data subject has the right to sue and receive compensation for violations of his data. The provisions regarding the remedy and compensation will be further detailed in the implementing regulations.

There has been no cross-border litigation regarding data protection and privacy in Indonesia yet. To date, litigations on this matter only pertain to domestic disputes.

B. Jurisdictional Issues Involving Cross-Border Data Protection and Privacy

Indonesian civil procedural law adheres mainly to the *actor sequitur forum rei* principle to establish a court's jurisdiction in civil cases.[95] A civil lawsuit is to be filed in the court of the defendant's place of residence or the court where the defendant's legal seat is situated if it involves a legal person. If the defendant's place of residence is unknown, the lawsuit is to be submitted to the court of the defendant's factual residence. If there are multiple defendants, the claimant has the right to select the court of one of the defendants' places of residence in order to lodge the legal suit. The court of the claimant's place of residence may have jurisdiction (*forum actoris*), provided that the defendant's place of residence or factual residence is unidentified. If the case concerns immovable goods, the court where such goods are located has jurisdiction over the case (*jurisdiction in rem*). In addition, the parties may choose a legal domicile in a written deed for their legal relationship beforehand. In this situation, the claimant has the option to lodge the legal suit in the court of the defendant's place of

[90] ibid, Art 57.
[91] ibid, Art 65.
[92] ibid, Art 66.
[93] As of 22 February 2024, it is equivalent to USD260,000 – USD390,000.
[94] PDP Law, Art 70.
[95] *Herziene Indonesisch Reglement*, S 1941 number 44 ('HIR'), Art 118; *Reglement tot Regeling van het Rechtswezen in de Gewesten Buiten Java en Madura*, S 1855 number 2 ('RBg'), Art 142. Indonesian civil procedural law still relies mainly on HIR and RBg, the regulations on civil procedural law inherited from the Dutch East Indies period.

residence or the court of the chosen legal domicile. It is certain that the Indonesian court would exercise jurisdiction following these provisions in settling cross-border disputes regarding personal data protection and privacy.

Indonesian civil procedural law is silent as to parallel litigation. Since no cross-border litigation has taken place regarding data protection and privacy disputes in Indonesia to date, the court's approach in this situation is unascertainable. Nevertheless, in case of parallel litigation, it is conceivable that the court would retain its jurisdiction and continue the proceeding taking place in Indonesia, regardless of an ongoing proceeding of the same matter in another country.

C. Applicable Law in Litigations Involving Cross-border Data Protection and Privacy

Indonesia has yet to codify its Private International Law (PIL) rules. Articles 16–18 of the *Algemene Bepalingen van Wetgeving voor Indonesië* ('AB'), inherited from the Dutch East Indies period, are preserved to date as the primary sources of PIL in Indonesia. Article 16 of the AB emphasises that the law of one's nationality shall determine the law applicable to natural persons.[96] Article 17 adheres to the *lex rei sitae* principle, which specifies that the law of the place where the goods are located shall apply. Article 18 reads that the law that governs legal actions is the law of the place where such activity is conducted. In general, these articles are the main rules in determining the applicable law in PIL cases in Indonesia. Nevertheless, these Articles are deemed far too limited and rudimentary to resolve PIL problems of a complex and mature legal system.[97] The aforementioned sources are complemented, to a limited extent, by the scattered national laws enacted after independence.[98]

In light of the limited statutory framework on PIL, the extent to which the Indonesian courts apply foreign law is uncertain. It is also interesting to note that the Indonesian courts tend to exhibit disinterest in PIL matters and foreign law.[99]

The PDP Law is silent concerning the law applicable to data or any connecting factor to be employed in determining the law applicable to data. However, bearing in mind the scope of application of the PDP Law as detailed earlier, Indonesian law would be applicable to any legal acts concerning personal data processing encompassed by the scope of the PDP Law. Another reference as regards the applicable law in the PDP Law pertains only to the procedural law. The PDP Law states that the procedural law that applies in dispute settlement or judicial process of personal data protection is carried out based on the applicable procedural law in Indonesia.[100]

[96] This rule is reaffirmed by Law Number 12 of 2006 on Nationality.

[97] These Articles pertain to the *statuta* theory of the Italian city-states in the 14th century. As the anchor of Indonesian PIL, Articles 16–18 AB concern only the matter of applicable law, leaving out the matters concerning establishing Indonesian court jurisdiction or recognising and enforcing foreign judgments.

[98] These laws, among others, are Law Number 1 of 1974 on Marriage, which provides rules concerning international marriage and Law Number 40 of 2007 on Limited Liability Company as amended by Law 6 of 2023, which provides rules concerning the law applicable to a limited liability company.

[99] See Priskila Pratita Penasthika, *Unravelling Choice of Law in International Commercial Contracts – Indonesia as an Illustrative Case Study* (Eleven International Publishing, 2022) 86–87, 111–66.

[100] PDP Law, Art 64(2).

It is worth noting that a stipulation touching upon applicable law to international electronic contracts is available in the EIT Law. Article 18 of the EIT Law stipulates that the law applicable to international electronic transactions is the law as chosen by the parties. However, choice of law in electronic transactions may only be exercised in contracts that bear a foreign element, and its application must be in line with PIL rules. The EIT Law further provides that in the absence of choice of law by the parties, the law applicable to their international electronic transaction shall be determined according to PIL rules.[101]

The amendments of the EIT Law in 2024 address the law governing electronic contracts. A new provision, Article 18A, is added to the EIT Law. This Article stipulates that an international electronic contract that uses standard clauses made by Electronic System Operators ('**ESOs**') shall be governed by Indonesian law in the situation of (i) the user of the ESOs' services, as a party to the electronic transaction, is from Indonesia and gives their consent from or within the Indonesian jurisdiction, (ii) the contract is performed in Indonesia, and/or (iii) the ESOs has a place of business or carries out business activities in Indonesia. The Official Elucidation of Article 18A specifies that Indonesian law shall also govern the settlement of any disputes that may arise between the ESOs and the users.

Due to the lack of statutory provisions on PIL rules, scholars' opinions play a significant role in the field of PIL. The late Sudargo Gautama, the most prolific Indonesian PIL scholar, was of the view that the application of foreign law should not be at variance with the public order and international mandatory rules of Indonesia. As to public order, Gautama firmly advocated it as being an *ultimum remidium* measure. Meanwhile, international mandatory rules are those with a significant social-economic function, so they have mandatory force and become imperative for international relations. According to Gautama, these rules usually deal with matters in public law but have an impact on private relations, including those in international settings.[102] Nevertheless, due to disinterest towards PIL matters and foreign laws, the Indonesian courts rarely invoke public order or international mandatory rules as grounds to set aside the application of foreign laws.

D. Recognition and Enforcement of Foreign Judgments Involving Data Protection and Privacy

Indonesia has a firm attitude that a foreign judgment is unenforceable unless it concerns damages arising from marine salvage (*averij grosse*). A foreign judgment must be tried afresh before the Indonesian court, and the foreign judgment may serve as prima facie evidence in the new proceedings.[103] However, the judges are at liberty to determine whether and to what extent the foreign judgment in question is taken into account as evidence.

[101] EIT Law, Art 18 and its Official Elucidation.

[102] Sudargo Gautama, *Hukum Perdata Internasional Indonesia [Indonesian Private International Law]* 2nd edn (Alumni, 2004) Vol 2 Part 4-Book 5, 133–45, 178–80.

[103] *Reglement op de Burgerlijke Rechtsverordering*, S 1847 number 52 ('RV'), Art 436(1)-(2). During the Dutch East Indies period, the RV was the civil procedural law applicable to civil disputes involving members of the European group before the European courts. In light of the absence of corresponding provisions in the HIR or the RBg, the judicial practice in Indonesia has recourse to the RV.

It is, nevertheless, interesting to point out that case law and doctrine have distinguished between the concept of recognition and the enforcement of a foreign judgment. Legal scholars consider that recognition does not require an active action by the court, while enforcement entails more active action.[104] Provided that it is valid and rendered by a competent foreign court as well as being subject to the Indonesian public order, a foreign judgment of a declaratory or constitutive nature is recognisable in Indonesia.[105] The rationale is that these types of judgments simply establish rights and obligations for the parties in a particular civil status or civil relationship. Thus, only foreign judgments of a condemnatory nature, regardless of whether it is monetary or non-monetary-related, will not be assisted in terms of execution by Indonesian courts.[106]

Following this stand, it is indisputable that the Indonesian courts would not assist in recognising and enforcing a condemnatory foreign judgment involving data protection and privacy matters.

E. Obstacles to Effective Data Protection

The lack of proper rules and statutory provisions on PIL poses an obstacle to effective data protection and privacy in Indonesia. As mentioned earlier, the prevailing primary sources of Indonesian PIL are considered outdated and concern only the matter of applicable law. None of them addresses the matters concerning the establishment of Indonesian court jurisdiction or the recognition and enforcement of foreign judgments. Therefore, the civil procedural laws for domestic cases, as regulated in *Herziene Indonesisch Reglement* ('HIR')/ *Reglement tot Regeling van het Rechtswezen in de Gewesten Buiten Java en Madura* ('RBg') and *Reglement op de Burgerlijke Rechtsverordering* ('RV'), are made applicable to both matters. Due to these circumstances, some questions related to data protection and privacy remain unanswered. The questions include, for example, matters concerning the basis of the Indonesian court jurisdiction over cross-border personal data disputes. It is unclear whether: (i) the place of residence of the defendant as stipulated in the HIR/RBg; (ii) the provision on the possibility of a non-resident foreigner to be sued before an Indonesian court for his obligations to an Indonesian national as provided in Article 100 RV; (iii) the location of a data centre or a server; or (iv) the legal consequences occurred in Indonesia, as prescribed in the scope of application of the PDP Law, would be the decisive factor for the Indonesian court in exercising its jurisdiction over the cross-border personal data disputes.

The absence of provisions concerning the connecting factor to determine the law applicable to data is another factor that poses a challenge to effective data protection in Indonesia. However, considering the scope of the PDP Law and the tendency of the Indonesian courts

[104] Sudargo Gautama, 'International Civil Procedure in Indonesia' (1996) 6 *Asian Yearbook of International Law* 87, 96–97.

[105] For example, a judgment regarding divorce, the validity or nullity of marriage, the ownership of goods, or the annulment of a contract.

[106] Sudargo Gautama and Robert N Hornick, *An Introduction to Indonesian Law Unity in Diversity* (Alumni Press, 1974) 177–78; Sudargo Gautama, *Hukum Perdata Internasional Indonesia [Indonesian Private International Law]*, 8th edn (Alumni, 2013) Vol III Part 2-Book 8, 282–83.

to be indifferent to foreign laws, it is conceivable that the court would apply Indonesian law to cross-border personal data disputes. In addition, as mentioned earlier, the Indonesian firm position of not recognising and enforcing foreign judgments also poses difficulties for an effective data protection.

There is no plan or ongoing discussion that Indonesia would take into account Lisbon Guidelines on Privacy.

VI. Topical Issues and Prospects

A. Artificial Intelligence or AI-Generated Data

Taking into account its position as the largest digital economy market in Southeast Asia, the GoI launched the Indonesia National Artificial Intelligence Strategy 2020–2045 (*Strategi Nasional Kecerdasan Artificial*) ('Stranas KA') in August 2020.[107]

According to the Ministry of Research and Technology and the National Research and Innovation Agency, Stranas KA aims to advance the Indonesian economy through leadership in AI from 2020 to 2045. It outlines five national priorities where AI is anticipated to have the most significant impact and outcomes: (i) health services; (ii) bureaucratic reform; (iii) education and research; (iv) food security; as well as (v) mobility and smart cities. As such, Stranas KA ties together many of the digital developments taking place in the country and aligns closely with Indonesia Vision 2045 (*Visi Indonesia 2045*), the national grand development strategy to commemorate the centenary of Indonesian independence.[108]

The realisation of Stranas KA, nonetheless, encounters challenges. Specific provisions to regulate the use of AI remain lacking. The provision that touches upon AI in the PDP Law is Article 10, which stipulates that a personal data subject has the right to submit an objection to the ADM, including profiling, which creates legal consequences or significantly impacts the personal data subject. The Official Elucidation of this Article explains that 'profiling' shall also encompass electronically identifying personal data subject's movements. Additionally, as noted earlier, Article 17 of the PDP Law allows the use of facial recognition technology or visual data processing devices in public places limited only for security, disaster prevention, or traffic information analysis. These provisions allude to the use of AI, but they do not provide details on handling such technology.

BSSN is currently the agency mandated to oversee AI's governance and ethical use in Indonesia. However, the Stranas KA guidebook advises the formation of a data ethics board to oversee AI development and regulate the national standards for AI innovation. In this regard, it remains to be seen how the data ethics board will join forces with BSSN and the

[107] 'AI Towards Indonesia's Vision 2045' (*AIIS*, 2024), available at https://ai-innovation.id/strategi; 'Indonesia Artificial Intelligence' (*Asia Society*, 2022), available at asiasociety.org/policy-institute/raising-standards-data-ai-southeast-asia/ai/Indonesia.

[108] 'President Jokowi Calls for Grand Strategy for Indonesia's 2045 Vision' (*Cabinet Secretariat of the Republic of Indonesia*, 2023), available at setkab.go.id/en/president-jokowi-calls-for-grand-strategy-for-indonesias-2045-vision/.

data protection authority, mandated by the PDP Law to be established, to protect personal data in the context of AI use in Indonesia.

B. Potential Cooperation under Belt and Road Initiative

Indonesia is one of the leading destinations of the Belt and Road Initiative (BRI). Consequently, Indonesia has also become China's strategic partner in the Digital Silk Road (DSR). In this regard, Indonesia has warmly welcomed numerous investments from China, especially in digital telecommunication infrastructure, financial technology, and e-commerce sectors.

Huawei, a Chinese telecom giant, is one of Indonesia's main partners in the DSR framework. In June 2015, Huawei and the MCI agreed to cooperate in building a training centre for innovation in Jakarta to accelerate human resources in Indonesia's information and communication technology sector.[109] Huawei is also partnering with Indonesia's Agency for the Assessment and Application of Technology (BPPT) in the fields of AI, cloud computing, and 5G networks in Indonesia. This collaboration is marked by a Memorandum of Understanding (MoU) signed by Huawei and BPPT in October 2020.[110] In addition, Huawei signed contracts with Indosat Ooredoo, Indonesia's second-largest telecommunication firm, for the installation of 5G network infrastructure in primary areas of Indonesia.[111] These collaborations are also followed by the plan to establish data centres in Indonesia, led by Tencent Cloud and Alibaba Cloud.

The materialisation of collaboration between Indonesia and China concerning the DSR also occurred at the state level. In January 2021, during a visit by the Chinese Foreign Minister, Indonesia and China signed the MoU to improve internet security and technological cooperation. The signing of the MoU is notable because Indonesia is the first foreign country with whom China has signed an internet security agreement. The MoU details the cooperation between the BSSN and the Cyberspace Administration of China (CAC) on the internet governance system, data security, and the cyberspace order.[112]

Nevertheless, there is no specific materialisation concerning data transfer management and protection for the aforementioned collaborations in Indonesia. There are concerns about the risk of surveillance and data leaking because most data would be transmitted and relayed by Chinese-designed base station technology and data centres. In this regard, it is conceivable that the newly enacted PDP Law will serve as the legal framework for the data protection and transfer of those collaborations.

[109] 'Huawei Bangun Pusat Inovasi Untuk Kembangkan SDM di Bidang ICT' (*Kominfo*, 2015), available at www.kominfo.go.id/content/detail/5022/huawei-bangun-pusat-inovasi-untuk-kembangkan-sdm-di-bidang-ict/0/sorotan_media.

[110] 'BPPT, Huawei Team up to Develop AI, Cloud and 5G' (*The Jakarta Post*, 2020), available at www.thejakartapost.com/news/2020/10/13/bppt-huawei-team-up-to-develop-ai-cloud-and-5g.html.

[111] 'Indosat Ooredoo Partners Huawei to Build 5G Transport Networks' (*IDN Financials*, 2020), available at www.idnfinancials.com/news/36871/indosat-ooredoo-partners-huawei-build-g-transport-networks.

[112] 'China, Indonesia Sign MoU on Internet Security Amid Washington Pressure on Beijing's 5G Technology' (*Global Times*, 2021), available at www.globaltimes.cn/page/202101/1212657.shtml.

C. Data Protection Post COVID-19 Pandemic

The change in data transfer and privacy regulation in Indonesia in the context of the COVID-19 pandemic occurred concerning the use of *PeduliLindungi*, the country's COVID-19 digital contact tracing application. The use of *PeduliLindungi* was established by Decree of the MCI Number 171 of 2020.

The security and protection of the personal data of *PeduliLindungi*'s users were heavily criticised. To respond to the criticism, the MCI held a press conference on 17 April 2020, ensuring the public about the application's security from phishing and malware.[113] Additionally, the MCI collaborated with the BSSN to enhance the security system of *PeduliLindungi*. In this regard, the BSSN assessed each version of the application prior to its release to the public.[114] The users' data in *PeduliLindungi* were also claimed secured since they are encrypted and stored in the national data centres.[115] Nevertheless, in September 2022, the personal data of at least 3.2 billion users of *PeduliLindungi* were leaked online, including the vaccine certificates of President Joko Widodo and his ministers.[116]

With the revocation of Community Activities Restrictions Enforcement, a cordon sanitaire policy imposed by the GoI to deal with COVID-19, starting on 1 January 2023, the Ministry of Health issued a statement that the use of *PeduliLindungi* is no longer mandatory in Indonesia.[117] It was reported that the personal data of *PeduliLindungi*'s users would be deleted once the COVID-19 pandemic ends. However, the procedure and handling of the deletion of personal data in *PeduliLindungi* remain unclear.

[113] 'Aplikasi PeduliLindungi Aman dari Phising dan Malware, Diunduh lewat App Store dan Play Store' (*Kominfo*, 2020), available at www.kominfo.go.id/content/detail/25866/siaran-pers-no-57hmkominfo042020-tentang-aplikasi-pedulilindungi-aman-dari-phising-dan-malware-diunduh-lewat-app-store-dan-play-store/0/siaran_pers.

[114] 'Siapkan Security System, Pemerintah Pastikan Data Pribadi Pengguna PeduliLindungi Aman' (*Kominfo*, 2021), available at www.kominfo.go.id/content/detail/31961/siapkan-security-system-pemerintah-pastikan-data-pribadi-pengguna-pedulilindungi-aman/0/berita_satker.

'Aplikasi PeduliLindungi, Lindungi Data Pribadi Penggunanya' (*Satuan Tugas Penanganan*, 2022), available at covid19.go.id/artikel/2022/04/19/aplikasi-pedulilindungi-lindungi-data-pribadi-penggunanya.

[115] 'PeduliLindungi Tetap Aman' (*Kominfo*, 2021), available at www.kominfo.go.id/content/detail/36894/pedulilindungi-tetap-aman/0/artikel.

[116] 'Care and Protect?: Apparent Govt Health App Breach Raises Deeper Data Concerns' (*The Jakarta Post*, 2022), available at www.thejakartapost.com/indonesia/2022/11/22/care-and-protect-apparent-govt-health-app-breach-raises-deeper-data-concerns.html.

[117] 'No Additional Rules after Lifting of All Covid-19 Restrictions: MoH' (*a.id*, 2022), available at www.theindonesia.id/news/2023/01/02/182059/no-additional-rules-after-lifting-of-all-covid-19-restrictions-moh.

13

Thailand

THAYA UTHAYOPHAS*

I. Introduction

The full implementation of the Personal Data Protection Act B.E. 2562 (PDPA) on 1 June 2022 marked a pivotal milestone for the international data transfer and protection regime in Thailand. Modelled after the European Union's General Data Protection Regulation (GDPR), the PDPA regulates the collection, usage, disclosure, and cross-border transfer of personal data, and is the first Thai law to comprehensively govern personal data protection. Many businesses and government agencies, some of whom are also subject to additional regulation in data privacy matters through sector-specific laws, have made major headway in terms of aligning their data practices for PDPA compliance.

However, there is still room for improvement for the international data transfer and protection regime in Thailand. First, although fully in effect, the PDPA itself has until recently remained somewhat incomplete. Various provisions in the PDPA rely on further specification by the Personal Data Protection Committee (PDPC), including the specifications on international transfer mechanisms, which recently took full effect in the first quarter of 2024,[1] after a period of great activity in late 2023 by the PDPC. Second, while certain provisions under the law are directly taken from the GDPR, others are independently drafted – a commendable action to adapt the GDPR to the local contexts but one that has also led to some unintended conflicts.[2] Third, the official guidelines of the PDPC itself sometimes adds on to the main text of the PDPA, no doubt for greater personal data protection measures, but nonetheless causing some confusion over which instructions to follow.[3]

* Special thanks to Chumpicha Vivitasevi and Jedsarit Sahaussrungs for providing their expertise. Thank you also to my research assistant Rawhiphutsagorn Chaiphairojn for her contribution.

[1] Announcement of the Personal Data Protection Committee on the Criteria for Protection of Personal Data Sent or Transferred Abroad according to section 28 of the Personal Data Protection Act B.E. 2019 and Announcement of the Personal Data Protection Committee on the Criteria for Protection of Personal Data Sent or Transferred Abroad according to section 29 of the Personal Data Protection Act B.E. 2019, which both took effect on 24 March 2024.

[2] See, eg, the issue with explicit consent mentioned in section II.C.i.

[3] For instance, the guidelines on providing notification to the data subject has noted that details concerning the transfer of personal data to foreign countries should also be included in the notice to the data subject, see PDPC's Guidelines on Notifying the Purpose and Details on the Collection of Data from the Data Subject according to the Personal Data Protection Act B.E. 2562, s 4.1 (9) ('PDPC's Guidelines on Notification'). This does not exist in the main law, see PDPA, s 23.

Fourth, issues broader than the PDPA such as the protection of non-personal data, the legal classification and nature of data property, and the classification between the content of data and data itself, remain. Finally, the initial delays and gradual implementation of the law has allowed non-compliance to continue.[4] With many businesses still unprepared, strict enforcement after the 2023 'transitional period' may prove challenging.[5]

The analysis begins with a broad background on the data protection landscape in section II, examining the constitutional, statutory and basic data protection framework. Section III delves into the PDPA in more detail, analysing the legal bases, mechanisms and exceptions for international data transfers. Section IV explores data security and localisation mandates under the PDPA and sectoral laws. Section V shifts the focus to private international law issues, discussing conflict of law rules, categories of litigation, and obstacles to data protection. Finally, section VI concludes by addressing topical issues and upcoming changes, such as regulations for artificial intelligence (AI)-generated data.

By evaluating the strengths and weaknesses of the existing legal framework, this chapter aims to provide policy recommendations for improving Thailand's data protection regime. A robust and consistent regulatory system is essential to engender trust in digital services and enable responsible cross-border data flows.

II. General Legal Framework of International Data Transfers and Data Protection

A. Constitutional Protection for Data Transfer and Protection

The right to privacy is recognised under section 32 of the Constitution of the Kingdom of Thailand B.E. 2560 (2017) (the 'Thai Constitution'), which states that: '[A] person has the right to privacy, honour, and family.'

An individual may claim for tortious damages under section 420 of the Civil and Commercial Code (CCC) for any personal data processing that violates his or her right to privacy under the Thai Constitution.[6] However, reported cases involving section 420 of the CCC and violation of the right to privacy under the Thai Constitution are rare, and mainly concern media reporting of private sexual acts.[7]

[4] Deloitte Thailand, 'PDPA Readiness Survey Report 2022' (2022), available at www.deloitte.com/content/dam/Deloitte/th/Documents/deloitte-private/th-deloitte-thailand-pdpa-readiness-survey-report-2022.pdf.

[5] Janine Phakdeethum, 'Explainer: What is PDPA, Thailand's New Data Law?' (*Bangkok Post*, 1 June 2022), available at www.bangkokpost.com/business/2319054/explainer-what-is-pdpa-thailands-new-data-law-.

[6] Civil and Commercial Code, s 420: 'A person who, willfully or negligently, unlawfully injures the life, body, health, liberty, property or any right of another person, is said to commit a wrongful act and is bound to make compensation therefore.'

[7] Supreme Court Decision No 4893/2558.

B. Statutory Frameworks for Data Transfer and Protection

i. Personal Data Protection Act

The PDPA acts as the main general regulation governing personal data transfer and protection in Thailand.

ii. Applicability of the PDPA

The PDPA applies to the collection, use, or disclosure of personal data by a natural or legal person in the role of a data controller or a data processor who is located in Thailand, regardless of whether such collection, use, or disclosure takes place in Thailand.[8] In addition, the PDPA also applies to the collection, use, or disclosure of personal data by a data controller or a data processor who is outside of Thailand in specific situations.[9]

iii. Exemptions from the PDPA

The PDPA, however, does not apply to:

1) the collection, use, or disclosure of personal data by a natural person for only the personal benefit or household activity of such person only;
2) operations of public authorities which are responsible for maintaining state security, including the financial security of the state or public safety, including with respect to the prevention and suppression of money laundering, forensic science and/or cybersecurity;
3) a natural or juristic person who uses or discloses personal data for activities involving mass media, fine arts, or literature, which are done in accordance with professional ethics or for the public interest;
4) the House of Representatives, the Senate, and the National Assembly, including the committee appointed by the House of Representatives, the Senate, or the National Assembly, which collect, use or disclose Personal Data under their duties and power;
5) trial and adjudication of courts and work operations of officers in legal proceedings, legal execution, and deposit of property, including work operations in accordance with criminal justice procedures;
6) data processing undertaken by a credit bureau company and its members, in accordance with the law governing the operations of a credit bureau business.[10]

Nonetheless, exempted entities aside from a natural person in (1) above must still put in place measures to protect personal data in accordance with specified standards.[11]

[8] PDPA, s 5, para 1. For the full definition and distinction between a data controller and data processor, please see section II.C. iv.

[9] ibid, s 5, para 2. For more on the extra-territorial application of the PDPA, please see section III.B.iii.

[10] PDPA, s 4, para 1.

[11] ibid, s 4, para 3. Announcement of the PDPC Re: Standards for Maintaining Personal Data Security of Data Controllers who are exempted from the enforcement of the Personal Data Protection Act B.E. 2562 (2019).

Importantly, a Royal Decree recently became effective on 14 January 2024 and provides exemptions on complying with certain aspects of the PDPA for organisations such as the National Anti-Corruption Commission, the Revenue Department, certain local government organisations, and the Cabinet secretariat, and for matters relating to international crimes.[12]

iv. PDPA and Other Laws

The PDPA serves as supplementary legislation with respect to any sector-specific law governing the protection of personal data in Thailand:

- In regards to provisions concerning the collection, use, or disclosure of personal data, as well as relating to the rights of data subjects including relevant penalties, these shall apply in an additive fashion, regardless of whether they replicate or overlap with the sectoral laws.[13]
- However, for provisions concerning complaints, orders from the expert committee to protect the data subject, and the power and duties of competent officials including penalties, the PDPA only applies under specific conditions. Specifically, it only takes effect where: (a) the specific sectoral laws contain no provision with respect to complaints; or (b) the sectoral laws grant complaint powers not equivalent to those of the PDPA's expert committee, and either the official requests the expert committee's involvement or the data subject files a PDPA complaint directly.[14]

Additionally, the PDPA allows sectoral supervisory authorities, professional councils, associations, and industrial groups to issue compulsory or voluntary standard forms for obtaining consent[15] and providing notice[16] to the data subjects.[17] These forms can be used as long as they align with the PDPA's requirements.

v. History of the PDPA

The PDPA was passed on 24 May 2019 and came into effect on 28 May 2019. However, its implementation faced delays. An initial one-year grace period was provided for most provisions. Subsequently, two Royal Decrees in 2020 and 2021 further postponed full enforcement and exempted many organisations and businesses from compliance.[18] These delays

[12] Royal Decree on the Characteristics of Businesses of Agencies Exempted from Certain Applications of the Personal Data Protection Act B.E. 2563 (2020).

[13] PDPA, s 3(1).

[14] ibid, s 3(2). For more on the sectoral laws, please see section III.C.ii.

[15] PDPC's Guidelines on Obtaining Consent from the Data Subject According to the Personal Data Protection B.E. 2562, ss 2.1, 2.2.

[16] PDPC's Guidelines on Notification (n 3), ss 2.1, 2.2.

[17] Examples include various guidelines passed by the Official of Insurance Commission on protection of the personal data of insurance businesses' customers, which cover both consent and notice.

[18] Royal Decree Stipulating Agencies and Businesses that the Personal Data Controller is not subject to the Personal Data Protection Act B.E. 2563 (2020) and Royal Decree Stipulating Agencies and Businesses that the Personal Data Controller is not subject to the Personal Data Protection Act B.E. 2562 (2019). As the name suggests, these exemptions only apply to Data Controllers. However, no enforcement actions have been commenced against data processors during the delay period.

stemmed from pushback from impacted sectors, under the backdrop of implementation challenges due to the complexities of the law and the impact of COVID-19.[19]

As a stop-gap measure prior to the full implementation of the PDPA, the Ministry of Digital Economy and Society announced minimum data security standards in 2020 ('MDES Data Security Standards') that applied to exempt data controllers until 31 July 2022. These include requirements such as implementing administrative, technical, and physical safeguards to ensure confidentiality, integrity, and availability of the personal data, as well as measures for access controls and audit mechanisms.

The PDPA has now been fully in force for all entities within its jurisdiction since 1 June 2022. Enforcement actions have been initially rare, with a member of the PDPC legal subcommittee having acknowledged that the PDPC will solely focus on issuing warnings to violators in the first year of the PDPA's implementation.[20] However, as of January 2024, 91 administrative actions have been taken by the PDPC from a total of 394 complaints with various complaints still in the consideration or fact-finding process,[21] and the expectation is that the PDPC will be even more proactive in monitoring PDPA compliance and taking enforcement actions for the rest of 2024.[22]

vi. Secondary Laws under the PDPA

The following are some of the secondary laws that have been announced by the PDPC:

a. Specification of Requirements for Data Controller and Processors

- Announcement of the PDPC Re: Security Measures of Data Controller B.E. 2565 (effective on 21 June 2022) ('PDPC Announcement on Security Measure').
- Announcement of the PDPC Re: Criteria and Methods for Reporting Personal Data Breach B.E. 2565 (effective on 15 December 2022) ('PDPC Announcement on Reporting Personal Data Breach').
- Announcement of the Personal Data Protection Committee on the Criteria for Protection of Personal Data Sent or Transferred Abroad according to Section 28 of the Personal Data Protection Act B.E. 2019 (effective on 25 March 2024) ('PDPC Announcement on International Data Transfer and Adequacy Decision').
- Announcement of the Personal Data Protection Committee on the Criteria for Protection of Personal Data Sent or Transferred Abroad according to Section 29 of the Personal Data Protection Act B.E. 2019 (effective on 25 March 2024) ('PDPC Announcement on BCR and SCC').

[19] ibid; The official reason given for the first delay was attributed to the lack of readiness of data controllers due to the 'complex procedures' required for compliance with the PDPA and the second delay was the effects of the Covid-19 virus on the overall economy and society.

[20] Phakdeethum (n 5).

[21] Baker McKenzie, 'Thailand: PDPA Compliance and Challenges – Development of the Insurance Industry in 2024' (*Baker McKenzie*, 9 February 2024), available at insightplus.bakermckenzie.com/bm/financial-institutions_1/thailand-pdpa-compliance-and-challenges-development-of-the-insurance-industry-in-2024.

[22] ibid.

- Announcement of the Personal Data Protection Committee regarding the Provision of Personal Data Protection Officers in accordance with Section 41 (2) of the Personal Data Protection Act B.E. 2019 (effective on 13 December 2023).
- Announcement of the Personal Data Protection Committee on the Criteria for Protection Measures for the Collection of Criminal Records that are not under the Control of Agencies having Authority under the Law (effective on 7 April 2024).

b. Exemptions

- Announcement of the PDPC Re: Exemption of Records of Personal data controller as a Small Business B.E. 2565 (2022) (effective on 21 June 2022).

c. Administrative

- Announcement of the PDPC Re: Criteria for Consideration of Administrative Fines Order of the Expert Committee B.E. 2565 (2022) (effective on 21 June 2022).

d. Data Protection

- Guidelines on Obtaining Consent from the Data Subject According to the Personal Data Protection B.E. 2562 (published on 7 September 2022).
- Guidelines on Notifying the Purpose and Details of the Collection of Personal Data from the Data Subject according to the Personal Data Protection Act B.E. 2562 (published on 7 September 2022).
- Guidelines for Risk Assessment and Notification of Personal Data Breach Version 1.0 (published on 16 December 16 2022) ('PDPC Guidelines on Data Breach').

vii. Other General Laws

In addition to the PDPA, data protection issues in Thailand are also covered under the Cybersecurity Act B.E. 2562 (2019), and the Computer-Related Crime Act B.E. 2550 (2007), which relate to preventing cybersecurity threats and computer-related crime respectively.[23]

C. Data Protection Frameworks

i. Influence of International Data Protection Frameworks

The PDPA was drafted to closely align with the GDPR.[24] However, while the PDPA contains data protection measures generally in line with the data protection principles of lawfulness,

[23] The Cybersecurity Act also provides specific duties to a certain list of organisations deemed to be Information Infrastructure Organisations under the law.

[24] Suchit Leesa-nguansuk, Somruedi Banchongduang, and Darana Chudasri, 'Personal Privacy in the Balance' (*Bangkok Post*, 11 March 2019), available at www.bangkokpost.com/business/1642336/personal-privacy-in-the-balance. The PDPA is also very much inspired by the requirement under free trade agreements with the EU on

transparency, purpose limitation, data minimisation, accuracy, storage limitation, integrity, and confidentiality, as well as accountability as emphasised under the GDPR, there also exist significant divergences from the GDPR. These include a generally more expansive list of exempted entities like public security agencies, different enforcement penalties, and a lack of data subject rights concerning automated decision-making. Furthermore, although concepts of adequacy decision, binding corporate rules (BCR), standard contractual clauses (SCCs), and derogations do exist under the PDPA as potential avenues for international data transfer, the PDPA provides a definition of international data transfer that specifically excludes the transfer of data outside of Thailand where the third party (such as a cloud service provider) cannot access the personal data.

It is also important to mention here that the effort to mimic the GDPR may have also led to inconsistencies within the PDPA itself. For instance, explicit consent is specifically required only for processing of special categories of personal data under section 9 of the GDPR. Under the PDPA, section 19 of the PDPA requires that all consent requests must be explicit for all personal data, despite the language of section 24 of the PDPA on general personal data using the language of normal consent only in contrast with section 26 of the PDPA on special categories of personal data's usage of the language of 'explicit consent'.

Beyond the PDPA, privacy rights in Thailand are also informed by international commitments. The International Covenant on Civil and Political Rights (ICCPR) provides in Article 17 that '[N]o one shall be subjected to arbitrary or unlawful interference with his or her privacy, family, home or correspondence, nor to unlawful attacks on his or her honour and reputation.'

Additionally, Thailand is a member state of the Association of Southeast Asian Nations (ASEAN), with the ASEAN Human Rights Declaration providing at Article 21 that 'Every person has the right to be free from arbitrary interference with his or her privacy, family, home or correspondence including personal data.'

However, these instruments have limited direct impact compared to the PDPA's provisions and do not influence the interpretation of privacy rights as so understood under the law.[25]

ii. Specific Provisions for Particular Sectors

Key business sectors are governed by sector-specific regulations for data transfer and protection that interact with the PDPA's data protection framework.

Entities regulated by the Bank of Thailand (BOT): These include financial institutions and payment services.[26] They are primarily governed by the BOT's Market Conduct rules[27] and the BOT's Announcement Re: Supervision of Designated Payment System Business.[28]

data privacy requirements, see Nguyen MH, 'Thailand Issues First Personal Data Protection Act' (*ASEAN Briefing*, 31 May 2022), available at www.aseanbriefing.com/news/thailand-issues-first-personal-data-protection-act/.

[25] See subsection iii below.

[26] Payment System Act B.E. 2560 (2017), s 7.

[27] Bank of Thailand Notification No SorKorSor. 2.4/2565 Re: Market Conduct ('BOT Market Conduct').

[28] Bank of Thailand Notification No SorNorChor 1/2561 Re: Supervision of Designated Payment System Business.

Entities regulated by the Security Exchange Commission of Thailand (SEC): These include securities companies that must comply with business standards and customer service announcements focused on investor protection.[29]

Entities regulated by the Ministry of Public Health (MPH): Healthcare providers like hospitals and clinics adhere to acts and regulations on medical facilities and personal health information, including the Ministry of Public Health Ministerial Regulations Relating to the Protection and Organization of Personal Health Information B.E. 2561 ('MPH Regulation on Health Information').

Entities regulated by the National Broadcasting and Telecommunications Commission (NBTC): These include entities in the telecom and broadcasting sectors and follow relevant business acts and personal data protection announcements, including the Announcement of the National Broadcasting and Telecommunications Commission Re: Measures to Protect the Rights of Telecommunication Service Users Regarding Personal Data, Right to Privacy and Freedom of Communication by Telecommunication ('NBCT Announcement on Personal Data').

In addition, there exist regulations geared specifically towards government agencies such as the Official Information Act, B.E. 2540 (1997) and Rule on the Maintenance of Official Secrets B.E. 2544 (2001). The National Credit Bureau governed by the Credit Information Business Act, B.E. 2545 (2002) handles personal credit data, and must abide by data usage rules.

However, potential gaps or conflicts between sectoral rules and the PDPA persist. The banking regulations predate the PDPA and may not fully align with its consent requirements. Healthcare protocols on data sharing for research purposes may not match PDPA disclosure principles.

More analysis is required to assess sector-specific regulations against PDPA standards and identify areas of divergence. A unified approach is needed to avoid contradictions and ensure sufficient protection across all industries handling personal data. Targeted guidance could help reconcile sectoral practice with national data protection law.

iii. Distinction and Interface between Data Protection and Privacy

Data protection and privacy are distinct concepts under Thai law. Data protection under the PDPA focuses on personal data handling practices. Privacy under the Constitution relates to tortious interference with private and family life. However, there is overlap in practice. Breaching PDPA data protection principles may violate constitutional privacy rights. For example, improperly disclosing personal data could harm privacy.

iv. Distinctions between 'Data Users', 'Data Subjects', 'Data Processors' and 'Data Sub-Contractors'

The PDPA defines key data roles, and sectoral laws may also cover these concepts under their own definitions.

[29] Notification of the Capital Market Supervisory Board No TorThor. 35/2556 Re: Standard Conduct of Business, Management Arrangement, Operating Systems, and Providing Services to Clients of Securities Companies and Derivatives Intermediaries, s 14.

Under the PDPA, data controllers are defined as '[A natural person] or a juristic person having the power and duties to make decisions regarding the collection, use, or disclosure of the personal data'.[30]

Data processors are defined as:

> [A natural person] or a juristic person who operates in relation to the collection, use, or disclosure of the personal data pursuant to the orders given by or on behalf of a data controller, whereby such person or juristic person is not the data controller.[31]

Sub-processors are not defined under the PDPA but may process data on behalf of data processors. Data subjects are defined under the PDPC's Official PDPA Guide for Citizens as '[N]atural persons with legal rights for which the personal data identifies to such persons either directly or indirectly'.[32]

v. Distinction between 'Personal Data' and 'Non-Personal Data'

Under the PDPA, personal data refers to '[A]ny information relating to a natural person, which enables the identification of such persons, whether directly or indirectly, but not including the information of deceased persons in particular.'[33]

Similar to the GDPR, personal data is divided into general personal data and sensitive personal data under the PDPA. Examples of general personal data include an individual's name, surname, address, phone number, national ID card number, email address, bank account number, etc.[34] Sensitive personal data includes personal data pertaining to an individual's race, ethnic origin, political opinions, cult, religious or philosophical beliefs, sexual orientation, criminal records, personal health data, disability, trade union information, genetic data, biometric data, or any data which may affect the data subject in the same manner, as prescribed by the PDPC.[35]

vi. Distinction between Anonymised, Pseudonymised, or Encrypted (if any)

The PDPA does not directly define the concepts of anonymised, pseudonymised, or encrypted data. However, anonymised data that can no longer identify the data subject is no longer considered personal data under the PDPA, and therefore is not regulated by the PDPA. Pseudonymised data that may still indirectly identify the data subject is still considered as personal data, and subject to regulation under the PDPA. Pseudonymisation and encryption can help demonstrate compliance with the PDPA.

vii. Distinction between Domestic and Cross-Border/International Transfers (if any)

The PDPA governs both the domestic and international disclosure of personal data, and international transfers of personal data. Disclosure of personal data under the PDPA

[30] PDPA, s 5.
[31] ibid.
[32] PDPC's Official PDPA Guide for Citizens, Guideline 2.
[33] PDPA, s 5.
[34] PDPC's Official PDPA Guide for Citizens, Guideline 2, 3.
[35] PDPA, s 26.

primarily refers to the disclosure of personal data by a data controller to another legal or natural person, regardless of whether the disclosure is conducted domestically or internationally. International transfer of personal data, on the other hand, refers to the sending or transferring of personal data to a foreign country.[36]

viii. Is there a Privacy Regulator? Does it have Sanctioning Powers?

The main privacy regulator of the PDPA is the PDPC.[37] Its key roles include determining measures and guidelines, issuing notifications and rules, providing recommendations to the Cabinet on the enactment of the Royal Decree or reforms, and interpreting and rendering rulings with respect to the enforcement of the PDPA.[38]

In addition, an Office of the Personal Data Protection Committee has been set up under the PDPA[39] to support regulatory operations. The Office of the PDPC has various duties and power, including to:

- analyse and certify the compliance with and accuracy of the standards or measures, or the supervision mechanism in connection with personal data protection, as well as to review and certify the personal data protection policy as part of the international data transfer mechanism for companies in the same affiliated business or in the same group of undertakings;
- establish course outlines and provide training in relation to the performance of the data controller, data processor, data protection officer, employees, service providers, or the general public; and
- follow-up on and evaluate compliance with the PDPA.[40]

Of note, in its mission to follow the development trends of the personal data protection,[41] the Office of the PDPC has established a centre called the 'PDPC Eagle Eye' with a mission to survey and monitor internet information, which may have an adverse effect on personal data protection. From November 2023 to January 2024, the PDPC Eagle eye has detected 5,273 issues of data breaches.[42]

Finally, the PDPC is tasked with setting up an Expert Committee, with the following powers and duties:

- to consider complaints and settle disputes under the PDPA;
- to investigate any act of the data controller or the data processor, including the employees or the contractors of the data controller or the data processor in connection with any personal data that causes damage to the data subject;

[36] Please see section III.A.ii for the definition of sending or transfer under the PDPA.
[37] Some sectors are primarily governed and sanctioned by the supervisory authority in charge of the sectors such as those mentioned in subsection C.ii above instead.
[38] PDPA, s 16.
[39] ibid, s 43.
[40] ibid, s 44.
[41] ibid, s 44 (4)(5).
[42] Lexology, 'Thailand's Cybersecurity Snapshot: Current Laws and Emerging Trends' (3 July 2024), available at www.lexology.com/library/detail.aspx?g=abb786e2-f9f4-4192-a364-046ab9f11bd5.

- to order any person to submit documents or information in connection with the complaint under the PDPA or any other matter related to the protection of personal data under the PDPA; and
- to request any person to provide a statement of facts.[43]

The Expert Committee also has the power to impose administrative fines for any violations of the PDPA that trigger any administrative liabilities under the law.[44] The potential violations are vast and includes failure to act in compliance with the order of the Expert Committee.[45] However, if it deems fit, the Expert Committee also has discretion to issue an order for rectification or a warning first before issuing any fines.

III. Legal Bases, Mechanisms and Exceptions for International Data Transfers and Data Protection

A. International Data Transfers

The law on International Data Transfers is covered under the two main requirements of the PDPA:[46] data disclosures and international data transfers.

i. International Data Transfer as Data Disclosures under the PDPA

Under the PDPA, a data controller is prohibited from disclosing personal data without the consent of the data subject unless certain exemptions, commonly known as 'legal bases', are applicable.[47] These exemptions are classed as either general personal data or sensitive personal data.

Exemptions for general personal data include the following cases:

- For the purpose of preparing historical documents or archives in the public interest, or for research or statistical purposes, provided suitable measures are implemented to safeguard the data subject's rights and freedoms in accordance with the PDPC's notification. To prevent or suppress a danger to a person's life, body or health.
- For the performance of a contract involving the data subject or to take steps at the data subject's request before entering into a contract.
- For the performance of a task carried out in the public interest by the data controller, or for the exercising of official authority vested in the data controller.

[43] PDPA, s 71.
[44] ibid, s 90.
[45] ibid, s 89.
[46] Note that the analysis in this chapter will focus solely on the PDPA. There may be further specific-sector requirements for the international transfer of both personal data and non-personal data.
[47] PDPA, s 27, para 1.

- For the legitimate interests of the data controller or any other persons or juristic persons, except when such interests are overridden by the fundamental rights of the data subject.
- For compliance with a law applicable to the data controller.[48]

Exemptions for sensitive personal data include the following cases:

- To prevent or suppress a danger to a person's life, body or health where the data subject is incapable of giving consent.
- For legitimate activities with appropriate safeguards conducted by foundations, associations or any other not-for-profit bodies for political, religious, philosophical, or trade union purposes, limited to their members, former members of the bodies, or persons having regular contact with them, without disclosing the personal data outside of these entities.
- When the data subject has given explicit consent for the disclosure to the public.
- For the establishment, compliance, exercise or defence of legal claims.
- For compliance with a law concerning various purposes, including medical treatment, assessment of employee working capacity, public health interests, social security, and scientific research.[49]

Reliance on the exemptions above must be documented as part of the recordings requirement under section 39 of the PDPA.[50] This typically takes the form of a Records of Processing Activities (ROPA) document.

Additionally, section 37(2) of the PDPA requires the data controller to take action to prevent any unauthorised or unlawful use or disclosure of the personal data when providing it to other individuals or legal entities, apart from itself.[51] Meanwhile, the entity that receives the disclosed personal data is required to only use or further disclose the personal data for the purpose previously notified to the disclosing party in its request to obtain the personal data from the disclosing party.[52]

To satisfy the requirements of section 37(2), many data controllers have entered into data disclosure clauses or agreements with the receiving party when disclosing personal data. In cases of international data transfers between two entities relying on appropriate safeguards[53] such as Standard Contractual Clauses, Codes of Conduct, or certifications, it is most likely that these safeguards will satisfy the requirements of section 37(2). If two entities in the same affiliated business or group of undertakings have a certified personal data

[48] ibid, s 24.

[49] ibid, s 26.

[50] ibid, s 27, para 3.

[51] ibid, s 37(2).

Note that there are two possible interpretations of section 37(2) of the PDPA: the data controller is required to take action where it provides personal data to any other person other than itself, or specifically where it provides personal data to non-data controllers (ie, data processors). The first interpretation is the broader and more likely reading of the law. The second interpretation is narrower and may be redundant in light of the PDPA's other requirement on data controllers having to enter into a data processing agreement with data processors to govern their actions as per section 40 of the PDPA. However, there is some uncertainty as to what 'taking action' means in the context of section 37(2) of the PDPA.

[52] ibid, s 27, para 2.

[53] ibid, s 29, para 3 and PDPC Announcement on BCR and SCC.

protection policy governing their relationship,[54] this policy is likely to suffice for satisfying section 37(2). When the data controller discloses personal data to a data processor, the existing data processing agreement required by the PDPA[55] is likely to be deemed sufficient for the purposes of section 37(2).

ii. International Data Transfer as the Sending or Transfer of Data to a Foreign Country under the PDPA

It must first be pointed out that the sending or transfer of data is specifically defined under the PDPA to provide a natural exemption for many companies who merely transfer or store data outside of Thailand where no other party, including a cloud storage service provider, can access the data.[56] This is in contrast with the standards of the GDPR, which does exclude data transit from its definition of a restricted transfer but does not similarly exclude the transfer of personal data to a cloud based IT system outside of the European Economic Area.[57]

Where the sending or transfer of personal data falls under the definition of the PDPA, the PDPA only allows for the sending or transfer of personal data by a data controller to a foreign country in the following circumstances:[58]

1. Where the foreign country or international organisation has in place adequate data protection standards as determined by the PDPC, and where the transfer is carried out in accordance with the rules for the protection of personal data as prescribed by the PDPC.

   (Note that the law on adequacy criteria came into effect in March 2024 with considerations for whether a foreign country or international organisation will have in place adequate data protection standards including the following factors:

   a) whether the country or organisation has mechanisms for data protection that aligns with the personal data protection laws of Thailand, especially on the duty

[54] ibid, s 29, para 1 and PDPC Announcement on BCR and SCC.

[55] ibid, s 40, para 3.

[56] Under section 3 of the PDPC Announcement on International Data Transfer and Adequacy Decision and PDPC Announcement on BCR and SCC, the sending or transferring of personal data refers to: 'the sending or transferring of personal data by the sender or transferor, regardless of whether the sending or transfer is via physical means or via computer system or wireless system to the personal data receiver, but not including the sending or receipt of personal data in the characteristics of an intermediary for data transit between computer systems or data storage network in both temporary and permanent basis where no third party can access the personal data aside from the data controller or the data processor who is the sender of such personal data or their personnel, staffs, or employee of such data controller or data processor' (for instance, the sending of data through a foreign network or the sending of data via the system of the cloud computing service provider which no individual other than the data controller or data processor who sent the data or their personnel, staff, or employees can access the personal data given the technical or legal measures involved).

A cloud computing service provider is further defined as: 'A service provider who stores data or put asides data for others in either a temporary or permanent format with system to manage data on the internet, which may be in various forms such as: Infrastructure as a Service (Iaas); Platform as a Service (Paas); Software as a Service (SaaS); Data Storage as a Service (DSaaS); and Serverless Computer or Function as a Service (Faas).

[57] 'International Transfers' (*Information Commissioner's Office*, 2 August 2018), available at ico.org.uk/media/for-organisations/guide-to-the-general-data-protection-regulation-gdpr/international-transfers-1-0.pdf.

[58] Note that there is some confusion as to whether a data processor is also specifically required to follow the same restrictions with regards to the international transfer of data in section 28 of the PDPA, which refer to only the data

of the data controller to have appropriate security measures for personal data and enforcement on the rights of the data subject as well as effective legal remedies; and

b) whether there is an entity with the power to enforce laws on personal data protection within the country or international organisation.[59]

The PDPC also has the power to designate a list of countries or international organisations that has adequate data protection standards (otherwise known as an adequacy decision).[60] **However, note that unlike the GDPR, the PDPC does not need to have made an adequacy decision for a data transfer to a particular country or international organisation to be deemed safe. Instead, the transfer can be considered safe so long as the destination country or international organisation fits the given adequacy criteria above, and any subsequent disputes on the matter can be then further considered by the PDPC. This has led to significant debates within the PDPC as to whether to explicitly make adequacy decisions for countries that have already been deemed safe by the European Council under the GDPR (left unstated, these countries would most likely already fit in with the adequacy criteria of the PDPA, given the fact that the PDPA was directly drafted based off of the GDPR)).**[61]

2. In the case that the transfer falls under certain exemptions, including:[62]
   a) compliance with the law: the transfer is necessary to comply with the law;[63]
   b) informed consent: the transfer is based on the informed consent of the data subject, provided that the data subject has been informed of the inadequate personal data protection standards of the destination country or international organisation;
   c) contractual performance: the transfer is necessary for the performance of a contract to which the data subject is a party, or to take steps at the request of the data subject prior to entering into a contract;
   d) contractual interests: the transfer is necessary for compliance with a contract between the data controller and other natural persons or juristic persons for the interests of the data subject;

controller. However, the exceptions on international data transfer requirements per section 29 of the PDPA also includes the role of the data processor in transferring personal data to a foreign country in exemption to compliance with section 28 of the PDPA. Regardless, the role of the data processor is to act on behalf of a data controller, and ultimately, it will be important for the data controller to demonstrate its compliance with the international data transfer rules of the PDPA.

[59] PDPC Announcement on International Data Transfer and Adequacy Decision, s 5.

[60] ibid, s 6.

[61] PDPC Thailand, 'Criteria for Protecting Personal Data Sent or Transferred Abroad According to Section 28 and Section 29', available at www.youtube.com/watch?v=z3rPxZI4XQA.

[62] It may be worth noting that prior to the recent passage of the PDPC Announcement on International Transfer and Adequacy Decision, as well as the PDPC Announcement on BCR and SCC, many companies have relied on specific exemptions for international data transfers, usually based on the necessity of the transfer for contractual performance or compliance with a contract, which are directly incorporated from Article 49 and in turn, Recital 111 of the GDPR. However, it remains unclear whether the PDPC will interpret these exemptions in the same manner as the GDPR.

[63] Note that this exception only applies to Thai law, as noted by the PDPC experts in their public consultation. PDPC, 'Subject: Bank Z Would Like to Discuss Guidelines for Submitting Personal Data of Directors in Accordance with ACRA Regulations in Singapore and/or the Regulations and Laws of other Countries'; www.pdpc.or.th/wp-content/uploads/2024/02/PDPC-consultation-18.pdf.

  e) protection of life, body or health: the transfer is necessary to prevent or suppress a danger to the life, body, or health of the data subject or other natural persons, when the data subject is incapable of giving its consent at such time;
  f) substantial public interest: the transfer is necessary for carrying out activities in relation to substantial public interest.[64]

3. Certification of Personal Data Protection Policy: The Office of the PDPC can review and certify a data controller's personal data protection policy regarding the transfer of personal data to another data controller or processor in a foreign country within the same affiliated business or group of undertakings[65] (BCR). The rules and method for review and certification of the BCR can be found in the PDPC Announcement on BCR and SCC, which has been in effect since 25 March 2024. Key considerations for the approval of the BCR includes:
  a) legal effectiveness of the policy on the affiliated companies, including relevant data processors and their personnel;
  b) provisions covering the protection of data subject rights and complaint mechanisms for the personal data that has been sent or transferred abroad; and
  c) security measures that aligned with the law.[66]

4. Appropriate Safeguards: The data controller or data processor can provide appropriate safeguards that enable the enforcement of the data subject's rights, including effective legal remedial measures, according to the rules and methods prescribed by the PDPC, found in the PDPC Announcement on BCR and SCC, which has been in effect since 25 March 2024.[67] The appropriate safeguards can be in any of the types below,[68] but must adhere to a list of suitable protection criteria, summarised as follows: effectiveness of the appropriate safeguards in terms of legal enforcement and remedial measures, protection of data subject rights for the data sent or transferred, and data protection and minimum security measures in accordance with the PDPA.[69]

  a) Standard Contractual Clauses on Data Protection with specific criteria[70] (PDPC SCC);

[64] PDPA, s 28.

[65] ibid, s 29, para 1 and PDPC Announcement on BCR and SCC.

The concept of having the same affiliated business or group of undertakings is defined as: 'businesses that has control and management power over businesses or businesses under control of other businesses in the form of a parent company, subsidiary company, associated company or natural person or juristic person who is legally related or related due to joint economic activities by using the criteria in accordance with generally accepted accounting standards' (PDPC Announcement on BCR and SCC, s 3).

[66] PDPC Announcement on BCR and SCC, s 7.

[67] PDPA, s 29, para 3 and PDPC Announcement on BCR and SCC.

[68] PDPC Announcement on BCR and SCC, s 8.

[69] ibid, s 9.

[70] The PDPC SCC must contain the following measures under the framework of the suitable protection criteria:

1. Collection, usage, and disclosure, including the sending or transfer of personal data to recipients in accordance with the PDPA;
2. Minimum security measures in accordance with the PDPA for the sender or transferer of the personal data as well as the recipient;
3. In the case that the recipient is a data processor, the recipient must
   a. process data in accordance with the command and purpose of the sender or transferer;

b) Standard Contractual Clauses on Data Protection made in compliance with specific foreign law or international organisation[71] and criteria[72] (International SCC);
c) Certification for the collection, use, and disclosure of personal data of the data controller and processor in respect of the sending or transfer of personal data across borders or foreign countries with accepted standards for personal data protection in accordance with the PDPC's specification (to be further announced);[73]
d) In the case where there is a sending or transfer of personal data between Thai and foreign government agencies, measures to protect personal data in terms of legal instruments or agreement that can be enforced against such government agencies.

iii. Asia-Pacific Economic Cooperation (APEC) Cross-Border Privacy Rules (CBPR) System

Thailand's membership in APEC does not automatically make it a participant in the APEC CBPR system. The APEC CBPR system is a government-backed data privacy certification that allows companies to demonstrate their compliance with internationally recognised

b. contact the sender or transferer at the first opportunity in the case of data subject requests, unless the data processor was assigned the duty to comply with the data subject rights on behalf of the sender or transferer;
c. return the personal data in accordance with the contract to the sender or transferer or delete, destroy, or anonymise the personal data in accordance with the conditions determined by the sender or the transferer and provide written confirmation to the sender or the transferer of such actions;
d. notify the sender or transferer of the personal data of any personal data breach in accordance with the PDPA as soon as possible but within 72 hours from knowledge.

4. In the case that the recipient is a data controller, the recipient must notify the data controller sender or transferer of the personal data of any personal data breach in accordance with the PDPA as soon as possible but within 72 hours from knowledge, unless such data breach does not pose any risk on the rights and liberties of individuals. (PDPC Announcement on BCR and SCC, s 10(1)).

[71] As of 28 January 2024, the International SCC can be based off the ASEAN Model Contractual Clauses for Cross Border Data Flows and the Standard Contractual Clauses for the Transfer of Personal Data to Third Parties that has been issued under Arts 36(1), 46(2)(c) and 28(7) of the GDPR, although the PDPC has the power to add to the list.

[72] The International SCC must contain the following measures under the framework of the suitable protection criteria:

1. Notification to the data subject of the sending or transfer of personal data;
2. Purpose limitation of the sending or transfer of personal data;
3. Options for the data subject to exercise their right to cancel the sending or transfer of personal data to third parties or cancel the usage of their personal data beyond the given purpose;
4. Responsibility for the sending or transfer of personal data for the appropriate protection of personal data, including on the sending or transfer of personal data to third parties;
5. Security measures on the sending or transfer of personal data to prevent data breach;
6. Data subject rights of access, right to accuracy, and right to deletion;
7. Legally effective remedial for damages, legal enforcement, and determination of liability for the unauthorised sending or transfer of personal data.

Note that the parties may edit or add on to the content in the International SCC but only where such edits or addition do not conflict with the measures above and do not have an impact on the rights and liberties of the data subject. (PDPC Announcement on BCR and SCC, s 12).

[73] PDPC Announcement on BCR and SCC, s 14.

data privacy protections.[74] Therefore, companies in Thailand cannot currently rely on this certification to facilitate international data transfers.

iv. Any Privacy Certification Schemes, Trustmarks or Privacy Seals (international)

The PDPC recognises certifications as a potential avenue for international personal data transfer.[75] However, the current lack of announcement by the PDPC on certification standards[76] means that there are currently no privacy certification schemes, trustmarks, or privacy seals recognised under the PDPA for the purposes of international data transfers, beyond the potential certification of the BCR by the Office of the PDPC.

B. International Data Protection and Liability

i. Specific Requirements or Policies for Data Processing and Retention

The PDPA imposes several requirements on data controllers in relation to data processing. These requirements include: providing notice to the data subject;[77] obtaining consent or other legal bases for the collection and usage of personal data, which align with the legal bases applicable to data disclosures;[78] providing appropriate security measures;[79] notifying the authorities and the data subject[80] of any data breaches; complying with data subject rights;[81] maintaining the accuracy of personal data;[82] maintaining records of data processing and other matters;[83] appointing and assisting the data protection officer;[84] appointing representatives for foreign companies.[85]

The duties of data processors' are governed by section 40 of the PDPA, and include carrying out data processing pursuant to instructions given by the data controller, and providing appropriate security measures for personal data protection including notifying the data controller of any breaches and maintaining records of data processing.[86] Data controllers are also required to enter into processing agreements with data processors to ensure the activities of the data processors are PDPA compliant.[87]

[74] 'Participation in the APEC Cross-Border Privacy Rules (CBPR) System Affords Asia-Pacific Economic Cooperation Members a Unique Opportunity to Work' (*Cross Border Privacy Rules System*), available at www.cbprs.org/government/.

[75] PDPC Announcement on BCR and SCC, s 8, para 2 (3).

[76] ibid, s 14.

[77] PDPA, ss 23 and 25.

[78] ibid, ss 19, 24, 25, and 26.

[79] ibid, s 37(1).

[80] ibid, s 37(4).

[81] ibid, s 19, para 5, ss 30–34, s 36, and s 73, para 1.

[82] ibid, s 35.

[83] ibid, s 39.

[84] ibid, ss 41–42.

[85] ibid, s 37(5).

[86] ibid, s 40, para 1. Note that the maintenance of some data processing records are exempted for certain small data processors.

[87] ibid, s 40, para 3.

In terms of data retention, the PDPA mandates that personal data should only be collected as necessary for lawful purposes.[88] The data controller must establish a system for erasing or destroying personal data when the retention period ends, or when the personal data becomes irrelevant or no longer necessary for the purpose it was collected.[89] The data subject's requests for erasure or destruction, as well as withdrawal of consent, must be honoured.[90] There are exceptions to the data retention requirements under the PDPA, such as when retention is allowed for freedom of expression, preparing historical documents, public interest, establishment, compliance, exercise or defence of legal claims, or compliance with law.[91] It is worth noting that the PDPC has the authority to stipulate additional rules for the erasure, destruction, or anonymisation of personal data in the future.[92]

ii. Regulations on Legal Ownership of Data Protection and Privacy Rights

The PDPA contains a comprehensive list of rights for data subjects. These include the right to withdraw consent,[93] the right to request access and obtain a copy of personal data as well as the right to disclosure of the acquisition of personal data obtained without consent,[94] the right to data portability,[95] the right to object to data processing,[96] the right to erasure,[97] the right to restrict the use of personal data,[98] the right to rectification,[99] and the right to file a complaint to the Expert Committee appointed by the PDPC.[100]

However, the rights of the data subject under the PDPA are not absolute, and are often subject to restrictions and/or exceptions. For instance, the right to request access to and obtain a copy of personal data is limited to data that is under the responsibility of the data controller.[101] The data controller may reject access requests in cases permitted by law or pursuant to a court order, or when access would adversely affect the rights and freedoms of others.[102]

While the PDPA does not explicitly specify response timelines for most types of data subject requests, the timeline outlined in section 30 of the PDPA, which pertains to the right of access, is commonly used as a general standard by data controllers. According to section 30, data controllers must fulfil the data subject's right of access request without undue delay, but no later than 30 days from the date of receiving such a request.

[88] ibid, s 22.
[89] ibid, s 37(3).
[90] ibid, s 33.
[91] ibid, s 37(3).
[92] ibid, ss 37(3) and 33, para 5.
[93] ibid, s 19, para 5.
[94] ibid, s 30.
[95] ibid, s 31.
[96] ibid, s 32.
[97] ibid, s 33.
[98] ibid, s 34.
[99] ibid, s 36.
[100] ibid, s 73, para 1.
[101] ibid, s 30, para 1.
[102] ibid, s 30, para 2.

The PDPA does not explicitly require legal ownership of data to invoke data protection, presumably because legal rights with regards to personal data are directly tied to the data subject.[103] Personal data may be considered as a type of property under Thai law.[104] However, the PDPA specifies that the authority over a minor below the age of 10, or a quasi-incompetent or incompetent individual lies with their parents, custodians, or curator, who can file complaints or exercise the data subject's rights on their behalf.[105]

Anti-doxxing measures against the non-consensual publication of personal data are present in the PDPA and other laws. Under the PDPA, personal data may only be disclosed with the consent of the data subject or under another appropriate legal basis.[106] In addition, in specific situations where a data subject makes a request related to the disclosure of personal data, the data controller is held responsible for taking appropriate actions, including implementing necessary technological measures and incurring associated expenses to fulfil the request. The data controller is also required to inform other relevant data controllers to obtain their responses regarding the actions to be taken in order to fulfil the request. This obligation arises when the data controller has made personal data publicly available and is requested to erase the personal data, and there are no exceptions that allow the data controller to refuse such a request.[107] In addition to the PDPA, an individual may claim for tort damages under section 420 of the CCC for any acts of doxxing that violate his or her right to privacy under the Thai Constitution. Furthermore, depending on the underlying acts, doxxing may also fall under the Computer Crime Act B.E. 2550 (2007) and the Criminal Code for Defamation.[108]

iii. Extraterritorial Effect of Laws on Data Protection and Privacy

The PDPA applies extraterritorially to the collection, use, or disclosure of personal data by a data controller or a data processor which is located outside of Thailand where the collection, use, or disclosure of personal data relates to (1) data subjects who are in Thailand and (2) where such activities occurring involve:

- the offering of goods or services to the data subjects who are in Thailand, irrespective of whether the payment is made by the data subject or
- the monitoring of the data subject's behaviour, where the behaviour takes place in Thailand.[109]

Note that foreign data controllers who are subject to the PDPA are also required to appoint, in writing, a representative in Thailand who is authorised to act on behalf of the data controller, without being subject to any limitation of liability with respect to the collection, use or disclosure of the personal data according to the purposes of the data controller.[110]

[103] Official PDPA Guide for Citizens, 2.
[104] Civil and Commercial Code, ss 138, 140.
[105] PDPA, s 20, para 4.
[106] ibid, ss 24, 26, and 27.
[107] ibid, s 33, para 3.
[108] Criminal Code, ss 326–28.
[109] PDPA, s 5, para 2.
[110] ibid, s 37(5).

iv. Data Breach Notification

Under the PDPA, a data breach is defined as:

> [A] violation of security measures that causes loss, access, use, change, correction or disclosure of personal data without authority or in a wrongful manner, whether due to intent, wilfulness, negligence, unauthorised or wrongful action, wrongful acts involving computer, cyber threat, mistakes, glitches or accidents or for any other reason.[111]

In the event of a data breach, data controllers are required under the PDPA to notify the Office of the PDPC of any personal data breach without delay, and, where feasible, within 72 hours after having become aware of it, unless such personal data breach is unlikely to result in a risk to the rights and freedoms of the persons concerned.[112] Additionally, if the personal data breach is likely to result in a high risk to the rights and freedoms of the persons concerned, the data controller must also notify the data subject of the personal data breach and the remedial measures it will take without delay.[113] Data processors, meanwhile, are required to notify the data controller of any personal data breaches that occur.[114]

Furthermore, the Announcement of the PDPC Re: Criteria and Methods for Reporting Personal Data Breach B.E. 2565 further specifies the steps that the data controller and processors should take once a data breach is discovered, regardless of whether the data breach has to be reported to the Office of the PDPC or the data subject by law.[115]

Note that the PDPC also has the power to further specify the rules and procedures for notification and exemption to the notification requirements under this provision.[116]

IV. Data Security and Data Localisation

A. Data Security and Localisation Requirements

Data security is generally addressed under the PDPA, which broadly includes the provision of appropriate security measures for preventing the unauthorised or unlawful loss, access to, use, alteration, correction or disclosure of personal data. This is in accordance with the minimum standards specified by the PDPC, which are primarily found in the PDPC Announcement on Security Measures.[117] These minimum standards include organisational,

[111] PDPC Announcement on Reporting Personal Data Breach, s 3.

[112] PDPA, s 37(4). Note that, if necessary, the data controller may also request the Office of the PDPC to waive the 72 hours requirement with justification within 15 days from the data breach, see PDPC Announcement on Reporting Personal Data Breach, s 7.

While the analysis for evaluating the personal data breach will ultimately be on a case-by-case basis, the PDPC has provided 10 key examples in its PDPC Guidelines on Data Breach.

[113] ibid.

[114] PDPA, s 40(2). Section 8 of the PDPC Announcement on Reporting Personal Data Breach further specifies that the data processing agreement between the data controller and data processor must include a provision for the data processor to notify the data controller within 72 hours after the data processor learns about the data breach.

[115] PDPC Announcement on Reporting Personal Data Breach, s 5.

[116] ibid, s 37(4).

[117] PDPC Announcement on Security Measures, s 4.

technical, and physical measures.[118] Data controllers must regularly review their data security measures, especially when the technology has changed[119] or a data breach occurs, unless the breach poses no risks to the rights and freedoms of individuals.[120]

Specific data security requirements exist for various sectors, such as entities regulated by the BOT,[121] SEC,[122] Ministry of Public Health,[123] NBTC,[124] the National Credit Bureau,[125] and government agencies.[126] While it is beyond the scope of this chapter to discuss these requirements in detail, each sector has its own security measures.

Data localisations, understood as the requirement to store and process data within Thailand, are only covered under the PDPA to the extent that the law imposes restrictions on the cross-border transfer of personal data, unless certain standards of data protection are met.[127]

Data localisation requirements are explicitly covered by the Credit Information Business Act. According to this Act, the National Credit Bureau and related information controllers and processors are prohibited from processing credit related data outside of Thailand.[128]

B. Data Security and Localisation Requirements for Particular Types of Data

The PDPA recognises the concept of sensitive data, which includes biometric information, religious beliefs, sexual orientation, criminal records, and health data.[129] The PDPA requires controllers and processors to maintain appropriate security measures for personal data, including both general and sensitive data, taking into consideration the types of data involved.[130] Violations related to sensitive data under the PDPA may result in harsher penalties, including the possibility of criminal convictions.[131] However, there is no special requirement for the transfer of sensitive personal data abroad beyond the general data transfer requirements under the PDPA. This is in keeping with the standards of the GDPR.

Health data is protected under both the PDPA and by the MPH (for entities regulated by the Ministry). The MPH has specific criteria for the collection, usage, and disclosure of health data electronically, including safeguarding the electronic data by controlling access,

[118] ibid, s 4(2).
[119] ibid.
[120] ibid, s 5, para 2.
[121] BOT Market Conduct, s 6.1.
[122] SEC Announcement on Business Standards, s 14.
[123] MPH Ministerial Regulations Relating to the Protection and Organization of Personal Health Information B.E. 2561(2018), s 25.
[124] Telecommunications Business Act B.E. 2544 (2001), s 50; NBCT Announcement on Personal Data, s 10.
[125] Credit Information Business Act, B.E. 2545 (2002), s 17.
[126] Official Information Act, B.E. 2540 (1997), s 23 and Rule on the Maintenance of Official Secrets B.E. 2544 (2001).
[127] See PDPA, ss 28 and 29.
[128] Credit Information Business Act, B.E. 2545 (2002), s 12.
[129] For the full list of sensitive data under the PDPA, see PDPA, s 26.
[130] PDPC Announcement on Security Measures, s 4.
[131] PDPA, ss 79–81.

backing up, and regular inspection and risk assessment.[132] Whilst there are no explicit data localisation requirements for health data under the MPH regulations, the disclosure of health data must comply with the consent of the data subject or authorised parties and adhere to the applicable regulations.[133] In addition, no disclosure of health data should cause damage to the data subject and data owner.[134]

State secrets are governed by the Rule on the Maintenance of Official Secrets B.E. 2544. Government agencies must keep state secrets in a safe location with specific procedures, following the advice of the relevant security organisation (such as the National Intelligence Agency, Thai Army, or National Police).[135] State secrets may be transferred outside of the government agency with the approval of the head of the agency or other authorised personnel, as well as registration with the appointed registrar on state secrets.[136] State secrets that are transferred outside of Thailand must additionally be conducted in accordance with the regulations of the Ministry of Foreign Affairs on diplomatic bags or carried by officials with diplomatic status.[137]

V. Issues in Private International Law

A. Litigations involving Cross-Border Data Transfer and Privacy

There are three forms of liabilities under the PDPA: administrative liabilities, civil liabilities, and criminal liabilities.

i. Administrative Liabilities

The data subject has the right to file a complaint to the PDPC's appointed Expert Committee in the event that the data controller or the data processor, including their employees or their contractors, violates the PDPA.[138] In addition, the Expert Committee also has the power to independently investigate the data controller, the data processors and their employees and service providers.[139]

If, after the Expert Committee's investigation, it is found that the complaint has reasonable grounds and may be settled, the Expert Committee shall proceed with the dispute settlement. However, if such a complaint is not amenable to settlement, or dispute settlement efforts fail, the Expert Committee has the power to issue orders prohibiting the data controller or the data processor from carrying out acts which cause damage to the data subject or to order them to carry out any acts to mitigate such damage.[140]

[132] MPH Regulation on Health Information, s 25.
[133] ibid.
[134] ibid.
[135] Rule on the Maintenance of Official Secrets B.E. 2544 (2001), s 44.
[136] ibid, s 37.
[137] ibid, s 39.
[138] PDPA, s 73.
[139] ibid, s 72(2).
[140] ibid, s 74, para 3.

Ultimately, administrative liabilities may attach to the data controller,[141] data processor,[142] the representative of the data controller or data processor,[143] or any person who fails to act in compliance with the order given by the PDPC's appointed Expert Committee,[144] or fails to provide a statement of facts to the Expert Committee,[145] or fails to facilitate government officials in their investigation.[146]

The Expert Committee has the power to render administrative fines ranging from 500,000 to five million Baht as penalties for any violations of the PDPA that trigger any administrative liabilities under the law.[147] This includes an administrative fine of not exceeding three million Baht (five million Baht for sensitive data) for a data controller or data processor's failure to transfer personal data in accordance with the certified group company policy or appropriate safeguards per the rules and methods as prescribed by the PDPC.[148] In determining whether to issue an order to impose an administrative fine, the Expert Committee must take into consideration the severity of the violation, size of the data controller or the data processor, or other circumstances according to the PDPC.[149] If it deems fit, the Expert Committee may also issue an order for rectification or a warning first, prior to issuing the administrative fines.[150]

In cases where a person ordered to pay an administrative fine by the Expert Committee refuses to pay such fine, the provisions concerning the execution of administrative orders under the administrative procedure law shall apply.[151] The Expert Committee shall also have the power to seize, attach, or sell by auction the property of such data controller or the data processor per the law on administrative procedures.[152] In cases where the administrative order cannot be executed for any reason, the Expert Committee can also file a lawsuit with the Administrative Court in order to demand payment of the relevant fine.[153]

ii. Civil and Criminal Liabilities

In addition to administrative liabilities, the PDPA also provides for the imposition of civil and criminal liabilities on breach via the civil and criminal courts in Thailand. Civil liabilities under the PDPA pertain to any violation of the PDPA that causes damage to the data subject, whether intentionally or negligently (strict liability).[154] Data subjects may sue the data controller or data processor whose use of their personal data violates the PDPA and causes damage to the data subject in civil courts. Such a controller or processor must then

[141] ibid, ss 82–84.
[142] ibid, ss 85–86.
[143] ibid, s 88.
[144] ibid, s 89.
[145] ibid.
[146] ibid.
[147] ibid, s 90, para 1.
[148] ibid, ss 83–84, 86–87.
[149] ibid, s 90, para 2. See also Announcement of the Personal Data Protection Committee Re: Criteria for Considering Issuing an Administrative Fine Order of the Expert Committee B.E. 2565 (2022).
[150] PDPA, s 90, para 1.
[151] Administrative Procedure Act, B.E. 2539 (1996); PDPA, s 90, para 2.
[152] PDPA, s 74, para 4.
[153] ibid, s 90, para 2.
[154] ibid, s 77.

compensate the data subject for such damages, which will include all necessary expenses incurred by the data subject for the prevention of the damages likely to occur, and/or which was spent to suppress the damages occurred.[155] Exceptions include cases where the data controller or the data processor can prove that the operation in violation of the PDPA was a result of an event of *force majeure*, the data subject's own act or omission, or an action taken in compliance with an order of a government official.[156]

The PDPA additionally provides for punitive damages to be awarded if the court deems fit for civil wrongs, taking into account the relevant circumstances, such as the severity of damages incurred, the interest obtained by and the financial status of the data controller or the data processor, the remedies provided to the data subject, or the data subject's own contribution to the damages.[157]

Data subjects may also go to the police to file a criminal complaint under the PDPA. Criminal conduct pertains to violations of the PDPA by data controllers relating to the unlawful use, disclosure, or international transfer of sensitive personal data, in a manner that is likely to cause another person to suffer any damage or reputation impairment, or which exposes such other person to scorn, hate, or ridicule (imprisonment of up to six months and fines of not exceeding 500,000 Baht or both) or in order to unlawfully benefit the data controller (imprisonment of up to one year and fines not exceeding one million Baht or both) (compoundable offences).[158] Criminal liability may also be incurred by any person who comes to know the personal data of another person as a result of performing their duties under the PDPA (eg the Data Protection Officer or PDPC officials), and who unlawfully discloses it to any other person.[159]

Note that per section 81 of the PDPA, in the case where the violator is a juristic person and the criminal offence is conducted as a result of the instructions given by or the act of any director, manager or person who is responsible for such act, or in the case where such person has a duty to instruct or perform any act, but omits to instruct or perform such act until the juristic person commits such offence, such a person shall also be punished with the punishment as prescribed under the PDPA for such offence.[160]

The Minister of Digital Economy and Society has publicly stated on 29 January 2024 his intention to propose the amendment of the PDPA to increase the criminal penalties for those who illegally trade in personal data.[161]

iii. Other Types of Liabilities

In addition to the remedies under the PDPA, an individual may also file a claim in a civil court for tort damages under section 420 of the CCC for any personal data processing that

[155] ibid.
[156] ibid.
[157] ibid, s 78.
[158] ibid, s 79.
[159] ibid, s 80.
[160] ibid, s 81.
[161] Komsan Tortermvasana, 'Data Protection Complaint Centre Opens' (*Bangkok Post*, 30 January 2024), available at www.bangkokpost.com/business/general/2732700.

violates his or her right to privacy under the Thai Constitution.[162] Additionally, the individual may also file a complaint with the relevant supervisory authority for specific sectors such as the BOT[163] and the SEC.[164]

Finally, the underlying acts relating to data transfer and protection may also fall under other types of criminal violations, such as computer crime,[165] defamation,[166] child abuse,[167] etc.

iv. Major Litigation

There has not been any major litigation with regards to data protection and privacy in Thailand.

B. Jurisdictional Issues involving Cross-Border Data Protection and Privacy

The jurisdiction of Thai courts under Thai law is broad and depends on the reason behind the breach. For civil cases involving a data breach, complaints may be filed at a court where the defendant has his or her domicile, or at a court where the cause of the lawsuit accrues, regardless of whether or not the defendant has his or her domicile in Thailand.[168] For criminal cases involving a data breach, the court with jurisdiction is the one in the district where the offence has or is alleged or believed to have been committed, where the accused resides or is arrested, or where an inquiry has been conducted.[169] Additionally, certain criminal wrongs relating to the security of the Kingdom may be punishable in Thailand[170] under the jurisdiction of the court in which the inquiry has been held.[171] Finally, the Administrative Court has jurisdiction over data breach cases involving administrative liabilities under the PDPA.[172]

While arguments for a stay of proceeding such as *forum non conveniens* are possible, Thai courts rarely, if ever, restrict their own powers if they have the jurisdiction to take on the case according to Thai law, even if there is a parallel lawsuit in relation to the same matter in other jurisdictions.

[162] Constitution of the Kingdom of Thailand B.E. 2560 (2017), s 32; Civil and Commercial Code, s 420.
[163] 'BOT Complaint Form' (*The Bank of Thailand*), available at app.bot.or.th/1213/Complaint/Complaint/Disclaimer.
[164] 'SEC Complaint Center' (*The Securities and Exchange Commission, Thailand*), available at www.sec.or.th/EN/pages/aboutus/sechelp.aspx.
[165] Computer Crime Act B.E. 2550 (2007).
[166] PDPA.
[167] Child Protection Act B.E. 2546 (2003).
[168] Code of Civil Procedure, s 4.
[169] Code of Criminal Procedure, s 22.
[170] Criminal Code, s 7.
[171] Conflict of Laws Act B.E. 2481 (1938), s 16, para 1.
[172] Act on Establishment of Administrative Courts and Administrative Court Procedure, B.E. 2542 (1999), s 9.

C. Applicable Law: In Litigations involving Cross-Border Data Protection and Privacy

The primary law governing the applicability of law in multi-jurisdictional cases appearing in Thai courts is the Act on Conflict of Law B.E. 2481 (1938) ('Conflict of Law Act'). For civil wrongs, the law of the place governing the dispute is that place where the facts constituting the wrongful acts have taken place.[173] For issues involving physical movable property (ex. a physical server), the laws of the location where the property is established governs.[174] However, in a case where the property has been transferred outside of the country, the national law of the property owner governs from the moment the property has been exported.[175] Additionally, for administrative and criminal issues, Thai laws will apply to the extent that the case is within the jurisdiction of the Administrative and Criminal Courts, respectively.[176]

Under the Conflict of Laws Act, Thai courts may also displace the application of foreign law if it is contrary to public order or the good morals of the people of Thailand.

D. Recognition and Enforcement of Foreign Judgments

Thai law does not provide for the direct recognition and enforcement of foreign judgments, including those related to data protection and privacy. There is no specific legislation in Thailand that deals with enforcement of a foreign judgment, and Thailand is not a party to any treaty that would allow for the recognition and enforcement of foreign judgments.

To enforce a foreign judgment in Thailand, a party must commence new litigation proceedings, where the foreign judgment and related documents (such as a settlement document) may be accepted as evidence. Importantly, as these are new proceedings, the Thai courts may review the merits of the case before rendering a judgment.

E. Obstacles to Effective Data Protection

The primary obstacles with regards to effective data protection in Thailand concerning cross-border transfer issues have less to do with the country's private international law regime, and more to do with the lack of clarity within the PDPA itself and its delays and general lack of enforcement.

For instance, there is still significant vagueness concerning the appointment of representatives for foreign data controllers and processors who are not based in Thailand under the PDPA. The PDPA requires foreign data controllers within the jurisdiction of the PDPA[177] to appoint a representative who is authorised to act on behalf of the data controller without any limitation of liability with respect to the collection, use or disclosure of the

[173] Conflict of Laws Act B.E. 2481 (1938), s 15.
[174] Conflict of Laws Act B.E. 2481 (1938), s 16, para 1.
[175] ibid, para 2.
[176] Please see the prior section.
[177] For more on the extra-territorial application of the PDPA, please see section III.B.iii.

personal data according to the purposes of the controller and processor.[178] This provision also applies to data processors of such data controllers.[179] However, there are exceptions to this provision for public authorities as prescribed and announced by the PDPC, controllers and processors who engage in the business of collecting, using, or disclosing personal data that are not of a sensitive nature and do not involve a large amount of personal data as prescribed by the PDPC. Without these exceptions, the provisions concerning the appointment of foreign representatives under the PDPA may be a form of regulatory overreach where there is little hope of enforcing the provision on such a scale for all foreign data controllers and processors, regardless of their size and type, who fall under the jurisdiction of the PDPA.

Additionally, the two-year delays and the relative lack of enforcement of the law means that many companies have not yet fully implemented the data protection mechanisms as required by the PDPA.[180] The lack of enforcement also means that there are little substantive case precedents for the PDPA, especially regarding more complex matters such as the international transfer of personal data.

Finally, in terms of jurisdictional issues, any concerns levied against the GDPR, such as its 'all-or-nothing approach' under Article 3[181] is also likely to be applicable to the PDPA, which is modelled after the GDPR.

It is highly unlikely that Thailand will be influenced by private international law guidelines in relation to data protection and privacy such as the Lisbon Guidelines on Privacy.

F. Data Scraping Cases and Classification of Data

In data scraping cases under the PDPA, data controllers are allowed to process sensitive data if it is information which has been disclosed to the public with the explicit consent of the data subject.[182] However, there is no equivalent exception for general personal data under section 24 of the PDPA. This is presumably because most processing of personal data that is disclosed to the public with the explicit consent of the data subject will fall under the legitimate interests exception under section 24(5) of the PDPA. There are no specific laws that tackle data scraping for non-personal data, and the Government itself may have even employed data scraping techniques to gather information from the general public.[183]

While there is currently no legal precedent, it may be the case that Thai courts will decide to treat data content, as opposed to the physical data itself, as distinct legal assets in the future. The closest parallel may be found in intellectual property law, where a Supreme Court decision determined that a Copyright is a special kind of legal property obtained through Intellectual Property law, that is separated from movable property as defined in the Civil and Commercial Code.[184]

[178] PDPA, s 37(5).
[179] ibid, s 38, para 2.
[180] Tharittawat Samejaidee, 'Unease as PDPA Comes into Force' (*Bangkok Post*, 27 May 2022), available at www.bangkokpost.com/life/tech/2316766/unease-as-pdpa-comes-into-force.
[181] Marta Requejo, 'Jurisdiction, Conflict of Laws and Data Protection in Cyberspace' (*Conflict of Laws*, 12 August 2018), available at www.conflictoflaws.net/2017/jurisdiction-conflict-of-laws-and-data-protection-in-cyberspace/.
[182] PDPA, s 26(3).
[183] Wichit Chantanusornsiri, 'Web Scraping a New Tool in Revenue Hunt' (*Bangkok Post*, 3 January 2019), available at www.bangkokpost.com/business/1604558/web-scraping-a-new-tool-in-revenue-hunt.
[184] Supreme Court Decision No 846/2534; Copyright Act B.E. 2521 (1978).

VI. Topical Issues and Prospects

A. Artificial Intelligence or AI-Generated Data

There is currently no legal regime in Thailand explicitly governing data produced by artificial intelligence (AI). Nonetheless, two draft legislations on AI, of seemingly different objectives, have been introduced for public consideration: The Draft Royal Decree on Business Operations that Use Artificial Intelligence System ('Draft Decree on AI Businesses') and the Draft Act on the Promotion and Support for AI Innovations in Thailand ('Draft Act on AI Promotion').

The Draft Decree on AI Businesses is based on the EU AI Act with a risk-based approach to AI governance, prohibiting certain dangerous usages of AI, and requiring risk control mechanisms for others. The Draft Act on AI Promotion aims to promote the development of an AI ecosystem in Thailand by introducing various mechanics such as sandbox testing and standardisation, including guidelines for data sharing and setting up criteria to qualify as a trusted data intermediary between a data buyer and seller.

B. Potential Cooperation under the Belt and Road Initiative

Thailand has signed a Memorandum of Understanding with China on the Belt and Road Initiative. In a joint statement issued on 5 November 2019, both countries agreed to explore as part of the framework of the Belt and Road Initiative framework,[185] projects involving:

> [C]ooperation in communication technology, open innovation centre, high-tech industrial park', and technology transfer centre so as to strengthen the cooperation in such fields as digital economy, smart city, ICT converged application, software and IT service, ICT infrastructure connectivity, digital transformation of industry, cyber security, cloud computing and artificial intelligence.[186]

C. Data Protection post COVID-19 Pandemic

The COVID-19 pandemic has delayed the enforcement of the PDPA for most businesses and organisations from 31 May 2021 to 31 May 2022. For more on the timeline of the PDPA, please see section II.B.vi.

[185] 'Joint Press Statement between the Government of the Kingdom of Thailand and the Government of the People's Republic of China Issued on 5 November 2019, Bangkok' (*Ministry of Foreign Affairs Thailand*, 5 November 2019), available at www.mfa.go.th/en/content/111092-joint-press-statement-between-the-government-of-the-kingdom-of-thailand-and-the-government-of-the-people%E2%80%99s-republic-of-china-issued-on-5-november-2019,-bangkok?page=5d5bd3da15e39c306002aaf9.

[186] ibid.

14

Sri Lanka

HEMAKA PERERA

I. Introduction

In today's globalised world, cross-border data flows have become an essential aspect of international trade and communication. The protection of personal data and privacy rights are crucial for individuals, particularly in the context of cross-border data transfers. Private International Law plays a crucial role in regulating these transfers, as it governs the interaction of different legal systems and provides a framework for resolving disputes. Sri Lanka, as a developing country with a growing digital economy, has recognised the importance of data protection and privacy rights and has taken action to regulate these issues through legislation and policy frameworks. This chapter explores the current legal framework of international data transfers and data protection in Sri Lanka, analysing the key legal instruments, key definitions, and the legal bases, mechanisms, and exceptions for international data transfers and data protection. The chapter will also discuss the Sri Lankan approach to data security and data localisation and how data protection intersects with Private International Law. Finally, this chapter will discuss topical issues and prospects concerning data protection in Sri Lanka.

II. General Legal Framework of International Data Transfers and Data Protection

A. Constitutional Framework

The foundation of the Sri Lankan legal system is the Constitution of the Democratic Socialist Republic of Sri Lanka of 1978 ('Constitution'). The Constitution does not expressly guarantee a right to privacy as a fundamental right or provide any protection for data transfers. It does, however, expressly vest in every citizen the right of access to information. Article 14A, which was introduced in 2015 through the Nineteenth Amendment to the Constitution, provides that '[e]very citizen shall have the right of access to any information as provided for by law, being information that is required for the exercise or protection of a citizen's right held' by inter alia any ministry or statutory body created by law.[1]

[1] Constitution of the Democratic Socialist Republic of Sri Lanka of 1978 ('Constitution'), Art 14A.

While the constitutional entrenchment of the right to access information, and the introduction of the supplemental Right to Information Act, No 12 of 2016 (RTI Act), was an important first step in recognising the value of data, the use of this right is not without restriction. Recipients of requests for information under Article 14A and the RTI Act, such as a ministry or government department, may refuse such requests on several grounds, including if the disclosure would: cause the unwarranted invasion of an individual's privacy unless disclosure is justified by the larger public interest;[2] undermine the state's defence, its territorial integrity, or national security;[3] or seriously prejudice Sri Lanka's economy in specified circumstances.[4]

B. Statutory Framework

i. The Enactment of the Personal Data Protection Act

The principal legislative instrument which addresses protection of personal data in Sri Lanka is the recently enacted Personal Data Protection Act, No 9 of 2022 (PDPA or the 'Act'). It was primarily introduced to regulate the processing of personal data and to identify and strengthen the rights of data subjects in relation to the protection of personal data. It is notably the first comprehensive law concerning data protection introduced in South Asia and is a significant piece of legislation to further improve inter-operability among personal data protection frameworks as well as to strengthen cross-border cooperation among personal data protection enforcement authorities as recognised in the PDPA's preamble.

The need for data protection legislation was first lobbied by the Central Bank of Sri Lanka ('Central Bank') in September 2018, which requested the then Ministry of Digital Infrastructure to initiate work on a data protection bill. The policy motivations behind the adoption of a data protection bill were inter alia to provide for mechanisms to protect personal data ensuring consumer trust and safeguarding privacy, to improve the interoperability among data protection frameworks, and strengthen cross-border cooperation among personal data protection enforcement authorities. In February 2019, a 10-member drafting committee, comprising of members from the public sector (such as members of the Legal Draftsman's Department) and private sector (such as members from leading telecommunications providers) was formed. The committee was chaired by the General Counsel of the Information and Communication Technology Agency of Sri Lanka.

The drafting committee first finalised a 'Data Protection Framework' containing proposals for a data protection legislation in June 2019. Subsequently, there were seven rounds of public stakeholder consultations, commencing with a public sector and private sector stakeholder dialogue held on 27 June 2019, supported by the International Trade Centre and European Union.[5] Based on over 30 submissions received from experts, international

[2] Right to Information Act, No 12 of 2016 (RTI Act), s 5(1)(a).
[3] ibid, s 5(1)(b)(i).
[4] ibid, s 5(1)(c).
[5] Jayantha Fernando and Sanduni Wickramasinghe, 'Sri Lanka Personal Data Protection Legislation – An Overview' (3 August 2022) ('PDPA Overview'), available at https://ssrn.com/abstract=4246818.

organisations and multinational corporations, several versions of the Personal Data Protection Bill were prepared by the Legal Draftsman's Department. A revised draft was submitted to the Cabinet of Ministers on 8 December 2019, and approval was granted, in principle, by the Cabinet to proceed with the next steps. The bill thereafter was the subject of further stakeholder consultations and underwent further scrutiny in 2020 by the Ministry of Justice, the Central Bank, the Telecommunications Regulatory Commission of Sri Lanka, and the Hon Attorney General of Sri Lanka, among others. The bill approved by the Cabinet of Ministers was published on 25 November 2021 in the Gazette Supplementary[6] and finally, the PDPA was adopted by the Parliament of Sri Lanka and was certified by the Speaker of the Parliament on 19 March 2022.

ii. Other Acts

In addition to the PDPA, there are several other acts which directly or indirectly concern data protection and/or privacy. These include, the RTI Act, Computer Crime Act, No 24 of 2007, Electronic Transactions Act, No 19 of 2006, Intellectual Property Act, No 36 of 2003, Telecommunications Act, No 25 of 1991, and Banking Act, No 30 of 1988.

While the PDPA's provisions supersede these other acts,[7] these acts continue to operate and compliment the PDPA. As mentioned previously, the RTI Act enables citizens of Sri Lanka to request information from Ministries, Government Departments and other statutory bodies. The Computer Crime Act is a particularly pertinent piece of legislation since it provides penal sanctions for unlawfully obtaining data,[8] dealing with data unlawfully obtained,[9] illegal interception of data,[10] and abetting an offence under the Act.[11] The Electronic Transactions Act is also significant since it permits information (including data) to be stored as data messages, electronic documents, electronic records, or other communication in electronic form if there exists a reliable assurance as to the integrity of the information, even if a law requires information to be presented or retained in writing[12] or its original form.[13] It also stipulates the requirements for how such electronic information is to be retained.[14]

In addition to the various statutes concerning data protection and privacy, it warrants mention that Sri Lanka is a mixed-legal system, incorporating both common law and civil law into their system. A right to privacy can be found within the Roman Dutch law. It takes the form of action against injury (wrongful aggression upon the person, dignity or reputation) under *actio injuriarum*.[15] In the case of *Nararajah v Obeysekera*,[16] the Court

[6] The Gazette of the Democratic Socialist Republic of Sri Lanka – Part II of 19 November 2021 (issued on 25 November 2021).

[7] Personal Data Protection Act, No 9 of 2022 (PDPA), s 3.

[8] Computer Crime Act, No 24 of 2007, s 3.

[9] ibid, s 7.

[10] ibid, s 8.

[11] ibid, s 12.

[12] Electronic Transactions Act, No 19 of 2006, s 4.

[13] ibid, s 5.

[14] ibid, s 6.

[15] TB Abeysekara and AE Ranasinghe, 'Holistic Approach in Introducing Proper Legal Framework to Regulate Data Protection and Privacy in Sri Lanka' (2022) *Vidyodaya Journal of Management* 8(1) 169–200.

[16] *Nararajah v Obeysekera* 52 NLR 76 (1971).

discussed the notion of invasion of privacy and recognised the right of an individual to personal space. Sri Lankan courts have also discussed the importance of an individual's right to privacy in subsequent cases such as *Chinnappa et al v Kanakar et al*,[17] *Abraham v Hume*,[18] *A.M.K Azeez v W.T Senevirathne (SI Police)*.[19] Notably, in *Sinha Ratnatunga v The State*, the Supreme Court recognised that 'to invade [an individual's] privacy is to assail his integrity as a human being and thereby deny him his right to remain in society as a human being with human dignity'.[20]

C. Data Protection Framework

i. *Influence of International Data Protection Frameworks*

At the outset, it is important to note that the PDPA is heavily influenced by existing international data protection frameworks. During the PDPA's drafting process, the drafting committee engaged international organisations and bodies such as the European Commission and the Council of Europe. The PDPA espouses international best practices, derived from instruments such as the Organisation for Economic Co-operation and Development Privacy Guidelines, Asia-Pacific Economic Cooperation (APEC) Privacy Framework, Council of Europe Data Protection Convention (Convention 108+), the European Union's General Data Protection Regulation (GDPR) and laws enacted in other jurisdictions such as the United Kingdom, Singapore, Australia and Mauritius, and the State of California.[21] The GDPR in particular has been a significant influence on the PDPA. Much like the former, the PDPA is based on similar fundamental principles, such as lawfulness,[22] accuracy,[23] transparency,[24] purpose limitation,[25] data minimisation,[26] retention limitation,[27] integrity and confidentiality,[28] and accountability.[29] However, these principles are utilised in different ways and to different degrees, as will be observed below.

ii. *Application of the PDPA*

Although the PDPA was certified by the Parliament in March 2022, the provisions of the Act come into operation on a staggered timeline. The pertinent date for commencing the time period is the date on which the Certificate of the Speaker was endorsed,

[17] *Chinnappa et al v Kanakar et al* 13 NLR 157, 158–60.
[18] *Abraham v Hume* 52 NLR 449, 453.
[19] *A.M.K Azeez v W.T Senevirathne (SI Police)* 69 NLR 209, 210.
[20] *Sinha Ratnatunga v The State* [2001] 2 Sri L.R 172, 213.
[21] PDPA Overview (n 5) 2; Regulation (EU) 2016/679 of the European Parliament and of the Council of 27 April 2016 on the protection of natural persons with regard to the processing of personal data and on the free movement of such data, and repealing Directive 95/46/EC (General Data Protection Regulation (GDPR)) [2016] OJ L119/1.
[22] PDPA (n 7) s 5.
[23] ibid, s 8.
[24] ibid, s 11.
[25] ibid, s 6.
[26] ibid, s 7.
[27] ibid, s 9.
[28] ibid, s 10.
[29] ibid, s 12.

ie, 19 March 2022. First, section 1, which stipulates the dates of operation, came into operation on the date the Certificate of the Speaker was endorsed, ie, 19 March 2022.[30] Second, Part V (Data Protection Authority) comes into operation on a date appointed by the Minister no later than the date appointed for all other provisions of the Act (save for section 1 and Part IV).[31] The Minister means, the Minister assigned the subject of data protection under Article 44 or 45 of the Constitution.[32] The PDPA provides that this date may be within the first 18 months of the Speaker's Certificate, but it may not be later than 36 months from the Speaker's Certificate. On 21 July 2023, pursuant to the powers vested under section 1(5) of the PDPA read with Article 44(3) of the Constitution, the Minister appointed 17 July 2023 as the date on which the provisions of Part V of the PDPA would come into operation.[33] The operation of Part V is seemingly tied with the other provisions because Part V provides for the establishment and operation of the Data Protection Authority, which the regulator created under the PDPA. Third, or concurrently with Part V, all other provisions of the PDPA (save for section 1 and Parts IV and V), come into operation on the date appointed by the Minister between 18 months and 36 months from the Speaker's Certification.[34] Fourth and finally, Part IV (Use of Personal Data to Disseminate Solicited Messages) comes into effect on a date appointed by the Minister between 24 months and 48 months from the Speaker's Certification.[35] On 8 January 2024, by the powers vested under section 1(3) of the PDPA and Article 44(3) of the Constitution, the Minister appointed: first, 1 December 2023 as the date the provisions of Parts VI, VIII, IX, and X of the PDPA come into operation; and second, 18 March 2025 as the date the provisions of Parts I, II, III, and VII of the PDPA come into operation.[36]

The PDPA does not distinguish its application to any particular sector. Rather, it applies to both private and public sector entities, small or large. One notable exception is that similar to the GDPR,[37] the PDPA does not apply to any personal data processed purely for personal, domestic or household purposes by an individual.[38] It is noteworthy that the Authority is empowered to make rules governing the sharing of personal data between controllers which are public authorities[39] and to appoint advisory committees to formulate, among other things, sectoral guidelines and rules.[40] While the door is left open for sectoral guidelines, they would have to operate within the confines of the PDPA. Thus, it is unlikely that such guidelines or rules would be less burdensome than the provisions of the Act.

It bears emphasis that the PDPA provides the framework for certain detailed matters to be prescribed by regulations. For example, technical and organisational measures may

[30] ibid, s 1(2).
[31] ibid, s 1(5) read with s 1(3).
[32] ibid, s 56.
[33] See Gazette Extraordinary No 2341/59 issued on 21 July 2023, available at www.documents.gov.lk/files/egz/2023/7/2341-59_E.pdf.
[34] PDPA (n 7) s 1(3).
[35] ibid, s 1(4).
[36] See Gazette Extraordinary No 2366/08 issued on 8 January 2024, available at www.documents.gov.lk/files/egz/2024/1/2366-08_E.pdf.
[37] GDPR (n 21) Art 2(c).
[38] PDPA (n 7) s 2(3)(a).
[39] ibid, s 33(n).
[40] ibid, s 33(o).

be prescribed for use by controllers to ensure the integrity and confidentiality of personal data.[41] It is the Minister, with the concurrence of the Authority that may make regulations under the PDPA and prescribe any matter so required by the PDPA.[42]

iii. Key Definitions

In order to understand the PDPA's framework, it is imperative that the key persons covered by the Act are identified. The PDPA provides comprehensive definitions and illustrations for the persons it applies to and/or regulates. A 'data subject' is defined to mean an identified or identifiable natural person, alive or deceased, to whom the personal data relates.[43] In turn, an 'identifiable natural person' is a natural person who can be identified, directly or indirectly, by reference to any personal data. The PDPA's definition of a data subject goes further than the GDPR in that it expressly includes deceased persons, while the GDPR leaves this to the discretion of member states.[44] Further, by virtue of data subjects being limited to natural persons, the personal data concerning legal persons, such as companies, falls outside the scope of the PDPA.

A 'controller' may be any natural or legal person, private or public, which alone or jointly with others determines the purposes and means of the processing of personal data.[45] At this juncture, it is also pertinent to note that 'processing' is defined broadly to mean 'any operation performed on personal data including but not limited to collection, storage, preservation, alteration, retrieval, disclosure, transmission, making available, erasure, destruction of, consultation, alignment, combination, or the carrying out of logical or arithmetical operations on personal data'.[46] Accordingly, a controller may be any natural or legal person that, among other things, decides what information to collect, from whom to collect information, how and/or where to collect and/or store information.

A 'processor' on the other hand is a natural or legal person, public or private, who acts on the instructions of the controller.[47] Notably, a processor must be a third party and not a person subject to the hierarchical control of the controller. This means that an employee of a controller would not be a processor.

iv. Distinction between Personal and Non-Personal Data

The definition of 'personal data' is comprehensive in that it includes 'any information that can identify a data subject directly or indirectly, by reference to: (a) an identifier such as a name,

[41] ibid, s 10.

[42] ibid, s 53(1).

[43] ibid, s 56.

[44] GDPR (n 21), Recital 27.

[45] PDPA (n 7) s 56 ('"controller" means, any natural or legal person, public authority, public corporation, non-governmental organization, agency or any other body or entity which alone or jointly with others determines the purposes and means of the processing of personal data').

[46] Ibid, s 56.

[47] Ibid, s 56 ('"processor" means, a natural or legal person, public authority or other entity established by or under any written law, which processes personal data on behalf of the controller.

For the avoidance of doubt, a processor shall be a separate entity or person from the controller and not a person subject to any hierarchical control of the controller and excludes processing that is done internally such as one department processing for another, or an employee processing data on behalf of their employer').

an identification number, financial data, location data or an online identifier; or (b) one or more factors specific to the physical, physiological, genetic, psychological, economic, cultural or social identity of that individual or natural person.[48] Such information could include names, telephone numbers, national identification numbers, and financial statements. It is imperative that at the outset, controllers identify whether information they are processing is personal data or not. While it may be readily apparent that some types of information could be used to directly identify a person, the context in which personal data is processed is an important consideration, since an individual may be indirectly identifiable based on other information available to a controller.

The PDPA's definition for personal data appears to be broader than that found in the GDPR, since Recital 26 of the GDPR requires the factoring in of all means reasonably likely to be used to identify the natural person, directly or indirectly, when determining whether a natural person is identifiable. A similar provision is not found in the PDPA.

Further, personal data only concerns natural persons. Therefore, while identifying information regarding a legal person, such as a company's financial statements, would not be considered personal data, the financial data concerning its employees would be considered personal data.

The PDPA also recognises 'special categories of personal data', meaning personal data revealing racial or ethnic origin, political opinions, religious or philosophical beliefs, the processing of genetic data, biometric data for the purpose of uniquely identifying a natural person, data concerning health or data concerning a natural person's sex life or sexual orientation, personal data relating to offences, criminal proceedings and convictions, or personal data relating to a child.[49] These types of data are special classes within 'personal data' which are specifically identified. They require a higher level of protection and care.

Notably, the PDPA does not apply to any data other than personal data.[50] Although the Act does not provide a definition, it is axiomatic that non-personal data would be data that cannot identify or is not capable of identifying a natural person including statistical or anonymous data, such as the average age of visitors to a website.

v. Distinction between Anonymised, Pseudonymised, or Encrypted

Under section 10 of the PDPA, controllers are required to ensure the security and confidentiality of the personal data that is being processed. The PDPA differentiates between different types of technical and organisational measures that can be taken by controllers, such as anonymisation, encryption, and pseudonymisation.

Anonymisation refers to the personal removal of any personal identifiers from personal data so that the personal data cannot be related to an identified or identifiable natural person.[51] Anonymised data does not fall within the scope of the PDPA since it cannot be considered 'personal data' relating to a legal person.

[48] Ibid, s 56.
[49] ibid, s 56.
[50] ibid, s 2(3)(b).
[51] ibid, s 56.

In contrast, 'encryption' means the act of ciphering or altering data using mathematical algorithms to make the data unintelligible to unauthorised users.[52] This means the encrypted data can only be used by authorised persons to identify a data subject. 'Pseudonymisation' relates to the processing of personal data in a manner that additional information is needed to use the personal data to identify a data subject. Such additional information is kept separately and is subject to technical and organisational measures to ensure the personal data is not attributed to a data subject.[53]

vi. Distinction between Domestic and Cross-Border/International Transfers

The PDPA specifically recognises cross-border data transfers. A 'cross-border data flow' means the movement of personal data out of Sri Lanka for the purpose of processing personal data in another country.[54] Since the PDPA adopts a broad definition of processing, this could involve, for an example, the collection of data in Sri Lanka and the storage, preservation, or analysing of data in another country. The processing may take place between controllers, controllers and processors, or processors and sub-processors. Cross-border data flows are subject to data localisation requirements for public authorities, such as government ministries or departments, as discussed below.

In contrast, domestic data flows are not specifically defined in the PDPA. They would however relate to the movement of personal data within Sri Lanka for the purposes of processing. This too can take place between controllers, controllers and processors, or processors and sub-processors and would be subject to the general data protection framework of the PDPA.

vii. Privacy Regulator

A key objective of the PDPA, specified in its preamble, is the establishment of the Data Protection Authority. This is provided for in Part V of the PDPA, which establishes the Authority and specifies its objectives and powers. The Authority is to be a body corporate having its own legal identity, meaning it can sue and be sued in its own name.[55] A Board of Directors, consisting of five to seven persons appointed by the President of Sri Lanka, is to administer, manage, and control the affairs of the Authority.[56] In addition to the Chairperson and the Board of Directors, the Authority consists of the Director General and the staff of the Authority. The Board of Directors consisting of seven persons was appointed by the Minister in October 2023.[57]

A notable feature is that, in the interest of ensuring the proper functioning of the Authority, the PDPA prescribes a qualification criterion to be considered when appointing

[52] ibid.
[53] ibid.
[54] ibid.
[55] ibid, s 28(2).
[56] ibid, s 29(1) and (3).
[57] Presidential Secretariat, 'Sri Lanka's Personal Data Protection Authority Progresses with Board of Directors Appointment' (October 2023), available at www.presidentsoffice.gov.lk/index.php/2023/10/09/sri-lankas-personal-data-protection-authority-progresses-with-board-of-directors-appointment/.

the Board and Director General. With regards to the Board, the PDPA specifies a three-tier qualification criteria for the members of the Board, such as reaching eminence, and having proven professional expertise in specified fields such as law and banking and finance, and experience and knowledge in specific fields and sectors such as regulatory matters, and privacy and data protection.[58] The Chairperson of the Board will be appointed by the President from among the Board members.[59] The Director General, who shall be the chief executive officer of the Authority, is to be appointed by the Board and must have achieved eminence and proven professional expertise in providing leadership to public sector or private sector ventures.[60] In this regard, the PDPA goes further than most other statutes that establish authorities in Sri Lanka, which generally do not prescribe any qualifications and permit the relevant minister to appoint persons.

The objects of the Authority are four-fold: (1) to regulate the processing of personal data;[61] (2) to safeguard the privacy of data subjects from any adverse impact arising from the digitalisation of the procedures and services in the public and private sector;[62] to provide mechanisms to ensure protection of personal data of data subjects engaged in digital transactions and communications;[63] and to ensure regulatory compliance with the PDPA.[64] The Authority is vested with wide ranging powers that may be exercised for the purposes of performing its duties and functions under the PDPA. These include, among other things, powers to take all steps to ensure controllers and processors carry out their duties and obligations under the PDPA and to inspect any information held by a controller or processor to ensure compliance,[65] direct controllers and processors to take steps to comply with the PDPA,[66] and to establish standards in relation to data protection and data storage, data processing, obtaining consent and such other matters as may be necessary for the PDPA's proper implementation.[67]

With regards to its function as a privacy regulator, it bears mention that the Authority has the power, among other things, to conduct inquiries and receive complaints, make directives and impose fines,[68] and to enter into the premises of any controller or processor and inspect or seize records and carry out investigations where the Authority has reasonable grounds to believe that processing poses an imminent risk to the rights of data subjects.[69] Sections 35, 38, and 39 of the PDPA provides a mechanism by which the Authority may impose penalties. The first step is that the Authority may conduct an inquiry if the Authority has reason to believe, on the basis of a complaint or otherwise, that any controller or processor has or is about to engage in any processing activity violating the PDPA or any rules, regulations, guidelines or orders made under the PDPA or any

[58] PDPA (n 7) s 29(3) and (4).
[59] ibid, s 30(1).
[60] ibid, s 36(1).
[61] ibid, s 31(a).
[62] ibid, s 31(b).
[63] ibid, s 31(c).
[64] ibid, s 31(d).
[65] ibid, s 32(b).
[66] ibid, s 32(d).
[67] ibid, s 32(q).
[68] ibid, s 32(e).
[69] ibid, s 32(g).

other law relating to processing personal data.[70] The procedure for conducting an inquiry is to be prescribed by the Authority. It is, however, required that the Authority gives the controller or processor an opportunity to be heard.[71] Pursuant to conducting the inquiry, the Authority may issue a directive to the controller or processor, requiring the violator to: (1) cease and refrain from engaging in the offending act or omission; (2) perform acts necessary to rectify the situation; or (3) to pay compensation determined by the Authority to an aggrieved person.[72] Such directive shall be in writing and shall be binding on the controller or processor.[73] The compensation is intended to cover the harm, loss, or damage suffered by the aggrieved party as a result of the controller's or processor's contravention. Notably, the PDPA does not specify the maximum amount of compensation that a controller or processor may be directed to pay.

Subsequently, in the event a controller or processor fails to comply with the Authority's directive under Section 35, the Authority shall, by notice, require the controller or processor to pay an administrative penalty under section 38 after taking into consideration the nature and extent of the non-compliances and the following factors:

- the nature, gravity and duration of the contravention taking into account the nature, scope or purpose of the processing concerned together with the number of data subjects affected and the level of damage suffered by them;
- any action by the controller or processor to mitigate the damage suffered by the data subjects;
- the effectiveness of the controller's data protection management programme;
- the degree of cooperation with the Authority to remedy the contravention or mitigate its adverse effects;
- the categories of personal data affected;
- the manner in which the Authority came to know of the contravention, particularly whether, and to what extent, the controller or processor notified the Authority of the contravention;
- previous non-compliance with the PDPA by the controller or processor;
- any other aggravating or mitigating factors such as financial benefits gained or losses avoided directly or indirectly due to the contravention.[74]

The penalty shall not exceed a sum of 10 million Sri Lankan Rupees for each non-compliance.[75] However, if a previously penalised controller or processor subsequently fails to conform to a directive, a further penalty may be imposed, which may result in the penalties exceeding 10 million Sri Lankan Rupees.[76] Further, the penalties are administrative in nature and can be imposed in addition to a directive for compensation. All penalties that are collected by the Authority must be credited to the consolidated fund of Sri Lanka

[70] ibid, s 35(1).
[71] ibid, s 35(2).
[72] ibid.
[73] ibid, s 35(3).
[74] ibid, s 39.
[75] ibid, s 38(1).
[76] ibid, s 38(2).

after deducting sums collected as compensation, if any, payable to aggrieved persons.[77] The imposition of a penalty does not prevent a regulatory body from taking any other regulatory measures in parallel under applicable laws, including suspending the controller or professor from carrying on a business or profession, or cancelling a licence or authority granted for carrying on a business or profession.[78]

In the event a penalty is imposed on a body corporate, every director and other officer responsible for the management and control of the body corporate at the time of non-compliance shall be liable to pay such penalty.[79] In the case of a firm, every partner shall be similarly liable,[80] and in the case of a body of persons that is not a body corporate, every person who at the time of non-compliance was the officer responsible with management and control of that body shall be similarly liable.[81] However, in all such circumstances, such person shall not be liable if he proves he had no knowledge of the failure to comply or that he exercised all due care and diligence to ensure compliance.[82]

If a controller or processor fails to pay a penalty within the period specified in the penalty notice, the Authority may make an ex parte application to the Magistrate Court of Colombo for an order requiring the payment of the penalty as a fine imposed by the court.[83] In the event a controller or processor is aggrieved by the imposition of a penalty under section 38, such controller or processor may appeal against such decision to the Court of Appeal of Sri Lanka within 21 working days from the date the notice of the penalty was communicated.[84] The controller or processor preferring such appeal is required to deposit in cash the sum equivalent to penalty before the registrar of the Court of Appeal.[85] The PDPA specifically provides that the burden of proof in the appeal shall be on the controller or processor as the case may be, to prove that he acted in compliance with the PDPA.[86]

III. Legal Bases, Mechanisms and Exceptions for International Data Transfers and Data Protection

A. International Data Transfers

i. Adequacy Findings or Whitelists (Jurisdictions to which International Transfers could be Made without Consent or Other Compliance Requirements) and Blacklists

The PDPA's approach to cross-border data transfers has been formulated in line with regional and international procedures. In the interest of maintaining sovereignty over data

[77] ibid, s 38(3).
[78] ibid, s 38(5).
[79] ibid, s 38(6)(a).
[80] ibid, s 38(6)(b).
[81] ibid, s 38(6)(c).
[82] ibid, s 38(6).
[83] ibid, s 38(4). The penalty may be imposed as a fine notwithstanding the penalty exceeding the sum which a court may impose as a fine in the ordinary exercise of its jurisdiction.
[84] ibid, s 38(7).
[85] ibid, s 38(9).
[86] ibid, s 38(10).

processed by public authorities, the PDPA prescribes data localisation requirements for public authorities that process personal data in the capacity of a controller or processor. Public authorities include ministries, governmental and statutory bodies.[87] However, this is not without exception. Public bodies may process or store certain categories of data, that have been classified as permissible by the Authority, in a third country which has received an adequacy decision from the Minister.

The adequacy decision-making process is similar to that found in the GDPR. The significance of the adequacy decision is that it signifies that the country that is the subject of the adequacy decision provides an adequate level of protection to personal data on a par with the PDPA. The adequacy decision must be made by the Minister in mandatory consultation with the Authority, taking into consideration, among other things, the relevant written laws and enforcement mechanisms in the third country.[88] The decision-making process shall also include how the principles of data processing and the rights of data subjects under Parts I and II of the PDPA can be enforced in the third country,[89] and the application of provisions concerning the designation or appointment of the Data Protection Officer (section 20), additional obligations of a controller (section 21), additional obligations of the processors (section 22), data breach notifications (section 23), personal data protection impact assessments (section 24), measures to mitigate risks of harm and requirements for prior consultation (section 25). Once an adequacy decision is made by the Minister, it shall be subject to periodic monitoring for developments in the third country that may affect the decision and the Minister may review the decision at least every two years.[90] The adequacy decision shall continue to be in force until it is amended or revoked by the Minister.[91] Once an adequacy decision is made, public authorities may process permissible categories of data in the prescribed third country.

The PDPA provides greater flexibility for controllers and processors that process personal data outside Sri Lanka that are not public authorities. Similar to public authorities, such controllers or processors may also process personal data in such prescribed third countries.[92] However, the personal data is not limited to permissible categories of personal data. In addition, non-public authority controllers and processors may process personal data in countries other than prescribed third countries, if the controller or processor ensures compliance with the obligations imposed under Part I, Part II and sections 20, 21, 22, 23, 24, and 25 of the PDPA.[93] To this end, the controller or processor must adopt appropriate safeguards in the form of instruments that may be specified by the Authority.[94] This is in order to ensure binding and enforceable commitments in the third country and thereby place appropriate safeguards to the rights of the data subjects. Such instruments may take the form of standard contractual clauses, binding corporate rules, and codes of conduct adopted in other jurisdictions.[95]

[87] ibid, s 56.
[88] ibid, 26(2)(a).
[89] ibid.
[90] ibid, s 26(2)(b)(i).
[91] ibid, s 26(2)(b)(ii).
[92] ibid, s 26(3)(a).
[93] ibid, s 26(3)(b).
[94] ibid, s 26(4).
[95] PDPA Overview (n 5) 8.

The PDPA further permits a controller or processor that is not a public authority to process personal data outside Sri Lanka in the absence of an adequacy decision or appropriate safeguards in limited circumstances, including: if the data subject has expressly consented after having been informed of possible risks; the transfer is necessary for the performance of a contract between the data subject and the controller; the transfer is necessary for reasons of public interest; or such processing is permitted under any other conditions as may be prescribed under the PDPA.[96]

These exemptions are largely aligned with the exemptions found in Article 49 of the GDPR with the exception of Article 49(1)(c) and (g). One notable difference is that the PDPA permits the Authority to prescribe any other conditions not already provided for in the exemptions under section 26(4). This provides further flexibility, enabling the Authority to consider the cross-border data transfers on a case-by-case basis in light of the controller's or processor's legitimate interests. Thus, the cross-border provisions found in the PDPA may be remarked as setting a novel standard in the region which upholds rights of data subjects whilst facilitating cross-border data processing in the modern data-driven economy which Sri Lanka is gradually embracing.[97]

While the PDPA provides for the issuance of adequacy decisions, it does not expressly provide for blacklisting third countries. This is consistent with the PDPA's approach of specifying the instances in which controllers or processors, both public and non-public, can make cross-border data transfers, as opposed to limiting the instances in which such parties are not permitted to effect such transfers. Therefore, in effect, unless a third country is prescribed in an adequacy decision, a public authority that is a controller or processor may not transfer data to such third country for the purpose of processing. A controller or processor that is not a public authority may still effect transfer to such third countries as explained above.

ii. Consent of Data Subjects as Exception to Existence of Privacy Safeguards Overseas

As previously discussed, the PDPA imposes data localisation requirements on public authorities in the interest of protecting national sovereignty. Accordingly, the PDPA does not recognise consent as an exception to cross-border data flows by public authorities. However, controllers or processors that are not public authorities may process data outside Sri Lanka with the data subject's consent.[98] The data subject's consent must have been informed of the possible risks of processing outside Sri Lanka for the data subject due to the absence of an adequacy decision and appropriate safeguard, and the data subject must have explicitly consented to the same.[99] This exception applies even if an adequacy decision has not been issued concerning the third country in question or appropriate safeguards have not been adopted pursuant to section 26(4).

[96] PDPA (n 7) s 26(5).

[97] Sanduni Wickramasinghe, 'White Paper: Sri Lanka's Personal Data Protection Act No. 9 of 2022' (*Friedrich-Naumann-Stiftung für die Freiheit*, 2023) 14, available at https://pdpa.economynext.com.

[98] PDPA (n 7) s 26(5)(a).

[99] ibid, s 26(5)(a).

iii. Contracts between Data

As discussed previously, in the context of cross-border data transfers, non-public controllers or processors must adopt instruments to ensure appropriate safeguards to the data subjects' rights and remedies under the PDPA.[100] In addition, when a processor, on behalf of a controller, processes personal data, the controller must ensure the processors are bound by a contract or a written law stipulating inter alia the duration, nature, purpose, and subject matter of the processing, the type of personal data and categories of data subjects, and the obligations of the controller.[101]

iv. APEC Cross-Border Privacy Rules System

Sri Lanka is not a member economy of the APEC. Therefore, the cross-border privacy rules (CBPR) system of the APEC, which is a voluntary framework for APEC members, does not apply to Sri Lanka.

v. Any Privacy Certification Schemes, Trustmarks or Privacy Seals (Domestic or International)

Under the PDPA, the Authority has the power to recognise certification and certifying bodies in relation to personal data protection.[102] Certifying bodies may be foreign or local bodies that provide certification services concerning processing of personal data or qualifications of data protection officers.[103] At the time of writing, no bodies have been certified. In addition, the Authority is empowered to appoint advisory committees to formulate sectoral guidelines, rules and to identify and define categories of controllers or processors that would require a licence for the purpose of regulating identity management and related services.[104]

B. International Data Protection and Liability

i. Specific Requirements or Policies for Data Processing and Retention

Every controller is required to process personal data in accordance with the obligations and principles set out in the PDPA.[105] The principles pertaining to data processing and retention are set out in Part I of the PDPA. Similar to the GDPR, the PDPA embodies

[100] See section III.A.i and ibid, s 26(4).
[101] PDPA (n 7) s 21(b).
[102] ibid, s 32(j).
[103] ibid, s 56.
[104] ibid, s 33(o).
[105] ibid, s 4.

principles of lawfulness,[106] purpose limitation,[107] data minimisation,[108] accuracy,[109] retention limitation,[110] integrity and confidentiality,[111] transparency,[112] and accountability.[113]

The first principle, lawfulness, is set out in section 5 of the PDPA. The lawfulness of data processing by a controller is dependent on the type of personal data being processed. With regards to personal data in general, the processing must satisfy *any* condition in schedule I. These conditions include, among other things, receiving the consent of the data subject,[114] the processing being necessary to perform a contract the data subject is party to[115] or for the controller or processor to comply with a legal obligation,[116] or the processing is required in order to perform a task in the public interest, or the exercise of powers conferred under law.[117]

For controllers processing special categories of personal data such as personal data relating to a child or revealing racial or ethnic origins, sexual orientation, religious or philosophical beliefs,[118] it is imperative they comply with *any* condition set out in schedule II. These conditions include, among other things, the data subject giving consent to processing for one or more purposes specified by the controller,[119] processing is necessary for the purposes of carrying out the obligations of the controller and exercising of the rights of the data subject,[120] processing is necessary to respond to an emergency that threatens the life, health, or safety of a data subject or another natural person where the data subject is incapable of giving consent,[121] the processing relates to personal data which is manifestly made public by the data subject,[122] or processing is necessary for archiving purposes in the public interest, scientific research or historical research purposes or statistical purposes in accordance with law.[123]

In the event the controller is processing data based on the consent of a data subject (further to condition (a) of schedule I or condition (a) of schedule II), the controller must satisfy *all* conditions in schedule III. Finally, in the case of processing data in respect of criminal investigations, *all* conditions in schedule IV must be satisfied.

The second and third principles, found in sections 6 and 7, deal with defining a purpose and confining processing to the defined purpose respectively. The controllers are also required under section 6 to process personal data for specific, explicit, and legitimate

[106] ibid, s 5.
[107] ibid, s 6.
[108] ibid, s 7.
[109] ibid, s 8.
[110] ibid, s 9.
[111] ibid, s 10.
[112] ibid, s 11.
[113] ibid, s 12.
[114] ibid, sch I(a).
[115] ibid, sch I(b).
[116] ibid, sch I(c).
[117] ibid, sch I(e).
[118] ibid, s 56.
[119] ibid, sch II(a).
[120] ibid, sch II(b).
[121] ibid, sch II(c).
[122] ibid, sch II(d).
[123] ibid, sch II(h).

purposes, and not further processed in a manner incompatible with the purposes.[124] It is noteworthy though that further processing for archiving purposes in the public interest, scientific research, historical research or statistical purposes would not be considered to be incompatible with the initial purposes, subject to the obligation to maintain integrity and confidentiality in section 10.[125] Under section 7, every controller is required to ensure that the personal data being processed is adequate, relevant, and proportionate to the extent that is necessary for the defined purpose the personal data was collected or processed.[126]

The fourth principle pertains to accuracy. Every controller is required to ensure that the personal data being processed is accurate and kept up to date, and that every reasonable step is taken to erase or rectify any inaccurate or outdated personal data without undue delay.[127]

In order to ensure retention limitation, all controllers must ensure that the personal data being processed is kept in a form which permits identification of data subject only for a period that is necessary or required to achieve the purposes for which it is being processed.[128] However, the personal data may be stored for longer periods for archiving purposes in the public interest, scientific or historical research, or statistical purposes, subject to obligations pertaining to integrity and confidentiality in section 10.[129]

The final three principles concern integrity and confidentiality,[130] transparency,[131] and accountability.[132] Controllers are required to use appropriate technical and organisational measures to ensure the integrity and confidentiality of personal data and prevent the unauthorised or unlawful processing or loss, destruction or damage of personal data.[133] The technical and organisational measures include encryption, pseudonymisation, anonymisation and access controls, and may include any other measures prescribed by the Authority in the future. In order to promote transparency, controllers are required to provide data subjects the information referred to in schedule V[134] and the information regarding any decision taken pursuant to a request made under Part II of this Act.[135] These requests include requests to access data,[136] to withdraw consent,[137] for the controller to refrain from further processing of the data subject's personal data,[138] to rectify or complete data,[139] and erasure of data.[140] The information is to be provided in writing or by electronic means and in a concise, transparent, intelligible and easily accessible form. Finally, controllers are required to be accountable in processing data by implementing internal controls and procedures,

[124] ibid, s 6(a).
[125] ibid, s 6(b).
[126] ibid, s 7.
[127] ibid, s 8.
[128] ibid, s 9.
[129] ibid.
[130] ibid, s 10.
[131] ibid, s 11.
[132] ibid, s 12.
[133] ibid, s 10.
[134] ibid, sch V.
[135] ibid, s 11.
[136] ibid, s 13.
[137] ibid, s 14(1).
[138] ibid, s 14(2).
[139] ibid, s 15.
[140] ibid, s 16.

referred to as the Data Protection Management Programme (DPMP) to comply with other processing principles.[141] The DPMP must:

- establish and maintain catalogued records demonstrating the implementation of the other principles;[142]
- be designed according to the structure, scale, volume, and sensitivity of the controller's processing activities;[143]
- provide appropriate safeguards based on data protection impact assessments;[144]
- integrated into the controller's governance structure;[145]
- establish internal oversight mechanisms;[146]
- set up a mechanism to receive complaints, conduct inquiries, and identify personal data breaches;[147]
- be updated after periodic monitoring and assessments;[148] and
- facilitate the exercise of data subjects' rights under the PDPA.[149]

ii. Regulations on Legal Ownership of Data Protection and Privacy Rights

The rights of data subjects are recognised in Part II of the PDPA. In essence, the Act recognises six rights. First, data subjects have the right to access their personal data and to be provided with a confirmation whether their personal data has been processed and the information set out in schedule V.[150] Data subjects may exercise this right by making a request in writing to the controller. Upon receiving a request, the controller is required to provide the information stipulated in schedule V.[151]

Second, the PDPA recognises the data subject's right to withdraw his/her consent. Data subjects may, in writing, withdraw their consent if the processing was based on their consent (under the grounds in item (a) of schedule I or item (a) of schedule II).[152] The withdrawal of consent does not affect the lawfulness of any processing prior to such withdrawal. Third, data subjects have the right to request a controller to refrain from further processing personal data relating to the data subjects. A data subject may effect this right by making a request in writing to the controller.[153] This right may only be exercised, however, if processing was based on public interest or legitimate interest grounds.[154]

[141] ibid, s 12.
[142] ibid, s 12(a).
[143] ibid, s 12(b).
[144] ibid, s 12(c).
[145] ibid, s 12(d).
[146] ibid, s 12(e).
[147] ibid, s 12(f).
[148] ibid, s 12(g).
[149] ibid, s 12(h).
[150] ibid, s 13(1).
[151] ibid, s 13(2).
[152] ibid, s 14(1).
[153] ibid, s 14(2).
[154] Either ibid, sch I, items (e) or (f), or sch II, item (f).

Fourth, a data subject is entitled under the PDPA to request a controller to rectify or complete the inaccurate or complete personal data relating to the data subject.[155] The controller is required, upon receiving a written request from the data subject, to rectify or complete the personal data without undue delay. However, the controller is not obliged to collect and process any additional personal data that is not required for the original purpose of processing. Further, if any incorrect personal data is the subject of an ongoing investigation or is being used for evidentiary purposes, the controller is required to refrain from processing that personal data any further without first rectifying the same.

Fifth, the PDPA recognises a data subject's right to erasure of personal data in the following circumstances: (1) the personal data is being processed in violation of sections 5 to 11;[156] data processing is based on consent and the data subject has withdrawn his or her consent;[157] erasure of personal data is required under a written law or court order to which the data subject or controller is subject.[158] This right must be exercised by the data subject requesting the erasure in writing from the controller.

Sixth, and finally, data subjects are vested with the right to request a controller to determine a decision based solely on automated processing without any human intervention.[159] The processing ought to have created or is likely to create an irreversible and continuous impact on the data subject's rights and freedoms under any written law. A review cannot be requested, however, in circumstances where the automated processing was authorised by law,[160] in a manner permitted by the Authority,[161] based on the data subject's consent,[162] or it is necessary for entering into or performing a contract between the data subject and the controller which does not concern the processing of special categories of personal data.[163] Further, in these instances, the controller must comply with the measures and applicable criteria specified by the Authority to safeguard the rights and freedoms of data subjects.

Notably, the rights recognised in sections 13 to 16 are subject to exceptions set out in section 17 of the PDPA. These exceptions do not apply to a request made under section 18. Upon receiving a written request from a data subject pursuant to any of sections 13 to 16, the controller is required to inform the data subject, within 21 working days of the request, whether the request has been granted, refused, or the controller has refrained from processing the subject personal data further under sections 14(2) or 15.[164] Other than when a request is granted, the controller must give its reasons, unless doing so is legally prohibited.[165] The controller must also inform the data subject of the right of appeal, in the event the request is not granted. A request need not be acted on if it is regarding:

- national security;[166]
- public order;[167]

[155] ibid, s 15.
[156] ibid, s 16(a).
[157] ibid, s 16(b).
[158] ibid, s 16(c).
[159] ibid, s 18(1).
[160] ibid, s 18(2)(a).
[161] ibid, s 18(2)(b).
[162] ibid, s 18(2)(c).
[163] ibid, s 18(2)(d).
[164] ibid, s 17(1).
[165] ibid, s 17(1)(b) and (c).
[166] ibid, s 17(2)(a).
[167] ibid, s 17(2)(b).

- any inquiry, investigation or procedure conducted under any written law;[168]
- the prevention, detection, investigation or prosecution of criminal offences;[169]
- the rights and freedoms of other persons under any written law;[170]
- the controller's technical and operational feasibility to act on the request;[171]
- the inability of the controller to establish the data subject's identity;[172] or
- the requirement to process personal data under any written law.[173]

In the event a controller is unable to identify a data subject that is making a request, the controller may request additional information from the data subject.[174] The controller must also keep records of the reasons for any requests that were refused and submit the same to the Authority upon request.[175] In a case where the data subject is a minor, the parents, guardian, or person having parental authority may make a request under Part II.[176] The requests under sections 13 to 16 would have to be accompanied by such fees as may be prescribed under the PDPA.[177]

A data subject may appeal against the decision of a controller refusing a request under sections 14 to 18.[178] The Authority may then determine whether the controller's decision was lawful.[179] After concluding necessary investigations, the Authority may determine whether the appeal is allowed or disallowed and inform the data subject and controller in writing of its determination with reasons thereof.[180] If the appeal is allowed, the controller must take steps to give effect to the data subject's request within such period the Authority may determine, and the controller must inform the data subject and authority of such steps being taken.[181] In the event a data subject or controller is aggrieved by the Authority's decision, he or she may prefer an appeal to the Court of Appeal no later than 30 days from the date of the decision.[182]

iii. Extraterritorial Effect of Laws on Data Protection and Privacy

The PDPA applies both territorially and extraterritorially. The Act applies to the processing of personal data:

(*a*) where the processing of personal data takes place wholly or partly within Sri Lanka; or

[168] ibid, s 17(2)(c).
[169] ibid, s 17(2)(d).
[170] ibid, s 17(2)(e).
[171] ibid, s 17(2)(f).
[172] ibid, s 17(2)(g).
[173] ibid, s 17(2)(h).
[174] ibid, s 17(4).
[175] ibid, s 17(3).
[176] ibid, s 17(5)(a). See also s 17(5)(b).
[177] ibid, s 17(6).
[178] ibid, s 19(1). The form, manner, and time period for appeal may be prescribed under the PDPA.
[179] ibid, s 19(2).
[180] ibid, s 19(3).
[181] ibid, s 19(4).
[182] ibid, s 19(5).

(*b*) where the processing of personal data is carried out by a controller or processor who–
  (i) is domiciled or ordinarily resident in Sri Lanka;
  (ii) is incorporated or established under any written law of Sri Lanka;
  (iii) offers goods or services to data subjects in Sri Lanka including the offering of goods or services with specific targeting of data subjects in Sri Lanka; or
  (iv) specifically monitors the behaviour of data subjects in Sri Lanka including profiling with the intention of making decisions in relation to the behaviour of such data subjects in so far as such behaviour takes place in Sri Lanka.[183]

The Act applies to controllers or processors ordinarily resident in Sri Lanka or incorporated under Sri Lankan law. In addition, instances where the processing is done wholly or partly in Sri Lanka are clearly covered by the Act, irrespective of the controller's or processor's location. Thus, an entity outside Sri Lanka would have to comply with the PDPA, if the processing is done wholly or partly in Sri Lanka. The PDPA also applies extraterritorially by applying to controllers or processors that: target data subjects in Sri Lanka to offer goods and services; or monitor the behaviour of data subjects in Sri Lanka (including profiling), where such behaviour takes place in Sri Lanka. Such controllers and processors need not be located in Sri Lanka for the PDPA to apply. The Authority is empowered to make rules determining the circumstances in which specific targeting or specific monitoring occurs.[184]

iv. Data Breach Notification

The PDPA provides a framework for personal data breach notifications which is specified by way of rules under the Act. A personal data breach is any act or omission that results in accidental or unlawful destruction, loss, alteration, unauthorised disclosure of, or access to, personal data transmitted, stored or otherwise processed.[185] This definition is broad and can cover instances from a hacker gaining access to a controller's data servers to an employee disclosing information for commercial benefit. In the event of a personal data breach, the controller is required to notify the Authority of the same.[186] The form, manner, and time period for notifying the Authority is to be determined by the Authority in the form of rules.[187] The Authority must also issue rules providing the circumstances in which the Authority should be notified of a data breach, when the affected data subject should be notified, and the information to be provided in the notification.[188] At the time of writing this chapter, no such rules have been issued. In addition to a controller's obligations to inform the Authority of a data breach, controllers are also required to have a mechanism to receive complaints, conduct inquiries, and identify personal data breaches in their DPMPs in the interest of accountability.[189]

[183] ibid, s 2(1).
[184] ibid, s 2(2).
[185] ibid, s 56,.
[186] ibid, s 23(1).
[187] ibid.
[188] ibid, s 23(2).
[189] See ibid, s 12(f).

IV. Data Security and Data Localisation

A. Data Security and Localisation Requirements

As discussed previously, the PDPA imposes data localisation requirements for public authorities, such as governmental ministries, departments, and statutory bodies in the interest of national sovereignty. Personal data may be processed outside Sri Lanka if the Authority, in consultation with the controller or processor and any relevant regulatory or statutory body, classify the categories of personal data that may be processed outside Sri Lanka and the processing is done in a location that receives an adequacy decision.[190] As discussed above, controllers or processors that are not public authorities have very limited data localisation requirements.

B. Data Security and Localisation Requirements for Particular Types of Data

The PDPA imposes, under section 10, a general duty on controllers to ensure the integrity and confidentiality of personal data that is being processed, by using appropriate technical and organisational measures. These include encryption, pseudonymisation, anonymisation or access controls or such other measures as may be prescribed.[191]

Additionally, the PDPA requires controllers processing particular types of data to carry out personal data protection impact assessments ('Impact Assessments') to ascertain the impact of the intended processing on the controller's obligations and the data subjects' rights. Such Impact Assessments must be carried out when processing involves: (1) systematic and extensive evaluation of personal data or special categories of personal data including profiling; (2) systematic monitoring of publicly accessible areas or telecommunication network; or (3) processing activities determined by rules, after considering the scope and risks of that processing.[192] Where such processing is carried out in relation to national security, public order and public health, the controller must consult the Authority.[193]

Impact Assessments must be carried out prior to the processing and must be in the manner and form as may be prescribed. They must contain among other things information regarding the measures and safeguards the controller has taken to mitigate any risk of harm caused to the data subject by the processing.[194] The controller must carry out a fresh Impact Assessment if there is a change in the methodology, technology or process adopted in the processing.[195] Impact Assessments must be submitted to the Authority, as must any further information the Authority requires to assess the compliance of the processing and any risks of harm to the data subjects.[196]

[190] ibid, s 26(1).
[191] ibid, s 10.
[192] ibid, s 24(1).
[193] ibid, s 25(7).
[194] ibid, s 24(2).
[195] ibid, s 24(4).
[196] ibid, s 24(5).

In the event an Impact Assessment indicates the likely risk of harm to data subjects' rights under the PDPA or another law, the controller shall take measures to mitigate the risk of harm prior to processing any personal data.[197] In the event the controller is unable to mitigate the risks of harm even despite taking mitigatory measures, the controller may consult the Authority prior to processing.[198] The Authority may then in writing, instruct the controller to take additional mitigatory measures or to cease such processing.[199] Any failure to comply with the Authority's instructions without reasonable cause shall result in the controller contravening the PDPA's provisions.[200] Further, when processing personal data referred to in items (b), (f), (g) and (h) of schedule II, such processing is considered to have provided such measures and appropriate safeguards to protect the data subject's rights.[201]

The PDPA does not specify any data localisation requirements for particular types of data, save for, as discussed above, public authorities only being permitted to process categories of personal data classified by the Authority in consultation with the relevant public authority and any relevant regulatory or statutory authority.

V. Issues in Private International Law

A. Litigations Involving Cross-Border Data Transfer and Privacy

In general, potential claimants in litigations involving data transfer and protection in Sri Lanka include individuals whose data has been transferred without their consent, or have suffered from any losses due to another party committing offences under the PDPA, Computer Crime Act etc, entities that have lost data due to breaches, and regulatory authorities responsible for data protection. Defendants may include companies, data controllers, data processors and any individual or entity that has breached personal data protection laws.

Remedies available to claimants may include injunctions to cease data transfer, damages, compensation or any other relief deemed necessary to rectify breaches of data protection regulations. Such remedies are set out in the following acts.

i. The PDPA

Under the PDPA there are several routes to commence litigation by various parties. First, under section 38(4), the Authority may make an ex parte application to the Magistrate Court of Colombo for an order requiring the payment of the penalty as a fine imposed by the Court. The Authority would be the claimant in such an application.

Second, a controller or processor aggrieved by the imposition of an administrative penalty under section 38 may prefer an appeal to the Court of Appeal of Sri Lanka, under

[197] ibid, s 25(1).
[198] ibid, s 25(2).
[199] ibid, s 25(3). Further, under PDPA, s 25(4), the Authority may request additional information.
[200] ibid, s 25(5).
[201] ibid, s 25(6).

section 38(7). The controller or processor would be the appellant and the Authority would be the respondent. An appeal would be passed to the Supreme Court of Sri Lanka from a decision of the Court of Appeal.

Third, remedies such as injunctions to cease data transfer, damages, compensation or any other relief deemed necessary to rectify breaches of data protection regulations, are available under the PDPA. Section 35 of the PDPA states that where on receipt of a complaint or otherwise, the Authority has reason to believe, that any controller or processor – (a) is engaged in, or is about to engage in any processing activity in contravention of this Act; or (b) has contravened or failed to comply with or is likely to contravene or, fails to comply with the provisions of the PDPA, the Authority may, conduct an inquiry in accordance with the procedure as may be prescribed. Thereafter, section 35(2) states that the Authority, after giving an opportunity to the controller or processor to be heard at any inquiry, may issue a directive to the controller or processor requiring such controller or processor within such time as may be prescribed:

a) to cease and refrain from engaging in, the act, omission or course of conduct related to processing; or
b) to perform such acts as in the opinion of the Authority are necessary to rectify the situation; or
c) to make a payment of such sum of money as compensation as determined by the Authority to an aggrieved person who has suffered harm, loss or damage as a result of any contravention by a controller or processor under subsection 35(1).

Fourth, a data subject or controller who is aggrieved by the decision of the Authority under section 20 of the PDPA may refer an appeal to the Court of Appeal within 30 days of the Authority's decision.[202]

ii. Computer Crime Act No 24 of 2007

In particular, through penal sanctions, the Computer Crime Act addresses matters that involve data that has been unlawfully obtained, the illegal interception of data, and the unauthorised disclosure of information. Section 25 of the Computer Crimes Act vests the High Court of Sri Lanka with the jurisdiction to hear, try and determine all offences under the said Act. However, where the provisions of the Extradition Law, No 8 of 1977 are applicable in relation to the commission of an offence under the Act, the High Court holden at Colombo shall have exclusive jurisdiction to hear, try and determine such offence.[203]

B. Jurisdictional Issues Involving Cross-Border Data Protection and Privacy

In Sri Lanka, the jurisdiction of courts of first instance are typically determined by the Code of Civil Procedure, the Code of Criminal Procedure and the Judicature Act, unless specially

[202] ibid, s 20.
[203] Computer Crime Act, s 25.

provided under a specific act. Section 09 of the Civil Procedure Code states that a court has civil jurisdiction over a case when;

> Subject to the pecuniary or other limitations prescribed by any Institution of law, action shall be instituted in the court within the local limits of whose jurisdiction –
>
> a) a party defendant resides; or
> b) the land in respect of which the action is brought lies or is situate in whole or in part; or
> c) the cause of action arises; or
> d) the contract sought to be enforced was made.

The jurisdiction of the lower courts may be limited by the amount in controversy, while the jurisdiction of the higher courts may be limited by appeal or the subject matter of the case.

As per section 09 the Criminal Procedure Code, a Magistrate Court shall have jurisdiction over an issue when:

> Subject to and in accordance with the provisions of this Code every Magistrate's Court shall have –
>
> (a) power and authority and is hereby required to hear, try, determine, and dispose of in a summary way all suits or prosecutions for offences *committed wholly or in part within its local jurisdiction, which offences by this Code or any other law in force are made cognizable by a Magistrate's Court or a District Court*;
> (b) Jurisdiction –
>
> (i) to inquire into all offences committed or alleged to have of been committed wholly or in part within its local jurisdiction or in relation to which jurisdiction is by this Code given to such court to inquire into, to summon and examine all witnesses touching such offences, and to issue warrants and other processes to apprehend and summon all criminals and offenders and deal with them according to law ....
>
> (Emphasis added)

Undoubtedly, the principles of territoriality under the PDPA give Authority and consequently the relevant courts, broad jurisdictional scope. As discussed above, the PDPA can apply to controllers and processors irrespective of their location if processing is done wholly or partly in Sri Lanka. Similarly, controllers and processors that are outside Sri Lanka would be covered by the PDPA if they target data subjects in Sri Lanka to offer goods or services or monitor the behaviour of data subjects in Sri Lanka. This expanded jurisdictional scope would permit the Authority to take action against such controllers and processors that are in breach of the PDPA. In this regard, it is pertinent to note that section 38(4) of the PDPA identifies that it is the Magistrate Court of Colombo that will have jurisdiction to pronounce an order requiring the payment of any penalties under directives issued under section 35 of the PDPA by the Data Protection Authority. This should be done by making an ex parte application to the Magistrate Court of Colombo by the Data Protection Authority as also set out in section 38(4) of the PDPA.

The exercise of jurisdiction over entities outside Sri Lanka can raise several concerns. First, there can be issues concerning whether controllers and processors fall within the ambit of the PDPA. Since the PDPA is in the process of being implemented in full, it is unable to conclude how the Authority and courts may interpret the territorial and jurisdictional provisions of the PDPA. It is not outside the realm of possibility that the Authority and courts may adopt broad and expansive interpretations on matters such as targeting or monitoring data subjects in Sri Lanka which could further expand their jurisdiction. There can also be practical issues in properly identifying the controller or processor.

Second, there may be ambiguities in determining the applicable data protection frameworks. It is wholly possible that the foreign controller or processor is covered by other data protection legislation in addition to the PDPA. In such circumstances, the Authority and courts may have to resolve issues arising from conflicting legal frameworks.

Third, issues may arise when it comes to enforcement on foreign controllers and processors. While the PDPA provides remedies against breaches by controllers and processors, including those outside the territory, it is unclear in practice how such remedies may be enforced. This would require the Authority to rely on inter alia cooperation between jurisdictions or enforcement actions in the foreign jurisdiction.

C. Applicable Law: In Litigations Involving Cross-Border Data Protection and Privacy

There is a lack of Sri Lankan authority and statutes to help answer the above question, however a carefully considered decision of the Sri Lanka Court of Appeal may shed some light on the issue relating to the applicable laws. In *International Science and Technological Institute (ISTI) v Rosa and Another*[204] the Court of Appeal was engaged in the search for the proper law of a contract made between a Sri Lanka citizen and a foreign company. When determining the proper law of that contract, the Court applied the private international law of England, including well established precedents followed by English courts.[205] In the legal systems of the Commonwealth countries, which were former colonial possessions of the United Kingdom, the applicable private international law has always been the private international law applied in the English Courts. In the said circumstances, Professor Marasinghe, an authority on Private International Law in Sri Lanka, in his treatise[206] agrees that pursuant to the aforementioned case, it is clear that the applicable private international law in the Sri Lankan courts, is the private international law applied in the courts of England.

Although Sri Lankan jurisprudence shows that connecting factors in relation to various areas of law and circumstances have been identified, Sri Lanka currently does not have specific laws or regulations concerning connecting factors for data, whether personal or non-personal data.

D. Obstacles to Effective Data Protection

It bears emphasis that legislation in connection with data protection is rather new in Sri Lanka. Further, the PDPA is set to come into effect on a staggered timeline. Thus, at this

[204] *International Science and Technological Institute (ISTI) v Rosa and Another* [1994] 3 Sri LR 233.

[205] *Adelaide Electric Supply Co Ltd, v President Assurance Co Ltd,* [1934] AC 122; *Chatenay v Brazilian Submarine Telegraph Company* [1891] 1 QB 79; *Rex v International Trustees* [1937] AC 500; *Mount Albert Borough Council v Australian Temperance and General Mutual Life Assurance Society* [1936] AC 224.

[206] L Marasinghe, *Private International Law*, 2nd edn (Vijitha Yapa Publications, 2021).

juncture, it is too early, and would be an assumption to state that Sri Lanka's private international law poses any obstacles to effective data protection in the country.

However, the delay in enacting data protection legislature has caused issues such as the evident lacuna in practical and technical know-how in dealing with data protection related disputes, and the lack of decided jurisprudence that could be relied on by the court system when an issue of private international law comes up in the context of data protection. With the enactment of the PDPA, the area of private international law concerning data protection would undoubtedly be subject to significant growth in the near future.

E. Major Litigations Regarding Data Protection and Privacy

Whilst there have been reported cases of data breaches and cyberattacks in Sri Lanka, the extent of litigation related to these incidents is not known. Regardless, the Government has taken steps to strengthen data protection and cybersecurity measures in the country.

VI. Topical Issues and Prospects

A. Artificial Intelligence or AI-Generated Data

Presently, Sri Lanka does not have any laws that expressly concern artificial intelligence (AI) generated data, however there have been efforts to regulate its use. In 2019, the Sri Lanka Association of Software and Services Companies (SLASSCOM) launched a draft policy framework to promote the use of AI in Sri Lanka.[207] However, to this date, a policy framework has not been finalised. Further, there is no legal authority at present concerning the ownership of AI-generated data.[208]

B. Potential Cooperation under the Belt and Road Initiative

While it is unclear whether Sri Lanka has signed a Memorandum of Understanding (MoU) and cooperation agreements with China concerning the 'Digital Silk Road' initiative, Sri Lanka and China have been closely engaged under the Belt and Road Initiative (BRI) since signing an MoU in 2014. For example, Sri Lanka is part of the Initiative for Belt and Road Partnership on Green Development, and the Initiative for Belt and Road Partnership on COVID-19 Vaccines Cooperation launched on 23 June 2021.[209] At this juncture, there is no available information regarding data transfer and data protection as part of the BRI.

[207] Hiyal Biyagamage, 'SLASSCOM Launches Sri Lanka's First AI Policy Framework' *Daily Financial Times* (27 June 2019), available at www.ft.lk/Front-Page/SLASSCOM-launches-Sri-Lanka-s-first-AI-policy-framework/44-680805.

[208] However, in March 2024 a White Paper on the National AI Strategy has been developed by the Committee on Formulating a Strategy for Artificial Intelligence, available at https://mot.gov.lk/assets/files/AI%20White%20Paper%20March%202024-c09aa49f7990358ad1442103b804511d.pdf.

[209] United Nations Department of Economic and Social Affairs, 'Progress Report on the Belt and Road Initiative in Support of the United Nations 2030 Agenda for Sustainable Development' (14 September 2022), available at www.un.org/sites/un2.un.org/files/progress_report_bri-sdgs_english-final.pdf.

C. Data Protection Post COVID-19 Pandemic

It is only in the aftermath of the COVID-19 pandemic that Sri Lanka's primary piece of legislation on Personal Data Protection was passed and enacted. In fact, it is only being enforced in a phased manner and is still in the process of being implemented.

Furthermore, a draft for an Act to Provide the Implementation of the National Cyber Security Strategy (2019) (the 'Cybersecurity Bill') was also formulated under the National Cyber Security Strategy (2019–2023), which is being finalised by the National Centre for Cyber Security, also known as Sri Lanka Computer Emergency Readiness Team.[210] The Cybersecurity Bill will provide a comprehensive framework to prevent and manage cybersecurity threats and incidents effectively and to protect critical information infrastructure.

[210] A draft of the Bill can be accessed at www.icta.lk/icta-assets/uploads/2020/06/Cyber_Security_Bill_2019-05-22_LD_Final_Version.pdf.

15

India

SAI RAMANI GARIMELLA AND HAARIS MOOSA

I. Introduction

India became a Constitutional Republic on 26 January 1950,[1] and gave itself an extensively articulated rights regime, inspired as it was from international and comparative law developments after World War II.[2] The Constitution of India, several amendments notwithstanding, remains a vibrant document and the foundation for a regime on data protection and privacy. Decades later, the rights regime within Part III of the Constitution continues to gain in expansiveness of its content and operation, including a statement on privacy law,[3] which will be discussed in the following pages. Suffice to say at this stage, the law has recognised a right to privacy of the individual, including a right to be forgotten, although the contours of these rights have been subject to the opinion of the court at various times. India has been at the forefront of the technological revolution, following the liberalisation era that began in the 1990s,[4] and has since moved ahead in effectively monetising the economy surrounding data management.[5] India is home to big tech companies providing products and services in fintech, edutech and such other domains, as well as from data warehousing and data management services to clients from across the world.[6] Such developments also raise curiosity on the extent of legal and regulatory support through data protection. Surprisingly though, India has only recently enacted a legislation in this regard, and much of it has been

[1] Following independence from British imperialism in 1947, India's constituent assembly was elected to draft a constitution. The Drafting Committee chaired by Dr BR Ambedkar adopted the Constitution on 26 November 1949 and India was declared a Republic with the Constitution coming into force on 26 January 1950.

[2] The Constitution drew inspiration from the UK's Parliamentary form of governance and the Constitution of the USA, Ireland 1922, amongst others. See, Madhav Khosla, *India's Founding Moment: The Constitution of a Most Surprising Democracy* (Harvard University Press, 2020).

[3] See, eg, Committee of Experts under the Chairmanship of Justice B N Srikrishna, A Free and Fair Digital Economy: 'Protecting Privacy, Empowering Indians, Ministry of Electronics & Information Technology, Government of India' (27 July 2018) 3, available at meity.gov.in/writereaddata/files/Data_Protection_Committee_Report-comp.pdf.

[4] Biswajit Dhar and Reji K Joseph, 'India's Information Technology Industry: A Tale of Two Halves' in KC Liu and Uday S Racherla (eds), *Innovation, Economic Development, and Intellectual Property in India and China*. ARCIALA Series on Intellectual Assets and Law in Asia (Springer, 2019).

[5] India is unique in that as an IT service hub, almost 40% of India's goods and services exports consist of data-related activities in software and IT services. See, A Mattoo and S Wunsch, 'Pre-empting Protectionism in Services – the GATS and Outsourcing (2004) *Journal of International Economic Law* 7(4), 765–800.

[6] Dhar and Joseph (n 4).

managed only through the contracts law and contractual obligations imposed via the private international law rules. The following narrative will discuss the legal regime governing data protection in India, including a comment on the Digital Personal Data Protection Act, 2023. This research in its first part presents the normative framework addressing data protection, including the extensive sectoral legal regimes in India. It is followed by a discussion on the regime governing cross-border data transfers. Within this part, given the absence of a specific law addressing such transfers, there is a recital of the basic private international law rules that are applied to contractual disputes involving a foreign element. Further, it explains the specific data-related provisions in the various policy regulations that impact data handling between contracting parties. This section also addresses the interaction of privacy rights with data regulation. Finally, the Digital Personal Data Protection Act, 2023 in the context of cross-border data management is discussed. The last part of this research leaves the reader with a few suggestions for law reform.

II. General Legal Framework of International Data Transfers and Data Protection

The Digital Personal Data Protection Act, 2023 ('DPDP Act 2023') has been primarily enacted to ensure transparency, accountability, minimal retention of data and privacy of individuals vis-a-vis digital personal data.[7] The recognition of the right to privacy as a fundamental right by the Supreme Court of India[8] proved to be an inflection point in the development of the data protection regime to its current form in India.[9] The rudimentary regime that existed until then was given a shake-up by the Government of India with the Data Protection Bill, 2019 ('DPB 2019').[10] The DPB 2019 was sent to a joint parliamentary committee for the necessary vetting and was the basis of an extensive report.[11] The DPDP Act 2023 is markedly different from the DPB 2019 in so far as it builds on the suggestions of the Sri Krishna Committee Report and the Joint Parliamentary Committee Report of December 2021.

Hitherto, the data localisation regime has been regulated by the Information Technology (Reasonable Security Practices and Procedures and Sensitive Personal Data or Information) Rules, 2011 ('2011 Rules'), Public Records Act, 1993, along with other sectoral regulations.[12]

[7] Digital Personal Data Protection Act, 2023 (No 22 of 2023) ('DPDP Act 2023'). Press release of the Ministry of Electronics & IT issued by the Press Information Bureau on the DPDP Bill 2023, dated 9 September 2023, available at pib.gov.in/PressReleaseIframePage.aspx?PRID=1947264.

[8] *Justice KS Puttaswamy and another v Union of India*, Writ Petition No 494 of 2012.

[9] Report of the Joint Committee on the Personal Data Protection Bill 2019 submitted to the 17th Lok Sabha, December 2021, p 4.

[10] IT Rules; Provisions of the Indian Evidence Act, 1872 (as amended); Indian Penal Code, 1856 (as amended).

[11] Report of the Joint Committee on the Personal Data Protection Bill, 2019 (n 9).

[12] Framework for Adoption of Cloud Services by SEBI Regulated Entities; IRDAI (Outsourcing of Activities by Indian Insurers) Regulations, 2017; IRDAI (Maintenance of Insurance Records) Regulations, 2015; Consumer Protection (Direct Selling) Rules, 2021; Reserve Bank of India Guidelines on Managing Risks and Code of Conduct in Outsourcing of Financial Services by Banks, November 2006; Reserve Bank of India directive vide circular DPSS.CO.OD.No 2785/06.08.005/2017-18 dated 6 April 2018 on Storage of Payment System Data; corporate.cyrilamarchandblogs.com/2023/08/a-fine-balancethe-dpda-and-data-localization/; www.pwc.in/assets/pdfs/consulting/cyber-security/data-privacy/data-localisation-norms-a-key-pillar-for-privacy-protection.pdf.

Data protection conditions created by the existing regulations include a ban on the outsourcing of core management functions including internal audit relating to banking transactions[13] and includes monitoring of the political situations in foreign countries involved in cross-border financial services with Indian banks.[14] It also includes provisions for encryption[15] and a certain insistence on storing the data in India.[16] However, the thrust in all these regulations is on protecting the concerned sector from financial and compliance risks rather than on ensuring individual privacy.[17] However, relaxations on data localisation can be made on a case-by-case basis in the existing regime. The relevance of the Data Protection Board of India in reviewing and granting such relaxations can only be understood after the notification of the rules in this regard under the DPDP Act 2023.

The regime of the DPDP Act 2023 is a triangulation between the rights and interests of the Data Principal (an individual), the Data Fiduciary and the Government of India. In other words, what it attempts is a compromise between the economic incentives provided by cross-border data flows, the privacy rights of an individual and the security interests of the state. This compromise is executed by persons designated as 'Consent Manager'[18] (CM) and 'Data Protection Officer'[19] (DPO). It is relevant to note that persons who are appointed as CM and DPO are at the cutting edge of enforcement and wield significant powers in the functioning of a Data Fiduciary (DF). However, at the time of writing, the 2011 Rules for the appointment of CM and DPO have not yet been framed. It is interesting to note that a DPO can only be appointed for 'Significant Data Fiduciaries'[20] (SDF). The DPDP Act 2023 allows the Central Government to classify certain DFs as SDFs based on certain parameters that include 'volume and sensitivity of personal data processed', 'risk to electoral democracy' and 'security of the State'. Such protean thresholds for such a classification makes it prone to abuse. Practically every email service provider and social media company can be categorised as an SDF. It is relevant to note that it was the delocalisation of all major email service providers and social media companies that kept them outside the ken of drastic regulation by the Indian state, but their categorisation as SDFs ensures state control through DPOs. It is interesting to note that rather onerous provisions have been made for legitimating subordinate legislations relating to data localisation and penalties to DFs/SDFs in the DPDP Act 2023.[21] Such subordinate legislations would require the approval of both houses of Parliament.[22] Furthermore, the exemptions under section 17 to certain DFs/SDFs at the discretion of the Government from complying with the right to be forgotten and with the

[13] Reserve Bank of India Guidelines on Managing Risks and Code of Conduct in Outsourcing of Financial Services by Banks, November 2006, Guideline 3.

[14] ibid, Guideline 7.

[15] Framework for Adoption of Cloud Services by SEBI Regulated Entities; IRDAI (Outsourcing of Activities by Indian Insurers) Regulations, 2017, 34.

[16] IRDAI (Maintenance of Insurance Records) Regulations, 2015, reg 3(9).

[17] There are just three references to the word 'privacy' in Reserve Bank of India Guidelines on Managing Risks and Code of Conduct in Outsourcing of Financial Services by Banks, November 2006; There are no references to 'privacy' in the Reserve Bank of India directive vide circular (n 12) and in the Public Records Act 1993; and just one reference to 'Privacy' in IRDAI Regulations.

[18] DPDP Act 2023 (n 7) s 2(g).

[19] ibid, s 2(l).

[20] ibid, s 10(2)(a).

[21] ibid, s 41.

[22] ibid.

principles of limitation and minimal data retention enjoyed by an individual, exemplifies the triangulated compromises in the DPDP Act 2023.

A. Influence of International Data Protection Frameworks

The General Data Protection Regulation, 2016[23] overlaps with the DPDP Act 2023 in its avowed objectives namely 'lawfulness, fairness and transparency',[24] 'data minimisation',[25] 'accuracy',[26] 'storage limitation',[27] and protection to children.[28] However, the DPDP Act 2023 has left many things hanging as rights are contingent on the yet to be framed 2011 Rules.[29] There are both points of convergence and divergence between the GDPR and the DPDP Act 2023. Both have rechristened individuals invested with rights of privacy as 'Data Subjects'[30] and 'Data Principals'[31] respectively. Such characterisations give these legislations an impersonal hue that is anti-republican.[32] Other points of major convergence include the exemptions given on the basis of protean terms like 'security of the state'[33] and 'National Security'[34] and the turnkey control mechanism in the form of a 'Data Protection Officer'.[35]

The points of divergence include the general regulatory framework. In the case of the GDPR, there is a European Commission on top of the European Data Protection Board, whereas in the case of the DPDP Act 2023, notwithstanding a provision for independent functioning,[36] the Board is a creature of the state, fully appointed by the Government. Further, the GDPR makes concrete measures for the independence of the Data Protection Officer[37] and the Board,[38] whereas the allowances under the DPDP Act 2023 are rendered meaningless because of the absolute control of the state in appointments.[39] The regulatory regimes in the GDPR and the DPDP Act 2023 are quite similar at the cutting edge, but when it comes to the supervisory functions they are quite distinct. The GDPR has four stakeholders[40]

[23] Regulation (EU) 2016/679, of the European Parliament and of the Council of 27 April 2016 on the Protection of Natural Persons with Regard to the Processing of Personal Data and on the Free Movement of Such Data, and Repealing Directive 95/46/EC (General Data Protection Regulation or GDPR) [2016] OJ L119/1.

[24] DPDP Act 2023 (n 7), Art 5.1(a).

[25] ibid, Art 25.1.

[26] ibid, Art 5.1(d).

[27] ibid, Art 5.1(e).

[28] ibid, Art 8.

[29] See generally, Anirudh Barman, 'Understanding India's New Data Protection Law' (*Carnegie Endowment for International Peace*, 3 October 2023), available at carnegieindia.org/2023/10/03/understanding-india-s-new-data-protection-law-pub-90624.

[30] GDPR (n 23).

[31] DPDP Act 2023 (n 7), s 2(j).

[32] Nupur Chowdhury, 'Data Appropriation, not Protection' (*Deccan Herald*, 27 September 2023), available at epaper.deccanherald.com/Home/ShareArticle?OrgId=279a3ec53f3.

[33] DPDP Act 2023 (n 7), s 17(2)(a).

[34] GDPR (n 23), Art 23.

[35] DPDP Act 2023 (n 7), s 2(l); GDPR (n 23), Arts 38 and 39.

[36] DPDP Act 2023 (n 7), s 28.

[37] GDPR (n 23), Art 38.6.

[38] ibid, Art 69.

[39] DPDP Act 2023 (n 7), s 19.

[40] GDPR (n 23), Art 40.1.

who have a say, namely Member States of the European Union,[41] European Commission,[42] Supervisory Authorities[43] and the European Data Protection Board.[44] This distinction can be accounted for by the fact that the GDPR was enacted by an Economic Union of 27 states and the DPDP Act 2023 by an independent nation state.

The principles like data minimalism[45] and localisation[46] are given considerable clarity in the GDPR. It can be salutary for the future rules in this regard under the DPDP Act 2023. The GDPR provides for rather exemplary penalties and further the member states are given a free hand[47] to decide the penalties for residuary violations.[48] This scheme of residuary and exemplary penalties is almost replicated by the DPDP Act 2023.[49]

The DPDP Act 2023 has a three-tier adjudication mechanism. Starting with the DPOs and CMs and proceeding to the Data Protection Board and then culminating in an appeal before the Telecom Dispute Settlement and Appellate Tribunal. It is relevant to note that what is punishable as per the DPDP Act 2023 are personal data breaches,[50] failure to protect the data by a DF,[51] lack of consent or other breaches relating to data involving children,[52] failure to appoint a DPO or conduct a Data Impact Assessment or any failure to comply with any other condition under section 10 and individuals can be made liable for suppression, false and frivolous complaints and impersonation.[53] There is also a residuary penal provision as per entry 7 of the schedule to the DPDP Act 2023. The launching of a grievance/complaint under the DPDP Act 2023 can be done by an individual first to the Consent Manager or the DF[54] and in case of non-settlement can raise it before the Data Protection Board of India.[55] The decision of the Board can be challenged before the Telecom Dispute Settlement and Appellate Board.[56] However, the Board as an institution has not been notified along with the rules of business and it can only start functioning after such notification and the publication of the 2011 Rules. Curiously only mediation and not arbitration has been referred as an alternate dispute resolution mechanism.[57] The question then is what is the validity of an arbitration agreement between a Data Principal and a DF? Are the public policy implications so grave as to make data breaches inarbitrable? The Board has powers to initiate actions based on the intimations from DFs, references from government and complaints from Data Principals.[58] It can be argued that if need be, the Board can also take

[41] ibid, Principle 3, Arts 62, 80, 84, 85, 87, 88 and 90.
[42] See commission.europa.eu/law/law-topic/data-protection/data-protection-eu/eu-member-states-notifications-european-commission-under-gdpr_en.
[43] GDPR (n 23), Art 51.
[44] ibid, Arts 68 and 69.
[45] ibid, Arts 5.1(c), 25.1, 47.2(d) and 89.1.
[46] ibid, Principle 81, Art 45.
[47] ibid, Art 83.7.
[48] ibid.
[49] DPDP Act 2023 (n 7), schedule to s 33(1).
[50] ibid, s 2(u).
[51] ibid, s 8(6).
[52] ibid, s 9.
[53] ibid, s 15.
[54] ibid, s 13.
[55] ibid, ss 27 and 28.
[56] ibid, s 29.
[57] ibid, s 31.
[58] ibid, s 27.

suo moto actions.[59] The penalties are dealt with in the schedule to the DPDP Act 2023, the upper limits range from 120 USD to 30 million USD.[60]

III. Data Security and Data Localisation

Quite literally data localisation refers to the restrictions on the cross-border movement of personal data. The DPDP Act 2023 deals with it through sections 16 and 17. Data localisation is situated at the trijunction of e-commerce, privacy and security interests of the state, and consequently is crucial for all the stakeholders.[61] A full picture of the data localisation regime can only be had after the notification of the 2011 Rules in this regard, until then the existing norms in the form of sector specific regulations will continue. Today data localisation requirements are sector and industry specific and are ensured through specialised sector legislations.[62] The violation of these legislations triggers the jurisdiction of specialised tribunals, for instance the violation of Securities and Exchange Board of India (SEBI) regulations on data localisation would trigger the jurisdiction of the Securities Appellate Tribunal. The issue here with the DPDP Act 2023 is the conflict of the non-obstante clause[63] in it with the non-obstante clause in the other sector specific legislations. It can be said that the rights granted by the DPDP Act 2023 can be enforced through other sector specific regulators or tribunals. The DPDP Act 2023 is very clear on the position that the stringent standards created by sector specialised statutes and institutions shall hold the field, notwithstanding the current provisions.[64]

IV. Issues in Private International Law

A. Cross-Border Data Transfers – The Normative Content

Given that much of the normative content regulating data in India is located within sectoral regulations with no specific address to the cross-border implications involved in the transfer of such data, it is necessary to recall here the private international law rules of India. Such recall is a complex task, given that the conflicts rules in India are in the jurisprudence of Indian courts and there is no legislative activity in this domain. The following part of

[59] ibid, s 27(2).

[60] As per the exchange rates on 13 October 2023.

[61] Report of the Joint Committee on the Personal Data Protection Bill, 2019 submitted to the 17th Lok Sabha, December 2021, 8–10.

[62] Framework for Adoption of Cloud Services by SEBI Regulated Entities; IRDAI (Outsourcing of Activities by Indian Insurers) Regulations, 2017; IRDAI (Maintenance of Insurance Records) Regulations, 2015; Consumer Protection (Direct Selling) Rules, 2021; Reserve Bank of India Guidelines on Managing Risks and Code of Conduct in Outsourcing of Financial Services by Banks, November 2006; Reserve Bank of India directive vide circular DPSS.CO.OD.No 2785/06.08.005/2017-18 dated April 06, 2018 on Storage of Payment System Data, available at corporate.cyrilamarchandblogs.com/2023/08/a-fine-balancethe-dpda-and-data-localization/.

[63] DPDP Act 2023 (n 7), s 38.

[64] ibid, s 16(2).

this research begins with a narrative on the conflicts rules and is followed by a discussion on the implications of the new data protection legislation for cross-border data transfers and contracts involving data-related operations. The legislation's content impacting cross-border data transfers is analysed via a comparative approach juxtaposing it against the data regime in the US and the EU. There is also an analysis of the judicial opinion.

B. The Syncretic Private International Law Rules in India

The law applicable to a foreign element in interpersonal conflicts[65] is largely derived from the jurisprudence developed by the higher judiciary, as contrasted with countries of the other geographies which have either used the legislation method to regulate conflict issues or subscribed to unified laws.[66]

Interpersonal conflicts, especially those related to contractual obligations and tortious liability, are subjected to a *de minimis* regime that includes legislative provisions on the recognition and enforcement of foreign judgments,[67] foreign arbitral awards[68] and the law related to limitation.[69]

C. Jurisdiction of the Indian Courts

It is a general rule of private international law that courts do not assume jurisdiction over foreign immovables. The Supreme Court, in *CtA.Ct. Nachiappa Chettiar v CtA.Ct. Subramaniam Chettiar*[70] concerning the division of certain immovable properties situated in Burma (Myanmar), reiterated its engagement with this general rule and held against the Indian courts' jurisdiction for determination of questions of title in respect of immovable properties in foreign countries or to direct division thereof. It observed 'where a court has no jurisdiction to determine any matter in controversy such as the question of tide in respect of the foreign immovable property it has no jurisdiction to refer it for the determination of the arbitrators.'[71]

[65] Interpersonal conflicts are conflicts involving two or more individuals or organisations where the legal systems that the parties are connected to view the same facts of the dispute differently. See, TS Rama Rao, 'Private International Law in India' (1955) 4 *The Indian Yearbook of International Affairs* 219; Sai Ramani Garimella, 'India' in Anselmo Reyes (ed), *Recognition and Enforcement of Judgments in Civil and Commercial Matters* (Hart-Bloomsbury, 2019).

[66] Early literature on the subject documented that the common law principles have had a significant impact on the handling of a foreign element within a dispute. See, PV Raja Mannar, 'The Future of Private International Law in India' (1952) 1 *The Indian Yearbook of International Affairs* 20; VK Thiruvenkatachari, 'Developments in the Field of Private International Law' (1953) 2 *The Indian Yearbook on International Affairs* 195; Sai Ramani Garimella, 'OBOR and the Syncretic Private International Law Rules in India: Time for Accession to Harmonised Legal Regimes' in Poomintr Sooksripaisarnkit and Sai Ramani Garimella (eds), *China's One Belt One Road Initiative and Private International Law* (Routledge, 2018).

[67] Code of Civil Procedure, 1908, ss 13 and 44A.

[68] Arbitration and Conciliation Act, 1996 (amended in 2019).

[69] Limitation Act, 1963.

[70] *CtA.Ct. Nachiappa Chettiar v CtA.Ct. Subramaniam Chettiar* AIR 1960 SC 307.

[71] ibid, 312.

i. Inbound Jurisdiction

The inbound jurisdiction of the civil courts in India, courts of first instance, is specified within the Code of Civil Procedure, 1908 (CPC). Section 9 of the CPC reads:

> 9. Courts to try all civil suits unless barred.
>
> The Courts shall (subject to the provisions herein contained) have jurisdiction to try all suits of a civil nature excepting suits of which their cognisance is either expressly or impliedly barred.
>
> [1][Explanation I].- A suit in which the right to property or to an office is contested is a suit of a civil nature, notwithstanding that such right may depend entirely on the decision of questions as to religious rites or ceremonies.
>
> [2][Explanation II].- For the purposes of this section, it is immaterial whether or not any fees are attached to the office referred to in Explanation I or whether or not such office is attached to a particular place.

This jurisdiction is normally subject to territorial and pecuniary limitations further set out in the Code and the concerned state law creating the civil court.

ii. Anti-Suit Injunctions – Indian Courts

Judicial opinion has indicated that anti-suit injunctions or restraining orders against foreign proceedings (flowing from the idea that such foreign forum could be a *forum non conveniens*) may be issued only if those proceedings seem vexatious and oppressive. In appropriate cases, proceedings in India may be stayed if the court could perceive that proceedings in the foreign court could better serve the ends of justice.[72]

The Supreme Court in *Modi Entertainment Network v WSG Cricket Pte Ltd*[73] clarified the position on anti-suit injunctions in disputes before foreign proceedings:

1. The defendant against whom an injunction is sought must be amenable to the personal jurisdiction of the court.
2. The said injunction may be granted, only if the absence of it would lead to frustrating the ends of justice and perpetration of injustice.
3. Respect for the principle of comity of courts.
4. Where there is more than one forum, the court in the exercise of its discretion to grant anti-suit injunction has to examine and determine the appropriate forum (*forum conveniens*) – ie the convenience of the parties and may grant an anti-suit injunction in regard to proceedings which are oppressive or vexatious or in a *forum non conveniens.*

iii. Anti-Anti-Suit Injunctions

Indian courts have also indicated their preference for ordering anti-anti-suit injunctions (A2SI). In *Interdigital Technology Corporation & Ors v Xiaomi Corporation & Ors*,[74] the

[72] See, eg, *Vanichand Rajput v Lakshmichand Manekchand* (1919) 21 Bom LR 955; *Jethabhai Versey & Co v Amarchand Madhavji & Co* AIR 1920 Bom 20.

[73] *Modi Entertainment Network v WSG Cricket Pte Ltd* AIR 2003 SC 1177.

[74] *Interdigital Technology Corporation & Ors v Xiaomi Corporation & Ors* A. 8772/2020 in CS(COMM) 295/2020.

Delhi High Court ruled in favour of the plaintiff with an injunction against the global anti-suit restraint in favour of the defendant ordered by the Wuhan People's Court, China. The plaintiff pleaded that the relief was necessary for complete justice, as the subject matter of the proceedings, in the suit before the Delhi High Court and in the Wuhan Court, were different and if the injunction granted by the Wuhan Court was allowed to remain in place, not only would the plaintiff be injuncted from prosecuting the proceedings before the Delhi High Court; no court, in the world, would be entitled to adjudicate on the issue of infringement of the plaintiff's technology. They also pleaded that where the order of a foreign court was in defiance of the public policy of the domestic court, no principle of comity could inhibit the domestic court from protecting itself against the assault on its public policy.[75]

The Court noted that the principles for the grant of an A2SI were broadly the same as those which applied to the grant of an anti-suit injunction.

Observing that it could exercise personal jurisdiction over the defendants, the Court also focussed on the territorial nature of intellectual property rights to reiterate its jurisdiction on matters related to patent infringement claims. Relying on *Magotteaux Industries Pvt Ltd*,[76] the Court observed that patent rights being territorial in nature, are granted by the sovereign state. Thus, any foreign court that crosses its own jurisdiction to encroach upon the sovereign functions of another state would undeniably warrant the grant of an A2SI.

iv. Forum Selection Clauses

The Indian law lends validity to the forum selection clauses. In *ABC Laminart Pvt Ltd v A.P. Agencies Salem*,[77] the Court outlined the rules explaining the validity of contracts ousting or conferring jurisdiction on courts:

a) Ousting jurisdiction of a court, which otherwise would have jurisdiction, by a contract, is void.
b) Conferring jurisdiction on a court, which otherwise does not have any jurisdiction, by a contract, is void.
c) Where two or more courts have jurisdiction to try a matter, then limiting the jurisdiction to a particular court is valid. However, such a contract should be clear, unambiguous and specific. Ouster clauses may use the words 'alone', 'exclusively' and 'only' and the same pose no difficulty in interpretation.

In *Modi Entertainment Network*[78] the Court held that preventing a party from approaching a contractually designated forum would amount to aiding a breach of contract. Further, if parties contracted, in a non-exclusive forum selection clause, to approach a neutral foreign forum and to be governed by the law applicable to it for the dispute resolution, ordinarily no anti-suit injunction will be granted in regard to proceedings in such a *forum conveniens* on the presumption that the parties have thought over their convenience and all other relevant

[75] Reliance was placed on *SAS Institute In v World Programming Ltd* (2020) EWCA Civ 599.
[76] *Magotteaux Industries Pvt Ltd & Ors v Aia Engineering Ltd* FAO (OS) No 280/2008.
[77] *ABC Laminart Pvt Ltd v A.P. Agencies Salem* AIR 1989 SC 1239. See, also, *British India Steam Navigation Co Ltd v Shanmughavilas Cashew Industries and Ors* [1990] 3 SCC 481.
[78] *Modi Entertainment Network* (n 73).

factors before submitting to non-exclusive jurisdiction of the court of their choice which cannot be treated just as an alternative forum.[79]

In *Kumarina Investment Ltd v Digital Media Convergence Ltd and Another*[80] the Court held that the question of jurisdiction is to be determined as per the jurisdictional clauses of the contract, especially when the petitioner is a foreigner and the parties have preferred a specific law as the applicable law to govern their contract and disputes. It, however, identified a few situations when a non-chosen court could exercise jurisdiction:

1. The contracting parties being subject to the municipal law of the country with which the case has the connection or where the cause of action may have arisen.
2. The governing law clause of the contract is violative of the public policy of the country and such clause does not confer exclusive jurisdiction on the forum chosen.
3. It is possible according to the chosen applicable law to override the chosen forum.

v. Choice of Law

In *Dhanrajamal Gobindram v Shamji Kalidas and Co*,[81] the Court held that the choice between the *lex loci contractus* or *lex loci solutionis* for the decision on a proper law of the contract is a matter of presumption. An expressed intention of the parties regarding the choice of law overrides any presumption.[82] In the absence of an express intention regarding the choice of law, the applicable law is to be inferred from the terms and nature of the contract and from the general circumstances of the case. In *Delhi Cloth and General Mills v Harnam Singh*,[83] the grouping of elements test was applied in order to ascertain the proper law of contract, thus endorsing the objective approach.

In *Rabindra N Maitra v Life Insurance Corporation of India*,[84] the Supreme Court listed the factors to be considered while imputing the objective choice of law by the court – the place where the contract was made; place of performance; place of domicile; residence or business of the parties; national character of corporation; subject matter of contract; and all other facts that help localise the contract. Amongst these, the Court underscored the importance of the law of the place of performance of the contract as a determinant factor because of the contract's closer connection with that law than any other.

Courts in India possess the residual power to strike down the wholly unconnected choice of law clauses. The Supreme Court in *National Thermal Power Corporation v Singer Company and Ors*,[85] explained that an express choice of law, to be considered valid, ought to be explicit, emphatic, unambiguous, *bona fide* legal, and not opposed to public policy. The decision addressed an important issue in private international law – the choice of the forum and its impact on the tacit choice of law. In the absence of an expressed choice of law, such

[79] ibid, [15].
[80] *Kumarina Investment Ltd v Digital Media Convergence Ltd and Another* (2010) SCC Online TDSAT 641.
[81] *Dhanrajamal Gobindram v Shamji Kalidas and Co* [1961] 3 SCR 1029.
[82] ibid, [37].
[83] *Delhi Cloth and General Mills v Harnam Singh* AIR 1955 SC 590.
[84] *Rabindra N Maitra v Life Insurance Corporation of India* AIR 1964 Cal 141.
[85] *National Thermal Power Corporation v Singer Company and Ors* [1992] 3 SCR 106.

choice may be clearly inferred based on the contract and the surrounding circumstances that include amongst the indiciae, a chosen forum for dispute resolution.[86]

In *Shreejee Traco (I) Pvt Ltd v Paperline International Inc*,[87] the Supreme Court, in a matter related to arbitrator appointment, referred to the *NTPC v Singer* decision and ruled in favour of a presumption of linkages between the choice of forum and a tacit choice of law.

vi. Recognition and Enforcement of Foreign Judgments

Section 2 of the Code of Civil Procedure, 1908 defined 'foreign Court' and 'foreign judgments' as:

> (5) 'foreign Court' means a Court situate outside India and not established or continued by the authority of the Central Government;
> (6) 'foreign judgment' means the judgment of a foreign Court.

The judgment of a foreign court imposes upon the defendant a legal obligation to fulfill, and Indian courts, as courts elsewhere, are under a legal obligation to enforce such judgments. The common law 'doctrine of obligation'[88] has been turned into a legal obligation within section 13, which specifies the instances where such judgment is considered inconclusive, and hence not creating an obligation.

As per section 44A, a decree of any superior court of a reciprocating territory shall be executed in India as a decree passed by the Indian district court.

A 'reciprocating territory' is defined in Explanation I to section 44A as 'any country or territory outside India which the Central Government may, by notification in the Official Gazette, declare to be a reciprocating territory for the purposes of this section' and 'superior courts', with reference to any such territory, as 'such courts as may be specified in the said notification'.[89] A judgment from a court of a reciprocating territory can be directly enforced in India by filing an execution application. Section 44A(1) of the CPC states that where a certified copy of a decree of any superior court of a reciprocating territory has been filed in a District Court, the decree may be executed in India as if it had been passed by the District Court, meaning that the entire scheme of execution of decrees as laid down in Order 21 of the CPC will be applicable. In *Marine Geotechnics LLC v Coastal Marine Construction & Engineering Ltd*,[90] the Bombay High Court observed that, in the case of a decree from a non-reciprocating foreign territory, the decree-holder should file, in a domestic Indian court of competent jurisdiction, a suit based on the judgment debt created by the foreign decree or based on the original underlying cause of action or based on both. Although the foreign

[86] Jan L Neels, 'Choice of Forum and Tacit Choice of Law: The Supreme Court of India and the Hague Principles on Choice of Law in International Commercial Contracts (An Appeal for an Inclusive Comparative Approach to Private International Law)' in *Eppur si Muove: The Age of Uniform Law Essays in Honour of Michael Joachim Bonell to Celebrate his 70th Birthday* (UNIDROIT, 2016) 358, 366.

[87] *Shreejee Traco (I) Pvt Ltd v Paperline International Inc* (2003) 9 SCC 79.

[88] According to this doctrine, when a foreign court of competent jurisdiction by its judgment creates a right in favour of a person, it becomes obligatory on the other party to comply with it.

[89] The List of Reciprocating Territories under the Civil Laws in India are the United Kingdom, Singapore, Bangladesh, UAE, Malaysia, Trinidad & Tobago, New Zealand, the Cook Islands (including Niue) and the Trust Territories of Western Samoa, Hong Kong, Papua and New Guinea, Fiji, Aden.

[90] *Marine Geotechnics LLC v Coastal Marine Construction & Engineering Ltd* [2014] 2 Bom CR 769.

decree is not by itself executable in India, a domestic decree obtained in a civil action based on the foreign judgment can be executed.

While filing the execution application, the original certified copy of the decree along with a certificate from the superior court stating the extent to which the decree has been satisfied or adjusted has to be annexed to the application.

A foreign judgment or decree should be conclusive as to any matter adjudicated by it. The test for conclusiveness of a foreign judgment or decree is laid down in the Code of Civil Procedure, section 13. A foreign judgment shall be deemed conclusive unless:

1. It has not been pronounced by a court of competent jurisdiction.
2. It has not been given on the merits of the case.
3. It appears, on the face of the proceedings, to be founded on an incorrect view of international law or a refusal to recognise the law of India in cases in which such law is applicable.
4. The proceedings in which the judgment was obtained are opposed to natural justice.
5. It has been obtained by fraud.
6. It sustains a claim founded on a breach of any law in force in India.

The scope of section 13 has been explained *in extenso* by the apex court in *R Vishwanathan v Rukn-Ul-Mulk Syed Abdul Wajid*:[91]

> A judgment which is the result of bias or want of impartiality on the part of a judge will be regarded as a nullity and the trial *corum non judice*.[92]
>
> A foreign judgment of a competent court is conclusive even if it proceeds on an erroneous view of the evidence or the law if the minimum requirements of the judicial process are assured; correctness of the judgment in law or on evidence is not predicated as a condition for recognition of its conclusiveness by the Municipal Court.[93]

The foreign court's competence in delivering the judgment in question under section 13 is to be understood in the international sense and not merely by the law of the foreign state under which the court functions. In *Hindupur v Bellur*,[94] the Delhi High Court reaffirmed that section13(e) requires that a foreign judgment is recognised in India only if it conforms with public policy (ie, good conscience and equity as reflected by the grounds in CPC, section 13.

Interlocutory orders indicated by foreign courts are enforceable in India, similar to decrees. The Supreme Court in *Alcon Electronics (P) Ltd v Celem SA of France*,[95] enforced a foreign court order that awarded costs with interest in an interlocutory order. The Court explained that the foreign court's order was 'conclusive' and 'on the merits' and the quantification of the costs could be characterised as a money decree. Interestingly, the Court noted that while the CPC does not provide for interest on costs, Indian courts are not prevented from recognising and enforcing an order for the payment of interest made by a

[91] *R Vishwanathan v Rukn-Ul-Mulk Syed Abdul Wajid* AIR 1963 SC 1.
[92] ibid, [25].
[93] ibid, [71].
[94] *Hindupur v Bellur* (2015) SCC OnLine Del 7484.
[95] *M/S Alcon Electronics Pvt Ltd v Celem SA of Fos 34320 Roujan, France* [2017] 2 SCC 253, [2017] AIR SC 1.

foreign court. The Court consequently upheld the plaintiff's right to have its entitlement interest at eight per cent under the UK Judgments Act 1838 recognised in India.

vii. Application of the Law of Limitation

The Limitation Act 1963 applies to the foreign judgments enforceable under the Code of Civil Procedure, the period of limitation being:

1. for the execution of a decree granting a mandatory injunction, three years from the date of the decree or the date fixed for performance; and
2. for the execution of any other decree, 12 years from the date of its enforceability; in decrees for payment of money or delivery of goods, the limitation period begins upon default of such performance (provided that an application for the enforcement or execution of a decree granting perpetual injunction will not be subject to any period of limitation).

Judgment-holders from a non-reciprocating territory are required to file a civil suit before the competent court in India within three years of the date of the foreign judgment or decree.

viii. Procedure of Enforcement of Foreign Judgments

A foreign judgment, recognised as conclusive according to section 13, could be enforced by either instituting a suit on such judgment, or by instituting execution proceedings.

A suit on a foreign judgment must be filed within a period of three years from the date of the judgment.

V. Legal Bases, Mechanisms and Exceptions for Cross-Border Data Transfers and Data Protection

A. Cross-Border Data Transfer: Pre-2023

Given the little progress and political will in achieving harmonised regimes for data and cyberspace governance,[96] states have indulged in creating domestic 'norms'[97] and norms founded upon insufficiently developed principles in other regimes like, for instance, the conflict of laws that offered primitive tools for complex problems. There was little clarity on how these regulations interacted with the data belonging to foreign business entities and handled by Indian corporates. The downside of activating domestic normative architecture – these norms were much conflicting in their content and purpose, leading some

[96] Nicholas Tsagourias, 'Law, Borders and the Territorialisation of Cyberspace' (2018) 18(4) *Indonesian Journal of International Law* 523, 539.

[97] Anna-Maria Osula and Henry Rõigas, 'Introduction' in Anna-Maria Osula and Henry Rõigas (eds), *International Cyber Norms: Legal, Policy & Industry Perspectives* (Tallinn, Estonia: NATO Cooperative Cyber Defence Centre of Excellence, 2016).

commentators to lament that cyberspace is in a moment of crisis.[98] India was no different. In the last two decades it extensively engaged in regulatory space that often clashed with privacy rights.[99] Under section 69(1) of the Information Technology Act, 2000 (IT Act) (which largely corresponds with section 5(2) of the Telegraph Act, 1881), the Government always had the power to authorise intelligence agencies to submit requests to intercept, monitor and decrypt information. Mass surveillance programmes like the Central Monitoring System, National Intelligence Grid, Lawful Intercept and Monitoring Project, Network Traffic Analysis System and Crime and Criminal Tracking and Network System form the surveillance landscape in India with minimal process addressing any grievance redressal. Similar to other jurisdictions, digital sovereignty has worked against the privacy landscape in an *ad hoc* manner, in what could only be described as the creation of regulatory divergence to frameworks such as the GDPR.

According to a recent paper from the Organization for Economic Cooperation and Development (OECD), regulatory divergence can add between 5 and 10 per cent to the cost of doing business.[100] However, empirical evidence also indicates that, where laws are harmonised, foreign direct investment can increase by as much as 15 per cent.[101] David Markus used the APAC privacy matrix to identify the challenges in implementing content similar to the harmonised law, for instance, the GDPR. The Matrix placed India on Category 3 along with a few other Asian emerging economies:[102]

> Category 3: The GDPR 'Push-Pull Late Adopters': 2018 onwards
>
> India, China, Thailand, and Vietnam – the focus with these recent reforms is on adopting a GDPR style framework to achieve data security in the eyes of EU regulators, with some attempts to opt out of data transfer through localised security assessments and onshore servers.[103]

[98] K Mačák, 'Is the International Law of Cyber Security in Crisis?' (2016 8th International Conference on Cyber Conflict (CyCon)), 127–39.

[99] Chaitanya Ramachandran, 'PUCL v. UOI Revisited: Why India's Surveillance Law Must Be Redesigned For The Digital Age' (*Manupatra*, April–June 2014), available at docs.manupatra.in/newsline/articles/Upload/E90FA90F-0328-49F2-B03F-B9FBA473964F.pdf; Further, on 21 December 2018, the Government of India passed an Order authorising 10 Central agencies to intercept, monitor and decrypt any information on the computer. This regulation and such others have been much discussed in the scholarship on the subject. See, Arushi Gupta, 'The Case against the Constitutional Validity of Mass Surveillance Programmes' (2019) *Indian Law Review*; 'All Computers Can Now Be Monitored by Central Agencies' (*The Hindu*, 21 December 2018), available at www.thehindu.com/news/national/all-computers-can-now-be-monitored-by-govt-agencies/article25792523.ece; Elonnai Hickok, Vipul Kharbanda, Shweta Mohandas and Pranav M Bidare, 'Is the New Interception Order Old Wine in a New Bottle?' (*The Centre for Internet Society*, 29 December 2018), available at cis-india.org/internet-governance/blog/newslaundry-elonnai-hickok-vipul-kharbanda-shweta-mohandas-and-pranav-bidare-december-27-2018-is-the-new-interception-order-old-wine-in-a-new-bottle.

[100] International Federation of Accountants, 'Regulatory Divergence: Costs, Risks, Impacts: An International Financial Sector Study by Business at OECD and the International Federation of Accountants' (2018), available at www.ifac.org/_flysystem/azure-private/publications/files/IFAC-OECD-Regulatory-Divergence.pdf.

[101] David Markus, Digital Trade and Digital Sovereignty: Navigating Best Practice for Cross Border Data Transfers, Working Paper 2020 (available on file with the authors). Also see, D Marcus, 'Digital Resilience in the Age of a Global Pandemic: How Can Privacy Assist in Risk Mitigation?" (2020) 17(1&2) *Privacy Law Bulletin* 2.

[102] ibid.

[103] See, generally, David Nguyen and Marta Paczos, 'Measuring the Economic Value of Data and Cross-Border Data Flows: A Business Perspective' (2020), available at www.oecd-ilibrary.org/docserver/6345995e-en.pdf?expires=1706782378&id=id&accname=guest&checksum=DDF353291BD51FAF55C68309B37248A6.

It is pertinent to contextualise the Indian law, including the jurisprudence, against the comparative law practice in the EU, and the US which have also confronted issues related to digital sovereignty and privacy.

Domestic responses to protecting personal data, varied as they are, demonstrate the need to identify the applicable law to transnational personal data. According to conflict of laws, in finding *lex causae*, there are three stages:

1. characterise the issue into one of the established choice of law classifications by identifying the nature of the subject matter,
2. select the rule of conflict of laws which lays down a connecting factor for the issue in question, and,
3. identify the system of law which is tied by the connecting factor found in stage two to the issue characterised in stage one.[104]

The connecting factors could relate to the parties (their nationality/place of business at the time of conclusion of the contract), the place of conclusion of the contract, the place of performance of the contract, amongst others. Therein lies the concern – identifying the appropriate connecting factors in any dispute, even in the traditional disputes. The problem is much accentuated in disputes concerning data and cyberspace wherein it is difficult to identify the place of performance of the contract, when the contract is performed through a web of sub-contracts, as seen in contracts related to the outsourcing of database management.[105] Given the scale and volume of data transfers across jurisdictions, the concern of addressing and complying with multiple regulatory regimes addressing a variety of asset classes and clients, conflicts in the nature and content of regulation pose a heightened challenge.[106] It becomes therefore necessary to ensure that the law, domestic as well as international, is up and ready to address the requirements of the digital society, and not be mired in sovereignty-related issues alone. Towards this, the conflict of laws mechanisms should be empowered to address beyond the traditional issues of personal law and civil and commercial matters that it is currently equipped to address. Disputes related to data technologies are characterised differently under the variety of regimes, national, regional, as well as the global norms.[107] While India, similar to the EU and US, commends its law on personal data protection to its territorial nature, hence the application of *lex fori*, it considers the personal data protection law as a mandatory law and as a curtailment of party autonomy.[108] However, the characterisation of the right to personal data is articulated differently. The EU

[104] *Macmillan Inc v Bishopsgate* [1996] 1 WLR 387 (Eng); Jeanne Ji Huang, 'Applicable Law to Transnational Personal Data: Trends and Dynamics' (2020) 21 *German Law Journal* 1283, 1286.

[105] Huang, ibid.

[106] James Manyika, 'Digital Globalization: The New Era of Global Flows' (McKinsey Global Institute, 2016), available at www.mckinsey.com/~/media/mckinsey/business%20functions/mckinsey%20digital/our%20insights/digital%20globalization%20the%20new%20era%20of%20global%20flows/mgi-digital-globalization-full-report.pdf. It is estimated some 900 million people have international connections on social media, and 360 million take part in cross-border e-commerce. While digital technologies significantly enhanced the response mechanisms in combating the pandemic, they are also of immense value to the economic recovery.

[107] Huang (n 104).

[108] Sai Ramani Garimella and B Parthiban, 'Ringfencing Data? – Perspectives on Sovereignty and Localisation from India' in Poomintr Sooksripaisarnkit and Dharmita Prasad (eds), *Blurry Boundary of Public and Private International Law – Towards Convergence or Divergence Still?* (Springer, 2022) 261.

has accorded protection to personal data as a fundamental human right,[109] a data subject's right to their personal data is characterised as a 'right to privacy with respect to the processing of personal data'.[110] Similarly, the Treaty on the Functioning of the European Union also provided for a right to data protection.[111]

In the US, privacy, a right, is a civil liberty, and a constitutionally protected right.[112] The Fourth Amendment to the US Constitution has implications for data-related activity, however it is limited to government and state institutions, and therefore has little relevance to the issues arising from transnational data-related activity, managed by corporate entities. state action.[113] However, the First Amendment's free speech provision allows for a free flow of information,[114] which could be characterised as a fundamental human right to privacy and data protection in the US. The right to free flow of information was reiterated in *Sorrell v IMS Health Care*,[115] wherein the Court held the Vermont law related to confidentiality as unconstitutional and did not advance the policy goals, however appropriate they were, in a permissible way. It observed that 'the fear that people would make bad decisions if given truthful information' cannot justify content-based burdens on speech.[116]

B. Indian Perspective: Pre-2023

Indian law seems to be in favour of territorialisation, and data localisation as well. While it could be founded on concerns like safeguarding privacy and security,[117] digital protectionism could also be at play. This is achieved by the promotion of local Information and Communication Technology (ICT) enterprise either directly, by providing preferential treatment to domestic cloud computing businesses, or indirectly coercing foreign companies to locate their servers domestically. These restrictions tend to reduce market access for foreign suppliers of digital services, impeding trade and investment opportunities and

[109] Cole David and Fabbrini Federico, 'Bridging the Transatlantic Divide? The United States, the European Union, and the Protection of Privacy Across Borders' (2016) 14 *ICON* 220, 223.

[110] GDPR (n 23) 31; Huang (n 104), 1287.

[111] Consolidated Version of the Treaty on the Functioning of the European Union (TFEU) Art 16, October 26 [2012] OJ C 326/ 47.

[112] US Privacy art 5 USC §552 (2018); Raul Alan Charles, Manoranjan Tasha D and Mohan Vivek, 'United States' in Alan Charles Raul (ed), *The Privacy, Data Protection, And Cybersecurity Law Review*, 1st edn (Law Business Research Ltd, 2014) 268, 269.

[113] *Roe v Wade*, 410 US 113, 153 (1973). In *Whalen v Roe* 429 US 589, 605–606 (1977) although the Supreme Court of the United States identified a general right to 'information privacy' in the Fourteenth Amendment, the Court upheld a New York statute requiring identification of physicians and patients in dangerous legitimate drug prescription records, available at supreme.justia.com/cases/federal/us/429/589/.

[114] *Liquormart, Inc v Rhode Island*, 517 US 484, 503, 116 S Ct 1459 (Opinion of Stevens J) ('The First Amendment directs us to be especially sceptical of regulations that seek to keep people in the dark for what the government perceives to be their own good.').

[115] *Sorrell v IMS Health Care*, 564 US 552, 561 (2011) wherein the Court heard a plea of first amendment violation by the Vermont Prescription Confidentiality Law that prohibited disclosure or otherwise allowing pharmacies to share prescriber-identity information with anyone except for marketing reasons, available at www.supremecourt.gov/opinions/10pdf/10-779.pdf.

[116] ibid, 560.

[117] Christopher Kuner, 'Regulation of Transborder Data Flows under Data Protection and Privacy Law: Past, Present and Future', OECD Digital Economy Papers, No 187 (OECD, 2011), available at www.oecd-ilibrary.org/docserver/5kg0s2fk315f-en.pdf?expires=1632583184&id=id&accname=guest&checksum=5B68A70E599A3E4DF254649D803CFD8B.

increasing the costs and service choice of individual businesses.[118] The India story will present two recent developments – an order from one of the constitutional courts of India with an emphasis on local holding of the data and jurisdiction to the *lex fori*, and the much-expected law reform on personal data protection.

In *Balu Gopalakrishnan and others v State of Kerala and others*,[119] the Kerala High Court was hearing a writ petition in the matter related to the handling of COVID-19 patient data contracted to a New York business entity Sprnklr (with its registered office located in Bangalore, India). The petitioners, *ad vindictam publicam*, contended that the Union of India, Government of Kerala contracted with Sprnklr LLC and its Indian entities to manage the patient data during the pandemic and that the said contract raised certain confidentiality concerns. It must be stated here that the contract had a forum selection clause, which vested the power of dispute resolution in the courts at New York. This fact was also the basis of petitioner apprehension, presented in their arguments to the Court.

The petitioners also project an apprehension – based on certain terms of the contract, a copy of which has been appended to some of these writ petitions as an exhibit – that, in the event of breach of data confidentiality or any other dispute, the Government of Kerala will obtain no legal recourse through any courts in Kerala – or for that matter in India – since it postulates that the jurisdiction with respect to such is exclusively vested in the courts in New York in the US.

In its interim orders, the Court observed: '2. Prefatorily, data confidentiality is, in its ultimate sense, about protecting data from unlawful, unauthorised as also from unintentional access and disclosure'.[120]

It may be noted that the petitioners primarily alleged that the contract in question has little or no safeguards against the commercial and unauthorised exploitation of the data entrusted to Sprinklr for processing by the Government of Kerala. This contention was refuted within the arguments of the counsel: '10. [...] Sprinklr is not in possession of any data at present and that they have re-transmitted all such to the Government of Kerala, which is presently in its full custody and control'.[121]

Regarding the apprehension related to access to justice given the existence of the forum selection clause, the counsel for the respondents averred:

> 11. [...] that 'the data resides in India' and therefore, that the breach of its confidentiality would expose Sprinklr to action in India, both at the hands of individual citizens and the State. They, however, expressly admitted that the 'mandate of the New York jurisdiction' binds the Government of Kerala with respect to the breach of the terms of the contract.

[118] Circular on Storage of Payment System Data issued by India's central bank, the Reserve Bank of India, dated 6 April, 2018, available at rbi.org.in/Scripts/BS_CircularIndexDisplay.aspx?Id=11244; Effective July 2021, the payments firm Mastercard has been barred from adding new customers in India thereby significantly impacting its business which otherwise covered a third of credit and debit card business in India, see theprint.in/economy/what-is-data-localisation-why-mastercard-amex-diners-club-cant-add-more-customers-in-india/703790/; see, generally, Mitchell Andrew D and Hepburn Jarrod, 'Don't Fence Me In: Reforming Trade and Investment Law to Better Facilitate Cross-border Data Transfer' (2017) 19 *Yale Journal of Law and Technology* 182, 186.

[119] Interim orders in *Balu Gopalakrishnan and others v State of Kerala and others* W.P.(C). Temp. No.84 of 2020, wherein the Kerala High Court exercised jurisdiction despite the presence of a forum selection clause that vested jurisdiction in the courts of New York.

[120] ibid, 12.

[121] ibid, 15.

> The petitioners further submitted [...] that the Government of Kerala, by ceding to the jurisdiction of courts outside India, has rendered recourse to law, both for the citizens and itself, illusory in the event of breach of the contract by Sprinklr.

The Court based its observation on the fact that the data is located in India and is in the possession of the Government of Kerala. Exercising jurisdiction on the substantive issue of confidentiality of data,[122] the Court ordered Respondents 1, 2 and 3 to ensure anonymisation of the data and take all necessary steps to prevent breach of the confidentiality clause in the Masters Services Agreement between Respondent 1 and Respondent 3, Sprnklr LLC.

The Court ordered,

> [..] injunct Sprinklr from committing any act which will be, directly or indirectly, in breach of confidentiality of the data entrusted to them for analysis/processing by the Government of Kerala under the impugned contract/s; and that they shall not disclose or part with any such data to any third party/person/entity – of whatever nature or composition – anywhere in the world.[123]

Note here in the context of India's tryst with regulating data protection and data governance, that the Court felt that the presence of data in India, attributed a jurisdiction to the courts in India, and secondly the data concerned the Indian population, and there is a vested interest in the local courts exercising jurisdiction. This interim order therefore demonstrates the tendencies of territorialisation of jurisdiction based upon localisation of data.

C. The *Puttaswamy* Judgment – A Watershed Statement on Digital Footprint

On 24 August 2017, a nine-judge bench of the Supreme Court in *Justice KS Puttaswamy v Union of India*[124] passed a historic judgment affirming the constitutional right to privacy. The key features derived from the ratio of the decision encapsulated hereinbelow, reiterate a recognition of privacy as an intrinsic right, and the judicial standards of review that would be applied to actions that allegedly impinge upon privacy.

1. Privacy is intrinsic to and inseparable from the human element in the human being.
2. Right to privacy is not just a common law right but a fundamental right guaranteed by Part III of the Constitution.
3. Privacy is not an absolute right, subject to permissible restrictions.
4. Action must be sanctioned by law, it must be necessary to fulfil a legitimate aim of the state and the interference must be 'proportionate to the need for such interference'.
5. Recognition and enforcement of claims for breach qua non-state actors will require legislative intervention by the state.
6. Right to privacy was grounded in rights to freedom under both Article 21 and Article 19 of the Constitution encompassing freedom of the body as well as the mind.

[122] ibid, 21.
[123] ibid, 23.
[124] *Justice KS Puttaswamy (Retd) v Union of India & Ors* 2017 (10) SCALE 1.

The four elements of the judicial review standard are as follows:

1. Legality: The existence of a law.
2. Legitimate Goal: The law should seek to achieve a legitimate state aim (per Chandrachud J). The proposed action must be necessary for a democratic society for a legitimate aim (per Kaul J). Justice Kaul's opinion can be read to espouse the EU narrow tailoring test.
3. Proportionality: There should be a rational nexus between the objects and the means adopted to achieve them (per Chandrachud J). The extent of interference must be proportionate to its need (per Kaul J).
4. Procedural Guarantees: To check against the abuse of state interference (per Kaul J).

Despite being a unanimous decision, there were differences with regard to the articulation of the review standards, as shown above, wherein Justice Kaul's opinion seemed to lean closer to the EU model.

Protection of data is addressed via the IT Act and the Information Technology (Reasonable Security Practices and Procedures and Sensitive Personal information) Rules, 2011 ('IT Rules').[125] Rule 2(i) defines personal information as follows: 'any information that relates to a natural person, which, either directly or indirectly, in combination with other information available or likely to be available with a body corporate, is capable of identifying such person'.

Further, following the *Puttaswamy* judgment, the Government of India in 2018 proposed a legislation that aims to provide a comprehensive regulation of data protection. The bill was a result of extensive research reports submitted by the Justice Sri Krishna Committee,[126] The Telecom Regulatory Authority of India Report,[127] and the Justice AP Shah Report.[128] The Personal Data Protection Bill[129] is now for consideration and scrutiny before a Select Committee of the Parliament, before being returned to the Parliament for vote. The following section discusses the rights envisaged under the Sensitive Personal Data or Information Rules (SPDI Rules) and how they compare with the content under the Data Protection Bill, 2018 ('Draft Bill').

The IT Act mandates that a body corporate is responsible for handling sensitive personal data or information liable for compensating loss based upon a fault liability arising from

[125] Other regulatory mechanisms addressing data governance in India include:

- Consumer Protection Act, 2019 and Consumer Protection (E-Commerce) Rules, 2020;
- rules made by the Reserve Bank of India;
- rules imposed by the Telecom Regulatory Authority of India;
- rules imposed by the Insurance Regulatory and Development Authority of India;
- rules imposed by the Securities and Exchange Board of India (SEBI);
- various decisions of Indian courts; and
- Unified Licence Agreements issued pursuant to the National Telecom Policy, 2012 by the Department of Telecommunications.

[126] The Committee of Experts on a Data Protection Framework for India, (2018).

[127] Telecom Regulatory Authority of India Recommendations on Privacy, Security and Ownership of the Data in the Telecom Sector (2018).

[128] Report of the Group of Experts on Privacy, 2012, available at https://cis-india.org/internet-governance/blog/report-of-group-of-experts-on-privacy.pdf.

[129] The Personal Data Protection Bill, 2019. The Bill, finally adopted by the Parliament of India in 2023, had been through four revision attempts.

negligence in implementing and maintaining reasonable security practices and procedures. Such practices and procedures have been specified in the SPDI Rules[130] as minimum standards of data protection for sensitive personal data. A non-exhaustive set of guidelines, these SPDI Rules require companies to have a privacy policy, to obtain consent when collecting or transferring sensitive personal data or information, and to inform data subjects of recipients of such collected data. The SPDI Rules identified the following rights for the data subjects:

1. Right to be informed – applicable for all personal information, including sensitive personal data. The SPDI Rules insist on a privacy policy that will address, apart from the information so collected, the security procedures adopted to prevent leakage and misuse of such information. In comparison, the Draft Bill requires data fiduciaries to provide notice to data principals, at the time of collection of personal data, including the procedure related to consent and its withdrawal, information about the processing of such data and any cross-border transfers as well as procedures related to grievance redressal.
2. Right to access – the SPDI Rules allow the individuals to review the information that body corporates possess about them. The Draft Bill further articulated that data principals could request copies or summaries of the personal data processed by the data fiduciaries, including about the data shared by such fiduciaries.
3. Right to rectification – the SPDI Rules and the Draft Bill allow for the data principals to rectify any inaccurate information about themselves in possession of the data fiduciaries including updating any such outdated data.
4. Right to erasure – while the SPDI Rules did not refer to a right to erasure, the Draft Bill empowered the data principal with a right to request erasure of any personal information that may no longer be required for the purpose for which it was procured. Further, the data principals have a right to be forgotten with regard to preventing any disclosure of data made by them if such disclosure is no longer necessary in the context of the purpose for which the data has been collected, or if such disclosure is contrary to the applicable laws.
5. Right to object/opt-out – withdrawal of the consent by the data principals is possible under the SPDI Rules as well as the Draft Bill.
6. The Draft Bill provides for a right to portability for the data principals with respect to personal data that is processed through automated means, including transfer of such data among data fiduciaries.
7. However, the Draft Bill does not provide for a right to the data principals not to be subjected to automated decision-making.

Indian law's protection regime is limited to sensitive personal data (a sub-set of personal data). Rule 5 of the IT Rules prescribes that no body corporate shall collect sensitive personal data or information unless (a) the information is collected for a lawful purpose connected with a function or activity of the body corporate; and (b) the collection of such information is considered necessary for that purpose. Rule 6 prevents disclosure of sensitive personal information to any third party without the permission of the data principal. Sensitive personal data is a subset of personal data that is subject to enhanced processing

[130] Sensitive Personal Data or Information Rules, 2011 (amended in 2021).

requirements. It includes health or financial data, biometric data, sex life, sexual orientation, and religious or political beliefs. The Draft Bill allows the Government to specify further categories of sensitive personal data.[131]

While the Draft Bill does not provide for processing of anonymised data (online and offline), data fiduciaries could be compelled by the Government to share anonymised or non-personal data to enable better targeting of delivery of services or formulation of evidence-based policies offered by the Government.[132]

D. The DPDP Act

The DPDP Act 2023 adopts a rights-based approach towards the privacy protection of the Data Principal. The right of Data Principals includes the right to confirmation regarding whether the Data Fiduciaries have used accurate data and the right to correct the data if the data held by Data Fiduciaries is incorrect. The right to be forgotten, which has been established as a significant digital right, has been provided as an important right of Data Principals. By providing a set of rights enumerated for the Data Principal, the legislation evolves a data protection right framework for individuals which could be equated with the international best practices. However, the legislation, conscious of terror threats and national security concerns, as well as the impact of cross-border data transfers on privacy, moved towards a localisation model, while obligating the data fiduciaries to a duty of care for data protection. Unlike the GDPR which regulates the cross-border flow of data through extension of jurisdiction to data processing which takes place outside the EU, the Indian law insists on data localisation. The major factors determining the data localisation requirement in the Indian context are: (i) Protecting Rights of Data Subjects; (ii) Preventing Foreign Surveillance; (iii) Easy Access of Data in Support of Law Enforcement; and (iv) National Security. However, it is interesting to see that the new legislation has moved away from mandatory localisation, and moved to a regulatory and supervision model of localisation. In this model the Government will notify countries to which personal data cannot be transferred.[133] However, there are no other means of transferring personal data to these countries, such as through the Standard Contractual Clauses (SCCs). The law will not affect data localisation requirements under sectoral laws, for example, the data localisation requirements in the payment space.[134]

The DPDP Act 2023 largely does not apply to foreign personal data processed in India. This is somewhat counterproductive, as one of the reasons for having an omnibus privacy law is to assure the world that it is safe to send personal data to India. It also means that the legislation will fail to obtain an adequacy ruling from the EU. Because India lacks

[131] Mathew Chacko and Aadya Misra, 'India – Data Protection Overview', available at www.dataguidance.com/notes/india-data-protection-overview.

[132] ibid.

[133] DPDP Act 2023 (n 7), Chapter VI, s 16(1). The Central Government may, by notification, restrict the transfer of personal data by a Data Fiduciary for processing to such country or territory outside India as may be so notified.

[134] ibid, s 16(2). Nothing contained in this section shall restrict the applicability of any law for the time being in force in India that provides for a higher degree of protection for or restriction on transfer of personal data by a Data Fiduciary outside India in relation to any personal data or Data Fiduciary or class thereof.

independent oversight over Government surveillance, Indian law does not fully comply with *Schrems II*. The extraordinary powers and exemptions granted to the Government under the DPDP Act 2023 would also make that seemingly impossible.

VI. Conclusion

SCCs could be a safe way of contracting, they could ensure safe and regulation-compliant data transfers, especially in jurisdictions that have concerns relating to legal adequacy. They could be reviewed periodically, and their scope needs to be limited or expanded depending on changes to projects or use of other vendors in different locations. Further, Binding Corporate Rules[135] are a mechanism which often complement SCCs and sit well alongside them.

Dispute resolution in matters related to data transfer could be exposed to various conflict of laws methods like comity, consistency, and predictability to international civil litigations and discourage forum shopping. It is suggested that law reform could address cross-border data transfers and data management with more clarity as well as ensure conformity with global adequacy standards. The increasing presence of artificial intelligence in data management should also find a place on the reform agenda. Given the increasing interaction of data management in dispute resolution practices, India should also consider effective cross-referencing of the data protection and arbitration laws. Credible legal regimes are the need of the hour.

[135] Markus (n 101).

16

Uzbekistan

ABDULAZIZ JURAJONOV, ABDUMALIK MUKHTOROV
AND AZIZBEK SUYUNBOEV

I. Introduction

The Republic of Uzbekistan, bearing the legacy of its Soviet past where governmental transparency was often overshadowed by state control, now confronts the challenge of fostering 'openness and transparency'.[1] The problem has roots in the legislative practices prevalent during the Soviet era of the 1920s–1950s, which were ultimately abolished in the 1970s as a result of the massive second wave of codification. The late Professor Makowskii described this period as the time of '*legal chaos*', where acts of the Government, numbered in the thousands (decrees) and tens of thousands (orders) annually, were not published but rather disseminated internally within ministries and government agencies. The result was a vast body of 'unknown' law, leading to instances where courts would rely on secondary sources like the 'Commentary on Labour Legislation' (1955 edn) due to the inability to formally cite unpublished governmental acts.[2] The Government now acknowledges that the lack of transparency led to excessive bureaucracy and various manifestations of corruption, thus creating the need for the administrative reforms.[3]

This task is particularly critical when shaping the framework for privacy and data protection legislation. Consequently, Uzbekistan has embarked on a comprehensive legislative journey that seeks to strike a prudent balance between the necessary oversight functions of the state and the safeguarding of individual privacy rights. In 2019, Uzbekistan witnessed the promulgation of its inaugural data protection statute.[4] Yet, it is more accurate

[1] In the civil law context the transparency relates to the institutional environment which requires official registration (disclosure) of legal persons, rights in, and transactions related to, immovable property. See Alexander Makovskii, 'The Russian Civil Code and its Impact Upon Commercial Transactions' in William Simons (ed), *Private and Civil Law in the Russian Federation* (Brill 2009) 4. Russian law and Uzbek law are obviously related to each other. However, we mostly use doctrinal sources of the Russian law.

[2] Alexander Makovskii, *О кодификации гражданского права* [*On Codification of Civil Law*] *(1922–2006)* (Statut 2010) 7. His further commentary on these years can be found in his interview. See 'Правовой чердак. Александр Маквоский. Гражданский кодекс 1922 и 1964. [Legal attic. Alexander Makovskii. Civil Code 1922 and 1964]' (*Youtube* 15 May 2015), available at https://youtu.be/W2XsyTSZZfM.

[3] The Concept of Administrative Reform in the Republic of Uzbekistan, Annex No 1 to Decree of the President No DP-5185 dated 8 September 2017.

[4] Eldor Mannopov, Bobur Shamsiev, Ulugbek Abdullaev, 'Uzbekistan Enacts First Data Protection Law' (*Dentons* 16 July 2019), available at www.dentons.com/en/insights/articles/2019/july/16/uzbekistan-enacts-first-data-protection-law.

to characterise 2019 as the year when the data protection law achieved some degree of maturity, having undergone a cautious evolution since its initial conceptualisation in 1993. Data protection matters emancipated from overgeneralised, overstretched legislation on information, acquired a certain civil (commercial) dimension and most importantly specified data subjects' consent requirements and their remedies against not only illegal, but against the undesirable use of their data. However, the philosophy and government policy remained the same because this branch of legislation was a sandbox without the proper standards (criteria) of failure or success of legislation, therefore it has been extremely difficult to test and find the court practice on the application of data protection matters. Such an understanding is vital for the proper interpretation and application of the current data protection laws and regulations.

In this chapter, we endeavour to delineate the current state of data protection in Uzbekistan through analysing the historical context and the exigencies which compelled the Government to establish a legislative framework replete with adequate safeguards. The outline of this chapter will encompass an examination of the constitutional underpinnings of data protection post-Soviet influence, the progression from early legislative efforts to the comprehensive data protection law enacted in 2019, and a critical analysis of the law's provisions, including the rights of individuals and obligations of data controllers. We will also scrutinise the data regime's private international law aspects, as well as the challenges and opportunities posed by technological advancements. Our exposition of the state of Uzbek law as discussed herein is current as of 1 January 2024.

II. General Legal Framework of International Data Transfers and Data Protection

A. Constitutional Framework

The Constitution of the Republic of Uzbekistan underwent significant revision with the promulgation of the Constitutional Law of 1 May 2023 No LRU-837 (the '2023 Constitution') replacing the Constitution of 1992 (the '1992 Constitution'). This extensive reformulation marks a paradigmatic transition in Uzbek constitutional jurisprudence, warranting a reassessment of extant legal frameworks.

The 2023 Constitution introduces the principle of direct application in contrast to the 1992 Constitution.[5] It stipulates that pre-existing laws and other regulatory legal acts in force as of 1 May 2023 remain operative to the extent they do not contradict the 2023 Constitution.[6] The Supreme Court's directive reinforces this stipulation, empowering courts to disapply subordinate legal norms in conflict with the Constitution.[7] This innovation ostensibly invites a more rigorous constitutional scrutiny of legislative norms. However,

[5] 2023 Constitution adopted with the Constitutional Law of 1 May 2023 No LRU-837 'On Constitution of the Republic of Uzbekistan', Art 4.

[6] ibid, Art 3.

[7] Para 3 of Item 1 of Resolution of Plenum of the Supreme Court dated 23 June 2023 No 16 'On some issues of direct application of the norms of the Constitution of the Republic of Uzbekistan in the administration of justice'.

there is a palpable scepticism about the judiciary's capacity or willingness to depart from entrenched mechanical and formalistic methodologies of legal interpretation. The shift necessitated by the 2023 Constitution may encounter resistance from a judiciary unaccustomed to such an activist role.

One must question, therefore, the status of extant laws that are derivative of the 1992 Constitution's provisions, which have been incorporated into the 2023 Constitution. Pertinently, the provisions relating to citizen privacy and freedom of information – Articles 27 and 29 of the 1992 Constitution – warrant close examination. These Articles have historically influenced the legislative discourse on data protection:

> [**Article 27 of the 1992 Constitution**] Everyone shall be entitled to protection against … interference in his private life … No one may … violate the privacy of correspondence and telephone conversations, except on lawful grounds and in accordance with the procedure prescribed by law.
>
> [**Article 31 of the 2023 Constitution**] Everyone shall have the right to inviolability of private life, personal … secrecy, protection of his honour and dignity. Everyone shall have the right to secrecy of correspondence, telephone conversations, postal, electronic and other communications …. Everyone has the right to protection of his personal data, as well as to demand correction of inaccurate data, destruction of data collected about him illegally or no longer having legal grounds ….
>
> [**Article 29 of the 1992 Constitution**]. … Everyone shall have the right to seek, obtain and disseminate any information, except that which is directed against the existing constitutional system and in some other instances specified by law … Freedom of opinion and its expression may be restricted by law if any state or other secret is involved.
>
> [**Article 33 of the 2023 Constitution**] Everyone has the right to seek, receive and disseminate any information. … Restrictions on the right to seek, receive and disseminate information shall be permitted only in accordance with the law and only to the extent necessary to protect the constitutional order … or other secrets protected by law.

There appears to be an absence of jurisprudence from the Constitutional Court elaborating on these Articles, particularly concerning the tension between access to bank-held commercial information and bank secrecy laws, as well as the interplay with tax and law enforcement's prerogatives in criminal investigations. The doctrinal development of these constitutional provisions has been predominantly legislative, without the benefit of Constitutional Court interpretation. As a result, these 'migrant' Articles continue to shape legislative enactments without the scrutiny of constitutional adjudication.

As discussed below, during the first decade of the 1992 Constitution, the *Oliy Majlis* (*Oliy Kengash*) of Uzbekistan adopted several laws that laid the foundation of data privacy and transfer. This legislative activity culminated in the promulgation of the Law 'On Personal Data' of 2 July 2019 No LRU-547 (the 'Personal Data Law'), a statute signifying the maturation of data protection regulation in the nation. The early legislative efforts can be characterised by an apparent lack of precision in delineating the scope of protected information. Legislators amalgamated various elements – ranging from data, freedom of information, cybersecurity, archives, mass media, defamation, commercial secrets, wiretapping, state (official) secrets – into a singular legislative framework[8] without clear demarcation. Subsequently, specialised

[8] Law of 7 May 1993 No 868-XII 'On Informatization'.

laws were gradually introduced to establish specific procedures and rules in different fields related to 'information'. Such laws succeeded in developing and specifying the overly broad and declarative public law related articles of the 1992 Constitution.

In the historical-critical analysis that follows, we endeavour to demonstrate the intended meaning of the 'migrant' Articles of the 1992 Constitution by inquiring the pertinent laws and government regulations. Reference to repealed acts facilitates in comprehending the evolutionary trajectory of the legal framework and underscores the dynamic nature of legal interpretation over time.

i. Disseminating Harmful Information, Defamation, Moral Damages

Article 27 of the 1992 Constitution predominantly addresses the public rather than private law dimension. It guarantees that the state and its law enforcement agencies work within the set procedural boundaries which allow interference with the individuals' privacy. This Article does not preclude the availability of civil law remedies, nor does it exempt individuals from criminal and administrative responsibility.

Article 100 of the Uzbek Civil Code (the 'Civil Code')[9] extended and specified the constitutional protections afforded by Article 27 upon a privacy infringement. The aggrieved party who has suffered harm due to the dissemination of injurious information could refute the harmful information and may seek redress, including compensation for moral damages.[10] Dissemination is considered to occur irrespective of the number of recipients or the mode of transmission, whether in private or public settings, except for cases where the information is communicated directly to the person whom it concerns.[11] Judicial interpretation of these provisions traditionally focussed on defamation in the context of mass media. In particular, Resolution of Plenum of the Supreme Court dated 19 June 1992 No 5-PL-92, Item 7 stipulates that claims to refute information containing criticism of shortcomings in work, behaviour in a public place, society or everyday life that corresponds to reality cannot be recognised as justified. In other words, truthful statements regarding an individual's conduct do not constitute defamation and do not fall under remedies of Article 100 of the Civil Code.[12] Conversely, both Article 27 of the Constitution and Article 1022 of the Civil Code (compensation of moral damages) do provide for injunctive relief and moral damages even when the disseminated information is accurate. This seems to suggest that the right to privacy can extend to the protection of sensitive personal information, raising a potential conflict between the principles of truthfulness and privacy.

[9] Law of 21 December 1995 No 163-I 'On Approval of Part One of the Civil Code of the Republic of Uzbekistan'.

[10] Item 7 of Resolution of Plenum of the Supreme Court, 28 April 2000 No 7 'On certain issues of application of legislation on compensation for moral damages'.

[11] Dilbar Axrarova in Rakhmankulov Khodji-Akbar, Asyanov Shamil (eds), *O'zbekiston Respublikasi fuqarolik kodeksiga sharh* [*Commentaries to Civil Code of the Republic of Uzbekistan*] (Vektor-Press 2010) 267; S Mirzaahmedova (ed), *O'zbekiston Respublikasi Konstitutsiyasiga sharh* [*Commentaries to Constitution of the Republic of Uzbekistan*] (O'zbekiston, 2001) 150–57.

[12] Dilbar Axrarova, ibid, 274.

ii. Creating Informatization System, Title of Ownership to and First Commandment of International Transfer of Information (Data)

The evolution of Uzbekistan's legal framework regarding informatization, particularly in contrast to the 1992 Constitution's Article 27, is evident in the subsequent legislative enactments. Article 29 of the 1992 Constitution was expanded upon by the Law of 7 May 1993 No 868-XII 'On Informatization' (subsequently repealed and restated with Law 11 December 2003 No 560-II) ('Repealed Law On Informatization'). While similarities between 'informatization' and 'digitalization' exist, it is critical to differentiate the terms within the Uzbek legal context. The term 'digitalization' has been predominantly associated with the upgrade of national telecommunication network infrastructures, rather than the creation and development of information systems. It was not until Decree of the President dated 5 November 2020 No PD-6079, that a comprehensive reform was initiated to encompass the broader aspects of informatization. The Repealed Law On Informatization aimed to regulate state bodies, legal entities and individuals in the field of:

- Collection, accumulation, *processing, transfer*, use and protection *of information* from unauthorised access;
- Creation, implementation and operation of *information systems, databases and data banks, other systems for processing and transmitting information.*

With the Repealed Law On Informatization, the Government intended to facilitate the establishment and integration of the information systems at the republican level. In hindsight, the repealed law served more to elucidate the concept of informatization than to strictly regulate it, considering the nascent market economy's need for clarity regarding state influence in information dissemination.

The Repealed Law On Informatization's definition of 'information' pertained to the documented forms, as stated in Article 2(2), excluding information governed by other laws (eg mass media) or 'undocumented information, as well as to relations regulated by copyright and patent law'. Documented information, as an object of ownership, encompassed various forms, including individual documents and collections like libraries or archives.[13]

Notably, the Repealed Law On Informatization included a significant amount of private (civil) law provisions which had not previously been distinguished from its public law counterparts. These provisions include:

1. Licencing requirements for private entities to create information systems at their own expense for further creating information products and services.[14]
2. Recognition of information, information products, and information services markets, with legal entities and individuals participating as equal partners, and the establishment of 'consumer quality' standards for information.[15]
3. The ability of private entities in the field of informatization to establish the legal regime for the use of information through their contracts and agreements.[16]

[13] Repealed Law on Informatization [Law of 7 May 1993 No 868-XII 'On Informatization' repealed and restated with Law of 11 December 2003 No 560-II], Art 23(2).

[14] ibid, Art 1.

[15] ibid, Art 17.

[16] ibid, Art 22(2).

4. The peculiarities of exercising ownership rights over information being governed by the copyright legislation, suggesting that information is considered a form of intellectual property.[17]
5. Introduction of ownership rights over information, with owners responsible for establishing the processing regime and usage rules. The transfer of ownership could be contractual, with the owner liable for providing unreliable or incomplete information.[18]
6. Personal information and its material carriers being property of citizens, with processing by non-governmental organisations requiring licences, and liability for misuse of personal information.
7. Rights of individuals and legal entities to access information to ensure its completeness and reliability, and the right to be informed about the usage of their information. Rights and compensation for violations could be sought through judicial avenues.[19]

The Repealed Law On Informatization recognised information as a product of a person's activity and potentially an object of material or intellectual property.[20] It is noteworthy that Law No 868-XII predates the Civil Code and was enacted when the only relevant legal framework was the Law On Ownership, which briefly recognised that information in the context of intellectual property is regulated by specialised legislation.[21] This gap was later addressed by the Law On Copyright and Adjacent Rights which pertained exclusively to information possessing characteristics of 'the creation and use of works of science, literature and art (copyright), productions, performances, phonograms and broadcasts by broadcasting and cable broadcasting organisations'.[22] Prior to the enactment of the Repealed Law On Informatization, information not qualifying as intellectual property was not recognised as a tradeable commodity within the marketplace.

The Repealed Law On Informatization was also pioneering in its explicit provisions on international transfer of information (data). Article 35 of the Law stated that entities have the right to include their information systems in international information networks through contracts, with the caveat that systems processing restricted-access information could only be included after implementing necessary protective measures.

The significance of the Repealed Law On Informatization is profound, given its role in shaping the understanding of information (data) circulation as an economic asset, facilitating the development of a nascent market. Nevertheless, the restated edition of the Law did not encapsulate the same breadth of innovation within the legislative regime. It is plausible to surmise that the Civil Code may have subsumed the private law provisions of the repealed Law, particularly in its general part, which pertains to any intangible asset.[23] It is worth noting that, to the best of our knowledge, providing justifications for repealing certain acts in the preamble of new laws was not a mandatory component of legislative technique at the time. Consequently, we can infer that the now-repealed Law on Informatization

[17] ibid, Art 23(5).

[18] ibid, Arts 27 and 28.

[19] ibid, Arts 26 and 30.

[20] ibid, Art 23(1).

[21] Law of 31 October 1990 No 152-XII 'On Ownership'. Art 3(2).

[22] Law of 30 August 1996 No 272-I 'On Copyright and Adjacent Rights' (which was repealed and restated with Law of 20 July 2006 No LRU-42) Art 2.

[23] Law of 21 December 1995 No 163-I 'On Approval of Part One of the Civil Code of the Republic of Uzbekistan' Art 81.

offered extensive directives on managing freedom of information in the context of civil and commercial transactions.

In the interest of maintaining a chronological approach, the discussion of the new edition of the Law on Informatization will be preceded by an analysis of the interplay between information protection and its freedom.

iii. Freedom of Information and its Limits

One of the first quasi data protection laws was Law of 24 April 1997 No 400-I 'On Guarantees and Freedom of Access to Information' that remains in force. This law, in comparison to the Repealed Law On Informatization, predominantly embodies principles of public law with a few notable exclusions. In particular, Article 5 affirms the right of any person to request information, either directly or via representatives, through oral or written form, which are then registered. In case a body or official does not possess the requested information, they are to inform the applicant about this, and, if possible, to provide the name of the body or official possessing such information.[24] Most important parts of this Law are encapsulated in the original edition of Article 7 (excluding its further amendment with Law of 15 December 2000 No 175-II) and Article 9, which state:

> Article 7. Ensuring access to information
>
> State bodies, citizens' self-governing bodies, public associations, enterprises, institutions, organizations and officials *shall be obliged to provide everyone with the opportunity to familiarize themselves with documents, decisions and other materials affecting their rights and legitimate interests.* Access to information is ensured through the publication and dissemination of relevant materials.
>
> Article 9. Information not subject to provision
>
> State bodies, self-governing bodies of citizens, public associations, enterprises, institutions, organizations and officials *may not provide [access to] information containing* state *or other secrets protected by law.*

A notable omission within Law No 400-I is the lack of specificity regarding '*other secrets*' protected by law. Remarkably this broad terminology is still used in government decisions even after 2019.

During this period, which might accurately be characterised as the era of 'rule of bylaw', legislative acts commonly employed principle-based regulation, with a considerable number of enabling provisions that culminated in ambiguous references to 'accordance with legislation', without clarity on whether such legislation was extant or yet to be established. As a result, the laws were succinct, affording the Government latitude to delineate precise procedures at its discretion through subsidiary legislation (regulations, rules, etc). As an anecdotal example, the fate of the Civil Code eloquently illustrates such rule. The misfortune of the last 25 years of Uzbekistan's legal development has been that the Civil Code has ceased to be an act of direct application. The scale of its role is not at all comparable to that once provided by the greatest European codes of the past two centuries. As a legacy of the bygone years, we have the Government which adopted bylaws without regard to the Civil Code to solve the tasks of economic management. Often these governmental acts freely

[24] Law of 24 April 1997 No 400-I 'On Guarantees and Freedom of Access to Information', Art 6.

invaded the sphere of regulation of the Code through strict monetary supervision of the Central Bank[25] and limiting the availability of credit, including foreign currency[26] and as a result, it *de facto* ceased to be a source of law.[27] Even the recognition by the Constitutional Court of Civil Code as an act of 'fundamental importance' did not in any way improve its position 'in the system of civil legislative acts'.[28] Freedom of contract seemed to be a norm 'for export'.[29]

In a context where the application and interpretation of laws is approached with a mechanical and formalistic[30] mindset, principle-based regulation appears incongruent, particularly when juxtaposed with the more precise, albeit unwritten, cautelary jurisprudence. One of these symptoms is the status quo effect which occurs with omission bias.[31] In 2018, the Government recognised the negative effect of this regulatory approach, stating that

> the prevalence of laws of framework nature, as well as the adoption of individual decisions without a specific mechanism for their implementation negatively affects the development of the state and society as a whole, leads to the regulation of social relations mainly [through] bylaws.[32]

Nonetheless, the process of repealing laws from that period is progressing slowly. Even after 2018, this trend of regulation of civil legislation through bylaws continued.[33]

[25] Examples are the repealed Procedure for the Implementation by Economic Entities of the Compulsory Sale of Proceeds in Foreign Currency, approved by Resolution of the Cabinet of Ministers Decision of 29 June 2000 No 245 and the Regulation on the Procedure for Certain Foreign Exchange Transactions Related to Capital Movement (MoJ reg No 2536 of 17 December 2013) which formally operates contrary to liberalisation in the industry. In effect it should be noted that the Central Bank itself was dependent on the Cabinet of Ministers, so it had subsequently to be excluded from the list of state bodies 'supervised' by the latter (item 6 (4) of Decree of the President dated of 9 January 2018 No DP-5296).

[26] Professor Belov's description of the USSR's foreign exchange policy almost exactly describes the state of foreign currency relations in Uzbekistan before the adoption of Decree of the President dated 2 September 2017 No DP-5177, which opened free conversion. See Vadim Belov, *Ценные бумаги в коммерческом обороте* [*Negotiable Instruments in Commercial Turnover*] (Urait 2018) 116–18. The non-market nature of foreign exchange relations was directly acknowledged in the preamble of the said Decree No DP-5177.

[27] Ilkhom Azizov, 'Роль и значение гражданско-правовых доктрин и институтов в гражданско-правовом законодательстве Узбекистана [The Role and Significance of Civil Law Doctrines and Institutions in the Civil Law Legislation of Uzbekistan]' in Maidan Suleimenov (ed), *Гражданское право в эпоху трансформации общественных отношений* [*Civil law in the Era of Transformation of Social Relations*] (Almaty 2022) 104.

[28] Decision of the Constitutional Court dated 17 January 2007 'On submission to the Legislative Chamber of Oliy Majlis of the Republic of Uzbekistan of the Draft Law of the Republic of Uzbekistan "On Introduction of Amendments and Additions to Article 74 of the Law of the Republic of Uzbekistan" "On Joint Stock Companies and Protection of Shareholders' Rights"'.

[29] By analogy with the Constitution of the Russian Soviet Federative Socialist Republic of 1937. See Vadim Belov, 'Найти среди наших современных юристов чистого "деликтника" если не невозможно, то очень проблемотично[Finding Among Our Modern Lawyers a Pure "Delictual" If Not Impossible, Then Very Problematic]' (2020) 3 *Zakon* 8, 9.

[30] Formalistic tendencies in codification led Prussian courts to impotence. See Reinhard Zimmermann, *Roman Law, Contemporary Law, European Law The Civilian Tradition Today* (Oxford University Press 2001) 181–82.

[31] Artyom Karapetov, *Экономический анализ права* [*Economic Analysis of Law*] (Statut 2016) 80–81.

[32] Preamble of Decree of the President dated 08 August 2018 № PD-5505, para 5.

[33] Even presidential acts with generally binding civil law norms were adopted. Item 3(b) of Decree of the President dated 14 September 2021 No DP-6313 'On Measures to Radically Improve Contractual Relations', which introduced the institution of confirmation of a voidable transaction without any reference to the text of Civil Code. In the original draft of this Decree there was also such an unusual norm which states 'when concluding, amending and terminating … contracts and fulfilling obligations, the principle of *pacta sunt servanda* … must be applied, the parties to the contract must ensure the good faith fulfilment of their obligations in accordance with the terms of the obligation and the requirements of the law'. See Draft Decree of the President No ID-30780, available at https://regulation.gov.uz/ru/d/30780.

The legislative landscape concerning the safeguarding of data and, more broadly, information, underwent significant developments with the enactment of Law of 12 December 2002 No 439-II 'On Principles and Guarantees of Freedom of Information'. Nonetheless, Law No 439-II was not immune to the prevalent legislative tendencies of its time. For instance, in Article 4, it provided restrictions to the freedom of and access to the information 'in order to protect human rights and freedoms, the foundations of the constitutional order, the moral values of society, the spiritual, cultural and scientific potential, and to ensure the security of the country'. Consequently, the legislation acknowledged certain exceptions to the principle of openness and publicity of information, identifying confidential information as one such exception. Article 6, in defining confidential information, explicitly excludes:

> acts of legislation on the rights and freedoms of citizens, the procedure for their implementation …; … [and]
>
> information available in open … information systems of legal entities operating on the territory of the Republic of Uzbekistan.

Such *e contrario* definition has also broadened the limits of the confidential information. While the second exclusion appears obvious, the first one formally prohibited echoing of the aforementioned 'legal chaos' through excluding dissemination[34] of acts of legislation only internally within ministries and government agencies.[35]

Even though Law No 439-II developed fundament provisions, it did not function as a directly applicable statute, given its predominantly declaratory and framework character.

The Law introduced notable innovations, among them the precise yet expansive scope of information protection. It articulated a series of definitions as follows:

> Information – *information about persons, objects, facts, events, phenomena and processes*, regardless of the sources and form of their presentation;
>
> information protection – *measures to prevent threats to information security and eliminate their consequences*;
>
> information security – *the state of protection of the interests of the individual, society and the state in the information sphere*;
>
> confidential information – *documented information, access to which is restricted in accordance with the law*;
>
> documented information – *information recorded on a material carrier, with details that allow it to be identified.*[36]

From these definitions, it remained unclear whether the information owned or operated by commercial legal entities, such as network operators and internet service providers, fell

[34] The mechanisms and guarantees of proper electronic dissemination of any 'legal information' which includes acts of legislation was further elaborated in the Law of 7 September 2017 No LRU-443 'On the Dissemination of Legal Information and Ensuring Access to It'.

[35] The contemporary list of ministries and agencies which can receive electronic forms acts of legislation (apart from legal acts constituting state secrets and acts labelled '*для служебного пользования* [*For internal use*]') is provided in Resolution of the Cabinet of Ministers dated 22 December 2017 No 1013, Annex No 1.

[36] Law of 12 December 2002 No 439-II 'On Principles and Guarantees of Freedom of Information', Art 3, paras 2, 4, 7, 9, 11.

within the ambit of the state's information security (*cybersecurity*) framework, potentially engaging the state secrets laws and the discretionary powers of secret services. No official guideline was published on delimitation of 'the interest of the individual, society and the state'.

Secondly, this Law first introduced the terms of '*information owner*' and '*information possessor*', though it does not confer a title of ownership or other proprietary rights *in rem* over the information (data). This approach deviates from the repealed Law No 868-XII, which will be revisited in subsequent discussions below. Under the same Article 3 of Law No 439-II, the 'information owner' refers to 'a legal or natural person who possesses, uses and disposes of information, at the expense of whom this information is acquired or obtained in another legal way'. This definition interestingly bestows the possessor with a similar trifecta of prerogatives of ownership (*usus, fructus, and abusus*) but '*within the rights established by law or the owner of information*'. This model of rights allocation has more similarities with the English trust law – entailing both legal and equitable title (bundle of rights) to the same property – rather than the civil law doctrine of *traditio*.[37] In other words, the owner and the possessor had equal prerogatives to the same information, unless the law or the owner decides otherwise. Such allocation of rights is alien to civil law in which one cannot split[38] ownership – neither temporally, nor by object, nor by content. A cannot own all of the olive trees on an agricultural holding and B own the fruit trees on it; nor can A be given the exclusive power to grant pledges over a thing and B the exclusive power to grant rights of way over it; the owner can only authorise one other person to undertake certain actions over the thing on his behalf.[39] In any case, this Law readily allowed commercialisation of information that does not fall under the definition of commercial secrets or know-how.

Thirdly, and most importantly, this Law states that personal data of physical entities (data subjects) is confidential information (Article 13(2)) and its processing, that is collection, storage, processing, dissemination and utilisation, requires the data subjects' consent (Article 13(3)). However, this Law did not elaborate further procedures of requesting the consent, its scope and the statutory cases when such consent was not a prerequisite.

[37] In general terms *traditio* is the acquisition of the right of ownership (*modus tradendi*), ie an *in rem* effect which is achieved only upon fulfilment of a contractual obligation (*solutio*) by either transferring a movable thing (or surrogates of transfer – documents for the thing, etc). See Evgenii Sukhanov, *Вещное право: Научно-познавательный очерк* [*Property Law Scientific and Informative Essay*] (Statut 2017) 154.

[38] Professor Gretton states that there is nothing mysterious or puzzling about an owner who undertakes, by way of obligation, to hold the whole benefit for someone else: to call that 'divided ownership' is mystification. See George Gretton, 'Trusts without Equity' (2000) 49 *International and Comparative Law Quarterly* 599, 607. On the opposing qualification of trusts as civil law special patrimony which is segregated from the general patrimony of the trustee, except for Gretton's cited work, see also Remus Valsan (ed), *Trusts and Patrimonies* (Edinburgh University Press, 2015).

[39] Christian von Bar, *Foundations of Property Law Things as Objects of Property Rights* (translated by Jason Grant Allen) (Oxford University Press 2023) para 2.32. Professor von Bar's example is illustrative for tangible things, but in relation to 'information' he does not even mention splitting, but states that it is not only incapable of being owned, but it is also incapable of being possessed, pledged, or inherited and in turn 'individual data' (ie the symbols recorded on some storage device) are not even objects of property rights. See ibid, paras 5.17–5.19.

iv. New Life of Law on Informatization and So-Called Title of Ownership

The Repealed Law On Informatization was restated with Law of 11 December 2003 No 560-II ('Restated Law On Informatization'). This restatement, having been enacted during the period characterised by the proliferation of bylaws, saw a reduction in the number of articles from the original 36 to a mere 23. Despite the contraction in quantity, the law clearly mandated that 'documenting information is a prerequisite for the inclusion of information in information resources'[40] and that personal data is regulated with a specific legislation.[41] One of the most important bylaws from this era is Decree of the Cabinet of Ministers dated 26 March 1999 No 137 'On Approval of the Regulation on the Procedure for Preparing and Distributing the Information Resources of the Republic of Uzbekistan on the Data Transfer Networks, including the Internet', which not only remains in force but also elaborates on the applicability of the Repealed Law On Informatization to online information transfer, including personal data.

The primary objectives of the Restated Law On Informatization were to facilitate the development of markets for information resources, IT, and information services markets. In pursuit of this aim, the Law:

1. repeated the provisions on title of ownership on documented informational resources and information systems (Article 9);
2. categorised information resources into publicly available and limited access (including confidential information);
3. obliged the owners of websites and webpages, including bloggers, on pain of public law liability, not to exploit their respective data subjects with a view to disclosing information that contains 'other secrets protected by law';
4. gave the right of unlimited access to individuals to the information resources which contain their personal data only with a view to making corrections to it; and
5. outlined the right to include information resources into the international information networks and the Internet.

A brief examination of the Civil Code's regulation on rights *in rem* is warranted to contextualise the issues surrounding ownership of information. Firstly, the absence of a provision which define tangible (corporeal) objects as things (*res*),[42] or a provision which emphasises the discretion of the owner of an object over their property within legal boundaries,[43] is notable. Instead, the Civil Code adopts a broad and somewhat abstract concept of 'property' which encompasses property rights, non-property rights, and other tangible and intangible benefits, without a specific criteria of tangibility.[44]

[40] Law of 11 December 2003 No 560-II 'On Informatization', Art 8(1).
[41] ibid, Art 13.
[42] Similar to § 90 of BGB (*Bürgerliches Gesetzbuch*), section 85 of the Japanese Civil Code.
[43] See Art 641 of ZGB (*Zivilgesetzbuch*), '[t]he owner of an object [*une chose*] is free to dispose of it as he or she sees fit within the limits of the law'. Only the Law of 19 August 1999 No 811-I 'On Appraisal Activity' defines the thing as an individual material object (Article 5(2)).
[44] Civil Code, Art 81.

Ownership is also defined as the comprehensive right to possess, use and dispose of one's property.[45]

This expansive definition raises questions about the applicability of the right to ownership to intangible property (patrimonial) *rights* (*res incorporales*), such as contractual claims. This suggests a so-called 'ownership in claims' (*Eigentum an der Forderung*)[46] and potential alignment with the economic value approach recognised in the European case of *Marckx v Belgium*, No 6833/74, [1979].[47] On the other hand, other provisions of the Civil Code seem to restrict the scope of ownership to tangible 'things' (*res, Sache*).[48] Thus the Civil Code uses the *thing* and the *property* as synonyms, creating ambiguity regarding the exact contour of the right of ownership.[49]

Secondly, the Civil Code lacks a schematic of property law, providing only a non-exhaustive list without clear parameters or application guidelines.[50] The principle underlying this list, whether it is *numerus clausus* or *numerus apertus*, remains unsettled in both court practice and civil law doctrine.

Thirdly, while the Civil Code recognises *traditio* as the default mechanism for acquiring ownership, it does not address alternative methods or their jurisprudential interpretations, such as *solo consensu* or the *Abstraktionsprinzip*.[51]

The provisions concerning property rights and the *erga omnes* nature of rights *in rem* suggest that information and data could potentially constitute a property right, subject to ownership claims.[52] However, this stance is contested, especially considering provisions that emphasise the indefiniteness and inviolability of ownership and the constraints imposed by the rights and interests of others.[53]

Against the above context of the Civil Code, the Restated Law On Informatization expressly states that information is an object of the title of ownership. But it does not define how the owner can protect such right against infringement once information is inadvertently disclosed to others. This oversight highlights the gap between traditional property law, designed for tangible assets, and the challenges posed by intangible ones.[54]

In conclusion, the legal policy rationale for recognising ownership rights over information may be rooted in the efficiency and merit-based distribution of resources. The concept is that society benefits when the owner determines the transactional value of information. However, the legal implications of such a stance necessitate further discussion beyond the scope of this commentary.[55]

[45] ibid, Art 164.

[46] On the critique of this notion with extensive reference to German civil law doctrine, see Evgenii Krasheninnikov, 'К вопросу о "собственности на требование"' ['On the Question of "Ownership in the Claim"'] (2005) 12 [Очерки торгового права *Essays on Commercial Law*] 31, 32.

[47] Sabrina Praduroux, 'Objects of Property Rights: Old and New' in Michele Graziadei, Lionel Smith (eds), *Comparative Property Law Global Perspectives* (Edward Elgar 2017) 57.

[48] See Civil Code, Arts 185 and 186.

[49] Even though their taxonomic subordination is apparently given in Civil Code, Art 81.

[50] Civil Code, Art 165.

[51] ibid.

[52] ibid, Art 81.

[53] ibid, Arts 164, 166, 172.

[54] Mirodil Baratov, *Mulk Huquqi* [*Property Law*] (Toshkent davlat yuridik instituti 2009) 302.

[55] Guido Calabresi and Douglas Melamed, 'Property Rules, Liability Rules and Inalienability: One View of the Cathedral' (1972) 85 *Harvard Law Review* 1089, 1099–1100.

B. Statutory Framework

i. Codification Efforts

The preceding discussion concluded that information is subject to regulation by various laws, among which the Personal Data Law is significant. In recent times, the Government has made multiple attempts to consolidate the existing laws on information within a single Information Code. The earliest proposal for such a code can be traced to paragraph 70 of the Road Map for the Implementation of the National Human Rights Strategy of Uzbekistan (Decree of the President dated 22 June 2020 No DP-6012), which called for

> the preparation of a draft Information Code … with a view to systematising access to information as one of the most important factors in the development of civil and information society, ensuring the protection of freedom of human rights in the information environment, cybersecurity, media culture and online hygiene.

This draft was slated for completion by January 2022. A subsequent reference appeared in paragraph 324 of the State Program on the Implementation of the Development Strategy of New Uzbekistan for the Years 2022–2026, known as the 'Year of glorifying human dignity and active neighbourhood' (*Decree of the President dated 28 January 2022 No DP-60*), which outlined a broad goal to improve legislation in the field of information in line with contemporary demands and unify the existing laws governing the information sector into the Information Code.

The Draft Information Code (*ID-72848*) was published on 14 December 2022.[56] Notably, this draft only reiterated the article of the Law On Informatization that designates personal data as confidential, without introducing any notable new stipulations concerning personal data – suggesting an exclusion of personal data from the scope of this law. The legal community's response to the draft's quality was predominantly critical, with the primary focus of critique being the freedom of information and the ambiguous restrictions proposed by the draft.[57]

From the perspective of codification of private law, we believe that personal data matters shall be in general terms codified in the Civil Code. Currently, the Civil Code lacks direct provisions regarding the processing and circulation of personal data in the commerce. Paradoxically, despite the Concept for Improving the Civil Legislation of the Republic of Uzbekistan (*Presidential Order dated 5 April 2019 No O-5464*) (the 'Concept Note') referencing 'innovative forms and procedures of regulation of civil-law relations, demanded in modern conditions', there is a conspicuous absence of regulation concerning big data in the Draft Civil Code (*ID-23955*). Moreover, several bylaws addressing administrative, taxation, and banking reforms have mentioned the adoption of big data technologies, yet the Concept Note did not propose to generalise civil law protection over personal data. Instead,

[56] Agency of Information and Mass Communications under the Administration of the President of the Republic of Uzbekistan, 'Draft Information Code' (*ID-72848, Portal for Discussion of Projects of Draft Legal Acts* 2022), available at https://regulation.gov.uz/ru/d/72848.

[57] Nozima Davletova, 'Проект Информационного кодекса: Расплывчатые формулировки, ограничения для СМИ и блогеров' (*Gazeta.uz* 2022), available at www.gazeta.uz/ru/2022/12/28/information-code/.

it limited such protection to the image of the person '*Ensuring reliable civil law protection of images of persons*, their personal non-property rights and other intangible benefits' [emphasis added].

This conservative stance likely stems from the codification of a person's image protection in the Russian and Kazakh Civil Codes. The Concept Note seemingly eschewed excessive innovation in this field.

The foregoing codification efforts do not address the Data Protection Law, nor is there any indication of plans to incorporate it into either the Information Code or the new Civil Code. It is our belief that the Data Protection Law's status quo, that is being the central normative legal act regulating personal data, will remain unchanged for the foreseeable future, pending any shifts in legislative approach that may result from the post-2023 Constitutional reform.

ii. Existing Framework

The current legal landscape is characterised by a mosaic of sector-specific statutes, which predate the enactment of the Personal Data Law. These laws regulate a range of entities, including commercial banks, telecommunication operators, information and investment intermediaries, and e-commerce vendors. During the period that preceded the Personal Data Law, governance was primarily declaratory with limited enforcement mechanisms.

The Personal Data Law, adhering to established legislative practice, mandates the Government to align its decrees with its provisions.[58] However, a comprehensive legislative review – or 'legislative guillotine' – has not been applied to reconcile all preceding laws and regulations with the new law. In cases of conflicts between the Personal Data Law and bylaws, undoubtedly the former has priority over the bylaws.[59] However for the cases of conflicts between two laws, the legislation formally uses the *lex posteriori* in place of the *lex specialis* principle.[60]

Despite this, the majority of existing laws and regulations align with the Personal Data Law. Some of these have been examined previously. Two notable exceptions are the Law On Electronic Document Management (the 'EDM Law')[61] and On Electronic Commerce (the 'E-Commerce Law').[62]

The EDM Law is significant for establishing parity between paper-based and electronic documents, recognising the latter as valid for executing various transactions and communications.[63] However, it lacks comprehensive protections for electronic documents, merely stating that they should be secured according to established legal procedures.[64]

[58] Personal Data Law, Art 35.

[59] Law of 20 April 2021 No LRU-682 'On Normative Legal Acts', Art 18(3).

[60] ibid, Art 18(4). The use of *lex specialis* principle is suggested by Law No LRU-682 and the Civil Code's *titre préliminaire* (Arts 1–7), more precisely Art 3. Hierarchy between these two principles is beyond the scope of this commentary.

[61] Law of 29 April 2004 No 611-II 'On Electronic Document Management' ('EDM Law').

[62] Law of 29 April 2004 No 613-II 'On Electronic Commerce' ('E-Commerce Law') was restated with Law of 29 September 2022 No LRU-792.

[63] EDM Law, Art 4(2).

[64] ibid, Art 17.

The E-Commerce Law obligates operators to implement necessary security measures and to define the use of personal data and other restricted information within their contracts.[65]

Subsequent regulations at the bylaw level have further developed these laws. For instance, Regulation No 1558[66] provided early definitions and regulations for personal data[67] and procedures for digitising paper-based information.[68] Another bylaw introduced the first sectoral localisation requirements for the data servers.[69] These provisions remain consistent with the Personal Data Law.

However, several other sectoral laws,[70] presidential decrees (resolutions),[71] government regulations[72] and ministerial orders and decrees[73] continue to be in force.

iii. Scope of Personal Data Law

Since its enactment on 1 October 2019, the Personal Data Law has served as the governing legislation for matters arising from the processing and protection of personal data. It articulates the jurisdiction over these issues 'regardless of the means of processing used, including information technology'.[74] The law delineates the roles of various stakeholders in the personal data ecosystem, including database operators, owners, as well as any representatives or third parties engaged in the process.[75] The definition of an owner and or operator

[65] E-Commerce Law, Art 12, para 7, part 2, Art 21(2)(4).

[66] Regulations on the Procedure for Documenting Information, Accounting and Registration of State Information Resources (*dated 10 February 2006 MoJ reg No 1558*).

[67] ibid, Items 42–49.

[68] ibid, Items 10–16.

[69] Item 23 of Resolution of the Cabinet of Ministers dated 2 June 2016 No 185. For summaries of similar localisation rules, see Graham Greenleaf, 'Personal Data Localization and Sovereignty along Asia's New Silk Roads' in Anupam Chander, and Haochen Sun (eds), *Data Sovereignty: From the Digital Silk Road to the Return of the State* (Oxford University Press 2023) 320.

[70] Laws on Cybersecurity (*15 April 2022 No LRU-764*), on AML/FT (*26 August 2004 No 660-II*), on Protection of Information in the Automated Banking System (*4 April 2006 No LRU 30*), on Payments and Payment Systems (*1 November 2019 No LRU-578*), on State Genomic Registration (*24 November 2020 No LRU-649*), on Exchange of Credit Information (*4 October 2011 LRU-301*).

[71] Decree dated 21 November 2018 No RP-4024 'On Improving the Control System for the Implementation of Information Technologies and Communications' and dated 2 February 2019 No DP-5653 'On Developing the Sphere of Information and Mass Communication'.

[72] The following government acts regulate different matters with different degree of importance related to the protection and transfer of the information (personal data). The Resolution of the Cabinet of Ministers dated 10 July 1998 No 293; 26 March 1999 No 137; 22 November 2005 No 256; 21 April 2009 No 116; 7 November 2011 No 296; 2 June 2016 No 185; 2 August 2016 No 249; 8 February 2020 No 71; 29 November 2021 No 717 (the 'Resolution No 717'); and 5 October 2022 No 570 (the 'Resolution No. 570').

[73] Additionally, the following ministerial orders and decrees have also been issued: Rules for the Provision of Data Network Services (*dated 30 June 2020 MoJ reg No 3275*); Regulation on Accounting Registers (*dated 11 December 2015 MoJ reg No 2739*); Regulation on the Protection of Information in Automated Systems of Commercial Banks (*dated 10 March 2020 MoJ reg No 3224*); Regulation on ensuring information security in payment systems of operators of payment systems and providers of payment services (*dated 30 June 2020 MoJ reg No 3268*); Model procedure for the organisation of the activity of the structural unit or authorised person of the owner and (or) operator of the personal data base, responsible for the processing of personal data and their protection (*dated 15 November 2023 MoJ reg No 3477*); and Model procedure of processing personal data (*dated 15 November 2023 MoJ reg No 3478*).

[74] Personal Data Law, Art 3.

[75] ibid, Art 9.

extends to state bodies, individuals, or legal entities, thereby broadening its personal scope to include virtually all entities.[76]

The Personal Data Law does not provide a clear delineation of its territorial scope, but it is implicitly understood to be enforceable throughout the entire territory of the Republic of Uzbekistan. A potential exception to this rule may be the special economic zones, which operate under a distinct legal regime as outlined in Article 37 of Law of 17 February 2020 No LRU-60:

> 'In special economic zones, a special customs and tax regime may be established, as well as a regime of entry, exit and stay of citizens, conditions of labour relations, the implementation of financial and credit activities, *and another regime aimed at attracting investments, stimulating the development of entrepreneurship and the socio-economic development of special economic zones.*
>
> The special legal regime is established by laws *or by resolution of the President of the Republic of Uzbekistan*' [emphasis added].

Questions of jurisdiction arise particularly when the special economic zone adopts legal frameworks following common law regimes, such as the proposed 'English law regime' in the Navoi Free Economic Zone. As per para 21 of Decree of the President dated 15 May 2019 No DP-5719:

> 'Ministry of Justice, Ministry of Investments and Foreign Trade together with FEZ 'Navoi' Directorate JSC and other interested ministries and departments, with attraction of foreign experts, within two months term to make proposals on establishing special legal regime on FEZ 'Navoi' territory, providing possibility to regulate relations between FEZ 'Navoi' participants *based on standards, principles, and norms of English law with use of English language in office work*' [emphasis added].

Sources near to Navoi FEZ have indicated that the implementation of such a regime has been impeded due the administrative and judicial irregularities which were not fully foreseen when the aforesaid Decree was enacted. In any case, the potential establishment of such a special legal regime raises questions about the applicability of laws which are neither purely public nor purely private in character, such as the Data Protection Law. We believe that in the event of a conflict between the special legal regime of a special economic zone and the Personal Data Law, the latter has primacy only in cases when the former does not directly regulate the issues related to protection of data.

In terms of the subject matter of regulation, the Personal Data Law covers the range of operations constituting 'processing of personal data', which include 'the implementation of one or a combination of actions of collection, systematization, storage, modification, supplementation, usage, provision, distribution, transfer, anonymization and erasure [destruction]'.[77]

Notably, rather than stipulating exemptions for specific types of processing, the law entirely excludes certain categories of data from its scope of application.[78] These categories are:

1. when an individual processes the personal data for personal, household purposes, and unrelated to their professional or commercial activity;

[76] ibid, Art 4.
[77] ibid, Art 4(5).
[78] ibid, Art 3.

2. the formation, storage, and use of documents of the National Archival Fund and other archival documents containing personal data (*which is carried out in accordance with Law of 15 June 2010 No LRU-252*);
3. the processing of personal data related to State secrets (*which is carried out in accordance with Law of 07 May 1993 No 848-XII*); and
4. the processing of personal data obtained during operational search, intelligence and counterintelligence activities, and law enforcement activities (*which are carried out in accordance with number of laws, including Criminal Procedural Code, Law of 25 December 2012 No LRU-344 'On operative-search activity'*).

This broad scope of the Personal Data Law is of course a merit in Uzbek law. However, there appears to be legal incongruence between three laws, which are the Data Protection Law, Law on Bank Secrecy (*30 August 2003 No 530-II*) and Law on Exchange of Credit Information (*4 October 2011 LRU-301*), concerning the exclusion of certain data categories from the scope of the Personal Data Law. Under the *lex posterior* rule,[79] the Data Protection Law, being a newer legislation, holds precedence over other older statutes. However, the *lex specialis* principle implies the exclusion of credit information from the material scope of the Data Protection Law.

Credit information, as defined in Article 4 of LRU-301, represents any information 'contributing to the determination of creditworthiness, financial standing, solvency, payment discipline and other qualities of the subject of credit information'. According to part 5 of Article 8 of Law No 530-II and part 6 of Article 16 of LRU-301, the provision of such information to credit bureaus does not infringe upon any legally protected commercial, banking, or other secrets, which includes personal data. It is worth noting that in practice, credit bureaus require a special consent form to be obtained from the data subject via the bank issuing credit. Moreover, banks tend to seek explicit consent for the transfer of client data to third parties (defined in Article 4 of Law No 530-II as any party other than the bank, its client, or the Central Bank). This practice suggests that parts of the aforementioned laws may have become obsolete or *lettres mortes* within the Uzbek legal system.

C. Data Protection Framework

i. *Influence of International Data Protection Frameworks*

The preceding analysis has focused exclusively on national legislation. It is imperative to discuss the relationship between national and international law to provide context for the Data Protection Law. International treaties, along with generally recognised principles and norms of international law, are integral to the legal system of Uzbekistan.[80] This integration suggests the recognition and prioritisation of treaties and generally accepted norms of international law within the domestic legal hierarchy.

[79] One iteration of this rule is stated in the Law of 20 April 2021 No LRU-682 'On Normative Legal Acts', Art 18(4).

[80] Law of 6 February 2019 No LRU-518, Art 3, the 2023 Constitution, Art 5(3) and Resolution of Plenum of the Supreme Court dated 20 November 2023 No 27, Item 42.

The 2023 Constitution further states that human rights and freedoms are recognised and guaranteed in accordance with the generally recognised norms of international law (Article 19), which generally hold precedence over domestic laws. The Supreme Court interprets 'generally recognized principles and norms' to include seminal international human rights instruments, such as the Universal Declaration of Human Rights, the Covenant on Civil and Political Rights, the Covenant on Economic, Social and Cultural Rights and others.

Under the 1992 Constitution, direct application of international treaties – except for a few international instruments adopted within the framework of the Commonwealth of Independent States – was not customary in judicial practice. However, recent directives from the Supreme Court have prompted lower courts to consider international law and Uzbekistan's international obligations more explicitly.[81] The courts are also guided by the Vienna Convention on the Law of Treaties when interpreting international agreements.[82] Although the direct application of these international norms has not been judicially tested following the adoption of the 2023 Constitution, this does not preclude parties from raising legal issues regarding not only the constitutionality of national laws but also their potential inconsistency with, or violation of, international law.

a. CIS Model Law

In 1999 the Interparliamentary Assembly of Member States of Commonwealth of Independent States (the 'CIS') adopted its Model Law on Personal Data (the 'CIS Model Law'). This legislative effort aimed to harmonise the personal data laws of its member states, including Uzbekistan. The Model Civil Code serves as a prime example of such harmonisation. While general principles of the CIS Model Law have influenced national laws, offering guidance for resolving legislative discrepancies through teleological interpretation, there are notable divergences in the Personal Data Law of Uzbekistan from the CIS Model Law. This section preliminarily examines areas where the Personal Data Law lacks clarity.

The CIS Model Law defines personal data as *information (documented on a tangible medium)* about a specific person that is or can be identified with that person (Art 2(1)). It further clarifies 'Tangible medium – material objects (including physical fields) in which personal data are reflected in the form of symbols, images and signals …' (Art 2(2)).

It also defines the holder of personal data as public authorities and local self-government bodies, legal entities and natural persons *who perform actions with personal data on lawful grounds* (Art 2(4)).

The CIS Model Law's use of the term 'documented' in defining personal data reflects a precision not found in Article 4(2) of the Personal Data Law. Similarly, the term 'personal

[81] By stating that 'at the same time, in cases where the rules of international treaties are applied in the consideration of cases, *reference should be made to the rules of the international treaty in question in the [judgement rationale] of the judicial act* [emphasis added]'. (Resolution of Plenum of the Supreme Court dated 23 June 2023 No 16, Item 2(4)).

[82] Resolution of Plenum of the Supreme Court dated 20 November 2023 No 27, Item 44.

data holder' is more precise than the terms 'owner' or 'possessor', which are used in the Personal Data Law and do not suggest ownership of personal data per se, thereby establishing a special regime for such information without employing established civil law terminology.

The CIS Model Law also includes a unique prohibition, stating that 'personal data bases collected by holders for different purposes may not be combined for automated information processing'.[83] This is not found in the Data Protection Law.

Furthermore, the CIS Model Law addresses the processing of personal data for high-ranking public officials and candidates for such offices, allowing national legislation to establish a special legal regime for their personal data that ensures only publicly relevant data is open.[84]

Additionally, the Model Law also delineates when personal data becomes archival documents, in contrast to the Personal Data Law. It states that 'from the moment of the death of the personal data subject, the legal regime of personal data shall be replaced by the archiving regime or other legal regime …'[85] It also allows for posthumous data protection by other parties, including heirs, according to national legislation.[86]

In contrast to the multifaceted approach to state regulation in Article 5 of the Model Law, the Personal Data Law specifies only the registration of personal data bases, omitting the registration of personal data holders or the licensing of data processing.[87] The Personal Data Law does not articulate the purposes of such registration, whereas the CIA Model Law identifies the purpose as ensuring public record of databases and informing citizens about access to their personal data.[88]

ii. Specific Provisions for Particular Sectors

a. Labour Relations

The new Labour Code, which came into force on 30 April 2023, introduced rules regarding the protection of employees' personal data. The Code defines the personal data of employees as 'information about facts, events and circumstances of the life of an employee, as well as members of his/her family, provided to the employer in connection with labour relations'.[89] The Code establishes the general conditions for the processing, storage, use and transfer of personal data, the rights of employees to protect their data, and the legal consequences of an employer's breach of the procedure for processing such data.

The Code further establishes guarantees of personal data protection regardless of the terms of the labour contract or local acts of the employer.[90] Terms of the employment

[83] Resolution of Interparliamentary Assembly of the Member States of the Commonwealth of Independent States of 16 October 1999 No 14-19 On Model Law 'On Personal Data' (CIS Model Law), Art 3(7).
[84] ibid, Art 3(8).
[85] ibid, Art 4(5).
[86] ibid, Art 4(7).
[87] Personal Data Law, Art 5.
[88] ibid, Art 7(1).
[89] Law of 28 October 2022 No LRU 798 'On approval of the Labour Code of the Republic of Uzbekistan', Art 175.
[90] ibid, Art 177.

contract, other agreements between the employee and the employer, as well as clauses of local acts that prevent the protection of the employee's personal data or worsen the employee's position in comparison with the requirements of the legislation shall be recognised as invalid.

In addition, the Code stipulates employers' liability in cases of violation of the procedure for processing and protection of employees' personal data. If such violations result in the unlawful deprivation of an employee's ability to work or in the reduction of his/her wages, the employer guilty of the violation is obliged to compensate the employee for the lost earnings. In addition, if an employer disseminates defamatory and untrue information about an employee, he is obliged to refute this information.

b. Genomic Data Law

The Law of 24 November 2020 No LRU-649 'On State Genomic Registration' regulates activities related to the selection, use, storage, and destruction of biological material, as well as the processing and protection of genomic information. The primary purpose of this law is the identification of individuals, unidentified corpses, and the establishment of biological kinship.

c. Banks and Payment Systems

The Law of 4 April 2006 No LRU-30 'On Protection of Information in the Automated Banking System' outlines rules for safeguarding information in automated banking systems. The law mandates that the Central Bank and banks establish a dedicated service for the protection of information within automated banking systems.

Moreover, the Law on Payments and Payment Systems (No 578 of 1 November 2019) and Central Bank Regulation (MoJ reg No 3268, dated 30 June 2020) provide specific regulations for personal data in payment systems. Law No 578 establishes requirements and procedures for information protection in payment systems, including responsibilities for operators, payment service providers, and initiators. The Central Bank oversees and enforces information security controls over payment system operators and payment service providers. Regulation No 3268 offers detailed instructions and guidance for the implementation of these measures in payment systems.

iii. Key Definitions

a. Data Protection and Privacy

The distinction between data protection and privacy is nuanced, and while there may be an overlap, Uzbek law treats these concepts distinctly. For instance, Article 31 of the 2023 Constitution recognises the right to privacy, which historically laid the constitutional foundation for data protection laws – primarily rooted in private law. However, the impact of the constitutional provision on data privacy remains somewhat ambiguous without interpretative guidance from the Constitutional Court, raising questions about the hierarchy and interplay between privacy rights and data protection norms.

b. 'Data Users', 'Data Subjects', 'Data Processors' and 'Data Sub-Contractors'

Uzbek legislation does not contain the concepts of 'data user', 'processor' and 'subcontractor'. Instead, it uses *in rem* terminology to define the subjects in data protection.

Article 9 of the Personal Data identifies *the subject, the operator, the subject's legal representative, the owner* and *third parties* as key players in data processing. Article 4 of the Personal Data Law defines them as follows:

- *Data subject* – a natural person to whom the personal data relates;
- *Data operator* – a public authority, individual and (or) legal entity carrying out the processing of personal data;
- *Data owner* – public authority, natural and (or) legal person who has the right to own, use and dispose of the personal data base;
- *Third party* – any person who is not the subject, owner and (or) operator, but is related to them by circumstances or relations of personal data processing.

Although the Law does not define a legal representative, it states that written consent must be given by such a representative in cases where the data subject is incapacitated or has restricted legal capacity (Article 21), and provides that the representative manages the data subject's data (Article 30). This aligns with Civil Code, which specifies guardianship for incapacitated citizens and trusteeship for those with restricted capacity (Arts 30 and 31).

It should be noted that an entity can be both a data owner and a data operator if it owns the personal data and also carries out the processing activities. This typically occurs when an organisation collects and manages its own employee or customer data.

c. Distinction between Personal and Non-Personal Data

As discussed, Article 4 of the Personal Data Law defines personal data as information recorded on electronic, paper and (or) other tangible carrier relating to a certain natural person or enabling his/her identification. While the law does not use specific terms like 'non-personal data', it does categorise certain types of information as not falling within the scope of the Personal Data Law, as stated earlier.

d. Anonymised, Pseudonymised, or Encrypted

Uzbek law does not contain concepts of 'anonymised', 'pseudonymised' and 'encrypted' data. While some regulations use terms such as 'data encryption' or 'encrypted data', formal definitions are still absent. For example, Resolution No 570 mandates the encryption and protection of biometric and genetic data stored electronically using cryptographic or other methods. Conversely, Uzbek law does introduce the concept of 'depersonalization', akin to the General Data Protection Regulation's 'pseudonymization', defining it as actions that preclude the attribution of personal data to a specific subject.[91] Uzbek law mandates depersonalisation of data for historical, statistical, sociological, or scientific research purposes.

[91] Personal Data Law, Art 16.

e. Domestic and Cross-Border/International Transfers

Domestically, data transfers are relatively unrestricted if the individual consents to the processing of his or her data. Even in the absence of consent, Article 18 of the Personal Data Law allow for domestic transfers under prescribed circumstances. However, cross-border transfers are governed by separate provisions.

iv. Privacy Regulator

Uzbekistan's regulatory framework for personal data protection is overseen by multiple authorities, each with distinct roles and responsibilities.

a. The Cabinet of Ministers

The Cabinet of Ministers, acting as the executive branch of the state, holds a pivotal regulatory position. Its primary responsibilities, outlined in Article 7 of the Personal Data Law, are fundamentally rule-making and include:

- implementing a unified state policy in the personal data field;
- approving the state programmes in the personal data field;
- determining the procedure of maintaining the State Register of personal data bases;
- approving the procedure of registration of personal databases in the State Register of personal databases;
- coordinating the activity of state and economic administration bodies, local public authorities in the field of personal data.

The Cabinet also collaborates with the Agency for Personalisation to set protective measures and requirements for personal data based on security threat assessments, including standards for biometric and genetic data carriers.

b. The Agency of Personalisation under the Ministry of Justice[92]

The Agency for Personalisation is the authority authorised, pursuant to Article 8 of the Personal Data Law, with several tasks, which include:

- implementing the state policy in the personal data field;
- participating in the development and implementation of state and other programmes in the personal data field;
- approving the Model procedure of processing personal data;
- approving the Model procedure for the organisation of the activity of the structural unit or authorised person of the owner and (or) operator of the personal database, responsible for the processing of personal data and their protection;

[92] Decree of the President dated 21 December 2022 No PD-269 'On measures to implement the administrative reforms of the new Uzbekistan', as part of the administrative reforms, the Agency of Personalisation under the Ministry of Justice was established on the basis of the State Personalisation Centre under the Cabinet of Ministers.

- maintaining the State Register of personal databases;
- issuing a certificate of registration of the personal database in the State Register of personal databases;
- exercising, within the limits of its powers, the state control over the observance of the requirements of the legislation on personal data;
- submitting to the Cabinet of Ministers of the Republic of Uzbekistan proposals on improvement of the legal framework in the field of personal data;
- sending to the state bodies authorised in the field of ensuring state security, in relation to the sphere of their activity, the established information;
- determining the required level of personal data protection;
- analysing the volume and content of processed personal data, the type of activity, the reality of personal data security threats;
- issuing binding injunctions to legal entities and individuals to eliminate violations of the legislation on personal data;
- co-operating with the competent authorities of foreign states and international organisations.

c. The Ministry of Digital Technologies

As the special authorised state body in the sphere of informatization, the Ministry participates in regulating the use of technologies for the collection, processing and storage of personal and biometric data.[93] The Ministry may also restrict internet access of the owner or operator of the personal database after its entry in the register of violators of the rights of personal data subjects (Annex 3 of Resolution No 717).

d. Inspection for Control in the Field of Communications, Informatisation and Telecommunication Technologies ('Uzkomnazorat')

Uzkomnazorat, the regulatory body for communications, informatisation, and telecommunication technologies, ensures adherence to data localisation mandates.[94] Its powers encompass:

- Inspecting and verifying compliance with data localisation standards;
- Issuing binding instructions to address violations, and drafting protocols for administrative offences pertaining to data localisation breaches;
- Providing the Cabinet of Ministers with reports on the activities of database owners/operators;
- Managing the Register of violators of personal data subjects' rights and cooperating with international entities in the personal data sphere.

[93] Resolution of the Cabinet of Ministers No 318 dated 1 May 2018, Annex No 1.
[94] Resolution No 717, Annex No 3.

III. Legal Bases, Mechanisms and Exceptions for International Data Transfers and Data Protection

A. International Data Transfers

Uzbek legislation uses the term cross-border transfer of personal data in the context of international data transfers. The term is employed to describe the process by which a database owner or database operator sends personal data beyond the territory of the Republic of Uzbekistan. Such transfers are subject to special regulation. The main law regulating international data transfers in the legislation of the Republic of Uzbekistan is the Personal Data Law, which dictates the conditions, requirements and grounds for such transfers.

i. 'Adequacy Findings' or Whitelists and Blacklists

Article 15(2) of the Personal Data Law permits the cross-border transfer of personal data to the territory of foreign states that ensure adequate protection of the rights of subjects of personal data. However, the criteria for determining whether states ensure the adequate protection is not set out in Uzbek legislation. This contrasts with the approach of the Russian Federation, a fellow CIS member state, which maintains explicit 'whitelists' of countries deemed to have adequate protection and 'blacklists' of those that do not.[95]

Despite the absence of formal lists, the regulatory body's administrative practice provides some guidance. According to this unofficial stance, a country is considered to provide adequate protection if it has enacted legislation governing personal data protection. Additionally, when registering a personal data database and completing the application form, registrants must indicate whether they engage in cross-border personal data transfer. If the answer is affirmative, they are then questioned whether the recipient country has established personal data protection laws.[96]

ii. Consent of Data Subjects

Article 15 of the Personal Data Law sets out certain conditions under which cross-border transfer of personal data to foreign countries that do not provide adequate protection of the rights of subjects of personal data can be performed. A primary exception to the requirement stipulated in Article 15 is the consent of the data subject to cross-border transfer of his/her personal data.

[95] Order No 128 of Roskomnadzor 'On approval of the List of foreign states providing adequate protection of the rights of personal data subjects' (5 August 2022), available at https://rulaws.ru/acts/Prikaz-Roskomnadzora-ot-05.08.2022-N-128/.

[96] Request for Database Registration to the Personalization Agency under the Ministry of Justice, available at https://pd.gov.uz/appeals/create.

Other circumstances under which such transfers might be permissible according to Article 15 include:

- The need to protect the constitutional order of the Republic of Uzbekistan, the protection of public order,[97] the rights and freedoms of citizens, health and morality of the population.
- In cases stipulated by international treaties of the Republic of Uzbekistan.

There is no special requirement with regard to the form of the consent. Consent may be taken in any form confirming the fact of its receipt. However, for transferring special categories of personal data abroad, the consent of the subject in writing is required, which may include the form of an electronic document.

Furthermore, while obtaining the consent of the data subject, the following information must be indicated in the consent form:

- name, tax identification number of the operator-legal entity (surname, first name and patronymic of the operator-individual, his/her personal identification number);
- surname, first name and patronymic of the data subject, details of his/her identity document;
- the purposes of personal data processing;
- the list of the subject's personal data, for the processing of which consent is given;
- term or period of validity of the consent to personal data processing;
- consent to the transfer of personal data to third parties and (or) cross-border transfer of such data [if any];
- consent to dissemination of personal data in publicly available sources [if any];
- other information [if any].[98]

Article 21 of the Personal Data Law determines procedure for consent and revoking consent to the processing of personal data. In the event of incapacity or limitation of the legal capacity of the subject, written consent, including in the form of an electronic document, to the processing of his personal data is given by his legal representative. For juvenile subjects, this consent must come from their parents or legal guardians, or in their absence, the appropriate guardianship and trusteeship authorities. In the event of the death of the

[97] The following provisions of the court practice give us the guidelines on the boundaries of the public order. 'When recognising a transaction made with a purpose known to be contrary to the foundations of law and order and [public] morality as [null and void ab initio], courts should determine whether the transaction violates the requirements of legal norms ensuring the foundations of law and order, that is, aimed at preserving and defending the foundations of the constitutional system, rights and freedoms person and citizen, defense capability, security and economic system of the state (illegal export of weapons, tax evasion, etc), or whether it contradicts the foundations of public morality, that is, it grossly violates the prevailing ideas in society about good and evil, good and bad, vice and virtue, etc.' (12(3) of Resolution of Plenum of the Supreme Commercial Court dated 28 November 2014 No 269 'On certain issues of application by economic courts of civil law norms on invalidity of transactions').

[98] Model Procedure of Processing Personal Data, Item 11.

subject, this consent can be provided by their heirs, if such consent was not previously given by the subject during their lifetime. The processing of personal data of a person declared dead by a court and recognised by the court as missing is carried out with the consent of the heirs.

Data subjects can withdraw consent to the processing of personal data in the same manner it was given, or in writing, including as an electronic document. In this case, the personal data of the subject are to be destroyed by the owner and (or) the operator not later than the working day following the day of receipt of such withdrawal of consent.[99]

iii. Contracts

While the Personal Data Law of Uzbekistan does not explicitly cite contracts as a foundation for the authorisation of cross-border personal data transfers, it is inferred from Article 18. This Article indicates that personal data processing is permissible in order to fulfil a contract of which the data subject is a party or to undertake actions at the data subject's request prior to entering a contract. Since cross-border data transfer is a form of data processing, this provision is likely applicable to such transfers as well.

It is worth noting that Uzbek law does not directly require the execution of a contract with a data subject specifically for the purposes of international data transfers. Nonetheless, a broader legal requirement exists which obligates database owners and operators to implement necessary measures, encompassing legal, organisational, and technical actions, to ensure the protection of personal data.[100] Taking legal actions might also include, inter alia, the execution of a contract with a data subject specifically for the purposes of international data transfers.

iv. Asia-Pacific Economic Cooperation Cross-Border Privacy Rules System

The Republic of Uzbekistan is not a member of the Asia-Pacific Economic Cooperation (APEC). Nor has the Republic of Uzbekistan joined or lodged a Notice of Intent to participate in the APEC Cross-Border Privacy Rules (CBPR) System.

v. Privacy Certification Schemes, Trustmarks or Privacy Seals (International)

Uzbek law does not recognise certification schemes, privacy seals or trustmarks delivered in third countries as valid means for parties carrying out cross-border data transfers to demonstrate compliance with local data protection laws.

[99] ibid, Item 10. On the above-mentioned consent requirements see Abdulaziz Jurajonov, Abdumalik Mukhtorov, 'Uzbekistan – Data Protection Overview' (Data Guidance, June 2023), available at https://www.dataguidance.com/notes/uzbekistan-data-protection-overview-0.

[100] Personal Data Law, Art 31.

B. International Data Protection and Liability

i. Specific Requirements or Policies for Data Processing and Retention

As per Article 17 of the Personal Data Law, personal data must be destroyed by the database owner and the operator, as well as by any third parties involved, in the following cases:

- upon reaching the purpose of processing of personal data;
- if there is a withdrawal of the consent of the subject to the processing of personal data;
- after the expiration of the processing of personal data determined by the consent of the subject;
- upon entry into legal force of a court decision.

In addition, the existing regulations impose the following obligations on the accounting of log files, without providing detailed mechanisms of implementation:

- the internet service provider of a public point of access is obliged to organise the accounting of the used internet web resources (log files) and their storage for three months;
- the organiser of the WiFi service is obliged, together with the operator and (or) provider, to take hardware and technical measures to identify the users, as well as to organise the accounting of used web resources (log files) in the manner specified by law;
- the operator and provider have the rights to organise the accounting of the web resources of the data transfer network used by the subscriber (maintaining log files); and
- when providing WiFi services, the operator and provider are obliged to take hardware and technical measures to identify users, as well as organise the accounting of used web resources (log files).[101]

ii. Regulations on Legal Ownership of Data Protection and Privacy Rights

As discussed, the right to data protection and privacy is recognised as a constitutional right of the citizens in the Republic of Uzbekistan.

Furthermore, Article 14 of the Personal Data Law defines the dissemination of personal data as actions aimed at the disclosure of personal data to an indefinite number of persons, including the publication of personal data in the media, posting on the Internet, or providing access to personal data in any other way. The dissemination of personal data in cases beyond the previously stated purposes of their collection must be carried out with the consent of the subject.

[101] Abdulaziz Jurajonov, Abdumalik Mukhtorov, op cit.

iii. Extraterritorial Effect of Laws on Data Protection and Privacy

The Personal Data Law does not explicitly define its territorial scope of application. According to Article 3, it applies to relations arising from the processing and protection of personal data, regardless of the means of processing used, including information technology.

Regulation 'On the procedure of state control over the observance of special conditions of personal data processing of citizens of the Republic of Uzbekistan'[102] establishes the procedure of keeping the Register of violators of the rights of personal data subjects[103] (the 'Register'). The Register is understood as a list of database owners and (or) database operators who do not comply with the special conditions of personal data processing of Uzbekistan citizens. After inclusion of the database owner and (or) operator in the Register, the Ministry for Development of Information Technologies and Communications of the Republic of Uzbekistan shall take appropriate measures to restrict their activity in the national segment of the Internet.

This measure was introduced as a sanction against entities that violate the provisions of the Personal Data Law. In 2021 a number of foreign entities, such as Twitter, TikTok and VKontakte (*ВКонтакте*) were included into the Register.[104] This suggests that the Personal Data Law, along with the relevant bylaws derived from it, may have an extraterritorial effect and may apply to any foreign entity carrying out processing of personal data of Uzbekistan's citizens.

iv. Data Breach Notification

Under the current Uzbek legislation, there is no explicit requirement for database owners or operators to notify the Regulator or the data subjects in the event of a data breach. The obligation to inform the Regulator arises only in instances where there are changes to the information necessary for the registration of the personal data database.

Article 23 of the Personal Data Law obliges database owners/operators to inform the data subject in writing about the purposes of data processing and their rights as outlined in Article 30 of the same law, upon the inclusion of their personal data into a database. Furthermore, if personal data is to be transferred to a third party, the database owner and (or) operator is required to notify the data subject in writing within three days of the transfer.

Exceptions to the written notification requirement exist under the following circumstances:

- exercise of authority by government bodies;
- transfer of personal data for processing for historical, statistical, sociological or scientific purposes;
- collection of personal data from publicly available sources.[105]

[102] Regulation 'On the procedure of state control over the observance of special conditions of personal data processing of citizens of the Republic of Uzbekistan' (Resolution of the Cabinet of Ministers dated 29 April 2021 No 255).

[103] Register of violators of personal data subjects' rights, available at https://pd.gov.uz/spoiler/.

[104] The SPC launched a register of violators of the law on personal data (26 July 2021), available at www.spot.uz/ru/2021/07/26/personal-data/.

[105] Model Procedure of Processing Personal Data, Item 19.

The database owner and database operators are also obliged to notify in writing the data subject, as well as other participants in the processing of personal data in cases of changes, destruction of personal data, or restrictions imposed on data access.[106] Beyond these specified situations, the Personal Data Law does not impose any other notification requirements.

IV. Data Security and Data Localisation

Data localisation is a relatively new requirement in Uzbek legislation, which was formally incorporated by the Law of the Republic of Uzbekistan No ZRU-666 dated 14 January 2021 (the 'Law No 666'). This law amended the existing Personal Data Law to include a data localisation mandate.

A. Data Security and Localisation Requirements

i. General Localisation Requirement

While there are no special localisation requirements for particular sectors in Uzbek legislation, there is a general localisation requirement for personal data which is applicable to all database operators and database owners operating in all sectors. Article 27-1 of the Personal Data Law sets out the localisation requirements for personal data in Uzbekistan. It states:

> The database owner and (or) database operator when processing personal data of citizens of the Republic of Uzbekistan with the use of information technologies, including the worldwide information network Internet, is obliged to ensure their collection, systematisation and storage in databases of personal data on technical means physically placed on the territory of the Republic of Uzbekistan and registered in the established order in the State Register of Databases of Personal Data.

From the provisions of Article 27-1 of the Personal Data Law, the following factors trigger the localisation requirement:

- The personal data being processed is related to citizens of the Republic of Uzbekistan.
- The processing is carried out with the use of information technologies, including the Internet.

Consequently, the localisation requirement is not applicable in cases where (i) the processing occurs without the use of information technologies or (ii) the personal data does not relate to citizens of the Republic of Uzbekistan.

The localisation requirement necessitates that the collection, systematisation and storage of personal data is carried out within the territory of Uzbekistan. This requirement is stricter than that in the Kazakh legislation, which only requires storing personal data within the territory of Kazakhstan.

Article 27-1 of the Personal Data Law requires that the initial collection of personal data must be carried out using technical means that are physically located within Uzbekistan.

[106] ibid, Item 25.

This effectively precludes the collection of personal data by foreign entities without physical presence in Uzbekistan.

With regard to the interpretation of Article 27-1 of the Personal Data Law concerning the storage of personal data, there are two potential readings hinging on the meaning of the term 'ensure'. On the first interpretation, only one party, either the owner or the operator, needs to store the personal data on technical means that are physically located within the Republic of Uzbekistan. This viewpoint hinges on the term 'ensure' within the Article, implying that one entity's compliance could fulfil the requirement for all involved parties. On the second interpretation, the term 'ensure' is taken to mean that all entities involved in storing the personal data of Uzbek citizens must do so on technical means physically located within the country. In this case, any party that stores personal data must use local technical means. As of now, the Regulator has not issued any guidance on that matter. It is submitted that the first interpretation makes more sense, as the second would severely limit the feasibility of cross-border data transfer.

Furthermore, Article 27-1 of the Personal Data Law requires the registration of the databases of personal data in the State Register of Databases of Personal Data (the 'State Register'). The registration process and required registration documents is stipulated in Resolution of the Cabinet of Ministers dated 8 February 2020 No 71 'On the Approval of the Regulation on the Procedure for Registering Personal Databases in the State Register of Personal Databases' 'Resolution No 71').

ii. General Data Security Requirement

The Resolution of the Cabinet of Ministers of the Republic of Uzbekistan dated 5 October 2022 No 570 'On the Approval of Some Regulatory and Legal Acts in the Field of Personal Data Processing' ('Resolution No 570') sets out general security requirements for personal data which must be complied with by database owners and database operators, irrespective of the sector in which they operate. The emphasis on database security arises from the principle in Uzbek law that data processing is inherently tied to databases. Resolution No 570 consists of the two following key regulations:

i. Regulation on determining the levels of protection of personal data in their processing ('Regulation No 1').
ii. Regulation on requirements for material carriers of biometric and genetic data and technologies for storage of such data outside of databases of personal data.

Regulation No 1 outlines the general data security obligations. It categorises personal data processed within databases into four distinct types: (1) special; (2) biometric; (3) genetic; and (4) publicly available data. The Personal Data Law does not provide for an exhaustive list of personal data types, suggesting that Regulation No 1 specifically addresses the security for these four identified categories.

To safeguard personal data, database owners and operators are required to implement an appropriate level of protection. This level is determined by assessing various factors, including the potential threats to data security, as well as the volume and nature of the data in question.

Regulation No 1 distinguishes three types of security threats:

- Type I threats – related to the presence of undeclared opportunities in the system software of the database of personal data;

- Type II threats – related to the presence of undeclared opportunities in the application software of the database of personal data;
- Type III threats – related to the presence of undeclared opportunities in the system and application software of the database of personal data.

Similar to the Russian framework, which includes a classification of data security threats and a certification scheme to verify the absence of such threats, Regulation No 1 recognises the need for identifying and mitigating potential security risks. The Russian approach also provides a comprehensive list of potential threats, such as the risk of cloud server breaches, cross-site scripting, cross-site request forgery, and the compromise of user data isolation within a virtual machine.

At present, Uzbek legislation does not feature an equivalent certification scheme or a detailed list of potential threats, as seen in the Russian model. Consequently, Regulation No 1 assigns the responsibility to database owners and operators to determine and address the specific types of threats to the security of personal data they manage. This approach requires entities to exercise a degree of discretion in identifying and mitigating risks to ensure compliance with the overarching data security mandates set forth in Resolution No 570.[107]

Regulation No 1 establishes a structured framework comprising four distinct levels of protection. Each level corresponds to a set of requirements and is triggered when a certain criterion is met based on the following Table:

Table 16.1 Protection Framework Established by Regulation No 1

Level of Protection	**Conditions for Each Level** (***each level of protection is needed when at least one of the conditions is present***)	**Requirements** (***to ensure each level of protection the following requirements must be met***)
Level 4	(1) The presence of type III threats to databases and processing of publicly available data in the database.	(a) Organisation of the security regime of the premises in which the databases are located, preventing the possibility of uncontrolled break-in or stay in these premises by persons who do not have the right of access to these premises. (b) Ensuring security of material media of personal data. (c) Approval by the head of the owner and (or) the operator of the document defining the list of persons whose access to personal data processed in databases is necessary for performance of their official duties.

(continued)

[107] Abdumalik Mukhtorov and Azizbek Suyunboev, 'Uzbekistan: Resolution on Personal Data Processing Overview' (*DataGuidance*, June 2023), available at www.dataguidance.com/opinion/uzbekistan-resolution-personal-data-processing.

Table 16.1 ***(Continued)***

Level of Protection	**Conditions for Each Level** (***each level of protection is needed when at least one of the conditions is present***)	**Requirements** (***to ensure each level of protection the following requirements must be met***)
Level 4		(d) Use of means of data protection, which have passed the procedure of evaluation of compliance with the legislation requirements in the field of information security, in case when application of such means is necessary for protection of personal data from existing threats.
Level 3	(1) The existence of type II threats for the databases and processing of publicly available data of the owner or operator's employees or publicly available data of less than 50,000 subjects who are not employees of the owner or operator. (2) The existence of type III threats to databases and processing of special data of the owner's or operator's employees or special data of less than 50,000 subjects who are not employees of the owner or operator. (3) The existence of type III threats to databases and the processing of biometric or genetic data.	(a) The fulfilment of the requirements specified for level 4 protection. (b) Appointment of an official employee responsible for ensuring the personal data security in the databases.
Level 2	(1) The existence of type I threats for databases and processing of publicly available personal data in databases. (2) The existence of type II threats for databases and processing of special data of employees of the owner or the operator or special data of less than 50,000 subjects who are not employees of the owner or the operator. (3) The existence of type II threats to databases and the processing of biometric or genetic data in the databases. (4) The existence of a type II threat to databases and the processing of publicly available data by more than 50,000 subjects who are not employees of the owner or operator in the databases;	(a) The fulfilment of the requirements specified for level 3 protection; (b) Providing access to the electronic journal of messages exclusively to the official employees or to the authorised person who needs the information contained in the mentioned journal for performing their job duties.

(continued)

Table 16.1 ***(Continued)***

Level of Protection	Conditions for Each Level (*each level of protection is needed when at least one of the conditions is present*)	Requirements (*to ensure each level of protection the following requirements must be met*)
Level 2	(5) The existence of type III threats to databases and the processing of special data of more than 50,000 subjects who are not employees of the owner or the operator in databases.	
Level I	(1) The existence of type I threats for the databases and the processing of special and (or) biometric and (or) genetic personal data in the databases. (2) The existence of type II threats for databases and processing of special personal data of more than 50,000 subjects who are not employees of the owner and (or) the operator.	(a) Fulfilment of the requirements specified for level 2 protection. (b) The automatic registration in the electronic security log of the changes in the owner's and (or) operator's employee's authorisation to access the personal data contained in the databases. (c) Establishment of structural subdivision, responsible for ensuring security of personal data in databases, or assigning to one of the structural subdivisions the functions for ensuring such security.[108]

B. Data Security and Localisation Requirements for Particular Sectors

i. Requirement for the Banking Sector

Data security in the banking sector is regulated by two primary laws; the Law of the Republic of Uzbekistan on Protection of Information in the Automated Banking System No 30 dated 4 April 2006 (the 'Law No 30') and the Law of the Republic of Uzbekistan on Bank Secrecy No 530-II dated 30 August 2003 (the 'Law on Bank Secrecy').

Under Article 3 of the Law on Bank Secrecy,[109] the following data constitute bank secrets:

- Data about operations, accounts and deposits of its clients (correspondents).
- Data about its client (correspondent) received by the bank in connection with rendering banking services to him/her.

[108] Requirements for Protection of Personal Data in Uzbekistan (*Azizov & Partners*, 28 November 2022), available at https://azizovpartners.uz/en/memos/requirements-for-protection-of-personal-data-in-uzbekistan/.

[109] Law of No 530-II 30 August 2003 'On Bank Secrecy', Art 3.

- Data on availability, nature and value of a client's property stored in the bank's safes and premises.
- Data regarding interbank operations and transactions made on behalf of a client or in his/her favour.
- Data about the client of another bank, which became known as a result of circulation of information constituting banking secrecy between banks.
- Data on participants of the funded pension system, the amount and movement of pension contributions, pension savings on individual funded pension accounts of citizens.

Article 6 of the Law on Bank Secrecy prohibits disclosing or using for personal purposes or in the interests of third parties the information constituting bank secrecy. Banks are obliged to take organisational and technical measures necessary for proper storage of information constituting bank secrecy.

Law No 30[110] outlines specific obligations for banks to protect information within the automated banking system. These measures include:

- Development and observance of information protection rules, as well as control over the implementation of measures aimed at protecting information processed in the automated banking system.
- Using certified technical means and information protection means.
- Creation of information protection service in the automated banking system.
- Coordination of activities on collection and use of information processing methods in the automated banking system.

C. Data Security and Localisation Requirements for Particular Types of Data

Apart from the general data localisation requirement, Uzbek legislation prescribes specific localisation and data security requirements for particular types of data.

i. Biometric and Genetic Data

The Regulation on Requirements for Material Carriers of Biometric and Genetic Data and Technologies for Storage of Such Data outside of Databases of Personal Data (the 'Regulation No 2') is approved by Resolution No 570.[111] This Regulation establishes extra security requirements for material carriers of biometric and genetic data and technologies for the storage of such data outside of databases of personal data.[112]

[110] Law of 7 April 2006 No 30 'On the Protection of Information in an Automated Banking System', Art 5.

[111] The Regulation on Requirements for Material Carriers of Biometric and Genetic Data and Technologies for Storage of Such Data outside of Databases of Personal Data (Resolution of the Cabinet of Ministers dated 5 October 2022 No 570).

[112] See Requirements for protection of personal data in Uzbekistan.

ii. State Secrets

The system for the protection of state secrets, including the procedure for classification, access and related restrictions, as well as the procedure for handling state secrets, is determined by the Cabinet of Ministers of the Republic of Uzbekistan. Termination or withdrawal of access does not relieve an Uzbek citizen of his or her obligations not to disclose state secrets known to him or her. As per the Law on State Secrets, an Uzbek citizen who works or has worked with information constituting a state or military secret may, with his or her written consent, be restricted in his or her rights until the expiry of the period of secrecy, but not for more than five years.[113]

V. Issues in Private International Law

A. Litigations Involving Cross-Border Data Transfer and Privacy

Uzbekistan offers a range of legal procedures to address data protection disputes, including administrative, criminal, civil, and even constitutional proceedings.

Administrative remedies, such as filing appeals to supervisory bodies in matters like database registration disputes as per clause 31 of Resolution No 71 of 2020, are formally recognised. However, in practice, these processes are seldom utilised. This is the case even though Uzbekistan has a specific Law on Administrative Procedures (No 457 of 2018). As one of the law's drafters observed, state bodies and courts tend to overlook this law when resolving administrative disputes.[114]

The Table below summarises the main categories of litigation, the potential parties to data protection litigation, as well as the remedies available to them.

Table 16.2 Summary of Main Categories of Litigation

Categories of Litigation	Claimant	Defendant	Remedies	Basis	Deciding Authority
Administrative	Data subject, Owner, Operator, Regulatory authorities	Data subject, Owner, Operator, Third parties, Regulatory authorities	Administrative fine, issuing binding injunctions, restricting access to the Internet, challenging decisions of regulatory authorities	Articles 46^1 and 46^2 of the Administrative Liability Code, Article 8 of the Personal Data Law, Resolution No 717	Administrative Court, Regulatory authorities (Agency of Personalisation, Uzkomnazorat, the Ministry of digital technologies)

(continued)

[113] Law of 7 May 1993 No 848-XII 'On Protection of the State Secrets', Art 8.

[114] Isa Hamedov, 'ЗАП: закон, ожидающий исполнения [ZAP: Law Awaiting Enforcement]' (*gazeta.uz*, 20 April 2021), available at www.gazeta.uz/ru/2021/04/20/administrative-procedures/ and Isa Hamedov, 'ЗАП: закон, который не исполняется [ZAP: A Law that is Not Being Enforced]' (*gazeta.uz*, 8 June 2020), available at www.gazeta.uz/ru/2020/06/08/legislation/.

Table 16.2 ***(Continued)***

Categories of Litigation	Claimant	Defendant	Remedies	Basis	Deciding Authority
Criminal	Detective, investigator, prosecutor and official of the body conducting the pre-investigative inspection	Owner, Operator, Third parties	Administrative fine and Criminal penalties (fine, correctional labour, restriction of liberty, imprisonment)	Articles 46^1 and 46^2 of the Administrative Liability Code, Articles 141^1 and 141^2 of the Criminal Code	Criminal Court
Civil	Data subject	Owner, Operator, Third parties	Compensation of moral and other damages, reimbursement of lost earnings to the employee	Articles 989, 1021, 1022 of the Civil Code, Article 180 of the Labour Code	Civil Court
Constitutional	State body or official, citizens and legal entities	N/A	Appeal or a complaint to review the constitutionality of a Law if, in their opinion, the Law violates their constitutional rights and freedoms, is inconsistent with the Constitution and has been applied in a specific case that has been concluded in court and all other judicial remedies have been exhausted	Article 27 of the Law on Constitutional Court	Constitutional Court

B. Jurisdictional Issues Involving Cross-Border Data Protection and Privacy

Uzbek law does not currently have specific provisions addressing multi-jurisdictional issues in data protection or privacy cases. Nevertheless, the existing frameworks within the Civil, Criminal, Administrative, and Economic Procedural Codes provide a foundational basis for determining court jurisdiction in such cases. Courts may decide on jurisdiction based on a combination of factors relevant to personal data matters, such as a subject matter of the dispute, based on the nature of a data, the location of a plaintiff, a defendant or a place where the data breach occurred.

Courts have an authority to order third parties to produce documents during litigation. a court handling the case can issue a court order directing a relevant court in another district or city to collect evidence (documents) from the third party. These orders detail the case specifics, the documents required, execution timeframe. (Civil Procedural Code – Article 103, Economic Procedural Code – Article 91).

If the documents reside in cloud storage outside Uzbekistan's jurisdiction, things get more complex. In such cases, Uzbek courts can rely on international cooperation mechanisms, where agreements are in place between Uzbekistan and other countries that establish frameworks for legal cooperation, including evidence gathering.

Below is an outline of jurisdictional competencies as per the various procedural codes:

- **Civil Jurisdiction**: Civil courts manage disputes connected to civil, family, labour, housing, and land legal relationships when at least one party is a citizen of Uzbekistan. These courts also have the authority to preside over cases involving foreign citizens, organisations, or stateless persons, provided there is no conflicting stipulation in the international treaties to which Uzbekistan is a party (Civil Procedural Code, Article 361).
- **Administrative Jurisdiction**: Administrative courts have jurisdiction over disputes similar to those of civil courts, with the inclusion of matters specifically of an administrative nature (Code of Administrative Procedure, Article 26).
- **Criminal Jurisdiction**: Criminal courts in Uzbekistan generally have the jurisdiction to adjudicate offences committed within the country by foreign nationals and stateless persons, except for those who possess immunity based on international treaties (Criminal Procedure Code, Article 4).
- **Economic Jurisdiction**: Article 239 of the Economic Procedural Code sets out the conditions for economic court jurisdiction in cases involving foreign entities. This includes considerations like the domiciles of the parties, location of property, place of contract execution, locus of damage, and particular dispute types.

Rules related to deference of foreign courts' jurisdiction are outlined in procedural codes for different courts. These codes establish how foreign court decisions are enforced and how foreign court jurisdiction is determined. Additionally, Uzbekistan's treaties within the CIS framework and bilateral agreements may also be relevant. For instance, the Minsk Convention of 1993 (Art 21) and the Chisinau Convention of 2002 (Art 24) to which Uzbekistan is a party allow courts to accept cases based on choice-of-court agreements, as long as it does not conflict with the exclusive jurisdiction of foreign courts. These Conventions provide that if there is a choice-of-court agreement, a court shall, on the application of the respondent, discontinue the proceedings.

In situations where there is a concurrent legal action in a foreign jurisdiction concerning the same issue, the Economic Court of Uzbekistan may respond as follows:

1. Refusal to hear the claim: The Economic Court may choose not to entertain a claim if it is already being processed by a foreign court, unless the matter falls under the Economic Court's exclusive jurisdiction.

2. Termination of proceedings: The Economic Court may halt its proceedings if a foreign court has already issued a final judgment on the same matter, unless the matter falls under the Economic Court's exclusive jurisdiction.

C. Applicable Law: Litigations Involving Cross-Border Data Protection and Privacy

The Uzbek legal framework surrounding personal non-property rights, which includes privacy, private and family secrets, the right to a name, the right to an image, is encapsulated within the Civil Code (Article 99 of the Uzbek Civil Code).

Article 1179 of the Civil Code provides for *lex loci delicti commissii* – the law of the place where the wrongful act, or tort, was committed, as an applicable law to personal non-property rights: 'The law of the country where the act or other circumstance giving rise to the claim for protection of such rights took place shall apply to personal non-property rights.'

This provision implies that in cases involving cross-border elements, the Uzbek courts will determine the applicable law based on where the harmful event that infringed upon personal non-property rights occurred. Consequently, if a privacy violation or a breach of data protection happens across national boundaries, the Uzbek legal system will look to the jurisdiction where the infringement took place to decide on the applicable legal norms.

D. Recognition and Enforcement of Foreign Judgments

The Constitution, Laws and Codes of Procedure generally recognise the primacy of Uzbekistan's international treaties over national laws. This primacy is particularly relevant in the context of recognising and enforcing foreign judgments and arbitral awards.

Uzbekistan is party to several international treaties on recognition and enforcement of foreign judgments and arbitral awards, including:

- United Nations Convention on the Recognition and Enforcement of Foreign Arbitral Awards, dated 10 June 1958 in New York ('New York Convention');
- Agreement 'On the Procedure for the Settlement of Disputes Related to the Exercise of Economic Activities' dated 20 March 1992 in Kiev ('Kiev Agreement');
- Convention 'On Legal Assistance and Legal Relations in Civil, Family and Criminal Cases', dated 22 January 1993 in Minsk ('Minsk Convention');
- Convention 'On Legal Assistance and Legal Relations in Civil, Family and Criminal Matters' dated 7 October 2002, Chisinau ('Chisinau Convention').

In addition to these multilateral treaties, Uzbekistan is also a participant in numerous bilateral legal assistance agreements that provide for the mutual recognition and enforcement of judgments.

E. Obstacles to Effective Data Protection

The essence of data protection law is intrinsically linked to its human rights foundation, as highlighted by Christopher Kuner, as it is fundamentally about safeguarding personal data from being compromised. This protective dimension is commonly expressed through the legislative, judicial, and regulatory efforts to maintain the application of a nation's data protection laws to the personal data of its citizens, even when these data are processed abroad. In practice, at least in the Uzbekistan context, the reach of domestic data protection authorities tends to be limited once personal data leaves their jurisdiction. Despite the assertion that foreign data processing should adhere to the authority's national law, actual enforcement becomes challenging.[115]

In the Uzbek legal context, this protective stance is evident by the implementation of the overriding mandatory rules. Article 1165 of the Civil Code imposes such imperative rules, particularly concerning data localisation. These rules dictate that owners or operators processing personal data of citizens of Uzbekistan are obligated to ensure the collection, systematisation, and storage of such data in personal databases physically located within Uzbekistan. Moreover, these databases must be duly registered in the State Register of personal databases. Such data localisation mandates can impose significant burdens on data owners and operators, both in terms of logistics and costs. While the intention is to exercise greater control and protection over the data of Uzbek nationals, the strictness of this requirement may lead to issues in compliance.

VI. Topical Issues and Prospects

A. Artificial Intelligence or AI-Generated Data

The advent of Artificial Intelligence (AI) has brought about significant transformations in data processing practices. Although the Personal Data Law of Uzbekistan, as well as its related bylaws, do not explicitly mention AI, their provisions have broad applicability that extends to AI-generated data. This is reflected in Article 3 of the Personal Data Law: 'This Law shall apply to relations arising from the processing and protection of personal data, *irrespective of the means of processing*, including information technologies [emphasis added].'

The legislative framework in Uzbekistan has begun adapting to the challenges and opportunities presented by AI. Specific bylaws have been developed to address personal data processing within designated 'special regimes'. Notably, in 2021, as part of the 'Digital Uzbekistan 2030' Strategy, a separate unit of IT park[116] dedicated to the application of

[115] Christopher Kuner, 'Data Protection Law and International Jurisdiction on the Internet (Part 1)' (2010) 18 *International Journal of Law and Information Technology* 176, 176–93.

[116] IT park – a hub for software and IT startups in Uzbekistan, provides an extraterritorial free zone with dedicated facilities and support for launching and scaling businesses.

AI technologies ('special regime') was introduced.[117] This special regime introduces a legal environment conducive to the processing of personal data by entities and scientific organisations that employ AI technologies, with key provisions including:

- The Strategy Coordination Commission is authorised to establish the procedure and conditions for the processing of anonymised personal data by the participants of the special regime (para 4 (a) of Decree dated 26 August 2021 No 5234);
- State bodies and organisations provide anonymised personal data in full compliance with the requirements of personal data legislation (para 4 (v) of Decree dated 26 August 2021 No 5234);
- Participants of the special regime are entitled to receive from ministries, bodies and organisations anonymised personal data necessary for the implementation of experimental projects (para 22 of Resolution dated 29 November 2021, No 717).

From these developments, it is evident that the special regime requires that the data be anonymised and comply with the overarching principles of personal data law (*lex generalis*).

B. Potential Cooperation under the Belt and Road Initiative

Uzbekistan's strategic vision for becoming a central IT hub and advancing its digital economy is closely tied to the Digital Uzbekistan 2030 strategy. This strategy aligns with the development of the Digital Silk Road, which is described as 'one of the key aspects of further development of Central Asian economies'.[118] Uzbekistan's IT advancements often involve leveraging Chinese technological expertise and infrastructure, with the Chinese tech conglomerate Huawei playing a significant role in the nation's telecommunications sector and digital transformation initiatives. A notable collaboration between Huawei and Uzbekistan is the construction of the unified E-Government data storage and processing centre, equipped with a Huawei data system of 20 petabytes capacity.[119] During a 2019 government delegation visit to China, Uzbekistan further cemented its technological partnership with Huawei by signing two cooperation agreements. The first agreement focuses on cooperation in the implementation of the 'safe city' project in Uzbekistan, including the intelligent video surveillance of public places. The second agreement aims to enhance the application of modern ICT technologies in the activities of emergency medical services in Uzbekistan.[120]

Despite these developments, it is noteworthy that Uzbekistan has not yet formalised any specific data transfer or protection agreements with China. This absence of formalised

[117] Decree of the President dated 26 August 2021 No 5234 and Resolution of the Cabinet of Ministers dated 29 November 2021 No 717.

[118] Vladimir Norov, 'Central Asian Countries and China are Developing a Strategic Partnership to Ensure Peace, Security and Sustainable Development in the Region' (*O'zbekiston Milliy Axborot Agentligi*, 19 May 2023).

[119] Official website of the President, 'The Unified Data Storage and Processing Center of "E-Government" System Launched' (*president.uz*, 27 August 2022), available at https://president.uz/en/lists/view/5463.

[120] 'Prime Minister of the Republic of Uzbekistan has Visited Huawei R&D Center in Shenzhen' (*huawei.com*, 29 August 2019), available at www.huawei.com/en/news/2019/8/uzbekistan-prime-minister-visit-huawei.

data agreements highlights a gap in the cooperative framework that could address concerns related to data sovereignty, privacy, and cross-border data flows between the two countries.

C. Data Protection Post COVID-19 Pandemic

The COVID-19 pandemic necessitated changes in data protection practices globally, including in Uzbekistan. To manage the pandemic, Uzbekistan established quarantine complexes and introduced detailed procedures for personal data processing via Resolution No 254.[121] The Ministry of Health set up a centralised information system to track quarantined individuals and ensure data integrity and security in compliance with the Personal Data Law.

The pandemic also highlighted the significance of international data exchange. On 18 December 2020 the 'Agreement on mutual legal assistance in administrative matters in the field of personal data exchange' was signed by the CIS states, including Uzbekistan. It was originally anticipated that Azerbaijan, the Russian Federation, Armenia, Tajikistan, Belarus, Turkmenistan, Kazakhstan, Uzbekistan, Kyrgyzstan, Ukraine and Moldova would be the Agreement's parties. According to Article 18, the Agreement shall be open for accession by any member state of the CIS by depositing an instrument of accession with the depositary. However, by 2024, Uzbekistan had not yet ratified the Agreement, unlike Russia, Kazakhstan, and Kyrgyzstan.

In conclusion, as Uzbekistan continues to develop its digital infrastructure and engage in international commerce, the need for a comprehensive and coherent legal framework that addresses the nuances of data protection and privacy in a globalised world becomes increasingly critical. This necessitates the development of a private international law regime that is thoroughly harmonised with the contemporary digital milieu.

[121] Regulation on temporary procedure for the implementation of anti-epidemic measures in the complex, adapted for temporary quarantine of persons suspected of infection coronavirus infection (Resolution No 254 dated 25 April 2020).

17

Kazakhstan

BOTAGOZ OMAROVA, ABDUMALIK MUKHTOROV
AND ARUBEGIM YERLANKYZY

I. Introduction

The advent of modern information technologies has created conditions for the collection and systematisation of large volumes of structured and unstructured information, including personal data of citizens derived from sources like the Internet, e-commerce, search services, social networks, as well as the ubiquitous distribution of smartphones and tablets.

Despite the relative effectiveness of the provisions of the legislation on personal data and their protection in relation to the established methods of processing arrays of data, big data technologies are incompatible with a number of basic principles underlying the legislation on personal data and their protection, which asserts the necessity of revision of this branch of legislation.

In this regard, Kazakhstan has pursued significant legal reforms since 2020 to strengthen the protection of personal data and regulate actors that amass, analyse, and share digital footprints. Key changes include tightened restrictions, enhanced oversight, and mandatory standardisation for private data usage. For instance, whereas firms previously designed consent forms independently, new rules impose uniform requirements to mitigate non-compliance risks. The state also compelled internal governance policies on data processing, defining the operator's policy regarding the collection, processing and protection of personal data. Ongoing litigation and prosecutions further shape legal boundaries in this rapidly developing arena of personal data.

With this context, the chapter proceeds to analyse Kazakhstan's constitutional principles, statutory provisions, data transfer rules, and private international law issues implicated by the big data revolution and demanding greater coherence between law and technology to safeguard individual rights.

II. General Legal Framework of International Data Transfers and Data Protection

A. Constitutional Framework

The Constitution of the Republic of Kazakhstan forms the seminal foundation for data protection, enshrining informational privacy as an inviolable right with privileged status throughout the legal hierarchy. Adopted by national referendum on 30 August 1995, the Constitution mandates direct nationwide applicability superseding contradictory laws and other legal acts. Regarding data protection, Article 18 of the Constitution provides that everyone has the right to privacy, personal and family secrets, protection of their honour and dignity. It delineates specific protections over correspondence, communications data, and personal information, shielding individuals from undue collection or disclosure absent expressly defined procedural limitations.

This constitutional entrenchment of data privacy reflects enduring principles, though fluid technological conditions demand ongoing legislative elaboration. The law grants individuals comprehensive state safeguards against infringements upon not just their physical, mental and spiritual autonomy, but also the conditions that create the opportunity for realisation of personal needs, as long as it does not contradict the interests of the individual, society and the state. Such safeguards for personal inviolability also includes matters of personal privacy of individuals. Accordingly, privacy, personal and family secrets are protected by the Constitution and laws of the Republic of Kazakhstan. Such protection is subject to information about a person, giving an assessment of his character, appearance, health, financial condition, marital status, lifestyle, individual facts of his biography.[1] Debates linger regarding rights contours and permissible restrictions. However, the Constitution's primacy requires strict statutory conformity and furnishes grounds to challenge data privacy encroachments.

A significant part of the guarantees of the constitutional rights of privacy, personal and family secrets are contained in sectoral legislation. These include provisions on the inadmissibility of collecting, storing, using and distributing information about the private life of a person without his consent and are regulated by the sectoral law on personal data and their protection, on informatisation and a number of by-laws that contribute to the creation of a legal regime in which the violation of privacy is difficult or disadvantageous. However, the diffusion of protections across disparate statutes risks inconsistent application absent comprehensive legislation attuned to the digital age. Courts nevertheless consistently invoke these data protections during rights adjudication.

B. Statutory Framework

The legislation of the Republic of Kazakhstan on personal data and their protection is based on the Constitution of the Republic of Kazakhstan and consists of a mosaic of legislative, subordinate regulatory legal acts governing specific sectors, data types, and institutional practices. If an international treaty ratified by the Republic of Kazakhstan establishes rules other than those contained in national legislation, then the rules of the international treaty shall apply.

The main document regulating the relations in the sphere of personal data protection is the Law of the Republic of Kazakhstan 'On Personal Data and Their Protection' dated

[1] Constitution of the Republic of Kazakhstan, Scientific and Practical Commentary (Constitutional Council of the Republic of Kazakhstan, 2015), available at.

21 May 2013 No 94-V (the 'Personal Data Law'),[2] as well as other laws defining cases and features of personal data processing.

The Personal Data Law regulates public relations in the field of personal data, and also determines the purpose, principles and legal framework for activities related to the collection, processing and protection of personal data. It spells out the basic principles and procedure for collecting, processing and protecting personal data, the rights and obligations of the participants of personal data processing, as well as state regulation in the field of personal data and their protection.

Since the adoption of the Personal Data Law, it has been amended 19 times. In 2015, it was amended to stipulate that personal data shall be stored by the owner and (or) the operator, as well as by a third party in a database located in the territory of the Republic of Kazakhstan. In other words, personal data shall be stored on the territory of the Republic of Kazakhstan. In 2020, the concept of a person responsible for organising the processing of personal data in case the owner and (or) operator are legal entities and its following duties were introduced:

1. to exercise internal control over the compliance of the owner and (or) operator and its employees with the legislation of the Republic of Kazakhstan on personal data and their protection, including requirements for the protection of personal data;
2. to bring to the attention of employees of the owner and (or) operator the provisions of the legislation of the Republic of Kazakhstan on personal data and their protection on the processing of personal data, requirements for the protection of personal data;
3. to exercise control over the reception and processing of complaints of subjects or their legal representatives.

If previously it was not clear what the consent form for the collection and processing of personal data should contain, the amendments have included the following items:

1) name (surname, first name, patronymic (if it is indicated in the identity document), business identification number (individual identification number) of the operator;
2) surname, first name, patronymic (if it is indicated in the identity document) of the subject;
3) the term or period during which the consent to the collection, processing of personal data is valid;
4) information on the operator's ability or lack thereof to transfer personal data to third parties;
5) information on the presence or absence of trans-border transfer of personal data in the process of their processing;
6) information on the dissemination of personal data in publicly available sources;
7) list of collected data related to the subject;
8) other information determined by the owner and (or) operator.

[2] Law of the Republic of Kazakhstan, 'On Personal Data and Their Protection' (No 94-V, 21 May 2013) ('Personal Data Law').

The last amendments to the Personal Data Law were introduced on 11 December 2023. The amendments concerned the prohibition of collection, processing of hard copies of identity documents, except in cases of lack of integration with the informatisation objects of state bodies and (or) state legal entities, impossibility to identify the subject using technological means. In addition, the concept of 'violation of personal data security' was introduced, which is understood as a violation of personal data protection, which results in illegal dissemination, modification and destruction, unauthorised dissemination of transmitted, stored or otherwise processed personal data or unauthorised access to them. The amendments also established the obligation of the owner and (or) operator, which are obliged to notify the authorised body about such breach from the moment of detection of a breach of personal data security, indicating the contact details of the person responsible for the organisation of personal data processing (if any).

At the same time, the Personal Data Law does not apply to relations arising from:

- formation, storage and use of documents of the National Archival Fund of the Republic of Kazakhstan and other archival documents containing personal data, in accordance with the Law of the Republic of Kazakhstan dated 22 December 1998 No 326-I 'On the National Archival Fund and Archives';
- collection, processing and protection of personal data classified as state secrets, in accordance with the Law of the Republic of Kazakhstan dated 15 March 1999 No 349-I 'On State Secrets';
- collection, processing and protection of personal data in the course of operational-investigative activities, in accordance with the Law of the Republic of Kazakhstan dated 15 September 1994 No 154-XIII 'On Operational-Investigative Activities', in the course of intelligence activities, in accordance with the Law of the Republic of Kazakhstan dated 22 May 2010 No 277-IV 'On Foreign Intelligence', in the course of counterintelligence activities, in accordance with the Law of the Republic of Kazakhstan dated 21 December 1995 No 2710 'On the National Security Bodies of the Republic of Kazakhstan'.

The above laws contain their own measures to protect personal data. Other statutes layer additional bespoke data protections in realms like telecommunications, statistics, biometrics, and payments, including:

- Law of the Republic of Kazakhstan dated 24 November 2015 No 418-V 'On Informatisation' (the 'Informatisation Law'), which regulates security measures and protective actions in the processing, storage, distribution and protection of personal information contained in electronic information resources;
- Law of the Republic of Kazakhstan dated 30 December 2016 No 40-VI 'On Fingerprint and Genomic Registration', which regulates the relations regarding restricted personal data;
- Law of the Republic of Kazakhstan dated 5 July 2004 No 567-II 'On Communications' (the 'Communications Law'), which contains the features of cross-border transmission of service information about subscribers and (or) users of communication services;
- Law of the Republic of Kazakhstan dated 19 March 2010 No 257-IV 'On State Statistics', which ensures the confidentiality of primary statistical data by state statistics bodies during collection, processing and storage; and

- Law of the Republic of Kazakhstan dated 26 July 2016 No 11-VI 'On Payments and Payment Systems' establishes the obligation of the payment service provider, when providing payment services, to obtain consent from the subject of personal data when collecting and processing personal data.

In addition, there are policy documents that determine the directions for the development of national law, law enforcement and judicial systems, foreign policy and foreign economic activity, as well as legal education and legal propaganda, which may also affect the protection of personal data. For example, the Decree of the President of the Republic of Kazakhstan dated 15 October 2021 No 674 approved the Concept of the Legal Policy of the Republic of Kazakhstan until 2030[3] (the 'Concept'). The Concept mentions the main aspects of the transformation of the legal regulation of relations related to the use of the digital space. These aspects relate to the development of transit and communication potential and trust in the digital environment, as well as ensuring widespread compliance with the requirements established by law in the field of information security and personal data protection.

This fragmented approach bred gaps and inconsistencies, while rapid technological change further outstripped existing rules. There is also a need to resolve issues of inadmissibility of discrimination when using big data technology and restrictions on the uncontrolled use of gadgets to track citizens.[4] Recognising mounting deficiencies, Kazakhstan plans to overhaul its data protection laws by 2030,[5] looking to models like the European Union's (EU) General European Regulation on the Protection of Personal Data (GDPR) for guidance. At the same time, taking into account international experience, the plans for codifying legislation in the field of information and communication technologies, communications, data processing, digital assets, industrial automation, information security, machine learning and artificial intelligence, and protecting the rights of personal data subjects will be worked out.[6]

C. Data Protection Framework

i. *Influence of International Data Protection Frameworks*

a. CIS Model Law

Kazakhstan's personal data protection framework reflects the influential interplay of European and regional policy models. Kazakhstan is a member of Commonwealth of Independent States (CIS). In 1999, the Interparliamentary Assembly of Member Nations of CIS adopted its Model Law on Personal Data (the 'CIS Model Law') and forwarded it to the parliaments of the CIS member states and recommended it for use in the development of national legislation in the sphere of personal data protection.[7] Kazakhstan's Personal

[3] Concept of legal policy of the Republic of Kazakhstan until 2030 (Decree of the President of the Republic of Kazakhstan No 674, 15 October 2021), available at https://adilet.zan.kz/rus/docs/U2100000674.

[4] Concept of the legal policy of the Republic of Kazakhstan until 2030 (Decree of the President of the Republic of Kazakhstan No 674, 15 October 2021), Art 4.13, available at https://adilet.zan.kz/rus/docs/U2100000674.

[5] ibid.

[6] ibid.

[7] Inter-Parliamentary Assembly of Member Nations of the Commonwealth of Independent States (CIS), Resolution No 14-19 of 16 October 1999, On the Model Law 'On Personal Data', available at https://docs.cntd.ru/document/901818152.

Data Law closely tracked the 1999 CIS Model Law, sharing definitional approaches and data localisation requirements. This mirrored regional standards. For example, the Data Protection Law replicates the term 'database of personal data' in the CIS Model Law, which was mainly based on the assumption that processing of personal data occurs in the databases of personal data, and can also be found in the legislation of the other member states of CIS. When the first draft of Personal Data Law was announced, some experts expressed their opinions based on the CIS Model Law.[8] Some other experts critiqued the CIS model as lagging behind modern international principles.

b. GDPR

Kazakhstan's Personal Data Law was drafted before the adoption of the EU's GDPR. However, GDPR has played a significant role in the further development of Personal Data Law in recent years.

Some legal experts in Kazakhstan consider that the CIS Model Law does not fully reflect all international principles of dealing with personal data and GDPR can now become a good example for Kazakhstan of European standards in this area and contribute to the harmonisation of national legislation.[9] The recent changes clearly indicate Kazakhstan's movement towards GDPR. For example, in 2020 and 2021, Kazakhstan has introduced amendments to the data protection regime in the country based on the GDPR. These include, for example, the introduction of a specialised agency responsible for personal data protection.[10] These recent reforms reveal significant EU GDPR policy diffusion, incorporating generalised data protection agencies and other adaptations of European standards.

ii. Specific Provisions for Particular Sectors

Beyond Kazakhstan's core data protection law, sector-specific statutes tailor privacy safeguards for discrete realms like family, healthcare, labour, and media, which will now be discussed in the following subsections.

a. Family Code

The Code of the Republic of Kazakhstan dated 26 December 2011 No 518-IV 'On Marriage (Matrimony) and Family', in order to maintain the secrecy of adoption, allows changing the personal data of an adopted child, about which a new act record is made on state registration of birth with the conditional exception of an individual identification number from the National Register of Individual Identification Numbers.[11]

[8] IYu Loskutov and others, 'Expert Opinion on the Draft Law of the Republic of Kazakhstan 'On Personal Data'' (2013) 115, available at https://online.zakon.kz/Document/?doc_id=31071716&mode=p&page=3&pos=112;115#pos=112.

[9] Soros Kazakhstan Foundation, 'Personal Data Protection in Kazakhstan: A Dysfunctional Law and Cautious Movement towards GDPR' (4 June 2019), available at www.soros.kz/ru/personal-data-protection-in-kz/.

[10] 'Kazakhstan – The Impact of the GDPR Outside the EU' (*Lexology*, 30 September 2019), available at www.lexology.com/library/detail.aspx?g=72284bb5-a33a-465b-ab62-82d4f865f1bd.

[11] Code of the Republic of Kazakhstan On Marriage (Matrimony) and Family (No 518-IV ZRK, 26 December 2011) Art 98, available at https://adilet.zan.kz/rus/docs/K1100000518.

b. Labour Code

The Labor Code of the Republic of Kazakhstan dated 23 November 2015 No 414-V provides for the competence of the authorised state body for labour to ensure the confidentiality and protection of the employee's personal data contained in the unified system of accounting for employment contracts. Also, the employee has the right to ensure the protection of personal data stored by the employer, and the employer is obliged to collect, process and protect the employee's personal data in accordance with the legislation of the Republic of Kazakhstan on personal data and their protection.[12]

c. Civil Code

The Civil Code of the Republic of Kazakhstan dated 27 December 1994 contains norms regulating the right to a citizen's name and image. A citizen has the right to demand a ban on the use of his name, when this was done without his consent, except for cases provided for by the laws of the Republic of Kazakhstan. Damage caused to a citizen as a result of the misuse of his name is subject to compensation in accordance with the Civil Code. According to the Civil Code, no one has the right to use the image of any person without his consent, and in the event of death – without the consent of the heirs. Publication, reproduction and distribution of a pictorial work (picture, photograph, film, etc), in which another person is depicted, is allowed only with the consent of the person depicted, and after his death with the consent of his children and surviving spouse. Such consent is not required if it is established by legislative acts, or if the depicted person posed for a fee.[13] So, for exam ple, according to the Law on mass media (mass media), the mass media do not need the consent of the depicted person when preparing, publishing, reproducing and distributing mass media products in cases where this person is present or participates in spectacular cultural, mass, socially significant in the field of culture, mass sports events, peaceful assemblies and other public events; if the disseminated information contains an image of a person and information related to the official and (or) public activities of this person, and is also published by the person himself, his legal representative or authorised person in sources, access to which is not restricted; if the use of the depicted person is carried out in order to protect the constitutional order, protect public order, human rights and freedoms, health and morality of the population.[14]

d. Health Code

The Code of the Republic of Kazakhstan dated 7 July 2020 No 360-VI 'On the Health of the People and the Healthcare System' contains provisions that electronic information resources containing personal data of individuals (patients) are classified as confidential electronic information resources, collection, processing limited to the purposes for which they are

[12] Labor Code of the Republic of Kazakhstan (No 414-V ZRK, 23 November 2015) Arts 16, 22, 23, available at https://adilet.zan.kz/rus/docs/K1500000414.

[13] Civil Code of the Republic of Kazakhstan (No 268-XIII, 27 December 1994) Art 145, available at https://adilet.zan.kz/rus/docs/K940001000.

[14] Law of the Republic of Kazakhstan on Mass Media (No 451-I, 23 July 1999) Art 14, available at https://adilet.zan.kz/rus/docs/Z990000451.

collected. Access of medical personnel to electronic information resources containing personal data of individuals (patients) should be allowed only for the purpose of providing medical assistance to an individual (patient).[15]

e. Administrative Offenses Code

The Code of the Republic of Kazakhstan on Administrative Offenses dated 5 July 2014 No 235-V provides for administrative liability for violation of legislation on the protection of personal data. Liability is established in relation to:

- officials, private notaries, private bailiffs, lawyers, legal entities for illegal collection and (or) processing of personal data;[16]
- owner, operator or third party for non-compliance with measures to protect personal data;[17]
- a unified accumulative pension fund, a voluntary accumulative pension fund for violating the procedure for accounting for pension savings on personal accounts of contributors (beneficiaries);[18]
- mass media for the dissemination in the mass media or over telecommunications networks of personal and biometric data, which makes it possible to identify the identity of a minor who has suffered as a result of an offence;[19]
- the owner and (or) operator of the database containing personal data, or a third party for failure to implement or improper implementation of measures to protect personal data;[20]
- officials and other persons for the use of electronic information resources containing personal data on individuals in order to cause them property and (or) moral damage, restrict their exercise of rights and freedoms.[21]

f. Criminal Code

The Criminal Code of the Republic of Kazakhstan dated 3 July 2014 No 226-V provides for criminal liability for:

- non-compliance with measures to protect personal data by a person who is entrusted with the obligation to take such measures, if this act caused significant harm to the rights and legitimate interests of persons;
- illegal collection and dissemination of information about the private life of a person, constituting his personal or family secret, without his consent, or causing significant

[15] Code of the Republic of Kazakhstan 'On the Health of the People and the Healthcare System' (No 360-VI, 7 July 2020) Art 62, available at https://adilet.zan.kz/rus/docs/K2000000360.

[16] Code of the Republic of Kazakhstan on Administrative Offenses (No 235-V ZRK, 5 July 2014) Art 79, available at https://adilet.zan.kz/rus/docs/K1400000235.

[17] ibid.

[18] ibid, Art 264.

[19] ibid, Art 451.

[20] ibid, Art 79.

[21] ibid, Art 641.

harm to the rights and legitimate interests of a person as a result of illegal collection and (or) processing (except for distribution) of other personal data.[22]

In sum, sectoral specificity also enables nuanced protections attuned to each domain's sensitivities. However, such dispersed, context-dependent measures can breed inconsistencies absent overarching principles. Kazakhstan's multifaceted statutory mixture thus presents trade-offs between coherence and tailored treatment. Ongoing reforms wrestle with integrating flexible responsiveness within systematic rights.

iii. Key Definitions

a. 'Data Users', 'Data Processors' and 'Data Sub-Contractors'

Such terms as 'data users', 'data processors' and 'data sub-contractors' do not exist in the legislation of the Republic of Kazakhstan. As per Article 7(1) of the Law on Personal Data and Its Protection, the collection and processing of personal data is carried out by database owners, database operators and third parties. Thus, it can be concluded that the participants of processing of personal data can be (1) a database owner, (2) a database operator, (3) a data subject, and (4) a third party. The Law on Personal Data and Its Protection gives the definition to all those terms, which is as follows:

> subject of personal data (hereinafter – subject) – individual, to which the personal data are referred;
>
> owner of the database containing personal data (hereinafter – the owner), – a state body, individual and (or) a legal entity, exercising in accordance with the laws of the Republic of Kazakhstan the right to own, use and dispose of the database containing personal data;
>
> operator of the database containing personal data (hereinafter – the operator) – a state body, individual and (or) legal entity that collects, processes and protects personal data;
>
> third party – a person who is not the subject, owner and (or) the operator, but is related to them (him) by circumstances or legal relationships for the collection, processing and protection of personal data.[23]

A database operator seems to be a concept close to the term 'data processors' by definition.

b. Personal and Non-Personal Data

Personal Data Law does not distinguish personal and non-personal data. Meanwhile, there is no such concept as 'non-personal data' in Kazakhstan's legislation. Personal Data Law only gives a definition of 'personal data' as 'information related to a determined or determinable, on the basis of such information, data subject, recorded on electronic, paper and (or) other tangible media'.[24] This umbrella term encompasses all data attachable to a data subject.

[22] Criminal Code of the Republic of Kazakhstan (No 226-V, 3 July 2014) Art 147, available at https://adilet.zan.kz/rus/docs/K1400000226.
[23] Personal Data Law (n 2) Art 1.
[24] ibid.

c. Anonymised, Pseudonymised, or Encrypted Data

Kazakhstan's legislation does not contain the concepts 'anonymised data' or 'pseudonymized data'. While these terms are absent, the Personal Data Law incorporates a related notion of 'depersonalised' data. This refers to actions that make it impossible to determine whether personal data belongs to the subject of personal data.[25] Even though depersonalised data are not excluded from the scope of Personal Data Law, the data owner, operator, as well as third parties are obliged to protect personal data finishes with depersonalisation of personal data.[26] Personal Data Law also specifies that when processing personal data for historical, statistical, sociological, scientific research, the data owner and operator, as well as a third party, are obliged to depersonalise such data.[27]

The term 'encryption of data' or 'encrypted data' arises in some legacy statutes which are no longer in force. The 'encryption of data' is defined as the process of converting the original data into encrypted data in order to conceal its content, using cryptographic keys.[28] Robust encryption could render data essentially anonymised absent decryption keys.

d. Domestic and Cross-Border/International Transfers

The law permits unfettered domestic data sharing given user consent or statutory exceptions specified in the Personal Data Law. Meanwhile, cross-border data transfers are subject to specific regulation different from domestic data transfers. The only distinction of cross-border transfers of personal data from domestic transfers, by definition, is that cross-border transfers of personal data occurs outside the jurisdiction of the Republic of Kazakhstan.[29]

iv. Privacy Regulator

Kazakhstan established a dedicated personal data protection regulator, the Ministry of Digital Development, Innovations and Aerospace Industry (MDAI), conferring expansive oversight authority.

The MDAI is authoried to:[30]

1) participate in the implementation of state policy in the field of personal data and their protection;
2) develop the procedure of implementation by the owner and (or) operator, as well as by the third party, of personal data protection measures;
3) elaborate the rules for determining by the owner and (or) operator the list of personal data necessary and sufficient for the performance of their tasks;

[25] ibid.
[26] ibid, Art 22.
[27] ibid, Art 17.
[28] Order No 86 of the Chairman of the National Security Committee of the Republic of Kazakhstan 'On Approval of the Rules for Depositing Cryptographic Information Security Tools in the Republic of Kazakhstan' (22 June 2001), available at https://adilet.zan.kz/rus/docs/V010001601.
[29] Personal Data Law (n 2) Art 16.
[30] ibid Art 27-1.

4) examine the requests of the subject or his/her legal representative on the compliance of the content of personal data and the manner of their processing with the purposes of their processing, and taking the appropriate decision;
5) take measures to bring the persons, who allowed violation of the legislation of the Republic of Kazakhstan on personal data and its protection, to responsibility, established by the laws of the Republic of Kazakhstan;
6) demand from the owner and (or) the operator, as well as the third party to clarify, block or destroy unreliable or illegally obtained personal data;
7) implement measures aimed at improvement of protection of the subjects' rights;
8) establish the Consultative Council on personal data protection and personal data protection, as well as determining the procedure of its formation and functioning;
9) approve the rules for the collection, processing of personal data;
10) approve the rules for security examination of the processes of storage, processing and distribution of the restricted personal data, contained in the electronic information resources, in coordination with the National Security Committee of the Republic of Kazakhstan;
11) approve the rules of functioning of the state service of control over access to personal data;
12) approve integration of the non-state objects of informatisation with the objects of informatisation of the state bodies and (or) state legal entities, under which personal data transfer and (or) access to personal data is provided;
13) approve rules of integration with the state service of access control to personal data; and
14) exercise other powers stipulated by laws of the Republic of Kazakhstan, acts of the President of the Republic of Kazakhstan and the Government of the Republic of Kazakhstan.

With regard to the sanctioning powers, the MDAI is responsible for considering cases in regards to administrative violations related to personal data protection. Upon the complaints of citizens and legal entities, the MDAI has the right to initiate an inspection against the violator in order to establish the offence and bring to responsibility. In case of confirmation of an offence, the MDAI initiates an administrative case and brings to responsibility for violations stipulated by Articles 79, 639, 640 and 641 of the Code of Administrative Offenses of the Republic of Kazakhstan.[31] For this purpose, the complaint must contain sufficient data indicating the signs of an administrative offence – materials confirming the fact of violation, the subject who committed the offence and the period of its occurrence. After consideration of the case on administrative offence, the MDAI makes a decision on imposing an administrative penalty or dismissal of the case. Anonymous complaints are not considered by the MDAI.

As per the statistical data published by the Portal of Legal Statistics and Special Records, in 2023 the MDAI considered overall 5,309 cases of administrative offences and applied sanctions with regard to 4,949 cases. With regard to the violations in the sphere of personal data protection, the MDAI handled 181 cases and applied sanctions for 168 cases for the entire year of 2023. As a result of the applied sanctions for the violations in the sphere of

[31] Code of the Republic of Kazakhstan on Administrative Offenses (n 16) Art 692-2.

personal data protection, fines in the overall amount of 3,436,280 tenge were paid to the state budget.[32]

This centralised regulatory concentration aims to further institutionalise data protections and provide firmer implementation after years of ambiguous dispersion across various agencies. Converting robust formal authorities into genuine on-the-ground effectiveness remains Kazakhstan's foremost data protection imperative.

III. Legal Bases, Mechanisms and Exceptions for International Data Transfers and Data Protection

A. International Data Transfers

The Kazakh data protection framework uses the term cross-border transfer of personal data, which is defined as transfer of personal data to the territory of foreign countries. They are regulated under specific provisions distinct from domestic exchanges. The main laws regulating international data transfers are (1) the Personal Data Law and (2) the Communications Law. While the Personal Data Law regulates cross-border transfer of personal data, requirements and grounds for such transfers in general, peculiarities of cross-border transfer of professional information about subscribers and users of communication services are laid down in the Communications Law.

i. Adequacy Findings or Whitelists (Jurisdictions to which International Transfers Could be Made without Consent or Other Compliance Requirements) and Blacklists

According to Article 16 (2) of the Personal Data Law, cross-border transfer of personal data to the territory of foreign states is carried out only if these states ensure the adequate protection of personal data. However, criteria for determining which states ensure the adequate protection of personal data are not set out in Kazakh legislation. Contrary to neighbouring Russian Federation, where there is a list of foreign states that provide adequate protection of the rights of personal data subjects,[33] Kazakhstan eschews common mechanisms like so-called 'whitelists' or 'blacklists' for the purposes of data transfers.[34]

Unofficially, the regulator endorses transfers to nations maintaining personal data protection treaties with Kazakhstan, implying these partnerships ensure acceptable standards. Kazakhstan has such an agreement with 28 European countries.[35] This agreement also

[32] Summary by the Bodies of Ministry of Digital Development, Innovations and Aerospace Industry (2023 January – December), available at https://qamqor.gov.kz/crimestat/statistics.

[33] Order No 128 of Roskomnadzor 'On Approval of the List of Foreign States Providing Adequate Protection of the Rights of Personal Data Subjects' (05 August 2022), available at https://rulaws.ru/acts/Prikaz-Roskomnadzora-ot-05.08.2022-N-128/.

[34] Kazakhstan – Data Transfers (*OneTrust Data Guidance*, October 2023), available at www.dataguidance.com/notes/kazakhstan-data-transfers.

[35] Enhanced Partnership and Cooperation Agreement between the European Union and its Member States, of the one part, and the Republic of Kazakhstan, of the other part, available at https://adilet.zan.kz/rus/docs/Z1600000475.

contains a reference to accession of the Republic of Kazakhstan to the Council of Europe Convention for the Protection of Individuals with regard to Automatic Processing of Personal Data and its Additional Protocol. But the lack of codified whitelists leaves compliance obligations unclear for both state and private actors.

ii. Consent of Data Subjects as Exception to Existence of Privacy Safeguards Overseas

While Kazakhstan lacks formalised whitelists, Article 16(3) of the Personal Data Law sets out certain conditions under which cross-border transfer of personal data to foreign countries that do not provide personal data protection can be performed. Consent offers a primary exception. Article 16(2) permits external sharing absent adequate overseas protections if the data subject or his/her legal representative consents.

However, governmental and non-governmental entities face differential consent requirements. Governmental organisations (including state entities) must utilise an integrated digital system to document consent. Private organisations can use independent platforms or formats to confirm consent.[36]

Beyond consent, other conditions provided for in Article 16(3) of the Personal Data Law are:

- in cases provided by international treaties ratified by the Republic of Kazakhstan;
- in cases provided by the laws of the Republic of Kazakhstan, if it is necessary for protection of the constitutional system, protection of public order, human and civil rights and freedoms, health and morality; and
- protection of constitutional human and citizen's rights and freedoms if obtaining consent of the subject or his legal representative is impossible.

iii. Contracts

Unlike some regional counterparts like the Russian Federation and the Republic of Uzbekistan, Kazakhstan does not recognise contracts as an independent basis for cross-border data transfers absent user consent.[37] There is a special norm in Kazakh legislation with regard to the cross-border transfer of personal data stating that processing of personal data in the form of cross-border transfer of personal data is carried out with the consent of the subject, except cases provided in Article 16 of the Personal Data Law.[38] Article 16(3) of the Personal Data Law omits contracts from exceptions to the adequacy requirement in foreign countries. Even when there is a contract with a data subject, including one for cross-border transfer, there is still a need for obtaining consent of the data subject for processing his/her personal data.

Furthermore, it is not required to conclude a contract with a data subject for the purposes of international data transfers. However, the law still obligates owners and operators to

[36] Personal Data Law (n 2) Art 8-2.

[37] Kazakhstan – Data Protection Overview (*OneTrust Data Guidance*, August 2023), available at < www.dataguidance.com/notes/kazakhstan-data-protection-overview.

[38] Personal Data Law (n 2) Art 7.

take necessary measures, including legal, organisational and technical, to protect personal data. Contractual clauses governing compliant transfers may provide advisable structure, if legally insufficient alone. So contracts can complement consent authorisations as a best practice, if not an outright exemption.

iv. Asia-Pacific Economic Cooperation Cross-Border Privacy Rules System

The Republic of Kazakhstan is not a member of the Asia-Pacific Economic Cooperation (APEC), nor has the Republic of Kazakhstan joined or lodged a Notice of Intent to participate in the APEC Cross-Border Privacy Rules (CBPR) System.

v. Any Privacy Certification Schemes, Trustmarks or Privacy Seals (International)

Kazakh law does not recognise certification schemes, privacy seals and trustmarks delivered in third countries as valid means for parties carrying out cross-border data transfers to demonstrate compliance with local data protection laws.

Kazakhstan has its own security certification scheme which is mandatory when transferring data through internet resources using .KZ and (or) .ҚAZ domain names.

B. International Data Protection and Liability

i. Specific Requirements or Policies for Data Processing and Retention

As a general rule, there are two conditions for the collection and processing of personal data:

- The consent of the data subject to the processing of his personal data is obtained. Consent must be given in writing or through verified digital platforms.
- The collection and processing must remain necessary and proportional for specified legitimate purposes detailed in approved lists. The data owner and operator must analyse proposed data activities,[39] determine the list of personal data necessary and sufficient to perform the tasks they carry out in a specially approved form, and indicate the purposes of their collection and processing within the framework of the tasks. The purposes should be unambiguous, legitimate and correspond to the tasks carried out by the owner and/or the operator.

In a special form where personal data is indicated, it is necessary to indicate:

- the name of the task, including functions, powers, responsibilities;
- the purpose of collection and processing within the framework of the task being carried out;

[39] On approval of the Rules for determining by the owner and (or) operator the list of personal data necessary and sufficient to perform the tasks they carry out (Decree of the Government of the Republic of Kazakhstan No 1214, 12 November 2013, available at https://adilet.zan.kz/rus/docs/P1300001214#z5.

- the name of personal data for a specific purpose;
- an indication of documents or regulatory legal acts that have direct indications of the tasks carried out by the owner and (or) operator.

At the same time, consent of the subject to the collection and processing of data is not required in the following cases:

a. implementation of the activities of law enforcement agencies, courts and other authorised state bodies that initiate and consider cases of administrative offences, enforcement proceedings;
b. implementation of state statistical activities;
c. the use of personal data by state bodies for statistical purposes with the obligatory condition of their depersonalisation;
d. implementation of international treaties ratified by the Republic of Kazakhstan;
e. protection of the constitutional rights and freedoms of a person and a citizen, if obtaining the consent of the subject or his legal representative is impossible;
f. carrying out the legal professional activities of a journalist and (or) the activities of television, radio channels, periodicals, news agencies, online publications or scientific, literary or other creative activities, subject to the requirements of the legislation of the Republic of Kazakhstan to ensure the rights and freedoms of man and citizen;
g. publication of personal data in accordance with the laws of the Republic of Kazakhstan, including personal data of candidates for elected public office;
h. non-fulfillment by the subject of his obligations to provide personal data in accordance with the laws of the Republic of Kazakhstan;
i. receipt by the state body that regulates, controls and supervises the financial market and financial organisations, information from individuals and legal entities in accordance with the legislation of the Republic of Kazakhstan;
j. receipt by state revenue bodies for tax (customs) administration and (or) control of information from individuals and legal entities in accordance with the laws of the Republic of Kazakhstan;
k. transfer for storage of a backup copy of electronic information resources containing personal data of limited access to a single national backup platform for storing electronic information resources in cases provided for by the laws of the Republic of Kazakhstan;
l. use of personal data of business entities related directly to their business activities for the formation of a register of business partners, subject to the requirements of the legislation of the Republic of Kazakhstan; and
m. other cases where the laws of the Republic of Kazakhstan provides that consent to the collection and processing of personal data from the subject is not required.

It should also be noted that upon the achievement of the purpose of the collection and processing of personal data, such personal data must be destroyed.[40] The processing which takes place in the above-mentioned cases is also subject to this requirement.

[40] Personal Data Law (n 2) Art 25.

ii. Regulations on Legal Ownership of Data Protection and Privacy Rights

Kazakhstan's Constitution enshrines informational privacy as an inviolable right, safeguarding individuals' control over personal data and dignity. Legal protections cover private life details, communications, reputation, home, and professional confidences.[41]

The constitutional right to privacy includes several key elements:

- a ban on the collection, storage, use and dissemination of information about the private life of a person without his consent;
- the right to control information about oneself;
- the right to protection of honour and good name;
- the right to protection of personal data;
- the right to secrecy of communication (sometimes formalised as a separate right);
- the right to the inviolability of the home (sometimes formalised as a separate right);
- medical secrecy, adoption secrecy, confessional secrecy and other types of professional secrecy, and more.

A citizen also has the right to demand a ban on the use of his name when this was done without his consent, except for cases provided for by the laws, according to Article 15(8) of the Civil Code.

The Personal Data Law and other laws delineates specific instances where the collection and processing of personal data may proceed without consent of the subject or his legal representative.[42] This includes certain bank customer data during corporate reorganisations.

Kazakh law provides various mechanisms to safeguard against illegal intrusions upon privacy and to compensate for harm caused by such actions, including administrative, civil, criminal, and international liability. These legal protections aim to uphold individuals' honour and dignity when rights are violated.[43]

For example, criminal procedure and administrative offence laws guarantee citizens' rights to private and family life during legal proceedings, restricting infringements absent explicit statutory basis. Article 16 of the Code of Criminal Procedure of the Republic of Kazakhstan states that no one has the right to collect, store, use and disseminate information about the private life of a person without his consent, except as otherwise provided by law. The criminal executive legislation also provides that the private life of a convict that has become known to certain classes of people may not be disclosed without the convict's consent. It is also considered an administrative offence for participants in the national preventive mechanism to disclose information about the private life of a person that became known to them during preventive visits, without the consent of this person, if this action does not contain signs of a criminally punishable act.[44]

Criminal penalties apply to the illegal collection of information about the private life of a person constituting his personal or family secret without his consent or causing significant harm to the rights and legitimate interests of a person as a result of illegal collection or

[41] Constitution of the Republic of Kazakhstan, Scientific and Practical Commentary (n 1).
[42] ibid.
[43] ibid, 167.
[44] Code of the Republic of Kazakhstan on Administrative Offenses (n 16) Arts 15, 16.

processing of other personal data, and non-compliance with measures to protect personal data by a person who is entrusted with the obligation to take such measures, if this act caused significant harm to the rights and legitimate interests of persons.[45] For the commission of the above criminal offences are punishable by a fine, or restriction of liberty or imprisonment from two to three years, depending on the gravity of the act committed.

More severe punishments attach where the abuse is committed by a person using his official position or special technical means designed to secretly obtain information, or through illegal access to electronic information resources, an information system or illegal interception of information transmitted over an information and communication network, or in order to derive benefits and advantages for oneself or for other persons or organisations, as well as the dissemination of information specified in section IV of this chapter in a public speech, publicly displayed work, in the media or using telecommunications networks (Article 147.3 of the Criminal Code).[46]

iii. Extraterritorial Effect of Laws on Data Protection and Privacy

The CIS countries concluded an Agreement on Mutual Legal Assistance in Administrative Matters in the Field of Personal Data Exchange dated 18 December 2020 to establish mutual legal assistance on administrative issues in the field of personal data exchange.[47] The 2020 Agreement between Azerbaijan, Russia, Armenia, Tajikistan, Turkmenistan, Kazakhstan, Uzbekistan, Ukraine, and Moldova allows member states to request specified categories of personal data, including on citizenship, residence status, property ownership, visa history, and criminal or administrative penalties.

The Agreement imposes confidentiality duties, prohibiting parties from disclosing the existence of a data request, its content or related actions absent consent. In the event that the requested party cannot comply with the conditions of confidentiality, it shall notify the requesting party of this before making the above information public. Requesting states cannot utilise personal data obtained on the basis of the agreement for purposes beyond the stated purpose without permission. Onward transfers to third parties or countries also require the requested state's authorisation, which may be granted or which may be refused in whole or in part.

Overall, the CIS Agreement establishes a mechanism for controlled cross-border data sharing while mandating protections for individuals' information. Member states must ensure the protection of information about an individual from unauthorised or accidental access to it, destruction, modification, blocking, copying, provision or distribution, as well as from other illegal actions in relation to such information. Once transferred abroad under the Agreement, personal data remains protected by both the Agreement and the recipient state's national law.

Kazakhstan's current data protection laws do not explicitly provide for their extraterritorial application. Generally, the laws of the Republic of Kazakhstan apply within the territory

[45] Criminal Code of the Republic of Kazakhstan (n 22), Art 147(1), (2), available at https://adilet.zan.kz/rus/docs/K1400000226.

[46] ibid, Art 147.

[47] The Agreement was ratified by the Law of the Republic of Kazakhstan (No 113-VII ZRK, 1 April 2022), available at https://adilet.zan.kz/rus/docs/Z2200000113.

of Kazakhstan, unless specific reference to their extraterritorial application are provided for in such laws. As per the Personal Data Law, it regulates the public relations in the scope of personal data, as well as determines the purpose, principles and legal bases of activity, related with collection, processing and protection of personal data.[48] However, the Personal Data Law does not determine its scope by territory and persons. The MDAI has not issued any official clarification on this matter either.

There have been two contradictory statements by two state bodies of Kazakhstan in this regard. On 10 December 2015 the Ministry of Industry and Infrastructural Development of the Republic of Kazakhstan (former Ministry for Investments and Development) suggested that personal data localisation requirements apply in any case, if the personal data of a Kazakhstan's resident are being processed. On the contrary, on 5 January 2016 the Ministry of Internal Affairs of the Republic of Kazakhstan publicly stated that the Personal Data Law, including personal data localisation requirements, applies only to relations connected with the collection, processing, and protection of personal data in the territory of Kazakhstan.[49]

However, it is generally considered that Kazakhstan's data protection laws apply to both individuals and legal entities in Kazakhstan and foreign individuals and legal entities located in Kazakhstan,[50,51] while the extraterritorial application of such laws cannot also be excluded.

iv. Data Breach Notification

Until 2024 Kazakhstan's data protection laws did not impose general notification duties to notify either the authorised body or the subject of personal data following a personal data breach. The exception was cases when data leakage occurs at e-government informatisation objects and is of decisive importance for state information and communication infrastructure objects, in which case the owners of the relevant objects notify the technical service of the state.

Under the Personal Data Law, the owners and operators are obliged to block personal data related to the subject, if there is information about a violation of the conditions for their collection, processing, to prevent unauthorised access to personal data. They must also delete personal data collected and processed in violation of the law, upon the request of the subject or his legal representative, or by decision of the court or other authorised state bodies.

The lack of a general data breach notification mandate was a gap in Kazakhstan's legal framework. Notification serves vital functions – curbing the growth of misconduct by the owners and operators of databases containing personal data, enabling individuals to take protective steps, and deterring negligent data handling. As databases expand, the risks of

[48] Personal Data Law (n 2) preamble.

[49] Kazakhstan – Data Protection Overview (n 37).

[50] Aset Shyngyssov and Bakhytzhan Kadyrov, 'Data Protection in Kazakhstan: Overview' (*Thomson Reuters*, 2023) 2, available at https://uk.practicallaw.thomsonreuters.com/w-007-8602?transitionType=Default&contextData=(sc.Default)&firstPage=true.

[51] Alexander Chumachenko, 'Problematic Issues of Localisation of Personal Data' (*Chambers and Partners*, 29 November 2016), available at https://chambers.com/articles/problem-issues-of-personal-data-localization-in-kazakhstan.

leakage of personal data due to circumstances such as violation by unrecognised persons and other human factors grow, with potentially serious consequences. Beyond direct individual harms, unreported breaches inhibit enforcement and accountability.

The latest amendments to the Personal Data Law compel data owners and operators to notify the competent authority about data breach immediately from the moment of detection of such personal data security breach, indicating the contact details of the person responsible for the organisation of personal data processing.[52] However, this amendment will become effective starting from 1 July 2024. Embedding this duty in law would modernise Kazakhstan's data protection regime consistent with global standards.

IV. Data Security and Data Localisation

A. Data Security and Localisation Requirements

i. Information Security

Kazakhstan's concept of 'Information Security' was approved by the President of Kazakhstan on 14 November 2011.[53] This concept provides a multidimensional definition of information security encompassing both technical and socio-political dimensions.

Technically, information security involves the protection of national information resources, information systems, information and telecommunication infrastructure from unauthorised access, use, disclosure, violation, alteration, reading, verification, recording or destruction to ensure the integrity, confidentiality and availability of information.

Socio-politically, information security means protecting Kazakhstan's national information space and mass information distribution systems from purposeful negative information and organisational impact that can harm the national interests. This aspect addresses risks from purposeful dissemination of detrimental content or coordinated informational actions.

a. Data Localisation

When the Personal Data Law was first adopted, it lacked data localisation requirements. In 2015, the data localisation requirement was introduced by way of amendment to Article 12(2) of the Personal Data Law, now requiring personal data storage within the country by owners, operators, and third-party processors.

It might be argued that under Article 12(2) if either the owner, the operator, or a third party stores the database in Kazakhstan, there is no need for others to also store such databases in Kazakhstan. This interpretation may be supported by the view that localisation mandates undermine data flows, increase costs, and encourage local data misuse while

[52] The Law of the Republic of Kazakhstan On Making Amendments and Additions to Certain Legislative Acts of the Republic of Kazakhstan on the Issues of Information Security, Informatization and Digital Assets (No 44-VIII ZRK, 11 December) Art 1, available at https://adilet.zan.kz/rus/docs/Z2300000044#z50.

[53] 'Kazakhstan – Octopus Cybercrime Community – Cybercrime Policies/Strategies' (*Council of Europe*, 2024), available at www.coe.int/fr/web/octopus/country-wiki-ap/-/asset_publisher/CmDb7M4RGb4Z/content/kazakhstan?_101_INSTANCE_CmDb7M4RGb4Z_viewMode=view/.

providing marginal security advantages over sound cybersecurity practices. On the other hand, the Personal Data Law does not expressly provide that fulfilment of obligation by one party releases the others from such obligation.

It is argued that such a localisation requirement imposes extra burden on foreign tech firms operating in Kazakhstan, because establishing and maintaining a localised data service requires staffing, training, engineering (ie, development, maintenance, debugging), backup, and local physical infrastructure that meets certain standards to physically store data. Data localisation requirements are also viewed as a weapon of the Government which is used against Big Tech companies to assert state authority and limit their autonomy.[54]

The Data localisation requirement is also considered to create new risks and challenges for foreign tech firms for a number of reasons. First of all, Kazakhstan's lack of safeguards for cybersecurity is noted given that in 2019, a database containing information pertaining to approximately 11 million people was leaked from the Central Election Commission, resulting in a massive scandal. One solution to this problem would be 'data sharding', or breaking up data into smaller chunks and distributing across data nodes. However, Kazakhstan's data localisation requirement is considered to block such 'sharding' of data.[55] Furthermore, there have also been concerns that data localisation makes data more vulnerable to security attacks, rather than more secure.[56]

Such a localisation requirement parallels the legislation of other countries of Central Asia but differs in scope. For example, Uzbekistan imposes broader localisation rules covering the collection, systematisation, and storage of personal data, while the Kazakh localisation requirement is only applicable to the focuses more narrowly on storage. Furthermore, Uzbek Law only requires owners and operators to comply with the localisation requirement, whereas Kazakh Law also requires third parties to store personal data in its territory.

B. Data Security and Localisation Requirements for Particular Sectors

Apart from the general data localisation requirement set forth in the Personal Data Law, there are various sector-specific data localisation requirements.

i. Communications Sector

The communications sector faces particular regulations under the Communications Law. According to Article 15(1)(2), service information on subscribers must be stored in Kazakhstan. Cross-border transfer is prohibited, except to serve customers located abroad. Covered service information includes subscriber numbers and IDs, device IDs, billing details, network locations, IP addresses, and other connectivity and traffic information. This law has also been supplemented by the Government Resolution of the Republic of Kazakhstan No 246 dated 30 March 2010 regarding subscriber details.

[54] Kenddrick Chan et al, *Against the Grain: The Data Regulatory Regimes of Kazakhstan and Uzbekistan vis-à-vis Russia, China, and Big Tech* (LSE IDEAS DIGITAL IR | WORKING PAPER 10/2022) 7, available at http://eprints.lse.ac.uk/117154/.

[55] ibid.

[56] ibid.

ii. Informatisation Sector

Kazakhstan's Informatisation Law also imposes data localisation requirements for certain digital systems. The law covers organisations that develop electronic databases, websites, software, and hardware for organisational, socio-economic, scientific, and technical purposes.

Article 56 requires organisations to store electronic databases containing personal data in the Republic of Kazakhstan. Article 56-1 which resulted from the 2020 amendment further requires internet resources with the registered domain names.KZ and/or.KAZ to be located in the Kazakhstan segment of the Internet.

The introduction of this new localisation rule, as the Information Security Committee of the MDAI explains, was necessitated by the need to maximise domestic data centre usage and network infrastructure, which has traditionally been underused. The Information Security Committee further explains that websites (website, web application, web service) using domain.KZ must be hosted on a computer server (rented, owned, cloud hosting, VDS hosting, virtual hosting) located in a data centre (server room, office) in any city of Kazakhstan. The server must be connected to a Kazakhstani internet service provider and use a Kazakhstani IP address (dedicated or shared).[57] This requirement can also be found in the approved domain registration application form.[58]

C. Data Security and Localisation Requirements for Particular Types of Data

In addition to sector-specific rules, Kazakhstan also imposes localisation requirements for specific types of sensitive data.

i. Personal Data of Limited Access

Apart from the general data localisation requirement set out in the Personal Data Law, regulations also mandate data localisation for the processing and storage for personal data of limited access carried out through informatisation objects.[59] This heightened protection covers categories like health, religious, and biometrics information. While the general localisation rule only requires storing databases of personal data on the territory of Kazakhstan, this rule also covers such acts as collection and processing.

a. Biological Information

Kazakh law defines 'biometric data' like biological and physiological characteristics as a form of personal information. Most biometric data are considered as publicly available

[57] Letter from the Information Security Committee of the Ministry of Digital Development, Innovation and Aerospace Industry of the Republic of Kazakhstan dated 20 December 2020 No 27-1-27/910-I (*Kazakh Center Network Information*, 20 December 2020) 36, available at https://online.zakon.kz/Document/?doc_id=32729960&pos=52;-36#pos=52.

[58] Order of the Minister for Defense and Aerospace Industry of the Republic of Kazakhstan 'On the Approval of the Rules for Registration, Use, and Distribution of Domain Names in the Area of Kazakhstani Segment of the Internet' (No 38/NK, as amended on 13 March 2018) (in Russian).

[59] ibid.

personal data, thereby being subject to general localisation requirements. However, highly sensitive biometric data such as fingerprints and genomic information,[60] are considered as personal data of limited access and face stricter in-country controls.

b. State Secrets

Kazakhstan's Law on State Secrets does not expressly mandate domestic storage of classified information. However, in practice, state secrets likely face residency requirements given national security sensitivities.

V. Issues in Private International Law

A. Litigations Involving Cross-Border Data Transfer and Privacy

Kazakhstan permits the cross-border transfer of personal data provided the destination countries ensure adequate protection.[61] Domestic laws establish administrative and criminal penalties for data protection violations, applicable to both citizens and foreign entities operating in Kazakhstan.[62]

[60] Law of the Republic of Kazakhstan 'On Fingerprint and Genomic Registration' (No 40-VI, 30 December 2016 with amendments and additions as of 1 January 2024) Art 8, 51, available at https://online.zakon.kz/Document/?doc_id=33276266&pos=146;-51#pos=146.

[61] Personal Data Law (n 2) Art 16.4.

[62] The Code of the Republic of Kazakhstan on Administrative Offenses (n 16) Art 79.1: '... Illegal collection and (or) processing of personal data, if these actions do not contain any signs of a criminal offense shall entail a fine on individuals in the amount of ten, on officials, private notaries, private enforcement agents, advocates, subjects of small entrepreneurship or non-profit organization – in the amount of twenty, on subjects of medium entrepreneurship – in the amount of thirty, on subjects of large entrepreneurship – in the amount of seventy monthly calculation indices ...';

ibid, Art 451.4: 'Distribution with violation of requirements of the legislation of the Republic of Kazakhstan in mass media or on networks of telecommunications of the personal and biometric data, other information allowing to identify the personality of minor, injured illegal acts (inaction) and also the suspect and (or) the administrative and (or) criminal offense accused of commission except for the minors found by court guilty of commission of heavy or especially serious crimes, including information on their parents and other lawful representatives subject to fine natural persons at a rate of five, on officials, small business entities or non-profit organizations – at a rate of twenty five, on subjects of average business – at a rate of fifty, on subjects of large business – at a rate of hundred monthly settlement indicators ...';

ibid, Art 641.1: '1. The violation of the law of the Republic of Kazakhstan about informatization made in a look: 1) failure or inadequate implementation by the proprietor or owner of the information systems containing personal data, proprietor and (or) operator of the base, containing personal data, as well as by the third party of measures for their protection; 2) violations of uniform requirements in the field of information and communication technologies and ensuring information security; 3) No. 237-VI is excluded by the Law of the Republic of Kazakhstan dated 18.03.2019 (shall be enforced upon expiry of ten calendar days after its first official publication); 4) non-presentations of the developed software, initial program codes (if available), a set of settings for licensed software of "electronic government" informatization objects to the service integrator of "electronic government"; 5) losses of originals of technical documentation on papers; 6) industrial operation of "electronic government" informatization object without an act of positive test result for compliance with information security requirements – subject to fine natural persons at a rate of ten, on officials, small business entities or non-profit organizations – at a rate of fifteen, on subjects of average business – at a rate of thirty, on subjects of large business – at a rate of hundred monthly settlement indicators ...'

Criminal Code of the Republic of Kazakhstan (n 22), Art 147.1: 'Non-compliance with measures for protection of personal data by a person, to whom an obligations of taking such measures is imposed, if this action has caused significant harm to the rights and legitimate interests of persons, – shall be punished by a fine in the amount of up

The common violations, as presented by representatives of the MDAI under the Information Security Committee on 5–6 April 2023,[63] include the lack of consent or legal grounds for the collection and processing of personal data, non-compliance with personal data protection requirements, illegal distribution of personal data in publicly available sources and its transfer to third parties, and non-use of cryptographic protection of information to encrypt personal data of restricted access.

Recent government enforcement data shows actions taken against businesses and individuals for such infringements. The latest data for 2022 and the first quarter of 2023 showed that 15 unscheduled inspections were carried out, 26 administrative cases considered, four officials have been held accountable, 24 legal entities have been held accountable, and 10 individuals have been held accountable. However, the representative of the governmental bodies added that even if there are few foreign persons among these claimants and defendants, cross-border complaints appear relatively rare so far.

Potential data protection claimants in Kazakhstan include individual data subjects along with public authorities. Defendants span private companies and government bodies engaged in unlawful data collection or handling.

Available remedies differ based on defendant status. Administrative penalties cover warnings, fines, and bans. Individual fines differ depending on the status of the violators, such as whether they are individuals, officials, agencies, private notaries, private bailiffs, lawyers, small business entities or non-profit organisations, medium-sized businesses, or large businesses. Criminal liability can entail stricter measures, including fine, correctional labour, community service, restriction of liberty, deprivation of liberty, and deprivation of the right to hold certain positions or engage in certain activities for a period of time or without it.

B. Jurisdictional Issues Involving Cross-Border Data Protection and Privacy

Kazakhstan's Constitution recognises that international agreements ratified by Kazakhstan have primacy over its laws.[64] Article 4.2 of the Personal Data Law also allows the data protection regime to expand through ratified accords.[65]

to three thousand monthly calculation indices or corrective labors in the same amount, or community services for a term of up to six hundred hours, or restriction of liberty for a term of up to two years, or deprivation of liberty for the same term with deprivation of the right to hold certain positions or engage in certain activity for a term of up to three years or without it.'

ibid, Art 211.1: 'Illegal distribution of electronic information resources, containing personal data of citizens or other details, an access of which is restricted by the Laws of the Republic of Kazakhstan or other possessor or owner, – shall be punished by a fine in the amount of up to two hundred monthly calculation indices or corrective labors in the same amount, or community services for a term of up to one hundred and eighty hours, or arrest for a term of up to fifty days, with deprivation of the right to hold certain positions or engage in certain activity for a term of up to three years or without it.'

[63] Presentation of the Ninth Key International Exhibition and Conference on Security in Kazakhstan and Central Asia Kazakhstan Security Systems 2023.

[64] Constitution of the Republic of Kazakhstan Scientific and Practical Commentary (n 1), Art 4.3: '... The legislation of the Republic determines the procedure and conditions of operation of international agreements in the territory of the Republic of Kazakhstan to which Kazakhstan is a party.'

[65] Personal Data Law (n 2), Art 4.2: 'If an international treaty ratified by the Republic of Kazakhstan establishes rules other than those contained in this Law, the rules of the international treaty shall apply.'

For civil litigations, the general territorial jurisdiction rule as found in Art 29 of the Civil Procedural Code applies – claims are brought to court at the place of residence of the respondent. This is also the case in civil litigations involving foreign parties, applying Art 466.1 of the Civil Procedural Code.[66] Consequently, the courts of Kazakhstan will consider cases where the respondent-organisation is located or the respondent-citizen has a place of residence in Kazakhstan.

An exception permits data protection suits by Kazakhstan residents against foreign entities in local courts regardless of defendant domicile, in the case of protection of the rights of personal data subjects, including compensation for damages and (or) compensation for moral damage.[67] Accordingly, this carve-out enables Kazakhstanis to pursue data harm claims domestically rather than abroad. It should be noted that Article 466.3 of the Civil Procedural Code also leaves the state the opportunity to further narrow or expand its jurisdiction through domestic laws or the ratification of international treaties in the scope of its competence.[68]

However, parallel proceedings may raise complexities around conflicting judgments and enforcement. If there is a parallel lawsuit on the same data protection or privacy issue in another jurisdiction(s), unless the governmental bodies of that state or claimant request assistance in execution or enforcement of the decision of its court, Kazakhstan lacks obligations to execute or enforce any foreign decisions contradictory to its public order. Moreover, if the case is subject to the jurisdiction of Kazakhstan, then the courts of Kazakhstan can adjudicate the case per Kazakh law regardless of any foreign legislations.

For example, according to Article 255 of the Civil Procedural Code, the court shall issue a ruling to refuse to issue a writ of execution to enforce an arbitral award if it finds that enforcement of the award is contrary to the public order of the Republic of Kazakhstan or that the dispute on which the arbitral award was made cannot be the subject of arbitration in accordance with the law.

C. Applicable Law: In Litigations Involving Cross-Border Data Protection and Privacy

Determining the governing law in multi-jurisdictional data disputes involves complex conflict-of-laws issues. Kazakhstan's framework lacks clarity on connecting factors for personal versus non-personal data matters.

Legal uncertainties exist regarding when cross-border data transfers constitute processing by one controller versus transmission to a separate entity. If the same controller handles data across national borders, breaches of Kazakhstan's localisation requirement may occur. Therefore, when personal data is transferred by the same owner or operator between its bases located in Kazakhstan and abroad (for example, between a Kazakhstani structural unit of a foreign company and its head office outside Kazakhstan or between a Kazakhstani subsidiary and its parent foreign company), potentially there is a risk of violating the

[66] Civil Procedural Code of the Republic of Kazakhstan (No 377-V ZRK, 31 October 2015) Art 466.1: 'The courts of the Republic of Kazakhstan consider cases involving foreign persons if the respondent-organization is located or the respondent-citizen has a place of residence in the territory of the Republic of Kazakhstan.'

[67] ibid, Art 466.2.10.

[68] ibid, Art 466.3: 'The courts of the Republic of Kazakhstan also consider other cases if they are referred to their competence by law and (or) an international treaty ratified by the Republic of Kazakhstan.'

requirement to locate bases on the territory of Kazakhstan. However, the legal implications remain unclear.

The stumbling block here lies between Articles 1103[69] and 1117[70] of the Civil Procedural Code of the Republic of Kazakhstan. Depending on the characterisation, a breach towards personal data is viewed as either a breach of personal non-property rights or an infliction of injury causing obligations. However, competing civil code provisions may apply to yield different results. Both Articles 1103 and 1117.1 refers to the application of *lex loci delicti commissi* (law of the place of wrong). However, Article 1117.2 suggests that *lex patriae* (law of common nationality) could govern in such instances. This causes uncertainty when both parties are citizens or legal entities of Kazakhstan while the breach took place outside of the territory of the Republic of Kazakhstan.

D. Recognition and Enforcement of Foreign Judgments

The enforceability of foreign court rulings in Kazakhstan depends firstly on international treaties on legal assistance between Kazakhstan and the state whose court issued the decision. Absent such international agreement, Kazakh courts may still recognise external data protection judgments, provided reciprocal treatment exists in the originating country.

This fallback principle of 'mutuality' by analogy to Article 1089 of the Civil Procedural Code means Kazakh courts will respect foreign decisions so long as Kazakhstan's own judgments receive reciprocal standing abroad. The assumption is mutuality applies unless proven otherwise.

However, uncertainties remain around the interpretation and application of this mutuality doctrine for data protection. Kazakh law lacks explicit provisions on enforcing foreign privacy and data rulings.

E. Obstacles to Effective Data Protection

Article 1117.3 of the Civil Procedural Code complicates effective personal data protection for foreign persons. It states the following: 'Foreign law shall not apply if an action or other circumstances that serve as the basis for claims to compensate injury in accordance with the legislative acts of the Republic of Kazakhstan is not unlawful.'

In effect, non-Kazakh claimants unable to pursue cases abroad could lack local recourse for data infringements not recognised under Kazakh law. This risks leaving certain cross-border complaints without viable avenues for redress.

However, an alternative basis for jurisdiction exists if personal data protection is characterised as a personal non-property right. Recourse could then be made to Article 1103 of the Civil Procedural Code. Nonetheless, the significant public policy exception in Article 1117.3 creates legal uncertainty.

[69] ibid, Art 1103: 'The law of the country where an action or any other circumstance has taken place which serves as the basis for claim to protect such rights shall apply to personal non-property rights.'

[70] ibid, Art 1117: '1. The rights and obligations under commitments which emerge in consequence of infliction of injury shall be determined in accordance with the law of the country where the action took place or any other circumstances which cause the basis for claims to compensate for injury.'

From a regulatory perspective, applying Kazakh law to all data claims adjudicated domestically, regardless of applicable foreign law, may appear sovereigntist. On the other hand, rigidly requiring unlawful acts under Kazakh statutes to allow any redress inhibits cooperative cross-border enforcement and remedies.

F. Major Litigations Regarding Data Protection and Privacy

Kazakhstan lacks prominent examples of foreign data protection litigation so far. However, domestic incidents reveal regulatory gaps, spurring legal reforms.

In one case, a contractor leaked the personal details of 11 million Kazakh citizens held by the Central Election Commission. A local cybersecurity firm discovered that the exposed database was publicly available on the Internet and notified the authorities.[71] Initially denying any breach, the Commission later admitted a developer's misconfigured server caused the leak.[72]

This mass-scale domestic incident highlighted insufficient safeguards and oversight around public sector data handling. It provoked strengthenings of Kazakhstan's data protection framework, including expanded breach notification requirements and centralised monitoring for violations.

VI. Topical Issues and Prospects

A. Artificial Intelligence or AI-Generated Data

Kazakhstan's current data protection framework does not directly address artificial intelligence (AI) or AI-generated data. As AI adoption increases domestically across sectors like e-commerce, finance, and healthcare, regulatory gaps around automated data processing present challenges.

For example, the company Kazpost is actively developing and applying AI technologies to improve the efficiency of service planning and quality interaction with the client. When using AI, a mechanism is provided for requesting consent to the collection and processing of personal data. These automated interactions raise novel consent, transparency, and accountability issues around data collection absent specific AI governance.

B. Potential Cooperation under the Belt and Road Initiative

Kazakhstan has explored potential engagement with China's Digital Silk Road initiative but has not yet entered data transfer or protection agreements under this framework.

[71] Vlast.kz, '*Утечка данных казахстанцев в сеть произошла из Центризбиркома – ЦАРКА*' (*Аналитический интернет-журнал Власть*, 8 August 2019), available at https://vlast.kz/novosti/34706-utecka-dannyh-kazahstancev-v-set-proizosla-iz-centrizbirkoma-carka.html.

[72] 'В ЦИК прокомментировали утечку данных' (*Profit.kz*, 12 August 2019), available at https://profit.kz/news/54565/V-CIK-prokommentirovali-utechku-dannih/.

On 17 July 2020, during the meeting of the Ministers of Foreign Affairs 'Central Asia – China', representatives of the Central Asian countries expressed their readiness to connect to the Digital Silk Road, as reported by the CIS Internet portal.[73] Proposed areas include developing 5G networks, smart cities, mobile payment systems, and IT platforms for cargo transportation. Central Asian countries paid special attention to transnational e-commerce.

There are about 84 completed and planned projects of the Digital Silk Road in Central Asia. Of these, 30 are in Kazakhstan, 26 in Uzbekistan. 10 projects each are being developed in Tajikistan and Kyrgyzstan, where attention is mainly paid to smart city and telecommunications networks projects. There are eight operating in Turkmenistan – they are mainly engaged in laying fiber optic cables along the bottom of the Caspian Sea. However, Kazakhstan has not signed any memorandums of understanding or cooperation pacts with China relating to cross-border data flows or governance.

C. Data Protection Post COVID-19 Pandemic

The COVID-19 pandemic accelerated Kazakhstan's focus on cybersecurity and data protection, but has not prompted major regulatory changes thus far.

Remote work and digitalisation trends of many companies and government agencies during the crisis increased cyber risks, especially around unauthorised access to confidential personal and corporate data. This highlighted pre-existing vulnerabilities in Kazakhstan's digital governance frameworks.

In response, Kazakhstan continues implementing its cybersecurity concept 'Cybershield of Kazakhstan', which has been in implementation since 2017, to enhance critical information infrastructure safeguards. The concept defines the main directions for the implementation of state policy in the field of protection of electronic information resources, information systems and telecommunications networks, ensuring the safe use of information and communication technologies. The concept is designed to ensure the unity of approaches to monitoring the information security of state bodies, individuals and legal entities, as well as the development of mechanisms for preventing and promptly responding to information security incidents, including the introduction of a state of emergency or martial law in emergency situations.[74] A new strategy called 'Cybershield-2' will be implemented in the country until 2027, which aims to further strengthen protections for citizens and businesses through upgraded security systems and coordinated responses.[75]

Looking ahead, Kazakhstan is currently at the stage of negotiations on signing the Convention for the Protection of Individuals with regard to Automatic Processing of Personal Data (Strasbourg, 28 January 1981) which will bolster the protection of the right to privacy in relation to automated processing of personal data. This reflects Kazakhstan's

[73] '"Digital Silk Road" in Central Asia' (*CIS Internet Portal*, 10 March 2023), available at https://e-cis.info/news/566/107475/.

[74] ibid.

[75] ibid.

continued efforts to modernise its digital governance amid growing reliance on data-driven technologies.

Overall, COVID-19 validated Kazakhstan's pre-pandemic policy priorities around cyber resilience and data protection. But concrete regulatory changes directly responsive to pandemic impacts are still evolving across Kazakhstan's complex digital landscape. Sustained governance upgrades will be vital to match Kazakhstan's accelerating digital adoption with appropriate data safeguards.

Conclusion

ADRIAN MAK

I. Overview

Asia's data protection landscape is a mosaic of evolving frameworks, shaped by rapid technological change, geopolitical tensions, and shifting societal expectations. The data protection and privacy landscape across the 17 Asian jurisdictions surveyed is a complex tapestry, reflecting the region's immense diversity in legal systems, socio-economic development, and digital maturity. Despite this heterogeneity, several overarching themes and trends emerge.

Firstly, there is a clear trend towards strengthening personal data protection, with jurisdictions adopting new laws or updating existing frameworks. While motivations vary, from fostering digital innovation to protecting individual rights, the recognition of data protection as a policy imperative is gaining ground. Core data protection principles like transparency, accountability, and individual empowerment are increasingly enshrined in law, even if specific applications differ.

Secondly, the influence of international frameworks, particularly the European Union's (EU) General Data Protection Regulation (GDPR), China's Personal Information Protection Law (PIPL) complemented by the Cybersecurity Law (CSL) and Data Security Law (DSL), and the Asia-Pacific Economic Cooperation (APEC) Cross-Border Privacy Rules (CBPR), is palpable. Many new laws draw inspiration from these models, with some like China's PIPL closely mirroring GDPR concepts. Adequacy decisions, contracts and binding corporate rules (BCRs), and CBPR certifications are also gaining traction as cross-border transfer mechanisms. However, local adaptations remain significant, reflecting distinct legal traditions, constitutional values, and economic priorities.

Thirdly, data localisation and cross-border transfer restrictions are emergent trends, especially in jurisdictions like China, Vietnam, and India. Motivations span from protecting citizens' data from foreign surveillance to promoting domestic digital champions. While some jurisdictions like Japan and Singapore maintain a more open stance, even they are not immune to localisation pressures in strategic sectors. These fault lines create new complexities for cross-border data flows.

Fourthly, enforcement is gradually gaining teeth, but challenges remain. While regulators in Hong Kong, Singapore, and South Korea are more active, enforcement is nascent in jurisdictions with newer laws. Regulatory capacity, resources, and coordination are common hurdles.

Fifthly, from a private international law perspective, the growing extraterritorial reach of data protection laws and the inherently cross-border nature of data flows present complex jurisdictional and conflict of law challenges. Questions around the applicable law, jurisdiction, and enforcement of judgments in cross-border data disputes remain thorny across the 17 Asian jurisdictions surveyed. While some jurisdictions are developing data-specific private international law rules, like China's provisions on the applicable law for data disputes, most still rely on general principles not tailored to the data context. The risk of jurisdictional overreach, inconsistent judgments, and enforcement gaps looms large. Harmonising private international law norms for data disputes, through regional or multilateral efforts, will be crucial for legal certainty and effective redress.

Sixthly, technological developments in AI, big data, and biometrics, as well as the impact of COVID-19, are testing the boundaries of personal data protection. Jurisdictions are starting to grapple with novel risks like algorithmic bias and profiling. Regulatory responses range from sectoral guidelines to binding laws, with challenges around effective oversight.

Despite these commonalities, significant divergences remain. The role of constitutional protections, the distinction between personal and sensitive data categories, the stringency of cross-border transfer rules, the centrality of individual consent, and the emphasis on collective versus individual rights vary considerably. Tensions between data protection and adjacent values like innovation, free speech, and public order are also balanced differently.

These commonalities and divergences will be explored in detail in the ensuing sections.

II. General Legal Framework of International Data Transfers and Data Protection

A. Constitutional Protection for Privacy and Personal Data

Constitutional protection for data privacy and personal data varies significantly among the 17 Asian jurisdictions covered. In some, it is explicitly recognised as a fundamental right, while in others it is implicit or absent from the constitution altogether.

India stands out as having one of the most robust constitutional protections.[1] In the landmark *Puttaswamy v Union of India* case, the Supreme Court of India unanimously held that the right to privacy is a fundamental right under Article 21 of the Constitution, which guarantees the right to life and personal liberty. The Court interpreted this expansively to include informational privacy and autonomy over personal data. This watershed ruling has shaped subsequent developments in India's data protection landscape.

Similarly, in South Korea, while privacy is not explicitly enumerated in the Constitution, the Constitutional Court has derived a 'right to informational self-determination' from the rights to dignity and pursuit of happiness in Articles 10 and 17.[2] This right encompasses control over one's personal data and has been instrumental in setting boundaries on data collection and use by the Government and private sector.

In the Philippines, the right to privacy is grounded in constitutional provisions on the inviolability of privacy of communication and correspondences.[3] The Supreme Court has

[1] See Sai Ramani Garimella and Haaris Moosa, 'India' in chapter 15 of this volume.
[2] Eung-Kyung Cho, 'South Korea' in chapter 4 of this volume.
[3] Lemuel Didulo Lopez, 'The Philippines' in chapter 11 of this volume.

interpreted these as creating a broader right to informational privacy. Similarly, section 357 of the Myanmar Constitution contains an express protection of the right to privacy, but only an oblique provision relating to the protection of personal data transfers.

In contrast, other jurisdictions have more limited or indirect constitutional protections. Hong Kong's Basic Law Article 30 safeguards privacy of communication, while Article 14 of the Bill of Rights protects against arbitrary or unlawful interference with privacy, family, home or correspondence.[4] However, courts have held these rights may be restricted if necessary for legitimate aims and proportionate.

China, Vietnam, Indonesia, and Cambodia's constitutions do not directly address data protection, arguably reflecting a legal tradition that has historically emphasised collective interests over individual rights. Singapore's constitution similarly does not explicitly mention privacy.[5] However, general provisions like China's Article 38 (protection of personal dignity) and Article 40 (freedom and privacy of correspondence)[6] and Vietnam's Article 21 (inviolability of private life, personal secrets, family secrets, and protection of honour and reputation) have been viewed as providing a basis for privacy and data protection legislation.[7]

Japan and Taiwan present additional nuances. While neither have explicit constitutional provisions, courts have interpreted other rights to encompass aspects of data protection. In Japan, Article 13's right to 'life, liberty and pursuit of happiness' has been construed to protect against undue disclosure of personal data.[8] Likewise in Taiwan, the Constitutional Court has ruled that the right to privacy, while unenumerated, is a fundamental right grounded in human dignity and free development of personality.[9]

The role of constitutional courts in shaping data protection jurisprudence is significant across the region. From India's *Puttaswamy* decision to South Korea's 'right to informational self-determination' cases to recent rulings in Japan and Taiwan, judicial interpretations have been pivotal in recognising data privacy as a fundamental value, influencing subsequent legislation. The ongoing interplay between courts and lawmakers will likely continue to define the constitutional contours of data protection in Asia.

At the same time, the absence of express constitutional protections in many jurisdictions underscores the important role of statutory law in establishing data privacy norms. As digital economies and societies evolve, there may be pressure to constitutionalise data protection more explicitly. However, the path will likely be gradual, as jurisdictions balance innovation, individual rights, public interest and consistency with global standards according to their own legal and political traditions.

Overall, while constitutional approaches to data protection in Asia remain diverse, there is an undeniable trend towards greater recognition and stronger protections, whether through direct provisioning, judicial interpretation or statutory gap-filling. Finding the right constitutional balance will be an ongoing challenge and opportunity for the region.

[4] Adam Au and Phoebe Woo, 'Hong Kong' in chapter 2 of this volume.
[5] Lanx Goh and Joshua Kow, 'Singapore' in chapter 5 of this volume.
[6] Yun Zhao, 'China' in chapter 1 of this volume.
[7] Mai-Thanh Le and Tien-Duc Nguyen, 'Vietnam' in chapter 8 of this volume.
[8] Nobuyuki Sato, 'Japan' in chapter 3 of this volume.
[9] Sung Huang-Chih, 'Taiwan' in chapter 6 of this volume.

B. Data Protection Frameworks

The 17 Asian jurisdictions exhibit a spectrum of approaches to data protection, reflecting their diverse legal systems, economic priorities, and cultural values.

At one end are comprehensive, omnibus laws like Singapore's Personal Data Protection Act (PDPA), South Korea's Personal Information Protection Act (PIPA), the Philippines' Data Privacy Act, and Hong Kong's Personal Data (Privacy) Ordinance (PDPO) which are relatively extensive, covering both the private and public sectors with detailed provisions. They provide an overarching framework with dedicated regulators like Singapore's Personal Data Protection Commission (PDPC), South Korea's Personal Information Protection Commission (PIPC), the Philippines' National Privacy Commission, and Hong Kong's Office Of The Privacy Commissioner For Personal Data (PCPD).

At the other end are more piecemeal approaches, with scattered provisions across various laws, as seen in Cambodia (eg the Law on Electronic Commerce, the Law on Telecommunications, financial sector regulations) and Sri Lanka. In between are hybrid models like PIPL complemented by the CSL and DSL, and Indonesia's draft Personal Data Protection Law combined with sector-specific rules.

Japan has transitioned from a segmented regime with the Act on the Protection of Personal Information (APPI) governing the private sector and separate laws for the public sector, to a more unified approach with the 2021 APPI amendments making the Personal Information Protection Commission the overarching regulator.[10] Taiwan's Personal Data Protection Act applies broadly, with some exceptions for specific sectors.[11]

Myanmar presents a unique case among the jurisdictions surveyed. Despite lacking a comprehensive data protection law, existing legislation such as the Electronic Transactions Law provides a rudimentary data privacy and protection regime. Given the current political situation, data protection cannot be a priority. However, as a member of the Association of Southeast Asian Nations (ASEAN), Myanmar must adopt best practices in data protection, aiding its development and integration into the ASEAN Economic Community (AEC). Monitoring this situation is crucial, as implementing data protection laws will significantly advance individuals' privacy and security rights.

The role of sectoral laws and regulations is significant in many Asian jurisdictions, particularly in areas like financial services, healthcare, and telecommunications. These sector-specific rules often impose additional or stricter requirements beyond the general data protection law. For example, Thailand's Cybersecurity Act sets detailed requirements for critical information infrastructure operators (CIIOs), while India's proposed data protection law would require 'significant data fiduciaries' to implement trust scores and data audits.[12] Vietnam's cybersecurity law has localisation provisions for certain providers.[13] Navigating this complex web of general and sectoral regulations can be challenging for businesses operating across multiple sectors and jurisdictions.

[10] Nobuyuki Sato, 'Japan' in chapter 3 of this volume.
[11] Sung Huang-Chih, 'Taiwan' in chapter 6 of this volume.
[12] Thaya Uthayophas, 'Thailand' in chapter 13 of this volume.
[13] Mai-Thanh Le and Tien-Duc Nguyen, 'Vietnam' in chapter 8 of this volume.

Most jurisdictions define personal data broadly as information relating to an identifiable individual, with some variations. Sensitive data categories like biometrics, health, and sexual orientation are common, but not universal. For example, South Korea's PIPA lists ideology, belief, union membership, political opinions, health, sex life, and criminal records as sensitive information.[14] China's PIPL treats biometric data, religious beliefs, specific identities, medical and health data, financial accounts, location tracking, and minors' data as sensitive.[15] In contrast, Singapore's PDPA does not explicitly distinguish sensitive data, though advisory guidelines recommend stronger safeguards for National Registration Identity Card (NRIC) numbers, financial data, insurance policy details, and minors' data.[16]

Data controller and processor concepts are increasingly adopted, but with variations. China's PIPL uses 'personal information handler', while Indonesia's draft law introduces 'data controller-processor' hybrids. Some jurisdictions like Japan differentiate duties based on entity type (eg business operators vs data intermediaries), while others like the Philippines' DPA impose more uniform obligations.

Newer laws align with the GDPR's principles-based model, with requirements like purpose limitation, data minimisation, and storage limitation. For example, South Korea's PIPA, the Philippines' DPA, and Thailand's PDPA all incorporate these principles. Legacy frameworks like Hong Kong's PDPO may be more prescriptive, centred around data protection principles. Accountability measures like Data Protection Impact Assessments (DPIAs) and Data Protection Officers (DPOs) are gaining traction in most of the jurisdictions surveyed, such as in Singapore, the Philippines, and South Korea, but remain less comprehensive than the GDPR.

Data protection bodies are set up with varying levels of independence. For example, Hong Kong's Office of the Privacy Commissioner for Personal Data is an independent body, whilst Singapore's Personal Data Protection Commission is a part of the Infocomm Media Development Authority under the Ministry of Communications and Information. The Philippines' National Privacy Commission is an independent body. In Japan, the PPC has been made the unified regulator for both the private and public sectors. South Korea's PIPC is under the Prime Minister's office.

Individual rights are expanding, with access, correction, and erasure rights widely recognised, but procedural barriers remain. For example, Singapore's PDPA grants access and correction rights, while South Korea's PIPA has rights of access, objection, deletion, and suspension. Some laws go further – Thailand's PDPA includes rights to portability and human review of automated decisions.[17] The Philippines' DPA has rights of access, objection, erasure, and data portability.[18] However, the right to data portability is still rare in Asia, only appearing in a few laws like Thailand and the Philippines, and the right to human review of automated decisions even more so, though China's PIPL is a notable exception. Jurisdictions are starting to grapple with algorithmic transparency and fairness, but clear regulations are nascent.

[14] Eung-Kyung Cho, 'South Korea' in chapter 4 of this volume.
[15] Zhao Yun, 'China' in chapter 1 of this volume.
[16] Lanx Goh and Joshua Kow, 'Singapore' in chapter 5 of this volume.
[17] Thaya Uthayophas, 'Thailand' in chapter 13 of this volume.
[18] Lemuel Didulo Lopez, 'The Philippines' in chapter 11 of this volume.

III. Legal Bases, Mechanisms and Exceptions for International Data Transfers and Data Protection

A. Cross-Border Data Transfers

Approaches to cross-border data transfers vary across Asian jurisdictions, with some common themes emerging.

Consent is a key basis for transfers in many countries. China's Personal Information Protection Law (PIPL) and South Korea's Personal Information Protection Act (PIPA) require specific, informed consent separate from general processing consent. Vietnam's sectoral regulations and the Philippines' Data Privacy Act (DPA) also mandate separate transfer consent in certain cases. However, Singapore's Personal Data Protection Act (PDPA) allows deemed consent where transfers are reasonably expected based on the original purpose. Hong Kong's Personal Data (Privacy) Ordinance (PDPO) and Malaysia's Personal Data Protection Act 2010 permit transfers with general processing consent.

Contracts and binding corporate rules (BCRs) are increasingly recognised as transfer mechanisms, particularly within ASEAN. Singapore and the Philippines expressly endorse model contractual clauses and BCRs. The ASEAN Model Contractual Clauses (MCCs) are designed to facilitate intra-ASEAN data flows. Novel contractual approaches are also emerging, such as the Greater Bay Area Standard Contract for cross-border data transfers between Mainland China and Hong Kong under specific conditions.[19]

Certifications like the APEC CBPR and Privacy Recognition for Processors (PRP) systems are gaining acceptance as interoperable transfer mechanisms. Japan and Singapore have updated their laws to recognise CBPR/PRP-certified entities as having adequate safeguards. The Philippines and South Korea are participating APEC economies. While voluntary, these APEC initiatives promote accountability-based transfers within the region and globally.

Adequacy decisions enabling streamlined transfers to approved countries are less prevalent in Asia compared to the EU model. Japan is a notable exception, having issued adequacy findings for EU/European Economic Area countries and the UK post-Brexit.[20] South Korea also allows consent-free transfers to countries deemed equivalent by the Personal Information Protection Commission (PIPC).[21] China and Indonesia's draft laws contemplate adequacy decisions but have not designated any countries yet. Most Asian laws emphasise case-by-case assessments of protection levels.

For example, Japan's amended Act on Protection of Personal Information (APPI) permits transfers to countries with protections equivalent to Japan, as designated by the Personal Information Protection Commission (PPC). It also allows transfers to foreign entities with substantially equivalent safeguards, like APEC CBPR certification.[22]

[19] Adam Au and Phoebe Woo, 'Hong Kong' in chapter 2 of this volume.
[20] Nobuyuki Sato, 'Japan' in chapter 3 of this volume.
[21] Eung-Kyung Cho, 'South Korea' in chapter 4 of this volume.
[22] Nobuyuki Sato, 'Japan' in chapter 3 of this volume.

Singapore's PDPA requires overseas recipients to provide a standard of protection comparable to the PDPA, without restricting transfers based on the destination country.[23]

The Philippines' DPA limits transfers to countries lacking adequate safeguards. The National Privacy Commission has issued guidance on assessing adequacy, looking at factors such as the general data privacy environment, specific protections for the transferred data, and enforcement mechanisms.[24]

Hong Kong plans to restrict transfers to places without adequate protection through section 33 of the PDPO, which remains pending as of 2024. Currently, cross-border transfer requirements are minimal, but the Privacy Commissioner encourages adoption of the 2022 model contractual clauses guidance.[25]

Malaysia's PDPA restricts prohibits the transfer of personal data outside Malaysia unless protection is guaranteed. No whitelisted countries have been designated to date.[26]

Thailand's Personal Data Protection Act (PDPA) restricts transfers to countries without adequate protection as determined by the Personal Data Protection Committee, subject to exceptions.[27]

South Korea's PIPA mandates specific consent for overseas transfers, separate from collection consent, with exceptions for transfers to countries deemed equivalent by the PIPC, such as the EU/EEA and UK.[28]

Taiwan's amended Personal Data Protection Act empowers central competent authorities to restrict transfers by non-government agencies to specified destinations under certain conditions, such as risks to major national interests.[29]

India's IT Rules allow transfer of sensitive personal data with consent if necessary for performance of a lawful contract or legally permissible. The proposed data protection bill aimed to expand transfer conditions, including adequacy decisions and approved mechanisms, before being withdrawn.[30]

Sri Lanka's draft PDPA would allow transfers to countries with adequate protection or appropriate safeguards.[31]

In summary, while specific requirements differ, there is a trend in the region towards increased regulation of cross-border data transfers, with a mix of consent-based, contractual, certification, and adequacy-oriented approaches emerging. It should further be observed that encryption and anonymisation are increasingly recognised as important tools for enabling cross-border data flows while protecting privacy. Anonymised data is not considered personal data in many jurisdictions, such as China and Singapore. However, the standards for anonymisation vary. For example, while Singapore's PDPA provides a detailed framework for anonymisation, China's PIPL has a broader concept of de-identification that may not meet the stricter anonymisation standards in other jurisdictions.

[23] Lanx Goh and Joshua Kow, 'Singapore' in chapter 5 of this volume.
[24] Lemuel Didulo Lopez, 'The Philippines' in chapter 11 of this volume.
[25] Adam Au and Phoebe Woo, 'Hong Kong' in chapter 2 of this volume.
[26] Noor Muzalifah Binti Shabudin and Chia Eng Yi, 'Malaysia' in chapter 7 of this volume.
[27] Thaya Uthayophas, 'Thailand' in chapter 13 of this volume.
[28] Eung-Kyung Cho, 'South Korea' in chapter 4 of this volume.
[29] Sung Huang-Chih, 'Taiwan' in chapter 6 of this volume.
[30] Sai Ramani Garimella and Haaris Moosa, 'India' in chapter 15 of this volume.
[31] Hemaka Perera, 'Sri Lanka' in chapter 14 of this volume.

B. International Data Protection and Liability

Purpose limitation, data minimisation, and storage limitation principles are common across many of the Asian jurisdictions surveyed, though the specificity of requirements varies. Some laws like Hong Kong's PDPO and Japan's APPI explicitly codify these principles, while others incorporate them more implicitly.

Security safeguards are universally required but diversely implemented. China has detailed requirements in its Multi-Level Protection Scheme (MLPS) and PIPL rules prescribing specific security controls.[32] Singapore takes a more flexible, risk-based approach, with the PDPA allowing organisations to determine reasonable security arrangements considering the nature of the data, among other factors.[33] The Philippines' DPA and South Korea's PIPA mandate appropriate technical, physical and organisational measures to protect personal data. Vietnam's cybersecurity law has security obligations for certain service providers.

Data breach notification is an area of increasing convergence, but thresholds, timelines and procedures still differ across jurisdictions. For example, the Philippines' DPA requires notification to the National Privacy Commission and affected individuals within 72 hours of becoming aware of a breach, while Singapore's PDPA mandates notification as soon as practicable, but no later than three calendar days after assessment. China's PIPL requires prompt notification to authorities and individuals, but does not specify a timeline.[34] Taiwan amended its PDPA in 2023 to add a data breach notification obligation with further details to be prescribed.[35] These differences can create challenges for companies operating across multiple jurisdictions. Recent major breaches like the Cathay Pacific incident in Hong Kong and the *SingHealth* case in Singapore have spurred regulator focus on this issue. Expect continued tightening of notification requirements and increased penalties for non-compliance.

Accountability measures like DPIAs and DPOs appointments are gaining traction across Asia, but implementation remains a work in progress. The Philippines and Singapore expressly require DPOs under their laws. South Korea mandates a Chief Privacy Officer (CPO) for certain personal information processors.[36] China's PIPL requires DPOs for large volume processors.[37] Hong Kong, Japan and Taiwan encourage DPO appointments as a best practice. Thailand's PDPA has a hybrid approach mandating DPOs for certain entities.[38] DPIAs are required in varying circumstances – China mandates them for high-risk processing, the Philippines for government agencies, and Vietnam's draft decree for cross-border transfers.

There is a growing trend towards enshrining individual rights over personal data, though the scope and implementation mechanisms differ. Access and correction rights are widely recognised, with some exceptions and procedural variations. The right to data portability is emerging in some of the newer laws like China's PIPL, the Philippines' DPA and

[32] Zhao Yun, 'China' in chapter 1 of this volume.
[33] Lanx Goh and Joshua Kow, 'Singapore' in chapter 5 of this volume.
[34] Zhao Yun, 'China' in chapter 1 of this volume.
[35] Sung Huang-Chih, 'Taiwan' in chapter 6 of this volume.
[36] Eung-Kyung Cho, 'South Korea' in chapter 4 of this volume.
[37] Zhao Yun, 'China' in chapter 1 of this volume.
[38] Thaya Uthayophas, 'Thailand' in chapter 13 of this volume.

Thailand's PDPA, but less consistently available in legacy frameworks. The right to explanation for automated decisions is even rarer, though China's PIPL notably includes it. As AI decision-making proliferates, we are likely to see more jurisdictions grapple with algorithmic transparency and incorporate rights to human review, building on early initiatives like Singapore's Model AI Governance Framework and Hong Kong's guidance on ethical AI development.

Overall, while the core tenets of purpose limitation, security, breach notification, accountability and individual rights are common themes across Asian data protection frameworks, the devil is in the detail of specific requirements and implementation. Substantial diversity persists in terms of the granularity of obligations, the procedures for exercising rights, and the exceptions carved out.

C. Extraterritorial Application

The extraterritorial reach of data protection laws is a significant trend in Asia. Most jurisdictions now assert jurisdiction over foreign entities that collect or process their citizens' data, regardless of physical presence. China's PIPL, in particular, has far-reaching extraterritorial application, covering any processing of Chinese citizens' personal information, regardless of where the processing takes place.[39] This is similar to the GDPR's extraterritorial scope, but potentially even broader. The PIPL is applicable to the handling of personal information of natural persons within China by overseas organisations for the purpose of providing products or services to natural persons within China, analysing or assessing the behaviour of natural persons within China, or other circumstances provided by laws and administrative regulations.

Other jurisdictions are following suit in extending the reach of their data protection laws. Vietnam's Law on Cybersecurity requires foreign enterprises providing telecommunications services, Internet services, or value-added services in cyberspace in Vietnam to establish a branch or representative office in Vietnam.[40] The Philippines' DPA has extraterritorial application to the processing of personal data by entities outside the Philippines if they use equipment located in the Philippines or maintain an office, branch, or agency in the Philippines.[41]

Thailand's PDPA also has extraterritorial scope, applying to the collection, use, or disclosure of personal data of data subjects in Thailand by a data controller or data processor outside Thailand.[42] India's proposed Personal Data Protection Bill, although currently withdrawn, had sought to extend its application to the processing of personal data by entities outside India if such processing is in connection with any business carried on in India, any systematic activity of offering goods or services to data principals within India, or any activity which involves profiling of data principals within India.[43]

[39] Zhao Yun, 'China' in chapter 1 of this volume.
[40] Mai-Thanh Le and Tien-Duc Nguyen, 'Vietnam' in chapter 8 of this volume.
[41] Lemuel Didulo Lopez, 'The Philippines' in chapter 11 of this volume.
[42] Thaya Uthayophas, 'Thailand' in chapter 13 of this volume.
[43] Sai Ramani Garimella and Haaris Moosa, 'India' in chapter 15 of this volume.

Similarly, Singapore's PDPC has taken the position that the PDPA applies to organisations collecting, using, or disclosing personal data in Singapore, regardless of their physical location.[44] Hong Kong's PDPO also applies to the processing of personal data by a data user who either has a link to Hong Kong or uses equipment located in Hong Kong.[45]

The enforcement of extraterritorial jurisdiction remains a challenge, particularly for smaller jurisdictions with limited resources. Regulators are increasingly assertive in claiming jurisdiction, necessitating greater cross-border enforcement cooperation. Mechanisms like the Global Privacy Assembly and bilateral agreements, will be increasingly important to address cross-border violations effectively. Mutual legal assistance treaties (MLATs) and memoranda of understanding (MOUs) between regulators will also be crucial for facilitating cross-border investigations and enforcement actions in Asia. However, many existing MLATs are outdated and do not adequately address questions of personal data protection and jurisdictional overlaps in the digital age. Updating these instruments and establishing new frameworks for regulatory cooperation will be essential to keep pace with the extraterritorial reach of data protection laws in the region.

As discussed below, this trend also raises knotty conflict of laws issues. Private international law norms will need to evolve in tandem to address these challenges, balancing convergence with respect for sovereign diversity. Clearer rules and principles for allocating regulatory authority over transnational data flows are needed. Contractual choice of law and forum clauses in data processing agreements can help mitigate conflicts, but may not always be dispositive.

IV. Data Security and Data Localisation

Data security and localisation requirements are becoming increasingly prominent features of data protection frameworks across Asia. While approaches vary, there is a growing trend towards more prescriptive security obligations and restrictions on cross-border data flows, particularly for sensitive sectors and data categories.

China has one of the most comprehensive and stringent data security and localisation regimes in the region.[46] The MLPS under the Cybersecurity Law imposes granular technical and organisational controls based on the criticality of information infrastructure. CIIOs must store personal and important data collected and generated within China locally, and undergo security assessments by the Cyberspace Administration of China (CAC) for any cross-border transfers. Moreover, the PIPL requires processors of personal information outside China to establish a special agency or appoint a representative in China. These requirements reflect China's emphasis on 'cyber sovereignty' and using data regulation as a tool for national security and economic development.

Vietnam has also introduced data localisation requirements through its Cybersecurity Law and guiding decrees.[47] Cross-border transfers are subject to Government approval, and

[44] Lanx Goh and Joshua Kow, 'Singapore' in chapter 5 of this volume.
[45] Adam Au and Phoebe Woo, 'Hong Kong' in in chapter 2 of this volume.
[46] Zhao Yun, 'China' in chapter 1 of this volume.
[47] Mai-Thanh Le and Tien-Duc Nguyen, 'Vietnam' in chapter 8 of this volume.

certain foreign service providers may be required to store data locally and establish a local presence. Enforcement has been relatively limited to date, but the legal framework signals a restrictive stance.

Elsewhere in Southeast Asia, data localisation mandates are sector-specific rather than economy-wide. Indonesia's Government Regulation 71/2019 requires 'electronic system operators' serving the public sector to process and store data domestically, with exceptions for international headquarters and cloud backup.[48] The previous requirement for all operators was softened after industry pushback. In the Philippines, the central bank imposes localisation for financial institutions as part of outsourcing registrations.[49]

Debates over data localisation have been particularly heated in India. The withdrawn Personal Data Protection Bill would have required sensitive and critical personal data to be stored only in India, with transfers subject to strict conditions and adequacy decisions. The Digital Personal Data Protection Act, 2023 allows for cross-border transfers to all jurisdictions unless otherwise restricted, but it remains to be seen whether future government bills will address this issue.[50]

South Korea maintains localisation requirements for geospatial data under separate legislation.[51] Japan's amended APPI similarly facilitates international data flows based on PPC adequacy decisions or APEC CBPR certification, without any general localisation requirements.[52]

Singapore and Hong Kong stand out for their lack of explicit data localisation mandates in their omnibus data protection laws – the PDPA and PDPO respectively. Both jurisdictions have thriving digital economies and have sought to position themselves as a regional data hub. However, even they are not immune to localisation pressures for sensitive sectors. Singapore's Monetary Authority imposes localisation as a licensing condition for certain financial institutions.[53] Hong Kong's pending amendment to introduce cross-border transfer restrictions in the PDPO has also sparked concerns about de facto localisation.

Finally, data security and localisation controls are often stricter for sensitive data categories like financial, health and children's data. China subjects personal financial information, health and biometric data to localisation and enhanced security requirements under the PIPL and sectoral rules.[54] Even the more open regimes of Japan and Singapore restrict international transfers of sensitive data like My Number and NRIC numbers respectively. Heightened protection for sensitive data reflects its greater potential for harm and discrimination if misused.

Overall, while the spectrum of approaches to data localisation in Asia remains wide, the direction of travel is clear. Restrictions on cross-border data flows are becoming more common, whether through explicit localisation requirements or strict conditions for transfers. Motivations range from protecting citizens' data from foreign surveillance to promoting domestic digital industries and exerting regulatory control. The economic and human rights impact of these measures remains hotly debated.

[48] Priskila Pratita Penasthika, 'Indonesia' in chapter 12 of this volume.
[49] Lemuel Didulo Lopez, 'The Philippines' in chapter 11 of this volume.
[50] Sai Ramani Garimella and Haaris Moosa, 'India' in chapter 15 of this volume.
[51] Eung-Kyung Cho, 'South Korea' in chapter 4 of this volume.
[52] Nobuyuki Sato, 'Japan' in chapter 3 of this volume.
[53] Lanx Goh and Joshua Kow, 'Singapore' in chapter 5 of this volume.
[54] Zhao Yun, 'China' in chapter 1 of this volume.

V. Issues in Private International Law

A. Litigation, Enforcement and Penalties

Litigations involving cross-border data protection and privacy can take various forms, with plaintiffs, defendants and remedies varying depending on specific laws and circumstances. Common scenarios include:

- Data subjects suing data controllers/processors: This can involve domestic data subjects suing foreign data controllers, foreign data subjects suing domestic businesses, or even foreign data subjects suing foreign businesses in the local jurisdiction's courts.
- Representative/collective actions: Some jurisdictions like China allow procuratorates, consumer associations or other designated organisations to bring public interest litigations on behalf of data subjects. This enables addressing mass infringements.
- Business-to-business disputes: Litigations may arise between data controllers and processors, such as contractual disputes over data processing agreements. The data subject may or may not be party to such proceedings.
- Regulatory enforcement actions: Data protection authorities may investigate and sanction entities for cross-border data protection violations, either on its own accord or upon complaints. Penalties can include fines, injunctions, and other corrective orders.

Remedies sought commonly include damages, injunctions to cease/rectify infringements, and other relief like public apologies. Applicable procedures can be civil, administrative or criminal, varying by jurisdiction and nature of violation.

The strength of enforcement varies widely. Established authorities like Hong Kong's PCPD, Singapore's PDPC and South Korea's PIPC have been more active in investigations and penalties. Enforcement is more nascent in jurisdictions with newer laws.

i. Jurisdiction and Applicable Law

Data protection presents a dynamic, thorny private international law (PIL) frontier. The transnational nature of data flows creates complex jurisdictional and applicable law questions.

As the 17 chapters show, Asian jurisdictions are grappling with when and how to apply domestic laws to foreign actors, platforms, and processing arrangements. Most laws assert extraterritorial reach over foreign entities processing citizens' data, even without physical presence. In dealing with extraterritorial assertions, common sense limits, restraint, and coordination are needed. Over-expansive claims would subject entities to a patchwork of conflicting obligations. If a data controller has no intention of targeting a country's residents and has little presence there, applying that country's law may be harder to justify. The practical enforceability of such long-arm jurisdiction also remains uncertain. Private international law norms will need to evolve in tandem to address these challenges, balancing convergence with respect for sovereign diversity. Clearer rules and principles for allocating jurisdiction and facilitating enforcement in cross-border data protection matters are needed.

Determining applicable law is equally thorny. Laws like China's PIPL and arguably South Korea's PIPA apply to foreign entities targeting or profiling local individuals. But detailed conflict of law rules are often lacking. It is frequently unclear which country's laws would govern, especially with data stored across multiple jurisdictions. Contractual choice of law clauses may not always be dispositive, as data protection laws are often considered mandatory overriding statutes. This is seen in South Korea, where the Supreme Court confirmed the PIPA's mandatory nature in a 2023 decision involving Google.[55] In many jurisdictions, forum selection clauses are further subject to public policy limits.

This issue is highlighted in the context of cloud services spanning multiple regions. Ascertaining which court has authority to compel production of data stored in the cloud, and on what basis, is a vexing challenge.[56] The surveyed jurisdictions currently give limited guidance on when the location of data, the provider, or the affected data subjects should control.

This applicable law quandary also arises with the 'equivalence' standard for data transfers found in many Asian laws and transfer instruments (eg the ASEAN Model Contractual Clauses, Hong Kong's Greater Bay Area Standard Contract). When courts interpret such standards, questions arise on the weight to give foreign regulatory guidance. Deference promotes consistency, but room for local adaptation is also important. While joint guides between jurisdictions (like the ASEAN-EU guide) can help, such coordination is still rare.

Therefore, in some ways, determining the traditional conflict of laws distinction between jurisdiction and applicable law can be blurry in the context of data protection. The real question is often whether a country's domestic law applies to a given processing situation. If so, the authority will likely assert jurisdiction and apply that law, not foreign law. This blurring stems from the public regulatory nature of data protection laws. Classical choice of law analysis becomes less relevant.

Fundamentally, a spirit of comity is essential. Excessive unilateral jurisdictional assertions and aggressive extraterritorial application attempts will likely backfire, undermining the cross-border cooperation vital for effective data regulation. Conversely, a web of interlocking, mutually-reinforcing jurisdictional and applicable law norms and practices can optimise data protection across borders while respecting legitimate sovereign differences. Striking this delicate balance will remain a pressing priority as data disputes proliferate across the Asian borders surveyed.

ii. Enforcement and Judgments

Cross-border enforcement cooperation on data protection matters remains ad hoc and limited across the surveyed Asian jurisdictions. While MLATs exist, they are rarely utilised for data disputes. Regulator-to-regulator MOUs, such as the bilateral partnerships between the Philippines' privacy regulator and those of Hong Kong and Singapore, are promising but represent a piecemeal approach. Formal adequacy decisions or transfer agreements can reduce friction but require substantial convergence of laws and practices.

[55] Eung-Kyung Cho, 'South Korea' in chapter 4 of this volume.

[56] See, eg, *United States v Microsoft Corp*, 584 US ___, 138 S Ct 1186 (2018).

Achieving consistency of data protection-related judgments across borders is a significant concern. Conflicting court decisions showcase the risks of jurisdictional clashes in an increasingly data-driven economy. As data litigation grows in volume and complexity, risks of forum shopping and incompatible rulings may proliferate absent clear private international law rules.

This issue is prominent when an injunction needs to have global effect to provide effective protection to the data subject. Courts in several of the studied jurisdictions have grappled with the problematic nature of orders with worldwide effect, as they effectively impose the applicable law on the rest of the world. Whilst this issue remains novel in the 17 Asian jurisdictions surveyed, the results suggests that prudence is vital. While cross-border delisting orders and global injunctions may sometimes be justified to vindicate privacy rights, unilateral assertions of universal jurisdiction should be the exception not the norm. Negative international comity and practical constraints warrant restraint. Cooperative approaches based on minimum harmonisation are preferable.

iii. Harmonisation of PIL Rules and International Interoperability

Substantive convergence and conflicts between national laws will shape cross-border enforcement. Closer alignment of data protection standards will mean fewer clashes for regulators and courts. Market forces and 'Brussels Effects' could promote convergence around leading models, reducing conflicts.

The PIPL's similarities with the GDPR illustrate this: both define personal data broadly, impose extraterritorial obligations, and grant individual rights. This could facilitate EU-China cooperation on violations affecting both markets. Conversely, divergence on issues like sensitive data definitions, consent requirements, or government access carve-outs may amplify PIL problems.

But some level of conflict is inherent in the decentralised global data regime. Pockets of difference will likely persist, rooted in domestic preferences, constitutional traditions, and geo-economic competition. For example, while China's PIPL shares many similarities with the GDPR, there are still notable differences such as China's more expansive government access provisions and the PIPL's emphasis on national security considerations.

China and India's growing influence adds another layer of complexity. The PIPL reflects China's distinct stance on data governance, with an emphasis on national security and government access. This may pose challenges for interoperability with more individual rights-focused regimes. However, China's framework also presents opportunities for shaping regional norms, especially through its Digital Silk Road initiative and cross-border data flow pilots with Hong Kong. India's proposed data protection framework could be another potential standard-setter, given the country's large population and digital economy. However, delays and disagreements over the contours of the law have impeded progress. When India finalises its approach, it could significantly shape the regional landscape.

Ultimately, perfect uniformity is unrealistic given Asia's diversity. The goal should be 'interoperability' – ensuring that different national frameworks can work together despite some variations. This includes agreeing to common principles, recognition of comparable safeguards, and harmonisation of rules jurisdiction, applicable law and enforcement cooperation. Both bilateral and multilateral efforts will be key.

Japan's adequacy decision from the EU demonstrates the potential for interoperability despite differences. Japan amended its APPI to introduce GDPR-like concepts and strengthen individual rights, paving the way for an adequacy finding. However, Japan's constitutional traditions and the APPI's separate regimes for regulating public and private sectors still shape a distinctive approach.

The APEC CBPR system is another important regional mechanism for promoting interoperability of privacy frameworks. It provides a voluntary certification scheme for companies to demonstrate compliance with common principles for cross-border data transfers. Japan, Korea, the Philippines, Singapore, and Taiwan are all participating APEC economies. However, the CBPR has limits as a voluntary, non-binding scheme. Uptake has been selective and SME participation is low. Bilateral and multilateral efforts like Singapore's Digital Economy Agreements with Chile and New Zealand, and the Singapore-Australia Digital Economy Agreement's data transfer chapter are promising, but fragmentation remains the norm.

Global mechanisms offer instructive models, but Asian participation is mixed. The Hague Conference's Judgments Convention could ease recognition of data rulings, but only South Korea and the Philippines have joined regionally. Similarly, Japan is the sole Asian party to the modernised Council of Europe Convention 108+ on data protection.[57] The ASEAN Framework on Personal Data Protection and Model Contractual Clauses are regionally tailored solutions, but implementation is nascent. Myanmar's situation where comprehensive domestic legislation is not yet a priority underscores the importance of such regional initiatives. The recently established Global CBPR Forum, which includes several Asian economies like Singapore, the Philippines, and Taiwan, aims to promote interoperability and cooperation on data transfer systems. The success of these initiatives will depend on finding the right balance between harmonisation and flexibility to accommodate diverse national approaches.

VI. Topical Issues and Prospects in Asia

Rapid development and adoption of artificial intelligence (AI), big data analytics, and biometrics, and the impact of COVID-19 are transforming the digital landscape across Asia. They offer immense potential for innovation and progress, but also pose complex challenges for data governance and privacy protection. As the surveyed jurisdiction chapters highlight, policymakers, regulators, and courts across the region are grappling with how to harness the benefits of these technologies while mitigating their risks.

A. AI

i. AI and Automated Decision-Making

The proliferation of AI systems that collect and analyse vast troves of personal data is a key concern. Automated profiling and decision-making algorithms are being deployed across sectors, raising questions about fairness, transparency, and accountability.

[57] Nobuyuki Sato, 'Japan' in chapter 3 of this volume.

Some jurisdictions are starting to address these issues. China's PIPL requires separate consent for automated decision-making and grants a right to explanation and objection.[58] Singapore's PDPA and Advisory Guidelines on Use of Personal Data in AI Recommendation and Decision Systems emphasise transparency, human oversight, and risk management. Hong Kong's PCPD has also issued guidance on ethical AI development, emphasising transparency, fairness and accountability. South Korea amended its PIPA in 2023 to introduce provisions on automated decision-making, including a right to reject decisions solely based on automated processing.

Other jurisdictions like India, Vietnam, and Indonesia are considering new rules on AI as part of their draft data protection bills. However, many existing laws in the region still lack clear provisions on AI decision-making safeguards.

Enforcement challenges remain significant given the complexity and opacity of many AI systems. Regulators often lack technical expertise and resources to audit algorithms effectively. Explainability requirements may also need to be balanced against IP protection and innovation incentives. Finding the right governance approach will require ongoing multi-stakeholder dialogue and capacity building.

ii. Big Data and Analytics

Big data practices can amplify privacy risks. Aggregation and analysis of data from multiple sources can reveal sensitive patterns and enable re-identification. Predictive analytics can lead to discriminatory profiling. The scale of data collection strains traditional notice and consent models.

Some regimes are evolving to address these challenges. China's PIPL and Singapore's amended PDPA impose stricter obligations for large-scale processing, like mandatory DPIAs and breach notification.

However, many Asian data protection laws still lack specific provisions on big data safeguards. Notice and consent requirements can be challenging to implement meaningfully given the complex data flows involved. Ensuring interoperability will be crucial for cross-border data flows and analytics.

iii. Biometric Technologies

The widespread deployment of biometric technologies is another key trend. Some jurisdictions are starting to regulate biometric data as a sensitive category. China's PIPL imposes limits on the collection and use of biometric information.[59] India's draft data protection bill would require explicit consent and local storage of biometric data.

However, gaps remain. Many data protection laws do not yet cover biometrics specifically. Exemptions for law enforcement and national security are often broad.

iv. Generative AI and Data Protection

The ease of use and wide accessibility of generative AI has raised significant data protection and privacy concerns. The potential misuse of personal data for model training, the

[58] Zhao Yun, 'China' in chapter 1 of this volume.
[59] ibid.

risk of algorithmic biases leading to discrimination, and the challenges of ensuring compliance with data protection regulations are key issues that need to be addressed. However, many existing data protection frameworks in the 17 surveyed Asian jurisdictions still lack clear provisions on AI governance. Regulators often face challenges in auditing complex AI systems effectively due to limited technical expertise and resources.

In this context, it is submitted that core data protection principles can serve as a valuable starting point for Asian jurisdictions to mitigate the risks posed by generative AI and other AI applications.[60] Adhering to principles such as data minimisation, purpose limitation, accuracy, and security can help ensure that personal data used for AI training and deployment is handled responsibly. Conducting DPIAs and implementing appropriate technical and organisational measures can further enhance AI governance. Transparency is particularly crucial for building public trust in AI systems. Providing clear information about how personal data is collected, used, and processed by AI models, along with meaningful human oversight and redress mechanisms, can help address concerns about algorithmic bias and accountability.

As generative AI continues to advance rapidly, it is essential for Asian jurisdictions to proactively develop comprehensive regulatory frameworks that balance innovation with robust data protection safeguards.

v. COVID-19

The COVID-19 pandemic has accelerated digital transformation across Asia, with increased adoption of remote work, e-commerce, and digital health solutions. This has also intensified data protection challenges, particularly around the collection and use of health data for contact tracing and pandemic response. Several jurisdictions, such as Singapore and South Korea, have introduced temporary measures or exemptions to enable data sharing for public health purposes. The long-term impact of these measures on data protection norms and public trust remains to be seen.

B. The Future of Data Protection and Privacy in Asia

The future of data protection in Asia will also be shaped by broader geopolitical and economic trends, such as the rise of digital trade agreements and the increasing importance of data flows in regional economic integration initiatives like the Regional Comprehensive Economic Partnership (RCEP) and the Comprehensive and Progressive Agreement for Trans-Pacific Partnership (CPTPP), on the one hand, and risks of digital conflicts such as cyber espionage and cyber warfare, on the other. Achieving interoperability amidst this diversity is a formidable but crucial challenge. As jurisdictions like Myanmar continue to develop their data protection frameworks, the influence of regional initiatives like ASEAN's data management framework and privacy principles, the APEC CBPR, and the Global CBPR Forum offer promising avenues. Bilateral efforts can also drive convergence. However, the risk of a fragmented data governance landscape, with conflicting obligations and forum shopping, looms large.

[60] Yeong Zee Kin, 'International: Clear and Present Harm of AI – How Data Protection Principles may Help' (*DataGuide*, 2024), available at www.dataguidance.com/opinion/international-clear-and-present-harm-ai-how-data.

Ultimately, striking the right balance will require not just legal harmonisation, but also sustained dialogue, capacity building, and mutual learning. Regulators, policymakers, judges, businesses, and civil society need to collaboratively find the right balance between data protection, innovation, and cross-border data flows. As the 17 Asian jurisdictions navigate this evolving landscape, they have much to learn from each other's experiences and international best practices. At the same time, they have valuable insights to contribute to the global discourse on data governance. With its rich diversity and dynamic digital transformation, Asia is poised to be a key crucible and innovation hub for the future of data protection and privacy.

BIBLIOGRAPHY

Introduction

Anu Bradford, Digital Empires: The Global Battle to Regulate Technology (Oxford University Press, 2023)
William Prosser, 'Privacy' (1960) 48 *California Law Review* 3, 384

Cambodia

Cambodia Digital Economy and Social Policy Framework 2021–2035 (2021) & Cambodia Digital Government Policy 2022–2035 (2022)
Fiona Kelliher, 'Leaked Law Proposal Would Give Cambodia Expanded Powers to Censor Critics' (*est of world*, 2020)
Gerald Flynn and Phuong Vantha, 'Cambodia's Online Freedoms under Threat from Draft Cybercrime Law' (*Cambodianess-ThmeyThmey in English*, 22 October 2020)
Keo Sothie, 'Cambodia's Culture and Laws on Privacy and Data Protection, and the Future' in the Law Talks Series 'Law in the Digital Age: Protection of Consumer Rights' (*Konrad Adenauer Stiftung*, November 2021)
Nov Sivutha, 'Draft Law on Cybercrime Fast-Tracked' *The Phnom Penh Post* (28 June 2022)
Royal Government of Cambodia, 'National Research Agenda 2025' (2023)
Sar Socheath, Ministry of Interior Finalising Draft Law on Cybercrime *Khmer Times* (27 October 2022)
Sovath Phin, 'Privacy and Data Protection in the Digital Age: A Holistic Approach to Privacy and Data Protection in Cambodia' (*Konrad Adenauer Stiftung*, 2021)

China

Bret Cohen, Britanie Hall and Charles Wood, 'Data Localization Laws and their Impact on Privacy, Data Security and the Global Economy' (2017) *Antitrust* 32, 107
Fa Guo, 'The State Council on the Issuance of Notice of the "Thirteenth Five-Year" National Informatization Plan' (2016) No 73
Hong Shen, 'Building a Digital Silk Road? Situating the Internet in China's Belt and Road Initiative' (2018) *International Journal of Communication* 12, 19
Jinhe Liu, 'China's Data Localization' (2020) *Chinese Journal of Communication* 13(1), 84–103
Joseph Lee Riccardi, 'The German Federal Data Protection Act of 1977: Protecting the Right to Privacy' (1983) *Boston College International and Comparative Law Review* 6
Paul de Hert and Vagelis Papakonstantinou, 'The Data Protection Regime in China' (2015) *Depth Analysis Brussels Privacy Hub Working Paper* 1(4)
'Xi Jinping to Host 37 World Leaders at Belt and Road Forum' (*The Straits Times*, 20 April 2019)

European Commission

European Commission, 'What Rules Apply if my Organisation Transfers Data Outside the EU?'

Hong Kong

Chor Kiu Woo, 'Doxxing in Hong Kong – Way Forward'
Constitutional and Mainland Affairs Bureau, 'The Legislative Council Panel on Constitutional Affairs: Section 33 of the Personal Data (Privacy) Ordinance' LC Paper No. CB(2)1368/16-17(03) (15 May 2017)
Constitutional and Mainland Affairs Bureau, 'Overview of the Greater Bay Area'
'Contact Tracing Apps: A New World for Data Privacy' (February 2012)
Dr Hon Kennedy WONG's motion on 'Promoting Data Interchange in the Guangdong-Hong Kong-Macao Greater Bay Area and Developing Cross-Border E-Commerce', LC Paper No. CB(3)811/2022(01)
Government of Hong Kong, 'Government Announces Establishment of Digital Economy Development Committee' (22 June 2022)
Government of Hong Kong, 'Facilitation Measure on "Standard Contract for Cross-boundary Flow of Personal Information Within the Guangdong-Hong Kong-Macao Greater Bay Area (Mainland, Hong Kong)" and its Early and Pilot Implementation Arrangements' (13 December 2023)
Ho M, 'Xi Jinping Sends Message on Growth through Innovation, Big Data in Guizhou' *South China Morning Post* (Hong Kong, 9 February 2021)
Law Reform Commission of Hong Kong, 'Report: Reform of the Law Relating to the Protection of Personal Data' (August 1994)
—— 'Report: Privacy and Media Intrusion' (December 2004)
Legislative Council Panel on Constitutional Affairs, 'Report on the Work of the Office of the Privacy Commissioner for Personal Data in 2019' LC Paper No. CB(2)815/19-20(04) (April 2020)
—— 'Review of the Personal Data (Privacy) Ordinance' LC Paper No. CB(2)512/19-20(03) (20 January 2020)
Office of the Privacy Commissioner for Personal Data, Hong Kong, *Data Protection Principles in the Personal Data (Privacy) Ordinance – from the Privacy Commissioner's Perspective*, 2nd edn (2010)
'Outline Development Plan for the Guangdong-Hong Kong _Macao Greater Bay Area'
PCPD, 'Transfer of Personal Data Outside Hong Kong: Some Common Questions' (1 April 1997) Fact Sheet No 1
—— 'Report Published under Section 48(2) of the Personal Data (Privacy) Ordinance (Cap. 486)' (18 October 2010) Report Number R10-9866
—— 'Outsourcing the Processing of Personal Data to Data Processors' (September 2012)
—— 'Guidance on Personal Data Protection in Cross-border Data Transfer' (December 2014)
—— 'Privacy Management Programme: A Best Practice Guide' (August 2018)
—— 'Response to Media Enquiry on Data Localisation' (15 April 2020)
—— 'Guidance on the Ethical Development and Use of Artificial Intelligence' (August 2021)
—— 'First Sentencing Case of the New Doxxing Offence' (15 December 2022)
—— 'The Use of Information on Social Media for Tracking Potential Carriers of COVID-19' (26 February 2023)
Research Office, Legislative Council Secretariat, *Information Note: Measures to Address Doxxing in Selected Places* (IN09/19-20)
Shirley Zhao, 'Hong Kong Scraps Contact Tracing App That Raised Privacy Concern' (*Bloomberg UK*, London, 9 January 2023)
Stephen Kai-yi Wong, 'Balancing Privacy Right Against Public Interests Amidst COVID-19 Pandemic' (2010) *Hong Kong Lawyer*

India

A Mattoo and S Wunsch, 'Pre-Empting Protectionism in Services – the GATS and Outsourcing' (2004) *Journal of International Economic Law* 7(4), 765–800
Anirudh Barman, 'Understanding India's New Data Protection Law' (*Carnegie Endowment for International Peace*, 3 October 2023)
Anna-Maria Osula and Henry Rõigas, 'Introduction' in Anna-Maria Osula and Henry Rõigas (eds), *International Cyber Norms: Legal, Policy & Industry Perspectives* (Tallinn, Estonia: NATO Cooperative Cyber Defence Centre of Excellence, 2016)

Arushi Gupta, 'The Case against the Constitutional Validity of Mass Surveillance Programmes' (2019) *Indian Law Review*

—— 'All Computers Can Now Be Monitored by Central Agencies' (*The Hindu*, 21 December 2018)

Biswajit Dhar and Reji K Joseph, 'India's Information Technology Industry: A Tale of Two Halves' in KC Liu and Uday S Racherla (eds), *Innovation, Economic Development, and Intellectual Property in India and China.* ARCI-ALA Series on Intellectual Assets and Law in Asia (Springer, 2019)

Chaitanya Ramachandran, 'PUCL v. UOI Revisited: Why India's Surveillance Law Must Be Redesigned For The Digital Age' (*Manupatra*, April–June 2014)

Christopher Kuner, 'Regulation of Transborder Data Flows under Data Protection and Privacy Law: Past, Present and Future', OECD Digital Economy Papers, No 187 (OECD, 2011)

Circular on Storage of Payment System Data Issued by India's Central Bank, the Reserve Bank of India, dated 6 April, 2018.

Cole David and Fabbrini Federico, 'Bridging the Transatlantic Divide? The United States, the European Union, and the Protection of Privacy Across Borders' (2016) 14 *ICON* 220, 223

Committee of Experts under the Chairmanship of Justice B N Srikrishna, A Free and Fair Digital Economy: 'Protecting Privacy, Empowering Indians, Ministry of Electronics & Information Technology', Government of India (27 July 2018)

Consolidated Version of the Treaty on the Functioning of the European Union (TFEU) Art 16 [2012] OJ C326/47

David Markus, 'Digital Trade and Digital Sovereignty: Navigating Best Practice for Cross Border Data Transfers, Working Paper 2020

—— 'Digital Resilience in the Age of a Global Pandemic: How can Privacy Assist in Risk Mitigation?' (2020) 17(1&2) *Privacy Law Bulletin* 2

David Nguyen and Marta Paczos, 'Measuring the Economic Value of Data and Cross-Border Data Flows: A Business Perspective' (2020)

Elonnai Hickok, Vipul Kharbanda, Shweta Mohandas and Pranav M Bidare, 'Is the New Interception Order Old Wine in a New Bottle?' (*The Centre for Internet Society*, 29 December 2018)

James Manyika, 'Digital Globalization: The New Era of Global Flows' (*McKinsey Global Institute*, 2016)

Jan L Neels, 'Choice of Forum and Tacit Choice of Law: The Supreme Court of India and the Hague Principles on Choice of Law in International Commercial Contracts (An Appeal for an Inclusive Comparative Approach to Private International Law)' in *Eppur si Muove: The Age of Uniform Law Essays in Honour of Michael Joachim Bonell to Celebrate his 70th Birthday* (UNIDROIT, 2016) 358, 366

Jeanne Ji Huang, 'Applicable Law to Transnational Personal Data: Trends and Dynamics' (2020) 21 *German Law Journal* 1283, 1286

K Mačák, 'Is the International Law of Cyber Security in Crisis?' (2016 8th International Conference on Cyber Conflict (CyCon)), 127–39

Madhav Khosla, *India's Founding Moment: The Constitution of a Most Surprising Democracy* (Harvard University Press, 2020)

Mathew Chacko and Aadya Misra, 'India – Data Protection Overview'

Mitchell Andrew and Hepburn Jarrod, 'Don't Fence Me In: Reforming Trade and Investment Law to Better Facilitate Cross-border Data Transfer' (2017) 19 *Yale Journal of Law and Technology* 182, 186

Nicholas Tsagourias, 'Law, Borders and the Territorialisation of Cyberspace" (2018) 18(4) *Indonesian Journal of International Law* 523, 539

Nupur Chowdhury, 'Data Appropriation, not Protection' (*Deccan Herald*, 27 September 2023)

PV Raja Mannar, 'The Future of Private International Law in India' (1952) 1 *The Indian Yearbook of International Affairs* 20

Raul Alan Charles, Manoranjan Tasha D and Mohan Vivek, 'United States' in Alan Charles Raul (ed), *The Privacy, Data Protection, And Cybersecurity Law Review*, 1st edn (Law Business Research Ltd, 2014) 268, 269

'Regulatory Divergence: Costs, Risks, Impacts: An International Financial Sector Study by Business at OECD and the International Federation of Accountants' (2018)

Report of The Joint Committee on The Personal Data Protection Bill, 2019 submitted to the 17th Lok Sabha, December 2021, pp 4, 8–10

Sai Ramani Garimella, 'OBOR and the Syncretic Private International Law Rules in India: Time for Accession to Harmonised Legal Regimes' in Poomintr Sooksripaisarnkit and Sai Ramani Garimella (eds), *China's One Belt One Road Initiative and Private International Law* (Routledge, 2018)

—— 'India' in Anselmo Reyes (ed), *Recognition and Enforcement of Judgments in Civil and Commercial Matters* (Hart-Bloomsbury, 2019)
—— and B Parthiban, 'Ringfencing Data? – Perspectives on Sovereignty and Localisation from India' in Poomintr Sooksripaisarnkit and Dharmita Prasad (eds), *Blurry Boundary of Public and Private International Law – Towards Convergence or Divergence Still?* 261 (Springer, 2022)
TS Rama Rao, "Private International Law in India" (1955) 4 *The Indian Yearbook of International Affairs* 219
VK Thiruvenkatachari, 'Developments in the field of Private International Law' (1953) 2 *The Indian Yearbook on International Affairs* 195

Indonesia

'AI Towards Indonesia's Vision 2045' (*AIIS*, 2024)
'Aplikasi PeduliLindungi Aman dari Phising dan Malware, Diunduh lewat App Store dan Play Store' (*Kominfo*, 2020)
'Aplikasi PeduliLindungi, Lindungi Data Pribadi Penggunanya' (*Satuan Tugas Penanganan*, 2022)
BPPT, 'Huawei Team Up to Develop AI, could and 5G' (*The Jakarta Post*, 2020)
'Care and Protect?: Apparent Govt Health App Breach Raises Deeper Data Concerns' (*The Jakarta Post*, 2022)
'China, Indonesia Sign MoU on Internet Security amid Washington Pressure on Beijing's 5G Technology' (*Global Times*, 2021)
'Huawei Bangun Pusat Inovasi Untuk Kembangkan SDM di Bidang ICT' (*Kominfo*, 2015)
'Indonesia Artificial Intelligence' (*Asia Society*, 2022)
'Indosat Ooredoo Partners Huawei to Build 5G Transport Networks' (*IDN Financials*, 2020)
'Kominfo Siapkan Sertifikasi Kerja dan Kompetensi PPDP' (*Kominfo*, November 2022)
'No Additional Rules after Lifting of All Covid-19 Restrictions: MoH' (*a.id*, 2022)
'PeduliLindungi Tetap Aman' (*Kominfo*, 2021)
'President Jokowi Calls for Grand Strategy for Indonesia's 2045 Vision' (*Cabinet Secretariat of the Republic of Indonesia*, 2023)
Priskila Pratita Penasthika, *Unravelling Choice of Law in International Commercial Contracts – Indonesia as an Illustrative Case Study* (Eleven International Publishing, 2022) 86–87, 111–66.
'Siapkan Security System, Pemerintah Pastikan Data Pribadi Pengguna PeduliLindungi Aman' (*Kominfo*, 2021)
Sudargo Gautama, 'International Civil Procedure in Indonesia' (1996) 6 *Asian Yearbook of International Law* 87, 96–97
—— *Hukum Perdata Internasional Indonesia [Indonesian Private International Law]*, 2nd edn (Alumni, 2004) Vol III Part 4-Book 5, 133–45, 178–80
—— *Hukum Perdata Internasional Indonesia [Indonesian Private International Law]*, 8th edn (Alumni, 2013) Vol III Part 2-Book 8, 282–83
—— and Robert N Hornick, *An Introduction to Indonesian Law Unity in Diversity* (Alumni Press, 1974) 177–78

Japan

Kunifumi Saito, 'Conflict of Law around the Right of Publicity' (2014) 32 *Jyoho Tsushin Gkkai Shi* 2
Mathias Audit, 'Le droit international privé confronté à la blockchain' (2022) 293 *Journal of Law and Politics* 135
Ministry of Health, Labour and Welfare (eds), *Guidelines for Security Management of Medical Information Systems (Edition 6.0) – Planning and Management* (May 2023) 27
National Center of Incident readiness and Strategy for Cybersecurity (eds), *Guidelines for the Formulation of Standards for Measures for Government Agencies* (4 July 2023) 164
Nobuyuki Sato, 'Saibansho ni your Intanetto Jyoho no Sekaiteki Kisei no Kanousei – Google Inc.v Equustek Solutions Inc Kanada Saiko Saibansho Hanketsu o Keiki to shite-' in N Sato (ed), *Kenpo Riron no Saikochiku* (Keibundo, 2019)

PPC, *Guideline on the APPI (Provision to the Third Party in Foreign Countries)*
—— *Q&A Concerning the Guideline for the APPI*
Secretariat Office of the PPC, *Sharing of Personal Information between Medical Institutions in Relation to New Coronavirus Infections and the APPI* (28 April 2020)
Takuya Shima, 'Online Service Provider o meguru Kokusaiteki na Ho Kiritsu: Teishoku Ho no Kanten kara no Kosatsu' (2022) 73(1) *Hokudai Hogaku Ronshu* 1
The Agency for Cultural Affairs, *On AI and Copyright (Tentative Draft)* (15 January 2024).

Kazakhstan

Aset Shyngyssov and Bakhytzhan Kadyrov, *Data Protection in Kazakhstan: Overview* (Thomson Reuters, 2023) 2
Alexander Chumachenko, *Problematic Issues of Localisation of Personal Data* (*Chambers and Partners*, 29 November 2016)
В ЦИК прокомментировали утечку данных' (*Profit.kz*, 12 August 2019)
IYu Loskutov and others, 'Expert Opinion on the Draft Law of the Republic of Kazakhstan "On Personal Data"' (2013)
Kenddrick Chan et al, *Against the Grain: The Data Regulatory Regimes of Kazakhstan and Uzbekistan vis-à-vis Russia, China, and Big Tech* (LSE IDEAS DIGITAL IR | WORKING PAPER 10/2022) 7
'Kazakhstan – The Impact of the GDPR outside the EU' (*Lexology*, 30 September 2019)
Soros Kazakhstan Foundation, 'Personal Data Protection in Kazakhstan: A Dysfunctional Law and Cautious Movement towards GDPR' (4 June 2019)
Vlast.kz, '*Утечка данных казахстанцев в сеть произошла из Центризбиркома – ЦАРКА*' (*Аналитический интернет-журнал Власть*, 8 August 2019)

Malaysia

Abu Bakar Munir and Siti Hajar Mohd Yasin, *Personal Data Protection in Malaysia Law and Practice* (Sweet & Maxwell Asia, 2010)
Akmar Annuar 'Threats and Challenges of AI' (*The Malaysian Reserve*, 5 June 2023)
Ali Alibeigi and Abu Bakar Munir, 'Malaysian Personal Data Protection Act, a Mysterious Application' (2020) *University of Bologna Law Review*
Atiqah Binti Azman and others, 'Privacy in the Era of Big Data: Unlocking the Blue Oceans of Data Paradigm in Malaysia' (2021) 6 *Malaysian Journal of Social Sciences and Humanities* 203
'Contract Tracing Apps in France' (*Norton Rose Fulbright*, 2 December 2020)
Janet Toh Yoong San, Boo Cheng Xuan, and Yee Yong Xuan, 'Data Residency and Retention Requirements in Malaysia' (2023) *Lexology*
Karen Cheah Yee Lynn, 'Press Release: Transparent and Protection of Privacy Crucial for Personal Data Collected through the MySejahtera Application' (*Malaysian Bar*, 27 February 2023)
Liew Jia Teng, 'Tech: Tencent Cloud offers path to China for Malaysians firms' (*The Edge Malaysia*, 17 April 2024)
Mahadhir Monihuldin, Ragananthini Methuselah, Martin Carvalho and Arfa Yunus, 'Amendments to Personal Data Protection Act in Final Stages, says Deputy Comms Minister' (*The Star*, 12 October 2023)
Mazwin Nik Anis and Ragananthini Vethasalam 'AG's Report: MySejahtera was Target of 1.12 million Cyber Attacks' (*The Star*, 2023)
Nurkhairina Binti Noor Sureani and others, 'The Adequacy of Data Protection Laws in Protecting Personal Data in Malaysia' (2021) *Malaysian Journal of Social Sciences and Humanities* 6, 10
'Public Consultation Paper No 01/2020' (*Personal Data Protection Commissioner*, 12 February 2020)
Sheila Ramalingam, 'The Case for the Tort of Privacy in Malaysia [2023] 1 MLJ xlv' (2023) *Malayan Law Journal*
S Joan Santani 'Malaysia Coming up with AI Governance and Code of Ethics' (*Business Times*, 9 January 2024)
Shahrin Aizat Noorshahrizam 'Deputy Minister: Three million MySejahtera Users' Data Downloaded to Protect them from Hackers' (*The Malay Mail*, 27 February 2023)

Tay Pek San, 'The Impact of the Personal Data Protection Act 2010 on Data Analytics in the Retail Industry' (2020) *The Malayan Law Journal* lxii-lxxxiii

'What You Need to Know' (*Ministry of Communications of Malaysia and Personal Data Protection Commissioner Malaysia*, 2019)

Myanmar

'ASEAN Model Contractual Clauses for Cross Border Data Flows' (2021)

'Joint Guide to the ASEAN Model Contractual Clauses and EU Standard Contractual Clauses' (2024)

Philippines

Aiken Larisa Serzo, 'Cross Border Data Regulation for Digital Platforms: Data Privacy and Security' (Discussion Paper No 2020-47, Philippine Institute for Development Studies, December 2020) [1.2.1].Asia Pacific Economic Cooperation, 'Data Privacy Framework' (Reports, December 2005)

Bangko Sentral ng Pilipinas, *BSP Circular No 982*, 2 November 2017, s 4

Bernie Cahiles-Magkilat, 'Lack of Legislation on Data Privacy Protection Worries Investors – JFC' (*Manila Bulletin*, 7 June 2011)

'CBPR System: An Overview' (*National Privacy Commission*)

Christopher Lloyd Caliwan, 'DOJ Chief Welcomes PH Inclusion to Cybercrime Convention' (*Philippine News Agency*, 4 March 2018)

Ivy Patdu and Jamael Jacob, 'The Data Privacy Act and the National Privacy Commission's Five Pillars of Compliance' (2018) 63(1) *Ateneo Law Journal* 120

Lemuel Lopez, 'The Right to Privacy in Inquiries in Aid of Legislation' (2003) 78(1) *Philippine Law Journal* 162

—— 'When Choice of Forum Clauses are Challenged: Key Lessons from Asian Jurisdictions' (PhD Thesis, The University of Melbourne, 2019) 195

Marck Joseph Macaraeg, 'From Atoms to Bits: Personal Data Privacy and Security in the Information Society' (2017) 62(1) *Ateneo Law Journal* 223

National Privacy Commission, *NPC Advisory Opinion No 2017-06* (5 January 2016)

—— *NPC Circular No 2016-01* (10 October 2016) ('Security of Personal Data in Government Agencies')

—— *NPC Circular 2016-02* (10 October 2016) ('Data Sharing Agreements Involving Government Agencies')

—— *NPC Circular No 2016-03* (15 December 2016)

—— *NPC Advisory Opinion No 2017-005* (5 January 2017)

—— *NPC Advisory Opinion No 2017-012* (6 February 2017)

—— *NPC Advisory No 2017-01* (14 March 2017)

—— *NPC Advisory No 2017-02* (3 April 2017) ('Access to Personal Data Sheets of Government Personnel')

—— *NPC Advisory Opinion No 2017-27* (23 June 2017)

—— *NPC Advisory Opinion No 2017-028* (23 June 2017) ('Data Sharing Agreement between Government Agencies')

—— *NPC Advisory Opinion No 2017-031* (28 June 2017) ('Consent on the Sharing of Mobile Number of Bank Clients for Credit Scoring')

—— *NPC Advisory Opinion No 2017-038* (14 August 2017) ('Data Sharing Agreement between Government Agencies')

—— *NPC Advisory Opinion No 2017-054* (11 September 2017) ('Data Sharing Agreement between Government Agencies')

—— *NPC Advisory Opinion No 2017-57* (3 October 2017)

—— *NPC Advisory Opinion No 2018-022* (30 April 2018)

—— *NPC Advisory Opinion No 2018-025* (4 May 2018) ('Request for Information from Law Enforcement Agencies')

—— *NPC Advisory Opinion 2018-029* (6 June 2018)

—— *NPC Advisory Opinion No 2018-060* (30 August 2018) ('Disclosure of Personal Information to the Bangko Sentral ng Pilipinas')
—— *NPC Advisory Opinion No 2018-057* (20 September 2018)
—— *NPC Advisory Opinion No 2018-58* (26 October 2018)
—— *NPC Advisory Opinion No 2018-68* (20 November 2018)
—— *NPC Advisory Opinion No 2019-006* (4 January 2019) ('Use of Clinical Data in Research')
—— *NPC Advisory Opinion No 2019-014* (5 March 2019) ('Proposed Bangko Sentral ng Pilipinas and Department of Interior and Local Government Join Memorandum Circular')
—— *NPC Advisory Opinion No 2019-017* (5 March 2019) ('Research and the Data Privacy Act of 2012')
—— *NPC Advisory Opinion No 2019-018* (11 March 2019) ('Data Collection Surveys by Government Agencies')
—— *NPC Advisory Opinion No 2019-040* (17 October 2019) ('Anti-Money Laundering Council Request')
—— *NPC Advisory Opinion No. 2019-041* (23 October 2019) ('Credit Card Fraud Investigation')
—— *NPC Advisory Opinion No 2020-002* (6 February 2020) ('Re: Publication of the Full Content of Bureau of Internal Revenue (Bir) Rulings in the Bir Website')
—— *NPC Advisory Opinion No 2020-012* (19 February 2020) ('Re: Disclosure of Insurance Policy Details to the National Bureau of Investigation')
—— *NPC Advisory Opinion No 2020-021* (29 May 2020) ('Re: Automated Retrieval of Bank Transaction History')
—— *NPC Advisory Opinion No. 2020-031* (6 August 2020) ('Re: Access to Files and Records of Anti-illegal Drugs Operations of the Philippine Drug Enforcement Agency')
—— *NPC Circular No 2020-01* (14 September 2020) ('Guidelines on the Processing of Personal Data for Loan-Related Transactions')
—— *NPC Advisory No 2020-03* (30 October 2020)
—— *NPC Advisory Opinion No 2020-039* (30 October 2020) ('Re: Disclosure or Sharing of Bank Transaction Information for Fraud Investigations')
—— *NPC Advisory Opinion No 2020-050* (26 November 2020) ('Re: Disclosure by Fintech, Digital Payment Platforms, and Telecommunications Entities of Personal Data for Fraud Investigation')
—— *NPC Advisory Opinion No 2020-051* (26 November 2020) ('Re: Request for Personal Data by the National Bureau of Investigation and the Philippine Army');
—— *NPC Circular 2020-03* (23 December 2020) ('Amending Certain Provisions of NPC Circular No 20-01 on the Guidelines on the Processing of Personal Data for Loan-Related Transactions')
—— *NPC Circular No 2021-01* (28 January 2021)
—— *NPC Advisory No 2021-01* (29 January 2021)
NPC Advisory No 2022 01 (29 January 2021) ('Guidelines On Requests For Personal Data Of Public Officers')
—— *NPC Advisory Opinion No 2021-007* (5 March 2021) ('Re: Data Sharing Arrangements of the Philippine Veterans Affairs Office With Other Government Agencies')
—— *NPC Advisory Opinion No. 2021-012* (16 April 2021)('Re: Documentary Requirements for Accreditation as Financial Institution')
—— *NPC Advisory Opinion No 2021-018* (18 June 2021) ('Re: PNP Request for Personal Information from Employers')
—— *NPC Advisory No 2021-02* (28 June 2021) ('Guidance for the Use of the ASEAN Model Contract Clauses and ASEAN Data Management Framework')
—— *NPC Advisory Opinion No 2021-023* (5 July 2021)('Re: Processing of Personal Data for Research Without Ethics Clearance');
—— *NPC Advisory Opinion No 2021-026* (12 July 2021) ('Re: Data Privacy Implications for Financial Services Industry Initiatives on Data Sharing')
—— *NPC Advisory Opinion No 2021-031* (5 August 2021) ('Re: Processing for due Diligence, Quality Control, and Compliance Checks Pursuant to the Requirements of the Government Procurement Reform Act')
—— *NPC Advisory Opinion No 2021-033* (13 August 2021) ('Re: Internal Dissemination of Information Regarding Bank-Related Crimes')
—— *NPC Advisory Opinion No 2021-036* (23 September 2021) ('Re: Disclosure of Loan Documents Pursuant to a Legal Claim')
—— *NPC Advisory Opinion No 2021-03* (5 November 2021) ('Guidelines On The Processing Of Personal Data For Election Campaign Or Partisan Political Activity')
—— *NPC Advisory Opinion No 2021-043* (16 December 2021) ('Re: Data Sharing with the Philippine National Police')

—— *NPC Advisory Opinion No 2022-025* (22 November 2022) ('Re: 201 Files of Government Employees')
—— *NPC Advisory Opinion No. 2022-026* (23 November 2022) ('Re: Disclosure of Personal Data Through the Database of Individuals Barred from Taking Civil Service Examinations and from Entering Government Service (DIBAR))
—— *NPC Circular No 2022-04* (5 December 2022)
—— *NPC Advisory Opinion No 2023-009* (27 February 2023)
—— *NPC Advisory Opinion No 2022-013* (21 June 2023) ('Re: Online Lending Mobile Application Permissions')
—— *NPC Circular 2023-05* (25 October 2023)
—— *NPC Circular No 2024-01* (26 January 2024)
National Privacy Commission and Department of Health, *Joint Memorandum Circular No 2020-0002* (24 April 2020)
'The APEC CBPR System: An Overview' *National Privacy Commission*

Singapore

AI Verify Foundation & IMDA, 'Proposed Model AI Governance Framework for Generative AI: Fostering a Trusted Ecosystem' (Issued 16 January 2024)
ASEAN, 'ASEAN Model Contractual Clauses for Cross Border Data Flows' (Final Copy Endorsed by the 2nd ASEAN Digital Senior Officials' Meeting, January 2021)
—— 'ASEAN Guide on AI Governance and Ethics'
Benjamin Wong, 'Confidential Information and Data Protection' (2021) 22 *Singapore Academy of Law Annual Review of Singapore Cases* 267
Explanatory Statement to the Personal Data Protection Bill (Bill No. 24/2012), Part I, Clause 3
Gary Kok Yew Chan and Pey Woan Lee, *The Law of Torts Singapore,* 2nd edn (Academy Publishing, 2015)
Goh Yan Han, 'S'pore Seeks International Feedback on New Governance Framework for Generative AI' (*The Straits Times*, 17 January 2024)
IMDA, 'The Full Composition of Singapore's Advisory Council on the Ethical Use of AI and Data (Advisory Council) was announced by Minister for Communications and Information Mr S Iswaran at AI Singapore's First Year Anniversary' (30 August 2018)
—— 'Enabling Data-Driven Innovation Through Trusted Data Sharing in a Digital Economy' (28 June 2019)
—— 'The Driving Force behind Personal Data Protection' (25 January 2022)
—— 'Singapore Welcomes Establishment Of The Global Cross-Border Privacy Rules (CBPR) Forum' (21 April 2022)
—— 'About the Trusted Data Sharing Framework' (4 April 2023)
—— 'Proposed Advisory Guidelines on use of Personal Data in AI Recommendation and Decision Systems' (Issued 18 July 2023), 8, [6.1]–[6.4]
—— 'Opening Remarks for PDPC Commissioner at IAPP Asia Privacy Forum' (19 July 2023)
—— 'DPTM Certification Checklist' 6, section D
—— and PDPC, 'Trusted Data Sharing Framework' (3 August 2023)
Janil Puthucheary, 'Parliamentary Debates, Official Report', Vol No 94, Sitting No 59 (6 February 2018).
—— Singapore Parliamentary Debates, Official Report of Parliament No 14 Session 2 Vol No 95 Sitting No 103 (9 May 2023)
Jeanette Tan, '40% of Singaporeans Use AI at Work, 76% of them Pass Results off as their Own: Survey' (*The Straits Times*, 20 September 2023)
Kasiviswanathan Shanmugam, Singapore Parliamentary Debates, Official Report, Session 1, Vol No 95, Sitting No 71 (5 October 2022)
Ken Chia, 'Jurisdictional Report: Singapore' in Asian Business Law Institute, *Regulation of Cross-Border Transfers of Personal Data in Asia* (2018), 317, [8]
Lanx Goh and Jansen Aw, 'Data Protection Law in Singapore' in Simon Chesterman (ed), *Data Protection Law in Singapore: Privacy and Sovereignty in an Interconnected World,* 2nd edn (Academy Publishing, 2018)
——, 'Data Localisation: The Way Forward or Backward for Data Innovation?' [2020] *PDP Digest* 63, 66
Lanx Goh and Nadia Yeo, 'Sensitive Personal Data in the Singapore Context' [2019] *PDP Digest* 37.
MAS, 'Guidelines on Outsourcing' (5 October 2018)

MCI, 'Singapore and the US to Deepen Cooperation in AI'
—— 'Speech by Minister of Communications and Information, Mrs Josephine Teo, at the Opening of the Personal Data Protection Week on 18 July 2023' (18 July 2023) [37]
Ministry of Law, 'Press Release: Quicker, More Effective Remedies Against Harassment with New Protection from Harassment Court from 1 June 2021' (31 May 2021)
Ministry of Trade and Industry Singapore, 'What are Digital Economy Agreements (DEAs)?'
PDPC, 'Data Protection Obligations' for an Overview of these Eleven Obligations
—— 'Advisory Guidelines on Key Concepts in the PDPA' (Revised 16 May 2022) ('Key Concepts Guidelines') 2, [2.2]
—— 'Do Not Call Registry & You'
—— 'Advisory Guidelines on the Personal Data Protection Act for NRIC and Other National Identification Numbers' (31 August 2018)
—— 'Data Protection Obligations'
—— 'PDPA Overview – What is the PDPA?'
—— 'Response to Feedback on the Public Consultation on Proposed Data Portability and Data Innovation Provisions' (20 January 2020) 12
—— 'Singapore's Approach to AI Governance'
—— 'Guidance for Use of ASEAN Model Contractual Clauses for Cross Border Data Flows in Singapore' (22 January 2021)
—— 'Advisories on Collection of Personal Data for COVID-19 Contact Tracing and Use of SafeEntry' (4 January 2022)
—— 'Guide to Basic Anonymisation' (31 March 2022)
—— 'Joint Guide to ASEAN Model Contractual Clauses and EU Standard Contractual Clauses Now Available' (24 May 2023)
—— 'Public Consultation for the Proposed Advisory Guidelines on Use of Personal Data in AI Recommendation and Decision Systems' (19 July 2023)
—— 'Two Guides Unveiled at ASEAN Digital Ministers' Meeting (ADGMIN) 2024' (2 February 2024)
Smart Nation Singapore, 'Government's Personal Data Protection Initiatives, online: Singapore Government'
—— 'Government's Personal Data Protection Laws and Policies'
—— 'The Next Frontier of Singapore's Smart Nation Journey'
—— 'Discontinuation of TraceTogether and SafeEntry'
William L Prosser, *Privacy* (1960) 48 *California Law Review* 383
Yaacob Ibrahim, 'Singapore Parliamentary Debates, Official Report', vol 89 (15 October 2012)

South Korea

Choi Kyung Jun et al, *Personal Information Protection Act* (Parkyoungsa, February 2024)
Go Hak Su et al., *Ingongjineung sidaeu geinjeongbo bohobeob* [*Personal Data Protection Law in the Age of Artificial Intelligence*] (Parkyoungsa, 2022) 8–9
Kim Ju Young and Son Hyung Seob, *Geinjeongbobobeu Ihae* [*Understandung Personal Data Protection Law*] (Beobmumsa, 2012) 112–128
Kim Hyun Sook, 'A Comparative Study on Scientific Research in the Data Protection Laws between EU and Korea' (2020) *Journal of Korea Information Law* 115–44
Kim Ju Young and Son Hyung Seob, *Geinjeongbobobeu Ihae* [*Understandung Personal Data Protection Law*] (Beobmumsa, 2012)
Kim Yong Hak, *Geinjeongbo Bohobob* [*Personal Information Protection Act*] (Chongho Books, 2021)
Lee He-Won, 'A Legal Research on The Scope of Application of the Personal Information Protection Act' (2022) *Journal of Korea information Law* 26-1
Lee Joo Hee, 'A Study on Personal Information Protection Measures in the Covid-19 Era' (2020) *Science, Technology and Law*, 11-2, 307–308
Lee Jong Hyeok, 'New Developments in Korean Private International Law' in Olivier Gaillard and Krista Nadakavukaren Schefer (eds), *Private International Law in East Asia, From Imitation to Innovation and Exportation* (Bloomsbury Publishing, 2024) 107–22, 114–15

—— 'A Preliminary Study on the Data Protection Litigations from the Perspective of Private International Law – With Focus on the Categories of the Data Protection Litigations and the Issue of International Adjudicatory Jurisdiction' (2019) *Journal of Korea International Trade Law Association*, 28-2, 139–72, 160–62

Ministry of the Interior and Safety, *Guidelines for the De-Identification of Personal Data* (2016)

PIPC, *Guide to the Interpretation of Data Protection Laws and Regulations* (2 December 2020)

—— *Handbook on the Psedonymisation of Personal Data* (5 February 2024)

Shin Jong Chul, *Geinjeongbobohobobhesol* [*Commentary of the Personal Information Protection Act*] (Jinhan M&B, 2020) 29–32

Suk Kwang Hyun, *Gukjejepangwanhalbob – 2022nyeon gejeong gukjesabob hesol* [*International Adjudicatory Jurisdiction Law – Commentary of the 2022 Revised PILA*] (Parkyoungsa, 2022)

Sri Lanka

Fernando, Jayantha and Wickramasinghe, Sanduni, 'Sri Lanka Personal Data Protection Legislation – An Overview' (3 August 2022) ('PDPA Overview') SSRN

Hiyal Biyagamage, 'SLASSCOM Launches Sri Lanka's First AI Policy Framework' (*Daily Financial Times*, 27 June 2019)

Marasinghe L, *Private International Law*, 2nd edn (Vijitha Yapa Publications, 2021)

Presidential Secretariat, 'Sri Lanka's Personal Data Protection Authority Progresses with Board of Directors Appointment' (October 2023)

Sanduni Wickramasinghe, 'White Paper: Sri Lanka's Personal Data Protection Act No. 9 of 2022' (2023) *Friedrich-Naumann-Stiftung für die Freiheit* 14

TB Abeysekara and AE Ranasinghe, 'Holistic Approach in Introducing Proper Legal Framework to Regulate Data Protection and Privacy in Sri Lanka' (2022) *Vidyodaya Journal of Management* 8(1) 169–200

United Nations Department of Economic and Social Affairs, *Progress Report on the Belt and Road Initiative in Support of the United Nations 2030 Agenda for Sustainable Development* (14 September 2022)

Taiwan

George E Edwards, 'International Human Rights Law Challenges to the New International Criminal Court: The Search and Seizure Right to Privacy' (2001) 26 *Yale Journal of International Law* 323

Huang-Chih Sung, 'Legal Risks and Management Implications of Big Data Transactions – Focusing on the Reidentification of Personal Data' (2018) 37 *Management Review* 121

J Angelo Corlett, 'The Nature and Value of the Moral Right to Privacy' (2002) 16 *Public Affairs Quarterly* 329

Kelly Freund, 'When Cameras Are Rolling: Privacy Implications of Body-Mounted Cameras on Police' (2015) 49 *Columbia Journal of Law & Social Problems* 91

National Development Council, 'The National Development Council is Promoting the Amendment of the Personal Data Protection Act, and is Seeking Recognition of GDPR Adequacy' (News Release, 29 December 2019)

—— 'Statement by the National Development Council in response to the News Report on the EU General Data Protection Regulation and the harmonisation of the Implementation of the Personal Data Protection Act' (News Release, 26 May 2021)

Zaied Shouran, Ahmad Ashari and Tri Kuntoro Priyambodo, 'Internet of Things (IoT) of Smart Home: Privacy and Security' (2019) 182 *International Journal of Computer Applications* 3

Thailand

Baker McKenzie, 'Thailand: PDPA Compliance and Challenges – Development of the Insurance Industry in 2024' (*Baker McKenzie*, 9 February 2024)

Deloitte Thailand, 'PDPA Readiness Survey Report 2022' (2022)

Janine Phakdeethum, 'Explainer: What is PDPA, Thailand's New Data Law?' (*Bangkok Post*, 1 June 2022)
'Joint Press Statement between the Government of the Kingdom of Thailand and the Government of the People's Republic of China Issued on 5 November 2019, Bangkok' (*Ministry of Foreign Affairs Thailand*, 5 November 2019)
Komsan Tortermvasana, 'Data Protection Complaint Centre Opens' (*Bangkok Post*, 30 January 2024)
Marta Requejo, 'Jurisdiction, Conflict of Laws and Data Protection in Cyberspace' (*Conflict of Laws*, 12 August 2018)
MH Nguyen, 'Thailand Issues First Personal Data Protection Act' (*ASEAN Briefing*, 31 May 2022)
PDPC Thailand, 'Criteria for Protecting Personal Data Sent or Transferred Abroad According to Section 28 and Section 29
Suchit Leesa-nguansuk, Somruedi Banchongduang, and Darana Chudasri, 'Personal Privacy in the Balance' (*Bangkok Post*, 11 March 2019)
Wichit Chantanusornsiri, 'Web Scraping a New Tool in Revenue Hunt' (*Bangkok Post*, 3 January 2019)

United Human Rights Committee

UN Human Rights Committee, 'CCPR General Comment No. 16: Article 17 (Right to Privacy), The Right to Respect of Privacy, Family, Home and Correspondence, and Protection of Honour and Reputation' (8 April 1988)

Vietnam

Anh Hoai Nguyen, Giang Thi Huong Tran and Waewpen Piemwichai, 'A Closer Look at Vietnam's First-Ever Personal Data Protection Decree' (*Tilleke & Gibbins*, 21 April 2023)
Bảo Hà, 'Đại Biểu Quốc Hội Tranh Luận về Dự Thảo Luật an Ninh Mạng' ['National Assembly Delegates Debate on Draft Law on Cyber Security'] (*Vnexpress*, 29 May 2018)
Bui Ngoc Son, 'Globalization of Constitutional Identity' (2017) 26 *Washington International Law Journal* 463
Chu Thi Hoa, 'Còn những khoảng trống pháp luật về bảo vệ dữ liệu cá nhân' (Ministry of Information and Communication, 1 June 2022)
'Đại Biểu Quốc Hội Tranh Luận về Việc Ban Hành Luật An Ninh Mạng' ['National Assembly Deputies Debate the Promulgation of the Law on Cyber Security'] (*Tạp chí Cộng sản*, 23 November 2017)
Danh Sách Hiệp Định Tương Trợ Tư Pháp Việt Nam Đã Ký Với Các Nước' ['List of Mutual Legal Assistance Agreements Vietnam Has Signed with Other Countries'] (*Luật sư Đà Nẵng – Luật sư FDVN*, 29 January 2019)
Đỗ Thoa, 'Quốc hội thảo luận về dự thảo Luật An ninh mạng' ['The National Assembly Discussed The Draft Law On Cyber Security'] (*Dang cong san*, 23 Nov 2017)
Dữ liệu người Việt đang bị rò rỉ như thế nào?' ['How Is Vietnamese People's Data Being Leaked?'] (Vnexpress Podcast, 31 March 2023)
Giang Thi Huong Tran and Thomas J Treutler, *Significant Aspects of Vietnam's New Consumer Protection Law* (*Tilleke & Gibbins*, 3 November 2023)
Giang Thi Huong Tran, Waewpen Piemwichai and Trung Bao Tran, 'Decree 53 Provides Long-Awaited Guidance on Implementation of Vietnam's Cybersecurity Law' (*Tilleke & Gibbins*, 12 October 2022)
Graham Greenleaf, *Asian Data Privacy Laws: Trade & Human Rights Perspectives* (Oxford University Press, 2017) 361–70
Hội thảo về bảo vệ dữ liệu cá nhân trên không gian mạng (*MPS*, 9 Dec 2020)
James Fox, 'How are Foreign Investors Responding to Vietnam's New Data Localization Regulation' (*Vietnam Briefing*, 23 September 2022)
James Q Whitman, 'The Two Western Cultures of Privacy: Dignity Versus Liberty' (2004) 113 *The Yale Law Journal* 1151
Lê Mạnh Hùng, 'Vấn đề áp dụng pháp luật nước ngoài trong giải quyết các vụ việc dân sự tại tòa án Việt Nam' ['The Issue Of Applying Foreign Law In Resolving Civil Cases In Vietnamese Courts'] (*Tap chi toa an*, 20 July 2021)

—— 'Áp dụng pháp luật nước ngoài trong giải quyết các vụ việc dân sự có yếu tố nước ngoài' ['Apply Foreign Law in Resolving Civil Cases With Foreign Elements'] (*Tap chi toa an*, 20 July 2021)

Lưu Quý and An Thu, '25 năm phát triển Internet Việt Nam' ['25 Years Of Vietnam Internet Development'] (*Vnexpress*, 13 February 2023)

Minh Nga, 'Vietnam Records Over 5,400 Cyberattacks In Five Months' (*Vnexpress*, 10 June 2022)

'Người dân nhiều địa phương xuống đường gây náo loạn' ['People In Many Localities Took To The Streets To Cause Chaos'] (*Vnexpress*, 10 June 2018)

Nguyen Hung Quang, 'Thực tiễn áp dụng pháp luật nước ngoài trong xét xử dân sự ở Việt Nam và những khó khăn, thách thức – Góc nhìn của luật sư' ['Practical Application Of Foreign Law In Civil Trials In Vietnam And Difficulties And Challenges – A Lawyer's Perspective'] (2020) *7 Thông tin Khoa học pháp lý*

Ngoc Son Bui and Jyh-An Lee, 'Comparative Cybersecurity Law in Socialist Asia' (2022) 55 *Vanderbilt Journal of Transnational Law* 631

Nguyen Anh Duong, 'Time for Vietnam to Get Cracking on CPTPP Reforms' (East Asia Forum, 13 January 2022)

Nguyễn Đình Hiệp, 'Tổ Chức Xã Hội Tham Gia Bảo vệ Quyền Lợi Người Tiêu Dùng Được Quy Định Như Thế Nào?' ['How Are Social Organizations Involved In Protecting Consumer Rights Regulated?'] (*Luật Hoàng Anh*, 31 January 2023)

Nguyen Ngoc Minh, Tran Ha Han and Nguyen Thi Thu Trang, 'Vietnam' in Anselmo Reyes (ed), *Recognition and Enforcement of Judgments in Civil and Commercial Matters* (Hart Publishing, 2019) 198–99

Oliver Massmann and Nguyen Thi Lang, 'Vietnam – Cybersecurity – Comparing Vietnam's Cybersecurity Law with Its Commitments Under the CPTPP, EVFTA' (*Duane Morris*, 22 September 2021)

Quoc-Tan-Trung Nguyen, Thi-Hong-Ninh Bui, and Hong-Thanh Phung, 'Human Right Concerns in Vietnam's Cybersecurity Law: From International Discourse to a Comparative Perspective' (2022) 14(3) *Journal of Human Rights Practice* 968

Thanh Chung, 'Dự thảo nghị định bảo vệ dữ liệu cá nhân 'mới, khó, cần xem xét tính cấp bách'' ['The Draft Decree On Personal Data Protection is "Novel, Demanding, And Necessity To Be Considered"'] (*Tuoi tre*, 13 February 2023)

Thanh tra toàn diện các nhà mạng về vấn đề bảo vệ dữ liệu cá nhân (Laodong) (4 Nov 2022)

Tien-Duc Nguyen and Pasquale Viola, 'Constitutional Rights in Socialist East Asia' (2022) 40(2) *Nordic Journal of Human Rights* 320

Tien-Duc Nguyen and Thu-Thuy Thi Tran, 'The Limits of Vietnam's Incrementalism towards the Abolition of Capital Punishment for Drug Offenses' (2022) 17(2) *Asian Journal of Comparative Law* 222

Tom Ginsburg and Alberto Simpser, *Constitutions in Authoritarian Regimes* (Cambridge University Press, 2014) 2–3

Trinh Hai Yen, 'Viet Nam' in Simon Chesterman, Hisashi Owada and Ben Saul (eds), *Oxford Handbook of International Law in Asia and the Pacific* (Oxford University Press, 2019) 492–95

Trong Dat and Van Anh, 'Personal Data Of 10,000 Vietnamese Offered For Sale Online' (*Vietnamnet*, 17 May 2021)

Truong Nhat Quang, Nguyen Duy Duong and Vu Tuan Duc, 'Foreign Court Judgments and Arbitral Awards in Vietnam' (*YKVN*, 6 January 2021)

'Vai trò quan trọng và một số kết quả đạt được của Hội Bảo vệ Người tiêu dùng Việt Nam (VICOPRO) trong công tác bảo vệ quyền lợi người tiêu dùng ở Việt Nam' ['The Important Role and Some Achievements of the Vietnam Consumer Protection Association (VICOPRO) in Protecting Consumer Rights in Vietnam'] (*Vietnam Competition and Consumer Authority*, 15 October 2021)

Van Anh, 'Important Transition For Digital Government As Public Services Go Online' (*Vietnamnet*, 8 February 2022)

VCCI, *The Flow of Business Law 2022* (Industry and Commerce Publisher, 2022) 35

Vedan: A Call for Class Action Suits in Vietnam' (*Vietnam Law Magazine*, 9 January 2010)

Võ Hải, 'Tranh Luận Việc Buộc Facebook, Google Đặt Máy Chủ ở Việt Nam' ['Debate on Forcing Facebook and Google to Set Up Servers in Vietnam'] (*Vnexpress*, 23 November 2017)

Waewpen Piemwichai, 'Socialist Republic of Viet Nam' in Clarisse Girot (ed), *Regulation of Cross-Border Transfers of Personal Data in Asia* (Asian Business Law Institute, 2018) 399

—— Giang Thi Huong Tran and Trung Bao Tran, 'Vietnam's Personal Data Protection Decree Takes Important Step toward Issuance' (*Tilleke & Gibbins*, 8 February 2023)

Yee Chung Seck and Thanh Son Dang, 'Vietnam: Regulatory Framework Regarding Reporting and Responding to Cyber Information Security Incidents – Decision No. 05 and Circular No. 20' (*Global Compliance News*, 24 November 2017)

Uzbekistan

Abdumalik Mukhtorov, Azizbek Suyunboev 'Uzbekistan: Resolution on Personal Data Processing Overview' (*DataGuidance*, June 2023)

Alexander Makovskii, 'The Russian Civil Code and its Impact Upon Commercial Transactions' in William Simons (ed), *Private and Civil Law in the Russian Federation* (Brill, 2009) 4

—— *О кодификации гражданского права* [*On Codification of Civil Law*] *(1922–2006)* (Statut, 2010) 7

Artyom Karapetov, Экономический анализ права [*Economic Analysis of Law*] (Statut, 2016) 80-1

Christian von Bar, *Foundations of Property Law Things as Objects of Property Rights* (translated by Jason Grant Allen) (Oxford University Press, 2023) fn 2.32

Christopher Kuner, 'Data Protection Law and International Jurisdiction on the Internet (Part 1)' (2010) 18 *International Journal of Law and Information Technology* 176

Dilbar Axrarova in Rakhmankulov Khodji-Akbar, Asyanov Shamil (eds), *O'zbekiston Respublikasi fuqarolik kodeksiga sharh* [*Commentaries to Civil Code of the Republic of Uzbekistan*] (Vektor-Press, 2010) 267

Eldor Mannopov, Bobur Shamsiev, Ulugbek Abdullaev 'Uzbekistan Enacts First Data Protection Law' (*Dentons*, 16 July 2019)

Evgenii Krasheninnikov, 'On the Question of "Ownership of the Claim"' (2005) 12 *Essays on Commercial Law* 31

Evgenii Sukhanov *Вещное право: Научно-познавательный очерк* [*Property Law Scientific and Informative Essay*] (Statut, 2017) 154

Graham Greenleaf, 'Personal Data Localization and Sovereignty along Asia's New Silk Roads' in Anupam Chander, and Haochen Sun (eds), *Data Sovereignty: From the Digital Silk Road to the Return of the State* (Oxford University Press, 2023) 320

Guido Calabresi, Douglas Melamed, 'Property Rules, Liability Rules and Inalienability: One View of the Cathedral' (1972) 85 *HLR* 1089

Ilkhom Azizov 'Роль и значение гражданско-правовых доктрин и институтов в гражданско-правовом законодательстве Узбекистана ['The Role and Significance of Civil Law Doctrines and Institutions in the Civil Law Legislation of Uzbekistan'] in Maidan Suleimenov (ed) *Гражданское право в эпоху трансформации общественных отношений* [*Civil Law in the Era of Transformation of Social Relations*] (Almaty, 2022) 104

Mirodil Baratov, *Mulk Huquqi* [*Property Law*] (TDYI, 2009) 302

Nozima Davletova, 'Проект Информационного кодекса: Расплывчатые формулировки, ограничения для СМИ и блогеров' (*Gazeta.uz*, 2022)

Reinhard Zimmermann, *Roman Law, Contemporary Law, European Law The Civilian Tradition Today* (Oxford University Press, 2001) 181–82

S Mirzaahmedova (ed), *O'zbekiston Respublikasi Konstitutsiyasiga sharh* [*Commentaries to Constitution of the Republic of Uzbekistan*] (O'zbekiston, 2001) 150–57

Sabrina Praduroux, 'Objects of Property Rights: Old and New' in Michele Graziadei, Lionel Smith (eds), *Comparative Property Law Global Perspectives* (EE, 2017) 57

Vadim Belov, *Ценные бумаги в коммерческом обороте* [*Negotiable Instruments in Commercial Turnover*] (Urait, 2018) 116

—— 'Найти среди наших современных юристов чистого "деликтника" если не невозможно, то очень проблемотично ['Finding Among Our Modern Lawyers a Pure "Delictual" If Not Impossible, Then Very Problematic'] (2020) 3 *Zakon* 8

Vladimir Norov, 'Central Asian Countries and China are Developing a Strategic Partnership to Ensure Peace, Security and Sustainable Development in the Region' (*O'zbekiston Milliy Axborot Agentligi*, 19 May 2023)

Conclusion

Sai Ramani Garimella and Haaris Moosa, 'India' in Adrian Mak, Ching Him Ho and Anselmo Reyes (eds) *Privacy and Personal Data Protection Law in Asia* (Hart Publishing, 2025)

Yeong Zee Kin, 'International: Clear and Present Harm of AI – How Data Protection Principles May Help' (*DataGuide*, 2024)

INDEX